ABC-CLIO LITERARY COMPANION

Encyclopedia of Traditional EPICS

ABC-CLIO LITERARY COMPANION

Encyclopedia of Traditional EPICS

Guida M. Jackson

ABC-CLIO

Santa Barbara, California
Denver, Colorado
Oxford, England

Library of Congress Cataloging-in-Publication Data

Encyclopedia of traditional epics / by Guida M. Jackson.
Includes bibliographical references and index.
1. Epic literature—History and criticism. 2. Epic literature—Encyclopedias. I. Jackson-Laufer, Guida M. (Guida Myrl) II. Title.
PN56.E65E64 1994 398.22—dc20 94-9303

ISBN 0-87436-724-7

00 99 98 97 96 95 10 9 8 7 6 5 4 3 2

ABC-CLIO, Inc.
130 Cremona Drive, P.O. Box 1911
Santa Barbara, California 93116-1911

This book is printed on acid-free paper ♾.
Manufactured in the United States of America

To Robert Daniel, Ashley Diane,
and Christopher Michael Ramos;
Mattie Rose Jackson;
Elizabeth Anne and Gregory Allen Jackson;
and Richard Harris Fish, M.D.

CONTENTS

PREFACE

The boundaries of this book range beyond oral epics captured and transcribed from live performance, although to me those are by far the most exciting. Also included are epics that have evolved from oral tradition and have been given literary form by a single poet or several poets, as well as a few classified as literary epics but incorporating some degree of traditional material. The latter category offers the most fertile ground for controversy: Why include the *Shāh-Nāmah* and omit the Luciads, for example. Each inclusionary decision in this category was a personal one based on my quavering judgment on how broadly to interpret the term *traditional* and how closely to tie at least some portion of the work to an underlying oral tradition.

One of the difficulties arises due to the various ways in which epics evolve. In the usual pattern an epic begins as an oral account that is added to by generations of bards until it is finally put into literary form, but sometimes the opposite occurs. Some epics, primarily in the Far and Middle East, began as literary works that have been altered and enhanced through repeated performances, so that the extant version is both more and less than its literary forebear.

Epics are often so closely bound to the religious beliefs and mythology of their milieu that including a certain number of entries devoted to mythological and religious figures will assist the reader in understanding the epics. Heroic epics are supposedly based—loosely—on history. Myth leads to history and explains it.

Some of the material that may have been sung as poetry in bygone years has come down to us as prose. In the broad sense of the term *traditional,* I have included it. This also explains the inclusion of a number of prose sagas, which have crept into the collection under the umbrella of the term *traditional,* as well as of a few shorter poems of great antiquity, whose length and scope hardly qualify them as epics, but whose development places them squarely in the "traditional" pigeonhole. In almost every questionable instance, I have erred on the side of inclusion rather than exclusion, on the grounds that this is to be a collection of information about "traditional" narratives that make up the heritage of the human race. There are also entries about major collections and literary works having some relevance to an older work. Because so much extraneous material has crept into the collection, I have included a categorical list of the various works among the appendixes.

In contemporary times we are indebted to the anthropological field-workers who have transcribed and translated oral performances in remote regions. Prior to the invention of the tape recorder we relied upon scribes, of whom even Homer might well have been one. Theirs were secondary renderings. Many, probably most, epics are not available from verbatim taped performances, even if we could understand the languages. In the sense that every written rendering is a secondary source, this collection is classified as being based on tertiary sources.

Further, it is a tertiary survey of readily available epics *only.* If one were able to scour the remote villages of South Asia alone, one could collect enough additional epics in 700 languages to fill a large volume. The same could be said for Southeast Asia or Africa. In fact, there are an estimated 190–627 million indigenous peoples speaking 6,250 languages where an oral tradition persists, according to Alan Thein Durning, Worldwatch Paper 112, December 1992. The present collection represents only a small part of a vast oral tradition, and obviously some of the epics are far from ancient and are in fact still evolving. A bibliography of sources used is included at the end of the book.

For those epics that I consider most significant, I have attempted to offer much more than a brief sketch such as might be found in a study guide. I have summarized the epic by "books" or subtitle or chapter, often quoting a sampling of the text, so that the reader could consult the original version and find the complete passage without too much trouble. The text samplings also serve to give the reader a flavor of the original style and, I hope, bring the summary to life.

Some attempt has been made to standardize the spellings of names of characters and even epics that appear in several different countries, as in the *Mahābhārata,* which is widely told throughout South and Southeast Asia. Even in India there are spelling variations. However, where a character, such as Siegfried, appears in the traditions of several countries in various languages, I have attempted to conform to the spelling appropriate for the specific work involved. Alternate spellings are noted in parentheses following the name.

Diacritical marks, particularly those in Indian and Arabic entries, have been standardized to conform to those used in the country of the epic's origin, even though a slightly different version, with varying diacritics, may be sung elsewhere. This will assist the reader in identifying and relating epics and characters appearing in more than one culture.

Dates, if known, are included for both epics and historical characters; however, bards, scops, and griots alike have shown a propensity for lumping historical elements of different eras into the same epic stew and attributing to their favorite heroes deeds separated by centuries. For the reader's assistance, a chronological table is included, but its value may be questionable because some epics, only relatively recently collected from oral tradition, may in fact have long, tenacious roots.

Also included is a listing of epics by geographical location so that the reader can locate and compare other epics of the region. In short, every effort has been made to make this material accessible to a wide range of readers of varying degrees of educational experience.

A few themes, such as flood, abandonment, savior, and quest, are treated as separate entries; however, I have confined most of my comments on the subject of themes to the introduction.

This is not a work of literary criticism: No interpretation is given of the epic entries. As a reader and the author of the condensations, however, I plead guilty to emphasizing certain elements over others. Because I anticipate use of this collection by some relatively young readers, I have chosen to deemphasize certain arbitrarily crude aspects and raw language (sinking in some instances into pornographic) in certain South American and Southeast Asian works as not adding significantly to the plot—in fact, seriously detracting from it in some instances. By the very elements I have included or excluded, I have in a sense interpreted the epic. This is inevitable in any condensation. Nevertheless, I have refrained from offering opinion in any section of the book outside the introduction.

In the preparation of this collection, which was the suggestion of my editor, Suzanne Chance, I have received, in addition to her invaluable assistance and support, help from William H. Laufer, Ruby C. Tolliver, Chi Chi Layor, Donna Wolfe, Veniece Standley, James Tucker Jackson, Mary Winzig, Mary Gillis Jackson, William A. Jackson, Dr. Jeffrey A. Jackson, Dr. Linda J. Jackson, and Annabeth Ramos. Special thanks to Amy B. Catala, development editor, who guided the book to completion.

INTRODUCTION

A romantic perception persists about the daring heroes of the ancient epics accorded such an elevated position in our literary heritage. But it is a garbled perception, probably because there is a tendency in the West to confuse "epic" with the medieval romantic tales such as those of Arthurian legend. Epics represent a much more elemental tradition. Heroic epics celebrating the exploits of forebears were sung before battle to instill courage in the warriors. The old stories defined heroism to the new generation. Unlike other predators, ordinary men didn't have fangs or talons or superhuman strength with which to defend their territories or acquire new ones. Their weapons were courage and wits, both of which to some extent could be engendered, if only briefly. So heroic epics often commemorate battles and glorify violent men who plunder, rape, murder, and make slaves of their captives. We are apt to question the relevance of such stories today and to ask, are age and beautiful language justification for perpetuating them?

As if it were a matter over which we have any control; as if, by any amount of rhetoric, they could be eradicated from the collective psyche. The possibility of ignoring the past is the greatest myth/legacy of Modernism, which had otherwise run its course by the middle of the twentieth century.

Modernism's one great illusion was that we could erase the influence of the past so as to be unfettered by the weight of tradition. It began as a Western artistic movement that quickly spread to philosophy, architecture, and literature and lasted until after World War II. During its heyday, we went about inventing our lives and the art of the day with the lean and cocksure arrogance that we had left the flaccid past of form and rule and convention.

But something happens to things that are buried: they come alive in their own composting heat. By happy synchronicity, the demise of Modernism in the West coincided with the decline of colonialist acculturation in Africa, India, Southeast Asia, and Oceana and with the decline of dictatorships and capitalist exploitation of the non-European populace—to some degree—in Latin America. The result was an eruption: a reemergence of indigenous culture at every level. These long-suppressed people had maintained an awareness of the importance of the encounter with the past and its resultant understanding of the tradition from which they had sprung. Further, it was a multilevel understanding dependent upon multilayered interpretations. Roberto Calasso reminds us that a myth that survives in only one version is "like a body without a shadow." In the long history of the human race, even the shadows have shadows.

Epics have played an important part in preserving identity in colonialist societies, where regimes often attempted to eliminate all vestiges of native culture: mode of dress, language, social mores, even religion. Oral tradition, passed on around village campfires, kept native cultures alive. When colonial governments withdrew from Africa, for example, the boundaries of states had been set with no regard for the tribal makeup of the residents. Tribal loyalties often span national borders, and many cultures may exist in one country. The epics have served to reunite people of like cultures, regardless of national boundaries, and to return to them their precolonial pride and sense of self, to say nothing of their history.

Aside from this and their poetic value, there are other lagniappes of the epics for people of other cultures. They offer graphic depictions of cultural differences that persist down to the present time. For example, if we examine the underlying differences between African and Arab or Viking heroes, we may discover how to deal more diplomatically with people of those cultures today. Arab and Viking heroes are usually portrayed as swooping down in terrorist raids upon their victims, whereas African warriors are very often depicted as sending polite messages to announce their forthcoming attack, as they considered it cowardly to strike without warning. An epic is always biased; it never tells both sides of a story, and usually the exploits of the conquering heroes are greatly exaggerated. In those rare instances where an oral tradition survives from both sides of the same conflict, as in the two epics of *Ezemu,* for example, it is noteworthy that the African epics are not so very different on many points.

Epics have been told not only to justify a hero's deeds but to glorify them, as in the case of the Assyrian epic of Tukulti Ninurta I, whose ravagement of Babylon is said to be the will of the gods. Gods, or magic, are frequently given credit for tipping the balance toward victory in epics. As Sophocles reminds us, "Mortal life can never have anything great about it except through átē (divine infatuation; hence, intervention)." In the sense that a tale attributes the deeds of one man to something larger than himself, the sin or weakness of hubris is avoided. If the message translates as the incomprehensible complexity of circumstance that prevents the nailing of effect to single cause, the epics reveal an important maxim of history.

This is not to excuse their faults, although many justifications for preserving and honoring the epics may be offered. One negative aspect is the frequent depiction of mistreatment of women and children, which unfortunately probably mirrored their cultures.

The abandoned child, prevalent in epics, is a universal archetype that had entered the human psyche even prior to the great classical epics. Cronus, it may be remembered, ate his young. In heroic epics, if the child-hero appears to spring from humble beginnings, it is usually because his father the king has heard a prophecy that the child will usurp the throne; therefore, he orders the child killed or banished. Like Cronus, each power-mad generation attempts to eat the next in the hubristic delusion that survival can somehow be divorced from continuity. John Berger has said, "Experience is indivisible and continuous, at least within a single lifetime, perhaps over many lifetimes."

The hero-child of myth and/or epic is usually rescued and reared by a peasant couple, benign animal, or bird. Although possessing superhuman strength at birth, the child may have one weakness, sometimes the result of a curse placed upon him even before birth, usually by a vindictive female figure. Great moral lessons sometimes accrue concerning the downfall of a great man or nation, usually as the result of someone's sin or weakness of hubris, leading to the attempt to destroy what has gone before or what is to come after. Berger says, "I never have the impression that my experience is entirely my own, and it often seems to me that it preceded me." He speaks of experience that "folds upon itself, refers backwards and forwards to itself through the referents of hope and fear...." Like his description of writing, the elements of the epic resemble a shuttlecock: "Repeatedly it approaches and withdraws, closes in and takes its distance."

The child, nevertheless, invariably becomes expendable. He is frequently blamed for the sins of his parents; unborn illegitimate children are as guilty as their mothers. Zulu courts are considered models of wisdom, yet in the epic of *Emperor Shaka the Great,* a man appears before the elders' council demanding justice because the woman given to him as a wife has already been impregnated by his brother. When an elder opines that the brother deserves death, Emperor Shaka indicates the woman and asks, "Has she not been the cause of this disintegration?" The elder answers, "A woman in Zululand is the mother of our nation; / In her is both the power of life and destruction /. . . This woman deserves even greater punishment than this man." The condemned brother pleads, "Let other nations who hear of our judgments / Say 'Punishments of death are meted out only to men.'" But Shaka, refusing leniency, commands that her womb be split open: "Let the monster that has destroyed the families be exposed."

Other cobwebs must be swept from the corners of the closet of epic-treasures. For example, women are routinely trivialized: A passage from the *Shāh Nāma* reminds men: "Refrain from describing masculine beauty when women are in earshot. In the heart of every female lurks a living devil. . . . When desire enters a woman's heart, wisdom flies out the window." A warning from the West African *Epic of Bakaridjan Kone* says, "Do not relate a matter of importance to a woman."

Women are often depicted as the troublemakers. In the *Rāmāyaṇa,* after a string of incidents and mishaps brought about by women, it is no surprise that Lakṣmaṇa lops off Śūrpaṇkhā's ears and nose for daring to propose herself as a wife for Rāma. Later, when Rāma's wife Sītā begs him not to leave her unguarded near the territory of the demon king Rāvaṇa, he chides her: "Wrong words are nothing new for a woman." He draws a circle around her and commands her not to step beyond it until he returns. As soon as he is out of sight, Rāvaṇa swoops in, kidnaps her, and takes her to his palace dungeon with the promise, "When winter comes...if you haven't come into my bed, I'll eat you minced for breakfast." Although Rāma goes to considerable trouble to rescue her, he later decides that if she has been violated by her captor she is no longer fit to be queen. So he turns her out to wander in the forest, alone and pregnant with his sons.

Men have been defining appropriate behavior for women at least since the time of the epics. The Japanese Ainu epic *Woman of Poi-Soya* is devoted entirely to delivering a lesson for women on the consequences of behaving in an unfeminine fashion. When the "exalted hero" hears that a certain woman goes hunting and fishing and even dresses in masculine clothing for the outings, he is furious, calling her behavior "self-exaltation,/ outrageous arrogance!" Whenever they meet, he slashes her; beats her violently; knocks her against trees, rafters, and walls; drags her around by the heels; and ties her mangled body to trees or posts. Each time, she is chastened and returns to her needlework. But soon she grows restless again. Once she decides to go on a trading mission to sell her needlework. The "exalted hero" says, "At the mere/ hearing of it,/ a frenzied rage/ burst over me." He tracks her down, slashes and mutilates her, ties her ankles, and drags her body to the beach where he tosses it into the boat with her servants, whom he also beats soundly. He returns home and throws himself down on his bed: "I was overcome/ with feelings of rage."

Abduction and the rape it implies were old hat before the time of Zeus and Apollo, so the epics merely perpetuate what had gone before. Although some early scholars, including Plato, decried such actions as Theseus "going forth to perpetuate a horrid rape," others, such as Herodotus, took the more universal view of rape victims: "Had they not wanted to be abducted, they would not have been." Roberto Calasso suggests that tales of rape can be seen as "a projection of the supposed triumph of patriarchal over matriarchal forms of society."

Indeed, the story of the African *Gikuyu,* or Kikuyu, tells how the men conspired to take over power in their matriarchal society by first making all the women pregnant. This same mentality prevails in the Finnish epic *Kalevala* when the hero Lemminkäinen, "the very finest of men," prepares to depart on a wooing escapade. His mother warns him that women may make fun of him, but he vows to make short work of their derision: "I will knock a boy into their wombs..../ There is an end to even good ridicule...." He sets off on his venture and manages to impregnate nearly every woman he finds. When one maiden spurns him, he drags her away and ties her to the slatted bottom of his sleigh. She is apparently charmed by this treatment, for she immediately consents to become his wife. We must bear in mind, however, that kidnapping a bride was legal even in England until the thirteenth century.

Not every epic celebrates a victory; sometimes it keeps old animosities smoldering. The ongoing political crisis involving Serbia, Croatia, and the Bosnian Muslims, seen against the backdrop of the burgarštica of the area, seems merely a continuation of what has gone before. For example, the *Battle of Kosovo* commemorates a tragic defeat of the Serbs at the hands of the

Muslims, marking an end to the great Serbian empire. The epic has kept alive the memory and bitter resentment of that humiliating defeat and surely must be given credit for at least exacerbating Serbian feeling against their neighbors in the mid–twentieth century. The horizon of the present does not take shape without the past. Hans-Georg Gadamer has talked of the "fusing" of horizons occurring constantly "in the working of tradition."

In Gadamer's metaphor, epics lose their "moment" and become supple, fluid, difficult or impossible to contain, awash in eddies of minutiae from a thousand distant horizons, soon to be overtaken and mingled with other horizons—indeed, "fused" seems entirely too concrete a term to apply.

Our own myths are so taken for granted as to be largely invisible. Without doubt epics have continued to influence models of manhood to the present time, for we have inherited the warrior psyche and at times are ruled by the warrior archetype. Warriors of both genders are good talkers, seldom listeners. They take a combative, aggressive approach to problems rather than a compromising or persuasive one. Their function is to do battle, either on the field of conflict or in the economic arena, where making money or coming out on top take precedence over sustaining relationships. Warriors are called upon to attack, kill, suffer, and die for the cause of nation, family, clan, team, or corporation. They may rape and be raped by the brutality of combat, because the war system begets systematic violence, and the end justifies the means.

But what is the war really about? We must find a more profound message beyond war for warfare's sake. And it is there. We need not go beyond *Gilgamesh* to find it.

Epics are indeed often about war, about fighting, kicking, and screaming—against extinction. Robert Graves contends that all myths are ultimately the same myth. If certain epics portray nothing else, they constantly keep before us the inexorableness of our own frail mortality. The lust for battle and renown stills for King Gilgamesh when his blood brother sickens and dies. Who can forget Gilgamesh's helpless raging over Enkidu's death "like a lioness deprived of her whelps," pacing around the deathbed, tearing out his hair and strewing it about in a frenzy: drastic histrionics staged in a desperate attempt to sway whatever gods might notice. But the inevitable signs of the body's advancing decay—"worms fastened upon him"—make the acquiescence to death's victory unavoidable.

The dilemma of Gilgamesh is now the dilemma of every soul: how to manipulate nature's laws so as somehow to escape decay and death. Gilgamesh's search for immortality in his futile, dangerous trip to the underworld, frittering away his own precious life with a fruitless scheme to bypass the natural laws by which the rest of mankind must abide, is equivalent now to spending irretrievable living time subjecting oneself to dehumanizing ordeals at the hands of the new gods we have made of science and medicine, lavishing upon them sacrificial offerings of time, money, and adoration in the same attempt somehow to beat death.

Certain epics remind us that making deals for immortality isn't going to work; perhaps this ultimately confers upon them their stature as the greatest literature of the world.

In a densely populated mobile society, the epic is a thread connecting one to homeland, tribe, or clan. The horizon of the present does not take shape without the past. The human spirit resonates to the ancient stories of proud and mighty heroes who uphold the honor of the clan by deeds of great courage, failing only when their pride threatens to overshadow that of the gods. But most of these stories leave the weaker, expendable members of the population—usually children and women—waiting to be used and/or ravished or killed. This is not a scenario that needs perpetuating.

If the fusing of horizons, due to long accretion, can be considered an apt metaphor for the epic's "moment," a suitable simile for the constitution of our human experience may be Jacques Derrida's paradigm of a collage or montage. There are, after all, layers of experience below the most weighty ones—ancient layers—as well as cross-cultural layers abutting and overlapping our own. So also, any epic may be considered less a narrative about one experience, regardless of how specific, than a "text" into which ancient elements bob up, "already written," into the story, and cross-cultural elements insinuate themselves unbidden. For example, when traditional stories, all but eradicated by colonialist "overcultures," re-emerge, they inevitably bear the imprint of the "overculture" as well. As Derrida points out, it is difficult to draw the boundary line between the text and what seems to lie beyond its fringe. To understand an epic, all the layers of human experience must be taken into account, even the bestial ones of the ancient past or of the moment. That which has been pushed aside inevitably makes its way into the story, regardless, so that, if preserving the brutality depicted in these epics carries some misgiving, we feel justified in perpetuating them because to deny the parts of which we disapprove would be to deny not only deep layers of our own psyche but also patterns of behavior still extant somewhere in the world today—possibly on the mean streets of our own cities.

Perhaps the reader will temper a full-blown sense of outrage at mankind's past insensitivities with the glad realization that we have, after all, made progress since the time of the epics. Our reverence for them is vindicated if they serve as a reminder, not only of humankind's courage and the progress we have made in the matter of human rights, but also of those injustices that persist to the present time.

A

AARON

(Also Aaron the Levite)

In the Jewish oral tradition, recorded in the Talmud and Midrash as well as the Pentateuch of the Old Testament, Aaron is the brother of Moses (ca. fourteenth century B.C.). He is three years older than Moses, born presumably before the pharaoh's edict that all Hebrew boy babies be cast into the Nile. Aaron is appointed by God to be spokesman for Moses, who has a speech impediment, in petitioning the pharaoh of Egypt for release of the children of Israel from bondage. Aaron, his older sister Miriam, and their families accompany Moses to lead the Israelites out of Egypt. After Aaron and his sons Nadab and Abihu are cleansed, robed, and their sins expiated by sacrifice, they are made priests, with Aaron as the head of Jewish priesthood. He wears bells on the hem of his robe, perhaps to ensure that he does not enter God's presence unannounced. But only six weeks after making solemn vows, Aaron, God's high priest, fashions a golden calf for the Israelites to worship while Moses is on Mount Sinai. (Exodus 4:14; Exodus 28–32ff.)

See also Moses.

ABANDONMENT

Abandonment is a common theme in epic literature where the hero often faces almost insurmountable odds very early in life, although he may possess superhuman attributes even as an infant with which to meet life's exigencies.

In the process of elevating the baseborn hero to an exalted position, it is often desirable to give him royal blood, particularly if he becomes a ruler. Often the story develops that he is actually a king's son, abandoned as an infant and reared by peasants; thus, he is truly fit to be king.

Epics often arise to fill a longing among the people for someone to look up to, someone who will save them and make their lives better. The king reared by peasants has a broad appeal, because such a ruler will have empathy for the common people.

Hero tales have always been told to instill courage, particularly among warriors. The archetypal hero must have endured more hardships, faced more sorrow, suffered more, and met greater foes than any of the listening warriors will have. The abandoned hero stands on his own from the cradle, a fitting example for the warrior of any age.

The hero Sargon I is placed in a basket sealed with pitch and cast adrift by his mother, a virgin. A gardener finds him floating in the river and takes him in. The story is similar to the story of Moses, whose mother places him in a basket that is found in the Nile by an Egyptian princess. Cyrus the Great, whose king has dreamed that the boy will grow up to kill him, has been ordered slain as a baby, but is given instead to a shepherd to rear. Perseus and his virgin mother are both set adrift when King Acrisius, informed by an oracle that his grandchild will kill him, seals his daughter Danai and Perseus in a chest that is thrown into the sea. A fisherman, Dictys, and his wife care for Danai and adopt Perseus. The medieval Danish hero-orphan Havelok, son of King Birkabegn, is set adrift at sea by his guardians. When the raft drifts to the coast of Lincolnshire, a fisherman, Grim, finds him and brings him up as his son. Siegfried (Sigurd), of the *Nibelungenlied* and Old Norse legends, is left in a glass vessel in the river and adopted first by a doe and then by a blacksmith. Later he becomes the king of Denmark. Karṇa, in the *Mahābhārata,* who was born with golden earrings and a hard gold armor, is the product of the immaculate union of Princess Kuntī and Sūrya, the sun god. His mother sets him adrift in the Yamuna River in a basket made waterproof with wax. The Yamuna carries the basket to the Ganges, where the charioteer Adheratha (Azirath) and his wife Radhā find it and raise the boy as their own. The Polynesian demigod Maui is thrown into the sea and adopted by sea spirits. Oedipus is left to die in the wilderness but is taken in by a shepherd. Bakaridjan Kone's father abandons his mother before he is born and goes off to live at the court of King Da Monzon in Mali. The *Epic of Sundiata* tells of a Mali prince, born stiff-legged and unable to walk as a child. He and his mother are banished by another of the king's wives after the king dies. They live in an old hut on the outskirts of civilization and have to beg for food, while the other wife's son is made ruler. A Seneca myth tells of a boy who becomes lost on the plains and is adopted by a family of buffalo. Many years later he is returned to his tribe and teaches a select few the secrets of the buffalo. This is the origin of the Buffalo Society (also referred to as the Society of Buffaloes) as it exists today among the Seneca. In an Indian legend Kaṃsa, king of the Yādavas, is warned that the infant Kṛiṣṇa will one day slay him and therefore seeks to kill the child. Kṛiṣṇa is spirited away and brought up by shepherds. Later he does indeed kill the king, and assumes the throne. T'u-chüeh, founder of the Turkish nation, whose deeds are recounted on the Orhon (Orkhon) monuments in Mongolia, is abandoned as a child. Zāl, a Persian hero in *Shāh-Nāmah,* is born with white hair and is taken to the mountaintop and abandoned. An Indian Simurgh bird adopts him, raising him as her own, and later assists him with the birth of his son Rostam. In the Mayan *Popol Vuh,* when the gods Hunahpú and Xbalanqué are born, they cannot sleep. The grandmother orders, "Go throw them out because truly they cry too much." They are placed on an anthill, where their jealous older brothers expect (even hope) that they will die. Instead, the two sleep peacefully. Because the older brothers and the grandmother refuse to receive them into the house, they are brought up in the fields. They are given nothing to eat, but they suffer silently because they know their rank and they understand everything clearly.

The Chinese *Book of Songs* tells the legend of Hau Ki (born after his mother Kian Yuan steps in the footprint of God), who "was placed in a narrow lane, / But the sheep and oxen protected him with loving care." The ode goes on to describe other places where he is abandoned: "in a wide forest," and "on the cold ice," but he survives and grows up to become a champion of husbandry. (Buck 1981; Civrieux 1980; Exodus 2ff.; Levy 1967; Graves 1955; Grousset 1970; Hatto 1969; Mackenzie 1990; Niane 1989)

See also Anius; *Bakaridjan Kone, a Hero of Segu, Epic of; Da Monzon, Epic of;* Hunahpú; Karna; Rostam; Siegfried; Sundiata; Tu'-chüeh.

'ABD ALLĀH IBN JA'FAR

He is the hero of a popular Tunisian folk epic, *Futūḥ Ifrīqiyya* (The Conquest of North Africa), which tells of the hero's adventures and of the conquest of Tūnis by Arab armies. (Connelly 1986)

See also *Futūḥ Ifrīqiyya.*

ABDUCTION

A common theme in epics, abduction usually involves a woman. Abductions were common among gods before humans began the practice. Zeus's abduction of Europa is among the best known of the myths involving gods. Among humans, Paris's abduction of Helen, causing the Trojan War, is the subject of the *Iliad.* In the Finnish *Kalevala,* the hero Lemminkäinen abducts Kyllikki and ties her onto his sleigh, but she apparently likes rough handling and eventually agrees to marry him. In the *Rāmāyaṇa,* the abduction of Sītā by the demon Rāvaṇa results in Rāma's attack upon Lanka, with the help of the monkey-king Hanumān. (Buck 1976; Graves 1955; Lattimore 1976; Lönnrot 1963)

See also *Iliad; Kalevala; Rāmāyaṇa;* Zeus.

ABO MAMA

Abo Mama is the war hero of a mvet epic, or heroic narrative, from the Fang of Cameroon, in which he successfully defeats Akoma Mba in battle. The mvet was recorded in 1966 by S. Awoona as "La Guerre d'Akoma Mba contre Abo Mama." (Westley *RAL* 1991)

ABU NUWAS

Abu Nuwas is the Arab lyricist (d. 810) celebrated in the "Arabian Nights." He appears in folk stories throughout the Arab world such as "Abu Nuwas and the Fur Cloak" from Tunisia, "Abu Nuwas and the Caliph's Queen" and "Abu

Abduction, a common theme in literary and oral epics, most often involves gods stealing goddesses away. This sixteenth-century Rajput illustration from the Hindu *Bhāgavata Purāṇa*, however, shows a demon king's daughter falling in love with Arjuna, friend of the god Kṛiṣṇa, and spiriting him to her room.

Nuwas and the Hundred Eggs" from Syria, and "Abu Nuwas Travels with the Caliph" from Iraq. (Bushnaq 1986; Dawood 1973)

ABU ZAYD EPIC

(Also *Sīrat Banī Hilāl)*

This is an Arabic epic about a black Arab hero, Abu Zayd, and the eleventh- to thirteenth-century wanderings of the Bani Hilal tribe from Arabia to Nigeria. (Connelly 1986)

See also Sīrat Banī Hilāl.

ACHILLES

(Also Achilleus)

In the *Iliad,* Achilles is the hero who fights under Agamemnon on the side of the Greeks. He is the son of Peleus, king of the Myrmidons, and the Nereid (sea nymph) Thetis. He is reared by his mother at Phthia with his cousin Patroklos. According to one legend, in order to render her son invulnerable, Thetis holds him by the heel and dips him into the River Styx. Only the heel by which she holds him remains dry and thus vulnerable. For the first nine years of the Trojan War, Achilles fights brilliantly, capturing 12 cities. But in the tenth year, Apollo visits a pestilence on Agamemnon's troops because Agamemnon has captured Chryseis, daughter of Apollo's priest, as a war prize. Agamemnon is obliged to return Chryseis to her father, and in her place he confiscates Achilles's prize, Briseis. Achilles is outraged and refuses to fight anymore. Patroklos begs to be allowed to impersonate him and go into battle, and Achilles agrees. When the Trojan warrior Hektor slays Patroklos, Achilles returns to battle to avenge his cousin's death. He kills Hektor, but an arrow shot by Hektor's younger brother Paris wounds him in his vulnerable heel. (Lattimore 1976)

See also Agamemnon; Ajax; Briseis; Chryseis; *Iliad.*

ADAD-NARARI, EPIC OF

This epic, celebrating the victory of Assyrian king Adad-narari I (1307–1275 B.C.) in a border clash with Babylonia, is one of the first Assyrian literary works. Adad-narari I gains fame for expanding the kingdom of Assyria from the Xagros Mountains down the Diyalo River southwest to the Tigris. The purpose of the epic was propaganda: to show that the action against Babylonia was in accordance with the wishes of the gods. (Saggs 1990)

ADAM

In Jewish, Christian, and Muslim belief, Adam is the first man, created from dust by Yahweh. According to Jewish legend, God takes dust from the four corners of the earth—black, red, white, and yellow—and adds a spoonful of dust from the site of the atoning altar so that man can be forgiven and endure.

Adam, with his mate Eve, is placed in the Garden of Eden. Because of his disobedience in eating the forbidden fruit of the Tree of Knowledge of good and evil, he brings on sin and death for the human race. When he is banished from Paradise, he receives permission to take saffron, calamus, and cinnamon so he can bring offerings to God. He also takes out seeds for his sustenance. He decides to fast for 40 days, hoping God will forgive him, and he convinces Eve to stand in the water of the Tigris up to her neck in penance. But Satan, fearing God will forgive them, again disguises himself and convinces Eve to come out. (Genesis 1–4ff.; Ginzberg 1992)

See also Eve.

ADANGME, THE NATIONAL EPIC OF THE

Part of a larger "Klama epic" still being performed in coastal Ghana, West Africa. The Adangme are seven groups of Ghanaians speaking variants of the Adangme tongue, a dialect of Ga-Adangme of the Kwa subgroup of Niger-Congo languages. The epic recounts the migration of these seven clans in search of fertile lands from Lake Chad through Nigeria to their present locations along the Volta River and the coast of Ghana. (Westley *RAL* 1991)

ADAPA
(Man)

In Akkadian mythology, Adapa is the hero of the Sumerian city of Eridu. His tale is related in four fragmentary accounts found in the Tell el-Amarna archives and the library of Ashurbanipal. The story of Adapa resembles that of *Gilgamesh* in that each is denied immortality. Adapa receives superior intelligence from Ea, the god of wisdom, but he breaks the wings of the south wind, and the god Anu summons him to heaven to receive punishment. Ea warns him not to accept bread or water while he is in heaven. The two doorkeepers, Tammuz and Ningishzida, take pity on Adapa and convince Anu not to punish him. Instead, the god offers him the bread and water of eternal life. Because Ea has told him to partake of nothing, Adapa refuses. From thenceforth, mankind has been mortal. (Pritchard 1973)

ADICHAWO

In the *Watunna* of the Makiritare Indians of Venezuela, Adichawo is the daughter of Sahatuma. Sahatuma is killed by her husband Mominaru for lying to him. (Civrieux 1980)

See also Attawanadi; *Watunna.*

ADU OGYINAE

He is a legendary Ashanti leader of West Africa celebrated in oral tradition. Ashanti lore says that on a Monday the first ancestors follow a worm from a hole in the ground to the earth's surface. They are very frightened as they look around. Only their leader, Adu Ogyinae, is not afraid. On Tuesday, he lays his hands on them and soothes their fears. On Wednesday, as they begin to build their houses, Adu Ogyinae is killed by a falling tree. A dog goes out to look for food and brings the food back to the starving humans. They cook it and try it out on the dog first. When he does not die, they eat the food and are nourished. As they work, the God of creation, who is out walking, comes upon these people. He takes one of them to act as his helper and spokesman; the man's staff is treasured by his relatives for many generations. (Parrinder 1982)

AENEAS

This Trojan warrior is the hero of Virgil's *Aeneid,* in which Aeneas carries his father out of burning Troy and sets out on a journey that ends in Italy, where he founds the settlement that later becomes Rome. He is the son of the goddess Aphrodite and the Trojan Anchises and the cousin of Hektor. According to Homer, after the war he rules The Troad. (Fitzgerald 1990)

See also *Aeneid.*

AENEID

This epic poem was written ca. 29–19 B.C. from earlier legends by the Roman poet Virgil at the request of the emperor of Rome. It is primarily Virgil's literary creation, but it has a place in this collection because it is the link to the oral tradition that provides the Roman portion of the myth. According to legend, Aeneas, son of the goddess Aphrodite and the Trojan warrior Anchises, founded Lavinium, the forerunner of Alba Longa and Rome. Legend also says that Aeneas had a son, Ascanius (or Iulus), from whom Julius Caesar was said to have descended.

The poem is composed of 12 books. In book I, Aeneas, his family, and his men flee Troy after their defeat by the Greeks, but he loses his wife. Her ghost instructs them to travel west toward present-day Rome. During a storm they are shipwrecked near Carthage, where they are welcomed by Queen Dido, founder of the city. In book II, Aeneas tells her his story: of the Greeks' wooden horse and the fall of Troy, of his family's escape and the loss of his wife. Book III recounts the adventures of their voyage from Troy to Sicily to Carthage and of the death of his father in Sicily. In book IV the queen falls in love with Aeneas and he returns the feelings, but Mercury reminds him of his intended goal, so he determines to continue his trip. When he leaves, Dido commits suicide. In book V, Aeneas and his party reach Sicily, where they hold funeral games to honor Anchises. In book VI, Aeneas visits his father in the underworld. There, he envisions the future of Rome. His father tells him, "Roman, remember that you shall rule the nations by your authority, for this is to be your skill, to make peace the custom, to spare the conquered, and to wage war until the haughty are brought low." In book VII, Aeneas continues his journey. Latinus, the Italian king, welcomes him and decides to offer his daughter Lavinia to Aeneas as a wife. But Tumus, Lavinia's betrothed, and her mother resist the idea of the match. Tumus raises an army among his Rutuli (the tribe that he rules on the coast of Latinum) and prepares to drive Aeneas away. Book VIII recounts war preparations and Aeneas's visit to Latium. In book IX, while Aeneas is gone, Tumus attacks his ship and camp. Two of Aeneas's men, Nisus and Euryalus, attempt to spy on the Rutuli camp, but they are captured and slain. War breaks out in book X, and Aeneas slays Mezentius and his son Lausas. The war continues in book XI, and in book XII, a confrontation between Aeneas and Tumus results in Tumus's death. Aeneas marries Lavinia and they found Lavinium, forerunner of Alba Longa and Rome. (Fitzgerald 1990)

See also Aeneas; Aeolus; Ascanius; Dido; Virgil.

AEOLUS
(Also Aiolos)

In the *Odyssey* (x), Aeolus is the ruler of the winds and the island of Aeolia. Aeolus gives Odysseus favorable winds for his return voyage and a leather bag containing the unfavorable winds. He warns Odysseus not to open the bag. Believing that he is hiding a treasure from them, Odysseus's men open the bag while he sleeps and allow the winds to escape, driving the ship back to Aeolia. However, Aeolus refuses to help them a second time. Aeolus appears in the *Aeneid* (i) as well.

Aeolus is also the name of the grandson of Deucalion, the Greek Noah. (Graves 1955; Rouse 1937)

See also *Aeneid; Deucalion's Flood;* Odysseus; *Odyssey.*

AESIR

In Scandinavian mythology, in the *Poetic Edda* and the *Prose Edda,* Aesir is one of two tribes of gods. The other tribe is the Vanir, with whom the Aesir are in continuous battle. Among the most famous of the Aesir are the chief Odin and his wife Frigg. Among the many others are Thór, Týr, Baldr, and Loki. (Hollander *Edda* 1990; Jones, G. 1990; Young 1954)

See also Baldr; *Edda, Poetic; Edda, Prose;* Loki; Óthin; Thor; Týr.

AETHIOPIS

Aethiopis is one of the epics in the *Epic Cycle,* or *Cyclic Epics* (poems other than the *Iliad* and *Odyssey),* that cover the Trojan and Theban wars and other myths. The five books of the *Aethiopis* are the work of Arctinus of Miletus. See *The Cyclic Epics* for a description of contents. (Finnegan 1978)

See also *The Cyclic Epics; Iliad; Odyssey.*

AFRĀSIYĀB

In the *Shāh-Nāmah,* Afrāsiyāb is the pretender to the throne whom the hero Rostam drives away. He is the son of Pesheng, king of Turān, who, hearing of the death of King Manuchehr, becomes ambitious to occupy the throne of Iran. Pesheng summons his son Afrāsiyāb, commander of the army, and orders him to begin a campaign against Iran. Although Rostam drives him away, Afrāsiyāb does not give up. Many years later, when Rostam's son Sohrāb goes off to find his father, it is Afrāsiyāb who instructs his chieftains to keep Rostam and his son apart, and to keep each from learning the identity of the other. The result is that Rostam kills his own son in battle. (Levy 1967)

See also *Shāh-Nāmah.*

AGAMEMNON

In the *Iliad,* Agamemnon is the leader of the Greek forces against Troy. He is the legendary king of Mycenae or Argos, possibly a historical figure. In the *Iliad,* he is the brother of Menelaus, whose wife Helen is carried off by Paris (Alexandrus), the son of Troy's king Priam. Agamemnon marshals forces from several principalities and is chosen commander-in-chief. But because he has previously killed a sacred stag and offended the goddess of hunting, Artemis, she manipulates the winds and prevents his ships from sailing. Agamemnon is forced to sacrifice his own daughter, Iphigeneia. He is forced to return his war prize, Chryseis, to her father, Chryses, a priest of Apollo; in her place, he takes Achilles's prize, Briseis. This causes Achilles to withdraw from the war in a fit of pique, a decision that not only prolongs the war, but almost costs the Achaeans' victory. Later, Agamemnon makes amends, offering to return Briseis, and Achilles rejoins the war to avenge the death of his friend Patroklos. After the surrender of Troy, Agamemnon receives Priam's daughter Cassandra as his war booty. When he returns home, he is murdered by his wife Clytemnestra's lover, Aegisthus. (Lattimore 1951)

AGASTYA

(Also Kumbhayoni)

Agastya is a legendary "wise old man" of the epic era (ca. 3000 B.C.) in Sanskrit and Tamil literature of South India. A dwarf, he is said to have been born in a jar. One of his pupils is Rāma, to whom Agastya presents Viṣṇu's invincible bow and his never-empty quiver of arrows. (Dimmitt and van Buitenen 1978)

See also Rāma; Viṣṇu.

AGDISTIS

Androgynous or hermaphroditic god of Asia Minor, he is the father, by Nana, of Attis; as the consort of Attis, he is worshiped as Great Mother of the Gods.

When Attis is about to be married, the jealous Agdistis causes a frenzy to overcome him, during which he castrates himself and dies. (Leeming 1990)

See also Attis.

AGENOR

In the *Iliad,* Agenor is a Trojan warrior who battles Achilles. The god Apollo takes Agenor's form to confuse Achilles, allowing time for the Trojans to withdraw.

Agenor is also the name of Poseidon's son and the father of Europa, Phoenix, Cilix, and Cadmus. When Zeus captures Europa, Agenor send his sons to the corners of the earth in search of her, and each son settles in a different area. (Graves 1955; Lattimore 1951)

See also Achilles; *Iliad;* Poseidon; Zeus.

AGGA OF KISH

In the Sumerian epic poem "Gilgamesh and the Agga of Kish," of which 115 lines are extant, Agga is the last ruler of the first dynasty of Kish, which is in conflict with the city-state of Erech to the south, of which Gilgamesh is the ruler. Agga sends envoys to Erech demanding that its inhabitants submit to Kish. When the Erechites resist, Agga besieges Erech, but Gilgamesh apparently finds some method to appease him so that the siege is lifted without a fight. (Kramer 1956)

See also Gilgamesh, Sumerian Poems.

AGNI

In Sanskrit literature, Agni is the Hindu god of fire, hearth, lightning, and sun, second in importance in the *Rāmāyaṇa* only to Indra. In the *Ṛg Veda,* he is occasionally identified with Śiva's forerunner, the storm god Rudra. He is described as having two faces, one good, one evil, with several tongues; seven arms and three legs; and hair that streams up like a comet's tail. Among his many forms are the brothers Vaísvānara (the digestive fire within man), Gṛhapati (household fire), Yaviṣṭha (fresh fire, ignited from wood), Pāvaka (purifying fire, such as lightning), and Sahaḥsuta and Saucīka (strength and sharpness). Like a bird, Agni carries fire or the elixir of immortality from heaven to earth, fleeing the gods who would harness him for the role of Hotṛ (hotar), or priest, who recites the *Ṛg Veda* at a sacrifice.

In the *Bṛhaddevatā,* he hides in the waters, dispersing himself into various plants and waters, and seeks the immortality of a full life span. He finally becomes benevolent and performs the office of Hotṛ tirelessly. In the *Tattirīya Saṃhitā,* he has three brothers who perish while carrying the oblation to the gods. Fearing that he too may perish, Agni disappears into the waters. The gods try to find him, and a fish reports his whereabouts. Agni curses the fish, "Since you reported me, they will slay you whenever they fancy." In the *Mahābhārata,*

Agni hides because he is afraid to carry the seed of Śiva, which is a multiform of the oblation to the gods. The fish who betrayed him in the *Tattirīya Saṃhitā* is replaced by a frog, an elephant, and a parrot, all of whom reveal his location to the gods. In the *Mahābhārata* Agni curses the frog, "You will have no tongue, nor will you know the sensation of taste." He curses the elephants, "Your tongues will be bent backwards." He curses the parrot, "You will be deprived of speech." The gods partially reverse these curses. To the frog they promise, "Although you have been made tongueless by the curse of Agni, and deprived of the knowledge of taste, you will utter many kinds of speech. Though you dwell in holes, without food, without consciousness . . . the earth will support you, and you will move about even at night when all is in darkness." To the elephant, they promise, "Although your tongue will be bent backwards, with it you will eat all foods and you will utter loud sounds with indistinct syllables." To the parrot they say, "You will have speech confined to 'ka,' sweet, indistinct, and wonderful, like the speech of a child or an old man." Agni is seduced by Svāhā, who takes the form of the wives of the Seven Sages, and Skanda, the six-headed son of Śiva, is begotten. (Buck 1976; Buck 1981; O'Flaherty 1975; O'Flaherty 1981)

See also *Mahābhārata; Rāmāyaṇa; Ṛg Veda;* Rudra; Śiva; Skanda.

AH KIN
(He of the Sun)

In the *Popol Vuh* of the Maya, Ah kin are the priests of the Mayan god. The Ah kin offered human heart sacrifices and served as diviners. (Recinos, Goetz, and Morley 1983)

See also *Popol Vuh.*

AH PUCH

In the *Popol Vuh* of the Maya, Ah Puch is the god of death. (Recinos, Goetz, and Morley 1983)

See also *Popol Vuh.*

AH TOLTECAT
(Toltec Lord)

In the Mayan *Popol Vuh,* Ah Toltecat is a Toltec deity. (Recinos, Goetz, and Morley 1983)

See also *Popol Vuh.*

AHĀDĪTH AL-BAṬṬĀL

These North African Arabic folk stories of al-Baṭṭāl from the epic *Sīrat al-Amīra Dhāt al-Himma* were told prior to the twelfth century. The epic tells of North African Arab conflicts with Christians (Byzantines). The hero is a warrior woman, Dhāt al-Himma, whose name means both "woman of noble purpose" and "wolf." She is the Amazon leader of the tribe, daughter of a female jinn. She gives birth to a black son who joins her as one of a trio of heroes defending Islam against the Christians. The epic spans three centuries of Islam and depicts encounters with the Franks and Berbers as well as the Byzantines. (Connelly 1986)

See also *Sīrat al-Amīra Dhāt al-Himma.*

AHIKAR, THE STORY OF
(Also "Ahiqar")

This Babylonian or Persian tale was written as a memoir about Ahikar, a wise and respected man who serves as counselor to King Sennacherib of Assyria (704–681 B.C.). According to the Jewish book of Tobit, Ahikar is Tobit's nephew and the cupbearer of Esarhaddon. As an old man, Ahikar, who has served Sennacherib, trains his nephew Nadin to take his place and serve Sennacherib's successor Esarhaddon. But the jealous Nadin fills the new king's ears with lies about Ahikar's loyalty, and the new king sends another chief, Nabu-sumiskun, to kill Ahikar. When Ahikar reminds him of a similar situation that occurred during Sennacherib's reign, Nabu is persuaded to kill a eunuch slave in Ahikar's place. Ahikar is sure that someday Esarhaddon will remember Ahikar's wisdom, desire his counsel, and tell his advisors, "I will give you riches as the number of the sands if you will find Ahikar." A fragmentary papyrus version of the story in Aramaic dating ca. 450–410 B.C. was discovered in Egypt. The story resembles that of Job in the Old Testament. Ahikar is a righteous man whose power-hungry son betrays him. He is ridiculed, imprisoned, tortured, even condemned to death before his good name is cleared and he is restored to his former eminence in the king's court. The work is classified as pseudepigraphical. Its widespread translation into Syrian, Ethiopian, Greek, Turkic, Armenian, and Arabic languages suggests the universality of the tale.

Wise sayings attributed to Ahikar include: "Withhold not thy son from beating, if thou canst not keep him from wickedness" and "A blow for a slave, rebuke for a maid, and for all thy slaves discipline." (Olmstead 1948)

AHISHAMA

In the *Watunna* of the Makiritare Indians of Venezuela, Ahishama is the Troupial, who is the first of the Star People to reach Heaven, where he is transformed into the planet Mars. (Civrieux 1980)

See also *Watunna.*

AHURA MAZDA
(Also Auramazda, Wise Lord)

In the *Avesta,* Ahura Mazda is the supreme god of Zoroastrianism. He creates the opposing spirits of Spenta Mainyu (beneficent; favoring light, life, and truth) and Angra Mainyu (malevolent; favoring darkness, death, and falsehood). Persian king Darius I and his successors worshiped Ahura Mazda under the name of Auramazda. (Olmstead 1948; Sproul 1991)

See also Angra Mainyu; Spenta Mainyu.

AIWEL LONGAR

Aiwel is a legendary hero of a Dinka people of the Upper Nile. Like so many heroes, Aiwel is a precocious infant: He is born with a full set of teeth. No ordinary man can claim fatherhood; Aiwel is a gift to his widowed mother from the river spirit. While he is still a baby, more than once he steals and drinks a full gourd of milk. When his mother discovers this, Aiwel warns her not to tell anyone, or she will die. But she cannot keep the secret, and she dies as he has predicted. Aiwel then lives with his spirit-father in the river until he is grown. When he returns to his mother's village as a man, he has with him an ox of many colors, representing great wealth. The ox is called Longar, and from then on the villagers call the man Aiwel Longar.

He tends the cattle that had belonged to his mother's late husband. A drought forces other villagers to move their cattle, but Aiwel's cattle remain fat and strong. The young men of the village spy on him to find out where he feeds and waters his stock. They follow him to his feeding ground, but Aiwel knows they are spying on him. When they reveal his secrets to others in the village, they all mysteriously die.

The drought grows worse. Aiwel Longar tells the elders to leave the parched land and follow him to a promised land where there is plenty of water and no death. The elders refuse to believe him and set off on their own in a different direction. Aiwel goes by himself, but after a few days some of the people attempt to follow him after all.

As they begin to ford a certain river, Aiwel waits on the opposite bank and kills them one by one with his fishing spear. One of the men, Agothyathik, thinks of a trick to fool Aiwel. He gives a friend a large ox bone to hold out on a pole in front of him as he goes through the reeds on the riverbank. Aiwel, thinking it is a human head, prepares to spear it. Meanwhile, Agothyathik sneaks up behind Aiwel and wrestles him to the ground.

The two men fight until Aiwel is exhausted. He tells Agothyathik to call the people across; they may come in safety. Some are still afraid, but to those who dare to come, Aiwel gives spears, divinities to worship, and a sky-colored bull whose thigh bone will later become sacred to them. The men who receive these gifts found the clans that are now called Spear-Masters. Aiwel leaves them to rule the country, promising that he will not interfere except in time of trouble. (Parrinder 1982)

AJAX
(Also Aias)

In the *Iliad* (i) and the *Odyssey* (xi), Ajax the Greater is a Greek warrior of colossal stature, second only to Achilles in courage and strength. He engages the Trojan warrior Hektor in combat and rescues the body of Achilles from the Trojans with the goddess Athena's help. He vies with Odysseus for Achilles's armor; when he loses, he dies of rage. A later version has him driving Hektor's sword through himself. From his blood springs a red flower that bears his initials in its leaves.

Ajax (Aias) the Lesser, or Locrian Aias, is the diminutive and arrogant son of King Oileus of Locris, who appears in the *Iliad* (ii and xxiii) and the *Aeneid* (i), and whose fate is told by Proteus to Menelaus in the *Odyssey* (iv). He ravages Trojan king Priam's daughter Cassandra after dragging her from Athena's statue. For his crime, his Greek allies try to stone him to death, but he escapes and sails for home. On the way, his ship is wrecked, but he is saved. Later, he boasts of his escape, and Poseidon casts him into the sea and drowns him. (Humphries 1951; Lattimore 1976; Rouse 1937)

See also *Aeneid; Iliad;* Menelaus; *Odyssey;* Teucer.

AKATO

In the *Watunna* of the Makiritare Indians of Venezuela, akato is the body's companion spirit or double, which descends from heaven to occupy the body at birth. At death, the akato returns to heaven. A principal cause of death is loss of the akato, which enjoys venturing forth at night and thus risks being captured by Odosha, the master of evil. (Civrieux 1980)

See also *Watunna.*

AKKAD, THE FALL OF

An epic from the time of Naramsin. ***See*** *The Fall of Akkad.*

ALANAUS

In the *Odyssey,* Alanaus, king of Phaeacians and grandson of Poseidon, entertains Odysseus when he is shipwrecked on the shore of Scheria Island. In the legend of the Argonauts, Alanaus lives on the island of Drepani, where he entertains Jason and Medea after their escape from Colchis. (Graves 1955; Rouse 1937)

See also Argonauts; Jason; *Odyssey.*

ALBERICH

In the *Völsunga Saga* and in the *Nibelungenlied,* Alberich is a dwarf who guards the treasure of the Nibelungs, who own a magic ring. In Wagner's opera *Der Ring des Nibelungen,* after Loki and Wotan steal the ring, Alberich puts a curse upon it that remains with it wherever it goes. (Hatto 1969)

See also Loki; *Nibelungenlied; Völsunga Saga;* Wotan.

ALCMENE

(Also Alcmaeon)

In the *Odyssey* (xi) and the mythology of Herakles, Alcmene is the daughter of Electryon, king of Mycenae. When Amphitryon, son of King Alcaeus of Tiryns, accidentally kills his uncle Electryon, he flees, taking Alcmene with him. She refuses to marry him until he avenges the deaths of her brothers, all but one of whom died battling the Taphians. Amphitryon defeats the Taphians with the help of the king's daughter, Comaetho, who cuts off her father's hair, which has kept him immortal. Alcmene marries Amphitryon, but while he is again gone to war, she becomes pregnant by Zeus, who has disguised himself as her husband. Later, she also becomes pregnant by her husband when he returns. Twin sons are born of these unions: Herakles, the son of Zeus, and Iphicles, the son of Amphitryon. (Graves 1955; Rouse 1937)

See also Amphitryon; Herakles; *Odyssey;* Zeus.

ALFONSO VI OF CASTILE AND LEON

(Also El Bravo)

In the *Poema del Cid,* Alfonso is the early adversary of the Spanish national hero El Cid, Rodrigo Díaz de Vivar (Bivar). Later the two are reconciled, and El Cid conducts raiding campaigns into eastern Spain against the Moors. (Merwin 1962)

See also *Cid, Poema del;* Rodrigo, Don.

ĀLHĀ EPIC

This epic cycle is sung throughout the Hindi-speaking area of northern India, where it is almost as widely known as the *Mahābhārata* and the *Rāmāyaṇa.* The setting is the late twelfth century A.D. on the edge of the Turkish conquest of the Chandel Kingdom, centered in the city of Mahoba.

As Kariyā, son of King Jambay of Mando, is leaving for a bathing festival on the Ganges, his sister asks him to bring her a souvenir. When he arrives at the festival, he looks in vain for a souvenir—a necklace that costs nine-lakh (900,000 rupees). Then he meets Māhil, son of the ousted king, who tells him that his sister Malhanā has a necklace such as he desires. Malhanā is the wife of the new king Parmāl, who took her as a prize when he overthrew her father, the Parihār king.

Kariyā arrives in Mahoba, finds Malhanā, and demands the necklace from her. When she refuses to give it to him, he gathers his private army and attacks the palace. But some visitors from Baksar and Benares join with the palace guard to defeat him. They are four brothers of the Banāphar clan of Baksar Rajputs and the Muslim Tālā Sayyid from Benares. He is so impressed by the brothers that he hires them to be a part of his private army.

Later, still stung by his defeat at the hands of the brothers, he decides to kill two of them in their sleep. He hangs their heads over the city gate, but apparently the men's families do not know who is responsible for their deaths. One day, the sons and brothers of the slain men are out hunting when the goddess Śāradā, disguised as a deer, leads one of the boys, Ūdal, into the garden of Māhil, son of the ousted king. There, after a scuffle with the gardener, Ūdal is ridiculed by Māhil for swaggering about like a great warrior when his own father's death has not been avenged. Ūdal demands to know the truth about his father's death.

When he learns that Kariyā is responsible, he, his brothers and their kinsmen, and the other brothers from Benares form an army. They march against Kariyā and kill both him and his brother. Then Ālhā, Ūdal's brother, with Śāradā's help, kills Kariyā's father, King Jambay.

The Banāphars and the other heroes all marry, winning princess brides in contests set by the princesses' king-fathers. Meanwhile, Māhil, who still wants his Mahoba kingdom back, plots with the warrior Prithvīrāj to march on Mahoba and present Queen Malhanā with an ultimatum. However, Malhanā learns of the plot and sends her nephew for help, so that when the army arrives from Kanauj, she is able to fend off a direct attack.

Later, when Prithvīrāj's daughter Belā is threatening sati (burning to death on a funeral pyre) after the murder of her husband Brahmā by Chaunṛā, Prithvīrāj rushes to Delhi to try to prevent it. A terrible battle with the people from Mahoba ensues, during which Belā lets down her hair. It bursts spontaneously into flame, lighting her pyre. When the battle is over, all the men of Mahoba are dead. Only Ālhā survives, having been granted immortality by the goddess Śāradā.

When news of the disaster reaches Mahoba, all the wives rush to the battlefield to look for their husbands. Sunwā, Ālhā's wife, meets their son Indal and asks, "Where is Ālhā?" thus committing the unforgivable sin for a Rajput wife of mentioning her husband to her son by name, thus destroying his Rajput honor. Ālhā is forced to reject her for this sin.

All the widows throw themselves on Belā's funeral pyre. In Mahoba, Malhanā, realizing the defeat is permanent and the city's glory is over, throws the Philosopher's Stone, the city's greatest treasure, into the lake. King Parmāl starves himself to death, and Malhanā becomes a sati. Since then, no king has ever ruled Mahoba. (Blackburn et al. 1989)

ALI

A ninth-century African Islamic hero of the Battle of Haiwara, Ali is the subject of the *Kayarwar Epic* of the present-day Borno State in northeastern Nigeria. However, the Kanuri did not become Muslims until the eleventh century. (Westley *RAL* 1991)

See also *Kayarwar Epic.*

ALIM EPIC

This epic of the Ifugao people of the Philippines, rice farmers on mountain terraces, describes life among the gods. It is part of a larger Ifugao cycle, the *Hudhud,* which includes the story of creation. The entire cycle takes two days to recite. (Dixon 1964; Preminger 1990)

See also *Hudhud.*

THE ALPHABET OF BEN SIRA

This is a collection of Jewish folklore and proverbs ca. the eleventh century, purported to be compiled by the sage who wrote the apocryphal book Ecclesiasticus, or Wisdom of Jesus the Son of Sirach. The author is a child prodigy who performs miraculous deeds. The work exists in two versions, one of which illustrates the proverbs with tales. (Charles 1913)

AMA-TERASU NO OHO-KAMI

In the ancient Japanese *Nihongi* chronicles, Ama-terasu is the goddess of the sun from whom the Japanese imperial family descends. The first story concerning her follows the description of how the creative deities Izanagi no Mikoto and Izanami no Mikoto bring the land, sea, rivers, mountains, trees, and herbs into being. The deities consult, saying, "We have now produced the Great-eight-island country, with the mountains, rivers, herbs, and trees. Why should we not produce someone who shall be lord of the universe [empire]?" Together they produce the sun goddess, who is called Oho-hiru-me no muchi, meaning Great-noon-female-of-possessor. She is also called Ama-terasu no Oho-kami, meaning Heaven-illumine-of-great deity. She is born of the left eye of Izanagi, her father. She and her brother, the fourth creation—the storm god Sosa no wo Mikoto (or Susa no wo, Impetuous Male)—mate and produce offspring by chewing a sword and jewels, spewing the pieces out in the form of children. But Sosa no wo has a fierce temper and is given to cruel acts. When his conduct becomes unbearable, Ama-terasu retreats into the Rock-cave of Heaven, bringing darkness upon the earth.

The other gods send Ama no Koyane no Mikoto to recite a liturgy. He uproots a true Sakaki tree and hangs upon its branches a mirror with eight hands, curved jewels, and mulberry paper. Then he begins his recitation, which is so beautiful that Ama-terasu says, "Though of late many prayers have been addressed to me, of none has the language been so beautiful as this." She opens the Rock-door and peeks out, whereupon the whole universe is filled with her light. (Aston 1972)

See also Izanagi and Izanami; *Nihongi.*

AMADÍS OF GAUL

(Also *Amadís de Gaula, El Doncel del Mar,* or *Child of the Sea)*

The first extant version of this prose romance of chivalry is written in Spanish, dated 1508, and incorporates Celtic Breton lays of the Arthurian cycle. Its origin, although obscure, is thought to be ca. late-thirteenth-century Portuguese. The extant Spanish version, compiled and "corrected and emended" in four books by Garci Gutierrez Rodriguez (Ordóñez) de Montalvo, depicts the hero Amadís as the illegitimate son of King Perion of Gaul (Wales). His mother, Princess Elisina of Brittany, abandons him, placing his crib in the sea. He is rescued by a chivalrous knight, Gandales, who takes him to the Scottish court, where he grows to be handsome and courageous. At the age of 12, he falls in love with the English king Lisuarte's daughter Oriana, who inspires him to perform great deeds. With his brother Galaor and his cousin Agrates, he battles villains, giants, la Desconocida (the Unknown), and the malevolent trickster Archelaus to win the princess's favor. (Ker 1957)

AMBA

In the *Mahābhārata* of ancient India, Amba is a princess who is rejected by Bhīṣma, the most perfect man. She vows to hound him for the rest of his life. Even after she kills herself, her ghost returns to Bhīṣma in a dream to inform him that she has been reborn as a man, Sikhandin. When the Pāṇḍavas convince Bhīṣma that unless he sacrifices himself in battle the war will continue indefinitely, he instructs them to "put Sikhandin in front of the line and tell him to strike me." But when Amba at last has the opportunity to kill him, she no longer remembers the reason for her hatred. Instead, Arjuna's arrow kills him. (Buck 1981)

See also Arjuna; Bhīṣma; *Mahābhārata;* Pāṇḍavas.

AMBIKĀ

(Little Mother)

In the Hindu *Vedas,* Ambikā is the supreme goddess Śakti. She is first described as the sister of Rudra ("the ruddy one"), the antecedent of Śiva. Later she is depicted as his wife. In the *Brahmāṇḍa Purāṇa,* Ambikā is a euphemistic epithet of Kālī ("the black goddess"). Agni, god of fire and the sun, says, "All this universe, moving and still, has Agni and Soma (ambrosia) for its soul. I am Agni of great energy, and this woman, my wife Ambikā, is Soma." (Dimmitt and van Buitenen 1978; O'Flaherty 1981)

See also Agni; *Ṛg Veda;* Rudra; Śiva.

AME-NO-UZUME NO MIKOTO
(Also Uzume no Mikoto)

In the *Nihongi* chronicles of ancient Japan, Amë-nö-uzume no Mikoto is the Japanese celestial goddess of great beauty who stands before the door of the Rock-cave of Heaven and performs a mimic dance to entice Ama-terasu to come out. Her dance is said to be the origin of the Kagura or pantomime dance now performed at Shinto festivals. Later, when the August Grandchild of Ama-terasu is to be sent to Earth to govern, Amë-nö-uzume is sent to confront the god who dwells at the eight crossroads past which the August Grandchild must pass. She bares her breast, pushes her garment down past her navel, and asks him, "Who art thou that dost thus remain in the road by which the child of Ama-terasu no Oho-kami is to make his progress?" The god, who introduces himself as Saruta-hiko, says he will go one way, if Amë-nö-uzume will accompany him, while the August Grandchild goes another. In gratitude for her service, the August Grandchild confers upon her the title of Sarume no Kimi. (Aston 1972)

See also Ama-terasu no Oho-kami; *Nihongi.*

AMINATA

In the *Epic of Bakaridjan Kone,* Aminata is the woman with whom Bakaridjan and two rival warriors become enamored. (Courlander 1982)

See also *Bakaridjan Kone, a Hero of Segu, Epic of.*

AMIS ET AMILES

This twelfth-century chanson de geste (heroic epic) is based on a much older legend, probably Oriental in origin, that was incorporated into the Charlemagne legends through Byzantium. It relates the friendship of two knights, Amis and Amiles. In an attempt to save his friend's reputation, Amis takes on a deception that is punished by the plague of leprosy. In a vision he learns that his leprosy can only be cured by the blood of Amiles's children. When his friend learns of this, he sacrifices his own children. However, they are resurrected when the treatment is completed. (Ker 1957)

See also Chansons de geste.

AMON
(Also Amen-Ra)

Egyptian deity who became king of the gods and patron of the pharaohs (ca. 1990 B.C.). (Budge 1969; Ceram 1990; Olmstead 1948)

See also *Battle of Qadesh;* Horus; Isis; Osiris.

AMOOGU BI

This oral heroic tale from the Igbo community of Ohafia people in Imo State, Nigeria, tells of a little-known warrior whose powers of endurance enable the Ohafia people to overcome their great adversary, the short-armed dwarf of Aliike named 'Miiko (Omiiko).

The dwarf repeatedly routs the people and packs their chopped-up parts in long-baskets. The war chiefs summon Okoro Mkpi, the medicine man of Ezhi Abaaba, who advises them to get into a nest of soldier ants. "Who among you can sit in the nest of soldier-ants and charge the guns, so the short-armed dwarf of 'Liike can be killed?"

Akwa, Iro, Awa, Mbu, Igbun, Mkpawe, Oke, Kamalu, Nkuma, Nkata—all warriors of renown—go into the ant beds and attempt to charge the guns, but when the ants begin to sting, each man "trembles off" and fails. Defeated, they all say, "Let us go home." But the little-known Amoogu asks to be given the guns, saying, "We should all go home if I try and fail! / Ohafia warriors, give me the guns!"

The others ask, "Of what patriclan are you?" When he tells them that he is a native of Amuma, they agree, "Let the guns be given to him."

Amoogu takes two guns and enters the nest, and although he is stung "in four hundreds," he is able to charge the guns. The warriors take the guns from him, kill the dwarf, and massacre the dwarf's Ishiagu people. But after the massacre, they begin to conspire against Amoogu, saying, "If we do not kill him, he shall become the leading hero of Ohagia!"

They lure him to a solitary corner to kill him, then bring his severed head home on a stake. His mother, great mother Ori Ukpo, weeps inconsolably. Now there is no one to protect her or her poultry. She dwells beside a silk-cotton tree. Kites and hawks from the tree prey on her chickens. Ori Ukpo cries, "O, if my son were alive, / He would have shot these kites away."

Amoogu's age-mates summon all the men of Amuma, give them two cases of palm wine, and tell them, "We plead with you, let this silk-cotton tree be felled, / That the chickens of my great mother Ori Ukpo may thrive. / That man we killed is the cause of her great grief."

The men agree to cut down the tree. For three days they drink wine and hack at the tree. On the third day, the tree begins to fall, and the drunken men, "shaken by the wine," try to catch the tree with their hands. Four hundred men are crushed to death. The tribal great mother Aja Ekeke divines, "Whatever it was that made you people agree to kill Amoogu, / It was the spirit of Amoogu that pushed that silk-cotton tree to crush you people!"

And that is why Amumu is still so thinly populated to this day: "It is the wrath of the spirit of Amoogu. . . ." (Azuonye *RAL* 1990)

AMPHION AND ZETHUS

In the *Odyssey*, Amphion and Zethus are the twin sons of Zeus and Antiope, daughter of Asopos. According to myth, they are abandoned on Mount

Cithaeron but are found and reared by a shepherd. Amphion becomes a musician and Zethus a hunter. According to Odysseus (xi), "These first established the foundations of seven-gated / Thebes, and built the bulwarks, since without bulwarks they could not / have lived, for all their strength, in Thebes of the wide spaces." (Rouse 1937)

See also Odysseus; *Odyssey.*

AMPHITEA

In the *Odyssey* (xix), Amphitea is the wife of Autolycus and mother of Anticlea, Laertes's wife. (Rouse 1937)

AMPHITRYON

In the *Aeneid* (viii), Amphitryon is the husband of Alcmene and the mother, by Zeus, of Herakles. In the *Odyssey,* Odysseus says, "I saw Amphitryon's wife Alkmene [Alcemene], / who, after lying in love in the embraces of great Zeus, / brought forth Herakles, lion-hearted and bold of purpose." (Humphries 1951; Rouse 1937)

See also *Aeneid;* Alcmene.

AN
(Also Anu, Sky)

An is the Sumero-Akkadian god of the sky, father of all gods, worshiped in Erech and found in the *Epic of Gilgamesh* and in *Enuma Elish.*

An is also a name for the Egyptian king of the gods, Amen-Ra, found in *The Egyptian Book of the Dead.* (Budge 1967; Sandars 1972; Sproul 1991)

See also *Enuma Elish, Epic of; Gilgamesh, Epic of;* Ishtar; Marduk; Tiamat.

AN-GIM DIM-MA

In this ancient Sumerian myth, Ninurta, god of thunderstorms, returns from battle with Enki to Nippur and is met by Nusku, Enlil's page, who orders him to calm himself before entering the presence of Enlil and the other gods so as not to frighten them. Ninurta makes long speeches boasting of his accomplishments, but Nusku perseveres and convinces him to enter Nippur peacefully. (Pritchard 1973)

ANATH
(Also Anat)

Although she plays a role in other legends, Anath is known first as the chief goddess in the Ugaritic epic cycle of Baal and Anath. She is the Canaanite (Ascalon, Palestine) goddess of love and war, the virgin sister of the storm god

Baal. Her role in the *Baal Epic* is that of avenger and savior of Baal. When the death god Mot devours Baal, Anath buries her brother, then searches out Mot and cuts him to pieces. It is only then that Baal is restored to life, and honey and oil flow in the land. Because of her brave and ferocious nature, Egyptian king Ramses II (reigned ca. 1304–1237 B.C.) designated her as his favorite. The *Aqhat Epic*, in which the sister is named Paqhat, bears many similarities to the *Baal Epic*.

Later, during the Hellenistic period, Anath and the Sidon Phoenician goddess Astarte (Ishtar) were merged into the Syrian fertility goddess Atargatis, whom the Greek queen Stratonice revived ca. 300 B.C. (Pritchard 1973)

See also *Aqhat Epic; Baal Epic;* Paqhat.

ANCAEUS

In the Argonautic legend, Ancaeus becomes the helmsman of the *Argo* after the death of Tiphys. Ancaeus is the king of the Leleges of Samos. A famous saying is attributed to an incident involving Ancaeus and a prophet who foretells that he will never drink wine from the vineyard that he is planting. At the first harvest, as Ancaeus prepares to taste the juice and prove the prophet wrong, the prophet says, "There is many a slip between the cup and the lip," at which time men rush up with the news that a wild boar is on the rampage. Alcaeus puts down his drink and rushes off to confront the boar, which kills him. (Morford and Lenardon 1977)

See also *Argonautica;* Argonauts; Jason.

ANDROMACHE

In the *Iliad* (vi), Andromache is the wife of the Trojan prince Hektor (son of King Priam), who is slain by Achilles. At the fall of Troy, Andromache becomes the war prize of Achilles's son Neoptolemus (Pyrrhus), according to Euripides's play named for her. She also appears in the *Aeneid* (iii). (Lattimore 1976)

See also Hektor; *Iliad.*

ANEIRIN

Aneirin is a sixth-century Welsh poet, whose (attributed) "The Gododdin" is one of the earliest surviving Welsh poems. His works have been preserved in a thirteenth-century volume entitled *The Book of Aneirin* (ca. 1250). The poem is written in praise of the 300 doomed heroes of the sixth-century Scottish army of Mynyddawg the Wealthy (Mynyddawg Mwynfawr) of Caereidyn, who are sent to Yorkshire to recapture the old Roman fort of Catraeth (Catterick) from the invading Saxons of Deira. (Chadwick 1976; Jackson, K. 1971)

See also "The Gododdin."

ANGRA MAINYU
(Also Ahriman)

In the Yashts of *Avesta,* Angra Mainyu is the chief of all demons and antagonist of the Wise Lord Ahura Mazda. (Olmstead 1948)

See also Ahura Mazda; Spenta Mainyu.

ANIUS

In Greek mythology, Anius is the son of Apollo and Rhoeo. When Rhoeo's father Dionysus learns that she is pregnant, she is put in a chest and cast into the sea. She floats to the island of Delos, where Anius is born. He grows up to be a priest of Apollo. His daughters Oeno, Spermo, and Elais (wine, grain, oil) are responsible, by the grace of Dionysus, for establishing these three crops such that they are supplied to Agamemnon's forces on their expedition to Troy in the *Iliad,* and to Aeneas's party on his escape to Italy in the *Aeneid.* (Graves 1955)

See also Abandonment; Apollo; Dionysus.

ANNALS OF THE CAKCHIQUELS

This narrative of the Cakchiquel Indians of Central America is meant to establish territorial rights of the members of Xahila. It begins with "the sayings of our earliest fathers and ancestors, Gagavitz . . . and Zactecauh . . . as we came from the other side of the sea, from the land of Tulan. . . ." The two ancestors bring the Obsidian Stone (Chay Abah), made when men were first created, and place it on the summit of a hill overlooking Iximche, the capital city. The Obsidian Stone becomes an oracular talisman.

The narrative continues with episodes that may be historical. Zactecauh is killed when he falls down a ravine. A being named Tolgom, "son of the Mud that Quivers," is captured. Galgavitz has two sons, Caynoh and Caybatz, who succeed him upon his death. These two go to war against a Quiche king, Tepeuh, and gain independence. (Alexander, H. 1964)

AṆṆAṈMĀR

This Indian martial folk epic of the Kongu area of Tamil Nadu has been sung since the fifteenth century. It is performed by professional bards at various festivals year-round, and parts of it are routinely chanted in the evenings around village courtyards. Some versions can take up to 18 nights to perform. It has oral versions and versions written on palm leaves, in chapbooks, and in full-length scholarly texts.

The story begins after a fifteenth-century famine when the grandfather of a family must leave home to seek work. A Chola king takes him in and assigns him agricultural duties, which he performs so well that he and his eight younger brothers are given land. However, the eight brothers are envious and threaten the holdings of their older brother, because his eldest son is childless. But Viṣṇu and Śiva intervene to produce a child, whom they hide under a pile of rock where the eldest son can find him and adopt him. However, when the child reaches age five his parents die, and the eight evil uncles force him off the land. The boy fends for himself in the wilderness, managing to survive with the help of Viṣṇu and his own magical powers.

Finally he reaches manhood and marries a girl named Tāmarai. He and his wife return to reclaim his ancestral lands. The children of his evil uncles are now in control of the lands, and they are eager to undermine his attempts to reestablish his home. Nevertheless, he works hard, prospers, and rebuilds the family palace. He invites the king to the ceremonies reinstating him as the family landowner.

After 21 years of penance to pay for her father's sins, Tāmarai finally becomes pregnant. The jealous cousins hire an evil midwife and instruct her to blindfold Tāmarai and kill any male child that is born. But Viṣṇu intervenes again and causes a magical birth in which twin boy-warriors, Poṉṉar and Caṅkar, step out and are quickly spirited away through a tunnel before the midwife can see. They are raised by the goddess Cellāttā and fed on tiger's milk. Only a girl baby, Taṅkāl, is born naturally. Since it appears that there is no male heir, the jealous cousins grab the family lands and force the parents into exile.

When the twins are five years old, they rejoin their parents, living in exile, and lead them back to their homeland. The parents die in their own palace soon afterward. This precipitates the first of several epic wars, lasting many years. The twins eventually kill their evil cousins and even the Chola overlord so that they can rule in their own right.

But the twins become involved in an altercation with some forest hunters, who turn a wild boar loose upon their lands. The twins organize a boar hunt and are eventually drawn into a war with the hunters. Although the boys are not killed, thousands of their followers are slain, and the boys feel very bad about going home to face their survivors. Viṣṇu reminds them that their predetermined span of 16 years is over, so the twins decide to fall upon their own swords. Their loyal minister does the same.

The sister learns of their deaths in a dream and goes to the forest to look for them. She revives them long enough for the three to exchange final words. Then she dies and the three are carried to heaven by Śiva's divine executioner.

Temples are built on the spot where the deaths are thought to have occurred, and annual rituals are held at the sites, where the epic is retold. (Blackburn et al. 1989)

ANTAEUS

In Greek mythology, and in the *Aeneid* (x), Antaeus is a friend of Turnus whom Aeneas kills. In the Herakles legend, Antaeus is a Libyan giant, son of Ge

(Earth) and Poseidon (Sea). Antaeus maintains his strength by remaining in contact with Earth, his mother. He challenges all strangers passing through Libya to wrestle with him, and he always wins. However, Herakles, who is required to fight Antaeus, discovers the secret of his strength. He lifts Antaeus above Earth, thus separating him from the source of his strength, and then kills him by squeezing him lifeless. (Fitzgerald 1990; Graves 1955)

See also Aeneas; *Aeneid;* Herakles.

'ANTAR, THE ROMANCE OF

This pre-Islamic Arabian cycle in prose and verse originated in the Bedouin tradition, and later incorporated the Persian and Byzantium traditions. Composed in rhymed prose (saj) interlaced with 10,000 poetic verses, the work consists of 32 tales related in separate books, the ending of each being left in suspense. The work is part of the larger collection of pre-Islamic writings entitled *al-Mu'allaqāt.*

The cycle relates the fantasy childhood and adult adventures of the poet and warrior Antarah ibn Shaddad in his quest to win the beautiful 'Ablah as a bride. He journeys backward through time to Iran, Iraq, Syria, and around the Mediterranean to Constantinople, Rome, Spain, North Africa, Sudan, and Egypt. He meets a Byzantine emperor, the king of Rome, by whose sister he fathers a son, Ghadanfar, who becomes a crusader; Frankish royalty, who provide a princess who bears him another son, Godfrey (Jufrān), who also becomes a crusader; and Spanish royalty.

In one place the romance names the author as al-Asma'ī, a ninth-century philologist, but it may have been composed as early as the eighth century or as late as the twelfth century. Scholars believe that it is the work of many authors. (Connelly 1986)

See also *Sīrat 'Antar.*

ANTARAGAṬṬAMMA

This Kannada folk epic of South Dravidian India, recorded in 1921 and 1977, is of the Akam, or "interior" or "domestic" variety. Akam also means "house." These tales are told within the house rather than at public performances.

The story describes a Brahmin custom of arranging marriages for girls before they come of age. If a girl comes of age before she is married, she is blindfolded and left in the forest to die. A certain Brahmin girl gets her period before she can get married, so her father blindfolds her and leaves her in the jungle. A Liṅgāyat man observes this; feeling compassion for the girl, he rescues and adopts her.

A mādiga (Untouchable) sees the girl and falls in love with her. He tells his mother, "Avva, you'd better learn to dress like a Brahmin. . . ." He too dresses like a Brahmin and goes to ask the Liṅgāyat for his adopted daughter's hand in marriage. The Liṅgāyat is eager for a Brahmin husband for the Brahmin girl and readily agrees to the marriage.

The girl moves into her mother-in-law's house, where she cooks for the family. She is mystified when the old woman complains about her Brahmin cuisine, but she is afraid to tell her husband about his mother's complaints.

As the years go by, she bears two sons who, as they grow older, become curious about their father's occupation. They secretly follow him to a secluded spot where they watch him making sandals for people. They return home and begin to play at making sandals with banyan leaves. Their mother sees them and is disgusted, so she scolds them for spending their time imitating the occupation of a lower caste. But they proudly tell her, "We are doing exactly what Daddy does . . . all day under that hill."

She realizes then that she has been duped into marrying an Untouchable and thus has been desecrated. She can no longer be part of any household or community. As a terrible rage comes over her, she begins to grow taller and taller, "joining heaven and earth in one body," becoming a Māri (terrifying goddess). With her tongue hanging out, she storms off in search of her husband, who flees in terror as he sees her coming. She turns her attention to her sons, saying, "I'll . . . finish off these children who were born to that man." The boys hide inside two goats, but she breaks off the goats' heads and drinks her own children's blood. Meanwhile, her husband hides in a buffalo. But Māri sees him and slits the beast open. She drinks her husband's blood and makes a vow, "I'll cut you down every year."

Disguised as an old woman, she meets a Dāsayya (religious mendicant), who does not recognize her at first. She asks him to help her put her basket on her head, but he only scolds her and orders her to get out of the way. But when he sees that the basket coil on her head is a seven-headed serpent, he knows that this is Māri. She orders him to walk in front of her and not to turn around. The Dāsayya agrees to do as he is told, and as they walk along, she changes into Māri, "joining earth and sky," and puts out "her lolling tongue." Finally the Dāsayya can stand it no longer; he turns to look and is struck dumb with fear. Furious that he has disobeyed, Māri lashes out her tongue, kills him, and drinks his blood.

She stalks on to the village of Alsande, where she kills the chieftain and all the residents. She destroys the village but leaves the calves untouched. She goes on to the village of Bēgūru and does the same. She eats all the stored fodder and water; then, still famished for water, she leaps onto a large boulder, where she throws off her sari and strikes the boulder with her fist. The Earth Goddess below makes water spring from the rock so that Māri can drink.

She hops and hops from place to place and arrives at Antaragaṭṭe, where she decides to stay, "showing her long lolling tongue." The epic tells us, "That is why she is called Antaragaṭṭamma." This story also explains why goats, sheep, and a buffalo are sacrificed to her when she is angry. (Blackburn and Ramanujan 1986)

ANU

(Also An)

Anu is an ancient Mesopotamian deity associated with the city of Erech, ruled by Gilgamesh. Anu (Danu) is also the name of a Celtic goddess. (Sandars 1972; Sproul 1991)

See also An.

ANUBIS

(Also Anpu)

In *The Egyptian Book of the Dead,* Anubis is the God of the Underworld, whose mother is Nephthys and whose father is said by some to be Osiris; by others, Set; by still others, Ra. His symbol is the jackal, and originally he may have been merely the jackal god. The face of the dead is said to be in the form of that of Anubis. In the Theban recension of *The Book of the Dead,* Anubis plays important parts in connection with the judgment and the embalming procedure. In some places in Egypt his rank and importance were as great as Osiris's.

In the Judgment Scene it is Anubis's duty to examine the tongue of the Great Balance. Anubis produces the heart of the deceased for judgment and guards the body from being captured by the "Eater of the Dead." In chapter XXVI the deceased receives a necklace and pectoral from Anubis. He shares with another god whose symbol is the jackal, Ap-uat, the duty of guiding souls around the Underworld and into the kingdom of Osiris. He appears even in the second century at Rome where the principal members of the old Egyptian ceremony of Osiris were represented: Osiris in two forms, Isis as the one who revived him, and Anubis as the one who embalmed him.

At least one scholar, C. W. King *(Gnostics and their Remains,* London, 1887), identified Anubis with Christ in Gnostic traditions. (Budge 1967; Budge 1969)

See also *The Egyptian Book of the Dead;* Osiris.

ANUKILI NA UGAMA

A West African Igbo epic purported to be a true story, it was recorded ca. 1980 from a three-hour performance recited by Bernard Chukwadi Nwabunwanne. It relates the story of a huge and ugly man, Anukili, who causes much destruction in Igbo villages and seems invincible, but who is eventually conquered. (Westley *RAL* 1991)

APHRODITE

In the *Odyssey,* this Greek goddess of erotic love and fertility is paired with the lame smith god Hephaestus, and has affairs with the handsome Adonis and with Ares, the god of war, from whence Harmonia is born. Among her many lovers is Anchises, who fathers her son Aeneas, hero of Virgil's *Aeneid.* When

Anchises reveals the identity of Aeneas's mother, she retaliates by calling down a lightning bolt upon him. (Fitzgerald 1990; Graves 1955)

See also Aeneas; *Aeneid.*

APOLLO

Apollo is a Greek god of many functions, including light, healing, music, poetry, dance, crops, herds, and archery. He and his twin sister Artemis, children of Zeus and Leto, are born on the island of Delos, where Leto has fled to escape the wrath of the jealous Hera (a story told in the Homeric *Hymn to Delian Apollo).* At a young age Apollo travels to Pytho, where he slays Python, the snake-dragon who guards the oracle. He then takes charge of the oracle himself, taking on the appearance of a dolphin (delphis), and Pytho is renamed Delphi (a story told in the Homeric *Hymn to Pythian Apollo).* Among Apollo's many liaisons is Coronis, mother of Asclepius. When she is unfaithful, Artemis kills her. Trojan king Priam's daughter Cassandra rejects him; in retaliation, she is doomed always to speak the truth but never to be believed. (Graves 1955)

APSU

In the *Enuma Elish,* a Mesopotamian creation epic, Apsu is the father of the gods, "first begetter." (Sproul 1991)

See also *Enuma Elish, Epic of;* Lahamu and Lahmu; Tiamat.

AQHAT EPIC

This fragmentary Canaanite epic (ca. fourteenth century B.C.) is concerned with the cause of the annual summer drought. Clay tablets containing the poem were discovered in the early 1930s during the excavation of the ancient Syrian city of Ugarit (now Ras Shamra).

The poem tells of the Haranamite king Danel, aggrieved because he has no son. He makes prayers and sacrifices to El, who eventually answers his prayers by giving him and his wife Danatiya a son, Aqhat. Later, in appreciation for Danel's hospitality, the Semitic god of crafts Kothar (or Kosharwa-Khasis) gives Aqhat a marvelous composite bow, originally intended for the war goddess Anath. Anath covets the bow and even offers Aqhat her favors in exchange for it, but he spurns her gifts of wealth and immortality, and even her favors. Anath arranges for him to be killed during a hunting party that she attends disguised as a falcon, which her servant Yatpan carries in a sack. At the appropriate moment Yatpan drops the sack on Aqhat; in the confusion that follows, he kills Aqhat and grabs the bow. However, later he carelessly breaks the bow and loses it by dropping it into the sea.

Aqhat's death causes drought and famine to spread across the land, lasting for seven years; thus, Danel and Aqhat's sister Paqhat realize that Aqhat is dead. Danel shoots down the eagles that circle about and finds his son's remains, which he buries. After seven years of mourning, Paqhat sets out to avenge her brother's death. She hides soldier's clothes and weapons under her dress and goes to see Yatpan, a professional assassin; besotted by drink, he reveals that he is Aqhat's killer. As Paqhat and Danel take steps to avenge Aqhat's death, the text breaks off. The similarity to the *Baal Epic* is obvious, so it may be surmised that, if this story is a seasonal myth, like Anath in the *Baal Epic,* Paqhat is able to bring her brother back to life and reverse the drought. (Pritchard 1973)

See also Anath; *Baal Epic;* Danel.

ARA AND SHAMIRAM

This well-known Armenian legend repeated by the fifth-century A.D. historian Movses Khorenats'i (Moses of Khoren) in his *History of Armenia* describes the unrequited love of Assyrian queen Shamiram (possibly Semiramis of Greek legend) for the legendary king of Armenia, Ara the Beautiful. The queen is the consort of King Shamshi-Adad, but she becomes enamored of the Armenian king. Upon being rebuffed, she sends her warriors against Armenia with explicit orders not to harm Ara. However, a stray arrow kills him, and the grief-stricken queen prays to the gods to restore him to life. The sacred dog-gods Aralez hear her prayers and lick him back to life.

The queen, referred to as "energetic and sensual," stays only a short time on the Plain of Armenia, called, after Ara, "Ararat." Then she travels southward, impressed by the beauty of the valleys, the purity of the air, "the limpid springs which gushed out everywhere in abundance," and "the gentle murmur of the rivers." She decides to build a palace in Armenia in which to pass the summer months, returning to Ninevah to spend the colder months. She selects a valley on the shores of the great salt lake Van upon which to build an entire city of palaces, which she names Shamiramakert. On one of the mountains rimming the valley she has palaces hewn from its side. "Over the whole surface of the rock, as if it were wax, she caused a great many characters to be traced. The sight of these marvels throws everyone into amazement."

Another tradition tells of the king of Assyria falling in love with and marrying a beautiful courtesan named Shammu-ramat, who persuades him to grant her kingly powers for five days. On the first day, she orders a feast; on the second, she imprisons the king or has him executed and becomes sole ruler. The historical King Shamshi-Adad died in 811 B.C. and King Menua did not accede to the Vannic throne until one year later, in which time the queen may have ruled Armenia. (She did in fact rule Assyria as queen regent for three years until her son Adad-nirari III came of age in 809 B.C.) Further, Menua ruled jointly with his son Inushpua, whose name is not mentioned again after 810 B.C. Scholars speculate that Inushpua may have been the Ara of legend. Plato tells the story of Er, son of Armenios, who is slain in battle but returns to life after a sojourn in the underworld. Another myth of Armenian heroes killed in battle and returned to life by the gods Aralez appears in the writings of Faustus of Byzantium and Pseudo-Agathangelus. (Chahin 1987)

ARES

Ares is the Greek god of war, the son of Zeus and Hera according to Homer. On some occasions he is Aphrodite's husband. In the *Iliad* Ares is depicted as being unpopular with the other gods, even with his parents. Among the children of Ares and Aphrodite are Phobos (Panic), Deimos (Rout), and Harmonia. His two sons and his sister Eris (Strife) go into battle with him. In the *Iliad,* Ares and Aphrodite are both allied with the Trojans, while his mother sides with the Greeks and his father remains neutral. In the Herakles legends, he is the father of both Cycnus and Diomedes of Thrace, two of Herakles's adversaries. (Graves 1955; Lattimore 1976)

See also Herakles; *Iliad.*

ARGONAUTICA

This epic, in four books written by Apollonius of Rhodes ca. 260 B.C., tells the story of the voyage of the Argonauts. (Graves 1955)

See also Argonauts.

ARGONAUTS

The Argonauts are a group of 50 legendary Greek heroes who travel with Jason aboard the *Argo* to recover the Golden Fleece of the ram, which had once borne his cousin Phrixus to safety. The quest is a condition imposed by Jason's uncle Pelias, who agrees to relinquish the throne he has usurped from Jason's father in exchange for the fleece. Scholars say the legend, which was known at the time of Homer, may have been the basis in part for the *Odyssey.* The legend is second only to the Trojan War as the inspiration for Greek literary epics, the most notable being Apollonius of Rhodes's four-book epic *Argonautica,* written ca. 260 B.C.

Jason's original crew consists of Minyans like himself, but later other well-known heroes—notably Herakles—are included. Among the Argonauts are Orpheus, Herakles, Polydeuces, Peleus, Castor, Meleager, Melampus, Mopus, Atalanta, Admetus, Telamon, Pelias's son Acastus, Lynceus (of the lynx eyes), Idas, Amphiaraus, and the winged sons of Boreas and Orithyia, Calais and Zetes.

The Argonauts stop at the island of Lemnos, occupied only by women. Having killed off their husbands the previous year, the women entice the heroes to tarry with them for several months. Their next port is the land of the Doliones, where King Cyzicus offers them hospitality. But after they sail away, they are blown back by a storm, and the Doliones, mistaking them for intruders, attack them. In the ensuing battle, Jason inadvertently kills their king. They sail on to the land of Bebryces, where King Amycus challenges them to a boxing match. Polydeuces accepts the challenge and kills the king. They meet the blind king Phineus at Salmydessus, and Zetes and Calais run off the Harpies, who have been contaminating the king's food. In gratitude, Phineus tells them how

Jason and his companions, heroes of a Greek literary epic that predates Homer's *Odyssey,* sailed on the *Argo* in quest of a ram's golden fleece.

to avoid being crushed by the Cyanean rocks, two boulder-cliffs that move together whenever a ship passes between them. Jason sends a dove ahead of the Argo, and after the rocks have moved together and rebounded, he sails the Argo through the pass. The crew is attacked by the birds of Ares, but they drive them away. Because they rescue the four sons of Phrixus from shipwreck, the men lead them to Colchis, where the fleece is located. King Aeetes, who has the fleece, will not relinquish it unless Jason harnesses two fire-breathing bulls, plows a field, then sows it with dragon's teeth, from which will sprout armed men that he must then battle. Jason succeeds in the task with the help of Aeetes's daughter, the sorceress Medea, who has fallen in love with him. When Aeetes refuses to honor his promise, Medea puts to sleep the dragon guarding the fleece, and Jason escapes with not only the fleece but Medea as well.

During their escape, they kill Medea's brother Apsyrtus, which enrages Zeus, and he causes them many hardships on the way home. When they reach Aeaea, Aeetes's sister Circe purges them of their sin of murder. Thetis, sea goddess and Achilles's mother, helps them maneuver the *Argo* past the Wandering Rocks. Orpheus, who sings even more beautifully than the Sirens, so disheartens the Sirens that they cause the Argonauts no trouble. Queen Arete secretly arranges for Medea and Jason to be married, and on Drepane, King Alunous protects them from pursuing Conchians.

Their ship is blown onto the African coast, where Hesperides and other mythical creatures help them become seaborne again. They head for Crete, where the bronze giant Tolus attempts to destroy the *Argo,* but Medea intervenes with sorcery. The Argonauts reach Iolcos, where Medea convinces Pelias's three daughters that if they cut their father to pieces, she can revive him. Two of the daughters do so, and Alcastes becomes king. Jason places the fleece in a temple of Zeus, while the *Argo* finds berth in the Isthmus of Corinth, under the care of Poseidon. (Graves 1955)

See also Herakles; Jason; Medea; Poseidon; Zeus.

ARJUNA

In the *Mahābhārata* of India, Arjuna is the third of the five Pāṇḍava brothers, sons of Kuntī and Pāṇḍu, who are the epic's heroes. Arjuna is the participant in the discourse on duty with Lord Kṛiṣṇa; it is called the *Bhagavadgītā,* India's most famous religious text. Arjuna is the finest archer in the world, with the possible exception of Droṇa. It is Arjuna who brings Draupadī home as a bride for all five brothers. He is the special friend of Kṛiṣṇa, whose sister Subhadra he takes as his second wife. As his best friend, he asks Kṛiṣṇa to drive his carriage into battle. An arrow from Arjuna's bow kills Bhīṣma. When Arjuna's son is killed by Jayadratha's magic after he has broken through Droṇa's "iron disk" formation, Arjuna vows to kill Jayadratha and, with the help of an eclipse provided by Kṛiṣṇa, he succeeds. Arjuna must face his own half brother Karṇa as his chief rival in a showdown, but a fantastic act of nature results in Karṇa's death. (Buck 1981)

See also *Bhagavadgītā;* Bhīṣma; Kṛṣṇa; *Mahābhārata.*

ARMES PRYDEIN

In this tenth-century Welsh poem an alliance of Celtic forces is pictured to oppose the Anglo-Saxon overlord, or mechdeyrn. The poem was inspired by the long subjection of the Welsh kingdoms by the English sovereigns, and most particularly by the appeasement of Athelstan of Wessex (d. 939) by Gwynned (South Wales) King Hywel ap Cadell (Howell the Good, d. 950), who agreed to become a subregulus of the West Saxons. *Prydwen* is the name of Arthur's ship in the *Mabinogion* story "How Culhwch Won Olwen." (Gantz 1976; Hubert 1980)

ARMINIUS

(Also Hermann)

This heroic chief (ca. 18 B.C. to A.D. 19) of the Germanic Cherusci tribe was the subject of a number of heroic lays. Tacitus called him the liberator of Germanics, since he led his people against their Roman oppressors under Publius Quinctilius Varus and in A.D. 9 dealt them such a resounding defeat in the Teutoburg Forest in Westphalia that the German culture was preserved for all time. (Bowder 1984)

ARTEMIS

Greek moon goddess of hunting and childbirth, Artemis is the twin sister of Apollo. She appears in the *Odyssey* (v) and the *Aeneid* (i). (Humphries 1951; Rouse 1937)

ARTHUR

A legendary British king revered for at least 1,400 years, Arthur is the hero of the medieval cycle of legends bearing his name. A historical Arthur who led Celtic resistance against West Saxons is indicated by sixth-century historian Gildas, ninth-century historian Nennius, and tenth-century *Annales Cambriae.* The latter source claims that he was mortally wounded at the Battle of Camlann (537). However, there may have been an even earlier Arthur who was possibly a Celtic deity. Early Welsh literature depicts him as a king of extraordinary talents—a wise, just, and magnanimous ruler whose persona, as Christian elements replaced Celtic ones, was adopted as the British ideal.

Now, since the time of Malory's *Le Morte d'Arthur* (ca. 1469), Arthur is seen as the natural son of Uther Pendragon who, with Merlin's magic, lies with Igraine disguised as her husband. He is reared by Sir Ector. By pulling the sword Excaliber from the stone, he shows his right to the English throne. He subdues 12 rebellious kings led by King Lot of Norway. He defeats invading Saxons in 12 crucial battles. Around his table he gathers those knights whose chivalrous deeds give luster to his court and add to his reputation as a just and generous ruler of great courage and strength. His most valiant knight is

Arthur, a legendary ruler in medieval Britain, provided grist for tales of chivalry and honor, battles, intrigue, a quest for the Holy Grail, and characters such as the Lady Guinevere, Sir Lancelot, and the magician Merlin. The epic, told and retold, inspired this 1917 illustration of knights fighting by N. C. Wyeth for the cover of *The Boy's King Arthur.*

Launcelot; his wife is Guinevere. In earlier tales, she and Mordred are the cause of his downfall. In later ones, her illicit love affair with Launcelot appears. Originally, Arthur's sons are born out of wedlock. When Arthur is mortally wounded and the barge comes to bear him away to Avalon, he directs Sir Bedivere to cast Excaliber into the lake. (Graves 1955; Hubert 1980)

ARTHURIAN LEGEND

This large body of medieval literature revolves around the legendary King Arthur and his court as first mentioned in the writings of the chronicler Gildas (ca. 540); the poem "Gododdin" (ca. 600); *Historia Britonum* by Nennius (ca. 800); the tenth-century poem "The Spoils of Annwn"; the Latin history of Wales, *Annales Cambriae* (ca. 955); "Kulhwch (Culhwch) and Olwen," a twelfth-century prose romance found in the *Mabinogion;* William of Malmesbury's *Chronicles of the Kings of England* (twelfth century); and, from the same period, Geoffrey of Monmouth's *History of the Kings of Britain.* This last work, which was taken to be an authentic chronicle, included Uther Pendragon, Merlin, Guinevere, Gawain, and Modred. According to Geoffrey, Cantii king Vortigern's chief magician is Merlin, who is fatherless because his mother has been seduced by a demon.

The Arthurian legend, the core of which derives from Celtic mythology, appears to have originated in the British Isles, particularly in Ireland and Wales, before being brought to the European continent in the sixth and seventh centuries. Many of the incidents parallel those of Irish heroes Cú Chulainn and Finn Mac Cumhail. The circumstances of Merlin's birth as reported by Geoffrey of Monmouth, for example, may have been a misconstrued reference to a miraculous birth such as that of Cú Chulainn.

The Norman poet Wace of Jersey took Geoffrey of Monmouth's work as the basis of his verse chronicle, *Roman de Brut,* which introduced the Round Table to the legends. In *Annales Cambriae* Arthur was reported as having been mortally wounded at the Battle of Camlann. Monmouth's version may be the first suggestion that the wounded Arthur was taken to Avalon, and Wace added the suggestion that Arthur might be healed at Avalon, with the expectation of returning to Britain one day. The first English-language version of Wace's work, by the English priest Layamon and entitled *The Brut,* returned to Celtic legends for a description of Arthur's journey to Avalon, where his sister Morgan le Fay would heal his wounds.

Late in the twelfth century the French poet Chrétien de Troyes returned to Celtic sources to compose five tales that recounted the chivalrous deeds of individual knights, the best known of whom is Lancelot (Launcelot, the Knight of the Cart). He also introduced the theme of the quest for the Grail in his *Perceval,* or the *Story of the Grail,* which he left unfinished at his death. His other Arthurian works are *Eric et Enide, Cliges,* and *Yvain,* or the *Chevalier of the Lion.*

During the thirteenth century, two German works appeared by Gottfried von Strassburg and Wolfram von Eschenbach. At about the same time, a prose romance entitled *Lancelot* (ca. 1225) became the core of a cycle of Lancelot stories known as *Vulgate Cycle.* Lancelot's son, the pure Sir Galahad (who is not tainted with sin as is his father due to his adulterous relationship with Guinevere) is the knight chosen to retrieve the Holy Grail. Another section of the *Vulgate Cycle* draws on Robert de Boron's poem "Merlin" to tell in prose form the story of Arthur pulling Excaliber from the stone. A third branch of the cycle tells of Arthur's battle with Mordred and of Lancelot's battle with Gawain as a result of the former's affair with Guinevere. A post-Vulgate romance (ca. 1240) includes material from the Tristan tradition.

In the fourteenth century, a revival of interest in England brought two important anonymous works, *The Alliterative Morte d'Arthur* (ca. 1360) and *Sir Gawain and the Green Knight,* a poem that ranks as one of the greatest Middle English works.

In the fifteenth century Sir Thomas Malory gathered the existing legends, particularly from the *Vulgate Cycle,* to produce the great prose version, *Le Morte d'Arthur.* Arthur also appears, much altered, in Edmund Spenser's *The Faerie Queene.* Tennyson retold the story in *Idylls of the King,* and it has been retold many times since. It is its resilience to the ravages of time that marks the Arthurian legend as great literature. (Barber 1961; Hubert 1980; Rutherford 1987)

ASA

In the *Ynglinga Saga* found in the *Heimskringla,* and in the *Ynglinga Lot* from which it is derived, Asa (also called "the Ill-minded" in one place and "every inch a royal lady" in another) is the daughter of the Swedish king Ingjald, who gives her in wedlock to King Gudrod in Scania (southernmost Sweden). According to the saga, "She was like her father in temper and she made him slay her brother Halvdan, who was father to Ivor the Widefathom." Asa also brings about the death of her husband Gudrod. Afterward, Asa returns to her father Ingjald's house, and soon Ivor the Widefathom appears with an army to avenge his father's death. Ingjald and Asa decide on "the well-known plan of making all their folk dead drunk and afterward setting fire to the hall." Everyone is burned to death, including King Ingjald. (Sturlason 1990)

See also *Heimskringla.*

ASCANIUS
(Also Iulus)

In Roman mythology, Ascanius is the son of Aeneas. In the *Aeneid* (i), Ascanius escapes with his father after the fall of Troy. They travel to Italy, where Aeneas and Lavinia establish Lavinium. After his father's death, Ascanius builds the capital, Alba Longa (ca. 1152 B.C.), near present-day Rome. However, according to Roman historian Livy, Ascanius could not have been present at Troy because he was the son of Aeneas and Lavinia. The family of Julius Caesar traced its descent from Ascanius. (Fitzgerald 1990)

ÁSGARD

In Scandinavian mythology, Ásgard is the dwelling place of the gods where Valhalla, the great hall for fallen warriors, is located. (Jones, G. 1990)

ASKIA MOHAMMED, THE EPIC OF

(Also *Askia Mohammad)*

This oral epic poem of 1,602 lines tells the history of the Songhay empire of West Africa. A recording was made in the 1970s from a performance by griot Nouhou Malio.

The Songhay empire was located in the central Saharan region. It was founded in the fifteenth century by Songhay raider Sunni Ali (1464), a man of the peasants whom Arabs and seventeenth-century Timbuktu writers villify as a tyrant. His successor was Askia Mohammed Turay, praised in Timbuktu records; he is the hero of the epic. The Tarikh el-Fettach and the Tarikh es-Soudan are chronicles about the same hero.

Askia Mohammed takes his title from a Songhay military rank and switches from reliance on the peasants to reliance on the new, strong, and prosperous towns of Songhay. Not content to control a wide region around the Middle Niger, he sets out on a journey of conquest in all directions. After his pilgrimage to Mecca in 1496, where he obtains authority to act as caliph of Islam in western Sudan, he takes an army west to Takur and exacts tribute from all non-Muslim rulers.

When Mossi and Dogon raiders attack the Middle Niger, he successfully fends them off. Then he turns his attention to the east and overruns the Hausa states of Gobir and Katsina. Later he takes Kano and places a governor there to collect tribute. He turns his generals north and they march to the great oasis of Aïr, where they attack the native Tuaregs and drive them away. A permanent colony of Songhay settles at Aïr.

Askia Mohammed rules long and well, bringing law and order to his empire. When he is 80 and almost blind, jealous factions (which may include the son who replaces him) see their leader's defenses weakening and have him deposed (1528). (Davidson 1991; Hale 1990; Panikkar 1963; Westley *RAL* 1991)

ASMODEUS

In the Jewish apochryphal book of Tobit, Asmodeus is the evil demon who falls in love with Raguel's daughter Sara and, one by one, kills each of her seven husbands on their wedding nights. Upon advice from the angel Raphael, Tobias uses a charm made of the heart and liver of a fish seared over perfumed ashes to drive Asmodeus away to Egypt. Tobias then marries Sara himself. Referring to Asmodeus as the king of demons, the Talmud states that while the first Temple of Jerusalem was being built, King Solomon captured Asmodeus and set him to work constructing the temple. (Charles 1976)

ASMUNDAR SAGA KAPPABANA

See Hildebrandslied.

ASSUR
(Also Ashur)

In Mesopotamian religion, Assur is the principal god of Assyria and the god of the city of Ashur. In the Urartu hierarchy of gods, he ranks below Khaldi. He is the consort of Ishtar. By 1800 B.C. he had become identified with the Sumerian Enlil. He is the Baal of the Assyrian capital of Ninevah. By 721 B.C. he had become identified with Anshar, the father of An in the Sumerian creation myth. By 700 B.C., he was awarded much of the dominant role that had been played by the Babylonian Marduk. (Chahin 1987; Saggs 1990)

ASTARTE

Great West Semitic goddess. ***See*** Ishtar.

ASTYANAX
(Also Scamandrius)

In Greek legend, Astyanax is the son of Trojan prince Hektor and Andromache. He appears in the *Iliad* (vi) as a baby, described as "the admired, beautiful as a star shining, / whom Hektor called Skamandrios, but all of the others / Astyanax—lord of the city. . . ." Andromache shows her husband the child and begs him not to go into battle and be killed, but Hektor refuses to listen. He takes the child in his arms, kisses him, and prays, "Zeus, and you other immortals, grant that this boy, who is my son, / may be as I am, preeminent among the Trojans, / great in strength, as am I, and rule strongly over Ilion; / and some day let them say of him: 'He is better by far than his father,' / as he comes in from the fighting; and let him kill his enemy / and bring home the blooded spoils, and delight the heart of his mother."

After the fall of Troy, Astyanax is hurled from the battlements by Achilles's son, the Greek warrior Neoptolemus; however, later legend has him surviving the war, establishing the Sicilian kingdom of Messina and the line of Charlemagne. He appears early in the *Aeneid* (ii). (Humphries 1951; Lattimore 1976)

ATE

In the Herakles legends and in the *Iliad* (xix), Ate is a malevolent Greek goddess who convinces Zeus to take an oath making Herakles the subject of King Eurystheus of Mycenae. Zeus repents of his hasty act and banishes Ate from Olympia. She continues to work her mischief on earth, which Zeus's old and crippled daughters, the Litai, attempt to rectify. (Graves 1955; Lattimore 1976)

ATHENA
(Also Athene)

Athena is the Greek goddess of war, wisdom, and handicraft, patroness of Athens. In the *Iliad,* her father Zeus assigns the arena of war to Ares and Athena. Athena comes to the aid of the Greeks against the Trojans, where she shows herself to be Ares's superior. In the *Odyssey,* Athena is the personal tutelary deity of the king. In the Herakles legends, she is the hero's helper. In *Theogony,* Hesiod tells how the motherless Athena sprang from Zeus's forehead. She had no consort and no offspring. (Graves 1955; Lattimore 1976; Rouse 1937)

See also Herakles; *Iliad; Odyssey; Theogony;* Zeus.

ATLI, LAY OF
(Also "Atlakviđa")

This Nordic heroic poem found in the *Poetic Edda* is one of two lays (the longer "Atlamál" is considered less authentic and aesthetically inferior) that preserve the grand theme of the fall of the Niflungs. As such, it is an older variation of the German epic *Nibelungenlied,* with important differences. In this version, Atli, or King Attila the Hun (known in the *Nibelungenlied* as Etzel), is cast as the villain, as opposed to his role in the *Nibelungenlied,* where he plays only a secondary role as Kriemhild's (Gudrun's) second husband. He also appears in the *Völsunga Saga* as Atli. The historical Attila was king of the Huns from 434 to 453.

In this version, the avaricious King Atli lures Gudrun's (Guthrún's) brothers Gunnar (Gunther) and Hogni (Hagen) to the Hunnish court to elicit information about their treasure. When the brothers refuse to divulge their secret, a battle ensues in the hall, but the Niflungs are outnumbered. Atli has Hogni's heart cut out, and Gunnar, who laughed at him, is thrown into a snake pit. Gudrun avenges their deaths by first slaying Atli's sons, then killing Atli himself: "To their bridal bed she gave blood to drink / with murderous hands, and the hounds she loosed; / into hall hurled she— the housecarls were waked— / burning firebrands. . . ." (Hollander *Edda* 1990)

See also *Edda, Poetic;* Etzel; Gudrun; Gunnar; Hagen; Kriemhild; *Nibelungenlied.*

ATRAKHASIS, MYTH OF

This Akkadian myth (ca. nineteenth century B.C.) tells about the wise Babylonian hero Atrakhasis. The god Enki orders that a rebellious god, who does not believe in toil, be killed and that the birth goddess Nintur (Ninmakh) mix his flesh and blood with clay. After Nintur does this, the mixture is gestated by 14 womb goddesses, who give birth to seven pairs of humans. The etemmu (ghost) of the slain god is left in the mixture and thus man's nature is part human and part divine. His divine part—his etemmu—will survive after death. The toil, formerly relegated to the gods, now becomes a human condition. After

Athena, Greek goddess of war and wisdom, featured in the *Iliad* and the *Odyssey,* is represented on a fifth-century B.C. relief on a boundary marker.

man is created, he begins to multiply too quickly and makes such a racket that the noise keeps Enlil awake. So he orders Namtar, the god of death, to cause a plague to wipe out a great portion of mankind. But the wise Atrakhasis, on advice from Enki, persuades men to offer sacrifices and prayers to Namtar, who is touched by their devotion and refuses to kill them. Enlil then has Adad, the god of rains, cause a drought and famine, but Atrakhasis tells the men to offer sacrifices to Adad, and again the god refuses to kill mankind. Enlil then plans a group-effort famine that lasts for seven years. The famine is so bad that people are eating their own children. After Enki takes pity and "accidentally" lets some fish escape from the sea, Enlil decides to wipe out the entire population with a flood. But Enki warns Atrakhasis to build a boat in which he saves himself, his family, and all the animals. When the floodwaters recede, Atrakhasis offers a sacrifice to the gods, who all—Enlil excepted—gather around in shame. Enki berates Enlil and suggests other methods of birth control. She and Nintur invent the barren woman and the demon Pashittu who kills babies at birth. A portion of the text is missing. (Pritchard 1973)

See also Enki; Enlil; Flood Myths.

ATREUS

In Greek legend, Atreus is the head of the royal house of the Mycenae. The father of Agamemnon and Menelaus, he appears in the *Odyssey;* however, his story and that of the downfall of his house have been a favorite topic for dramatists since the time of Aeschylus, Sophocles, Euripides, and Seneca. (Graves 1955; Rouse 1937)

ATTAWANADI

In the *Watunna* of the Makiritare Indians of Venezuela, Attawanadi is the third incarnation (damodede) of Wanadi (God) to be sent to earth. He is also called "House Wanadi" because he constructs the first houses and creates the first people, instructing them in their most important ritual and material skills. (Civrieux 1980)

See also Watunna.

ATTIS
(Also Atys)

Phrygian vegetation or fertility god, Attis is the consort of the Great Mother. His worship spread throughout the Roman empire, where he became, by the second century A.D., a solar deity. According to legend, Attis is the son of the river goddess Nana and the hermaphrodite Agdistis. Agdistis was also worshiped as the Great Mother. Attis, a handsome youth, becomes her lover, and when he prepares to marry someone else, the jealous Agdistis reacts by striking him with frenzy. Attis is overcome with madness, castrates himself, and dies. Filled with remorse, Agdistis pleads with Zeus to preserve Attis's body so that it will never decay. Agdistis's priests continued the practice of self-castration upon entering the priesthood. (Frazer 1963; Graves 1955; Olmstead 1948)

See also Agdistis.

AU CO

In Vietnamese mythology, Au Co is a Chinese woman, the queen of the fairy race. From her union with Lac Long Quang 100 sons are born. (Terada 1989)

See also *Lac Long Quang and Au Co.*

AUCASSIN ET NICOLETTE

This French chante-fable was told in alternating verse (sung) and prose (recited), probably by an early-thirteenth-century minstrel of northeastern France. However, scholars detect both Moorish and Byzantine roots in the work, and there is some belief that both it and an earlier work on the same theme called *Floire et Blancheflor* may spring from a common source, now lost. The story involves the noble son of Count Gavin of Beaucaire, Aucassin, who falls in love with the Saracen captive Nicolette. To prevent the two from marrying, the count imprisons Nicolette, but she escapes and takes flight. Aucassin follows; after he has endured many hardships, including capture by the Saracens, he is shipwrecked near his home. He learns that his father has died and that he is now the count. Meanwhile, Nicolette is taken to Carthage, where it is learned that she is in reality the daughter of the king and is betrothed to a noble Saracen. But she escapes once again and, disguised as a wandering minstrel, makes her way to Beaucaire, where she and Aucassin are reunited. (Preminger 1990; Siepmann 1987)

AUDUMLA

In Norse mythology, Audumla is a cow who nourishes the giant Aurgelmir with her milk. She herself feeds on salty stones, which she licks into the shape of a man. The man is Bur (Buri), grandfather of Óthin and other gods. (Hollander *Edda* 1990; Young 1954)

See also Aurgelmir; *Edda, Poetic; Edda, Prose;* Óthin.

AUGEAS

(Also Augias or Augeias)

In the Herakles legend, Augeas is a son of the sun god Helios, and the king of the Epeians. King Eurystheus imposes upon Herakles the task of cleaning out Augeas's immense stables in one day, in exchange for which Augeas promises Herakles a tenth of his herd. The hero accomplishes the task by diverting the river Alpheus through the stables, but Augeas refuses to honor his part of the bargain. In retaliation, Herakles leads an army against the king, slaying him and his sons. (Graves 1955)

See also Herakles.

AURGELMIR

(Usually Ymir in the *Poetic Edda)*

In Norse creation mythology, Aurgelmir, or Ymir, is a giant fashioned by melted ice created when the ice of Niflheim meets the heat of Muspelheim. He is nourished by the cow Audumla, and produces a male and female giant from his armpits and a six-headed son from his groin. The race of gods whom Audumla licks into being eventually kill Aurgelmir, whose blood drowns all but one frost giant. His body is cast into the void where, according to the "Lay of Vafthrúthnir" the gods fashion the earth from his flesh, the seas from his bones, the sky from his skull (held aloft by four dwarfs), and the fence surrounding Midgard (Middle Earth, the home of mankind) from his eyebrows. (Hollander *Edda* 1990; Young 1954)

See also Audumla; *Edda, Poetic; Edda, Prose.*

AUŠRINẸ

(Also Auseklis)

Aušrinẹ is the Baltic god, or goddess, of the dawn, heroine of perhaps a thousand Lithuanian folktales, a typical one being *Saulė and Vẹjụ Motina* (the Sun and the Mother of the Winds). According to the story, there are three brothers. One brother, Joseph, always sees two suns at breakfast and vespers. He asks his brothers to allow him to search for the second sun, which disappears except for those times. They bless him and send him off. He has many adventures and is transformed into various animals. He is aided by the North Wind to find Aušrinẹ. He ascends into the sky with her and remains with her forever. (Greimas 1992)

AVESTA

(Also *Zend-Avesta)*

The sacred book of the Zoroastrians and Parsees (ca. third century A.D.), this is a fragmentary collection drawn from oral tradition and the writings of Zoroaster before 800 B.C. One of the five extant parts is called the *Yashts,* which are said to be the inspiration for the epic *Shāh-Nāmah.* (Zaehner 1955)

AWANG SULONG

This is the title of a Malay folk narrative delivered in rhythmical verse and containing stock phrases inserted with frequency as the reciter waits for inspiration. (Preminger 1990)

AZI DAHĀKA

(Also Ažhdahāk, Azhdahak, Azhdahāk, or Azhi Dahaka)

Iranian half-man, half-monster, in the Persian epic *Shāh-Nāmah* he is described as having two serpents growing on either side of his head. In the *Yashts* of the sacred book of Zoroastrianism, *Avesta,* he is described as a three-headed dragon with six eyes who slays Yima, the first man, and carries off Yima's two wives. Afterward, as the epitome of evil, he reigns from Babylonia for a thousand years until the hero Keresāspa (or Thraētaona) binds him to the underside of the mountain of Damāvand. At the end of time he will be loosed to wreak devastation upon the world until, in the Great War, Keresāspa will slay him with his mace. The belief is also held by the Manichaeans; a similar story, involving the dragon Ahi (also Vṛtra) who is killed by Indra, exists in Indian tradition. (Levy 1967)

See also *Shāh-Nāmah.*

B

BAAJANKARO EPIC

This is a Fulani epic from Sudan. ***See*** the related *Bambara Epic.* (Courlander 1982)

BAAL EPIC

(Also *Poem of Baal)*

This is a Ugarit (Syrian) Canaanite myth (ca. early second millennium B.C.). Ugarit (Ras Shamra) was a city on the Syrian coast opposite Cyprus. The epic survives in Ugaritic texts on clay tablets unearthed since 1929 at Ras Shamra, Syria. The tablets date from the fourteenth century B.C., the Late Bronze Age, but scholars believe the mythological texts may have been composed many centuries earlier. Only fragments of the epic remain. Its content suggests the yearly cycle of fertility and infertility.

The epic begins with a fragment in which the dragon Yamm (or Yam), god of the sea and inland waters, is vying for dominance over the young Ashtar, god of irrigation. Ashtar ignores warnings from the sun goddess Shapash and demands that El, the supreme Bull God, depose Yamm. But El upholds Yamm's supremacy on the grounds that Ashtar is not able to fulfill the requirements of Yamm's office. However, El's son Baal, the rain or storm god and spirit of fertility (also called Hadad and "cloud rider"), is challenged to a battle by the sea god Yamm, who has sent emissaries to the assembled gods with the intent of frightening them. Kothar, or Koshur-wa-Khasis ("Deft"), the god of crafts, fashions special weapons for Baal—two thunderbolts—that enable him to defeat Yamm.

Although he has overcome the sea, Baal has no abode of his own on the earth, which he now rules. The war goddess Anath accompanies him to see his mother Asherat, mother of the gods and El's consort, in order to convince her to intercede in Baal's behalf. They bring her rich gifts, and after a great feast, Asherat agrees to speak to El about a palace for Baal. El consents, so upon Mount Zaphon (also called Khazzi and Kasios), the Canaan Olympus, Kothar constructs for him a magnificent house furbished with silver and gold. At first Baal fears that Yamm will try to steal his brides, so he refuses to allow Kothar to put windows in the palace. Finally, when he has disposed of Yamm, he agrees to the windows, which, when opened, will allow rain to fall upon the earth, fertilizing it. There is a break in the epic at this point.

Filled with hubris, Baal decides to challenge an even more formidable foe: Mot, god of aridity, death, and the underworld. He sends two messengers, Gupan and Ugar (Vine and Field), to Mot with the demand that Mot henceforth confine himself to the deserts and the underworld. Mot replies with an invitation to a banquet in the underworld, which Baal feels he cannot refuse. He arms himself against demons by painting his body with red ochre and multiplies his strength by mating 88 times with a heifer and fathering a son. He then descends to the underworld and is declared dead.

When Baal's consort Anath, goddess of love as well as war, and the god-king El learn that Baal has descended into the jaws of Mot, god of death, they mourn greatly, and a drought settles over the land. El grieves by donning sackcloth and ashes and mutilating himself, and Anath follows suit. With the aid of Shapash, Anath recovers Baal's body and attends to his burial. Meanwhile, Ashtar sits on Baal's throne; when his feet will not reach the footstool, he realizes that he is inadequate to the position. Adorned with human heads and hands, Anath tracks down Mot and with ferocity cuts him to bits. El dreams that his son is alive and makes plans for his return. He instructs Anath to send Shapash to find Baal. Baal is then resurrected, and the drought over the land is ended. "The watercourses flow with honey." (Ben Khader and Soren 1987; Pritchard 1973)

See also Anath; *Aqhat Epic;* Dagon; Yam.

BACABS, THE RITUAL OF THE

This early Mayan document, written ca. the seventeenth century in Yucatec Maya, contains religious symbolism, medical incantations, and other rituals. It was written after the Spanish conquest by Indians who transcribed earlier hieroglyphic works. In Mayan myth, Bacabs are four gods who hold up the sky, or four manifestations of a single deity. (Bierhorst 1989)

BADB

(Also Bodb)

In pre-Christian Celtic literature, Badb is the goddess of battle, one of three Gaulish goddesses concerned with death who appear in Irish tales. (Chadwick 1976; Markdale 1986; Rutherford 1987)

BAKARIDJAN KONE, A HERO OF SEGU, EPIC OF

This epic is taken from the oral tradition of the Bambara, one of the most important West African tribes and the founders of the kingdom of Segu.

Located in the present-day country of Mali, Segu was a group of city-states that existed in the seventeenth century along the upper Niger River. Djeli (called griots in most other African societies), the bard-historians attached to the noble families, have preserved the history of actual and mythological events for more than 300 years. They accompany their recitations on the ngoni, a plucked-string musical instrument.

Before Bakaridjan Kone is born, his father leaves his wives in the village of Disoro Nko and moves to Segu City where he attaches himself to the court of the great king Da Monzon. When the man receives word that one of his wives, Kumba, has given birth to a male child, he does not go home even though it is his duty to be on hand for the naming ceremony. However, he informs the king that he is the father of a newborn son in hopes of receiving a gift from the king. But the king does not respect him for having left his wives, and refuses to give him anything. Instead, he sends cowries to the wives so that they can conduct a proper naming ceremony, and he requests that the child be named Bakaridjan. The wives gladly honor his request, and thus the king has in effect adopted the boy.

As years go by, the king wonders which of his sons will succeed him, and worries that one of the other heroes of the kingdom might try to overthrow him before his sons grow to manhood. So he consults his morike (diviner), who tells him that he need not fear any man, but there is a boy who would someday be capable of taking his throne if he wishes. He advises the king to call in every boy and ask him to hold the king's horse while the king mounts. The king is then to press his spear into the boy's foot, and the boy who does not cry out is the one destined to be the hero capable of overthrowing the king.

The king tests all his sons, then all the other boys in Segu, and everyone cries out. Eventually Bakaridjan is summoned, and he travels to Segu and shows great courage in not crying out. From the beginning, the child speaks with the authority of a great warrior, and he learns from the court djeli that he is descended from noblemen.

The king keeps Bakaridjan in court where he can keep an eye on him, but his oldest son offers to kill the boy and thus end the problem. Bakaridjan survives several insidious attempts on his life and eventually, in a one-on-one encounter with the king's son, Bakaridjan kills him. The king cannot punish Bakaridjan, for everyone knows that Bakaridjan acted in self-defense, so he decides to send the boy back to his village. There, in Disoro Nko, he remains, gaining fame throughout the land as a child-hero.

Soon other boys flock to his village, seeking his friendship. A prestigious club is formed of boys who wish to be heroes like Bakaridjan. Bakaridjan sends word to the king that the boys are ready for their circumcision ceremony, marking them as men. However, before the ceremony day, a large party of Fula launches a cattle raid and takes the entire livestock of the land back to Massina.

The king dispatches all his warriors to battle the Fula for the return of his country's cattle. When Bakaridjan learns of the theft, he sets out to join the warriors, but he meets them returning, having failed. Bakaridjan, who has borrowed the king's horse and stolen his spear and gun, sets out alone and rescues all the livestock and drives them back to Segu.

As the years pass, Bakaridjan continues to perform acts of courage, and his prestige grows. He conquers many cities in the name of his king, bringing the deposed kings' heads back as trophies. But he meets his match when an outcast water jinn named Bilissi comes to live in Segu and begins appropriating a portion of all Cows of Heroes, which are slain to provide meat for the warriors. Bakaridjan challenges Bilissi and, despite the jinn's magical power, eventually kills him. Nevertheless, Bakaridjan cannot escape completely; he falls prey to Bilissi's magic and becomes paralyzed on one side. His son Simbalon appeals to the king for help. The ruler, who both reveres and fears the great warrior, sends for 40 filelikelas (Bambara practitioners of mystic sciences) and 40 morikes (Muslim practitioners of mystic sciences). With the magic of 80 practitioners, Bakaridjan is finally cured.

Later Bakaridjan and two other popular heroes, Madiniko and Bamana Diase, all become "in conversation" with the same woman, Aminata, who can't decide which one she likes best. The king decides to intervene and assigns the djeli to resolve the dilemma of which man will win Aminata. The djeli suggests a test: The winner will be the one who brings the gun of a famous and dangerous hunter-hero named Dosoke Zan. Zan has never been defeated in battle, and it is said that his mystic strength has been given to him by water jinns. Dosoke Zan tricks the first two men with the help of magic, and Bakaridjan realizes he can never defeat Zan. So he turns from combat and goes home, disgraced.

Things are not the same in court without Bakaridjan. The djeli, in an effort to entice the warrior out of seclusion, visits and asks him to capture some fat cattle from the region of Samaniana. A noble cannot refuse the request of a djeli, so Bakaridjan accepts the challenge.

The king of Samaniana, upon learning that the great Bakaridjan is coming, rounds up all the cattle behind Samaniana's walls and locks the gate. Bakaridjan has the rumor spread that he has died and lies low, waiting to catch the Samanianans off-guard. Eventually he entices the warriors from behind the walls, kills them, and returns to Segu with all their fat cattle.

Once again he has become a great hero, and his past disgrace is forgotten—even by himself. In some of his boastings, which reach the king's ear, he indicates that he is greater than the king.

Considering Bakaridjan's boasts treasonous, King Da Monzon devises a plot to kill him. But he makes the mistake of confiding his plan to his favorite wife. The epic quotes a Bambara saying: "Do not relate a matter of importance to a woman. Her stomach is not a secret treasure box." The wife tells an elderly slave woman who has been treated generously by Bakaridjan's son. The slave woman alerts the two men to the plot, and it fails. The king promises never again to try to kill Bakaridjan and gives him a permanent place of honor in court. Bakaridjan lives many years as a hero, and so does his son. (Courlander 1982)

See also Aminata; *Da Monzon, Epic of.*

BAKUNGU

In the *Mwindo Epic* of eastern Zaire, Bakungu is the son of Shebankungu, the Chief Counselor. When Mwindo's father, Chief Shemwindo, relinquishes the chiefdom, Bakungu remains behind as Mwindo's counselor. (Biebuyck 1978)

***See also** Mwindo, Epic of.*

BALAM-ACAB

In the Mayan *Popol Vuh,* Balam-Acab is the second man, one of the founders of the Quiché nation. Along with the other three "first men," he is called an "admirable" man. His wife is Chomihá. He is the grandfather and father of the nine great houses of Nimhaib. His god is Avilix. He and Balam-Quitzé are the first to see fire and to ask for it for their people. (Recinos, Goetz, and Morley 1983)

See also Ah Kin; Ah Puch; Ah Toltecat; *Popol Vuh;* Quetzalcóatl, Topiltzin.

BALAM-CONACHÉ

In the Mayan *Popol Vuh,* Balam-Conaché is a Quiché king, son of Qocaib and grandson of Balam-Quitzé. In the manuscript "Título de los Señores de Totonicapán" (chapter III), the story is told that Qocaib and his brother Qocavib are elected as ambassadors to go to the land of their grandfather to ask for support against future attacks. Qocaib is sent east, to the coast of Guatemala and Yucatán, in order to go to the metropolis of Chichén Itzá, location of the court of Quetzalcóatl (also Acxitl or Kukulcán). Qocavib, "encountering some obstacles on the shores of the Lake of Mexico," returns "without doing anything." However, on his return, "finding a weak soul he illicitly knew his sister-in-law, the wife of Qocaib." When Qocaib returns and finds his wife holding a newborn, he asks whose it is. She answers, "It is of thy blood, of thy flesh and thy same bones." Qocaib accepts this explanation and says, "From today on, and forever this child shall be called Balam-Conaché." Balam-Conaché later founds the House of Conaché and Iztayul. He is the third king of the Quiché, ruling with Beleheb-Queh, king of the fourth generation of the House of Nihaib, and, with Ahah-Galel, first of the lords of the House of Nihaib. The rank and office of Ahpop-Camhain (Ahpop-Camhá), second title of the House of Iztayul, has its origin with him. (Recinos, Goetz, and Morley 1983)

***See also** Popol Vuh.*

BALAM-QUITZÉ

In the *Popol Vuh* of the Maya, Balam-Quitzé is the first man and Quiché chief, founder of the House of Cavec. His god was Tohil, which was said to be the same as Quetzalcóatl. The name Tohil is associated with rain and thunder. The *Cakchiquel Manuscript* calls "Tohohil" the principal god of the Quiché. Balam-Quitzé and Balam-Acab are the first to see fire and ask Tohil to supply it for their people. According to the "Título de los Señores de Totonicapán," Balam-

Quitzé and his companions were "beginning to rub wood and stones, those who first made fire." By offering Balam-Quitzé their daughters, the tribes of Vukamag are able to obtain from him "a little" of their fire. At the end of his reign, he and the other three "first men" tell their sons good-bye and disappear on the summit of the mountain Hacavitz. (Recinos, Goetz, and Morley 1983)

See also *Popol Vuh.*

BALARĀMA

In Hindu mythology, as in the *Mahābhārata,* Balarāma is the elder half brother of Kṛiṣṇa. Originally he may have been an agricultural deity, because second-century B.C. images depict him holding a plowshare. In contrast to Kṛiṣṇa, who is traditionally depicted with a blue face, Balarāma is shown with a white face. He was known for his great strength and his love of wine. In the *Mahābhārata,* as Arjuna nears Dwaravati he meets Kṛiṣṇa, who takes him to meet Balarāma. Dressed in blue robes and wearing a garland of wildflowers, he is carrying his ever-present great earthen wine jar. Balarāma sways tipsily and tells Arjuna that he once moved a city wall with his plow. Kṛiṣṇa explains, "He likes you. He is my brother, and the plow is his weapon, and he means to tell you—peace, or else!" When Arjuna waylays Balarāma's sister Subhadra, Balarāma reaches for his trumpet to call his bowmen. He tells Kṛiṣṇa, "This one, made welcome as your guest, has stolen your car and our sister!" Kṛiṣṇa assures his brother that he lent Arjuna his chariot. "Why should there be doubt where love is concerned?" Balarāma drinks more wine and complains, "Words!" But he adds, "This time. If they will be happy." (Buck 1981; O'Flaherty 1975)

See also Kṛṣṇa; *Mahābhārata.*

BALDR

(Also Balder and Baldur the Good)

In Nordic mythology, Baldr is the god of light, the son of Óthin (Odin) and Frigg (Frigga). In the *Poetic Edda,* Baldr appears in "Völuspá," the "Lay of Vafthrúdnir," the "Lay of Grímnir," the "Lay of Skírnir," the "Flyting of Loki," and "Völuspá him skamma," as well as in "Baldrs draumar" (Baldr's dreams). The last, which gives no new information, purports to be a supplement to the "Völuspá," in which the seeress foretells the death of Baldr.

Several myths surround his death. According to one version, he can only be wounded by Míming's (Mímir's) sword. He is slain with the sword by his rival Höder (Hodur or Höd) for the love of the beautiful Nanna. Another version says that he can only be slain by mistletoe, and that he is killed by mistletoe thrown by his blind brother Höd at Loki's instigation. After Baldr, "the blameless god," is killed, evil enters the world. The seeress foretells the downfall of the gods and the end of the world, after which a new world will emerge where Baldr and the other good gods will reign. (Hollander *Edda* 1990; Jones, G. 1990)

See also *Edda, Poetic.*

BALLAD OF MULAN

This northern Chinese folk poem composed during the domination of the Wei Tatars in the sixth century sings of a girl, Mulan, who is older than any of her brothers, who are not yet grown men. She buys a gallant horse and steals away from her parents' house, disguised as a warrior. She tramps a thousand leagues "on the errands of war," crossing frontiers and hills "like a bird in flight." After she has gained glory on the battlefield for 12 years, the emperor, or khan, asks her what reward she will take. She does not want to be made a counselor at court. She says, "I only beg for a camel that can march / A thousand leagues a day, / To take me back to my home." After she has donned her old dress and "bound her cloudy hair," she leaves the house and meets her messmates on the road. They are "startled out of their wits," having "marched with her for 12 years of war / And never known that Mulan was a girl." (Waley 1982)

BALLAD OF THE HIDDEN DRAGON

In this medieval ballad, written down during the Chin dynasty (1115–1234), verses were sung alternating with prose narrative. The form, chu-kung-tiao (meaning "various modes"), became popular in the eleventh century. Ballads were performed on the streets and also in theatrical shows. Often the professionals who told the stories were also prostitutes. The common people learned the literature and history, as well as new ideas, from these recitations. The original *Ballad of the Hidden Dragon* consisted of 12 chapters and an epilogue added by the storyteller, but only parts of it remain: the first, second, and twelfth chapters, plus parts of the third and eleventh.

The hero is Liu Chih-yuan, who became emperor during the Later Han dynasty (947–950); however, this work is an account of the years before his ascendancy, hence the name "Hidden Dragon."

The first three chapters describe the hardships and sufferings of Liu and his family. After his father is killed in battle, his poverty-stricken mother takes her two small sons from the famine-plagued land. Later she remarries and has two more sons, Chin-erh and Chao-erh.

When they are older, Liu's half brothers mock him for having a different surname, and Liu eventually quarrels with them and leaves home. He goes his way, "lacking money," and during his lonely wanderings he suffers, in the understated words of the bard, "trials and hunger." One day while he is sleeping under the trees, an old man sees him and knows that this homeless beggar will someday be king. When Liu awakens, the old man asks him about himself. Tears flow down Liu's cheek and he answers, "I am so poor I wear only a hempen singlet, / Who will believe me if I speak of honored ancestors?"

After the old man hears his life story, he offers Chih-yuan a six-month job working in his fields. He takes the youth home with him and gives him a place to sleep. That night, the farmer's 15-year-old daughter San-niang, "just a country maid, / yet beautiful beyond compare," finds Chih-yuan sleeping in the house. He is "seven feet tall and fair of face," and his "imperial body" is as awesome as a god's. Red glow and violet mist cover his body. She knows that he will someday be emperor and that she will be his wife. When he awakens, she breaks her silver pin and gives him half as a sign of their eventual betrothal.

Later, after an argument with San-niang's brothers, Chih-yuan and his betrothed part, grief-stricken. Chih-yuan continues on his way and has many more adventures. He is forced to marry Lady Yueh, the daughter of a military dignitary.

Meanwhile, bandits descend upon San-niang and carry her away. When Chih-yuan learns of it, he sends an expedition, led by Hung-chao, to rescue her. But the bandits capture Hung and drag him away. Another army led by Kuo Yen-wei also is no match for the bandits.

After both armies have failed, Chih-yuan himself rides out to confront the bandits. But when they appear, he sees that they are his half brothers, leading their old mother. They tell him, "We did not know that we had seized your wife San-niang."

Overjoyed, Chih-yuan calls for San-niang, whom he hasn't seen in 13 years, to be brought forth. Lady Yueh herself respectfully offers the golden headdress and rainbow robe to San-niang. But her captors have cut off her hair, so it is impossible to pin on the golden headdress. She asks Heaven, "If it is [my lot] to become the Emperor's first wife, let my hair grow long. . . . If gods agree I am only to be the Emperor's second wife, let my hair remain as it is now."

Miraculously, her hair begins to grow until it sweeps the ground. Liu Chih-yuan is ecstatic. He has won fame and wealth, he has his wife back, and he is joined again by his mother and brothers. (Finnegan 1978)

BAMBARA EPIC

This Mandé epic concerns the reassertion of power of the non-Muslim Bambara against the wealthy Muslim Marka clan to form the Segu state. The Bambara is a tribe of the Mandé group of West Africa, which also includes the Soninke, Mandinka, Bozo, and others. The Bambara interacted with these tribes, the Fula, and others in the empires of Mali and Ghana. In the seventeenth century the Bambara founded the kingdom of Segu, and later the kingdom of Kaarta as well. (Courlander 1982)

See also *Bakaridjan Kone, a Hero of Segu, Epic of; Bassadjalan Zambele, Epic of;* Biton Koulibaly; *Da Monzon, Epic of; Ngolo Diara.*

BANĪ HILĀL EPIC

(Also *Abū Zayd Epic, Hilāliyya,* or *Sīrat Banī Hilāl)*

This Arabic folk epic has been told for 900 years throughout Arabic-speaking lands. It is the story, told in verse, of a black Arab hero, Abū Zayd, and of the wanderings of the Banī Hilāl tribe of northern Africa.

The first story, called "Birth of Abū Zayd," tells of Prince Rizq ibn Nāyil, of the Banī Hilāl tribe. Although rich and powerful, he has no son and heir from his marriage to Princess Khaḍrā, daughter of the Sharīf of Mecca. The princess goes with the women on their annual fertility pilgrimage to the lake where, as is the custom, she prays to God for a son and wishes on a bird. She wishes on a large black bird because it routs all the other birds. That same day she conceives, but when the child is born, he is black. The tribe accuses her of adultery, and her husband tells her, "My anger is because of you, / You mother of earrings! / . . . Was it fair, Khaḍrā, to beget me a black slave ['abd]? / Now—leave, go to your father's house!" And with that he banishes her and her "bastard" son to her father in Mecca.

Along the way, Khaḍrā meets 'Aṭwān the Outlaw, who guards the border lands dividing the Hilāl and Zaḥlān tribes. Zaḥlān Prince Fāḍil intervenes in 'Aṭwān's plans, rescues Khaḍrā, and takes her and Abū Zayd back to his tribe. The boy is schooled within the tribe by a teacher who casts frequent aspersions upon both mother and child. In retaliation, the boy kills the teacher. The teacher's brother meets him in battle, and Abū Zayd triumphs. The tribe acquits the boy of all charges and declares him a hero. As time goes on, his fame as a Zaḥlān hero-warrior grows.

It has been the custom of the Banī Hilāl to demand a land tax from the Zaḥlān tribe. But one year, the tribe refuses to pay it; instead, they send Abū Zayd to meet a member of the rival tribe in man-to-man combat. But when Abū Zayd meets his adversary, who is Rizq, the two recognize each other as father and son. A joyous reconciliation brings father and son together, and as soon as Abū Zayd is recognized as his father's legitimate son, he unites the two tribes as well. Risq, Khaḍrā, and Abū Zayd return home.

The merger of two tribes occurs over and over in the convoluted cycles that make up the *Hilāliyya*, or total tale.

After the birth tale, the next large episode concerns Ḥandal of the 'Uqaylī, who kills off the older Hilāl generation, leading Abū Zayd to wreak vengeance upon the enemy. While he is pillaging and ravaging, he discovers the beautiful 'Aliyya al-'Uqaylīyya, "One for the wounding of hearts, a dame of illustrious lineage," whom he takes home to be his bride. Once again he merges tribes, the Hilāl and 'Uqaylī, through marriage.

In the third and final tale of the large cycle of episodes, entitled "Taghrībat," or Westward Migration, Abū Zayd and his comrade Diyāb ibn Ghānim wage many battles against the Zanātī Khalīfa, the Berber ruler of Tūnis and the Maghrib, in the name of the Hilāl heroine al-Jāziyya (Zāziya). But as time passes, inner tensions within the tribe lead to discord and disintegration. Abū Zayd quarrels with his kinsman Diyāb ibn Ghānim; it was Ghānim upon whom Khadira placed a curse years ago for being the instigator of the gossip that drove her and her newborn infant from the tribe. Now Khaḍrā's curse is fulfilled.

The Jordan and Palestinian versions of the cycle include: (1) the birth of the hero, the tribe's experience in Nedj, and migrations in search of green pastures; (2) the "Riyāda," account of a scouting expedition to Tūnis the Green by Abū Zayd and his three nephews; (3) the "Taghrībat," or immigration to Tūnis, via Iran, Ethiopia, Syria, and Gaza, including conflicts with Zanātī Khalīfa, Christians, and Jews; (4) the "Seven Thrones" cycle in which Diyāb the Herdsman, also called the Wolf, lusts for power; he puts a spear through the eye of the Berber ruler of Tūnis, kicks Zāziya to death, bludgeons Abū Zayd with an iron club, and cuts Ḥasan's throat; and (5) the "War of the Orphans" in which the survivors break Dihrāb's hold and the tribe disperses.

Dihrāb, as the Wolf, is known to "eat girls." A Nigerian version of the epic, in which he is known in Shuwa Arabic as Ḍiyāb, focuses on the tribe's fear of cannibalism, and of being devoured by its leader. (Connelly 1986)

See also *'Antar, The Romance of; Abu Zayd Epic; Dhū al-Himma.*

BANTUGAN

Bantugan is a darangan, or epic, of the Moro people of the Philippines. Combined with the darangan of *Bidasari* and others, it takes a week to perform. It is valued for its absence of Western influences. (Preminger 1990)

BARD

In *Orkneyinga Saga,* Bard is a farmer at Voluness on Sanday who gives Svein Asleigarson shelter. In *Egil's Saga,* Bard of Atley Isle in Norway is King Eirik's steward, who fills Egil full of ale and is killed by him. Also in *Egil's Saga,* Bard the White (Brynjolfsson) of Torg Island in Norway marries Sigrid, inherits land when his father Brynjolf dies, joins King Harald's forces, and is killed in battle. In *Laxdaela Saga,* Bard Hoskuldsson of Iceland marries Ástrid and shares his inheritance with his half brother Ólaf. (Pálsson and Edwards 1988)

See also *Egil's Saga; Laxdaela Saga; Orkneyinga Saga.*

BARDI GUDMUNDSSON

In *Laxdaela Saga,* Bardi is one of the men who join in the attack on Bolli Thorleiksson. (Magnusson and Pálsson 1969)

See also Bard; Beinir the Strong; *Laxdaela Saga.*

BARDO THÖTRÖL

(Also *Bar-do Thodol* or Tibetan: *Bar-do'i-thos-grol)*

The *Tibetan Book of the Dead,* attributed to the founder of Tibetan Buddhism, describes the gateway to levels or dimensions of experience encountered by the soul during the bardo (intermediate state between death and rebirth). The Tibetan Buddhist instruction of six types of liberation is said to have been composed by Tantric master Padmasambhava and written down by his wife, Yeshe Tsogyal (ca. eighth century). Padmasambhava is said to have buried the texts in the Gampo Hills of central Tibet. They were later discovered by Karma-Lingpa, said to be the incarnation of one of Padmasambhava's original 25 chief disciples. They are read to the dying or recently dead as a guide, or "The Great Liberation through Hearing," through the realm of Bardo. Bardo means gap; it indicates the interval of suspension between death and rebirth and includes the moment before death. This state lasts as long as 49 days.

According to the *Bardo,* upon death the soul often lingers around the body for several days, during which time it experiences three stages of Bardo: 'Chi-kha'i Bardo, Chonyid Bardo, and Sidpa Bardo. During the first stage, visions appear of a Being of Clear Light with which the soul should try to identify and release all attachment to its former body. The soul remains in 'Chi-kha'i Bardo for several days in order to reach the realization of its death.

If it is unable to do so, it passes onto the second stage, acquiring a psychic body resembling its physical one, in which to meet seven divine beings. If it cannot identify them, it meets seven demons, which it should attempt to identify as projections of its own unconscious.

In the third stage, the soul travels freely in the physical world, able to observe its mourning loved ones but unable to comfort them. It remains in misery until it meets the Lord of the Otherworld, with whom it reviews its former life. It then "experiences the torture of its own desires and fears as demons." (Fremantle and Trungpa 1987)

See also Heruka, Great.

BARṢĪṢĀ, THE LEGEND OF

This is an Islamic story whose hero from the tenth century is said to be Barṣīṣā, a hermit monk. Three brothers, who are leaving on a journey, place their sick sister in his care. The devil tempts him to seduce the woman, who becomes pregnant. When Barṣīṣā discovers this, he kills her and buries her body. But the devil reveals her death to her brothers, so Barṣīṣā renounces God in order to save his own skin. Satan mocks him, reminding him he need only fear God now. The legend is also associated with the first Egyptian Coptic ascetic, St. Anthony. (Jackson, G. 1991)

BASIL DIGENES AKRITAS, EPIC OF

This Byzantine epic and epic cycle concern the heroic figure Digenes, who symbolized the Greek ideal of manhood in the medieval period. The cycle apparently originated in the eastern provinces during the tenth century and spread from the Syrian deserts to the Russian steppes, and even to southern Italy where Greek colonists had settled. All that remains of the cycle are the *Akritic Ballads* and several twelfth- to seventeenth-century versions of the *Epic of Basil Digenes Akritas.* The extant remains show both Hellenistic and Greek elements mixed with confusing historical elements and Eastern references. (Ostrogorsky 1969; Preminger 1990)

BASSADJALAN ZAMBELE, EPIC OF

In this heroic cycle (seventeenth century) of the kingdom of Segu in West Africa, young Bassadjalan asks his father's permission to go to a faraway place to prove his valor. His father refuses to allow him to leave until he has made a talisman for his son to wear that will protect him from bullets.

Bassadjalan receives his talisman and leaves, journeying for days until he comes to the town of Kala. He learns that the heroes of Kala spend their time in the company of heroes, but Bassadjalan likes to spend his time with two women he has just met. Their brothers say of him, "Is he a man or a woman? He only sits and gossips with my sisters. . . ."

They invite him to join them drinking wine so that, "When he has drunk enough wine, he may say something offensive and then we can deal with him." But Bassadjalan declines to drink with them.

The heroes divide a Cow of Heroes to see if he has the courage to claim a portion. Bassadjalan first takes the head because, "I, Bassadjalan Zambele, am the head of everything. If war comes, I will be the leader." He then takes the chest, saying, "If war comes, I will be . . . the heart of Kala." He takes the foreleg, saying, "If war comes, I will be the foremost in battle." His boasts infuriate the brothers. They tell him to be ready the following morning for a battle against the town of Koble, whose chief is Zanke.

The sisters warn him that their brothers only want to humiliate him. For years they have tried to defeat Zanke, but they can't because he has 12 sons and a future son-in-law, Ntchi, who is twice the size of an ordinary man. But Bassadjalan goes to the numuke of the town and has him forge a weapon and endow it with magic powers. As payment, he promises to bring the numuke a cow from Koble.

When he rides alone into Koble, Zanke tries to kill him with gunfire and spears, but Bassadjalan strikes him down with his magic weapon. He then takes on Ntchi, subdues him, and takes him and his bride-to-be and 400 cattle back to Nala. He returns to the numuke to pay him the cow he has promised, and he vows to rid the town of false heroes by fighting the worst. The numuke tells him that the man he should best is Didiya Tiekele, because "His arrogance is greater than his honor."

Bassadjalan sends the numuke to deliver his challenge to Didiya Tiekele, and the man accepts. On the day of the confrontation, Bassadjalan quickly bests Didiya Tiekele and leaves him crying. He does not kill him because "It is not honorable to kill a man who is afraid."

Bassadjalan takes his cattle and goes back to the village of his parents. In later years, he goes to another place and founds a city and a kingdom of his own. (Courlander 1982)

See also *Bakaridjan Kone, a Hero of Segu, Epic of; Bambara Epic; Da Monzon, Epic of.*

BATTLE OF BRUNANBURH

See "Brunanburh, The Battle of."

BATTLE OF KADESH

See *Battle of Qadesh.*

THE BATTLE OF KOSOVO

This Serbian epic cycle (ca. the fourteenth century), in part recorded from the oral tradition by 1555, was collected before 1720 in the *Erlangen Manuscript.* It was recorded singularly by Alberto Fortes in 1774, and by Goethe, Alexander Pushkin, Wilhelm Gerhard, Sir John Bowring, Adam Mickiewicz, V. G. Belinsky, and even Bela Bartok, who transcribed actual performances by guslari, who chant their poems accompanied by the one-string gusli. The definitive collection, a four-volume work by Vuk Stefanovic Karadzic, appeared in the nineteenth century, and it is this version upon which the translators of the cited text have relied. By unusual happenstance, many of Karadzic's best-known poems were recorded from recitations, not of traditional guslari, but by old blind women, some associated with monasteries in Srem, who have now become the custodians of the oral tradition.

The cycle chronicles in decasyllabic poems a battle between the Serbs, with the Croats' help on one side and Turks on the other. The battle had its decisive end on Kosovo Field, the Field of Blackbirds, on St. Vitus's Day, 1389. Although the Kosovo Battle resulted in heavy losses on both sides, the Serbs received a blow from which they never fully recovered because most of their leaders and nobility were either slain or driven into exile. The struggle continued for another 70 years, but it is Kosovo that has survived in epic poetry as the end of the Serbian empire, the moment of defeat and enslavement.

The Serbs are apparently unique among peoples in that their national epic poetry celebrates the empire's defeat rather than victory. The Serbs embrace the tragic sense of life, in which long-held ambitions of the clan are of no importance, and even statehood would be tragic.

According to Serbian scholar Charles Simic, the ten-syllable line combined with Serbian literary idiom make finding English equivalents difficult. The succession of poems does not follow a linear pattern; we are told early of the death of Tsar Lazar, but again and again we are taken back to events occurring prior to that death or occurring elsewhere at the same time.

The historical characters behind the epic are the Turkish sultan Murad; Captain Milosh; the three claimants to the Serbian throne following the 1371 death of King Uros: Marko (son of Vulasin), Tvrtko (king of Bosnia), and Lazar (nobleman and leader of the armies at the Battle of Kosovo); and Lazar's son-in-law Vuk Brankovic and his wife Militsa. With time and retelling of the epic songs, Lazar has been transformed into a Christlike tsar and Marko has become the epic hero Marko Kraljevic.

The epic begins with a fragment in which Sultan Murad sends a message to Lazar: "We cannot both / together rule here. / Therefore send me / every tax and key. . . ." If Lazar does not comply, Murad advises him, "Bring your armies. . . ."

The outcome is foretold in the second poem, "The Downfall of the Kingdom of Serbia," when a falcon delivers a letter from the Blessed Mother to Lazar, asking him to choose either a heavenly crown or an earthly one. If he chooses the earthly one, he is to have his knights make a dawn attack against the Turks, in which the enemy will be destroyed. If he chooses a heavenly crown, he is to build a church, "O not of stone / but out of silk and velvet." If he chooses a heavenly crown, she advises him to "take the bread and wine, / For all shall perish, / perish utterly. . . ." He meditates on what to do and comes to the realization that "Earthly kingdoms / are such passing things." He chooses the heavenly crown, and the Turks begin to pour over the plain of Kosovo.

In "Supper in Krushevats" the knights assemble in the fortress of Krushevats. Tsar Lazar offers a toast "to noble Captain Milosh," whom he calls both friend and traitor, saying, "Tomorrow you'll betray me / on the field of Kosovo, / Escaping to / the Turkish Sultan, Murad!" Milosh springs up and protests that he has never been unfaithful to his tsar: "But Treason, Lazarus, / sits beside you now— / The traitor sips his wine / right up your sleeve. / It's Brankovich. . . ."

In "Captain Milosh and Ivan Kosanclich," Ivan, who has been spying on the Turkish army, returns to describe to Milosh the army's vastness: "If all the Serbs / were changed to grains of salt / We could not even / salt their wretched dinners!" He has traveled for 15 days and has found no beginning and no end to the Turkish hordes. Milosh wants to know the location of the sultan's tent, "For I have sworn / to noble Lazarus / To slaughter like a pig / this foreign Tsar. . . ." Ivan calls him mad, saying the tent is in the middle of the vast encampment. Milosh makes him promise not to reveal to the tsar what he has seen, for fear the army might grow afraid.

"Musich Stefan," a Serbian nobleman, directs his servant to ready the battle horses while he sleeps, preparing for battle. His wife, who has dreamed of the Serbs' defeat, begs the servant Vaistina not to wake his master, but the loyal servant cannot disobey Stefan. He wakes him, and the two of them ride off to Kosovo. There a lovely maiden appears carrying two empty golden goblets and a bloody helmet, which she has found floating in the river. Stefan recognizes the helmet and begins to weep. He rides quickly into battle and kills three pashas before he himself is cut down. We are told that Tsar Lazar also dies on that day.

"Tsar Lazar and Tsaritsa Militsa" takes up the story in the tsar's fortress on the eve of the battle. His queen, Militsa, begs him not to take every man with him. She wants him to leave one of her nine brothers behind. "Give me Boshko Jugovich!" she pleads. The tsar consents, but Boshko refuses to remain behind: "What would all / my comrades say of me?" he asks her. She stands beside the gate as the men ride out. One by one she implores the other men of her family to remain with her. Finally, her brother Voin comes riding past, and she throws her arms around him, begging him to stay with her. He answers, "Go back, my sister, / To your castle tower— / . . . Nor would I leave / these horses of the Tsar / Even if I knew / that I would perish." The queen is so stricken with grief that she faints, and the tsar commands his dear and faithful servant Goluban to remain behind with her. Goluban is deeply disappointed; he weeps as he carries the queen to the castle tower. "But yet his heart / torments him: He must go / And ride to battle." As morning dawns two ravens fly to the castle tower to report to the queen what they have seen on the battlefield: Few Turks are left alive, and even fewer Serbs. "And all of them / have cruel bleeding wounds." The servant Milutin rides up carrying his own severed hand. The queen helps him dismount and bathes his wound. Then he tells her that the tsar and all her brothers except Boshko have been slain. Boshko remains upon the battlefield still, "Where he chases / Turks in frightened herds." Milosh, he reports, has killed the sultan Murad and many of his soldiers. "But ask me nothing / of Vuk Brankovich! / . . . For he betrayed / the Tsar of Kosovo, / And led away twelve / thousand men, my Lady. . . ."

"Tsaritsa Militsa and Vladeta the Voyvoda" returns to the time a few hours earlier before the queen has learned the outcome of the battle. She is walking on the grounds with her two daughters, Vukosava and Mara, when Vladeta, a warrior returning from the battlefield, rides up. The queen asks him if he has seen the tsar. Vladeta answers that he saw only the tsar's war-horse being chased by many Turks: "And thus I think / our noble Lord is dead." She asks about her father and her nine brothers. He answers that he has seen them all in the midst of the fighting. "And their arms were bloody / clear up to their shoulders, / their tempered swords / clear up to the hilts. . . ." She asks of news of the husbands of her daughters and is told of Milosh: "I saw him lean / upon his battle lance / . . . And the Turks / were swarming him. . . ." As to the other son-in-law, Vuk Brankovich, "I did not see him— / let the sun not see him either! / For he betrayed the Tsar. . . ."

"The Kosovo Maiden" tells of the maid who goes onto the battlefield seeking the wounded. "On her back she carries / warm, white bread . . . " and goblets of water and of wine. She "turns the warriors / over in their blood. . . ." If one is still breathing, she bathes him with the water and offers him the bread and wine "as if in sacrement. . . ." She comes to Pavle Orlovich, the tsar's standard-bearer. His hand and leg are cut off, and his chest is so crushed that she can see his lungs. After she has ministered to him, he asks her for whom she is searching. She tells him that as the warriors were riding out to battle, Milosh promised to give her as a bride to Milan Toplitsa when he returned; Ivan Kosanchich promised to be best man at the wedding, and Milan himself promised to come back and marry her. Pavle tells her to go on home; all three men have fallen in battle. She returns to her "white" (fair or good) village, wailing that she is so utterly cursed "that if I touched / a greenly leafing tree / it would dry and wither, / blighted and defiled."

A fragment follows extolling the exploits of three fine heroes: Banovich Strahinja, Srdja Zlopogledja, and Boshko Jugovich.

"The Death of the Mother of the Jugovich" tells how the queen's mother prays that God will give her the eyes of a falcon and the wings of a swan so that she may fly over the battlefield and see the fate of her husband, Jug Bogdan, and her nine sons. God grants her wish, and she flies over the Kosovo Plain to find that her sons and husband have all been slain. "And still her heart / is cold as any stone / And no tears rise at all, / and no tears fall." She returns to the castle where her sons' widows weep, but she does not weep. She asks her son Damian's wife why his stallion screams, and the daughter-in-law explains that the horse is grieving. At dawn two ravens fly over and drop a severed hand in the mother's lap. Damian's wife recognizes it as her husband's hand by its wedding ring. Now the mother can endure no more. Her heart "swells and breaks with sorrow."

"The Miracle of Lazar's Head" tells how, when the Turks beheaded the tsar, not a single Serb witnessed it. But a Turkish slave boy, son of a Serbian woman who was enslaved, asks the Turks to have pity. "Here before us lies / a sovereign's noble head!" It would be a sin to allow it to be trampled by horses or pecked at by crows, he says. He takes the head and puts it in a spring, where it remains for 40 years. One day three young carters from Skoplje stop for the night at Kosovos. They discover the "holy head" in the spring, and one man dives in and retrieves it, placing it on the grass while he gets some water in a jug. When they look around, the head has rolled away, moving toward the body to rejoin it. The next morning the young carters send a message to 300 priests, who summon 12 bishops, who summon four old patriarchs. They all put on holy vestments and come to read prayers and question the saint as to which great church or monastery he would like to be taken. But he wishes to stay "at lovely Ravanitsa," which he endowed during those years when "he walked upon this earth."

"The Death of Duke Prijezda" tells of "message after message," which arrive at the white castle of Prijezda, duke of Stalach. They are from the Turkish sultan Mehmed, demanding three treasures: the duke's "deadly tempered sword" that will cut through stone or even cold iron; his gallant war-horse Zhadral that leaps the height of double rampart walls; and third, the duke's faithful wife Jelitsa. The duke sends a reply that the sultan may raise as large an army as he likes, but he will never get any of the three treasures. The sultan and his army begin a bombardment of Stalach that lasts for three years but does not dislodge a single stone. One Saturday morning Jelitsa goes to the top of the wall and gazes down into the muddy river Morava. She tells the duke that she fears the Turks will get into the castle underground. The duke assures her that no one can tunnel under the river. After Sunday mass, he sends her to the cellar for wine and proposes to his men that after they have eaten and drunk their wine, they open up the castle gates and "make a flying raid / against the Turks." But when Jelitsa goes to the cellar, she finds it full of Turkish soldiers, toasting her health and the death of her husband. She runs to tell the duke, who springs into action against the intruders. Sixty lords die in the fray, but thousands of Turks die. When he has chased them away temporarily, he locks the castle, cuts off his horse's head, breaks his sword, and asks his wife if she will choose to die with him. The two climb to the top of the walls where Jelitsa says, "The waters of the Morava / have nursed us; / The waters of the Morava / should bury us!" Holding hands, they leap into the river. Sultan Mehmed conquers Stalach, but there are no treasures left. He curses and complains that he had 3,000 men when he arrived, but he starts home with only 500. (Matthias and Vučković 1987; Miletich 1990)

See also Marko Kraljevic; Milosh Obilich, Captain.

BATTLE OF MALDON

See *Maldon, The Battle of.*

BATTLE OF QADESH

(Also *Battle of Kadesh)*

This Egyptian epic describes a battle fought in 1296 B.C. between Ramses II and Hittite king Muwatallis before the Syrian town of Qadesh. According to the epic, Ramses is unperturbed as waves of Hittites, fresh from an invasion of Palestine, arrive at Qadesh and camp overnight. Possessed of great courage and bolstered by confidence in his father/god Amon, Ramses decides to attack and single-handedly drives the hordes away. The poem, which is filled with wild exaggerations as to the number of men vanquished by Ramses, is preserved in a papyrus and on five temple inscriptions in three temples. The poet is unknown. (Ceram 1990)

BATTLE OF UHUD

(Also *Utenzi wa Vita Vya Uhud)*

This Swahili utendi, or epic poem, was compiled in the 1950s from an oral tradition in Paje by Haji Chum. The work has the advantage of psychological insight and the recorder's knowledge of artistic form. (Westley *RAL* 1991)

BAU

(Also Gula, Nininsina, or Ninkarrak)

Bau is a Sumero-Akkadian deity (ca. twenty-second to twenty-first century B.C.), goddess of healing and of the dog. Bau is the daughter of An, the king of the gods. She is the wife of the rain god Ninurta, also called Pabilsag, or Ningirsu, the earlier form, which is how he appears in the *Epic of Gilgamesh.* She is the city goddess of Urukug in the Lagash region. (Pritchard 1973)

BEINIR THE STRONG

In *Laxdaela Saga,* Beinir the Strong is one of Olaf Hoskuldsson's smiths, who supports Halldor Olafsson against Thorstein Kuggason and Thorkel Eyjolfsson. (Magnusson and Pálsson 1969)

See also Bard; Bardi Gudmundsson; *Laxdaela Saga.*

BEL

(Also Baal)

Mesopotamian god. ***See*** *Baal Epic.*

BEOWULF

This early (ca. eighth century) Anglo-Saxon work, which J. R. R. Tolkien termed a heroic-elegaic poem, of 3,182 lines in alliterative verse, is the earliest lengthy written work in Teutonic literature. It combines mid-sixth-century Danish historical events with Nordic legend. The Germanic peoples of the Dark Ages shared an oral tradition reaching from Iceland to Austria. This is one of the earliest surviving works. Old English scholar Robert P. Creed has suggested a scenario by which the pagan poem came to contain written Christian elements. The tale may have been carried to Anglo-Saxon England by a Dane, Geat, or Anglo-Saxon seafarer sometime after the events depicted took place. After St. Augustine's arrival in England in 597, the story was recast by a scop who was a singer.

The poem opens with a prologue concerned with the mythic ancestor of Danish kin, Scyld Scefing, and the founding of the Scylding dynasty. Scyld (or Shild) is an abandoned baby who is rescued by the Danes and later becomes their king. Late in life he has a son, Beo, not to be confused with the hero of the poem. When Scyld dies, Beo succeeds him as king.

Part 1 relates that Beo rules for a long time and is succeeded by his son, "the great Healfdane, a fierce fighter." Healfdane has a daughter, Yrs, given in marriage to the king of Sweden, and three sons. The middle son, Hrothgar, a superior warrior, eventually becomes king of the Danes on the island of Zealand. Hrothgar builds a great mead hall called Herot (Heorot) for entertaining his "mighty band," but he does not count on "that demon, that fiend, / Grendel, who haunted the moors. . . ."

In part 2, while the Danes are sleeping, Grendel slips into the hall and snatches up 30 men. Eventually all men must abandon the hall because of the monster's murderous ravages.

In part 3 Beowulf, "greater / And stronger than anyone anywhere in this world," son of Edgetho and Hrethel, and nephew of King Higlac (Hygelac) of the Geats (residing just across the water from the Danes on the coast of Sweden), hears of Hrothgar's trouble and determines to come to his aid. He chooses 14 warriors and sails toward the land of the Danes. In part 4 Beowulf and his men land on the Danish shore. He introduces himself to the watchman and explains his mission. In part 5 they reach the king's court and wait while the Swedish prince Wulfgar asks the king to receive them. Wulfgar notes their fine mail and assures the king, "These men are no beggars."

In part 6 Beowulf is ushered into King Hrothgar's presence. He explains that he has come to "purge all evil from this hall" and promises that, like Grendel, he will use no weapons: "My hands / alone shall fight for me." In part 7 Hrothgar recounts to Beowulf something of their shared past history, including how he had come to the throne and how he had helped Beowulf's father. He welcomes Beowulf's help and proposes a banquet in his honor.

During the feast, in part 8, a Danish warrior, Unferth, insults Beowulf by saying that he once lost a swimming match with Brecca and has only been lucky with his battle exploits so far. In answer, Beowulf describes the swimming contest. In part 9 he continues his description of his fight with sea monsters off the Finnish shore in the swimming match, during which he saved Brecca's life. When he has finished, Queen Welthow passes the mead cup and thanks Beowulf for coming to help her afflicted people. Pleased with "his bright-tongued boasts," she repeats them to her husband. At the evening's end, Hrothgar tells Beowulf, "No one strange to this land / Has ever been granted what I've given you." He gives over the hall to Beowulf and retires.

In part 10 the Geats settle down to spend the night in the mead hall, but Beowulf lies wakeful, watching. In part 11 Grendel rises "out from the marsh / From the foot of misty / Hills and bogs, bearing God's hatred. . . ." In part 12, in mighty bare-handed combat, Beowulf confronts the monster, wrenches its arm from its body, and hangs the arm from the rafters as a trophy. The monster runs off in a rage of pain.

In part 13, the next morning the crowd follows Grendel's bloody footprints down to the lake's edge but finds no trace of him. On the way back to Herot, one of the king's thanes sings some of the old lays, weaving Beowulf's deeds among those of Siegmund's. In part 14 the king comes to Herot, sees the monster's arm swinging from the rafters, and cries out thanks to God and to Beowulf. He makes Beowulf his son and tells him to take whatever he wishes. Even Unferth no longer feels like boasting or challenging the hero.

In part 15 Hrothgar orders the hall festooned and he gives a triumphant feast, during which a scop sings the tale of Finn and Hildeburgh (parts 16 and 17). In part 18, after the minstrel has finished singing, Queen Welthow offers Beowulf blessings and asks him to spread his protection on her son. The men enjoy a fine celebration lasting far into the night, and then both Danes and Geats lie down to sleep in the hall. Beowulf, however, is given other quarters.

In part 19, as the men lie sleeping, Grendel's mother comes to avenge her son, taking Hrothgar's closest friend and stealing the severed claw ripped from her son's body. The next morning, in part 20, Hrothgar tells Beowulf of the new calamity that has befallen them and says, "Our only help, / Again lies with you. . . ."

In part 21, Beowulf readily accepts the challenge to go to the lake and kill the monster, even if he himself may not survive the encounter. He tells the king, "fame after death / Is the noblest of goals." Unferth gives up "that chance to work wonders, win glory, / And a hero's fame." Instead, he lends his weapon to Beowulf. The warriors travel to the lake's edge where monsters now swarm on every side.

In part 22, Beowulf plunges into the demon-infested lake and wrestles with Grendel's mother, who drags him down to her den. The sword Hrunting, which Unferth has lent him, cannot dent her tough hide. In part 23, on the cave's wall Beowulf finds a sword crafted by the giants. With this he is able to behead her, although the blow melts the sword up to its hilt. He sees the corpse of Grendel and beheads it so that he can carry the head back by the hair as a trophy.

In part 24, Beowulf describes the battle to the king and gives him what remains of the giant-crafted sword: its golden hilt. The king praises him but warns him about becoming vainglorious like Hermond. In part 25 they enter

Herot, and the Danes and Geats again feast together. After a night's sleep, Unferth offers his sword to Beowulf as the Geats prepare to sail homeward.

In part 26, as they depart, Beowulf and the Geats receive many gifts and lavish praise from Hrothgar. In part 27, they reach their Geatish shore and Beowulf orders his treasure carried up to the king's hall. In part 28 he is received by Higlac, to whom he begins to relate his adventures among the Danes. He also mentions that King Hrothgar plans to give his daughter Freauw to Ingeld of the Hothobards, hoping to put an end to an old quarrel. However, in part 29, Beowulf predicts, "The friendship can't last, / The vows are worthless." He then returns to his tale of his struggle with Grendel. In part 30 he tells of his struggle with Grendel's mother, ending with, "Healfdane's great son heaped up / Treasures and precious jewels to reward me." He explains, in part 31, that he has almost no family, "almost no one, now, but you." He orders the treasures brought in for Higlac, who in turn rewards him with his grandfather's sword, 7,000 "hides of land, houses, and ground." The narrative moves rapidly forward to the time when both Higlac and his son are dead, killed in wars with the Swedes, and Beowulf becomes king, ruling long and well for 50 winters. Then a fire-breathing dragon, who has slept in a stone tower for ages, awakes, angered because a man has stolen a gem-studded goblet from his hoard.

Part 32 explains how the treasure came to be in there, how the dragon came upon it unguarded, and how the beast, finding his treasure violated, begins to ravage the land. In part 33 Beowulf, whose own home is consumed by the dragon's fire, orders a battle-shield of iron to protect him from "the flaming heat, / Of the beast's breath." A flashback describes Higlac's war with the Frisians, Beowulf's escape and swim to freedom, and his initial refusal of the crown offered him by Higlac's widow. In part 34 he recalls coming at age seven to live with his grandfather, King Hrethel. He tells how Hrethel's son Hathcyn accidentally killed his brother Herbald, but no vengeance could be enacted that would not deprive him of his one remaining son. "Pleasure is gone, / The harp is silent, and hope is forgotten," he says.

In part 35 Beowulf describes Hrethel's death from grief. He then says farewell to his companions and strides off alone to face the dragon. In face-to-face combat his shield begins to melt, and his spear breaks against the dragon's scaly hide. His followers—all but Wiglaf—run for their lives as Beowulf is wrapped in flames.

In part 36 Wiglaf, remembering Beowulf's past kindness, rushes in to help, but his shield quickly melts. Beowulf strikes the dragon in the head, but his sword, Naegling, shatters. In part 37 Wiglaf strikes the dragon with his sword, and Beowulf drives a knife into the beast. Together, the two noblemen are able to bring the monster down, but Beowulf has been mortally wounded. He tells Wiglaf to fetch him the dragon's treasure, that he may see it before he dies.

In part 38 Wiglaf rushes into the dragon's lair and drags out as much treasure as he can carry. Gasping for breath, Beowulf says with satisfaction, "I sold my life / For this treasure and I sold it well." Then his soul "leaves his flesh, flies to glory."

As Wiglaf grieves, in part 39, the cowards creep back out of the wood "like shamefaced jackals." He tells them, "death / Would be better for . . . you, than the kind / Of life you can lead, branded with disgrace!" In part 40 Wiglaf sends a messenger to tell the Geats that their king is dead. The herald rides off with dire predictions to the crowd that, once the Franks and Frisians have heard the news, "the people can expect fighting."

In part 41 the messenger tells the people that they should hasten to build a pyre for their king. The Geats follow him to where their king lies dead, beside the dragon and the treasure that has lain hidden in the earth for a thousand winters.

In part 42 Wiglaf commands the warriors to bring wood for the pyre. He chooses seven thanes who go with him to drag the carcass of the dragon to the edge of a cliff and drop it into the sea. Beowulf's body, along with the treasure, is put on a wagon and brought to the pyre. As Beowulf has requested, the pyre is hung with shields and helmets. His body is placed atop it and burned, amidst much lamenting and moaning by his subjects. Then, as Beowulf has also requested, the Geats work for ten days building a tower in which to seal his ashes and the treasure as well, which is now "forever hidden and useless to men." (Hieatt 1967; Raffel 1963)

See also Dagref; Grendel; Herbald; Higlac; Hrothgar.

BERA

In the Viking *Egil's Saga,* Bera is the daughter of Yngvar, wife of Skallagrim, and foster mother to Asgerd, whose son is Egil. (Pálsson and Edwards 1988)

See also Bard; Berg-Onund; *Egil's Saga.*

BERG-ONUND

In the Viking *Egil's Saga,* Berg-Onund marries Gunnhild, Asgerd's half sister. He prevents Egil from claiming Asgerd's share of her father's inheritance and is killed by Egil. (Pálsson and Edwards 1988)

See also Bard; Bera; *Egil's Saga.*

BERGTHORA

In the Icelandic *Njal's Saga,* Bergthora is Njal's wife. She quarrels with Gunnar's wife Hallgerd and dies with Njal in the burning. (Magnusson and Pálsson 1960)

See also *Njal's Saga.*

BERLE-KARI

In the Viking *Egil's Saga,* Berle-Kari is Egil's great-grandfather. (Pálsson and Edwards 1988)

See also Bard; Bera; Berg-Onund; *Egil's Saga.*

BHAGAVADGĪTĀ
("The Lord's Song")

This is part of book VI of the *Mahābhārata,* presented in the form of a dialogue between Kṛiṣṇa, who takes the shape of the avatāra of the god Viṣṇu, and his friend, the Pāṇḍava warrior Arjuna. The poem consists of 700 Sanskrit verses divided into 18 chapters. It is considered one of the most beautiful of all Hindu scriptures. Scholars consider it of a later date than most of the *Mahābhārata,* having been composed ca. the first or second century A.D.

The scene is the battlefield just prior to the confrontation between the Pāṇḍavas and the Kauravas. Arjuna has misgivings about engaging in brutal conflict against his brothers, even though the cause is just. He asks his friend and charioteer for advice. The Lord Kṛiṣṇa answers that man must act with right motive but must not be attached to the outcome. The work gives a detailed description of the three paths of the Hindu tradition that lead to mystic union with God. (Mascaró 1962)

See also Arjuna; Kṛṣṇa; *Mahābhārata;* Pāṇḍavas.

BHĀRĀTAYUDDHA

This ancient Indian epic forms the basis for the Javanese epic by the same name. In the twelfth-century reign of King Jayabhaya of the kingdom of Kadiri, the epic was rewritten in Javanese with story changes to reflect the occurrences in the country since Jayabhaya's father, the powerful King Airlangga, divided his kingdom into two parts—Kaḍiri and Janggala—for his heirs (1049). His son was able to recapture Janggala and reunite the kingdom, which is the essence of the epic. (Preminger 1990)

BHĪṢMA

In the *Mahābhārata,* Bhīṣma, the most perfect man, in order to allow his father Śaṇtanu to marry a second time, renounces his own opportunity ever to love a woman. As a reward for his unselfish vow, the gods allow him to choose the day of his death. The five Pāṇḍavas and their 100 Kaurava cousins are all brought up together under his guidance. True to his vow, Bhīṣma must reject the love of Amba, who promises revenge and pursues him all over the world throughout most of the story. In the end, he is almost 100 years old, having outlived Amba, who returns as Sikhandin, a man, and is still bent on revenge. On the front line of battle, however, Sikhandin forgets Amba's former bitterness and fails to kill Bhīṣma. (Buck 1981)

BHOMAKĀWYA

The *Bhomakāwya* is a Javanese kakawin of the eleventh century. The kakawin, an old Javanese genre, includes epic, lyric, and erotic poetry. The *Bhomakāwya* was discovered by invading Dutch in the nineteenth century, and was edited and published at the time. (Preminger 1990)

BHUZA

In the Zulu epic of *Emperor Shaka the Great,* Bhuza is the general of the Mthethwa regiment of Izichwe, to which Shaka belongs. (Kunene 1979)

See also *Emperor Shaka the Great.*

BIDASARI

The *Bidasari* is a darangan, or epic, of the Moro people of the Philippines. Along with the *Bantugan* and others, it takes a week to perform. It is valued for its absence of Western influence. (Preminger 1990)

BIDPAI, THE FABLES OF

Named after the narrator, Bidpai, this Indian animal lore (ca. 500–100 B.C.) was intended for instruction. The original is a mixture of Sanskrit verse and prose. The stories have traveled throughout Arabia, Europe, and Asia, reaching Indonesia possibly through the oral tradition and old Javanese literature. (Siepmann 1987)

See also Gellert; *Pañcatantra.*

BISHERIA
(Flashes)

In several versions of the *Mwindo Epic,* Bisheria appears as the son of Mwindo's sixth wife, Mweri. He receives the status of prince in some versions. Bisheria is also an epithet for lightning in some versions. (Biebuyck 1978)

See also *Mwindo, Epic of.*

BITON KOULIBALY
(Also Mamari, Mamari Kouloubali, Biton Mamari, and Mamari the Biton, the Commander)

He is the subject of an eighteenth-century Mandé epic of Mali. In 1712 the small Bambara state of Segu comes under Mamari's rule. He is the son of a non-Muslim farmer and is originally the captain of a raiding band that raids and hunts, using the proceeds from their raids to buy slaves. He becomes powerful enough to force the Muslims (Markas) to split off from the tribe. He builds an army of several thousand and a "navy" of canoes to patrol the Niger, manned by his slaves or prisoners of war. With his powerful force, he subdues his neighbors, Fulani, Mossi, and Soninke.

The king of Kong to the south resents his interference with trade routes and attacks (1730); however, Mamari beats back the invasion. Briefly he is able to gain control of Timbuktu and makes Segu a powerful, if small, kingdom.

The wealthy Muslim Marka clan eventually goes to war against Mamari (1740), but he bests them as well. After he defeats them, he tries to gain the support of other clan leaders. They snub him, so he has them executed.

He becomes such a stern ruler that the Massasi group leaves Segu and migrates northwest to form a new Bambara state in Kaarta and Nioro (1753) shortly before his death (1755). (Courlander 1982; Lipschutz and Rasmusson 1989)

See also *Da Monzon, Epic of.*

BJARKAMÁL

This Old Viking heroic poem, a call to arms of which only fragments remain, was often recited before a campaign. In "The History of St. Olav" from the *Heimskringla,* on the day of the Battle of Stiklarstadir against the Norwegians (1013), King Olav awakens early and calls for his bard Tormod the Scald to "Say before us a poem!" Tormod recites the old *Bjarkamál* to rouse the forces. It tells of the doomed, legendary Danish king Hrolf Kraki (fl. sixth century) and his warriors at Lejre. Before the poem begins, Hrolf, whose life is told in Iceland's *Hrolfs Saga Kraka* (ca. fourteenth century), has been successful in his attack at Uppsala upon Swedish king Athils. But when he encounters his brother-in-law Hjorvarther at Lejre, he meets a heroic death. After Tormod has recited the poem, the men call it "the egging on of the huscarls." The poem begins: "The day is sprung up, / The cock's feathers rustle; / . . . I wake you not for wine, / Or the chatter of women, / But rather for battle. . . ." (Jones, G. 1990; Sturlason 1990)

See also *Heimskringla; Hrolfs Saga Kraka.*

BJARNI BRODD-HELGASON OF HOF

In the Icelandic *Njal's Saga,* Bjarni is a member of Flosi's forces opposed to Njal. In *Orkneyinga Saga,* Bjarni the Gold-Brow Poet's work is quoted. (Magnusson and Pálsson 1960)

See also *Njal's Saga.*

BJORGOLF

In the Viking *Egil's Saga,* Bjorgolf is a landholder in Norway, father of Brynjolf. (Pálsson and Edwards 1988)

See also Bard; Bera; Berg-Onund; Brynjolf; *Egil's Saga.*

BJORN

In the Icelandic *Njal's Saga,* Bjorn the White of Mork takes vengeance on the Burners. In the great Icelandic *Laxdaela Saga,* Bjorn is a farmer and the father of Jorunn, wife of Hoskuld Dala-Kollsson. Also in *Laxdaela Saga,* Bjorn Buna (Grimsson) is the father of Ketil Flat-Nose and ancestor of Osvif Helfason, and Bjorn Ketilsson (Bjorn the Easterner) is the son of Ketil Flat-Nose. In the Viking *Egil's Saga,* Bjorn Brynjolfsson (the Yeoman) is a chieftain's son in Norway who abducts Thora Lace-Cuff and takes her to Iceland. He has a daughter, Asgerd. Later he makes a Viking expedition with Thorolf, loses his wife, marries again, and has another daughter, Gunnhild. (Magnusson and Pálsson 1960; Magnusson and Pálsson 1969; Pálsson and Edwards 1988)

See also *Egil's Saga; Laxdaela Saga; Njal's Saga.*

BLOOD MARKSMAN AND KURELDEI THE MARKSMAN

This Tatar oral narrative poem was recorded in the nineteenth century from nomadic Turkic-speaking inhabitants of the steppes of southeastern Siberia. The poem is typical of heroic poems in its mingling of gods with humans, and in its use of talking animals—in this case, as in so many others, a horse and a bull.

"Blood Marksman" is Kan Mirgan, the lord of all the land. As yet, Kan Areg, his dear wife of many years, has given him no heir. One day a golden arrow flies from the sky and lands in a post near him. A message is carved on the arrow: "Tomorrow morning you must come to us." Kan Mirgan knows the message is from the nine gods, but he throws the arrow into the camp flames and cries, "I owe nothing to the gods / I have nothing to give them!"

The next morning "the greatest of all warriors," Alten Kus, rides into camp to challenge Kan Mirgan. "At the sound of his voice stones on the ground are shattered / the sea-flood rises / mountains fall apart." The two warriors wrestle for seven days until Kan Mirgan bests Alten Kus and cuts him in two. His stallion escapes and gallops up to the sky.

Kan Areg asks her husband, "Why do you struggle with the gods / why fight the gods who live up in the sky?" She reveals that she is six months pregnant and predicts, "Even now the nine Kudais (gods) are forging / nine strong warriors to a single warrior / named Buidalei Mirgan. / Tomorrow morning they will send him here to fight you." She is very fearful, but Kan Mirgan goes to bed and sleeps peacefully.

The next day another warrior rides into camp: the dreaded Buidalei Mirgan. At the sound of his voice, "mountains fall asunder / . . . all the earth is shaken / the high peaks bow to the ground." As before, the two warriors clash; they "bellow like great bulls / they bend, crush, drag one another / neighing like wild foals." For nine days they wrestle, then they fight on for seven more. Finally Buidalei cuts Kan Mirgan into six pieces and stamps them underfoot. Kan Mirgan's stallion gallops to the fair Kan Areg, who has just borne two children, a boy and a girl.

The stallion takes the children in its nostrils and gallops far away, making no sound. Buidalei runs to Kan Areg's yurta and shouts so loudly that she falls to the ground weeping in fear, "Where have you hidden the two children?" Kan Areg answers, "Youth left me barren / and shall old age make me a mother?" Buidalei drags her by her plaits out of the yurta and whips her until she dies. Then he mounts his horse and flogs it "till the whip strikes on bare bones," following Kan Mirgan's stallion.

The stallion reaches the brave warrior Ai Mirgan and says, "I have come to you / because men say that you are full of pity / . . . that you may take these orphans in your care. . . ." But Ai Mirgan, who is middle-aged, says, "My time of flowering strength is past / . . . you must not put your trust in me!" He sends the stallion to find the mighty warrior Kartaga Mirgan. After the stallion leaves, Buidalei arrives, still pursuing the stallion, and strikes Ai Mirgan dead.

Meanwhile, the stallion arrives in Kartaga's homeland and finds the great man seated on his couch of gold with his wife standing beside him holding "a beaker of fine gold." He does not answer the stallion's plea for help; he says nothing at all. The stallion stands there weeping until evening, then it runs on. After the stallion leaves, Buidalei arrives at the homeland of Kartaga, who aims an arrow at Buidalei's horse. The arrow strikes the beast in the neck and "springs back as if from a rock / it clangs as if it hit hard iron."

Buidalei rides on after the stallion, who has run through 40 lands and has arrived at a shore where a large blue bull stands by the sea. The bull tells the stallion, "For all my strength / I cannot save these children's lives." The stallion gallops on to the home of the Khan-Maiden, to whom 60 khans pay tribute.

Meanwhile, Buidalei arrives at the seashore and meets the bull, which he wrestles for nine days and fights for seven more. He finally defeats the bull and rips open its belly.

The stallion, who has been ignored completely by the Khan-Maiden, has no land left. From its eyes "tears fall like drops of blood / the water from its nostrils is like hanging ice." Beyond the 40 lands lives the warrior Katai Mos and his wife Kezil Dyibak the Fair. The stallion decides to leave the 40 lands and appeal to Katai Mos.

He gallops up to the warrior and begs him to save the children. Katai Mos answers, "Give both the children to . . . my wife / and she will take them in her care." The stallion races down the mountainside where Kezil meets him, takes the children from him, and hurries to her yurta to feed them.

Buidalei arrives and straightaway attacks Katai Mos. The two wrestle for seven days and fight for nine more, but neither can prevail. The boy child, now five years old, comes to the battle scene and drags Katai to one side so that he himself can fight Buidalei. (The arithmetic of the number of years involved does not compute accurately. It is presumed that what is meant here and in the following fight scene is "a long time.")

The boy and the warrior wrestle for seven days, then fight on for seven years. They wrestle for nine days, and then fight for nine years, until Buidalei's strength fails and he falls. The boy cuts off Buidalei's head and returns with Katai to the yurta for a feast.

The boy wants to go back to the land of his birth, but years go by, and he is nine years old before a stallion appears to take him home. Katai orders a feast in his honor and gives him the name of Kureldei Mirgan and his sister the name of Kumus Areg. Kureldei kisses Katai on the mouth, and Kezil presents a robe with eagle wings to Kumus. The two start for home: Kureldei on his fine stallion and Kumus flying overhead with her garment of eagle wings.

When they arrive at their former yurta, they find it overrun with weeds. Kureldei rides off and shoots six elk with one arrow, and with the hides he builds a yurta. From the meat, the two have a fine meal.

The next day he rides out and sees seven black warriors standing on a rock. He shoots the largest warrior, and the rock opens. All of Kureldei's people and the herds rightfully belonging to him come streaming out of the rock. He takes them back home and has a great feast. To this day, "The valiant warrior Kureldei Mirgan / still lives on his own land." (Cohn 1946)

BOBBILI KATHA

(Also *Bobbili Yuddha Katha*)

This Telugu folk epic (ca. eighteenth century) is still performed orally. The word *katha* means "narrative" in Telugu. Two printed versions exist: One palm-leaf text bears the name of a lesser-known poet, Peddāḍa Mallēśam, and the other has no date or name. A printed version, called *Pedda Bobbilirāju Katha* (The Big Story of the Bobbili King), or *Bobbili Yuddha Katha,* edited and published in 1956 by Mallampalli Somasēkhara Śarma, includes the account of a cockfight between the Bobbili and Vijayangar kings that is obviously taken from an earlier Telugu epic. *(See Palnāḍu, The Epic of.)* The epic is a martial epic whose heroes are of the Velama caste of Bobbili, in northeastern Andhra Pradesh.

According to Telugu scholar Velcheru Narayana Rao, after the British took control of the area, the Bobbili chiefs lost interest in preserving their Velama heritage and aspired instead to a "Kṣatriyalike status" and a Westernized lifestyle. They seemed to prefer a literary version of the epic written by eighteenth-century scholar/poet Dittakavi Narayana Kavi. That version is called *Rangarāyacaritramu.*

The Velama are land-owning peasants whose ruling family Bobbili chief is Ranga Rao. The main rival of the Bobbili is the chiefdom of Vijayanagar, a Kṣatriya clan. When a French commander named Bussy arrives in the region, the Vijayanagar king bribes his interpreters to convince Bussy to order Ranga Rao to vacate the Bobbili fort and move southward. When the zamindar, or chief, of the Bobbili refuses to surrender his fort, the Vijayangar king, with the help of French troops, attacks the fort. To the last man, the Velama warriors of

Bobbili remain to defend their fort, and all are slain. To escape capture, their wives jump into a fire. (Blackburn and Ramanujan 1986)

BOLLI BOLLASON

In the Icelandic *Laxdaela Saga,* Bolli Bollason is the son of Bolli Thorleiksson and Gudrun, born after his father's death. He takes vengeance for his father's death. He marries Snorri's daughter Thordis and reconciles with the Olafssons. Later he travels to Norway, Denmark, and Constantinople, returning in triumph to Iceland. (Magnusson and Pálsson 1969)

See also Bolli Thorleiksson; *Laxdaela Saga.*

BOLLI THORLEIKSSON

In the great Icelandic *Laxdaela Saga,* Bolli Thorleiksson is Gudrun's third husband; he is attacked by the Olafssons and killed. (Magnusson and Pálsson 1969)

See also Bolli Bollason; *Laxdaela Saga.*

BOOK OF ANEIRIN

This collection of Welsh poems, ca. 1250, contains works believed to be the work of the poet Aneirin, ca. 600, to whom "The Gododdin" is attributed. (Chadwick 1976)

See also Aneirin; "The Gododdin"; Hengerdd.

THE BOOK OF LEINSTER

This collection of Gaelic Irish verse and prose was drawn from the oral tradition and older manuscripts extant at the time it was written (ca. 1160; completed ca. first part of the thirteenth century). Its beautiful calligraphy is thought to be the work of Abbot Hun Crimthaind of Terryglass, Tipperary. It contains legendary and historical accounts of battles; genealogy of pre-Norman kings and heroes; history and name-origin of nearly 200 places; the oldest extant version of the legend of Deirdre, *The Fate of the Sons of Usnech;* and a version of *The Cattle Raid of Cooley.* (Chadwick 1976; Evans-Wentz 1990; Gantz 1988; Hubert 1980; Kinsella 1969; Rutherford 1987)

BOOK OF SONGS

(Also *Shih-Ching)*

This Chinese anthology (ca. 1000–600 B.C.), comprised of 305 poems and traditional songs from antiquity, was drawn from several levels of Chou society. Although early China has no epic in which the people's central myth is woven over the centuries into a narrative whole, the *Book of Songs* occupies the position held in other cultures by the epic. It is the oldest collection of poetry in world literature. Although military heroism and glorification of military power abound, there is very little violence in the poems.

Among the oldest in the collection are some of the 18 dynastic legends. In a cycle of poems that might be entitled "Origin of the Chou Tribe," the hero, Hou Chi (Lord Millet), is born of a mother, Chiang Yuan, whose barrenness is removed by a miracle when she treads on the big toe of God's footprint. Successive attempts to destroy Hou Chi by exposure while he is still an infant fail. He is protected by oxen, sheep, birds, even woodcutters. He grows up to become a successful planter.

His son Pu-k'u settles in the "land of the barbarians," north of the Wsi. Pu-k'u's grandson, Liu the Duke, returns with his descendants to Pin. Liu the Duke is described as "stalwart . . . Not one to sit down or take his ease." He establishes a large, prosperous citadel.

Another culture-hero is Tan-fu, a duke and, according to tradition, descendant of Hou Chi. He marries Lady Chiang and builds many houses at the foot of Mount Ch'u. The couple has two children. The elder, T'ai-po, refuses the throne. The other, Wang Chi, marries T'ai-jen and their son becomes King Wen, who is "very diligent" and "august." He "harries the lives" of the rebels of Tu and Jui, until they are brought to justice. King Wen marries T'ai-ssu, and she "carries on the fair name of Lady Chiang of Chou" by "bearing a multitude of sons." One becomes King Wu and the duke of Chou. Wu's son is King Ch'eng.

The poems in the *Songs* concerning warriors and battles are of two kinds: Battles in the north and northwest are to protect farmland from raids by nomads from the steppe; conflicts in the southeast are wars of conquest and annexation. (Waley 1960)

See also Hou Chi; *Shih-Ching.*

BOOK OF THE DEAD, EGYPTIAN

See *The Egyptian Book of the Dead.*

BOOK OF THE DEAD, TIBETAN

See *Bardo Thötröl.*

THE BOOK OF THE DEAN OF LISMORE

This is the oldest extant collection of Gaelic poetry in Scotland (ca. 1512–1526). The Scottish and Irish poems were collected by the dean of Lismore, James MacGregor, who died in 1551, and his brother Duncan, who lived until at least 1579, since the work also contains the *Chronicle of Fortingall* to that date. The work begins with a partial genealogy of MacGregor chiefs and also contains a list of Scottish kings to 1542, plus tales and ballads from both the *Ulaid* (Ulster) and *Fenian* cycles. Twenty-one Irish authors are included. Works by 44 Scottish bards date from ca. 1310–1520 and include two women: Isabella, countess of Argyll, and Aithbhreac Inghean Coirceadail. The most distinguished bards included Lord of the Isles Giolla Coluim mac an Ollaimh, member of the 500-year-old bardic line of MacMhuirich; Fionnlagh Ruadh, bard to Gregor clan chief John (d. 1519); and Griolla Criost Bruilingeach. One poem, of unknown origin, is a stirring call to battle addressed to the earl of Argyll before the Battle of Flodden (1513). It recounts the legendary invasion of Ireland by the Fomorians. (Watson 1937)

See also Fomórians.

THE BOOK OF THE DUN COW

(Leabhar na h-Uidhre)

This old Irish literary collection (ca. 1100) compiled by Irish monks of Clonmacnoise from older works and oral tradition was so named because the original text was said to have been written on the hide of the cow of St. Ciarán. Among its contents are the partial text of the *Cattle Raid of Cooley (**see** Taín Bó Cúailnge),* the longest tale of the *Ulster Cycle;* a poem attributed to Finn MacCool *(**see** Fenian Cycle);* a romantic saga about the court of Da Derga *(**see** Destruction of Da Derga's Hostel); Bricriu's Feast;* and a part of *The Voyage of Brân.* (Chadwick 1976; Evans-Wentz 1990; Gantz 1988; Hubert 1980; Kinsella 1969; Rutherford 1987)

See also *Bricriu's Feast; Destruction of Da Derga's Hostel; Fenian Cycle; Taín Bó Cúailnge; The Voyage of Brân, Son of Febal.*

BORK STARKADARSON

In the Icelandic *Njal's Saga,* Bork Starkadarson is one of three sons of Starkad of Thrihryrning who are on Njal's side of the feud that leads to the burning of Njal's home. He is killed by Gunnar in the Knafahills battle. (Magnusson and Pálsson 1960)

See also *Njal's Saga.*

BOTOLF THE STUBBORN

In *Orkneyinga Saga,* Botolf, called "a good poet," is an Icelandic farmer at Knarston who gives shelter to Earl Rognvald during a blizzard. Botolf offers to keep a lookout while the men get some sleep. Earl Erlend and his men learn that Rognvald has made it ashore and walked as far as Knarston, so they do the same. Botolf meets them at the door with a poem, saying they are "Out after eating-birds! / Fine archers, the Earl's men. . . ." Erlend's men race out to find them, while Botolf goes inside to wake Rognvald and his men, who escape. (Pálsson and Edwards 1978)

See also *Orkneyinga Saga.*

BOW SONG

This Tamil folksong tradition of southern India dates from the seventeenth century and possibly from the dawn of Christian times. The bow song tradition comprises hundreds of shorter narratives sharing many features with Indian oral epics. The bow song performance includes icons for local deities and a hunting bow, with bells hung from its frame, used as a musical instrument. The lead singer, who is sometimes a woman, plays the bow by striking the string with sticks, causing the bells to shake. All the other performers, playing clay jugs, drums, cymbals, and wooden blocks, are men. The singers are from lower and middle castes.

The bow song tradition is the backbone of annual festivals, which last for three days and nights. Some bow songs, concerning widely worshiped hero-gods, are sung throughout southern India; others who have local hero-gods as their subject are known only in a small area. The songs are classified in two groups: birth stories, which begin at Mount Kailāsa and often include cosmology relating to a local deity, and death stories, which are historical accounts of local heroes.

An example of the latter is named for its protagonist, Muttuppaṭṭaṉ, the pampered youngest son of a Brahmin family. When he is asked to recite the *Rāmāyaṇa* at a village gathering, he deliberately jumbles it, humiliating his family, who turn him out. He travels to Kerala and becomes minister to a local raja. In time his parents, having arranged a marriage for him, send his brothers to find him and convince him to return. They do so, but on the way home they stop to rest, and Muttuppaṭṭaṉ begins meditating.

Elsewhere, two girls, abandoned as infants by their Brahmin mother and reared by an Untouchable cobbler couple, leave home to take food to their father at work. As they near the meditating Muttuppaṭṭaṉ, he hears their singing and falls in love. He chases after them until the girls' father comes after him with a knife. Muttuppaṭṭaṉ tries to convince the father that his intentions are honorable. The cobbler demands proof: He must remove his topknot and Brahmin clothes, and then stitch a pair of leather sandals. In addition, he must obtain permission from his parents to marry Untouchables.

Muttuppaṭṭaṉ returns home where his brothers, believing him to be mad, put him in chains. But he breaks the chains and runs out to buy leather with which to sew a pair of sandals. The cobbler is impressed by the Brahmin's sincerity and grants his permission for the wedding. The marriage celebration begins.

While the guests are still present, an alarm signals that someone is stealing the father's cattle. Muttuppaṭṭaṉ goes into battle against the rustlers in his father-in-law's place and is mortally wounded. The family dogs roll in his blood and return to the house to show the family what has happened. The new brides rush out to find his body, sing a long lament, and become satis on his funeral pyre. (Blackburn et al. 1989)

BRÂN

(Brân the Blessed Son of Llyr)

Legendary ruler of Ulster, in "Branwen Daughter of Llyr" in the *Mabinogion,* Brân is a giant Celtic god; he is the hero of *The Voyage of Brân, Son of Febal* (Imran Brain) as well (ca. seventh century). His story probably inspired later tales such as *Bricriu's Feast* and *Sir Gawain and the Green Knight,* as well as *The Legend of Sleepy Hollow.* According to the most important myth concerning Brân, when he is mortally wounded he asks his companions to cut off his head—the head being the seat of the soul according to Celtic belief. He has previously promised them that if they will take his head with them, it will keep them entertained and uncorrupted for so long as they do not open a certain door. Once that door is opened, they will return to the world and all its troubles. For 80 years, his former companions enjoy an idyllic life and, according to Brân's instructions, bury the head on White Mount in London, where it remains for centuries thereafter. Brân, whose name means "raven," is described in the *Mabinogion* as being so tall that no house ever built is tall enough to contain him, and his feasts are held in tents. At his court at Harddlech, he sits on a rock overlooking the sea. *The Voyage of Brân* tells in verse and prose the otherworld journeys of Brân and his 27 men. This story is preserved in *The Yellow Book of Lecan.* (Chadwick 1976; Gantz 1976; Markdale 1986; Meyer 1987)

See also Brian; *Mabinogion; Ulster Cycle; The Voyage of Brân, Son of Febal.*

BRIAN

In *Orkneyinga Saga,* Brian is King of the Irish. He meets Dublin king Sigtrygg Silk-Beard and Sigurd, earl of Orkney, in the Battle of Clontarf, in which his forces prove to be superior. There is no one else to carry the raven banner, so Sigurd carries it and loses his life. King Sigtrygg runs away, and Brian's forces win. But Brian himself is also killed. (Pálsson and Edwards 1982)

See also Brân; *Orkneyinga Saga.*

BRICRIU'S FEAST

(Fled Bricrenn)

This Irish Gaelic hero tale (ca. eighth century) is one of the longest of the *Ulster Cycle.* It is preserved in *The Book of the Dun Cow.* Bricriu Nemthenga, the trickster, promises the hero's portion of his great feast for Conchobar to three different champions: Cú Chulainn, Lóegure Búadach, and Conall Cernach. The day of the great feast arrives, and Bricriu throws down the challenge concerning the champion's portion: "Let it be given to the best warrior in Ulaid." The three warriors argue violently over who is most deserving of the portion, and a series of contests is planned to settle the dispute.

Meanwhile, Bricriu, waiting in his bower with his queen, ponders how he can incite the women as he has the men. He flatters the wife of each of the warriors, telling Fedelm Noíchride (Lóegure's wife), Lendabair (Conall's wife), and Emer (Cú Chulainn's wife) that each is the most deserving to be queen. He tells each woman that the first to enter the royal house will be queen. All three women and their entourages gallop toward the royal house, making such a din that the house shakes. The warriors inside spring for their weapons and try to kill one another before Senchae says, "Wait! This is not the arrival of enemies—rather, Bricriu has incited the women outside to strife." Emer reaches the door first, but the doorkeepers have closed them. Each husband tries to open the door so that his wife will enter first. Finally, Cú Chulainn lifts the side of the house so high that stars are visible beneath the wall, and Emer enters easily.

The warriors undergo a number of contests, but no decision can be reached concerning who is the greatest champion. They ask a giant, Úath, to decide which of them is the winner, promising that they will abide by his judgment. Úath takes his ax and challenges the knights to behead him in exchange for the chance to behead them in return. First Conall Cernach, then Lóegure, beheads Úath, but the giant puts his head on his chest and rides away to his lake. When he returns later to behead them in return, his adversaries have fled. On the third night, Cú Chulainn beheads the giant, and when the giant later returns, Cú Chulainn keeps his word and puts his own head on the block. Three times the giant draws his ax down on Cú Chulainn's neck, and three times the blade is reversed. The giant then proclaims Cú Chulainn the winner and first hero of Ulster. But the other two heroes do not accept the judgment and the same argument continues. Upon advice of the Ulaid, the three go to the wizard Cú Ruí for the final judgment.

The wizard is not at home when they arrive, but they are welcomed by his wife Blathnnait. They wait for three nights, and each night a different warrior keeps watch. Each night a giant appears and throws tree trunks at the watchman. The first night Lóegure, the oldest, is left half-dead by the giant and is dropped over the wall. The next night Conall, the next oldest, watches, and the same thing happens to him. The third night Cú Chulainn stands watch and, when the giant appears, he engages him in such a fierce battle that the giant is forced to grant him his requests. Cú Chulainn asks for supremacy over the warriors of Ériu, the champion's portion, and "precedence for my wife over the women of Ulaid forever." The giant grants his request and disappears. Later Cú Ruí returns and eventually reveals himself to be not only the giant, but also the churl who proclaims Cú Chulainn the winner and first hero of Ulster. (Gantz 1988)

See also Cú Chulainn; *Ulster Cycle.*

BRIGID

(Also Brigit or Brigantia)

Goddess of poetry, crafts, and divination of the ancient Celts, Brigid is the equivalent of the Greek Athena and the Roman Minerva. In Ireland, she was one of three daughters of the great god Dagda. Her two sisters were goddesses of healing and smithcraft. She was worshiped by the aristocratic professional class called the filid. In northern Britain she was known as Brigantia, for whom the Brigant tribe was named. (Chadwick 1976; Evans-Wentz 1990)

BRISEIS

In the *Iliad* (i), Briseis, daughter of Briseus, is the war prize of Achilles. When Agamemnon takes Briseis for himself, Achilles refuses to go into battle on the side of the Greeks. (Lattimore 1967)

See also Achilles; Agamemnon; *Iliad.*

BROT

This old Norse poem, ca. 1100, is an offshoot of the sixth-century Frankish "Lay of Siegfried and Brunhild" and of the ninth-century Norse "Atlakviða," all part of the cycle that ultimately contributed the *Nibelungenlied.* (Hatto 1969)

BRUNANBURH, THE BATTLE OF

This Old English narrative poem of 74 lines was included in the *Anglo-Saxon Chronicle* under the year 937. It recorded the important Saxon victory, after a historic daylong battle between the forces of West Saxon king Athelstan (grandson of Alfred), his brother Edmund Atheling, and allied Scots, led by King Constantine, against Norse Viking (Strathclyde Briton) invaders led by Dublin king Olaf Guthfrithson, who laid claim to the throne of York. Athelstan is glorified as "Lord among Earls, / Bracelet-bestower and / Baron of Barons." With obvious satisfaction, the poem counts "five young dead kings put asleep by the sword stroke, / seven strong Earls" fallen on the battlefield and the Norse leader fleeing to his warship, leaving "Many a carcase . . . to be carrion / . . . for the white tailed eagle to tear it, and / . . . for the horny-nibbed raven to rend it, and / . . . the garbaging war-hawk to gorge it. . . ." The poem claims, "Never had huger / Slaughter of heroes / . . . Hapt in this isle. . . ." (Alexander, M. 1991; Hieatt 1967)

BRUNHILD

In the *Völsunga Saga,* the *Poetic Edda* and the *Nibelungenlied,* Brunhild is a beautiful Amazonlike princess. Some Norse sources depict her as a valkyrie. Brunhild vows to marry only a man of great courage, who can best her in a test of strength. Siegfried is the only man able to qualify, but he is acting on behalf of Gunther. When Brunhild discovers the deception, she takes vengeance,

Brunhild, an Amazon-like princess, appears in the *Völsunga Saga, Poetic Edda,* and *Nibelungenlied.* British artist Arthur Rackham portrayed her as a romantic character for Richard Wagner's *The Rhinegold and the Valkyrie,* published in 1911.

which results in Siegfried's death. Her role is greatly diminished in the *Nibelungenlied,* in which she stubbornly adheres to the notion that Siegfried is Gunther's liegeman, regardless of evidence to the contrary. In persuading Gunther to invite Siegfried and Kriemhild to Worms, she reiterates her still-friendly position: "Whatever heights of power a royal vassal might have reached, he should not fail to do his sovereign's bidding." Although later she wishes him dead, in the *Nibelungenlied* Hagen replaces her as the inciter to murder, and Brunhild fades from the story. (Hatto 1969; Hollander 1990)

See also *Edda, Poetic;* Gunther; Hagen; Kriemhild; *Nibelungenlied;* Siegfried.

BRUSI SIGURDARSON

In *Orkneyinga Saga,* and in the Icelandic medieval *Book of Settlements,* Brusi is an earl of Orkney, one of three sons of the first earl, Sigurd the Powerful, among whom the earldom is divided after Sigurd's death. A fourth son, Thorfinn, age five and living with his grandfather, King Malcolm of Scotland, at the time, is later given Caithness and Sutherland and the title of earl. Thorfinn becomes a greedy man. Einar, whose subjects complain of his high taxes, is "ruthless and grasping," while Brusi is "gentle, restrained, . . . and a fine speaker." Sumarlidi, the eldest, dies young. Thorfinn claims Sumarlidi's share of Orkney; Einar opposes him, but Brusi is willing to give the land to him, saying, "I have no wish to take more of the earldom than the third that belongs to me by right." He spends much of his life reconciling the brothers. When Einar (Wry-Mouth) is killed by Thorkel Amundason the Fosterer, Brusi is awarded Einar's third by King Ólaf. But the islands are under constant attack, and Brusi complains to Thorfinn that despite all the tribute that Thorfinn collects, he is not contributing to the defense of the islands. By this time Brusi's mentor, King Ólaf, with Brusi's son Rognvald in his charge, is a fugitive, and Canute is ruler of Norway. So Thorfinn makes Brusi an offer: If he will give up one of the thirds, Thorfinn will take over defense himself. Brusi agrees. After Brusi dies, Thorfinn takes over his share as well. (Pálsson and Edwards 1982)

See also *Orkneyinga Saga.*

BRUT THE TROJAN

(Also Brutus or Brute)

Legendary great-grandson of Aeneas, founder of Rome, and hero of the *Aeneid,* Brut is banished from Italy. He emigrates to Britain where he founds the city of New Troy (Troia Nova, London) and gives his name to Britain. He is the hero of *The Brut,* ca. 1205, a Middle English verse by Layamon, which was inspired by Wace's Norman French *Roman de Brut. The Brut* relates the mythical and legendary history of Britain from the time of its founding by Brut down to the year 689. It includes stories of legendary kings including King Leir (Lear) and Cymbeline. (Brook and Leslie 1963; Graves 1966; Jones, G. 1990)

See also Corineus; Layamon; Wace.

BRYNJOLF

In the Icelandic *Njal's Saga,* Brynjolf the Unruly is a kinsman of Hallgerd, Gunnar's wife, who starts the feud. He is killed by Thord Freedmansson. In *Orkneyinga Saga,* Brynjolf, a member of Jon Petersson's household, gets into an argument with Harvard during a drinking session and later kills him. Harvard's brother Hallvard avenges his death by killing Brynjolf. Brynjolf Bjarnason, a chieftain in Norway, appears in *Egil's Saga,* as does Brynjolf Bjorgolfsson, a farmer at Torg Island in Norway. (Magnusson and Pálsson 1960; Magnusson and Pálsson 1969; Pálsson and Edwards 1988)

BUDDHACARITA

This second-century poetic narrative of the life of Buddha, Siddhartha Gautama, by northern India Sanskrit poet Aśvaghoṣa incorporates many of the myths and legends integral to early Buddhism. (Ashvaghosha 1936)

BULONGO

Among the Ila peoples of Zambia, Bulongo is the arch-demigod, "earth only, not a person." The name means "clay." It is speculated that originally Bulongo was the name of a very ancient prophet who came with other emigrants from the Sala country farther north, introduced the impande shells used in bartering, and gained such widespread influence that after his death he continued to be revered. (Smith and Dale 1968)

BUNGLING HOST

(Also *Bungling Guest)*

Myth of the American Indians of the Northwest Coast in which the main character, Trickster, attempts to emulate his host by producing food magically. When he fails, he narrowly escapes death. (Parker 1989; Walker 1983)

BURIRU

In some versions of the *Mwindo Epic* of eastern Zaire, Buriru appears as the seventh wife of Mwindo, mother of Utundo and Mwishi, and daughter of Kandobefu. (Biebuyck 1978)

See also *Mwindo, Epic of.*

BURNT NJAL

(Brennu-Njal)

Njal Thorgeirsson is the hero of the early Icelandic *Njal's Saga* (The Story of Burnt Njal, ca. 1280), called by scholars the mightiest of all the classical Icelandic sagas. He is on one side of a blood feud between two landholders and former friends, Njal and Gunnar. The disagreement, instigated by Gunnar's wife Hallgerd, culminates in Njal's death, with his family, inside his burning home. (Magnusson and Pálsson 1960)

See also *Njal's Saga.*

BYLINY

Byliny are epic poems of the Russian peasantry presented in song form and ranging from the earliest mythological period up to the eighteenth century. Throughout these songs a number of heroes reappear, their feats recounted in cycles. These feats are often unrealistically fantastic, sometimes humorous, and frequently ingenuous. Among them are the cycle of Novgorod, the cycle of Ivan the Terrible, and the cycle of Kiev. (Preminger 1990)

See also Ilya of Murom.

C

CALAIS AND ZETES

(Also Zethes)

In Greek mythology, Calais and Zetes are the twin sons of Boreas and Orithyia. In the Argonaut legend, they accompany Jason to Colchis, and upon their arrival at Salmydessus in Thrace, they free their sister Cleopatra, who has been imprisoned by her husband, King Phineus. In another legend they clash with the Harpies in Bithynia in order to deliver Phineus from their persecution, and as a result they are awarded wings. After Herakles slays them near Tenos, they are transformed into birds. (Graves 1955)

See also Argonauts; Herakles; Jason.

CALCHAS

According to Homer in the *Iliad* (i), Calchas is the wisest soothsayer, "most excellent of augurs, who knew of things that were and that should be and that had been before." His father Thestor is an Argonaut and a priest of Apollo. At the time of the Trojan War, Calchas accompanies the Greeks and foretells the ten-year length of the siege of Troy. He also predicts that Troy cannot be taken without Achilles's help and that, unless Agamemnon returns Chryseis to her father, the plague in the Greek army will not abate. He advises Agamemnon to sacrifice his daughter Iphigeneia to Artemis in order that the Greek fleet might be able to sail from Aulis to Troy. He advises the construction of the wooden horse with which the Greeks finally penetrated Troy's defenses. After the Trojan War is ended, a prophecy is fulfilled that Calchas will die when he meets a superior prophet. When he meets Mophus, who is able to tell exactly how many figs hang upon the branches of a certain tree, he dies. (Lattimore 1976)

See also Achilles; Agamemnon; Chryseis; *Iliad;* Iphigeneia.

CALLIOPE

(Also Kalliope)

Calliope is the chief of the nine Greek Muses, the Muse of epic or heroic poetry. She is the daughter of Mnemosyne and Zeus, who requests that she judge a dispute between Aphrodite and Persephone over Adonis. One of her sons, by King Oeagrus of Thrace with help from Apollo, is Orpheus. (Graves 1955)

CALYPSO
(Also Kalypso)

In the *Odyssey*, Calypso, the nymph of the island of Ogygia and daughter of Atlas, detains the shipwrecked Odysseus, offering him immortality if he will remain with her. He declines on the grounds that he is faithful to his wife Penelope, but he dallies for seven years and has two sons by her. Finally, Zeus sends Hermes to convince Calypso to release Odysseus, and she relents. Although she is inconsolable at the thought of his leaving, she assists him in resuming his journey homeward. (Lattimore 1967; Rouse 1937)

See also Odysseus; *Odyssey;* Zeus.

CAMILLA

In Roman mythology Camilla, the daughter of Metabus, becomes a Volscian queen and virgin warrior favored by Diana. In the *Aeneid* (vii, xi), Metabus is fleeing from his enemies with his infant daughter when he comes to the Amisenus River. He ties the baby to a javelin, dedicates her to the service of Diana (Artemis), and hurls her across the river. Then he swims across and takes the baby to the woods, where he teaches her the arts of hunting and fighting. She becomes a fearless warrior, a swift runner, and the leader of a band of warriors, a number of which are women. She fights with one breast bared so as not to encumber her bow arm. The band fights in a battle against Aeneas, but she is killed by the spear of Aruns, who in turn is killed by a dart of Artemis. (Fitzgerald 1990)

See also Aeneas; *Aeneid;* Artemis.

CANDAINĪ EPIC
(Also *Lorik-Candā Epic)*

This Indian oral epic of the central region of Chhattisgarh is performed in two styles: git (song-recitation) and naca (dance-drama). Traditional git performers are male members of the Raut, or cowherding caste, who may also use musical instruments. Although the audience tends to be men of any caste, women are permitted to stand along the sidelines and listen.

Candainī, daughter of Raja Mahar of Gaura Garh, leaves her husband Bawan Bīr because the goddess Pārvatī has cursed him with 12 years of impotence for a transgression of propriety. On her way back to Gaura Garh through the jungle, she meets an Untouchable, Battuā Camār, who makes advances toward her. He follows her home and becomes such a nuisance to the whole village that Candainī's mother asks a local man, Lorik, to fight him. But Lorik's wife, Dounā Manjar, fearing her husband will lose, suggests that the two be buried up to their necks in dirt, each by the other's wife, and whoever gets out and beats the other is the victor. As Camār's wife prepares to bury Lorik, Dounā throws gold coins around the area, and the greedy woman, in her haste to pick up the coins, only packs dirt loosely about Lorik's legs. He digs out easily and beats Camār.

Candainī watches his performance and falls in love. She decides to seduce Lorik, and he is easily convinced to casual dalliances, disguising himself in her sari as he leaves her palace. After a few trysts, she wants to elope; although Lorik balks, he finally agrees. Candainī's husband Bawan Bīr learns of the elopement plan and attempts to intervene, but Lorik's brother Sānvar foils his plan. He doctors Bīr's pipe tobacco with a sleeping potion and, while Bīr sleeps, breaks all his arrows.

Candainī and Lorik have many adventures on their journey to Hardi Garh. They pass through the all-woman kingdom of Candravali, where Lorik is almost stolen by a pān (betel leaf) seller. Candainī rescues him from the woman by playing a game of dice with Lorik as the stake.

Once they reach Hardi Garh, a Gond king asks that Lorik avenge the death of his father, whose head the king of Patan Garh keeps as a football. Lorik borrows a swift horse from the king, rides off to Patan Garh, and retrieves the head. Sometime later, Candainī gives birth to a son, Candrākar.

When Lorik hears from his wife Dounā that his brothers have been killed and his estate confiscated, he and Candainī hurry back to Gaura Garh. They find Dounā reduced to selling yogurt in order to make a living. Lorik is so overcome by the sight that he tries to leave unnoticed, but Dounā recognizes him and pulls him to her. Candainī rushes in and the two women begin to fight while Lorik looks on. After the fight is over, with Dounā the apparent victor, Lorik promises to recover the family cattle. This time he disguises himself as a beggar and roams the country until he has found all his cattle. He returns to Gaura Garh, but he is very sad, and one day he leaves his house and never returns. (Blackburn et al. 1989)

CANDĪ

(Also Mahāmāyā or Abhayā, meaning "she who is without fear")

This Hindu goddess, the demon-destroying form of Śakti, is the central figure in hundreds of Middle Bengali folktales devoted to her, known as Caṇḍīmaṅgal. The most widely known is *Mukundarama Cakravartī*. In the *Purāṇas* she is known as Caṇḍikā, who "raining down her own striking and throwing weapons, cut down . . . her enemy as if in play." (Dimmitt and Van Buitenen 1978)

CASSANDRA

(Also Alexandra)

In Greek mythology, Cassandra is one of the 12 daughters of Trojan king Priam and queen Hecuba, and the twin of Helenus. Apollo, who loves her, promises to grant her the gift of her choice if she will accept his favors. She chooses the gift of prophecy, but as soon as she receives the gift, she reneges on her promise to grant him favors. Apollo ordains that she will be able to foretell the future, but none of her prophecies will ever be believed. After the fall of Troy, Cassandra becomes Agamemnon's prize. Later he murders her. Cassandra appears in the *Iliad* (vi, xiii), the *Odyssey* (iv), and the *Aeneid* (ii), as well as in Chaucer's *Troilus and Crisyede,* Shakespeare's *Troilus and Cressida,* Byron's *Don Juan,* and others. (Fitzgerald 1990; Lattimore 1967; Lattimore 1976; Rouse 1937)

See also *Aeneid; Iliad; Odyssey.*

CATAKAṆTARĀVAṆAṈ

This Katai Tamil folk epic, with a woman as heroine, is an anonymous version of Sītā's battle against the demon Śatakaṇṭharāvaṇa, a story that is found in the Sanskrit Adbhuta *Rāmāyaṇa.*

The story begins in the palace of King Catakaṇtarāvaṇaṉ ("Rāvaṇa of the 100 heads"). A messenger, Cukacāraṇaṉ, arrives and relates a synopsis of the *Rāmāyaṇa (see Rāmāyaṇa).* The king is furious to learn that Rāma and Lakṣmaṇa, with the help of a monkey, have destroyed his relatives in Laṅkā. He sends messengers to Ayodhyā to inform Rāma that he will be attacked the following day. Rāma speaks in anguish of the strength of Catakaṇtarāvaṇaṉ, explaining, "It will be extremely difficult to overcome him." But his wife Sītā reminds him, "Śiva gave you the boon of immortality. No one in the triple universe can destroy you. . . ." Then she asks, "Give me the boon of achieving victory over him!"

After some discussion, Rāma allows Sītā to handle the battle. He sends a message back to Catakaṇṭaṉ to the effect that the king need not bother coming to Ayodhyā; Rāma and his forces will come to him.

Meanwhile, Sītā asks the monkey, Hanumān, to assemble the forces of the kings of 56 countries at the entrance to Catakaṇṭaṉ's fort on the shore of the Ocean of Milk. Hanumān assumes his gigantic body, filling the entire universe, in order to transport all the forces and their leaders to the battle site. As they pass Mount Kailāsa, home of the gods, Pārvatī sees them, and her husband Śiva tells her that Sītā is on her way to destroy Catakaṇṭaṉ. They and the 33 crores of deities, along with the 48,000 sages, all follow to watch the battle.

Sītā asks Rāma for his bow Kodaṇḍa, his quiver, and his magic arrows. Rāma instructs her on the mantras to be used with his weapons and agrees to act as her charioteer. Rāma and the other kings are made to swear not to interfere in her battle with the king.

Hanumān is sent to the fortress to call the king to battle. First he must slay the gatekeeper and guards in order to reach the king. The king and his minister fear neither the monkey nor the woman. The king's army, led by his brother Makāpalavāṉ, marches to the entrance of the fortress, where Hanumān now waits. The army surrounds the monkey, but he warns them against taking him prisoner: "I am the messenger of . . . Sītā, the Mother of the World. It is not dharma to capture me. . . . Do not die like a fool." But the king scoffs, "So you think a woman is something substantial!" He orders Hanumān's arms bound, but the monkey breaks free, tramples hundreds of troops, and destroys forests and gardens on his way back to Sītā's camp.

A nine-day battle ensues. Makāpalavāṉ is the first to fall. On the second day, the king's younger brother, Makāmāyaṉ, advises Catakaṇṭaṉ to fall at Sītā's feet. When the king refuses, Makāmāyaṉ seeks out Hanumān to explain that he is on the side of Rāma and Sītā, and that he hopes to go to the heaven of heroes by being slain by Sītā. Sītā refuses to kill him, because he is virtuous; however, she cuts off all but one of his 59 heads and all but one pair of his 118 arms.

The next day Akkiṉikkaṇṇaṉ, with 30 heads and 60 arms, dies. The king's younger son, Yamakaṇṭaṉ, a great magician with 25 heads and 50 arms, fights Sītā on the fourth day, and when he cannot defeat her, he says, "How masculine is this woman!" He employs magic and tries to run off with Rāma, Sītā, and the other kings, but Hanumān rescues them. He strikes Yamakaṇṭaṉ on the head but allows Sītā to finish him off. On the fifth day, Sītā slays the five-headed, ten-armed Pañcakaṇṭaṉ; on the sixth, Niṣkaṇṭaṉ; on the seventh, Nicācuraṉ. Finally, on the eighth and ninth days, Sītā battles Catakaṇṭaṉ. On the night before the last battle, Makāmāyaṉ advises him to fall at Sītā's feet and seek mercy, but he ignores the advice. He asks his brother, if he is defeated and slain, to request Sītā's help in gaining entrance into heaven for his warriors. After Sītā kills Catakaṇṭaṉ, she grants Makāmāyaṉ's request and also sends Hanumān to help him push all the warriors' widows into a huge pyre so that they can all enjoy bliss together. Sītā crowns Makāmāyaṉ the new Rākṣasa king.

The conquerors return to Ayodhyā, where Hanumān asks a boon of Rāma: he wants to have Brahmā's title. Rāma promises that when the present Brahmā reaches the age of 100, Hanumān will receive his title. Rāma reigns virtuously in Ayodhyā while Sugrīva returns to rule Kiṣkindhạ. (Blackburn and Ramanujan 1986)

CATH RUIS NA RÍG

(The Battle of Ros na Ríg)

This Old Irish tale continues the story of *Taín Bó Cúailnge.* It describes the Ulsters' war of revenge for the Taín, in which Cú Chulainn kills King Coirpre of Temair. (Kinsella 1969)

See also *The Cattle Raid of Cooley; Ulster Cycle.*

THE CATTLE RAID OF COOLEY

(Irish Gaelic: *Taín Bó Cúailnge)*

This Old Irish prose epic-saga (ca. seventh and eighth centuries), the centerpiece of the *Ulster Cycle* of heroic tales, is composed in prose with verse passages. It is the nearest work to a great epic that Ireland has produced, and the oldest vernacular epic in Western literature. It is found in part in the *Book of the Dun Cow* (ca. 1100), and in complete form in *The Book of Leinster* (ca. 1160) and the *Yellow Book of Lecan* (late fourteenth century); however, the work itself is much older. The *Ulster Cycle* was traditionally believed to refer to the time of Christ, but because of Ireland's remote location, the customs described could have remained until the introduction of Christianity in the fifth century.

The cattle raid is hatched during pillow talk between Queen Medb (Maeve) and her husband Ailill in Cruachan Fort in Connacht, in which the two begin to argue over who is the wealthiest. They begin by comparing lands, then jewels, and finally sheep and other livestock. At length, it is determined that Ailill has the finest bull in the land, called Finnbennach. Medb cannot find in her herd the equal of this bull, so she calls the messenger Mac Roth to ask where she might find a better bull. Mac Roth tells her that there is one such bull in the province of Ulster, in the territory of Cúailnge, in Dáire mac Fianchna's house. The bull is Donn Cúailnge, the Brown Bull of Cúailnge.

Medb sends word asking for the loan of the bull with the promise of 50 yearling heifers, land, a chariot, "and Medb's friendly thighs on top of it all." At first Dáire agrees to the bargain, but later he overhears the messengers bragging that they would have taken the bull if Dáire had not agreed to lend it. He is furious and refuses to give up the bull. When the messengers report this to Medb, she decides to steal the bull. Ignoring poetess-soothsayer Fedelm's warning, she sends the Connaught warriors against the Ulstermen, who are suffering pangs caused by a curse. However, young Cú Chulainn and his father Sualdam are not affected by the curse.

Fergus mac Roich, an Ulster warrior living in exile with Ailill, sends a warning for the men of Ulster, which Cú Chulainn sends his father to deliver while he spends the night with Fedelm. Fergus is given the position of head of the army, and he makes a great detour in order to give Ulster time to gather an army. When Medb notices the detour and accuses him of treachery, he tells her he is trying to miss Cú Chulainn. Young Cú Chulainn single-handedly defends the territory and holds off the warriors of Connaught until the Ulster army can be rallied. In the process, he engages in a three-day battle with Ferdia (Fer Diad), his foster brother and friend, who is also living in exile with the Connaught men. In the end he is forced to use the gae bolga (possibly meaning lightning spear), and Ferdia is mortally wounded. Before he dies, Ferdia tells Cú Chulainn, "Hound of the bright deeds, / you have killed me unfairly. / Your guilt clings to me / as my blood sticks to you."

Cú Chulainn is nearly dead from his own wounds when the Ulster army arrives and routs the men of Connaught. When Cú Chulainn is able to rejoin the battle, he confronts Medb. "If I killed you dead," he says, "it would only be right." But he spares her, for he is not a killer of women. Medb tells Fergus, "We have had shame and shambles here today, Fergus," to which he answers, "We followed the rump of a misguiding woman. It is the usual thing for a herd led by a mare to be strayed and destroyed."

However, the bull has been captured, and it easily defeats Ailill's white-horned bull. Then Ailill and Medb make peace with Ulster and Cú Chulainn. (Kinsella 1969)

See also Cú Chulainn; Medb; *Ulster Cycle.*

THE CATTLE RAID OF FROECH

(Taí Bó Froech)

Irish epic tale that is part of the *Ulster Cycle,* preserved in the *Book of Leinster* (ca. 1160). It is a companion story to *The Cattle Raid of Cooley,* because the same cattle raid appears in both stories. It tells of the handsome young warrior Froech, who learns that Findabair, the daughter of King Ailill and Queen Medb, hearing stories of him, has fallen in love with him. He sets off to woo her with his retinue of fine musicians. In fact, Froech himself is a fine musician who charms Queen Medb with his fiddle-playing. The queen becomes so entranced with his playing that when Ailill orders food prepared for the guests, she answers, "I have no wish but to go and play fiddle with Froech."

After many days at court, Froech finally attempts to woo Findabair, but she has become coy, refusing to elope with him and insisting that he bargain for her with the king. However, she gives him her thumb ring as a token of her devotion. When Froech asks Ailill and Medb for their daughter, they demand such a large bride price that he leaves in outrage, saying, "I would not give such a bride price for Medb herself."

Ailill and Medb, fearing that Froech will elope with their daughter, plot to have him killed. They invite him to bathe in a monster-inhabited river, flattering him about his fine swimming. After Froech removes his clothes and enters the water, the king opens Froech's wallet and finds Findabair's ring, which he throws into the water in a rage. He does not see a salmon leap up and swallow the ring, but Froech does see, and he quickly catches the salmon, swims for land, and hides the fish. Ailill insists that Froech swim to the opposite bank and bring him some berries. At midstream a monster seizes Froech, who calls out for a sword.

Findabair, who has been standing on the bank admiring his white body, throws off her clothes and jumps into the water with a sword. Ailill throws a spear at his daughter, but Froech catches the spear and hurls it back. Once Findabair has given him the sword, Froech slays the monster. Ailill and Medb, impressed with his bravery, regret their evil against him, but they decide that their daughter must die for giving away her ring. They order a bath prepared for Froech; it is made of "a broth of fresh bacon and the flesh of a heifer chopped up." As Froech's horn players precede him into court, their music is so sweet that 30 of Ailill's "dearest ones" die "of yearning."

A retinue of women bathe Froech, and he is desired by all. Later he sends for the salmon, which he has hidden. Ailill confronts Findabair about the missing ring, threatening death unless she produces it. She claims to have lost it. Froech opens the salmon and makes up a story about having earlier found the ring and placed it in his wallet, intending to return it to Findabair. Ailill and Medb believe this story and decide that Froech may marry Findabair as soon as he uses his own cattle to help drive the cattle from Cúailnge.

Froech's cattle are stolen, along with his three sons and his wife. He asks Conall Cernach, the best warrior in Ulaid, for help in finding them. They set off across northern England, cross the Channel and Normandy, and eventually reach the Alps. There they locate the cattle, guarded by a serpent. Conall (who appears in several Irish epics and whom scholars believe to be the same as the horned god Cernunnos) overcomes the snake and restores the cattle. The scene is apparently depicted on the Gundestrup Cauldron, an old Irish relic.

They return to Ulaid with the cows, Froech's wife, and his sons. Froech then accompanies Ailill and Medb to drive the cattle from Cúailnge. (Gantz 1988; Rutherford 1987)

CAVE OF THE JAGUA

This is a cycle of myths of the pre-Columbian inhabitants of the Caribbean, the Taínos of Hispañola. The stories were recorded at the request (ca. 1495) of Christopher Columbus by a Catlán missionary, Friar Ramón Pané, who had mastered the Taíno language. The cycle is recorded in free-verse form and is named for the hero myth that comprises the first two chapters.

Jagua is a plant that produces an edible fruit whose black juice was used by the Taínos to color their bodies. According to the first chapter, on Hispañola are two caves (cacibas): Cacibajagua (Cave of Jagua, symbolizing the Taínos who paint their bodies) and Amayauna (Without Importance, symbolizing the rest of humanity). Before the first people emerge from the cave, they put Mácocael (He of the Eyes that Do Not Blink) in charge of keeping watch at night. He returns to the door late one day, having been carried off by the sun, and when he cannot get inside the closed door, he is turned into stone, which evermore stands near the entrance. Now when people go out to fish and are made prisoners of the sun, they are turned into cherry plum trees.

One day a man named Guahayona (Our Pride) suggests to Cahubaba (the Ancient One) that they go harvest the digo (soap plant). Cahubaba goes out before daybreak, and the sun overtakes him. He is turned into a nightingale, now called Cahubabael (Son of the Ancient One). When he does not return, Guahayona decides to leave the cave and travel.

In chapters III and IV, "The Flight of the Güeyo Women," Guahayona tells the women of the tribe, "Leave behind your husbands and let us go / to other lands and carry off much güeyo. / Leave your children . . . and / later on we shall return for them." (Güeyo may be an ash to mix with tobacco to remove the bitter taste.) All the women leave with Guahayona and travel to the island of Matininó (No Fathers), where he leaves them. Meanwhile, the children become hungry and begin crying to be nursed. Their fathers, unable to feed them, want their women to come home. The children cry with "deep desire" and "great voice" and are turned into frogs, which evermore are the voice of springtime.

Chapter V, "The Betrayal," is a flashback of sorts to the time when Guahayona and the women leave. His brother-in-law Anacacuya (Light of the Center) begins the journey with them as they set out to sea in a canoe. Guahayona points out a beautiful seashell in the water, and when Anacacuya looks into the sea, Guahayona takes him by the feet and throws him overboard. Thus he has all the women for himself. After he leaves them on Matininó, he sets off for another island called Guanín. (Guanín is also the name of a gold alloy prized by the Taínos.)

In chapter VI, "The Healing by Guabonito," while Guahayona is in Guanín, he sees that he has left a beautiful woman in the sea. He dives down to get her and takes her back home to the mountain from which he originally took the women. He is pleased with the woman, whose name is Guabonito. He wants to cure himself of his sores ("the French Disease") so that she will find him attractive. She places him in a guanara (a place apart), where he is cured. After she has healed him, she asks permission to continue her own journey, and he grants her request. Before she leaves, she gives him many ornaments for his body. He changes his name to Albeborael Guahayona, meaning not deciphered. He remains in the land with his father Hiauna (He Who Was Made Brilliant), and his story is completed.

In chapters VII and VIII, "The Tale of Inriri," the men go to bathe, and while they are in the water, rain begins to fall. As they often do when it rains, they look for traces of their women, for they are very anxious to find them. This day, as it rains, they see four people falling through the trees—asexual people, neither male nor female. The men cannot catch the slippery creatures, so they call for four men who are caracaracol (scabby and rough-skinned from a syphilitic condition). These rough-handed men capture the creatures, and a council convenes to study how to make them into women. They seek the bird Inriri (woodpecker), formerly Inriri Cahubabayael (the Son of the Ancient One), and tie it to the creatures. The birds peck holes in the creatures, thus turning them into women.

Part of chapter IX deals with the banishment of Yayael. Yaya (Spirit of Spirits) has a son, Yayael (Son of Yaya), who is banished for four months for wanting to kill his father. Then Yaya kills him and puts his bones in a gourd, which he hangs from the rafters in his home. Finally one day he tells his wife, "I want to see our son Yayael." She is pleased to hear this, and she takes down the gourd. But the bones have turned into fish, so the couple decides to eat them.

The rest of chapter IX and part of chapter X deal with Deminán and the Great Flood. One day while Yaya is gone to the lands of his inheritance, four sons are born to a woman, Itiba Cahubaba (the Bleeding Ancient One). She is not identified as Yaya's wife or as the same woman who appears in the previous episode; no other identification is made. The woman dies in childbirth, and her belly is cut open to remove the children, called "twins." The first is caracaracol (the Scabby One) and is named Deminán. The others are not named. While they are eating, presumably the same fish mentioned in the previous episode, they sense that Yaya is returning, so they hastily try to hang up the gourd. But it falls and breaks apart, spilling so much water that the whole earth is covered, and many fish swarm in the sea. The flood sweeps the brothers away to new shores.

Chapter X continues with a fragment: "Conel, the Mute Listener." The brothers, who have left the land of Yaya, come upon a mute man named Conel (Son of the Listener). No explanation is given for their encounter with Conel. They continue their wanderings, ranging farther and farther from their primordial home. Their journey brings them closer to human society, so that they are no longer able to communicate with their former world.

In chapter XI, which Stevens-Arroyo divides into two sections, the first being named "Gifts of Bread and Herbs," the brothers arrive at the door of Bayamanaco (the Old Man). Seeing that he carries cassava (yucca bread), they recognize the man as their grandfather. Deminán Caracaracol follows his brothers into Bayamanaco's house, hoping to get some cassava too. But the old man, who is a shaman, puts his hand to his nose and blows out a spittle containing a purifying powder, cohoba, upon Deminán's back. The old man leaves, indignant because the boys have had the poor manners to ask for cassava.

The second part of the chapter, "The Wondrous Guanguayo-Made Female," tells of Deminán's return to his brothers to tell them what Bayamanaco has done to him. His back hurts terribly, and his brothers see that it is swollen. He almost dies. They try to cut the swelling off, but when they open it, a female turtle comes out. Miraculously, Deminán becomes well, apparently freed of his syphilitic condition. The brothers build a house and live there with the turtle, each in turn using her as a mate. From her their sons and daughters are born. (Stevens-Arroyo 1988)

See also Flood Myths; Guahayona.

CERBERUS

In Greek mythology, Cerberus is the three-headed dog (according to Hesiod's *Theogony,* he has 50 heads) that guards the entrance to the infernal regions. He appears in the *Odyssey* (xi) and the *Aeneid* (vi), as well as in the Herakles stories. The Sybil who conducts Aeneas through the lower regions puts Cerberus to sleep with a poppy-and-honey cake. Herakles's twelfth labor is to bring the monster to earth, show him to the king of Mycenae, then return him to the underworld. (Fitzgerald 1990; Lattimore 1959; Lattimore 1976; Rouse 1937)

CHAC

Chac is the Mayan rain god, especially in the Yucatán region. In *The Cuceb,* under "First Year/13 Kan," he is also called T'ul Caan Chac (Chac of the Dripping Sky), which is considered an evil aspect of Chac. Literally, T'ul Caan Chac means "rabbit sky," meaning a sky that produces nothing but useless, dripping rains. In *The Cuceb* under "Eleventh Year/10 IX" and "Twelfth Year/11 Cauac," Chac appears as Ah Siyahtun Chac, whose soul is "comforted at the coming of the new Katún. (Bierhorst 1974)

CHAKA

(Also Shaka and Tshaka)

This Zulu hero (ca. 1787–1828) is the subject of the epic *Emperor Shaka the Great.* His father Senzangakhona was chief of the Zulu clan, a small state in northern

Nguni at the time. His mother Nandi conceived out of wedlock but married the chief before Chaka was born. Nevertheless, she and her son were not well treated, and she returned with him to her own people while he was young. They also scorned him as illegitimate, and the two eventually went to live with cousins in the Mthethwa tribe, under whose chief Dingiswayo Chaka distinguished himself as a warrior. When Chaka's father died (ca. 1815), Chaka seized the Zulu throne using Mthethwa troops. During the next decade, he unified the northern Nguni to build one of the most powerful kingdoms in Africa at the time. The kingdom he founded remained a powerful force in South African history for more than a half century following his death. (Kunene 1979; Lipschutz and Rasmussen 1989)

See also *Emperor Shaka the Great.*

CHALCHIUTLICUE

(Also Chalchihuitlicue and Matlalcueye)

This Aztec goddess presides over rivers, lakes, and other freshwater bodies. The word *chalchuitl* may denote any precious or semiprecious green stone. *Chalchihuitlicue* means "she who wears a jade skirt," and *Matlalcueye* means "she who wears a green skirt." In Aztec creation myth, she is the sister-wife of the rain god Tlaloc. Corn is first used during her reign. It is interesting to note that in fragment C ("The Transformation") of the *Quetzalcóatl Cycle,* in an account of Quetzalcóatl's birth, the mythical amazon Chimalma (meaning "shield hand") usurps the role of earth mother and swallows a chalchuitl, (translated "jade stone" or "emerald"), from which the child grows. The version found in *Codex Vaticanus 3738* says that when the seminal "message" comes down from the sky, the earth mother faints in fright, leaving Chimalma to take her place. Thus the conception is regarded as immaculate, and the male parent is identified as Citlallatonac (Light of Day).

A similar connection between goddess and green stone occurs in the Navajo creation myth *Diné bahanè,* in which a figure of turquoise becomes Asdzą́ą́ nádleehé, or Changing Woman, the most revered of Navajo goddesses. The birth of Changing Woman's child takes place after she lies in the sun for four days with her legs spread. The father of her child, although she says there is none, is the Sun. (Bierhorst 1974; Toor 1947)

See also Changing Woman; *Diné bahanè; Quetzalcóatl, Topiltzin.*

CH'ANG O

(Also Heng O)

In Chinese mythology, Ch'ang O is the goddess of the moon. She steals the potion of immortality from her husband Hou Yi, who has received it from the "Royal Mother of the West." She flees to the moon, and Moon-Hare prevents her husband from following until he promises to forgive her. T'ang dynasty poet Li Shang Yin (787–858) writes concerning the episode: "Is Ch'ang O sorry that she stole the magic herb, / Above the green sea, beneath the blue sky / thinking night after night?" (Birch 1965; Mackenzie 1990)

CHANGING WOMAN

(Also Estsánatlehi and Asdzą́ą́ nádleehé)

In *Diné bahanè*, the Navajo creation myth, Changing Woman is the most revered of Navajo deities. She is the daughter of Long Life Boy and Happiness Girl. Her name signifies one who changes or rejuvenates. She grows to be an old woman, then becomes a young girl again, passing through a never-ending cycle of lives but never dying. As such she represents Mother Nature and the seasons. She is in charge of giving birth to all vegetation. She first comes into being by being transformed from a figure of turquoise. She is the sister of Yoołgai asdą́ą́, or White Shell Woman. Both sisters become pregnant at the same time. Changing Woman delivers her son first, followed quickly by Shell Woman's. Throughout the story the boys are referred to as brothers. Each asks his mother the identity of his father and is told, "You have no father." Later, Spider Woman tells the boys, "Your father is in reality Johonaa'ei the Sun." They set out to find him, and when they do, they are given the task of slaying a monster. After they accomplish this feat, they decide to name themselves Naayee neizghani (Monster Slayer) and Na'idigishi (He Who Cuts the Life Out of the Enemy). In another place, White Shell Woman's son is referred to as Born for Water.

Changing Woman appears in the Navajo restorative ritual Night Chant as Estsánaitlehi. (Bierhorst 1974; Zolbrod 1984)

See also Chalchiutlicue; *Diné bahanè.*

CHANSON DE ROLAND

(*Song of Roland* or *Song of Orlando*)

This Old French (Brittany) chanson de geste, ca. mid-eleventh century, is comprised of 4,002 decasyllabic lines employing assonance rather than rhyme, and separated into lays of varying lengths. The probable author was a Norman poet, Turold, whose name appears in the poem's last line. Roland's personality is based on the historic Hruotland of Brittany, who led Charlemagne's rear guard in the Battle of Roncesvals (778) against the Basques. In the poem (which depicts the battle as being against the Saracens), Roland is the most famous of Charlemagne's paladins, and tradition makes him the son of Charlemagne's sister. Over 300 years separate the event depicted in the poem from the only remaining manuscript, preserved on 72 small leaves of parchment at Oxford University. It is France's first great work of literature, and scholars speculate that it is based upon an earlier version, a proto-Roland, possibly an oral legend or folktale. It has influenced the literary works that followed, including *El Cid,* Boiardo's *Orlando Innamorato,* and Ariosto's *Orlando Furioso.*

As the chanson begins, Charlemagne has been in Spain for seven years and "has won that haughty land down to the sea." Only Saragossa remains unconquered. The wisest of pagans, Blancandrin, advises the Saracen king Marsilla to send word to Charlemagne asking for a meeting to discuss terms by which Charlemagne will leave Spain. "If he should ask for hostages," Blancandrin says, "then send them / to gain his confidence. . . . / We'll send the sons of our own wives to him; / . . . Much better they should lose their heads . . . / than we should lose our honor. . . ."

Although the Franks advise Charlemagne to accept Marsilla's overtures, Count Roland, who is there with his friend Olivier, warns King Charles against a plot: "You are wrong to trust Marsilla!" But the Frankish count Ganelon, Roland's stepfather, tells the king, "You're wrong to trust a lackey. . . ." The king accepts Ganelon's advice to dispatch a favorable message to Marsilla, but Roland manages to convince the king to make the messenger Ganelon himself. Ganelon angrily goes to Saragossa with Blancandrin, believing that he may be killed, and Roland tells his uncle, "His arrogance will be the end of him. / . . . If someone killed him, we might all have peace."

Ganelon and Blancandrin soon discover that they have one thing in common: a hatred of Roland. As they ride to Saragossa, each promises the other "that he will see to it that Roland dies." Ganelon's initial meeting with Marsilla is unpleasant, but the king quickly recants. He points out that Charlemagne is almost 200 years old. Only Roland and Olivier stand between Spain and victory. Ganelon decides to accept Marsilla's bribe and betray Roland. Ganelon returns to Charles with the keys to Saragossa, lavish gifts, and 20 hostages to show the king's good faith. Ganelon convinces Charles to assign his stepson Roland to command the rear guard of 20,000 men through the narrow pass of Roncesvalles. It is there that Roland's men are ambushed by 400,000 Saracens. Olivier begs his friend to sound the oliphant so that Charles can hear and come to their rescue, but Roland flings back, "May God forbid . . . / that it be said by any man alive / I ever blew my horn because of pagans!" Deeds are recounted of the various paladins during the bloody battle that follows. When only 60 men remain, Roland finally sounds his ivory horn, cracking the horn and bursting the veins in his neck in the process. But they are doomed; the two friends say farewell and are blessed by Archbishop Turpin. By the time Charlemagne arrives with his army, the men are all dead.

Charlemagne avenges their deaths by defeating the Saracens, but he is nearly overcome with grief at the loss of Roland. After the defeat of the pagans, he sends a thousand Frenchmen through the town to hunt out all the synagogues and mosques, and "they smash the effigies and all the idols; / no sorcery or magic will be left." A hundred thousand souls are baptized as Christians—"save the queen, / for she is to be led captive to sweet France. / The king desires that she recant through love." The king mounts up, along with his men, "and Bramimonde—he takes her as his captive. / He only plans to do what's good for her." Once they return to Aix, Olivier's sister Alde, who is betrothed to Roland, learns from Charlemagne that Roland is dead. She drops at the king's feet. The king believes that she has fainted and takes her by the hands to lift her up. But he sees that she is dead. Ganelon is brought before the assembly and charged with treason. Although the barons recommend leniency because of Ganelon's past service, Charlemagne decrees that a duel be fought by Pinabel and Thierry, representing relatives of Roland and Ganelon. Thierry cracks open Pinabel's skull, and thus the matter is settled: not only is Ganelon to be hanged, but his 30 relatives as well.

Charlemagne has his highborn prisoner, the Spanish queen, baptized as Juliana after she has heard many parables and sermons and decided to become a Christian. Having satisfied "his enormous rage," he lies down to rest. When Gabriel comes down from heaven to call him into service once more—to invade the land of Bire, where "the Christians there call out and cry for you"—the emperor has no desire to go. He cries out, "God, how tiring is my life!" He sheds tears and tugs at his white beard. (Harrison 1970)

See also Chansons de Geste; Ganelon; Olivier.

CHANSONS DE GESTE

These medieval Old French metrical epic-romances divided into lays, or stanzas, of varying length recount the heroic deeds of Charlemagne and his barons, as well as deeds of other legendary and historical knights of the Carolingian era (principally the twelfth and thirteenth centuries). Some 70 works in the *Charlemagne Cycle* have been preserved. The early chansons were usually comprised of ten-syllable assonant or single-rhyme lines. About 80 of the chansons, originally sung by jongleurs, recount the escapades of Frankish king Charlemagne (742–814) and his paladins. The earliest chansons, in which women played little or no part, glorified chivalry in battle. By the thirteenth and fourteenth centuries, romantic love became a factor in many of the chansons, which are characterized by 12-syllable rhyming lines (the alexandrine). Among the well-known chansons are "Le Chevalier au Cygne," *Huon de Bordeaux*, and *Renaud de Montauban*. (Harrison 1970; Preminger 1990)

CHARLEMAGNE CYCLE

See Chansons de Geste.

CH'ENG HUANG

In Chinese mythology, Ch'eng Huang is the guardian deity of cities. Although he is first mentioned in sixth-century literature, T'ang dynasty (618–907) elders gave him a much older lineage, identifying him with Shui Jung, one of the Eight Spirits of prehistoric times to whom Emperor Yao is said to have done obeisance. (Birch 1965; Mackenzie 1990)

CHENREZI

This Tibetan deity took earthly form as the first Dalai Lama and is reincarnated in each subsequent holy ruler. When each Dalai Lama dies, regents search for the child believed to have received Chenrezi's spirit. (Ward *Ntl Geo* 1980)

CHICOMECÓATL

(Seven-Serpent; also Chicomolotzin, meaning Seven Ears of Maize)

This ancient Aztec goddess of maize is one of several maize deities. In *Quetzalcóatl,* fragment E, the birth of Cintéotl, who calls himself "the variegated maize," is described. (Bierhorst 1974)

CHIH NU

In Chinese mythology, Chih Nu is the goddess who weaves seamless brocade robes from clouds for her father, the Jade emperor Yu Ti. She receives permission to visit earth and falls in love with a cowherd, Niu Lang, whom she marries. The couple lingers for a long time on earth before Chih Nu begins to pine for her heavenly home. When the couple returns to heaven, the irate father puts them at opposite ends of the Milky Way, or Celestial River. They are allowed to meet only once every seven months, at which time the magpies form a bridge over which the lovers can cross to be together. Rain on the seventh day of the seventh month is said to be caused by the couple's happy tears at being reunited. (Mackenzie 1990)

CH'IH YU

In Chinese mythology, Ch'ih Yu is a deity who revolts against authority and enlists the support of humans in overthrowing Shang Ti (Lord on High). The humans who refuse to help are slain; they complain to Shang Ti, who sends his troops to put down the rebellion. Then he decrees that a barrier be set up between heaven and earth, with Ch'ung administering heaven and Li administering earth. Heaven is kept from earth by four pillars at the four corners of the world. (Mackenzie 1990)

See also Ch'ung Li.

CHILAM BALAM, BOOKS OF

(Also *Secrets of the Soothsayers)*

This is the only principal sacred text of the ancient Mayas to survive. It is one of two major works written down in Yucatec Maya in the late sixteenth or early seventeenth century, the other being the *Book of the Songs of Dzitbalche.* Chilam means priest or prophet of the gods; balam means jaguar. (A similar word, the

Semitic ba'alim, is mentioned on numerous Roman inscriptions in Carthage.) The documents were written in Yucatec Maya using an orthography adapted from the Spanish. Because of their archaic language, they are generally considered to be compilations from memory of material from older hieroglyphic books containing myth, history, prophecy, and calendrical information. Despite the fact that the *Chilam Balam* was written, it was probably seldom read. Early Spanish conquerors mentioned it being sung, danced, and chanted to the accompaniment of drums and wind instruments. The poetic sections are primarily those dealing with prophecy.

The first recounts the arrival of five great priests, including Chilam Balam, the prophet of Mani, at the small house of Nacom Balam. Also the greatest of gods, Hunab-Ku, comes with his awesome escorts—the 13 gods (Oxlahun-Ti-Ku) and the 1,000 gods (Hun-Pic-Ti-Ku). Nacom falls into a trance in which he foretells the downfall of the clan and the end of history: "The new governors / will lie and cheat and steal. / Girls will have children / like chickens." The land will fall to foreign priests, alien gods, and barbarous rulers. The prophets go forth and repeat the prophecies. These are followed by the Katún prophecies of Chilam Balam. A katún is an era of time of 20 years. During Katún 13 Ahau, for example, "For five years / the crops will not grow, / even the locusts / will starve. . . ." The governors and prophets will always be drunk. Foreign men "with big boots" will "lounge all day in bed / ignorant and perverted . . . " and "the cry of the deer / will be long and tender / echo through the forest / until it too is finally / and forever stilled."

The flight of the Itzás from the village of Nacom Balam is described following the arrival of foreign lords from the east who take "the town and the people / and the fields and the trees / and even the great black crows." Before the conquerors came, "there was no sin, / . . . no fevers, no pox. / The foreigners stood / the world on its head." Nothing is left, "no more sound judgment, / no more great vision." Nothing is left, "just death and blood / and sorrow, sorrow, sorrow!" (Sawyer-Lauçanno 1987)

***See also** The Cuceb.*

CH'I-LIN

(Also ch'i-lung, hornless dragon, and k'iu-lung, horned dragon)

In Chinese mythology, the ch'i-lin is the fantastic one-horned creature who appears to signal the approaching birth or death of an important leader or sage and who is a protector of saints and sages. A gentle unicornlike creature with the body of a multicolored deer, it does not tread on nor eat living plants. The name has the qualities of yin-yang in that ch'i is the character for male and lin for female. According to legend, the first manifestation of a yellow-bellied ch'i-lin appeared in the palace garden ca. 2697 B.C. to note the arrival of Huang Ti, called the Yellow Emperor. In ca. 2400 B.C., two ch'i-lins appeared to herald the reign of Emperor Yao. In the sixth century B.C. a ch'i-lin, or dragon, appeared to a pregnant woman, who then spat up a jade tablet inscribed with the news of her illustrious child to be born: Confucius. Near the end of Confucius's life, a ch'i-lin was reportedly injured by a chariot. (Mackenzie 1990)

CHIMALMA

(Shield hand; also Chimalman)

In the *Quetzalcóatl,* fragment C, and elsewhere in Mayan lore, Chimalma is a mythical amazon who usurps the role of earth mother to become the female parent of Topiltzin. There is a similarity between her name and Chilmalmat, the wife of Vucub-Caquix, the evil and arrogant "being" in the *Popol Vuh.* (Bierhorst 1974)

CHIRON

In Greek mythology, Chiron is a gentle and learned centaur, noted for his wisdom and knowledge of medicine, music, and shooting. By some accounts he is the son of the sea nymph Philyra and the god Cronus. He teaches mankind the use of herbs. He instructs many of the greatest heroes, including Achilles, Aeneas, Asclepius, Herakles, Jason, and Peleus. When he is wounded by Herakles's poison arrow, he yields his immortality to Prometheus and goes to dwell in the heavens as the constellation Sagittarius. He appears in the *Iliad* (xi) and the *Aeneid* (vi). (Fitzgerald 1990; Graves 1955; Lattimore 1976)

See also *Aeneid;* Argonauts; Herakles; *Iliad.*

CHRONICLE OF NESTOR

(Also the *Kiev Chronicle)*

This account (ca. twelfth–thirteenth century) of the Slavic state of Kiev enumerates the seven pagan deities of Russia as being Perun (the lightning god), Volos, Khors, Dazhbog, Stribog, Simargl, and Mokosh. (Georgieva 1985)

CHRONICLES OF JERAHMEEL

This legendary history of the Jews was written in the fourteenth century in the Rhineland. The work, which includes several books of the *Apocrypha* in both Hebrew and Aramaic, is taken from an earlier Greek work mistakenly attributed to the first-century Alexandrian Jewish philosopher Philo. (Ginzberg 1956)

CHRYSEIS

In the *Iliad* (i), Chryseis is the daughter of Chryses, a priest of Apollo. When she is taken by Achilles as a war prize and later given to Agamemnon, Apollo sends a plague upon the Greeks and Agamemnon is forced to release her. He then takes Achilles's captive, Briseis, angering Achilles to the point that he refuses to fight with the Greeks. (Lattimore 1976)

See also Achilles; Agamemnon; Briseis; *Iliad.*

CH'U TZ'U

(Songs or Elegies of Ch'u)

This early collection of Chinese poetry originated in the Yangtze River basin of southern China during the period of the Warring Kingdoms, after the time of Confucius. It is believed that they were recorded by a minister of the king of Ch'u named Ch'u Yuan, China's first known poet (ca. fourth–third centuries B.C.), who drowned himself in the Mi-lo River after jealous courtiers accused him of disloyalty. The work includes the "Nine Songs," incantations used by shamans for calling up various deities and written as dance lyrics. Among the 25 elegies attributed to Ch'u Yuan, the most important is a long personal poem employing a new technique: seven-word lines divided into two three-word segments separated by the same character of hsi throughout, giving the effect of a mid-line caesura representing a sigh. This poem, "Li Sao" (On Encountering Sorrow), concerns the poet's vain journey to distant regions and all the way to the gates of heaven in order to rid himself of his disillusionment with his king, and to find himself a suitable love object. (Birch 1965)

CH'UNG LI

In Chinese mythology, Ch'ung Li is a deity, or two deities, assigned by Shang Ti the duty of setting up a barrier between heaven and earth. Ch'ung administers heaven; Li, earth. (Mackenzie 1990)

See also Ch'ih Yu.

CID, POEMA DEL

(Also *Cantar de Mio Cid)*

This Spanish epic poem (ca. 1140) consists of 3,735 lines about the exploits of military leader Rodrigo Díaz de Bivar (ca. 1043–1099). Soon after his death many anonymous epics, legends, and ballads sprang up that exaggerated his role in history. The historical Cid was born into a family of the landed aristocracy in Bivar and became an alferez (marshal) in Castilian king Sancho II's army in 1065. Later he served under Sancho's successor, Alfonso VI, who in 1081 exiled him for raiding Toledo, which was under Castilian protection at the time. The Cid then swore allegiance to the Moorish rulers of Saragossa, while preparing to invade Valencia. In 1094 he became the ruler of Valencia, which remained a Christian stronghold until his death, when it again fell to a Muslim army. The name Cid is from the Arabic "Sidi," meaning "lord." He was also known as El Campeador (the champion).

The *Poema del Cid* is the work of an unknown Castilian bard. It is divided into three sections, or cantares. The opening pages of the poem are lost, but the beginning may be assumed from another document, *Chronicle of Twenty Kings*, that had originally been translated from the poem into Latin prose. In the first cantar King Alfonso sends the Cid to collect tribute from the Moorish king of Seville, who is attacked by Count Ordóñez of Castile. The Cid defeats Ordóñez at Cabra, imprisons him, and returns to Castile with the tribute. But his envious enemies speak against him to the king, who believes the stories and sends letters to the Cid telling him that he has nine days in which to leave the kingdom. Saddened, the Cid calls his family and vassals together to see who will go with him and who will stay behind. The party leaves Castile and reaches Burgos, where no one will give him lodging because the king has warned them not to help him. Only one little girl will speak to him. She tells him that he must leave. The Cid camps outside the town, sleeping on the shingle of the riverbed. A man of the town, Martin Antolínez, brings the Cid food. Impoverished, the Cid negotiates with the Jews whom Antolínez has brought to supply him with provisions. He tricks them, filling their coffers with sand.

He travels on to Cardeña to say good-bye to his family, his wife Doña Jimena and his two daughters, all of whom he is leaving destitute. A hundred Castilians arrive from Burgos to join the Cid in exile. The company sets off and eventually arrives in the Moorish kingdom of Toledo, a tributary of King Alfonso. Taking the Moors by surprise, the Cid attacks and defeats them, but he takes no booty for himself, not wanting to anger King Alfonso further. He travels on to the lands of Zaragoza, dependencies of the Moorish king of Valencia. He defeats a number of provinces, taking booty for his king, but Alfonso refuses to forgive him.

The second cantar describes the Cid's drive against Valencia, which he soon conquers. The king of Seville attempts to retake Valencia but fails. The Cid sends new gifts to Alfonso, who relents and pardons the Cid's family. His wife and daughters travel to Valencia, where they are met with a great celebration and installed in a fine castle. The Moors under Yúsuf plan a new attack against Valencia, but they are defeated and Yúsuf's enormous wealth is divided as spoils of war. Again the Cid sends a gift to Alfonso, and the king shows benevolence toward the Cid. The Heirs of Carrión, the infantes, ask Alfonso if they can marry the daughters of the Cid, and the king agrees. Alfonso and the Cid meet on the banks of the Tagus, where the king pardons the Cid and then asks him for the hands of his daughters for the Heirs of Carrión. The Cid gives his daughters to the king, who marries them and commends the Heirs to the Cid.

The third cantar recounts the cowardly conduct of the Heirs, Fernando and Diego Gonzalo, who are afraid of a lion and fear battle. In addition, they beat their wives and ultimately abandon them. The Cid avenges his daughters' honor by defeating his worthless sons-in-law in a trial by combat between Pedro Bermúdez and Fernando and Martín Antolínez and Diego. The Heirs of

Carrión leave in shame and deep disgrace. The poet says, "May whoever injures a good woman . . . and abandons her afterwards / suffer as great harm as this . . . and worse, besides."

The Cid then marries his daughters, Doña Elvira and Doña Sol, to the princes of Navarre and Aragon. (Merwin 1962)

See also Rodrigo, Don.

CIHUACÓATL
(Snake-Woman)

She is the Aztec earth goddess, identified in Central Mexican myth as "a woman called Quilaztli." She is Quetzalcóatl's consort, half of the universal duo, also known as Ometecuhtli and Omecíhuatl, inventors of men (Teyocoyani). (León-Portilla 1982)

See also Coatlicue; *Quetzalcóatl, Tipiltzin.*

CIHUATETEO
(Divine women; also cihuapipiltin)

In Aztec cosmology, cihuateteo is a retinue of divinized women who bear the solar disk Tonatiuh from the zenith down to the western horizon. These women all died while giving birth to their first child and were thus singled out as one of two categories of the dead to go up to heaven as companions of the Sun. (The other category includes warriors killed in battle or by sacrifice, and merchants killed while traveling in another country.) Cihuateteo were said to appear on the roadways at night and haunt passersby at the crossroads, striking them with epilepsy. (Toor 1947)

CILAPPATIKĀRAM
(The Jeweled Anklet; also *Śilappadigāram, Shilappadikaram)*

This classic Tamil folk epic (ca. 500) exists in many versions and forms. One version was written ca. 600 by Iḷaṅkō (Iḷaṅkovaṭikaḷ), based on a folk epic, but possibly adulterated to some extent by Jaina beliefs. The story has continued to be transmitted to the present day in folk song, narrative, and drama. There are both written derivations from oral sources and oral derivations from written sources.

The epic has three parts. The three books, set in the capitals of three Tamil kingdoms, provide a rich description of Tamil culture. The work is a combination of the ancient Tamil caṇkam (literary academy) narrative tradition and Sanskrit poetry.

The story concerns a Pandyan man, a young merchant named Kōvalaṉ, who is unjustly accused of a crime and executed by the Pandyan king. The injustice is a result of misdeeds by Kōvalaṉ in a former life. Kōvalaṉ's virtuous wife, Kaṇṇaki, is described in the beginning as "quiescent, even colorless," until she learns that Kōvalaṉ has been brutally executed for an offense of which he had been falsely accused. She flies into a furious rage, flinging her breast on the towers of Maturai and burning it down. The Pandyan king is likewise destroyed because of his act, as is Mātavi, the concubine who temporarily entices Kōvalaṉ away from his virtuous and long-suffering wife and who takes the husband and wife's wealth. Kaṇṇaki and Kōvalaṉ are reunited in heaven, and Kaṇṇaki is deified as the goddess of chastity. (Blackburn and Ramanujan 1986; Daniélou 1965)

CIRCE

In Greek mythology, Circe is the daughter of the sun god Helos (Hyperion) and the sea nymph Perse (Perseis). She is the sister of Aeetes and Pasiphae, and the widow of a prince of Colchis, whom she murdered. To escape the wrath of her subjects, she is taken by Helios to the island of Aeaea. Circe is a sorceress who appears in the *Odyssey* (x), *Aeneid* (iii), the Argonaut cycle, and Hesiod's *Theogony.* When Odysseus and his men land on Aeaea, Circe changes the sailors into swine. Odysseus remains unaffected by the spell because Hermes has given him the magic herb moly, which protects him. Eventually he is able to persuade Circe to restore his men. In the Jason story, Circe, an aunt of Medea, exonerates Jason and Medea for slaying Absyrtus and sets them on their way. (Schwab 1974)

See also *Aeneid;* Argonauts; *Odyssey; Theogony.*

CLYTEMNESTRA

In Greek literature, Clytemnestra is the wife of Agamemnon and the mother of Orestes, Electra (Laodice), Iphigeneia, and/or Chrysothemis. She appears in more than a dozen works of Greek literature, including the *Iliad, Odyssey,* and *Aeneid,* as well as in works by Chaucer, Shakespeare, Milton, Byron, (T. S.) Eliot, O'Neill, and Rossetti. When Agamemnon goes off to the Trojan War, Clytemnestra becomes the lover of Aegisthus. When Agamemnon returns, she and her lover murder him. Agamemnon's death is later avenged by Orestes, who kills the adulterous couple. (Graves 1955; Lattimore 1976; Rieu 1961)

See also *Aeneid;* Agamemnon; *Iliad;* Iphigeneia; *Odyssey.*

COADIDOP
(Grandmother of Days)

Coadidop is the heroine of the oral creation cycle of the Tariana of Brazil, a version of the widely known Yuruparí myth. Coadidop is depicted as a young virgin who lives alone in empty space before the earth is formed. She is lonely and says, "I want earth and people." From her own legs she takes two bones with which to make a cigar holder, and from her body she draws the tobacco leaves with which to roll a large cigar. She squeezes her milk onto it, places it in the holder, and smokes. She also creates the coca plant (ipadu), which she takes as she smokes.

From the smoke come a flash of lightning, a clap of thunder, and the image of a man. But the image vanishes, as does the lightning. Once more she puffs, only to have the same thing happen. The third time, the smoke forms a human body, whom Coadidop calls Thunder, or Enu. She tells him, "You are son of Thunder and Thunder itself. You are my grandson. . . . I will give you power." He will be able to make everything he wants in the world. He will be able to do everything, both good and evil. She commands him to make companions for himself and says that she will make companions for herself. Enu creates three brother Thunders, and Coadidop makes two female companions for herself.

Then she takes a cord, circles her head with it to make the shape, and puts the circular cord on the ground. She squeezes her milk into the circle and forms the earth. A large field later takes shape on the earth. She gives it to the women and says, "With this earth you can live."

In time one of the females mates with one of the Thunders and gives birth to the demon-hero Yuruparí. He is born with no mouth, but grows so fast that, according to some versions, he reaches the age of six in a single day. His body is covered with hair like a monkey's, and only his head, arms, and legs are human. When his mouth finally forms, he lets out a roar heard around the world.

He goes into the forest, following three children who are going to look for and eat the forbidden fruit. When they find and eat it, Yuruparí calls down Thunder to frighten them, at the same time opening his mouth so wide that the children mistake it for a cave and run inside to escape the Thunder. Yuruparí eats them alive, then returns to the village and vomits the children, filling four baskets.

Yuruparí flees to the sky to escape the wrath of the creator and the vengeance of the children's parents. But he is lured back to earth with a dish of ants, smoked fish, and tobacco fumes. Before the people can annihilate him, he proclaims, "No one can kill me, for I am the wood, I am the water, I am the knife, I am the weapon." But he neglects to include the fire. He is thrown into a bonfire, and he cries out, "Because you have killed me, henceforth people must die before they rise to the heavens." He explodes and his soul rises up with a roar to the sky, where he becomes shining white. From his ashes spring both the palm tree and a poisonous plant. From his intestines come the first snakes and mosquitoes. (Bierhorst 1988)

COATLICUE

(She of the Serpent Skirt; also Teteoinnan, Mother of the Gods, and Toci, Our Grandmother)

Coatlicue is the Aztec earth goddess who gives birth to 400 Southerners and to the night goddess Coyolxauhqui, after which, according to legend borrowed from the Toltecs, she gives birth to the war and sun god Huitzilopochtli. The earth goddess also appears as Cihuacóatl (Snake Woman) and Tonantzin (Mother), goddess of childbirth, and as Tlazoltéotl, goddess of impurity. In fragment C of *Quetzalcóatl*, as Quetzalcóatl is leaving the city forever, preparing for his death, he sings a song to Coatlicue: "She will nurse me no more, / She, my mother, an ya'! / She of the Serpent Skirt, / Ah, the holy one! / I, her child, alas, / Am Weeping, iya', ye an'!" (Bierhorst 1974; León-Portilla 1982)

See also Quetzalcóatl, Topiltzin.

CONLE, THE ADVENTURE OF

This is an eighth-century Irish Celtic story about Conle the Redhead, son of Conn of the Hundred Battles, who is approached one day by a woman who tells him that she is from the Lands of the Living, where there is neither death nor sin. The land is located in a great fairy hill, and thus its inhabitants are called the People of the Fairy Hills.

She tells him that she has fallen in love with him, and she invites him to go with her to the Plain of Delights, where Boadhagh is king of a land without woe. She promises him everlasting youth and beauty until Doomsday.

Conn, Conle's father, consults his druid Corann, telling him that his son "is carried off from my royal side through the spells of women." Corann sings a charm against the woman's voice, and she is unable to make herself heard. As she leaves him, she throws him an apple. For a month afterward, he eats nothing but the apple, which remains whole no matter how much he eats.

A longing for the woman seizes him, and when the month is up, he sees the woman coming for him in a crystal boat, begging him to accompany her. The father Conn calls for his druid, but the woman tells him that soon a righteous man (St. Patrick) will come and "scatter the spells of druids. . . ."

Conle is torn between two desires: "It is not easy for me, for I love my people; yet longing for the woman has seized me." The woman tells him, "You are struggling . . . against the wave of your longing which tears you from them. . . . There is a land which rejoices the heart of everyone who explores it; there is no other sort there but women and girls."

With that, Conle springs away from his people and jumps into the woman's crystal boat. The two row away so fast that those on the shore can scarcely see. The couple has not been seen since. (Jackson, K. 1971)

CONTE D'ILBONIA

This Malagasy epic, translated into French in 1939, is considered to be one of the finest of the African epics. The Malagasy-speaking people of the island of Madagascar are of Indonesian origin, migrating across the Indian Ocean ca. the fifth century. Traders from Borneo traveled to the previously uninhabited island and settled there, later mixing with Africans from the mainland. Malagasy is a version of the Austronesian language of Merina. The Merina people comprise the largest and most dominant population on the island. The name "Imerina" means "Elevated People."

The epic treats the period prior to and just after the arrival of the French in the seventeenth century. The Merina kingdom is founded late in the sixteenth century in central Madagascar. In the eighteenth century it breaks into four warring kingdoms. They are reunited late in the century by King Andrianampoinimerina (1797), who divides the society into three classes: Andero (slaves), Hova (freemen), and Andriana (nobility). At length the entire Merino population is called Hova. When the king dies (1810), he tells his son, "The sea will be the boundary of my rice field."

Radama makes incursions into the northern and eastern parts of the island and the area is renamed the kingdom of Madagascar. When he dies in 1828, his wife Ranavalona succeeds him. She successfully fights off the French and British (1845) and remains in power until her death in 1861. Her son Radama II succeeds to the throne, but his policy of admitting foreigners leads to his overthrow (1863), led by the Hova head of the army, Rainilaiarivony. In order to maintain legitimate power as prime minister, Rainilaiarivony marries three queens of the royal line in succession: Rasoherina, Ranavalona II, and Ranavalona III. When the French invade in 1895, Ranavalona is forced to allow her kingdom to become a French protectorate. She remains on the throne as a figurehead.

The Merino literary output has thrived since the introduction of printing by the London Missionary Society in the early nineteenth century. (Davidson 1991; Westley *RAL* 1991)

CORINEUS

According to Geoffrey of Monmouth in his *Historia regum Britanniae* (1135–1139), this legendary Trojan warrior accompanies Brutus, the legendary great-grandson of the Trojan Aeneas and founder and first king of Britain, to England. Corineus confronts Gogmagog, the giant monster of present-day Cornwall, and slays him by throwing him from a cliff. Thereafter, he gives his name to the land. (Graves 1966)

THE CREATION OF THE HOE

In this ancient Mesopotamian myth, the god Enlil separates heaven and earth to make a space for seeds to grow. He then invents the hoe to dig a hole in the earth in the Temple of Inanna. From the hole, man springs forth, and Enlil gives him the hoe to work the soil. (Pritchard 1973)

CRONOS

(Also Cronus or Kronos)

In Greek myth and religion, Cronos is a Titan, the youngest son of Uranus (Heaven) and Gaea (Earth), and the husband and brother of Rhea. The two are parents of six of the 12 Olympians: Zeus, Poseidon, Demeter, Hera, Hades, and Hestia. Cronos appears in the *Iliad,* the *Homeric Hymns,* and Hesiod's *Theogony.* He is frequently identified with foreign gods such as Ba'alim. (Schwab 1974)

See also *Iliad;* Rhea; *Theogony.*

CÚ CHULAINN

(Also Cúchulain; originally Sétanta)

In ancient Irish Gaelic literature, he is the chief hero of the *Ulaid (Ulster) Cycle* (ca. first century B.C.), sometimes referred to as "Achilles of the Gael." He is the son of the god Lug of the Long Arm (although he has an earthly father, Sualdam) and of Dechtire, the sister of King Conchobar mac Nessa, king of the Ulaids of northeast Ireland. Originally named Sétanta, he is born with seven fingers on each hand, seven toes on each foot, and seven pupils in each eye.

Even as a child he gains a reputation for his prowess; when he is attacked by a ferocious dog belonging to Culainn, he kills it. When he sees how grieved the dog's master is, he himself takes the role of watchdog until a replacement can be found. In "The Death of Aife's Only Son," Cú Chulainn goes to the isle of the woman warrior Scathach nUanaind (Skye), where Scathach instructs him in weaponry. When Scathach is attacked by another woman warrior, Aoife (Aife), Cú Chulainn defeats her and then makes love to her. When he leaves the island, he directs Aoife to send their son Conlaoch (Condlae) to Ireland when he reaches maturity, but he is to tell no one his name.

After seven years the boy comes to Ireland in search of his father, but he is so ferocious that he strikes Cú Chulainn with his sword and leaves him bald. The two wrestle in the water, and the boy ducks Cú Chulainn twice. Cú Chulainn is forced to use the gae bolga, a spear-throwing technique that Scathach has taught no one else. He mortally wounds the boy before he realizes his identity.

At the age of 17, Cú Chulainn is called upon by Fergus, in *The Cattle Raid of Cooley (Taín Bó Cúailnge),* to defend Ulster single-handedly from the forces of Connaught of Queen Medb. He is the chief young warrior of the Knights of Red Branch and is involved in many heroic adventures. He marries Emer "of the yellow hair."

But in "The Wasting Sickness of Cú Chulainn," he is seduced by the sea god Manandan's (Mananaan) beautiful wife Fand. Emer tells him, ". . . what's familiar is stale. The unknown is honored, the known is neglected—until all is known." Cú Chulainn tells Emer that she still pleases him, and it is evident to Fand that he will never leave his wife, so she returns to Manandan, telling him, ". . . there is a man I would prefer as husband. But it is with you I will go . . . good person, you have no other worthy queen, but Cú Chulainn does."

The druids give Cú Chulainn a drink of forgetfulness, and he can no longer remember Fand. Then they give a drink to Emer as well, so that she can forget her jealousy. Manandan shakes his cloak between Cú Chulainn and Fand, so that they might never meet again.

At the age of 27, Cú Chulainn is felled by trickery when Queen Medb creates an illusionary army that he battles until exhausted. He lashes himself to a pillar so that he can face Medb's army standing. After he dies, his widow Emer throws herself into his grave. (Chadwick 1976; Jackson, K. 1971; Kinsella 1969; Markdale 1986; Rutherford 1987)

See also *Ulster Cycle.*

THE CUCEB
(That Which Revolves)

A Mayan ritual epic of prophecy, it is the finest of three found in the *Books of Chilam Balam.* It is preserved in the *Chilam Balam* of Tizimin and, with minor variations, in the *Chilam Balam* of Mani. Cuceb, meaning "that which revolves," refers to the life cycle of the katún lord. Although it is rooted in pre–Spanish Conquest sources, the extant version belongs to the colonial era, as evinced by the allusions to Christianity. It is written in phonetic Maya using the alphabet of the Spanish missionaries.

The word "katún" that appears throughout the work is the name of the 20-year life cycle of the katún lord. When capitalized, the word refers to the deity known as Lord of the Katún, who both represents the 7,200-day period and in a sense is the period. The Katún is not a one-time god who dies and is replaced, but an eternal being who is killed and resurrected over and over. The prophecy is told as a book of years, covering ten years in part I and ten in part II.

In the beginning of *The Cuceb,* after a brief introduction in which the prophet of Cuceb has a vision, seeking deliverance from the ruling Itzá, he imagines the inauguration of Katún 5 Ahau, when there is an invasion by the Itzá people, coming to dominate the people of the Yucatán. He sees the katún as one of warfare and scourge brought about by the sexual sins of the people, ending with a solar eclipse. In the time of drought and alien rule, the Maya must pay a surcharge to the Itzá of food, water, and clothing. In addition, the Itzá introduce unwelcome sexual practices and even sell the Maya as slaves. War and drought fires are predicted, and screech-owls will call for death. The people will be plagued by insects. Eventually the spirit of a new katún will remove the Itzá people.

The waning of Katún 5 Ahau will be accompanied by war, but the guilty will be punished with floods and drought fires. Forced to hide in the wilderness during the Itzá reign, the Maya return to the "well" and "grotto" when the spirit of the new Katún, Buluc Ch'abtan, vanquishes the Itzá by depriving them of their water supplies. The new Katún will mount his throne. At the close of the katún the old lord will be disgraced, and the Maya must suffer a drought in payment for his sins. During the ceremonies marking the close of 5 Ahau, the deliverer Lord Serpent looks down from the sky as a human victim representing the old Katún is purged and humiliated. The heavens open and welcomed rains fall.

The new lord, Amayte Ku (Angular Lord), is installed. He is an aspect of the great androgynous god Itzam Na (Iguana House).

The second half of *The Cuceb,* although containing some fresh details, is primarily an elaboration of the material in the first half of the book. (Bierhorst 1974)

See also *Chilam Balam, Books of.*

CULHWCH AND OLWEN

This Welsh prose romance (ca. 1100), the earliest known Arthurian romance, is preserved in the *Red Book of Hergest* (ca. 1375–1425). It appears in the *Mabinogion* as "How Culhwch Won Olwen." It recounts the adventures of King Arthur's cousin Culhwch, who refuses to marry his stepmother's daughter. The vengeful woman tells him that he can never marry until he is able to woo and win the hand of the beautiful Olwen, daughter of the giant Ysbadadden Pencawr. King Arthur dispatches a band of knights to help Culhwch find Olwen, but the giant, who has been told by a prophecy that if his daughter weds he will die, attempts to kill Culhwch. Eventually he agrees to allow the marriage if Culhwch completes 40 difficult tasks. Culhwch solves 16 of the tasks, or problems, then slays the giant and marries Olwen. Culhwch also appears in other Welsh tales such as "A Cursed and Undutiful Son-in-Law" and "Culhwch's Arrival at the Court of King Arthur." (Gantz 1976; Jackson, K. 1971; Markdale 1986; Rutherford 1987)

See also Arthurian Legend; *Mabinogion.*

CYBELE

(Also Magna Mater and Ops)

In the *Aeneid* (ix), Cybele is the Titan earth goddess. Cybele is the Phrygian name for Rhea. She is the daughter of Gaea and the wife of Cronos. (Humphries 1951)

See also Cronos.

CYCLE

In literature, a cycle refers to a group of poetic or prose narratives, usually evolving from a number of sources, about a legendary hero or an event such as the creation.

THE CYCLIC EPICS

A body of epics (ca. seventh and sixth centuries B.C.) concerning figures and actions connected with the Trojan War, no longer extant, that supplements the *Iliad* and the *Odyssey.* (Godolphin 1964; Hammond 1986)

See also *Cypria; Epic Cycle.*

CYCLOPS

(Also Cyclopes)

In the *Odyssey* (ix), Cyclops are one-eyed sons of Poseidon, shepherds and cannibals. When Polyphemus eats one of his men, Odysseus blinds him. Other myths give their names as Arges, Brontes, and Steropes, and cite their parents as Uranus and Gaea. (Graves 1955; Lattimore 1976)

CYPRIA

Cypria is one of the *Cyclic Epics,* or *Epic Cycle,* told in 11 books; its action precedes that of the *Iliad.* Nothing remains of the epic except a prose paraphrase made by the fifth-century Athens scholar Proclus and preserved by Photius.

It begins with the marriage feast of Peleus, during which a dispute arises among Hera, Athena, and Aphrodite as to who is the fairest. They go to Paris on Mount Ida to settle the dispute. Lured by a promise of marriage to Helen, Paris chooses Aphrodite. She directs him to build his ships, and he sets sail to win Helen. He arrives at Sparta, where Menelaus entertains him. Then Menelaus leaves for Crete, instructing his wife Helen to entertain his guests. When he is gone, Paris and Helen steal away to Troy. When Menelaus learns what has happened, he plans an assault on Ilium to get Helen back. He goes on to Nestor, who tells him several stories: of Epopeus and the daughter of Lycus, of Oedipus, of Herakles, and of Theseus and Ariadne. The two set off, traveling around the country, gathering leaders for the attack against Troy. When Odysseus pretends to be mad to avoid joining them, they seize his son Telemachos for punishment.

They set out for Ilium and land in Teuthranea, sacking it in error. Achilles wounds Telephus, who has come to the rescue. They leave and are scattered by a storm. Achilles lands at Scyros and marries Deidameia, then heals Telephus, who has been led there by an oracle.

As the troops muster again at Aulis, Agamemnon makes a boast that angers Artemis, who sends stormy winds that prevent them from sailing. In order to appease the goddess, they try to sacrifice Agamemnon's daughter Iphigeneia, but at the last minute Artemis substitutes a goat and makes Iphigeneia an immortal.

The men sail to Tenedos, where Achilles quarrels with Agamemnon because he has been invited late. The Greeks go on to Ilium, but the Trojans prevent them from landing. In the clash that follows, Achilles kills Poseidon's son Cycnus, and the Trojans are driven back. From the spoils of battle Achilles gets Briseis and Agamemnon receives Chryseis. (Godolphin 1964)

See also *Epic Cycle.*

DA MONZON, EPIC OF

This heroic oral-narrative cycle about a king of Segu in present-day Mali, West Africa, has been preserved for over 300 years by djeli, bard historians attached to noble families.

"Da Djera and Da Monzon against Samaniana Bassi" begins when Da Djera is king of Segu and Da Monzon is the oldest of his 22 sons. Da Djera sends a message to a neighboring Fula king, Samaniana Bassi, asking for his daughter as a wife. Bassi sends back an insulting refusal that includes the remarks that the Segu king is not of a noble line, is not a believer in Allah, and furthermore is ugly. Da Djera is furious and calls in his filelikelas (shamans) and morikes (shamans who also use Koranic knowledge), commanding them to make protection for his fighters, whom he plans to send against the Fula king. The wise men tell him, "We can give protective magic to your fighters, but Bassi's fighters will also have magic. . . ." Nevertheless, Da Djera is anxious for satisfaction. He sends his fighters against Bassi's, and the battle lasts for a very long time, with neither side able to gain victory.

At length Da Djera falls ill and knows that soon he will die. He sends word to his 22 sons to come to his bedside, each bringing a stick. When they arrive, he orders them to break their sticks in half, which they do easily. Then he takes the 44 halves, ties them into a bundle, and challenges anyone to break the bundle. His moral is: "This is what happens if you each go your way alone. Your enemy will break you. But if you stay bound together, the enemy can never break you." He extracts promises from them that they will always remain united. He makes Da Monzon promise to continue the war until he takes Bassi's head.

After the king dies, Da Monzon, the oldest, refuses to take the throne until all the brothers have agreed that he should be king. With their strong support, he sets about fulfilling his pledge to his father. He consults the morikes, who tell him that to make potent magic against Bassi they need Bassi's shoes, belt, and hat.

The elders ponder how to acquire these items and realize they have no hero who can accomplish the task. One of the elders says, "Certain things are beyond the powers of men, but history teaches us that sometimes a woman can accomplish what a man cannot."

A certain beautiful young woman, Djero, volunteers for the job of stealing Bassi's shoes, belt, and hat. She takes a maidservant and some paddlers and sets off on the river Jobba to Samaniana. She stops outside the city to bathe nude in the river. She continues her bathing until reports of her beauty reach Bassi. He comes out to see her for himself, is immediately smitten, and asks her to be his wife. She will not agree to be his wife at once, but says, "Let us go at it another way. I will agree to be your consort for a time. We will see how it goes. . . ."

She moves in with Bassi and stays until she and the maidservant are able to obtain a hat, shoes, and belt. Then they steal away and return to Segu with the paddlers, who have been waiting for them in the brush.

The morikes tie Bassi's belongings to a large rock and say, "If we have done good (magic), this rock will float." The men place the rock in the water, and it floats—a signal to Da Monzon that he can now wage a successful war against Bassi.

As is the heroic custom, he sends Bassi a courteous greeting informing him of the impending attack. Before the battle begins, he sends a Tonjon officer, Korote Masigi, into the city to bribe Bassi's favorite wife to pour water on their gunpowder. When the two sides clash, the battle is evenly matched until Bassi's men have to replace their ammunition and discover that their gunpowder is ruined. Bassi and his son persuade his wife to hide them under the floor, but she betrays them to Da Monzon by revealing the hiding place. Bassi comes out and explains that he did not hide out of fear, but out of the desire to discover who betrayed him by ruining his gunpowder. He asks Da Monzon to execute his wife first so that he can witness her punishment.

Da Monzon executes them in turn and then sends for Korote Masigi, who risked his life by slipping into the city to bribe Bassi's wife. Da Monzon praises him: "You are a valorous and artful man. You accomplished a great thing for me. . . . You are a true hero of Segu. But I cannot let you live, for I would never be sure that you would not do a similar thing against me. . . ." So he orders Korote Masigi executed as well. He does not execute Bassi's son out of respect for the bravery of the father. (Courlander 1982)

DAGDA

(Celtic: Good God; also Daghdhae, Euchaid Ollathair, Echu Ollathir, and In Ruad Ro-Fhessa)

In the Irish myth *The Wooing of Étaín,* and its continuing tale *The Dream of Óengus,* as well as *The Cattle Raid of Froech* and *The Intoxication of the Ulaid,* Dagda is a leader of the Túatha Dé Danann, a mythological Irish race springing from the goddess Danu. He is married to Mórrígan, war goddess. Because he is in charge of weather and the harvest, he is called the "Good God." He possesses a magic caldron of plenty and a staff with power both to kill people and to restore them to life. He has a son, Óengus, by Elcmar's wife Bóand. Stories about him are found in *The Book of the Dun Cow* (twelfth century), *The*

Book of Leinster (ca. 1160), and *Yellow Book of Lecan* (fourteenth century). *The Wooing of Étaín* was a part of the missing *Book of Druimm Snechtai* (eighth century). (Gantz 1976; Rutherford 1987)

See also *Óengus, The Dream of; The Wooing of Étaín.*

DAGON
(Also Dagan)

In the *Baal Epic,* Dagon is the father of Baal. He is the Western Semitic god of grain or crop fertility (ca. 2500 B.C.). (Pritchard 1973)

See also Anath; *Baal Epic;* Yam.

DAGREF
(Also Daeghrefn)

In *Beowulf,* Dagref is a Frankish warrior, the killer of Higlac, who in turn is slain by Beowulf. (Hieatt 1967; Raffel 1963)

See also *Beowulf;* Higlac.

DAIKOKU
(Also Dai-koku-sama)

Japanese god of prosperity and protector of farmers, Daikoku is one of the Shichi-fuku-jin, or Seven Gods of Happiness or Luck, identified in the *Nihongi* as Oho-kuni-nushi no Kami. (Aston 1972; Mayer 1948)

DAKIKI

Dakiki was the initiator of the Persian epic *Shāh-Nāmah* ca. the tenth century. (Levy 1967)

See also *Shāh-Nāmah.*

DAMAYANTĪ

In the Hindu epic *Mahābhārata,* Damayantī is a princess who chooses Nala as her husband, even though four gods have attempted to foil her by taking his appearance. A slightly different version is told in the *Ḍholā Epic,* where she also appears as the wife of Raja Nal, hero of Ḍholā. (Blackburn et al., 1989; Buck 1981)

See also *Ḍholā Epic; Mahābhārata.*

DAN

This eponymous hero of Danish legends is the son of Ypper, king of Uppsala in Sweden. Dan leaves Sweden to conquer Zealand and the surrounding isles, as well as Jutland, Fyn, and Skane. The whole area was named Danmörk after him. (Jones, G. 1990)

DANEL
(Also Daniel)

In the Semitic epic fragment *Aqhat* (fourteenth-century B.C.), Danel is a sage who prays to El for a son and is given Aqhat. Danel gives his son a magnificent bow crafted by the god Kothar. When the goddess Anath kills Aqhat for the bow, Danel and his daughter Paghat plan to avenge the murder. The text breaks off before the outcome is known. The character is also mentioned in the fourteenth chapter of the Old Testament book of Ezekiel. (Pritchard 1973)

See also Anath; *Aqhat Epic;* Paghat.

DANU
(Also Dana and Anu)

Danu is the earth mother in Celtic religion. In the *Ṛg Veda,* Dánu is the mother of the Dānavas (demons) and of Vṛtra, the demon slain by Indra. See also Tuatha Dé Danann, meaning "People of the Goddess Dana." (O'Flaherty 1981; Rutherford 1987)

***See also** Ṛg Veda.*

DAOINE SIDHE

In Gaelic folklore, Daoine Sidhe (literally, "People of the Mounds") are a fairy race as large as humans, living in castles hidden by mounds of earth. (Evans-Wentz 1990)

See also Túatha Dé Danaan.

DARDANUS

In Greek legend Dardanus is the son of Zeus and Electra and the founder of the royal house of Troy. He built a city named Dardania near the foot of Mount Ida in Phrygia. He appears in the *Iliad* (xx) and the *Aeneid* (v). (Graves 1955)

DARES PHRYGIUS

In the *Iliad,* Dares is a Trojan priest of Hephaistos described as "blameless and bountiful." He has two sons, Phegus and Idaios. Phegus is killed by Diomedes, while Idaios is rescued by Hephaistos. (Lattimore 1976)

DAŚARATHA

In the Hindu epic *Rāmāyaṇa,* Daśaratha is the king of Kosala, which he rules from Ayodhyā, and the father of Rāma. Daśaratha's three chief queens are all childless until he performs the horse sacrifice ritual ashvamedha. Then his wife Kausalyā bears a son, Rāma; Queen Sumitrā bears two sons, Lakṣmaṇa and Śatrughana; and Queen Kaikeyī bears a son, Bhārata. After Daśaratha is tricked into ordering Rāma into exile for 14 years, he dies of a broken heart. (Buck 1976; O'Flaherty 1975)

See also Rāma; *Rāmāyaṇa.*

DAVID OF SASSOUN

(Also Sasuntzi Davith)

This tenth-century Armenian folk epic, now lost, tells of the battles of David the Great of Tayk against Arab invaders. Some of the same period is covered in the Turkish cycle of *Dede Korkut.* (Chahin 1987; Preminger 1990; Suny 1988)

See also *Dede Korkut, The Book of; Sasuntzi Davith.*

DEDE KORKUT, THE BOOK OF

This heroic cycle of 12 stories and a "preface" set in the heroic age of the Oghuz Turks (ca. the thirteenth to fourteenth centuries) is presented as coming "from the tongue of Dede Korkut." Although the tales were given their present form relatively recently and are tinged with Islamic touches, they are basically much older pre-Islamic tales filled with references to ancient practices dating to shamanistic Turkey. The stories are heavily sprinkled with poetry; in fact, as much as half of the text in the cited work is poetry.

"Dede (Grandfather) Korkut" of the stories is the soothsayer, high priest, and ozan, or bard, of the Oghuz, Turkish nomads who flourished under that name ca. the eighth to twelfth centuries. They were also known as Ghuzz and, by Byzantine chroniclers, as Ouzoi. The Seljuks made up one clan of Oghuz. Fourteenth-century historian Rashid al-Din claimed that Dede Korkut lived for 295 years, and central Asian legend says that he died at age 300. Legend also credits him with inventing the kopuz, a lute that he played at Oghuz gatherings. The stories do not purport to come firsthand from him; in fact, he appears as a participant. In four stories, the reader is told that Dede Korkut "strung together this tale of the Oghuz."

The collection survives in two sixteenth-century manuscripts: one in the Royal Library of Dresden and another, containing only six of the tales, in the library of the Vatican. At the beginning of both manuscripts is a five-part section, at least some of which is, according to Turkish scholar Geoffrey Lewis, clearly of later origin than the stories themselves. In the cited reference, this newer section is entitled "The Wisdom of Dede Korkut" and is presented last.

Story 1, "Boghach Khan, Son of Dirse Khan," tells that once a year the Great Khan of Khans, Bayindir Khan, son of Kam Ghan, makes a feast to entertain the Oghuz nobles. One year he has three tents—white, red, and black—erected and instructs his servants to put the nobles who have sons in the white tent seated on silken rugs, the nobles who have daughters in the red tent, also on silken rugs. Those who have neither sons nor daughters have been humiliated

His bow drawn, a Turkish warrior turns in his saddle and steadies himself in the stirrups to deliver a Parthian shot. Horsemen such as this fought, loved, and raced throughout the 12 stories of *The Book of Dede Korkut.*

by God Most High and are relegated to the black tent, seated on black felt, and fed nothing but mutton stew made from black sheep.

A certain Dirse Khan comes with his 40 warriors to the tents of Bayindir Khan and asks, "What is my offense that he puts me in the black tent?" When he learns the humiliating reason, he tells his men, "Up, my warriors; rise from your place. This mysterious affliction of mine is due either to me or my wife." By the time he reaches home, he has obviously laid the blame upon his wife, who is never dignified with a name in the story. He threatens to cut off her head if it is her fault that he has no offspring. But she tells him that God is the reason that they have no child. She advises him to set up many tents and feed the hungry, clothe the naked, and pay the debts of the debtors, so that God may see fit to grant them a child. Dirse Khan follows her advice, and in a few months his wife delivers a fine son.

When the son reaches the age of 15, Dirse Khan goes to join Bayindir's horde. Twice a year the Khan of Khans holds an entertainment for his nobles: a fight between a bull and a camel. On this occasion, the son of Dirse Khan and three boys of the army are playing knuckle-bones in the arena when the bull is released prior to the fight. Although the other boys run, the son of Dirse Khan faces the bull and kills him, cutting off his head. The Oghuz nobles praise the boy and insist that Dede Korkut be summoned to give the boy a name. Dede Korkut arrives and sings the boy's praises, naming him Boghach, Bull-Man. Dede Korkut tells Boghach's father to make him a prince and give him a throne.

After the boy ascends to the throne, the 40 warriors are forgotten. They grow jealous and devise a plan to get rid of Boghach by telling his father lies about the terrible things his son has done. They convince the father that he must kill the wicked son while they are hunting. Dirse Khan, believing that his son has become a scoundrel, strikes him down with an arrow and leaves him for dead.

But his mother goes looking for him and, finding him half-dead, curses whatever caused this disaster to befall him. Boghach raises his head and tells her, "If you must curse, curse my father. / This crime, this sin is my father's." According to his instructions, she mixes a poultice of mountain flowers and her own breast milk and applies it to his wound, healing him.

Although Dirse Khan knows nothing of this, the 40 treacherous scoundrels learn that Boghach has survived, and they decide to save their own skins by absconding with Dirse to the land of the bloody infidel. But Dirse's wife learns of her husband's capture. She goes to her son and begs, "Bestir yourself, son; if your father showed no mercy to you, / Do you show mercy to your father!"

Boghach obeys his mother, girds on his black steel sword, takes up his bow and spear, and rides off on his Arabian horse to confront the scoundrels with their prisoner. When Boghach reaches their camp, the father, not recognizing his own son, tells him, "If it is for me that you have come, I have killed my own dear son. / I deserve no pity, warrior; turn back!"

But Boghach answers, "I have an old father too among them. / His mind is wandering, he's lost his wits, / But I shall not leave him to the forty cowards." So saying, he and his 40 warriors charge the 40 traitors, slay them, and free Dirse Khan.

Thereafter the Great Khan Bayindir gives the boy a principality and a throne, and Dede Korkut composes verses about the brave deeds of the son of Dirse Khan.

Story 2, "How Salur Kazan's House Was Pillaged," tells of a son-in-law of Bayindir Khan named Salur Kazan. He is described as "son of Ulash, chick of the long-plumed bird, hope of the wretched and the helpless, lion of the Emet river, tiger of the Karajuk, master of the chestnut horse, father of Khan Uruz, luck of the teeming Oghuz, prop of forsaken warriors." One day he has his 90 gold-capped pavilions set up and spread with silken carpets. He tells his nobles, "Our sides are sore with too much reclining." He suggests a hunting trip, after which they will come back, "eat and drink and have some fun." Although his warriors think this is a splendid idea, one Uruz Koja points out, "You are living in the mouth of foul infidel Georgia; whom will you leave to look after the camp?"

Kazan replies that his son Uruz with 300 men will stand guard. The warriors all mount up and ride off in splendid array. The infidels' spy sees them leave and brings the news to the "wild infidel beast," King Shökli. Seven thousand infidels, "men of foul religion," gallop into the camp at midnight, sack the golden pavilions, loot the treasure, and take into captivity "forty slender-waisted maidens and Lady Burla the Tall," Kazan's wife. Prince Kazan's old mother is also taken, "hanging round the neck of a black camel." Prince Uruz and his men go with their hands and necks tethered.

Then the infidels ride out to take Kazan's 10,000 sheep. But they are met by "that dragon among warriors," Karajuk, the shepherd, who warns them, "Come over here from far and near, / See the beating your men will get; and then be off." The infidels shower him with arrows, but he loads his sling and kills 300 infidels before he runs out of stones. Then he picks up sheep and goats and loads them into the sling and continues to kill infidels until the rest turn and flee.

Karajuk piles the corpses into a huge mound and weeps bitter tears, saying, ". . . Prince Kazan, are you dead or alive? Don't you know anything of this?"

Meanwhile, Kazan has a dream in which rabid wolves destroy his tent. He tells his companions to continue on the hunt while he makes the three-day journey back to his pavilions in a half-day. Along the way, he comes upon Karajuk, who tells him the devastating news that his whole family has been captured. He tells Kazan that he too was attacked and that two of his own brothers were also killed. He asks for Kazan's chestnut horse, his lance, shield, sword, and bow and arrows, promising, "I shall go to the unbeliever, / I shall rise again and kill, / I shall wipe the blood off my forehead with my sleeve. / If I die I shall die for your sake; / If God Most High allows, I shall deliver your family."

But Kazan, jealous for his honor, thinks that if he allows the shepherd to help, the Oghuz nobles will shame him, so he ties the shepherd to a tree and rides away, intent on rescuing his family himself. The shepherd says to himself,

"Now, shepherd, you'd better uproot this tree before you feel hungry and faint, or the wolves and birds will eat you here." So he uproots the tree and runs after Kazan with the tree on his back. Kazan sees the shepherd coming and asks, "What's the idea of the tree? . . ." The shepherd says, "While you're fighting the unbeliever you might feel a bit peckish, so I'll use this tree for firewood and cook you something to eat." The answer pleases Kazan, who unties him and promises him that, if God delivers his family, he will make the shepherd Master of the Horse. The two continue on their way together.

Meanwhile, King Shökli has decided to bring Lady Burla to his bed and make her his cupbearer. Lady Burla overhears his intent and instructs the 40 slender-waisted women, "Whichever of you they . . . ask if she is Kazan's wife, you must all forty of you call out together, 'That's me!'"

When the infidels cannot determine which is the wife of Kazan, King Shökli instructs them to bring her son Uruz, hang him on a hook, roast him, and offer all 41 ladies a piece to eat. The one who refuses it will be Lady Burla. When Lady Burla overhears this plan, she goes to her son to ask what she should do. He tells her, "I should seize you by your collar and your throat, I should cast you beneath my hard heel, I should trample your white face into the black earth, I should bring the blood gushing from your mouth and nose. . . ." He tells her to eat his flesh, lest she have to go to bed with the infidel and thus defile the honor of his father Kazan.

When Uruz is dragged out to be slaughtered, he begs the tree upon which he is to be hanged not to support him. He weeps and invokes the intercession of Muhammad. At that moment, Kazan and Karajuk the shepherd gallop up. The shepherd, preparing to shoot a hundredweight of stone, causes the whole world to go dark. Kazan asks him to hold off until he can ask the infidel for his mother. He calls to King Shökli, "Infidel, give me my mother. With no fight, with no battle, I shall retrace my steps, / I shall turn back and go. . . ."

When the king refuses, the shepherd suggests that, if he would like to improve his breed with the help of an Oghuz sire, "if you have a black-eyed daughter, fetch her, give her to Prince Kazan."

The Oghuz nobles have by this time heard of the disaster and, following Kazan's tracks, they arrive upon the scene. A glorious battle "like doomsday" ensues, in which the field is "full of heads." Heads are "cut off like balls." Twelve thousand unbelievers are put to the sword, while 500 Oghuz fall. Kazan frees his son, mother, and wife, and he makes the shepherd Karajuk his Master of the Horse. As a thank-offering for his son Uruz, he frees 40 male slaves and 40 female slaves. To the brave young warriors, he gives castles, lands, and treasures. Dede Korkut comes and declaims, stringing together this tale of the Oghuz.

Story 3, "Bamsi Beyrek of the Grey Horse," tells of the day that the Great Khan Bayindir Khan pitches his white pavilion and his many-colored tents and spreads 1,000 silken rugs. He assembles the Oghuz nobles, including the princes Kara Budak, son of Kara Göne; Uruz, son of Kazan; and Yigenek, son of Kazilik Koja. Prince Bay Büre sees them and sinks to his knees in tears, because he has no sons and no brothers; when he dies, there will be no one to inherit his crown and throne. So the nobles face heavenward and pray that Bay Büre be granted a son. Immediately, Bay Bijan asks the nobles to pray that he be granted a daughter, whom he will betroth in the cradle to Bay Büre's son.

Both prayers are answered, and Bay Büre sends the merchants off to the land of Rum (eastern Roman empire) for splendid gifts for his son. The merchants set out for Istanbul, where they buy a grey horse, a strong bow, and a mace. It takes many years for them to reach home again. By that time, Bay Büre's son is 15, a fine, handsome young man, brave as an eagle, "swaggering as he glared about him." In these times, until a boy has cut off heads, he is not given a name.

As the merchants near home, they are set upon by "the damned accursed infidels from the castle of Avnik" who rob them and capture all but one merchant. This man runs to a many-colored tent pitched nearby and begs the princely young man sitting with his 40 warriors to help him. The prince gladly goes after the infidels, kills the "contumacious unbelievers," frees the merchants, and restores their treasure to them. In gratitude, they tell him to take whatever merchandise that he fancies. He immediately chooses the horse, the mace, and the bow, much to the dismay of the merchants. When they explain that these are for the son of Bay Büre, he rides away, telling them that they should hurry and deliver them.

When Bay Büre learns from the merchants that his son has spilled blood, he calls for a great feast to be prepared, and Dede Korkut is summoned to give his son a name. The ozan comes, and after he praises the boy, he says, "Your pet-name for your son is Bamsa; / Let his name be Bamsi Beyrek of the grey horse. / I have given his name; may God give him his years."

Following the feast, the party goes hunting. Suddenly a herd of deer appears and Bamsi Beyrek, wearing a veil over his face, chases after one. He comes upon a red tent and fells his quarry in front of the tent, which belongs to the Lady Chichek, his cradle-betrothed. This lady peeks out and instructs her handmaiden Kisirja Yenge to go out and ask for a share of the kill. Bamsi Beyrek replies to this request by giving the handmaiden the whole deer. He asks whose tent it is and, learning it is the tent of his betrothed, he feels his blood inflamed. But like a gentleman, he withdraws.

When Kisirja Yenge describes the young prince to her mistress, Lady Chichek recalls that her father has told her that she is betrothed to Beyrek of the veiled face. She asks the handmaiden to call the prince to come back, and she herself dons a veil. When the prince arrives, she presents herself as a servingwoman of Lady Chichek and suggests that the two of them go riding together. "We shall shoot our bows and race our horses and wrestle. If you beat me in these three, you will beat her too." The prince agrees, and they ride out. The prince's horse surpasses hers, and his arrow splits hers. Then they wrestle, and after a hard struggle, he throws her on her back. It is then that she reveals her identity. He kisses her three times and puts a gold ring on her finger. They part company and he goes back to his tents.

He learns from his father that Lady Chichek has a brother called Crazy Karchar who kills anyone who asks for her hand. They assemble "all the nobles of the teeming Oghuz" to ask for their advice. The nobles suggest that Dede Korkut be sent to ask for Lady Chichek's hand on Beyrek's behalf. Dede Korkut is willing to undertake the mission, if he is provided with two horses: one for running away, and one for chasing.

Dede Korkut rides off to Crazy Karchar's camp, where Karchar, foaming at the mouth, tells him that just for setting foot on his land, on his "white forehead God has written doom . . . has your appointed hour come?" But the old bard bravely states his mission, whereupon Karchar calls for his black horse. Dede Korkut gallops off quickly, with Karchar in hot pursuit. When Karchar catches him and raises his sword, Dede Korkut, being a saint whose wishes are granted, warns, "If you strike me, may your hand wither." When Karchar sees what is happening to his hand, he promises to give his sister to Prince Beyrek if only Korkut will heal him. But once he is healed, he demands a huge dowry before he will give his sister away: 1,000 camels that have never seen a female camel, 1,000 horses that have never mounted a mare, 1,000 rams that have never seen a ewe, 1,000 dogs with no tails or ears, and 1,000 huge fleas. He adds, "Otherwise, don't let me see you again, for if I do—I haven't killed you this time but then I shall kill you."

When Dede Korkut returns to Prince Bay Büre's tents, the prince asks, "Dede, are you a boy or a girl?" meaning, have you been successful or not? Korkut reports that he has been successful, but enumerates Karchar's demands. The two assemble the items, and Dede delivers them all to Karchar, who immediately wants to know where the fleas are. The old sage tears off the man's clothes and throws him into a pen of flea-infested sheep and tells him to take the fat ones and leave the rest. Covered with fleas, Crazy Karchar promises to cause no more trouble once he is released. After he has bathed off the fleas in the river, he goes home to prepare for a lavish wedding.

When a young man marries, he shoots an arrow, and where it falls, he sets up his marriage tent. Beyrek shoots his arrow and pitches his tent where it falls. His betrothed sends him a crimson caftan as a wedding gift. All is in readiness.

A spy of the infidel lord of Bayburt reports the upcoming marriage of Beyrek to the woman whom the infidel wants. So "that damnable unbeliever" rides out with 700 infidels, kills one groomsman, and takes the other 39 and the groom Beyrek as prisoners. They march the men in chains back to Bayburt Castle, where they remain for 16 years.

Beyrek's parents, his betrothed, and his friends wear black in mourning for 16 years, until Crazy Karchar goes to the court of the Great Khan Bayindir, offering riches to anyone who brings news that Beyrek is alive, and offering his sister's hand to anyone who brings news that he is dead. Yaltajuk, son of Yalanji, happens to have a shirt of Beyrek's, which he dips in blood and offers as proof that Beyrek is dead. While Yaltajuk prepares for his wedding to Lady Chichek, Beyrek's father, Prince Bay Büre, sends off a caravan of merchants to find out exactly what happened to his son.

The merchants, on reaching the infidel lord Parasar's castle of Bayburt, are entertained by the prisoner Beyrek playing his lute. When they tell him that his betrothed is about to be married to the traitor Yaltajuk, he is heartbroken.

He confides his sorrow to the infidel lord's daughter, who has kept him company nightly for all these years. She offers to help him escape so that he can go and stop the wedding. She asks him, "If I let you down from the castle by a rope . . . will you come back and marry me?" Beyrek swears that he will.

After his escape, Beyrek finds his big grey horse, which takes him to the wedding site. Before approaching, he borrows a lute from a minstrel and dons an old camel-cloth. He enters the wedding feast and, during an archery match, he calls out a curse at Yaltajuk and even breaks the traitor's bow. When Beyrek's own bow is brought out as a replacement, Beyrek uses it to shatter Yaltajuk's wedding ring with an arrow. As a reward for his archery skills, Prince Kazan offers him whatever he wants. He asks to be fed at the banquet and is granted a place in the marriage tent.

But after he has eaten his fill, he overturns the cauldrons and hurls stew meat right and left. He storms off to the women's tent and calls for the bride to come out and dance. Lady Burla the Tall summons the maid Kisirja Yenge to go out, saying, "How will the crazy minstrel know the difference?" But Beyrek recognizes her and sends her away, as well as the next substitute who is sent out. Finally Lady Chichek herself comes out, heavily veiled. When Beyrek spies the gold ring that he gave her, he knows she is his betrothed. After he has convinced her of his identity, she rushes off to tell his parents. His father, now blind, says, "Let him draw blood from his little finger . . . and wipe my eyes with it. If they are open, he is indeed my son." Beyrek does so, and his father's sight is restored.

Beyrek goes after the traitor Yaltajuk, but when he catches him, he spares his life at the last minute and forgives him. Then he calls the nobles to arms and asks them to help him free his 39 men, still held captive in the castle. They saddle up and ride off to raid the infidel's castle. They free the captives, and Beyrek gives his seven sisters to seven of the men and finds mates for the rest. True to his promise, he marries the infidel king's daughter. They have a great wedding feast that lasts for 40 days and nights, during which Dede Korkut comes, plays music, and tells stories of the adventures of the heroic fighters of the Faith.

As for the Lady Chichek, she appears to have been left out in all but one version of the story, in which she too marries Beyrek. In this particular rendition, once she informs Beyrek's parents that he is alive, she is heard from no more.

Story 4, "How Prince Uruz Son of Prince Kazan Was Taken Prisoner," begins with the usual pitching of tents and calling in the young Oghuz nobles—9,000, in this instance. The host is Salur Kazan, who looks around the assemblage and weeps. When his son Uruz asks him why he weeps, he says, "You have reached your sixteenth year / . . . A day will come when I shall die and you be left, / You have not drawn bow, shot arrow, cut off head, spilled blood. / Among the teeming Oghuz you have taken no booty." He knows that when he dies, they will not give Uruz his crown and throne. But the son asks, "When have you ever taken me to the infidel frontier, brandished your sword and cut off heads? . . . What am I supposed to learn?" Kazan realizes that the boy is right, so he plans a week's outing to show him how to kill infidels.

Kazan takes with him 300 warriors with jewel-studded mail. Uruz takes his 40 chestnut-eyed young men. After several days on the steppes, 16,000 black-mailed infidels charge down upon Uruz. When Kazan sees their dust, he tells his son, "That which comes surging like the black sea / Is the host of the unbeliever / . . . the enemy, of savage religion." The boy asks the meaning of the word "enemy" and is told that "enemy" is "people whom we kill when we catch them, and when they catch us they kill us." He tells Uruz, "I shall dart hither and yon, . . . / Watch me wielding the sword and cutting off heads, and learn!"

He sends Uruz to the crest of the high mountains to watch. But after a while Uruz grows restive, and he charges into the battle. His horse is shot out from under him, and he is taken prisoner by a horde of infidels. Kazan does not know this, and he believes that Uruz has run off to his mother. His face grows dark, and he says, "God has given me a worthless son. I shall go and take him from his mother's side and hack him with my sword. I shall chop him into six pieces. . . ."

But when he arrives home without their son, Lady Burla the Tall, who has prepared a feast for her son's homecoming from his first hunt, is furious with Kazan for coming home without him: "I have not eaten garlic, Kazan, yet I burn within." She tells him, "If you have left my only son a captive / . . . I shall take a great army with plentiful treasure. / Until I am hacked down from my Kazilik horse, / Until I wipe away my red blood with my sleeve, / Until I fall dismembered to the ground, / Until I have news of my only son, / I shall not return from the roads of the infidel." She curses Kazan, and his inward parts shake.

Kazan calls out 90,000 young Oghuz to help him find Uruz. They return to the battlefield and find the corpses of Uruz's 40 chestnut-eyed young men and the corpse of his son's Arabian horse. He knows that his son is a prisoner.

Meanwhile, in the infidel camp, Uruz has been dressed in a black shepherd's cloak and placed across the threshold so that all who come in or out step on him. In this way he will die a slow and painful death. But the infidels are startled when Kazan gallops into the camp. Uruz asks to be freed so that he can beg his father to leave him to his fate. But Kazan will not allow his son to sacrifice himself for his sake. He says his prayers, blesses Muhammad, foams like a camel, roars like a lion, screams and shouts, and rides all alone into the infidel horde. He charges three times, but then a sword touches his eyelid and blood gushes into his eyes. He falls to the ground.

Lady Burla the Tall cannot wait at home. With her 40 slender maidens, she rides after Kazan. When she finds him wandering around, he does not recognize her through the blood, and he asks for her horse to ride. But she berates him and finally tells him, "Your loins are dead. / . . . You have fallen into dotage; what ails you? / To sword, Kazan, I am here!"

The Oghuz nobles have also heard of Uruz's captivity, and they mass and come riding out by the thousands. A bloody conflagration follows during which Lady Burla brings the infidel's black standard down with a blow of her sword, and the Oghuz nobles scatter the landscape with 15,000 infidel corpses and captives, while the Oghuz lose only 300. Kazan and Lady Burla untie their son and embrace him. The fight for the Faith is a success, and the nobles have their fill of plunder.

The whole party stops for a seven-day celebration. Kazan has 40 tents pitched, and he frees 40 male slaves and 40 female slaves. He awards the brave officers with castles, lands, and treasures. Dede Korkut comes and plays joyful music and strings together this tale.

In story 5, "Wild Dumrul Son of Dukha Koja," the man Wild Dumrul has a bridge built over a dried-up stream and he charges 33 pieces of silver to everyone who crosses. One day a portion of a tribe camps on the slope of the bridge. The tribe is loudly mourning the death by illness of a fine, handsome warrior. Wild Dumrul hastens up and asks, "What is this uproar by my bridge?" When they explain that "Azrael (the Muslim angel of death) has taken that man's life," Wild Dumrul tells God, ". . . Show me Azrael, that I may fight and struggle and wrestle with him and save that fine warrior's life. . . ."

Dumrul's words are not pleasing to God, who says, "This crazy pimp knows not My Unity. . . . Let him swagger and vaunt himself in My great court!" He tells Azrael, "Go . . . appear before the eyes of that crazy pimp; turn his face pale, make his soul yelp and bring it here."

So Azrael appears to Wild Dumrul while he is feasting with his 40 warriors and tells him, ". . . I have come to take your soul. Will you give it up or will you fight me?" When Dumrul discovers Azrael's identity, he orders the gates closed to trap Azrael. But the angel of death becomes a dove and flies out of the smoke hole. Dumrul mounts his horse and takes out after the dove with his falcon. But Azrael shows himself to the horse, frightening him, and the horse throws Dumrul to the ground.

Azrael settles on Dumrul's breast, and Dumrul begs, "I was full of wine; I was out of my mind; / I did not know what I said. / I have not tired of being a prince; I have not had my fill of being a warrior. / Do not take my soul, Azrael, mercy!"

When Azrael explains that it is God Most High who takes souls, Dumrul says, "Then what good are you, you pest? Get out of the way and let me talk to God Most High." He makes a most flattering speech that pleases God Most High, who offers to let Dumrul go free if he can find a soul to replace his.

Wild Dumrul goes to his father and tells him the whole sad story. He asks his father to give up his soul in his place. But the father insists that his mother is fonder of Dumrul than he is, and so Dumrul goes to his mother with the same request. But his mother also refuses to give up her life. Dumrul goes to his wife, tells her the sad story, and gives her all that he owns. But she tells him that her life would be meaningless without him, and she offers to let her life be sacrificed for his.

But Dumrul cannot bring himself to let her suffer. He supplicates God Most High, "If You will take, take both our lives. / If you will spare, spare both our lives. . . ."

His words are pleasing to God, who orders Azrael to take Wild Dumrul's parents instead. He then grants Dumrul and his wife 140 years more of life. Dede Korkut comes to declaim the story for all the brave bards who come after to remember.

Story 6, "Kan Turali Son of Kanli Koja," tells of a stout-hearted warrior, Kanli Koja, who has a grown daredevil son named Kan Turali. The father decides that it is time for his son to marry, but the young man asks, "How can there be a girl fit for me? Before I rise to my feet she must rise; before I mount my well-trained horse she must be on horseback; before I reach the bloody infidels' land she must already have got there and brought me back some heads." His father answers, "You don't want a girl; you want a daredevil hero to look after you, and you can eat and drink and be merry."

Kan Turali goes out looking for a girl, but he comes home without one because he has very high standards. His father leaves him to look after the property while he himself sets out with his white-bearded old men to find a suitable girl. Eventually the party reaches the land of the infidel king of Trebizond, who has a beautiful daughter. It is said that she can draw two bows at once and that when she shoots, her arrows never fall to earth. To win her, a suitor must first kill three beasts. If he fails, the king cuts off his head and hangs it on a stake beside those of all the others who have thus far failed.

Kanli Koja returns to tell his son about the girl, and Kan Turali is immediately aflame with desire for such a maid. He goes to Trebizond and slays the bull, the lion, and the camel, thus qualifying as a suitable mate for the princess Saljan. But when it is time to enter the marriage tent, he says that first he must see the faces of his parents. So he takes his betrothed and his entourage back toward home. They pitch tents not far from home and he goes to sleep, but the princess, fearing that some of her suitors may try to seize her, dresses for battle and mounts her horse.

As she suspected, her father the king has had a change of heart. He chooses 600 infidels to ride after Kan Turali's party and bring his daughter back. She sees them coming and wakes Kan Turali in time for him to mount up and ride out to meet them. The princess also rides out into battle.

Kan Turali's horse is shot, and he himself is wounded. The princess begins to fight off his attackers, but Kan Turali, not recognizing his rescuer, is enraged. He says, "In my land it is counted shame to attack another man's enemy without his leave; / Be off with you! / . . . Shall I nonchalantly cut off your head?" The two of them run off the enemy, but afterward he tells her, "When everyone says her say, / You will stand there and boast, / . . . Anger consumes me, the heart has gone out of me. / I shall kill you."

She begs to be spared, reminding him, "If a man will boast, let him boast; he is a lion. / For a woman to boast is scandalous. / Boasting does not make a woman a man." After calling him a "pimp and son of a pimp," she challenges him to a duel of sorts. But she cannot bring herself to use a pointed arrow, and she removes the tip. He invites her to shoot first, and her shot parts his hair and sends the "lice in his hair scuttling down to his feet." He comes forward, embraces her, and says, "My own soul I might sacrifice, but never yours; / I was but testing you." She admits that she was testing him as well.

The father pitches many tents and a gold-decked pavilion and makes a wedding feast. Dede Korkut comes, plays joyful music, and recounts the adventures of "the gallant fighters of the Faith."

In story 7, "Yigenek Son of Kazilik Koja," during a gathering of nobles, Bayindir's minister, Kazilik Koja, being full of wine, asks the Great Kahn's permission to go on a raid. He and his men ride off to the castle of the gigantic King Direk, who rides out with his men to meet them, decimates the warriors, and takes Kazilik Koja captive.

Kazilik remains a prisoner for 16 years, during which time Emen, his wife's brother, makes six or seven unsuccessful attempts to rescue him.

Meanwhile, Kazilik's son Yigenek, who was only one year old when his father left (although later in the story the poet states that he had not yet been born when his father left), comes of age and learns for the first time that his father is being held prisoner. He asks the Great Khan to give him some soldiers so that he can rescue his father. Bayindir obliges by dispatching the heroic lords of the 24 tribes to accompany him.

The finest men of the Oghuz ride up against the giant king and are driven back. Yigenek says a prayer to his god and rides in alone against the infidel. He succeeds in mortally wounding the king and then beheads him. Hoping to put an end to the fighting, the infidels release Kazilik Koja. He comes out of the castle and says, "I left my beautiful chestnut-eyed wife heavy with young. / Boy or girl the child? Would that I knew! / Tell me, warrior princes. . . ."

Yigenek goes up to his father and falls at his feet. The two embrace and then go off together to talk and howl "like wolves in the wilderness." The nobles advance upon the castle, sack it, reduce it to rubble, and build a mosque in its place. Then they return home and Dede Korkut comes to declaim to "the generous heroes of untarnished honor."

Story 8, "How Basat Killed Goggle-Eye," tells of the time when, while the Oghuz are sitting in their encampment, an enemy falls upon them. As they flee into the night, the baby son of Uruz Koja falls. A lioness finds him, carries him off, and nurses him for several years.

Eventually the Oghuz return to the area and learn that there is a lion who "walks with a swagger, like a man." He is known to attack horses and suck their blood. Uruz knows that it is his little son. The nobles mount up and find the lioness's lair, drive her off, and capture the boy. Dede Korkut comes and gives him the name of Basat, meaning "Attack-Horse."

A certain Oghuz shepherd captures and violates a peri (a winged demon borrowed from Persian legend). A year later when the shepherd returns, the peri appears and says, "Come shepherd, take back your property. But you have brought ruination on the Oghuz." She leaves a monster on the ground that grows every time he hits it with a stone. He becomes frightened and runs away.

Later the nobles come upon the monster, whom they kick until its belly splits open. Out comes a child with one eye at the top of its head. Uruz names the child Goggle-Eye and takes him home to rear with his son Basat.

Uruz hires a wet nurse for the child, but in one suck it takes up all her milk; with the second suck, all her blood; with a third suck, her life. The baby destroys several other wet nurses in the same way. They feed him on milk, but they cannot produce enough to satisfy him. He grows quickly and begins to eat the nose of one child, the ear of another. The whole camp begs Uruz to do something, so he finally drives Goggle-Eye from his house.

Goggle-Eye's peri mother appears and puts a ring on his finger that will protect him from arrows and swords. He travels beyond Oghuz lands and becomes a notorious menace, eating people until no shepherd is left. When he returns to Oghuz lands and begins to eat Oghuz people, the warriors assemble and march out against him. But he cannot be hurt by their swords and arrows, and he easily bars their escape.

The people back at camp call Dede Korkut to make peace with Goggle-Eye. The sage rides forth and asks the villainous giant to name his terms. Goggle-Eye says, "Give me sixty men a day to eat." Dede Korkut protests, "You'll (soon) exhaust the supply. Let us give two men and five hundred sheep a day." Goggle-Eye agrees to these terms, and the Oghuz set about choosing the men who will be sacrificed.

A woman who has already lost one son and who will soon have to sacrifice another to Goggle-Eye goes to the camp of Basat, who has just returned from a raid. She asks for and receives a captive, whom she can ransom for her remaining son.

Basat returns to his father's house and learns that it is his time to be delivered to Goggle-Eye. He goes forth willingly and attempts in vain to kill the giant. Goggle-Eye captures him and stuffs him into a boot, preparatory to having him put on a spit for roasting. But Basat escapes and sticks the hot spit in Goggle-Eye's eye, blinding him. He then dresses in a ram's skin to escape the giant's clutches. The giant gives him his ring, hoping then to be able to locate him, but this only enables Basat to cut off his head.

As soon as the news of Goggle-Eye's death spreads through the lands of the Oghuz, Dede Korkut comes and plays joyful music, relates the adventures of the brave, and invokes blessings upon Basat.

In story 9, "Emren Son of Begil," as Bayindir Khan has all his nobles assembled under his white pavilion, a tribute comes from Georgia that greatly displeases the Great Khan: a horse, a sword, and a mace. Dede Korkut comes and plays joyful music, asking, "My Khan, why are you displeased?" Bayindir describes the gold and silver that usually come as tribute, which he gives out to the nobles and warriors. Indicating the meager tribute, he asks, "Now whom can we satisfy with this?"

Korkut advises him to give all three things to one warrior and name him warden for the Oghuz land. Bayindir looks right and left, but no warrior is willing to take such an assignment. Finally a warrior named Begil consents, so Dede Korkut bestows the sword, mace, and bow upon him.

Begil mounts his horse, takes his family and his people, strikes his tents, and leaves Oghuz land. He reaches Barda, then Ganja—both in Azerbaijan—where he takes some grazing land before moving on to Georgia. There he stays as warden, sending the heads of passing strangers and infidels back to the Oghuz as presents. Once a year he travels back to attend Bayindir Khan's court.

Once while he is in court, he is insulted when the nobles claim that his hunting prowess is due primarily to his horse's skill. He leaves in a fury and goes back to Georgia. Seeing his distress, his wife suggests a hunting trip "to ease your soul." While hunting, he and his horse take a fall, and Begil breaks a leg. Lamenting that he has no grown son and no grown brother, he binds his own leg, remounts, and somehow makes it back to camp. His young son Emren meets him and cares for him, while an infidel spy reports to King Shökli that Prince Begil is down and it is a good time to attack. But Begil also has a spy, who reports the infidels' plans.

Begil tells his son to ride quickly back to the Oghuz court to beg for help. But young Emren is indignant. He asks for his father's own horse and says, "I shall just cut some heads off for you. / . . . Give me your three hundred chestnut-eyed warriors to bear me company, / I shall fight the cause of Muhammad's religion for you."

The boy is arrayed for battle and rides out against the infidel king, who merely scoffs at the idea of "a boy, skinny as a bird," riding out to defeat his best. He himself confronts young Emren. The boy fights valiantly, and when he is overpowered, he calls upon God Most High. The king, who has 72 temples full of idols, is dumbfounded by the boy's faith. God Most High orders Gabriel to give Emren the strength of 40 men. The boy picks up the infidel king and hurls him to the ground, causing blood to spurt from his nose like a fountain. The king instantly accepts the religion of Emren; the rest of the infidels, witnessing their king's conversion, flee the field with Emren's men in pursuit. Emren's men ravage their territory and take their daughters and daughters-in-law.

As the conquerors return, Begil comes out to greet them. He calls for a great feast and finds his son a nice wife. He sets aside a fifth of the booty for Bayindir Khan and takes his son to the court, where the emperor gives Emren fine robes and an honored seat. Dede Korkut plays joyful music and strings together this tale, which he calls "Emren Son of Begil."

Story 10, "Segrek Son of Ushun Koja," begins with an account of the conduct of the elder son of Ushun Koja, Egrek. He is a reckless warrior who defers to none, visiting Bayindir Khan's court whenever he pleases. Although he has not earned a seat of honor, he pushes aside the nobles and sits where he pleases.

A noble warrior challenges him, "Everyone . . . here has won the place where he sits with his sword and his bread. Have you cut off heads and spilled blood? Have you fed the hungry and clothed the naked?" Egrek asks, "Is cutting off heads and spilling blood a clever thing to do?" The answer comes, "Of course it is."

So Egrek asks the Commander of Commanders Prince Kazan's leave to go out on a raid. He assembles 300 warriors and for five days they hold a great feast and drinking bout. Then they set out to raid the land from Shirakavan (the Armenian name of the fortress known during the Ottoman period as Shuregel) to Blue Lake, or Lake Sevan in Armenia.

Along the way, near the Iranian border, is Alinja Castle, where the Black King sets a trap for the Oghuz by stocking a walled park with geese, elk, deer, and hare. Egrek and his men smash the park's gate, kill the beasts, and unsaddle their horses to prepare for a feast. Then 600 black-mailed infidels descend upon them, slay the warriors, and throw Egrek into the castle dungeon.

Years pass and Ushun Koja's younger son Segrek grows up to be a brave, reckless warrior. One day at a party, Segrek gets drunk and goes outside to relieve himself. He sees two orphan boys fighting and gives each a rap upon the head, whereupon one boy challenges him: "If you're so clever, your brother is a prisoner in Alinja Castle; go and set him free." Segrek leaves the party and rides to his mother's tent to verify the boy's claim and to ask her if he should attempt a rescue. When she gives him her blessing to go on a rescue mission, he knows that it is true that he has a brother. He tells her, "I should casually cut off your lovely head, / I should spill your red blood on the earth's face, / Mother, wicked mother!" His father denies that the man imprisoned is Segrek's brother, but Segrek insists on launching a rescue mission anyway.

His parents send a message to Kazan asking what they can do to prevent their son from embarking on this dangerous endeavor. Kazan answers, "Hobble him." He is already betrothed, so they quickly prepare a wedding feast and put the boy in the bridal bower. But Segrek tells his bride, "Daughter of a pimp, may I be sliced by my own sword . . . if I enter the bridal bower before I see my brother's face." He instructs her to wait for him for three years. When his parents learn that his bride has not been able to deter him, they give him their blessing to go.

Segrek rides three days and nights without stopping for sleep to reach the park where his brother was captured. Exhausted, he lies down to sleep in the park, and his presence is reported to the infidel king. The king sends 60 men out to capture him but his horse alerts him, and he quickly mounts and drives the men back into the castle. Again he lies down to sleep. The king sends 100 infidels out to capture him, but again his horse alerts him, and again he drives the infidels away. The king decides to release Egrek, give him a horse and armor, and send him out with 300 men to capture the intruder. But when the two men meet, they discover that they are brothers, and they turn on the infidels and chase them into the castle. Then they return to their parents, who celebrate with a great feast. The parents bring a beautiful bride for Egrek as well. Dede Korkut comes, tells stories, and declaims.

Story 11, "How Salur Kazan Was Taken Prisoner and How His Son Uruz Freed Him," tells of the time that the king of Trebizond, a Greek state on the Black Sea, sends Khan Kazan a falcon, which prompts the Commander of Commanders to decide on a hunting trip. But the falcon flies away and lights on Tomanin Castle, about 40 miles from Tiflis, Georgia.

As they set out to recover it, Kazan and his men are overcome by sleep; while they sleep, the infidel king of Tomanin is informed of their presence on his land. He leads his army out and kills Kazan's men and captures Kazan. They put Kazan into a pit in Tomanin Castle, which is the passageway down to their underground burial area. They seal the pit with a large stone with a hole in it, through which they pass him food and water.

The infidel queen becomes curious and goes to converse with the prisoner. He tells her that he is taking the food that is passed through the pit intended for the dead, and that he is riding the dead as if they were horses. The queen, who has lost a seven-year-old daughter, cannot bear for Kazan to be riding her daughter, so she demands that he be brought out of the pit. The infidels insist that Kazan must first praise them and insult the Oghuz.

Kazan asks for a lute, and he sings several long songs about his deeds. The first ends, "Drive your black sword at my neck; cut off my head. / I shall not flinch from your sword, / I do not defame my own stock, my own root." A second time he sings, and ends, "So long as Oghuz heroes stand, I do not praise you." A third, fourth, and fifth time he sings, ending with, "I do not defame my own stock, my own root." Finally he sings once more, ending with, "So if you will kill me, infidel, kill me. / If you do not kill me, infidel, God willing I shall kill you." But the infidels assemble and say, "This man has a son and a brother; we cannot kill him." So they imprison him in the pigsty.

In a few years Kazan's baby son grows into a young man who believes that his father is Bayindir Khan, his mother's father. One day he learns the truth from his mother about his real father's imprisonment, and he tells her, "I should casually cut off your lovely head, / I should spill your red blood on the earth's face!" His mother explains that she was afraid to tell him the truth for fear he would go after the infidels and be killed. She suggests they ask his father's brother for advice about what to do. When the uncle is summoned, it is agreed that they should mount a rescue party and ride to Tomanin Castle.

On their way is the infidels' great church, whose walls are very difficult to get through. They disguise themselves as merchants, but the priests are not fooled and they bar the gate. The warriors smash the gate with their maces and kill everyone inside. After they have plundered their treasure, they continue on and make camp.

When word reaches the king of what the Oghuz have done, he decides that the only one who can defeat them is Kazan himself. So they release Kazan, telling him that they are being attacked, and that if he defeats the attackers, he will be set free. The Oghuz advance, regiment after regiment, with their great war drums thundering. When Kazan rides out and meets his own son, Uruz charges his father and wounds him. Only then does Kazan identify himself, crying out, "My hero Uruz, my lion Uruz, / Spare your white-bearded father, son!"

Uruz's black almond eyes fill with tears of blood. He snatches his father from the infidels' grasp, and his men charge the infidel forces, routing them completely. Uruz sends the news to his white-skinned mother, and when the triumphant army returns, Kazan gives a feast that lasts for seven days and nights. Dede Korkut comes, plays his lute, and recounts the adventures of the gallant fighters of the Faith.

Story 12, "How the Outer Oghuz Rebelled against the Inner Oghuz and How Beyrek Died," describes a strange but well-established Turkish custom whereby once every three years Kazan assembles the nobles for a feast and afterward lets them pillage his tent, taking the gold and silver table appointments.

One year the Inner Oghuz begin the pillaging before the Outer Oghuz tribes arrive. When Uruz, Emen, and other Outer Oghuz nobles hear about this, they are furious and swear to salute Kazan no longer; in fact, they swear enmity to him.

Hearing rumors of their dissatisfaction, Kazan sends an emissary, Kilbash, to Uruz with a fictitious story that his camp is under siege and he needs his uncle Uruz's help. Uruz replies that, since Kazan allowed the Inner Oghuz to pillage his tent before the Outer Oghuz arrived, he will not come to Kazan's aid. Then Kilbash admits, "No enemy at all has attacked us; / I came to test whether you were friend or foe. / Now I know you are Khan Kazar's enemy." Kilbash leaves to report this to Kazan.

"Mightily displeased," Uruz sends for all the nobles of Outer Oghuz, and they swear loyalty to him and enmity to Kazan. Since Uruz's daughter is married to Kazan's minister, Beyrek, the Outer Oghuz nobles decide to trick Beyrek by summoning him to make peace between them and Kazan.

But when Beyrek arrives at Uruz's camp, the nobles bring out the Koran and demand that he swear to rebel against Kazan as they have done. Beyrek says, "Oft have I enjoyed Kazan's bounty; / . . . I shall not desert Kazan, be sure of that." Whereupon Uruz grabs Beyrek by the beard, intending to kill him, but the nobles cannot bring themselves to join in. Beyrek derides him, "To take a man by deceit is woman's work; / Have you learned this from your woman, pimp?"

Uruz strikes him with his sword, dealing him a mortal wound. The nobles load him onto his horse and send him back to Kazan. Beyrek lives long enough to demand that Kazan avenge his death, so the Inner Oghuz join Kazan to march upon Uruz and his allies. When the two sides meet, Uruz chooses Kazan as his target. He drives his horse at Kazan, but his sword misses. Kazan then aims his 60-span larice at Uruz's chest and pierces him through. Kazan's brother Kara Göne cuts off Uruz's head, and immediately the other Outer Oghuz nobles throw themselves at Kazan's feet, begging his forgiveness.

Kazan forgives them, allows Uruz's house to be sacked and his lands to be ravaged, pitches many tents, and sets up his pavilion. Dede Korkut comes to play joyful music and tell stories of the gallant fighters of the Faith.

The last section, "The Wisdom of Dede Korkut," written at a later date, includes as a beginning passage an almost verbatim paragraph taken from the *History of the Seljuks of Yazijizate Ali* (ca. the fifteenth century) that identifies Korkut Ata (Dede Korkut) as a soothsayer of the tribe of Bayat.

The "Wisdom" itself includes a number of short proverbs ("To the warrior who knows how to wield it, a club is better than arrow and sword.") and ends with a treatise on the four kinds of women: the pillar that upholds the house, the withering scourge who complains about her husband, the ever-rolling ball who scurries about eavesdropping and gossiping, and last, "she who whatever you say to her it makes no difference": she does not obey at all. Korkut ends with: "May God protect you from her also, my Khan; may such a wife never come to your hearth." (Lewis 1974)

DEFEAT OF THE YOONS

(Also "Defeat of the Yunnan" or "Yoon Pai")

This is one of the earliest (ca. 1475–1485) poems in the Thai language. It celebrates the fall of the Mongol control of Tali, or Yunnan, north of present-day Burma, following the reign of Toghan Temür, descendant of Jenghiz-khan. (Grousset 1970)

DEIANEIRA

(Also Deianira or Dejanira)

In Greek mythology, Deianeira is the second wife of Herakles. She unwittingly kills him by sending him a robe soaked in the blood of the centaur Nessus, who tainted it in order to reclaim husbands from unlawful liaisons. (Graves 1955)

See also Herakles.

DEIOCES

Deioces is a wise hero of an ancient Iranian cycle who acts as an unpaid justice for his neighbors. When he threatens to stop unless he is paid, he is made king of Medea. But instead of continuing to judge, he builds a palace at Ecbatana, where he retreats into seclusion. The historical Deioces was a petty village chief whom King Sargon deported to Syria. (Olmstead 1948)

DEIRDRE

(Also Deirdriu or Derdriu)

Deirdre is the beautiful heroine in the great love story of the *Ulster Cycle*, "Oidheadh Chloinne Uisneach" (Fate of the Sons of Usnech, ca. the eighth century). In most versions, Deirdre is the daughter of Felim, storyteller to Ulster king Conchobar. When she is born, a druid prophesies that she will become the most beautiful woman in Ireland, but that she will bring much bloodshed to the land.

To circumvent the prophecy, Conchobar sends her into the woods to be raised in seclusion by the nurse Lavarcham (Lebarcham), who tells the girl tales about her cousin Naisi (Noisi), son of Usnech. Deirdre begs Lavarcham to bring him to see her, and when he comes, she falls in love with him. With Naisi's two brothers, the lovers flee to Alba (Scotland) to avoid her father's ire. They are finally persuaded to return to Ireland, but the sons of Usnech are killed.

In some versions, Deirdre kills herself at Naisi's grave; in others, she lives for a year as a captive of Conchobar before dashing her brains on a rock. The story bears parallels to the elopement tale in "The Pursuit of Diarmuid and Grainne," and to the legend of *Tristan and Iseult.* (Kinsella 1969)

See also Cú Chulainn; *Taín Bó Cúailnge; Ulster Cycle.*

DEMETER

In the *Homeric Hymns,* Demeter is the goddess of agriculture and marriage. She is the mother, by Zeus, of Persephone, and by Iasion of Plutus, god of wealth. (Ben Khader and Soren 1987; Graves 1955; Perera 1980; Smith 1968)

DEMINÁN

Deminán is the hero of the mythological cycle of the Taíno Indians of the Caribbean. (Stevens-Arroyo 1988)

See also *Cave of the Jagua.*

DEOR

(Also *Deor's Lament* or the *Complaint of Deor)*

An Anglo-Saxon heroic poem, *Deor* is one of two surviving Old English poems (ca. ninth century) that end with a refrain. It is comprised of 42 lines written in alliterative verse and divided into seven stanzas of unequal length. Each stanza encapsulates a famous story and ends with the line: "That has passed; this will too." The narrator, Deor, is a scop (minstrel) of the Hedenings who is ousted by his lord in favor of another scop, Heorrenda, and deprived of his lands and holdings. He describes the misfortunes of other German heroes and heroines: the capture and mutilation of Weland (Wayland), the rape of Beadohild by Weland, the misfortune of Maethhild and Geat, the exile of Theodoric, and the tyranny of Ermanaric. Each is an example of misfortune overcome. (Alexander, M. 1991; Hieatt 1967)

See also Wayland.

DERGRUATHER CHONAILL CHERNAIGH

(Also "Conall Cernach's Red Onslaught")

In this Old Irish tale, part of the *Ulster Cycle,* Conall Cernach avenges the death of Cú Chulainn. (Kinsella 1969)

See also Cú Chulainn; *Ulster Cycle.*

DESCENT TO THE UNDERWORLD

A common motif in mythology worldwide, the purpose of the descent (usually made by the hero) may be to discover the answer to a secret, rescue someone, or steal a treasure. Gilgamesh makes such a journey to discover the secret of immortality. In the Babylonian tale, Ishtar descends to rescue Tammuz. In Norse mythology, Hermod descends to Hel to bring back Balder. Among Greek

Demeter, left, the Greek goddess of agriculture, figures in Homeric hymns. A fifth-century bas relief shows her with young Triptolemos, behind whom stands the goddess of the seasons, Persephone, Demeter's daughter by Zeus, king of the gods.

mythological stories of descents are those of Orpheus and Eurydice, Odysseus, Aeneas, Demeter and Persephone, and Herakles's rescue of Alcestis, as well as his bringing the three-headed guard dog Cerberus to earth as his Twelfth Labor. In Japanese mythology, Izanagi visits Yömï, the Japanese subterranean Hades, in search of his deceased wife Izanami. (Duerr 1985; Perera 1981; Philippi 1968)

See also *Gilgamesh, Epic of;* Herakles; Izanagi and Izanami; *Kojiki.*

DESTRUCTION OF DA DERGA'S HOSTEL

(Also *Destruction of Ûa Dergae's Hostel)*

This Early Irish heroic saga, found in *The Book of the Dun Cow* (Leabhar na H-uidre), bears the name of its scribe, Maelmuiri, known to have died in 1106. The story is also known to have been included in an early-eighth-century work, *Book of Druimm Snechtai,* of which only the list of contents remains. "Da Derga" means "the red god," while "Ûa Dergae" means "the nephew of the red goddess." (Gantz 1988)

See also *The Book of the Dun Cow.*

DESTURI ZA WASWAHILI

(Customs of the Swahili People)

This account of the Swahili civilization (ca. 1890s) ranks among the world's great literary achievements. It is not an epic per se, but its influence on African peoples has had the force of an epic. A major cultural document, it is written by "pure Swahili persons" in prose of classic beauty despite the fact that Swahili literature of the period is primarily poetry. Over 70 of the tenzi, or tendi (short epic poems), are now in print, and many more exist; only a smattering of verse appears in perhaps half of the chapters of the *Desturi.*

It is much more than a listing and description of customs. It conveys, in beautiful language, a deep universal philosophy of life and a profound respect for civilization in which greatness does not depend on industrialization. Much of the final work on the collection was apparently done by a master of Swahili prose named Bwana Mtoro bin Mwinyi Bakari of Bagamoyo. (Allen 1981)

See also Mtoro bin Mwinyi Bakari, Bwana.

DEUCALION'S FLOOD

In Greek legend, *Deucalion's Flood* is the story of the Great Deluge. When, at the end of the Iron Age, Zeus sends a flood, Phthian king Deucalion, son of Prometheus and Clymene, builds a boat. He and his wife Pyrrha are the only mortals saved. The ship comes to rest on Mount Parnassus, the only land that tops the waves. The oracle Themis instructs the couple to restore the human race by casting behind him the bones of their mother (the stones of Mother Earth). Those thrown by Deucalion become men; those thrown by Pyrrha become women. (Leeming 1990; Siepmann 1987)

See also Flood Myths.

DEVĪ

An Indian goddess called "mother of the universe" and worshiped from prehistoric times, she was assimilated into the Hindu pantheon long after Śiva and Viṣṇu. Durgā, Pārvatī, Umā, and Gaurī are all manifestations of the goddess.

The *Skanda Purāṇa* describes Devī's creation from the great angers of Viṣṇu's mouth and from the energies of the other gods: She is formed in order to kill the buffalo demons. Her head appears from the energy of Śiva, her arms from Viṣṇu, her feet from Brahmā, her waist from Indra, her hair from Yama, her breasts from the moon, her thighs from Varuṇa, her hips from the earth, her toes from the sun, her fingers from the Vasus, her nose from Kubera, her teeth from the nine Prijāptes, and her eyes from the Oblation-bearer. She is called Durgā, the fierce aspect of Devī.

In another version found in the *Skanda Purāṇa,* the goddess is not created in order to kill the buffalo demon but already exists. The gods entreat her to take the form of a nymph, to seduce and weaken the demon.

The tale of the goddess's bloody slaying of the demon appears in the *Mārkaṇḍeya Purāṇa.* When she throws a noose over the demon and binds him, he becomes a lion. When she cuts off his head, a man with a sword appears. She pierces the man with arrows, but he becomes a great elephant. She takes her sword and cuts off his trunk, at which point the demon assumes his buffalo shape again. Furious, the goddess drinks celestial wine until she is intoxicated. Now crazed, she leaps up, mounts him, and drives her foot through his neck. She cuts off his head with his own sword and goes on to destroy his army and her own friends, whom the demon has bewitched. All creatures in three worlds rejoice.

The *Devībhāgavata Purāṇa* tells how the goddess, as Satī, is dismembered and Śiva dances erotically with her corpse.

The *Bṛhaddharma Purāṇa* tells of the goddess (as Pārvatī, Śiva's wife) convincing Śiva to beget a son in her, whom she names Gaṇeśa. But Śiva severs the child Gaṇeśa's head and is unable to make it grow on again. Eventually the child is given the head of an elephant; in this version, by Nandin. (Dimmitt and van Buitenen 1978; O'Flaherty 1975)

See also Gaṇeśa; Pārvatī; Śiva.

DEVNĀRĀYAṆ

This oral epic of the desert region of Rajasthan in northwestern India celebrates the heroic deeds of the hero-god Devnārāyaṇ, or Devjī, an incarnation of Lord Viṣṇu. The epic is performed by and for agricultural castes. Two singers with a painted scroll called a par travel from town to town to perform at ceremonies and religious functions, during which the audiences take some responsive part. Lower-caste Nayak singers also perform the epic as an addition to their specialty in the epic of *Pābūjī.* These Nayak singers may be a husband-and-wife team. Women are allowed in the audiences of these performances, but they are not allowed to make offerings to the gods.

The epic consists of two parts. The first concerns the 24 Bagaṛāvat brothers of the Gujar cowherding caste to whom Lord Śiva gives a large amount of wealth. They spend it on the poor, and their resultant notoriety angers the king of the underworld, Raja Bāsak, who convinces Lord Viṣṇu to destroy them. But Viṣṇu finds the brothers devoted to Lord Śiva, and their sister Sādū so virtuous, that he decides to become incarnated in her household. He calls upon the goddess to uphold his pledge to Raja Bāsak, and she accomplishes this by taking incarnation in a Rajput household, openly marrying the Rajput king, but secretly marrying the chief Bagaṛāvat brother, Bhoj. When Bhoj carries her away from the Rajput's palace, a war breaks out in which all the brothers are slain by the goddess herself. Only Sādū and her four sons survive.

Lord Viṣṇu becomes incarnated as the infant Devnārāyaṇ, with whom Sādū flees to her father's home in Malwa. When the child grows older and learns the fate of the 24 brothers, he leaves to unite with the surviving four sons and avenge the Bagaṛāvat brothers. After a series of battles, the enemies are defeated. Devnārāyaṇ establishes his cult among the cowherders and returns to heaven. (Blackburn et al. 1989)

ḌHOLĀ EPIC

This epic of the history of the kingdom of Navargarh in northwestern India is performed by low- and middle-caste singers who travel between villages singing for religious functions and weddings. The epic consists of 50 or more episodes, one of which makes a night's performance. Because women are seldom permitted to attend public nighttime functions, the audiences are almost entirely land-owning men.

The epic covers three generations of the kings of Navargarh beginning with Raja Pratham, who is heirless until a guru provides a grain of rice, which causes his queen Manjhā to become pregnant. His 100 other wives are jealous and convince him that the son-to-be will kill him. He orders a servant to take Manjhā to the forest and slay her, but instead the servant kills a deer and brings its eyes to the king as proof that his queen is dead.

Meanwhile, Manjhā gives birth to a son, Nal. A wealthy merchant, Lacchī Baniyā, finds mother and child, adopts Manjhā, and takes them home with him. Later, he and his sons Pannā and Phūlā go on a business trip and find a cowrie shell, used in gambling, which they decide to present to the king. But the greedy king throws them in prison when they cannot produce 15 more shells.

Nal, now grown, travels to the capital and begs the release of his adopted grandfather, promising the king that he will get the 15 shells. The king agrees, and Nal, Lacchī, Pannā, and Phūlā set out to find the shells.

Nal goes ashore on the island where the original shell was found and meets an old woman who tells him the other shells are in the possession of Motinī, daughter of the island's demon ruler Ghūmāsur. Nal goes to the castle and defeats Motinī in a game of dice. She agrees to marry him and, in order to conceal him from her father, turns him into a fly, which she puts into her hair. After several more days of gambling, Nal learns that the secret of Ghūmāsur's strength lies in the health of a certain duck that is surrounded by snakes. If the duck dies, Ghūmāsur dies. Nal manages to get to the duck, which he tortures and kills, thus destroying the demon king and freeing Motinī to marry him.

The two return to the shore where the other three men wait in the boat. As they sail onward, both Pannā and Phūlā fall in love with Motinī and throw Nal overboard while he sleeps. Nal is able to reach the snake kingdom of Bāsik, while Lacchī sails home to tell his adopted daughter Manjhā the sad news that her son has drowned.

Because the time has elapsed in which to find the 15 cowries, Lacchī takes Motinī to the king and offers her in their stead. Raja Pratham is bewitched by her beauty and wants to marry her, but she refuses to marry anyone unless someone tells the *Nal Purāṇa* (Story of Nal).

Nal makes his way home from the snake kingdom and, disguised as an old pandit, goes to court to tell the *Nal Purāṇa* himself. When he hears the tale, the king realizes that Nal is his own son. He sends for his wife Manjhā, the family is reunited, and Nal is reunited with his wife Motinī. He has a son, Ḍholā.

A marriage proposal from Raja Bhīm, offering his daughter Damayantī to the god Indra, falls into Nal's hands in error. Thinking the proposal is meant for him, Nal decides to accept the invitation to marry the raja's daughter. Meanwhile, the raja learns of the error and sends a second invitation to Indra. Both Nal and Indra arrive in Samal Sikal to claim the bride. When Damayantī expresses a preference for Nal, Indra is so angered that he causes Nal's kingdom 20 years of disasters.

Conditions in the kingdom become so bad that Nal and Damayantī are eventually forced to flee naked and take refuge with an oil presser, Ragghu. Nal works for the oil presser for five years, making him a wealthy man. While Ragghu is away visiting the king, Raja Bhud, Nal has an argument with the king's men.

To settle the dispute, Raja Bhud and Raggha gamble, and Ragghu loses all his wealth. Nal proposes to gamble with the king, with the raja's daughter Mārū as the stake. Nal wins, but he must prove his royal status before he can accept Mārū as a bride for his son Ḍholā. He battles and defeats the demons of Lakhiyaban, enabling Ḍholā to marry Mārū.

But Ḍholā becomes bewitched, forgets his wife, and leaves her alone in Pengal. Eventually the grieving wife is able to send a message to Ḍholā, reminding him of their marriage, and they are reunited. (Blackburn et al. 1989)

See also Damayantī.

DHŪ AL-HIMMA

(Also *Delhemma)*

Dhū al-Himma is an Arabic folk epic. ***See*** *Ahādīth al-Baṭṭāl; Sīrat al-Amīra Dhāt al-Himma.*

DIALOGUE OF THE ANCIENTS

Gaelic saga. *See Interrogation of the Old Men.*

DIANA

In Roman religion, Diana was originally a woodland goddess, later moon goddess, synonymous with the Greek goddess Artemis. (Duerr 1985; Frazer 1963)

See also Artemis.

DIDO

(Also Elissa)

The legendary founder of Carthage, she is the daughter of King Mutton or King Belos of Tyros and Queen Acerbas. After her brother Pygmalion slays her husband Sichaeus, she flees to Africa where a local chieftain, Iarbas, offers to sell her all the land that can be covered by a buffalo hide. She cuts the hide in strips and lays them end to end so that they encompass a large piece of land. On this land she founds the city of Carthage and becomes its queen. According to one legend, after the city prospers, Iarbas demands her hand in marriage, and she stabs herself to avoid marrying him. According to Virgil's *Aeneid,* when Aeneas lands in Africa, she falls in love with him; when he spurns her and leaves for Italy, she utters a curse against the Trojans and kills herself with her sword. (Ben Khader and Soren 1987; Bullfinch 1962; Humphries 1951)

See also Aeneas; *Aeneid;* Iarbas.

DIETRICH VON BERN

(Also Thidrik)

This heroic figure appears in the Icelandic *Thiđrekssaga,* or Thidrik's Saga (thirteenth century), and in a number of South German songs. His character is possibly based in part on Ostrogoth king Theodoric the Great, ruler of Italy from 493 to 526, although many of the incidents related in the Dietrich cycle do not have any connection with the historical Theodoric. The wise and just Dietrich is driven from Verona (Berne) by King Ermanaric and flees to the court of Attila the Hun, where he remains for many years. His weapons master is the elder warrior Hildebrand, hero of the Old High German heroic ballad *Hildebrandslied.* With Hildebrand and Dietrich's own nephews, Alphart and Wolfhart, Dietrich marches with the Huns to Ravenna to confront Ermanaric, who is routed in the Battle of Ravenna. However, during the battle, Attila's two sons, Heime and Biterolf, are killed by Dietrich's treacherous vassal Wittich. Later Dietrich meets Ermanaric again and kills him. In the *Nibelungenlied,* Dietrich is lord of the Amelungs, living in exile at Etzel's court, and betrothed to Herrat (Herrad), daughter of Nantwin. (Hatto 1969; Heer 1962)

See also Etzel; *Hildebrandslied; Nibelungenlied; Thiđrekssaga.*

DIEVO SUNELIAI

(Also Dieva deli)

These Lithuanian gods, Heavenly Twins, are sometimes considered the morning and evening stars; however, Dievas is the name of God (Sky God), as in the Lithuanian mythic tale of *Aušrinę* (Morning Star). Dievas and his wife Saulė (Sun Maiden) are the parents of the twins. In the *Aušrinę* story, Aušrinę and Saulė are rivals, for Aušrinę is the most beautiful creature ever born. The word is Deivas in Old Prussian, and the word "deivé" refers to female mythic beings (also laumas). The use of the word in the plural means a number of secondary nonsovereign deities belonging to the category of household gods who are guardians of every family and farm separately. (Greimas 1992)

See also Aušrinę; Saulė.

DIGENES AKRITAS

This Byzantine epic poem (tenth century) is a historical romance containing material about the Byzantine struggle against the Muslims. At one point, Digenes wins the hand of his beloved, but he refuses to marry her until he takes her to meet his parents to receive their blessing. As her father makes wedding preparations, Digenes insists: "Let me first go hence to my own mother, / That my father may see his daughter-in-law to be, / And may praise God, and I will soon return." (Mavrogordato 1956; Ostrogorsky 1969)

DINÉ BAHANÈ

In this Navajo creation cycle, insectlike Niłch'i dine'é, or "air-spirit people," emerge from a primal domain deep within the earth and make their way to the earth's surface. There they become nihookáá' dine'é, or "earth surface people," who finally divide into a number of human clans. The First Man is Áłtsé hastiin; the First Woman is Áłtsé asdzą́ą́. The central theme is the aspiration to attain hózhǫ́, meaning a combination of beauty, harmony, and balance. This is achieved through the relationship between male and female. However, First Man and First Woman do not get along, which causes evil to enter the world, and for one generation the world is ruled by the Naayéé', or Alien Gods, and the people are pursued by evil monsters. Then Asdzą́ą́ nádleehé (Changing Woman) and Jóhonaa'éí (the Sun) appear, giving hope that the Naayéé will be destroyed. But Jóhonaa'éí is a philanderer, and full hózhǫ́ cannot be established until Changing Woman and the Sun achieve a balanced relationship. When they do, the Navajo people come into being. Ćsdzą́ą́ nádleehé has a sister,

Naayéé neizghání (White Shell Woman). These two bear sons, one of whom is called Monster Slayer after the two boys destroy the monster Yé'iitsoh.

The story is told in four parts. The first, "The Emergence," covers the story to the point where First Man and First Woman lead their people through a hole up to the Fifth World, the surface of the earth.

The second part, "The Fifth World," relates many adventures of early men and creatures such as Coyote, and ends with people fleeing the Binaayéé', the Alien Giants.

By now, in part three, "Slaying the Monsters," only First Man, First Woman, and four other persons remain. Then Haashch'ééłti'í (Talking God) and Niłch'i (the Wind) appear and cause a figure made of turquoise to be transformed into Changing Woman and a figure made of white shell to become her sister, White Shell Woman. The two give birth to sons who, on the advice of Spider Woman, set out to find their father, the Sun. They eventually kill a monster and throw him off the cliff.

They continue on and find their father, who tells them that he wants "a home where I can relax with [Changing Woman] and enjoy the pleasure of her company." The son says, "I will order her to find a suitable place in the west and to make a home for you." But the other boy says, "No. You cannot order her to do anything! Asdzą́ą́ nádleehé the Changing Woman is under nobody's power. . . . For she is her own mistress and no one else's." They promise, however, to relate his request to her.

He gives them four great hailstones, five hoops, and five knives and says, "Take these. Your mother will know what to do with them. Simply tell her to do what must be done. Then your victory over the remaining monsters is all but assured."

But when the boys give Changing Woman the objects, she says, "I know nothing of hailstones and knives. . . . And I care nothing for any of his possessions." But she listens as they relate the Sun's request and looks wistfully up at the sky. She says, "Once I felt the warmth of him. Deep within my body I felt his loving warmth."

She weeps and takes the hoops, knives, and hailstones and flings them in all four directions and overhead. The weather becomes so violent and lasts so long that most of the monsters are destroyed. Monster Slayer sets out to slay the last of the Naayéé'. Then Jóhonaa'éí comes and tells her, "Each day I labor long and hard alone in the sky. I have no one to talk with. I have no companion for my nights."

She says, "You have a beautiful house in the east I am told. I want just such a house in the west. . . . And I want all sorts of gems. . . . I will be lonely while you are gone each day. So I will want animals to keep me company. . . ."

He says, "What do you mean by making such demands of me?" and she answers quickly, "I will tell you why. You are male and I am female. You are of the sky and I am of the earth. You are constant in your brightness, but I must change with the seasons. . . . As dissimilar as we are, . . . we are of equal worth . . . there can be no harmony in the universe as long as there is no harmony between us." He agrees, and the two of them are betrothed. The earth thrives, and the Navajo people are born.

Part four, "Gathering of the Clans," tells the names, locations, and history of the various clans. (Zolbrod 1984)

DINGANE

In the Zulu epic *Emperor Shaka the Great,* Dingane is the brother of Shaka and chief organizer of his assassination. He also kills his own co-conspirators. He later becomes king of the Zulu. (Kunene 1979)

See also Chaka; Dingiswayo; *Emperor Shaka the Great.*

DINGISWAYO
(Also Godongwana)

In the Zulu epic *Emperor Shaka the Great,* Dingiswayo is king of the Mthethwas and founder of the Mthethwa empire where Shaka receives his early training. (Kunene 1979)

See also Chaka; Dingane; *Emperor Shaka the Great.*

DIOMEDES

In the *Iliad* (ii, v, vi, x, xxiii) and the *Aeneid* (i), Diomedes is the son of Tudeus and Deipyle, king of Aetolia; he is an Epigoni and one of the bravest leaders in the Trojan War. Diomedes is a favorite of Athena and second only to Achilles in bravery. He wounds Aeneas, but Aphrodite saves him. He also wounds Aphrodite and Ares, kills Dolon and Rhesus, and with Odysseus brings Philoctetes from Lemnos and seizes the Palladium, the sacred image of the goddess Pallas that protects Troy; he enters Troy in the wooden horse with Phoenix.

In the Herakles story, he is the son of Ares and Cyrene, and the king of Thrace, who feeds his horses human flesh. The Eighth Labor of Herakles is to destroy the mares of Diomedes. Herakles first kills Diomedes and feeds him to the horses. In some versions he captures and tames the mares, consecrating them to Hera. In some versions she frees them; in others, they escape and roam on Mount Olympus, where they are torn to pieces by Apollo's wild beasts. (Graves 1955; Humphries 1951; Lattimore 1976)

See also *Aeneid;* Herakles; *Iliad.*

DIONE

In the *Iliad* (v) and the *Aeneid* (iii), Dione is the mother, by Zeus, of Aphrodite. When Diomedes wounds Aphrodite, Dione comforts her and foretells Diomedes's death for waging war against the immortals. (Humphries 1951; Lattimore 1976)

DIONYSUS

(Also Bacchus)

In Greek religion, Dionysus is the youngest of the 12 Olympian gods—a nature god, the god of wine and revelry. (Graves 1955)

DIU NÔT

(Last Stand)

This Austrian epic poem (ca. 1160), now lost, concerns the fall of the Burgundians, which preceded and formed a basis for the *Nibelungenlied* and portions of *Thiðrekssaga.* German scholar A. T. Hatto concludes that by inference *Diu Nôt* "must have been a powerful poem, fierce, ruthless, with a gaunt beauty. . . ." (Hatto 1969)

DIULADJAN DIABI

This heroic narrative concerns a Soninke hero of Kiban from the oral tradition of the Soninke in the West African kingdom of Segu along the Upper Niger River in modern-day Mali. It has been preserved for more than 300 years by the djeli, bard historians attached to the noble families.

Before the greatness of the city of Kiban, there is a large Bambara town called Djekoro Bugu, whose chief is also named Djekoro. Some Soninke people led by the Diabi family come to town wanting to settle, but Chief Djekoro tells them, ". . . are you not Muslim? And we Bambara, are we not Bambara? . . . Our ways conflict with one another. There would be dissension." However, he gives them a piece of land upon which to build their own village, to be called Kiban.

The Soninke plant fields and build a mosque. At prayer time the muezzin mounts to the top and gives his azan so loudly that it annoys the Bambaras in the nearby town. The chief sends word for the muezzin to stop, so the Soninke, who are weak and not able to defy his command, instruct the muezzin to call the azan very softly.

In time, more and more people come to settle in Kiban, and the chief grants them more land. But soon the Soninke begin spreading the beliefs of Islam to the surrounding towns. Chiefs in small villages become Muslims; even ordinary people become Muslims. The chief thinks, "If these things go on, we Bambara will become nothing but islands with the water of Islam surrounding us."

He begins to deal harshly with the Soninke, meting out large taxes, and even threatening to destroy their mosque. By now, however, the Soninke have become strong, and they send word that they want to be treated as equals, or else they will come to the Bambara town with weapons. The chief tells their emissary, ". . . Because they hunt, that does not make them heroes. Even a bush rat can hunt. . . . They cannot fight. If your people decide to come . . . let them bring their own jokes, because we will give them nothing to make them laugh."

The warriors of Kiban, among them Diuladjan Diabi, Bakore Samassa, and Madine Diani, arrive in Bambara territory and by nightfall they defeat the people of Djekoro Bugu. The few survivors flee to a far-off place and build new villages.

At one time Diuladjan Diabi's favorite wife quits eating bassi, a food made with millet, because she does not like the milk given by the cows of Kiban. Diuladjan becomes concerned for her health: "Unless you eat bassi you will grow weak and die." She is convinced that what she needs is milk from the cows of Woro. Diuladjan remembers the saying, "The wish of a woman is the will of Allah," and he sets off for Woro with only his slave for company.

He finds the Woro herd guarded by two Fula herdsmen, whom he commands to drive the cows from their pen. One of the men raises his spear, and Diuladjan draws his sword and strikes him down. The second herdsman drives the cattle out. Diuladjan sends his slave back to Kiban with the cattle and, with true heroic ethics, instructs the herdsman to report what has happened to his chief. He spreads his blanket and lies down to wait.

When the Bambara chief hears the news of the theft of his cattle, he sends three brave warriors, one by one, to deal with the rustler. But Diuladjan has been treated by a morike (shaman), and the warriors' blades do not hurt him. One by one he kills them. He goes into town to ask for a great hero to challenge him for taking the cattle of Woro, but the chief tells him, "We have no one better to give you. . . . Let it rest there." So Diuladjan returns to Kiban and presents the finest of the cows to his favorite wife. One again she can eat bassi.

In the nearby town of Niare, the chief receives a visitor—the fierce and ruthless Siribi Ntiyi, who has come with his personal djeli and his company of Bambara fighting men to issue a demand: "I am looking for the . . . hero Kiuladjan. . . . I do not care where he lives. . . . Get him for me. . . . If you do not give Diuladjan Diabi to me, I will destroy your town. . . . I give you five days. . . ."

To save themselves, the chief of Niare and his counselors abandon their honor. They conspire to bring Diuladjan to Niare. They send a message asking for help in defending their town against an attack due to occur in five days. Diuladjan responds to the plea for help by bringing 99 of his finest warriors, refusing the council's offer to send 1,000. They arrive on the fourth day. The Niare greet the men with a great feast and dance, and afterward put the drunken men to bed in ten separate houses without their weapons.

The Niare go out to where Siribi Ntiyi and his men are hiding and tell them where they can find Diuladjan and his men. Siribi Ntiyi also abandons his honor when he takes his fighters and slaughters sleeping men.

But Diuladjan, who has slept with his cutlass made with mystic metal, hears the noise and rides out of town with the Siribi warriors in pursuit. He stops at a certain place and waits for them, then kills them one by one as they pass by. He rides back toward Kiban in darkness, and at sunrise the people see him coming alone. He tells them, "My brothers and sisters, he whom you see is alive. He whom you do not see is dead." The people wail and lament: "We have lost an entire generation. . . . Kiban will never again be what it is."

Another of the Seven Cities of the Soninke, Tuba, has always envied the city of Kiban because it has become the first city. Now that Kiban is in disarray, the chief of Tuba goes to the king of Segu, King Amadu, and asks to be appointed the new representative of the Seven Cities. When news of this reaches Kiban, the people are angry. Diuladjan goes to Tuba and tells the people, "Naire maimed us and you rushed forward to lick the bones. . . . Kiban is not dead. . . . Let us test each other."

They pick out two Bambara towns to attack: Tuba will attack Tara, and Kiban will attack Koniba. Both armies are successful, but the Tubans contend that the force they met at Tara was superior to the Koniba force. They want to fight the Kibans. But Diuladjan visits an old morike and tells him, "I want you to prepare me. I am going alone to conquer Tara."

The morike prepares him for battle, and the next day Diuladjan eludes two warrior friends who want to come along. He goes off alone to Tara, where he fights for five days, defeating 20 challengers each day. When he has killed 100 men, he makes the chief say three times, "Tara applauds your valor. We want it to end." Satisfied, he rides home, to be greeted with all the djeli singing songs of praise.

But he remains bitter against Tuba, who started the whole challenge. Of Tara he thinks, "They fought me one by one and observed the rules of honor. It is Tuba that should be punished." He decides to mount an expedition against Tuba. That night, when the counselors come to his house, they find him crying. He tells them, "I am crying because of the consequences of what we are about to do. . . . This war will bring the Seven Cities to their downfall. . . ." The counselors discuss it, and at last the chief says, "Diuladjan is right. . . . We must call off the expedition."

Meanwhile, news of Diuladjan's victory over Tara reaches King Amadu in Segu City. He decides that Kiban is still a great power whose heroes are still champions. He sends word to Kiban that it will continue to be his chief administrator for the region. Tuba is not happy. Because of Kiuladjan, Kiban is still foremost of the Soninke cities in the kingdom of Segu. (Courlander 1982)

DJANGGAWUL

This is a song-cycle of 188 songs, 2,921 lines in translation, of the Australian Aborigines of Arnhem Land. The *Djanggawul* is a collective name for three ancestral beings, creator figures, spirit beings in human shape, who travel over wide areas. The basic story concerns the journeys of the three Djanggawul: Bildjiwuraroiju, the Elder Sister; Miralaidj, the Younger Sister; and Djanggawul, the Brother. Accompanied by Bralbral ("another being"), and carrying sacred objects, they leave Bralgu, the Land of Eternal Beings, located far out in the sea, and paddle toward the mainland in their bark canoe, guided through the twilight by the Morning Star.

Sometimes the waves roar, "spraying like rain, churning to foam." At one point their path is blocked by a whale; another time they come across "lines of sea eggs spreading across the sea!" At another point driftwood, "revealed in the shine of the Star," blocks their path. They hear a plover, "its screeching cry . . . mingling with the roar of the sea, spreading across it." They see a sea gull, and then a pigeon; finally, the sun, "leaving its home beneath the water," warms their backs. Eventually they reach the beach at Port Bradshaw.

They plant their sacred pole, the mauwulan, in the ground to make wells. After they explore the land around the port, they resume their journey around Arnhem Bay. They see a parakeet, "drying its red feathers in the glow of the sun," watching the sinking sun. They describe every bird, every sight they come upon. Along the way, people are removed from the wombs of the two Sisters, who are perpetually pregnant. Sacred string, made from the parakeet's breast feathers, are laid out "carefully, reverently," pointing the way to the various Djanggawul sites.

The cycle includes songs in which the Djanggawuls reenact their voyage in the nara ritual with dancing. Originally the Sisters possess the sacred emblems, making them controllers of the ritual, but the men steal the emblems and take control. The major theme is fertility, expressed not only in human sexuality, but also in the relationship between human sexuality and fecundity in the wider world of nature. (Finnegan 1978; Sproul 1991; Wilde et al. 1991)

DJARADA

An Australian aboriginal song collection of 65 short, self-contained songs, the *Djarada* does not possess the mythological narrative thread of other aboriginal cycles. (Wilde et al. 1991)

DÔN, CHILDREN OF

In Celtic mythology, the Children of Dôn are a family of Welsh gods, powers of light, in an unending struggle with the Children of Llŷr, the powers of darkness. Dôn's children are Gwydion, poet, musician, magician, and warrior; Aranrhod, fertility goddess and mother by Gwydion of twin sons Dylan, a sea god, and Lley of the Dexterous Hand (Lley Llaw Gyffes). Dôn is an approximate equivalent of the Irish goddess Danu. (Gantz 1976; Rutherford 1987)

DOON DE MAYENCE

In the Old French medieval epic chansons de geste, Doon de Mayence is the hero baron of a chanson that is part of the cycle *Geste de Doon de Mayence,* which is named for him. The first half of the poem relates Doon's childhood, and the second half recounts his activities in wars in Saxony. (Preminger 1990; Ruland n.d.)

DRAUPADĪ

In the *Mahābhārata,* Draupadī is the wife of all five Pāṇḍava brothers, because their mother has told her sons, "You must share everything with your brothers." So Arjuna takes his bride Draupadī home to marry his brothers as well. She gives each of her husbands a son. When the oldest Pāṇḍava, Yudhiṣṭhira, loses the kingdom to the Kauravas in a game of dice, he also loses Draupadī. She is commanded to remove her garments before the Kaurava court, but she calls upon the aid of Kṛiṣṇa, who performs a miracle and produces a new layer of clothing each time she removes one.

During their long years of exile, the brothers and Draupadī make their way, disguised, to the court of King Virāṭa. When a general at the court becomes enamored of Draupadī, the second Pāṇḍava, Bhīma, takes her place in bed and pulverizes the unsuspecting general. When the Kauravas attack Virāṭa's kingdom in an attempt to steal his cattle, Draupadī proposes Arjuna as charioteer for Virāṭa's commander. After the Kauravas have been driven out, the king offers the Pāṇḍavas his kingdom, but they refuse. However, Arjuna does accept the king's daughter as his bride.

After the long war with the Kauravas, Draupadī and her husbands live peacefully for more than three decades before they all meet again in Indra's paradise. (Buck 1981)

DREAM OF CYRUS

This ancient Iranian legend is one of a cycle of dream legends in which Cyrus the Great, just before he is slain by the Massagetae queen, dreams that he sees Darius with wings on his shoulders, a portent that Darius will soon become king. Prior to this story, Cyrus's mother Mandane dreams, before Cyrus is born, that a vine grows from her womb that casts a shadow over all of Asia. (Olmstead 1948)

DRIED MILLET BREAKING

This is a Woi epic of the Kpelle of Liberia. (Stone, R. 1988)

See also *Woi-mene-pele.*

DUḤŚĀSANA AND DURYODHANA

In the *Mahābhārata,* they are the eldest of the Kauravas, cousins of the five Pāṇḍava brothers. It is Duḥśāsana who, after winning Draupadī in a dice game, orders her to disrobe in the palace court. Although Kṛiṣṇa provides her with an infinite number of garments to prevent her exposure, the incident precipitates the great war between the two families. (Buck 1981)

See also Draupadī; Kaurava; *Mahābhārata;* Pāṇḍavas.

DUMUZI
(Also Tammuz)

In Mesopotamian religion, Dumuzi is the Sumerian shepherd-god, the god of fertility who marries "the pure Inanna," the queen of heaven and goddess of love (also Ishtar). The story of his wooing of Inanna is told in two versions on the tablets of Sumer. One involves his having a dispute with a rival for her affections—the farmer-god Enkimdu, whom Inanna prefers. In another version, Dumuzi is the only suitor. He comes to Inanna's house, dripping with cream, and demands to be admitted. Inanna adorns herself in her finery and opens the door for him. They embrace and he carries her off to the city of his god. In *Inanna's Descent to the Nether World,* Inanna descends to the nether world to see her older sister Ereshkigal, instructing her minister Ninshubur that if she has not returned in three days, he is to go to Nippur and beg the chief god Enlil not to let her die. If Enlil refuses to intervene, he is to go to Ur and beg the moon god Nanna not to let her die. If Nanna refuses to help, he is to go to Eridu and beg the god of wisdom Enki. When Inanna reaches the gate to the nether world, she is made to pass through seven gates, at each one losing some of her finery. When she finally reaches Ereshkigal, she is stark naked. Her sister and the Anunnaki, the seven judges of the nether world, turn her into a corpse and hang her on a stake. When she doesn't return after three days, Ninshubur goes to the gods for help; Enki is the only one willing to help. He brings her to life, but she is still a prisoner of the underworld unless she can produce a substitute. She travels to Dumuzi's city of Kullab and, when he will not prostrate himself before her as have the other city deities, she fastens "the eye upon him, the eye of death," and she gives Dumuzi over to the demons to return to the underworld. Dumuzi weeps and his face turns green. He pleads to Inanna's brother, "O Utu, you are my wife's brother, I am your sister's husband, / I am one who brings cream to your mother's house, / . . . Let me escape my demons, let them not seize me." (Kramer 1956; Perera 1981; Wolkstein and Kramer 1983)

See also *Inanna's Descent to the Nether World.*

DUMUZI-ABZU
(Dumuzi of the Watery Deep)

In Sumerian mythology, Dumuzi-Abzu is the goddess of the marshland city of Kinirsha near Lagash. She is the equivalent of the god Dumuzi (Tammuz) of the central herding area and thus viewed as male, the son of Enki. (Wolkstein and Kramer 1983)

See also Dumuzi.

DUMUZI-AMAUSHUMGALANA

(Dumuzi the One Great Source of the Date Clusters)

This Sumerian fertility god of the orchard region is one of the forms of Dumuzi (Tammuz). He is the husband of Inanna, Goddess of the Date Clusters. (Wolkstein and Kramer 1983)

See also Dumuzi.

DURGĀ

(The Inaccessible)

In Hindu mythology, Durgā is one of the forms of Śakti, the wife of Śiva. Born fully grown, she represents the creative force or feminine strength. She is the benign aspect of Kālī, goddess of misfortune and destruction. (Another benign aspect is Pārvatī, also Devī.) In the *Rāmāyaṇa,* Rāma evokes Durgā so that he can conquer the demon king Rāvaṇa. Durgā manifests as a great warrior. (Buck 1976; O'Flaherty 1975)

See also Kālī; Pārvatī; *Rāmāyaṇa;* Śiva.

DURYODHANA

See Duḥśāsana and Duryodhana.

DWIN ÜLÛGAT-IT TÜRK

This Turkish dictionary and grammar was compiled between 1071 and 1077 by Kaşgârli Mahmut and contains fragments of pre-Islamic epics of Turkey. (Preminger 1990)

DYAUS

(Also Dyaus-Pitr or Dyava-Prthivi)

In Vedic mythology, Dyaus is Father Sky, the equivalent of Zeus in Greek mythology. Dyaus is usually paired with earth as Dyāvā-Pṛthivī. In the *Ṛg Veda,* sky and earth, referred to in the dual, are alternately characterized as male and female, parents of the sun, or as two sisters, the "two world-halves" who are "as bold as two wonderful girls when their father [Tvaṣṭṛ, or the creator] dresses them in shapes and colors." They are referred to as "these two who are good for everyone," and are asked to "hold the Order and bear the poet of space (the sun)." (O'Flaherty 1981)

Armed with a bow and arrows and mounted on a tiger, Durgā, a ferocious aspect of Śakti, wife of the Hindu god Śiva, represents strength as she battles the scimitar-wielding Mahisha in this Indian illustration from about 1700. Her deeds are related in the *Mārkaṇḍeya Purāṇa.* In the *Rāmāyaṇa* she manifests as a warrior to help Rāma defeat Rāvaṇa.

DZITBALCHE, BOOK OF THE SONGS OF

This is one of two major works, along with the *Books of Chilam Balam,* written down in Yucatec Mayan in the late sixteenth and early seventeenth centuries. The songs are ritual verses sung at Dzitbalche, located on the Yucatán peninsula in the present state of Campeche. They are preserved in Yucatec language using an orthography adapted from the Spanish. (Schell and Freidel 1990)

E

EBISU

(Also Yebisu)

In Japanese mythology, Ebisu is the patron of fishermen, one of the Shintō Seven Gods of Luck. He is identified in some shrines with Hiru-ko. In the *Nihongi* he is a firstborn child, born a leech and therefore abandoned, set adrift in a reed boat by his parents, the creative deities Izanami and his sister Izanagi. The *Nihongi* lists Izanami and Izanagi as the seventh generation of the age of the gods. Ebisu is also the patron of tradesmen, and his image frequently appears in shops. (Aston 1972; Mayer 1948)

See also Izanami and Izanagi.

EBULU IJEOMA

This migration legend of the Ohafia people of Nigeria, West Africa, is still being performed today. It concerns the foundation of the Aro-Ndi-Izuogu in eastern Nigeria by an Aro trader named Ebulu Ijeoma. (Azuonye *RAL* 1990)

EDDA, POETIC

(Also *Elder Edda)*

This early (thirteenth century) Icelandic collection consists of 34 much older lays recounting adventures of Old Norse heroes and gods. The poems were composed over a period of some 300 years, from 800 to 1100.

The first half of the *Edda* contains mythological poems. The opening one, "Völuspá" (Prophecy of the Seeress) (ca. 1000), furnishes an introduction to Old Norse cosmogony, from the origin of the world to its destruction with the death of the gods. Óthin (Odin), the supreme deity of the Teutons, summons Völuspá from her grave to appear before the Aesir (gods) in Ásgard to prophesy the fates of the world. She begins with a history of the world's beginnings, when there was "but a gaping nothing. . . ." She tells how the gods gathered, but "Sense they possessed not, / soul they had not," until Óthin gives them soul and other gods give them other attributes. She tells how man is given life and how the innocence of the gods comes to an end with the coming of the Norns (Fates) and the slaying of Gullveig, sent by an older race of gods, the

Vanir. In the war that follows, Baldr (god of light) is slain, and evil enters into the world. Völuspá foretells how, as a result of the moral depravity of the gods, they will be destroyed, and "'Neath the sea the land sinketh, / the sun dimmeth, / from the heavens fall / the fair bright stars; . . ." But out of the ruins she sees a new world arise, where Baldr and other good gods "all guiltless throne, / and live forever / in ease and bliss."

"Hávamál" (The Sayings of Hár, or Worlds of the High One), the longest of the poems in the *Edda,* is actually at least six didactic poems that propound the wisdom of Óthin. The first section, consisting of 79 stanzas, gives laws of social conduct for generosity in hospitality, decent conduct, circumspection in dealings with men, moderation in eating and drinking habits, the vanity of wealth, and the desirability of home ownership and of a good name. The next ten stanzas are largely proverbs and form a bridge to the second main section comprised of 20 stanzas known as "Examples of Óthin," a first-person account of two love affairs of Óthin that is an excuse for a cynical discussion of woman's gullibility, treachery, and fickleness: "Many a good maid, / if you mark it well, / is fickle, though fair her word. . . ." Following this is a 27-stanza unrelated poem, "Lay of Loddfáfnir," containing advice on various subjects supposedly given to the bard Loddfáfnir by Óthin. The next stanzas, called "Rune Poem," deal with the magical power of the runes (alphabetical characters) bestowed upon Óthin after he hangs himself "on the wind-tossed tree / all of nights nine, / wounded by spear. . . ." The work concludes with 18 magic charms to use with the various runes to dull the swords of deadly foes, break fetters, stay a flying spear, beat down fire, settle strife, calm wind and waves, heal wounds, and charm maidens.

"Vafthrúđnismál" (The Lay of Vafthrúdnir) is a didactic poem describing a contest, senna, or flyting between Óthin and the wise giant Vafthrúdnir. Óthin, hearing of the giant's wisdom and disregarding his wife Frigga's objections, goes to Vafthrúdnir's hall to match "lore" with him. When Óthin arrives, he insists on remaining standing during the initial match. Vafthrúdnir insists that Óthin occupy the high seat for the next round, and suggests that the loser of the match forfeit his head. Now Óthin becomes the interrogator and asks Vafthrúdnir the question, ". . . what did Óthin whisper / in the ear of his son, / ere Baldr on bale was laid?" Only then does the giant recognize Óthin, and he admits, "of all beings thou art born wisest."

"Grímnismál" (The Lay of Grímnir) is another didactic poem of two princes, Agnar and Geirroeth. They are sons of King Hrauthung, but fostered by Frigga and Óthin, respectively, who sail to an island inhabited by monsters. Geirroeth abandons Agnar to drift out to sea so that he can inherit the kingdom. One day when Frigga and Óthin are looking down upon the world, Óthin points out that her foster son Agnar "begets children with an ogress in a cave," while his foster son Geirroeth is king. Frigga retorts that Geirroeth is stingy with his food, a cardinal sin in a king. Óthin denies the accusation, and the two make a wager. Frigga sends her chambermaid Fulla to tell Geirroeth that a warlock is on his way who can be recognized as such because no dogs will approach him. When the man comes, Geirroeth takes him captive. The mysterious man, who is Óthin in disguise, gives his name as Grímnir, meaning "the Masked One." The king tortures him by setting him between two fires, in an attempt to make him tell more about himself. The king's son, whose name is also Agnar, gives the prisoner water and tells him his father has done wrong to torture him. Óthin tells him about the holy land of the Aesir and describes some of the 500 halls "and forty withal" that house the various gods. He gives a lengthy cosmogony before revealing his own name. When Geirroeth hears who his prisoner is, he rises to release him, but stumbles and falls upon his own sword. Óthin vanishes, but Agnar becomes king and reigns for a long time.

"Skírnismál" (The Lay of Skírnir), a romantic love-myth, probably originated in Norway ca. the tenth century or before Iceland was settled by Norwegians since the thistle, a plant mentioned in the poem, is not indigenous to Iceland. In the poem, Frey (Freyr), son of Njorth and god of the world, is sitting on Óthin's throne looking out over the world of giants. He spies a fair maiden, Gerth, with whom he falls deeply in love. Frey dispatches his devoted servitor and friend, Skírnir ("the Resplendent"), to her father Gymir's castle to win her. After Gerth refuses Skírnir's offer of gifts of golden apples—possibly of everlasting youth—and of Draupnir, the ring presented to Óthin by a dwarf, Skírnir threatens to cut off her head if she does not come with him. But Gerth answers, "Nor gold nor sword / will gain it over me / any wight's will to do." Skírnir then threatens to use rune magic to make a magic wand with which to bewitch her so that she is doomed forever to sit on a hill where imps will nip her, where weeping will be her pastime, and where she will live with three-headed thurs—a curse scratched on a tree three times. Gerth relents and agrees to meet Frey in a trysting glade. Skírnir returns to tells Frey of the proposed meeting in the trysting glade where "After nights nine / to Njorth's son there / will Gerth grant her love."

"Hárbarzljóđ" (The Lay of Hárbarth), another tenth-century poem originating in Norway, concerns a confrontation between Óthin (Hárbarth) and Thór in a senna, or flyting, and a mannjafnađr (matching wits, accomplishments, and prowess). Óthin, or Hárbarth, represents the warring, cruel, restless Viking who abhors work, while Thór represents the good-natured, simple but hard-working yeoman. Óthin, appearing in the poem as a ferryman for the dead, boasts of the many wars he has fought just for the sake of fighting, and of winning giantesses by overpowering or outsmarting their spouses and fathers. Thór, who can boast only of slaying the giant brood to make the earth safer for the race of men, sounds dull-witted and boring by comparison. It is soon obvious that Thór is no match for the clever, arrogant, knightly Óthin, with whom the sympathies of the poet lie. Thór loses the match, and the "ferryman" tells him, "Get thee gone now / where all trolls may take thee!"

"Hymiskviđa" (The Lay of Hymir) is pieced from at least four Thór myths. Thór is dispatched by the brewmaster AEgir to fetch a larger caldron. The war god Týr gives Thór the helpful hint that a certain Hymir, who lives "at Heaven's end," keeps a very "roomy caldron." Thor travels to see Hymir, who sends him out to sea to fish for the Mithgarth-Serpent. He makes various attempts to hook the serpent, finally catching it, only to have his line break (another version,

"Gylfaginning," says that Hymir cuts the line), allowing the serpent to sink back into the sea. Hymir challenges Thór to shatter his crystal cup, and after he fails to shatter it by throwing it at the granite walls, Hymir's leman gives Thór a helpful hint: "Strike Hymir's head! / That harder is, / the slothful etin's, / than any cup." Thór throws the cup at Hymir's head, shattering it. Hymir keeps his word and gives Thór the kettle, which he hauls home in triumph.

"Lokasenna" (The Flyting of Loki) tells of a flyting, or matching of wits, proposed by the crafty and mischievous god Loki to the various gods and goddesses because they have denied him a seat at the feast. Loki manages to uncover the sinful and embarrassing deeds of the various gods: Óthin and his wife Frigga, Thór's wife Sif, Týr, Njorth, Skathi and his wife Frey, Freya, Uithar, and others. Then Thór, who has been away, arrives and threatens to silence Loki with his hammer. Loki leaves and hides in the Fránangr waterfall, taking the shape of a salmon. There the gods find him and bind him with the guts of his son Nari. Skathi hangs a poisonous snake over him so that its venom will drip on his face. Loki's wife Sigyn sits holding a bowl to catch the drips. When the bowl is full, she carries it away to empty it. While she is gone, the dripping poison causes Loki to writhe so violently that the whole earth shakes. Men call these "earthquakes."

"Đrymskviđa" (The Lay of Thrym) is the best-known and best-loved poem of the *Edda* and is considered by scholars to be one of the great ballads of world literature. As it begins, Thór awakens to find his mighty hammer gone. He calls to Loki to inform him that his hammer has been stolen. They go to Freya, goddess of fertility and love, to ask her to lend them her feather coat, which she gladly gives them. Loki dons the coat and flies to the world of etins (giants), where he confronts Thrym, sitting on a mound making halters for his hounds. Thrym admits taking the hammer and hiding it deep in the ground. He tells Loki that he will return the hammer if Loki brings Freya to him for a bride. Loki hurries back to the land of gods where he and Thór approach Freya with Thrym's proposition. She reacts by flying into a rage. The halls literally shake with her wrath. Since she refuses to be a party to any scheme to retrieve the hammer, the other gods and goddesses convene to devise a plan. Heimdall suggests that they dress Thór as a bride and send him down to steal his own hammer. Although Thór protests, "A craven wretch / may call me the gods / if I busk me / in bridal linen," Loki overcomes his objections. Dressed in bridal attire and accompanied by Loki as the bride's attendant, Thór goes to etin-world, where Loki introduces Thór to Thrym as Freya, his bride. A feast is laid, and Thrym is astounded at the bride's appetite: She eats an ox and eight salmon, and drinks three barrels of mead. He is equally astounded at the fierce look in her eyes. The "handmaiden" explains that, so eager was the bride to come, she has not eaten nor slept in eight days or nights. A giantess-sister steps forward and begs a bridal gift from the hefty bride in exchange for her friendship. At that moment Thrym calls for the hammer so that it can be blessed by Freya. When the hammer is laid in the bride's lap, Thór unmasks himself and slays Thrym and all his kin, including the giantess-sister who, for a bridal gift, gets "a shock of the hammer."

"Alvíssmál" (The Lay of Alvís) is a didactic poem in which Thór, returning from the world of giants, meets the dwarf Alvís making away with Thór's daughter, whom he has convinced the gods to give him during Thór's absence. Thór tells the dwarf that he will consent to the marriage providing Alvís can answer a series of questions. He proceeds to ask the dwarf to explain the earth, the heaven, the "Upper World," the moon, the sun, the clouds, the wind, the calm, the sea, fire, wood, the night, seed, and beer, all of which Alvís explains. Finally the night comes to an end, and at daylight Thór turns Alvís into stone.

In "Baldrs draumar" (Baldr's Dreams), the god Baldr dreams that his father Óthin, fearing for his son's life, summons a seeress from Hel to tell him his son's fate. He asks her for whom the benches are covered and the dais decked in gold. The seeress answers that the decorations are in honor of Baldr, who will be slain by the blind god Hoth. Óthin asks her who will avenge the hateful deed and send Baldr's slayer to Hel. She answers that Váli will slay Baldr's killer. The seeress then recognizes Óthin, who has disguised himself as Vegtam. He tells her that she is no seeress but rather the mother of three thurses. She sends him on his way, telling him that no one else will charm her until Loki is loose from his bonds, at which time the gods will be doomed.

The conclusion to "Rígsþula" (The Lay of Ríg) has been lost, as have some of the intermediate verses; however, the lay's intent to reinforce the notion of divine right to rule in Scandinavia is evident in the extant portion. Experts disagree as to the lay's origin and to whom the poem's character of Kon refers—whether to Norwegian king Harald Fairhair, Danish king Gorm, or Harald Bluetooth, or to someone on one of the Scottish islands.

In this poem and no other place, the god Heimdall calls himself Ríg. He rides forth to a farm where, as was common practice at the time, his host offers him his wife Edda for his three-day stay. Later, Edda gives birth to a swarthy boy whom she calls Thrall, who grows to be exceptionally strong. When Thrall grows older, a "crook-legged wench" named Thír comes to sleep in his cot. The happy couple has a brood bearing such colorful names as Sluggard, Stumpy, Stinky, Lout, and Slattern. Again, Ríg rides forth and comes to a weaver's house, where the host offers him the hospitality of his wife, Amma. Ríg stays with Amma for three days, and later she gives birth to a ruddy son, Karl. This child grows and gains in strength such that he can tame oxen and timber houses and barns. A bride is chosen for Karl named Snoer, who bears a large brood with such names as Man, Yeoman, Crofter, Smith, Husbandman, Gentlewoman, and Dame. Ríg rides on to the south, where good and noble people live. He is treated to a fine meal and offered the hospitality of the wife, whose name is Mother. Nine months later, Mother bears a flaxen-haired son named Earl, who becomes an excellent bowman and hunter. Ríg meets him, teaches him runes, and gives him his own name as heir and son. Earl rides across the countryside, brandishing his sword, winning 18 manors for himself, and sharing his new-gained wealth with the people. When his heralds come to the hall where the chieftain Hersir dwells, in Earl's name they ask for Hersir's fair daughter Erna in marriage. She is driven home and given to Earl, and the two love each other and bear many children, among whom are Boy, Bairn, Issue,

Offspring, and others. The youngest is named Kon, and as the children grow, only Kon can carve runes. Kon can understand the speech of fowls, heal sick minds, soothe sorrows, and quench fires. He has the strength of eight men and rivals Earl himself in runes. One day as Kon rides through the woods snaring birds, a crow asks him why he is not instead brandishing swords and slaying heroes, particularly Dan and Danp (probably kings of Denmark). The poem breaks off here, but the poem suggests that Earl takes the crow's advice and takes the lands of Dan and Danp. According to another legend, King Ríg (Kon) marries Danp's daughter Dana, and their son Dan is the mythical king who unites all of Denmark.

"Hyndluljóđ" (The Lay of Hyndla) is a garbled poem meant to give the genealogy—perhaps exalted—of a man named Óttar, who may have been Óttar Birtingr, a man of low birth who married the widow of Norwegian king Harald Gilli and was assassinated in 1146. In the poem the goddess Freya is out riding on a boar and comes across her sleeping friend, the giantess Hyndla. Freya wakes her and invites her to ride with her on one of her wolves to Valholl. There, Óthin and Thór will favor the hero Óttar over Angantýr, with whom he has a wager about who is of nobler descent. As they ride, they will discuss genealogies. Hyndla is aware that the boar is really Óttar in disguise and she gives him the genealogical information he desires. Although a few of the lines are missing in this section of the poem, Hyndla ties Óttar to the kings of Horthaland; to Hálfdan the Old, mythical ancestor of Norwegian kings; and to a number of legendary heroes. Freya demands that Hyndla give him "memory ale," so that he will be able to remember his genealogy at least until after the match three days hence. When the giantess refuses the request, Freya threatens to hedge her with fire. Hyndla then puts a curse on the drink, wishing that it be brewed with venom. But Freya negates the wish, proclaiming it "a goodly draught."

In the middle of the previous manuscript appears "Völuspá hin skamma" (The Short Seeress's Prophecy), containing cosmogony paralleling that in the first poem (*see* "Völuspá," above).

Two late (seventeenth century) versions of earlier poems appear next under the common heading of "Svipdagsmal" (The Lay of Svipdag). In the first, "Grógaldr" (The Spell of Gróa), an evil stepmother gives young Svipdag the task of making "the dreaded journey" to giantland to win the hand of Mengloth, whom he loves but has never seen. He goes to his mother Gróa's grave, wakes her from death, and asks that she now fulfill her promise to help him in his time of need. She chants nine spells to speed him on his way and protect him from danger. In the second poem, "Fjölsvinnsmal" (The Lay of Fjolsvith), Svipdag, who has apparently made the journey safely, stands before a castle that is surrounded by flames. Fjolsvith, the giant watchman, commands him to begone, but Svipdag, concealing his name and purpose, is able to elicit the information that this is the castle where Mengloth lives, and that only Svipdag will be able to enter. Svipdag then reveals his name, and Fjolsvith calls for the gates to be opened. Mengloth welcomes Svipdag, saying, "Full long sat

I on Lyfja Mount, / bided thee day after day. . . ." She promises that "we two shall live / our life and lot together."

"Grottasöngr" (The Lay of Grotti) tells of two giantess sisters, Fenja and Menja, who are slaves of King Fróthi. Their task is "to moil at the mill," grinding gold. As the chained sisters turn the millstones, they chant their song. They have had many adventures, including going to Sweden, where they "fought among men" as Valkyries. Menja thinks, after having ground gold, peace, and happiness, that she has served as a slave long enough, for Fróthi no longer lets them rest. Fenja declares, "The stone must not stand," and the mighty maids strain their young limbs until the heavy slab bursts. At that, the maids say, "we have toiled enough at the turning mill."

"Völundarkviđa" (The Lay of Volund [Wayland] the Smith) concerns three Finnish princes—Slagfith, Egil, and Volund—who marry the Valkyries Hlathguth the Swanwhite, Olrun, and Hervor, respectively. After seven years, the three Valkyries fly away to battle and, when they do not return, Slagfith and Egil go off in search of their wives. Volund, however, stays at home in the Wolfdales, waiting for his bride to come home. When King Níthoth hears that Volund is at home alone, he sends his men to take one of Volund's rings and capture him. Volund comes home from hunting and lies down to sleep while his bear meat boils. He wakes to find his hands and feet in heavy shackles. The scene shifts to Níthoth's palace, where the king presents his daughter Bothvild with the gold ring. He has also taken Volund's sword, which he keeps for himself. But his queen is not satisfied. She commands him to hamstring Volund and force him to sit on an island not far offshore and make wondrous things. From there, Volund sees his sword at Níthoth's side and his bride's arm ring on Bothvild. He makes wondrous things for Níthoth both day and night, without sleeping. One day the young sons of Níthoth come to see him, and in that moment he plans his revenge. He tells them that if they return after the next snowfall and walk backward to his door, he will give them the keys to a chest containing much gold. The two sons agree eagerly, but when they come, Volund cuts off their heads and buries their bodies beneath the bellows' pit. He sets their scalps in silver and sends them to Níthoth. He makes shining beads of their eyeballs and gives them to the queen. Of their teeth he makes beautiful brooches that he sends to Bothvild. Níthoth is inconsolable at the disappearance of his sons, whose footprints show that they left Volund's house. He asks Volund what became of the boys, and Volund first reveals that he has fathered a child within Níthoth's walls. Then he reveals the sons' fate to the horrified king. Níthoth confronts Bothvild, who admits to having been with Volund on the isle.

The rest of the *Poetic Edda* consists of lays leading to or connected with the hero Sigurd (Siegfried). Three Helgi lays begin this cycle. "Helgakviđa Hjörvarþssonar" (The Lay of Helgi Hjorvarthsson) begins with a genealogy of sorts of Helgi, son of the fair Sigrlinn and King Hjorvarth. Sigrlinn's father, King Sváfnir, is killed by King Hróthmar, who has sought the hand of Sigrlinn and lost. Helgi receives no name at birth, but later a stately Valkyrie, Sváhā, names him and thereafter often shields him in battle. When Atli (Attila), king of Hunland, sets off to avenge the death of Sváfnir, Hjorvarth gives Helgi an army so that he can go along. Together, the two heroes fell Hróthmar and do "many a great deed." Helgi also kills the giant Hati, and Hati's daughter Hrímgerth approaches Atli during his night watch and offers to forgo vengeance in exchange for one night with Helgi. Helgi wakes and instead offers her Lothin ("Hairy") for a mate. The giantess accuses him of loving the Valkyrie who has protected him. Helgi learns that Sváhā has led "thrice nine" Valkyries to protect him. By this time it is dawn, and Atli is able to turn her into stone to be used as a harbor marker. King Helgi becomes a mighty warrior. He and Sváhā swear oaths to each other in observance of their great love. One day during a winter solstice festival, Prince Hethin, Helgi's brother, drinking from a hallowed cup provided by a troll woman, vows that he will have Sváhā. But he soon regrets the vow and hurries to find his brother and confess. Helgi believes that the old woman is in reality his fylgja, which is a tutelary spirit that attaches itself to a person until that person is "fey," at which time it chooses another person to protect. There is a great battle in which Helgi is mortally wounded. He sends for Sváhā and bids her to share his brother's bed, but she refuses. Hethin goes off to avenge his brother's death, and it is said that Helgi and Sváhā are born again as Helgi the Hunding-Slayer and Sigrún.

"Helgakviđa Hundingsbana I" (The First Lay of Helgi the Hunding-Slayer) begins with Helgi's birth to King Sigmund's wife, Brálund Borghild. At his birth the Norns come and spin his fate-thread, attaching it to heaven. From early childhood Helgi knows his duty is to avenge the death of his father. During one of his battles he meets Hogni's daughter Sigrún, whom he eventually wins for himself, along with the lands of the Hundings. This poem is considered to contain the truest expression of the warrior spirit of the Vikings.

"Helgakviđa Hundingsbana II" (The Second Lay of Helgi the Hunding-Slayer), probably by a different author, covers the same story as "The First Lay of Helgi"; however, more emphasis is placed on the love of Helgi and Sigrún. When Helgi dies, Sigrún lives on but a short time, succumbing to grief and sorrow. Helgi and Sigrún are said to have been born again as Helgi Haddingjaskati and Kára, as told in "The Lay of Kára," now lost.

A short prose selection follows entitled "Frá dauđa Sinfjǫtla" (Sinfjotli's Death), so placed as to explain Sigurth's origin and to lead into the Sigurth lays that follow. Sigurth is the son of King Eylimi's daughter Hjordís and King Sigmund, who is killed fighting the Hundings. Hjordís then marries Álf, son of King Hjálprek (West Frankish king Chilperic), and Sigurth grows up in the king's court. He becomes the noblest of men and the greatest leader in war.

"Gripísspá" (The Prophecy of Grípir) is considered by translator Hollander to be "poetically worthless" and "utterly lacking" in originality. It contains two contradictory versions of Sigurth's relation with Brynhild and Guthrún.

"Reginsmál" (The Lay of Regin) is a combination of fragments of poems originating before 1000. It begins with an introductory prose section that introduces Regin, a dwarf-wizard who is Sigurth's counselor. Regin traces the source of the Niflung gold back to antiquity when gods walked the earth and, through Loki, became involved in guilt. Loki is sent by the other gods to the waterfall of the dwarf Andavari to fetch the gold he possesses. Loki borrows a net from the sea goddess Rán, snares Andavari, and takes all his gold, including a gold ring, the Ring of the Niflungs. The gods give the gold to Hreithmar, who is Regin's father. But when Hreithmar dies, Regin's brother Fáfnir takes the gold, transforms himself into a dragon, and settles down to guard his treasure. Regin makes a sword for Sigurth named Gnita and urges Sigurth to slay Fáfnir. But first Sigurth wants to avenge his father's death at the hands of the Hundings, and the king provides him with a fleet and men for that purpose. As they sail away, a great storm arises. A man named Hnikar, standing on a nearby cliff, asks to be taken aboard. When they take him on, the storm abates: He is Óthin in disguise. He gives Sigurth several signs concerning the best time to do battle. Sigurth later fights a great battle with Lyngvi and his Hunding brothers, after which the defeated are sacrificed to the gods; their ribs are severed from their backbones and the lungs pulled out: "carving the blood-eagle."

"Fáfnismál" (The Lay of Fáfnir) continues the story of Sigurth's adventure. He and Regin go up to Gnita Heath and find Fáfnir's tracks leading to the water. Sigurth digs a ditch in which to hide until Fáfnir comes out. Although the dragon spews poison on him, Sigurth is able to thrust his sword into Fáfnir's heart. In response to the dying dragon's questions, Sigurth gives his history. Fáfnir warns him, "Ride thou home from hence: / the glistening gold / and the glow-red hoard, / the rings thy bane will be." He tells Sigurth that Regin once betrayed him and that Regin will betray Sigurth too. Regin cuts out the dragon's heart, which Sigurth places on a spit to broil. To see if it is done, he touches it and burns his finger. When he puts the finger in his mouth and Fáfnir's blood touches his tongue, he is able to understand the speech of birds. He hears some titmice saying that Regin is racking his brain as to how to betray Sigurth. Realizing that Fáfnir has told him the truth about Regin's treachery, he cuts off Regin's head, then eats Fáfnir's heart and drinks the blood of both Regin and Fáfnir. The titmice give him some advice, telling him to gather the golden rings and ride to the castle of Gjúki, who has a fair daughter, Guthrún. The castle is surrounded by fire, and near the fire is a Valkyrie, Brynhild. Sigurth follows Fáfnir's tracks to his lair, where he finds a great hoard of gold. He loads as much as he can on his steed Grani and rides away.

"Sigrdrífumál" (The Lay of Sigrdrífa) continues the story. Sigurth finds a sleeping woman whom he wakes. She is the Valkyrie Sigrdrífa, whom Óthin has pricked with a sleep-thorn; he has decreed that she will never again do battle but instead will wed. However, she has vowed that she will never be wed to a man who has known fear. In response to Sigurth's request that she teach him wisdom, she gives him a number of runes and some rules of conduct.

There is a break in the manuscript and a gap of eight pages, followed by what remains of a "Lay of Sigurth," known as "The Great Lacuna," in which Gunnar (Sigurth's friend who wants to wed Brynhild) attempts to ride through the flames surrounding the castle of Gjúki but fails. Sigurth, however, is able to urge his steed Grani through the fire. The next fragment concerns Guthrún telling Brynhild that it was Sigurth who slew the dragon, a deed more heroic than anything her husband Gunnar has done. The final fragment concerns Sigurth's failure in his attempts to console Brynhild.

Another fragment of a Sigurth lay, "Brot af Sigurþarkviđu," follows, which may originally have been a part of one of the longest of the Sigurth lays. Hogni is returning to the Gjúki's hall, he and Gunnar having slain the sleeping Sigurth because he deprived Brynhild of her virginity, breaking his promise to Gunnar. Hogni is sure that Brynhild's brother Atli (the historical Attila the Hun) will kill Gunnar because of what they have done. Guthrún, waiting outside the hall, asks them where Sigurth is, and they tell her that they have slain him. Brynhild hears this and laughs, praising the two for accomplishing the deed. But later that night, while everyone else sleeps, Gunnar tosses and turns. Brynhild wakes from a gruesome dream and tells Gunnar she has seen him led off in chains for killing his blood brother.

In "Guđrúnarkviđa I" (The First Lay of Guthrún), Guthrún sits beside Sigurth's body and mourns, but she is unable to weep. She is comforted by three women who try to get her to cry. The third, Gullrond, sweeps the sheet from Sigurth's corpse, and Guthrún, seeing him, burst into tears. She blames her brothers for his death and calls out an oath against them: "May ye lose your land / and lieges also. . . ." Brynhild then speaks up and curses Gullrond: "May that hag ne'er have / husband nor children / who again taught thee / thy tears to shed. . . ." Gullrond answers, telling Brynhild that she is hated by all. Brynhild blames Atli, whom the Nibelung treasure has corrupted. Guthrún leaves and journeys to Denmark where she stays "seven half-years" with Thóra, the daughter of Hákon. Brynhild no longer wants to live after Sigurth's death. She has 13 of her servants slain and then kills herself with her sword.

"Sigurþarkviđu hin skamma" (The Short Lay of Sigurth) is one of the longest poems in the *Edda.* It begins as Sigurth rides to Gjúki's hall after having slain the dragon Fáfnir and, in this version, having already been given Guthrún in marriage by her brothers Hogni and Gunnar. Sigurth goes to woo Brynhild on behalf of Gunnar, having taken an oath not to kiss or hold her. After Sigurth wins Brynhild for Gunnar, Brynhild is full of envy as Sigurth sleeps with his wife Guthrún. She urges Gunnar to kill Sigurth for the Nibelung gold. Although Gunnar has sworn a blood oath to Sigurth, he decides to summon Hogni to ask him, "Wilt betray Sigurth / for the sake of gold?" Hogni is reluctant, having also sworn an oath of loyalty to Sigurth. He knows who is responsible for such a scheme: He blames "Queen Brynhild's unbridled hate." Gunnar suggests they urge their stepbrother Guthorm, who has sworn no fealty oath, to kill Sigurth for them. In this version, Sigurth is sleeping with his wife when Guthorm makes three attempts to kill him, succeeding on the third try in mortally wounding him. Sigurth does not suspect Hogni or Gunnar; he knows that this foul deed is Brynhild's doing. When Brynhild hears Guthrún wailing, she laughs. She tells Gunnar that she loves only Sigurth and wanted only his gold, no other's. She plans to follow Sigurth to Hel. Gunnar tells Hogni to summon all the heroes in order to stop Brynhild from killing herself. But Hogni refuses, saying, "Hinder her not. . . . / Wicked left she / her mother's womb. . . ." Brynhild prophesies that Guthrún will marry Jónakr and have two sons. She instructs them to build a pyre and burn all of those "who after Sigurth . . . did seek their death." She wants to be placed beside Sigurth on the pyre.

"Helreiđ Brynhildar" (Brynhild's Ride to Hel) is a later (ca. twelfth century) poem in which, after Brynhild's death, she comes to a giantess's cave on her way to Hel. The giantess warns her not to hanker after Guthrún's husband in Hel. Brynhild justifies her behavior by telling the giantess the story of her life; how, after a happy childhood at Heimir's court, she comes to the aid of a young hero against an old suitor and thus angers Óthin, who kills the young man and imprisons her, sleeping, behind a wall of flames. There she remains until Sigurth wakes her. Then, because she is tricked by Sigurth into marrying Gunnar, she is compelled by fate to seek the death of her only true love. Now she will live with Sigurth in Hel.

"Dráp Niflunga" (The Fall of the Niflungs) is a brief prose exposition summarizing the action of the lays that follow.

"Guđrúnarkviđa II (hin forna)" (The Second [or Old] Lay of Guthrún), ca. early tenth century, does not mention Brynhild at all; rather, Sigurth's death is the result of Gunnar and Hogni's jealousy. The character Thjóthrek, historically Ostrogothic king Theodoric (reigned toward the end of the fifth century), has been with Atli and has lost most of his men in battle against the Burgundians. Guthrún, now Atli's wife, and Thjóthrek relate their sorrows to one another. She tells him of Sigurth's death and of her wanderings since. Her mother Grímhild sends for her brothers Hogni and Gunnar and instructs them to make amends for their sister's loss. They offer her gold and other gifts, but she does not trust her brothers. Her mother gives her a goblet of forgetfulness mead so that she can put Sigurth's death out of her mind. But she still wants her brothers to pay for their crime. She journeys to the realm of Atli and marries him, and her kinsmen are slain. The poem breaks off abruptly, and there are gaps in the section having to do with her marriage to Atli and the slaying of her brothers.

"Guđrúnarkviđa III," or "The Third Lay of Guthrún," is regarded by scholars as a relatively late addition to the *Edda.* A maidservant, Herkja, reports to Atli that she has seen Thjóthrek and Guthrún lying "in love . . . 'neath linen cover." When Atli tells Guthrún this, she swears that she has not even kissed the Gothic king. To prove that she speaks the truth, she calls for a caldron of boiling water into which she plunges her hand, bringing up "flashing gems" without burning herself. The servant Herkja is brought forward to take the same test. When Atli sees that Herkja's hands are badly burned by the water, he knows that Guthrún is blameless.

"Oddrúnargrátr" (The Plaint of Oddrún) is of late origin (late twelfth century) and deals with material not in the Niflung legend. Oddrún, Atli's sister, tells her story to another woman, Borgný. She claims that before her father Buthli died, he expressed the wish that Brynhild become a Valkyrie rather than marry, and that Oddrún be given in marriage to Gunnar. After

Sigurth rescues Brynhild and is slain, and after Brynhild kills herself, Oddrún gives her love to Gunnar. Atli finds out about the affair from Guthrún, who has meanwhile married Atli. He invites the Gjúkungs back to his court, where he kills both Hogni and Gunnar.

"Atlakviđa" (The Lay of Atli) is considered to be the older of two lays about Atli. This lay and the one that follows, "Atlamál hin groenlenzku" (The Greenlandish Lay of Atli) are treated in a separate entry. *(See Atli, Lay of.)*

"Guđrúnarhvöt" (Gudrún's Incitement, or Gudrún's Lament) concerns Guthrún's fate after she slays Atli; it is the newer of the two lays dealing with the subject (ca. eleventh century). Guthrún attempts to drown herself, but the waves carry her to King Jónakr's court, where her daughter Svanhild, by Sigurth, is already living. Guthrún marries the king and has three sons: Sorli, Erp, and Hamthir. The lay that follows indicates that Erp is a stepson. Her daughter Svanhild is given in marriage to King Jormunrekk the Mighty (historically, Ostrogothic king Ermanarich, fourth century), but the king's son Randvér also loves Svanhild, and his love is returned. When the king is told about the lovers by his counselor Bikki, Randvér is hanged and Svanhild is killed by trampling horses. When Guthrún learns of her daughter's death, she urges her three sons to avenge their sister. She praises Hogni and Gunnar, holding them up as examples for the boys. But Hamthir reminds her how she felt about them following Sigurth's murder. He also reminds her that she has already slain her sons by Atli—Erp and Eitil—to avenge the death of the Niflungs. Nevertheless, the three reluctantly leave to do their mother's bidding. After they are gone, she reflects upon her sad life—from Sigurth's murder to her brothers', to her second husband Atli's and her sons', to her daughter's. Now she foresees the deaths of her last begotten sons, with no one left to console her.

"Hamđismál (hin fornu)" (The Lay of Hamthir) is the older (sixth century) of the lays regarding Guthrún and her sons by Jónakr. It survives in fragmentary form only. It begins, as does the preceding lay, with Guthrún approaching her sons to avenge Svanhild's death. She compares her sons unfavorably to Hogni and Gunnar, until Hamthir reminds her that they slayed Sigurth. He reminds her also that she herself slayed her sons by Atli, and he predicts the death of her surviving sons during this latest act of vengeance. The sons, Hamthir and Sorli, ride off with Erp, "of another born," whom Hamthir refers to as "this brownish bastard." Erp wants to help them, "as one hastens . . . to help another." But the two kill Erp in a fit of jealousy, only to regret their rash deed. They come upon Randvér's corpse still swinging on the gallows. Inside the hall, Jormunrekk and his "ale-gay . . . throng" are making so much noise they don't hear the brothers approaching. The brothers burst in and attack, cutting off Jormunrekk's hands and feet. The king roars a command to stone the two to death. Again Hamthir regrets having slain Erp, whose task it was to cut off the king's head. The two brothers call in a hail of stones.

The last entry in the *Edda,* "Dvergatal" (The Catalog of Dwarfs), is made up of stanzas 9 through 16 from "Völuspá." It is a list of all the dwarfs who rose from the giants Brimir and Blain. (Hollander *Edda* 1990)

EDDA, PROSE
(Also *Younger Edda)*

This Icelandic compilation was written ca. 1220 by Snorri Sturluson. For the mythical portions, he drew from still-extant Eddaic and scaldic poetry as well as from sources that are now lost. The collection includes the "Gylfaginning" (The Beguiling of Gylfi), which is a retelling of Norse mythology; the "Sayings of Bragi" (god of poetry), which contains more stories of the gods; the "Skalda," which gives rules for prosody; and the "Hattatal," which is an instructional treatise about poetry. (Young 1954)

See also "Gylfaginning."

EGBE NRI ADIGHI

This heroic narration of the Ohafia people of Nigeria, West Africa, is still being performed today. It concerns a famous hunter, Inyima Kaalu, whose newborn baby is struck and killed by an unloaded gun that fires itself. (Azuonye *RAL* 1990)

EGBELE

This heroic narration of the Ohafia people of Nigeria, West Africa, is still performed today. It is believed to be the origin of and basis for Ohafia war songs. It concerns a mother who, having lost three sons to war, tries in vain to keep her last son from going into battle. When he returns victorious, she sings a joyful song. (Azuonye *RAL* 1990)

EGIL'S SAGA

This Icelandic saga (ca. 1230), rich in poetry, concerns five generations of the family of a Viking lawyer/farmer who lived in the ninth century. Although it is anonymous, it is usually attributed to Snorri Sturluson.

It begins in Norway with Egil's grandfather Kveldulf (Evening Wolf), who in early years goes on Viking raids, then marries the daughter of his Viking friend Berle-Kari and settles down to become a farmer. His sons Thorolf and Skallagrim are born ca. 858 and 863. Thorolf goes on a Viking raid and decides to join King Harald's forces. He fights in the Battle of Hafursfjord, marries the widow Sigurd, and makes three expeditions to Lapp territory to collect tribute for the king. He sends his overseer Thorgils on a trading voyage, but on the way, Thorgils is robbed by King Harald's envoys, Hallvard and Sigtrygg. In retribution, Thorolf attacks their farm and kills them both. King Harald then kills Thorolf, and Ketil Trout, Kveldulf, and Skallagrim avenge Thorolf's death by killing the king. Skallagrim and his wife Bera escape with Kveldulf to Iceland and settle in Borg. Bera has several children who die, then a son, Thorolf; two daughters, Saeunn and Thorunn; and finally Egil, who is "just as black-haired and ugly as his father."

When Egil is three, he is entertained by his maternal grandfather, Yngvar. By the time he is six, he has killed the boy Grim, and at age 12, he kills his father's overseer as punishment to his father for having killed Egil's friend Thord and his favorite slave-woman, Thorgerd.

He wants to go abroad with his brother Thorolf, but when Thorolf refuses to take him, he cuts the anchor ropes and sets Thorolf's ship adrift. After this prank, Thorolf lets Egil sail with him to Norway.

Thorolf gets married, but Egil falls ill and does not attend the wedding. Instead, he is entertained in the mead hall by Bard, King Eirik's steward, who fills him with ale, then informs the queen that Egil is mocking them. She and Bard poison his drink, but Egil becomes suspicious and runs his sword through Bard. He rushes out of the hall with the king's men in pursuit.

As soon as he can, he rejoins his brother on an expedition to the Baltic, followed by expeditions to Sweden and England, where his brother, assisting King Athelstan, dies in the Battle of Vin Moor. Egil buries his brother, accepts compensation from King Athelstan, and marries his brother's widow Ásgard.

However, when Ásgard's father Bjorn dies, Egil is unable to collect her inheritance from his brother-in-law Onund. King Eirik has already declared him an outlaw before he kills Onund and makes matters worse. As he is sailing away, he is confronted by the king's son, Rognvald, with 12 men. Egil kills them all.

He is back in Iceland when his father dies. Although the two have argued earlier because Egil has not given Skallagrim his share of the money from King Athelstan, Egil buries his father as a son should. He leaves for York and goes on to fight Atli (950), then returns to Iceland. He makes a fourth journey abroad before returning to Iceland in 957 for good. He is becoming mellow in his old age. He composes "Lament for My Sons" (ca. 961) and "Lay of Arinbjorn" in 962.

After his wife dies (ca. 974), he moves to Mosfell to live with his niece Thordis and her husband Grim. In his eighties, he falls one day and hits his head, to the amusement of the women of the house. They tell him, "You're really finished now, Egil, when you fall without being pushed." He composes another verse: "My bald pate bobs and blunders, / I bang it when I fall; / My cock's gone soft and clammy / And I can't hear when they call."

Eventually he becomes totally blind and does nothing but lie around underfoot by the fire. The women fuss at him for being in the way. He complains, "It's a bore to be blind." He composes another verse: "Time passes tediously, / I tarry here alone, / An old, senile elder / With no king to aid me. . . ."

One autumn he falls ill and dies. When Christianity comes to Iceland, Grim is baptized, builds a church at Hrisbru, and has Egil's bones moved to the church. When a church is built at Mosfell, the bones are moved again. The people can tell which bones are Egil's because they are so huge, and his skull cannot be cracked with an ax.

The last section (87) tells of Egil's son Thorstein and his descendants. (Pálsson and Edwards 1988)

See also Bard; Bera; Berg-Onund; Bjorgolf; Bjorn; Brynjolf.

THE EGYPTIAN BOOK OF THE DEAD

(Also *The Chapters of Coming-Forth by Day)*

This collection of magic spells for protecting and assisting the deceased in the afterlife was placed in Egyptian pyramids from ca. 2400 B.C. and in Egyptian coffins ca. 200 B.C. Four great versions of the text have been rendered. The first, written in hieroglyphics and called the Heliopolitan version, was edited by priests of the college of Annu. It contains inscriptions from pyramids of kings of the fifth and sixth dynasties at Sakkara, and from coffins and tombs from the eleventh dynasty to ca. A.D. 200.

Some of the gods included are: Nut, Nu, Ptah, Nefer-Tmu, Khnemu, Kheperȧ Tum, Rā, Shu, Tefnut, Seb (Qeb), Osiris Isis, Horus, Heru, Set, Nebt-het, Anpu (Anubis), Hu, Sȧa, Thoth, Maāt, Hathor, Net, Sekhet, Meḥ-urt, Bast, neḷob-ka, Sebȧk, and Amen.

The Theban version, written in hieroglyphics on papyri and divided into chapters in no particular order, was used from the XVIIIth to the XXth dynasty. A third version, approximating the Theban version, was used ca. the XXth dynasty. The fourth version, the Saite version, used from the XXVIth dynasty to the end of the Ptolemaic period, arranged chapters in a definite order.

The various chapters were numbered in 1842 by Lepsius in his edition of the Turin papyrus. Their contents are as follows. IA: "Going in to the divine chiefs of Osiris on the day of the burial and of going in after coming forth," meaning going into and coming forth from the underworld. A vignette shows the funeral procession from the house of the dead to the tomb. IB: Making the mummy to go into the underworld, the tuat, on the day of "the union with the earth." A vignette shows Anubis standing by the bier holding the deceased's mummy. II: "Coming forth by day and of living after death." A vignette shows a man holding a staff. III: Like Chapter II. It has no vignette. IV: "Passing along the way over the earth." V: "Not allowing the deceased to do work in the underworld." A vignette shows the deceased kneeling on one knee. VI: "Making the ushabti figures (akin to clones) to perform work for a man in the Neter-khert," or underworld. Vignette is an ushabti figure. VII: "Passing over the back of Apep, the evil one." A vignette shows the deceased spearing a serpent. VIII: Another chapter about the underworld and coming forth by day. A vignette shows the deceased kneeling before a ram. IX: "Passing through the underworld." A vignette also shows the deceased kneeling before a ram. X: Now chapter XLVIII. XI: The deceased coming against his enemies in the underworld. XII: "Entering and coming forth from the underworld." XIII: Going into and coming forth from Amentet, or the cemetery. XIV: "Driving away shame from the heart. . . ." XV: Hymn of praise to Ra, sun god, as he rises. A vignette shows the deceased "adoring Ra." XVB 1: Hymn of praise to Ra as he sets "in the land of life." A vignette shows the deceased worshiping Ra. XVB 2: Hymn of praise to Ra-Harmachis when he sets in heaven. A vignette shows the deceased adoring Ra. XVB 3: Passing through the secret places of the tuat, or underworld. A vignette shows the deceased spearing a serpent. XVIA has no text. A vignette shows mythical beings worshiping the rising sun. XVIB has

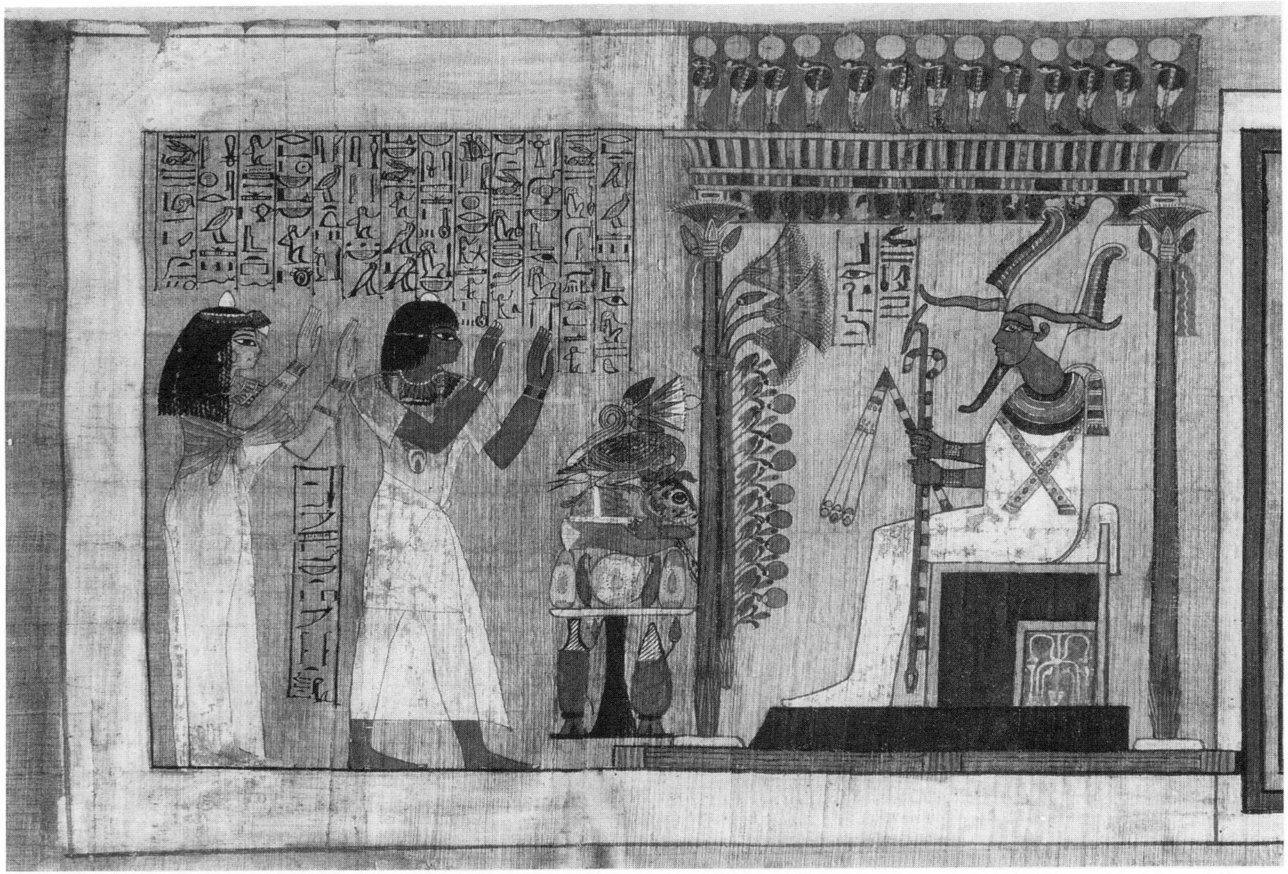

Two deceased Egyptians stand before Osiris, god of the dead, enthroned under a canopy. Egyptians began to include a copy of *The Book of the Dead,* a collection of spells to assist in the afterlife, within tombs beginning in about 2400 B.C.; the practice lasted nearly 2,000 years.

no text. A vignette shows mythical beings worshiping the setting sun. XVII: Praises of coming out from and going into the underworld, and "making transformations . . . into any form which he pleaseth," playing at draughts and "coming forth in the form of a living soul." A vignette shows the deceased playing draughts, adoring the lion-gods. It also shows the bier of Osiris with Isis and Nephthys at its foot and head, and mythical beings from the text. XVIII: No text. A vignette shows deceased adoring city gods. XIX: About the crown of victory. XX: No title and no vignette. XXI: Giving a mouth to a man in the underworld. XXII: Giving a mouth to the deceased in the underworld. A vignette shows guardian of the scales touching deceased's mouth. XXIII: Opening the mouth of the deceased. A vignette of priest touching deceased's mouth with an instrument. XXIV: Bringing magic words to the deceased in the underworld. XXV: Causing a man to remember his name in the underworld. A vignette shows priest holding up an ushabti before the deceased. XXVI: Giving a heart to the deceased in the underworld. A vignette shows Anubis holding out heart to deceased. XXVII: "Not allowing the heart of a man to be taken from him in the underworld." A vignette shows a man tying a heart to the statue of the deceased. XXVIII: Same title as above. A vignette shows the deceased touching his heart, kneeling before a demon with knife. XXIXA: "Not carrying away the heart of a man." XXIXB: A heart of carnelian. A vignette shows deceased sitting in a chair before his heart, which rests on a stand. XXXA: "Not allowing the heart . . . to be driven away. . . ." A vignette shows a heart. XXXB: Same title as above. A vignette shows deceased being weighed against his heart in the presence of Osiris. XXXI: Repulsing the crocodile who comes to take the magic words. A vignette shows deceased spearing the crocodile. XXXII: Coming to carry the magic words from the man. XXXIII: Repulsing reptiles. A vignette shows deceased attacking four snakes with knives in both hands. XXXIV: "Not being bitten by a serpent. . . ." XXXV: "Not being eaten by worms. . . ." A vignette shows serpents. XXXVI: "Repulsing the tortoise." A vignette shows the deceased spearing a beetle. XXXVII: Repulsing the two merti (from Mert, lover of silence). A vignette shows two representations of the eyes of Ra. XXXVIIIA: Living on air in the underworld. A vignette shows deceased holding a sail, symbolic of air. XXXVIIIB: Living on air and repulsing two merti. A vignette shows the deceased with knife in one hand, sail in the other, attacking three serpents. XXXIX: Repulsing the serpent. A vignette shows deceased spearing a serpent. XL: "Repulsing the eater of the ass." A vignette shows the deceased spearing a serpent that is biting the neck of an ass. XLI: "Doing away with the wounding of the eyes." A vignette shows the deceased holding a knife and a roll. XLII: "Doing away with slaughter in Suten-henen," an ancient Egyptian city. A vignette shows a man holding a serpent. XLIII: Not allowing a man's head to be cut off. XLIV: Not dying a second time. XLV: Not seeing corruption. XLVI: Not decaying; living in the underworld. XLVII: Not carrying off the throne from a man. XLVIII: A man coming against his enemies. XLIX: A man coming against his enemies in the underworld. A vignette shows a man with a staff. L: "Not going in to the divine block a second time." A vignette shows a man with his back to the block. LI: Not walking upside down.

A vignette shows a man standing. LII: Not eating filth in the underworld. LIII: "Not eating filth or drinking tainted water in the underworld." LIV: Giving air in the underworld. LV: Same as above. A vignette shows deceased holding two sails. LVI: "Snuffing the air in the earth." A vignette shows deceased kneeling and holding a sail to his nose. LVII: Snuffing the air and gaining mastery over the waters. A vignette shows man standing in a running stream, holding a sail. LVIII: Snuffing the air and gaining power over the waters. A vignette shows the deceased holding a sail. LIX: Same as above. A vignette shows man with hands extended. LX, LXI, LXII: Drinking water. Vignettes show deceased holding lotus, holding his soul, and scooping water from a pool. LXIIIA: "Drinking water and not being burned by fire." A vignette shows the deceased drinking from a stream. LXIIIB: Not being scalded. A vignette shows deceased standing by two flames. LXIV: Coming forth by day. A vignette shows the deceased worshiping the sun, which stands on the top of a tree. LXV: Coming forth by day and gaining mastery over foes. A vignette shows the deceased adoring Ra. LXVI: Coming forth by day. LXVII: Opening the doors of the tuat and coming forth. LXVIII: Coming forth by day. A vignette shows deceased kneeling by a tree before a goddess. LXIX, LXX, LXXI: Chapters of coming forth. Vignette shows the deceased kneeling before Meḥ-urt, cow-goddess of judgment. LXXII: Coming forth and passing through the hall of the tomb. A vignette shows the deceased worshiping three gods. LXXIII: Now chapter IX. LXXIV: Lifting the legs and coming upon earth. A vignette shows the deceased standing. LXXV: Traveling to Annu, Egyptian city of the sun, and receiving an abode. A vignette shows deceased before tomb door. LXXVI: Changing into whatever form one pleases. LXXVII: Changing into a golden hawk. A vignette depicts a golden hawk. LXXVIII: Changing into a divine hawk. A vignette depicts a hawk. LXXIX: Being in the company of gods, becoming a prince among the divine. A vignette shows the deceased worshiping three gods. LXXX: Changing into a god, sending forth light into darkness. A vignette depicts a god. LXXXIA: Changing into a lily. A vignette depicts a lily. LXXXIB: Same as above. A vignette shows a head rising from lily. LXXXII: Changing into the god Ptah, "father of fathers and power of powers," eating cakes, drinking ale, "unloosing the body," and living in Annu. A vignette shows Ptah in a shrine. LXXXIII: Changing into a phoenix. A vignette depicts a phoenix. LXXXIV: Changing into a heron. A vignette depicts a heron. LXXXV: Changing into a soul, not going to the place of punishment: "Whosoever knoweth it will perish." LXXXVI: Changing into a swallow. A vignette depicts a swallow. LXXXVII: Changing into serpent Sa-ta. A vignette depicts a serpent. LXXXVIII: Changing into crocodile. A vignette depicts a crocodile. LXXXIX: Uniting the soul with its body. A vignette shows the soul visiting its body, lying on a bier. XC: Giving memory to man. A vignette shows a jackal. XCI: Not allowing the soul to be shut in. A vignette shows a soul standing on a pedestal. XCII: Opening the tomb to a man's soul and shadow, that "he may come forth and gain power over his legs." A vignette shows the soul flying through the tomb door. XCIII: Not sailing to the east in the underworld. A vignette shows a buckle grasping the deceased's arm. XCIV: "Praying for an ink jar and palette." A vignette shows deceased seated before stand holding ink jar and palette. XCV: Being near Thoth, god of earth, air, sea, and sky. A vignette shows the deceased standing before Thoth. XCVI, XCVII: Being near Thoth and giving. A vignette shows the deceased standing near Thoth. XCVIII: Title of chapter incomplete. XCIX: Bringing a boat to underworld. A vignette depicts a boat. C: Making perfect the khu, a "transluscent casing" of the body something like the spirit, making the khu enter Ra's boat, with his divine followers. A vignette shows a boatful of gods. CI: Protecting Ra's boat. A vignette shows the deceased in the boat with Ra. CII: Going into Ra's boat. A vignette shows deceased in the boat with Ra. CIII: Being in the goddess Hathor's following. A vignette shows the deceased standing behind Hathor. CIV: Sitting among gods. A vignette shows deceased sitting between two gods. CV: Satisfying the ka, the free-moving personality, which could separate itself from the body at will. A vignette shows the deceased burning incense before his ka. CVI: "Causing joy each day to a man in Het-ka-Ptah [Memphis]." A vignette shows an altar holding meat and drinks. CVII: Going in and out of the gate of the gods of the west, knowing the souls of Amentet. A vignette shows the gods Ra, Sebek, and Hathor. CVIII: Knowing the souls of the west. A vignette shows the deities Tmu, Sebek, and Hathor. CIX: Knowing the souls of the east. A vignette shows the deceased worshiping Ra-Heru-khuti. CX: "Beginning . . . chapters of the Fields of Peace. . . ." A vignette shows the Fields of Peace. CXI: Now chapter CVIII. CXII: Knowing the souls of Pe, a district of the town Per-Uatchet, in the Egyptian delta. A vignette depicts Horus, Mestha, and Hapi. CXIII: Knowing the souls of Nekhen, shrine of the goddess Nekhebet. A vignette depicts Horus, Tuamautef, and Qebhsennuf. CXIV: Knowing the souls of Khemennu (Hermopolis). A vignette depicts three ibis-headed gods. CXV: "Coming forth to heaven, passing through the hall of the tomb, and knowing the souls of Annu." A vignette shows the deceased worshiping Thoth, Sau, and Tmu. CXVI: Knowing the souls of the city of Annu. A vignette shows the deceased worshiping three ibis-headed gods. CXVII: Taking a way in Re-stau, passages in the tomb leading to the other world. A vignette shows the deceased ascending the western hills with a staff in his hand. CXVIII: Coming forth from Re-stau. A vignette shows the deceased holding a staff. CXIX: Knowing the name of Osiris, going into and coming out from Re-stau. A vignette shows the deceased worshiping Osiris. CXX, CXXI: Now chapters XII and XIII, respectively. CXXII: Going in after coming forth from the underworld. A vignette shows the deceased bowing before his tomb. CXXIII: Going into the great house (tomb). A vignette shows the soul of the deceased standing before a tomb. CXXIV: Going to the princes of Osiris. A vignette shows the deceased worshiping Mestha, Hapi, Tuamautef, and Qebhsennuf. CXXV: Words to be said by the deceased when he comes to the hall of Maati, "which separateth him from his sins, and . . . maketh him to see God. . . ." A vignette shows deceased being weighed in the presence of gods in the hall of Maati. CXXVI: No title. A vignette shows a lake of fire with an ape sitting at each corner. CXXVIIA: Praise of the gods of the qerti. CXXVIIB: "Words to be spoken on going to the chiefs of Osiris," praise to gods, leaders in the tuat. CXXVIII: Praising Osiris. Vignette shows the deceased worshiping three gods. CXXIX: Now chapter C. CXXX: Making perfect the khu. A vignette shows the deceased standing between two boats. CXXXI: Making a man go to heaven beside Ra. CXXXII: Making a man go "round about" to see his house. A vignette depicts a man standing before a tomb or house. CXXXIII: Making the khu perfect in the presence of gods. A vignette shows the deceased adoring Ra, seated in a boat. CXXXIV: Entering Ra's boat and being among those in his train. A vignette shows the deceased worshiping Shu, Tefnut, Seb, Nut, Osiris, Isis, Horus, and Hathor. CXXXV: To be recited at the waxing of each moon. CXXXVIA: Sailing in Ra's boat. A vignette shows the deceased with hands raised in adoration. CXXXVIB: Sailing in Ra's boat, "to pass round the fiery orbit of the sun." CXXXVIIA: Kindling the fire in the underworld. CXXXVIIB: Same. A vignette shows deceased kindling a flame. CXXXVIII: Making the deceased enter Abydos. A vignette shows the deceased adoring the standard. CXXXIX: Now chapter CXXIII. CXL: To be recited in the second month of pert. A vignette shows the deceased adoring Anpu, utchat, and Ra. CXLI, CXLII, CXLIII: To be recited by a man for his father and his son at the festivals of Amentet. A vignette shows the deceased making offerings to a god. CXLIV: Going in. A vignette shows seven pylons. CXLVA: No title, no vignette. CXLVB: "Coming forth to the hidden pylons." CXLVI: Knowing the pylons in the house of Osiris. A vignette shows pylons guarded by gods. CXLVII: "To be recited by the deceased when he cometh to the first hall of Amentet." A vignette shows doors guarded by gods. CXLVIII: Nourishing the khu, removing him from every evil. CXLIX: No title. A vignette shows divisions of the other world. CL: No title. A vignette depicts the mummy chamber. CLIA: Hands of Anpu, who dwells in the sepulcher, upon the mummy. A vignette shows Anubis standing by the bier. CLIB: "Chief of hidden things." A vignette shows a head. CLII: Building a house in the earth. A vignette shows the deceased standing by his house's foundations. CLIIIA: Coming forth from the net. A vignette shows a net drawn by many men. CLIIIB: Coming forth from the fishing net. A vignette shows three apes drawing a fishing net. CLIV: Not allowing man's body to decay in the tomb. CLV: Placing a Tet of gold on the khu. A vignette depicts a Tet. CLVI: Placing an amethyst buckle on the neck of the khu. A vignette depicts a buckle. CLVII: Placing "a vulture of gold" on the neck of the khu. A vignette depicts a vulture. CLVIII: Placing a gold collar on the khu. A vignette depicts a collar. CLIX: Placing a scepter of mother-of-emerald on the khu. A vignette depicts a scepter. CLX: Placing a plaque of mother-of-emerald. A vignette shows a plaque. CLXI: Opening the doors of heaven. A vignette shows Thoth opening four doors. CLXII: "Causing heat to exist under the head of the khu." A vignette depicts a cow. CLXIII: Not allowing man's body to decay underground. A vignette shows two utchats and a serpent with legs. CLXIV: No title. A vignette shows a three-headed, winged goddess standing between two Pygmies. CLXV: Arriving in port, not becoming invisible, "making the body to germinate, satisfying it with water from heaven." A vignette shows the god Min or Amsu with a beetle's body. CLXVI: Of the pillow. A vignette depicts a pillow. CLXVII: Bringing the utchat. CLXVIIIA and B: No titles. Vignettes show boats of the sun and men pouring libations. CLXIX: Setting up the offering chamber. CLXX: Roof of the offering chamber. CLXXI: Tying the abu. CLXXII: Praises to be recited to the underworld. CLXXIII: Horus's addresses to his father. A vignette shows the deceased worshiping Osiris. CLXXIV: "Causing the khu to come forth from the great gate of heaven." A vignette shows the deceased coming from a door. CLXXV: Not dying a second time in the underworld. A vignette shows the deceased worshiping an ibis-headed god. CLXXVI: Same as above. CLXXVII: Raising the khu, making the soul live in the underworld. CLXXVIII: Raising up the body, making the eyes see, the ears hear, giving the head powers. CLXXIX: Coming forth from yesterday, praying with the hands. CLXXX: Coming forth by day, praising Ra. A vignette shows the deceased adoring Ra. CLXXXI: Going in to the chiefs of Osiris, who are the leaders in the tuat. A vignette depicts the deceased adoring Osiris. CLXXXII: "Establishing the backbone of Osiris . . . giving breath to him whose heart is still," repulsing by Thoth of Osiris's enemies. A vignette shows deceased on a bier surrounded by gods. CLXXXIII: Hymn of praise to Osiris. Vignettes show the deceased, hands raised in adoration, and the god Thoth. CLXXXIV: Being with Osiris. A vignette shows the deceased standing beside Osiris. CLXXXV: Praise to Osiris. A vignette shows the deceased adoring Osiris. CLXXXVI: Hymn of praise to Hathor, mistress of Amentet, and to Meḥ-urt. A vignette shows the deceased nearing the mountain of the dead, from which Hathor appears. (Budge 1967)

See also Horus; Isis; Osiris.

EIDOTHEA

(Also Idothea)

In the *Odyssey,* Eidothea is a daughter of Egyptian king Proteus, who advises Menelaus how to get back to Sparta safely (iv). Also in the *Odyssey* (xi), Eidothea is a daughter of King Proetus of Argos whom Melampus restores to her senses. (Rieu 1961)

EILEITHYA

(Also Ilithya)

Eileithya is an early goddess of childbirth whom Homer describes as the daughter of Hera. During the births of Herakles, Apollo, and Artemis—all enemies of Hera—Eileithya attempts but fails to neutralize birth pains caused by Hera. (Graves 1955)

EIRIKS SAGA RAUDA

One of many "Vinland sagas," it tells of the colonizing of Greenland ca. 986 by Eirik, father of Leif Eriksson. (Jones, G. 1961; Jones, G. 1990)

EKENGBUDA

He was the oba (king) of the kingdom of Benin, in present-day Nigeria, during the eighteenth century. According to some oral versions, Ekengbuda was the oba of Benin during the war with Ubulu, which is depicted in the epic of *Ezemu*. (Okpewho 1992)

See also *Ezemu*.

EL

In ancient Ugarit texts from Ras Shamra, Syria, El is the chief deity of West Semites. He is the husband of Asherah and father of all gods except Baal. (Pritchard 1973)

ELECTRA

In Greek mythology, Electra is the daughter of Agamemnon and Clytemnestra. She is the sister of Orestes, whom she incites to avenge their father's murder by slaying their mother and her lover Aegisthus. Electra is also one of the Pleiades, daughter of Atlas and Pleione. By Zeus she is the mother of Dardanus, founder of the Trojan royal family. She is also the wife of Thaumas and mother of Iris and the Harpies. Electra is the name of Cadmus's sister and of one of Helen's attendants. (Graves 1955)

ELIBE AJA

This heroic narrative of the Ohafia people of Nigeria, West Africa, is still performed today. It concerns a fearless hunter who stalks and slays a leopardess that has been ravaging the Aro region. Later, while attempting to kill a bush hog that has been destroying farms at Amuru, Elibe Aja is killed. (Azuonye *RAL* 1990)

ELISSA

(Also Elisa and Dido)

In the *Aeneid* (i, iv), Elissa is the daughter of King Belus of Tyre and sister of Pygmalion. When her brother murders her husband Sichaeus, she flees to Africa, where she founds Carthage and becomes its queen. She falls in love with Aeneas when he stops there on his way to Italy. When he leaves, she pronounces a curse against the Trojans and stabs herself. (Ben Khader and Soren 1987; Humphries 1951)

See also Dido.

EMMA-Ō

In Japanese Buddhist mythology, Emma-Ō is the overlord of Jigoku, 16-tiered fire-and-ice region of the dead. He judges the souls of men and sentences them to one of the tiers, where they must stay unless rescued through prayers offered by the living. One legend concerns a wife, Hana-no-maguzumi, who descends to the afterworld to save her husband's soul and returns with him. (Mayer 1948)

EMPEROR SHAKA THE GREAT

This Zulu epic is based on the life of Emperor Shaka (or Chaka), who reigned from 1816 to 1828. Much of the epic's material, preserved by Maizisi Kunene, derived from the oral accounts of a number of abalandi bezindaba zabadala, highly trained oral historians. These national historians have preserved not only details of various periods but also specific incidents from each period. Some specialized in recounting only one incident, one battle. One of the sources for the epic was Kunene's uncle, A. Ngcobo.

The epic contains fragments of praise poems, poems of excellence, or heroic poems. They must of necessity be fragmentary, because their full meaning can only be realized in a performance format.

As with many epics, the circumstances of Shaka's birth in 1787 and his early years shape his heroic character and provide the impetus for his powerful personality and political genius. Book 1 of the epic opens with a brief history of the tribe and a scene from the time of King Jama, Shaka's grandfather. An oracle foretells of a great era that is to come in succeeding generations: "The generation to come shall rule the earth." Jama tries to silence her, and his followers whisper, "The greatness . . . should have been ours." Jama looks at his son Senzangakhona, "wondering if these prophecies would fall on his shoulders." But Senzangakhona is "not like the wild ones who open the paths of men."

Later Senzangakhona meets the beautiful Langeni princess Nandi and forbids her and her followers to proceed across his land. But "as she walked she shook the earth. / She was the fear of the timid ones." Although she thinks to herself, "I have now met my soulmate," she tells him, "You have been spoiled. / You have listened to those who know only one side of you. / They have not seen the hidden rottenness of your bones." Senzangakhona is stabbed with pain by her words, but she quickly apologizes, and they fall together behind the bushes: "They loved as though to celebrate their final day on earth." The child Shaka is conceived from the union, and Senzangakhona takes Princess Nandi for a wife.

The women of the village curse Senzangakhona for violating the customs of their ancestors. They seclude Nandi "in the dark recesses of his father's villages" as a secondary wife.

Meanwhile, King Jama dies and Senzangakhona becomes king. Nandi gives birth to a son but continues to live like an orphan, removed from the king's presence. The people of Langeni are angered when they learn of their princess's treatment, and vow retribution.

In book 2, Senzangakhona's main and favorite wife, Mkhabi, advises him to send Nandi—who now also has a daughter, and continues to boast of her son and complain of her treatment—back to her own people. The king agrees to do so and adds, "I shall nip Nandi's beast in the bud; / I shall throw her troublesome son to the wild." But Mkhabi, realizing how "other women would denounce this hideous act," steals away to the camp of the chief commander, Prince Mudli, to beg him to intervene. Knowing that such an act of violence by the king to his son would destroy the very roots of the nation, Mudli agrees to act. He hides the boy in a sack, which he plans to deliver to the child's mother when she is safely out of the village.

Senzangakhona orders the official executioner to kill his son, and then he takes a walk. He encounters Mudli carrying a bag, which he claims contains the young of a pig. The king tests his spear-tossing skill on the bag, but he cannot strike it, so he allows Mudli to continue. Mudli delivers the bag, containing the one-year-old Shaka, to Nandi on the mountainside where she waits.

Nandi and her children set out on their journey. Learning of Nandi's plight, the Langa army sets out to avenge her. Senzangakhona quells the attack but abandons booty; he does not finish the battle or interfere with Nandi's escape. His aunt, Princess Michabayi, the most influential figure in Zululand, hears of the king's "ignominious return" from battle and rushes out to denounce him for coming home empty-handed: "True manhood must complete what it has begun! / Those like you earn only derision of friend and enemy alike."

Prince Shaka's reputation for power grows as he reaches boyhood, causing jealousy among the king's favorites, who plan an expedition to kill him.

Book 3 begins as Zulu warriors pillage and plunder the village of the Langeni, but Shaka has been forewarned by the Ancestors, and he escapes. Nandi's clan expells her and her children because their presence has been the cause of much bloodshed. The three of them undertake a long and hazardous journey to find asylum among their cousins of the Quabe clan. For Shaka the journey is also a ritual journey into manhood.

Book 4 begins with a history of how King Dingiswayo comes to power on the Mthethwa throne. It is with the Mthethwas that Shaka comes into his own, learning the crafts of military tactics and statesmanship from their warriors. He becomes a trusted favorite of the king as he brings more and more states into his confederation.

Once Senzangakhona visits and, after seeing the young warrior dance, asks his name and learns that he is Shaka, his own son. Shaka asks permission to return home with his father, but Senzangakhona reminds him, "Two bulls cannot live in one field"; his half brother, Prince Sigujana, has grown to manhood and is the heir apparent. Later, when Shaka asks his father for the gift of his spear, the king claims that he has already promised it to Sigujana. Shaka is hurt and angered but respectful of his father, and they shake hands. The king leaves the encounter, trembling from his son's power: a premonition of his own end.

When word reaches the kingdom that Senzangakhona has died, King Dingiswayo advises Shaka to return home and save his ancestral kingdom from strife.

In book 5 Shaka returns to his country prepared to implement his new ideas of sleek, streamlined warfare and his strict moral code for his people. In a battle against Phungashe, king of the powerful Buthelezi nation, Shaka surprises everyone by defeating him handily. He incorporates the Buthelezi into the Zulu nation. But Nandi rebukes him for leaving her alone with no grandchildren.

Book 6 brings Shaka to a new place. He advises Dingiswayo to wage war, with Shaka's army, against Matiwane, the nomadic ruler of the Ngwanes, who is feared and hated by many nations for his raids. Dingiswayo captures Matiwane, but releases him. This leads Zwide, the powerful king of the Ndwandwes, to attack Dingiswayo with the aim of bringing his territory into the Ndwandwe domain. During the conflict, Zwide needlessly murders Dingiswayo, and this cowardly act brings an end to all hopes for peace between the peoples of the region. It assures a direct confrontation between Shaka and Zwide.

In book 7 Zwide and his sons, epitome of a powerful but decadent aristocracy, are confronted by the cunning of Shaka, employing a network of agents who infiltrate the enemy's organization and send advance reports on all strategy. General Mzilikazi, leader of the Khumalos, who knows Zwide's court intimately, supplies Shaka with much military intelligence. The first battle between the two forces results in a rout of Zwide's army.

Book 8 leads to the second war against Zwide. Shaka has refined his espionage network such that he is able to initiate events in the enemy camp at the opportune moment. He plans a strategic retreat. He is able to anticipate his enemy's moves and conteract them.

But he cannot anticipate his mother's. She has learned that Mbuzikazi, of the enemy Cele clan, may bear Shaka a child and makes elaborate plans to save it by feigning ill health and requesting that Mbuzikazi alone attend her. Thus she is able to keep Mbuzikazi's pregnancy concealed.

When the nation's counselor, Mbopha, reports this to the king, Shaka is angered, knowing that he will be a target of blame among the Zulu people. He goes to Nandi to ask why she has concealed this child of an enemy clan from him. Nandi, who wants a grandchild at any cost, tells him, "It is not out of evil that people act against others, / But love sometimes obscures itself in acts of cruelty."

She goes on to tell him that she fears Mbopha as being treacherous, but Shaka explains that he cannot remove him from office. He seeks the advice of Mkhabayi, who quells his suspicions and restores peace, admonishing him, "You should only laugh at whatever talk is reported to you. / Words often assume a fierceness when reported by others."

In book 9 King Macingwane, a brother of Shaka's father and ruler of the fierce Chunu nation, hears of Zwide's defeat and vows, "However many kings may flee from the Zulu upstart, / There is one ruler who shall never surrender. / It is I, who am born of the ancient rulers. . . ." Shaka concentrates on shoring up the internal structure of the Zulu nation, forming alliances along ideological lines.

An example of his new ideas of justice occurs when a man appears before the assembly demanding justice because his brother had previously impregnated the woman the man had been given as a wife. An elder from a distant region steps forward and makes it clear to all that the brother deserves the punishment of death. Then Shaka questions the elder concerning the fate of the woman involved: "Has she not been the cause of this disintegration?" The elder replies, "A woman in Zululand is the mother of our nation; / In her is both the power of life and destruction / . . . the dignity and greatness of women / Speaks loudly through the Queen Mother and the Princess Mkhabayi. / Thus this woman deserves even greater punishment than this man."

The assembly gives its judgment, but the condemned brother pleads on behalf of the woman, "Let other nations who hear of our judgments / Say 'Punishments of death are meted out only to men.'" But Shaka refuses leniency. In fact, he decrees that the woman's womb be split open: "Let the monster that has destroyed the families be exposed."

The Zulus are challenged by both the Chunus and the Thembus, but the attacks are repelled.

In book 10 Shaka meets a delegation of white traders, whose habits and weapons he studies. When he is wounded in an assassination attempt, the white men tend his wounds and ask for land in return. Shaka accedes to their request with the intention of keeping them close enough to learn from them. He sends a delegation to negotiate an agreement with King George that will define the Englishmen's sphere of influence.

King Moshoeshoe of the Sothos, whose people have been terrorized by the roving Matiwane, asks for help, and Shaka dispatches an army led by General Mdlaka. The army of Matiwane is destroyed once and for all.

In book 11, General Mdlaka and his men are treated royally by the Sothos. As the conquering army returns home, plans for a welcoming feast are almost canceled because of the illness of Nandi. But Shaka decides to put aside his own troubles and go ahead with the celebration for the returning heroes. However, "Throughout the land there were poisonous rumours, / Claiming the Queen Mother's illness was caused by her unhappiness, / Or else that Shaka had exaggerated the whole event / To retrieve his sinking popularity." Shaka's close friends are dying off, and his brothers, particularly Dingane, begin to plot his assassination.

In book 12, Shaka is saddened when his old fighting companion, Mgobhozi, is killed in the battle against Zwide's successor, Sikhunyona. He remains in a dark mood for some time and emerges from the mood in a more reflective frame of mind.

Book 13 is concerned with Dingane's ceaseless plots against his brother Shaka. Shaka moves his capital from Bulawayo to Dukuza, not only to keep closer tabs on the white settlement, but also to leave behind the sadness of the past. He visits Zihlandlo, head of the Mkhize clan, upon whose friendship he now relies.

In book 14 Shaka continues to agitate for an emissary to King George, although he now knows that military confrontation is inevitable. The Zulus engage in a number of hunting expeditions, bullfights, dances, and poetry competitions until Nandi falls ill and dies; "Suddenly a fearful mourning exploded throughout Zululand." Shaka calls together the great counselors of the land and orders that the nation express its grief with dignity. He tells them, "There have been two rulers in Zululand: / One gentle, who excelled in her kindness and generosity; / Another who rules with wisdom and plans with wisdom. / Such duality has never been known in all history."

In book 15, the Zulus make a punitive strike against the Mpondos, only to learn that the Mpondos employ only guerilla tactics and do not want to fight an open war. Shaka calls off the war, but not before the great Zulu hero Manyundela is killed.

Shaka disapproves of the occupation of the Cape region by white invaders, but his emissaries' attempts to learn the intentions of the white men have netted nothing. His brothers continue to plot against him, and he leans heavily upon the friendship of Zihlandlo as the only man he can trust.

In book 16, Mbopha ("the puff-adder," whom Nandi feared as a traitor) spreads rumors concocted by Princess Mkhabayi that Shaka had actually killed his own mother. Shaka's brothers Dingane and Mhlangana, sent on a campaign against Soshangane, feign illness, abandon the campaign, and return. Several plots against Shaka fail. He awaits news of his northern campaign to look for iron, led by his uncle Nxazonke. Shaka gives his great friend Zihilandlo his spear as a symbol of their friendship.

In book 17, Shaka's brothers and Mbopha undertake to assassinate him themselves. When the campaign led by Nxazonke is late in returning, Mbopha intervenes, defying protocol, and berates the delegation for its tardiness. In the confusion that follows, Dingane and Mhlangane appear armed. Mbopha pretends to stab the intruders, but instead he turns and stabs Shaka. The intruders then stab him from all sides, making him the scapegoat. Later, the new king, Dingane, suspects plots against him and kills his brothers.

Shaka's last words are a warning about the whites: "No, you shall never rule. Only the swallows shall rule. . . ." The epic ends with a short poem, "Dirge of the Palm Race." (Kunene 1979)

See also Bhuza; Chaka; Faku; Isaacs, N.; Macingwane; Senzangakhona.

EN-URU

Mesopotamian god. *See* Enki.

ENKI

In Sumero-Akkadian religion, Enki is the son of Enlil and Nammu, god of fresh waters and of wisdom. Sumerian tablets refer to him also as king of the abyss, or abzu. In the myth *Inanna's Descent to the Nether World,* it is Enki who devises

Enki, a Sumerian figure from the myth of *Inanna's Descent to the Nether World,* is represented in this modern impression from an Akkadian-era seal made circa 2100 B.C.

a plan to restore Inanna to life. He fashions two creatures, kurgarru and kalaturru, and sends them to the nether world to sprinkle Inanna's corpse with "food of life" and "water of life." (Kramer 1956; Pritchard 1973; Wolkstein and Kramer 1983)

See also *Atrakhasis, Myth of;* Enlil.

ENKIDU

In the *Epic of Gilgamesh,* Enkidu is the wild man molded from clay by Aruru, goddess of creation, in the image of and "of the essence of" the sky god Anu and the war god Ninurta. He lives among the animals until he is called to challenge Gilgamesh. After the two clash, they become fast friends and engage in many adventures together. After he slays Inanna's Bull of Heaven, he is condemned to death. (Sandars 1972)

See also Anu; *Gilgamesh, Epic of;* Inanna.

ENLIL

Enlil is the Sumero-Akkadian god of wind, earth, and the "universal air," or spirit, the son of the sky god An and earth god Ki. In the *Epic of Gilgamesh* he is the patron god of the city of Nippur. (Kramer 1956; Sandars 1972; Sproul 1991)

See also Anu; *Enuma Elish, Epic of; Gilgamesh, Epic of;* Marduk; Tiamat.

ENMERKAR AND ENSUKUSHIRANNA, EPIC OF

This Sumerian epic (ca. 2400 B.C.) is about a rivalry between the Lord of Aratta, Ensukushiranna (also Ensuhkeshdanna), and the ruler of Erech, Enmerkar. Ensukushiranna issues a challenge through a herald to Enmerkar, demanding that Enmerkar should recognize Ensukushiranna as his overlord, and furthermore, that the goddess Inanna should be brought to Aratta. Enmerkar not only refuses but demands that Ensukushiranna become his vassal. The lord of Aratta calls in his council members for advice but when they advise him to submit, he refuses. The mashmash-priest of Aratta boasts that he can subdue all the lands around Erech, so Ensukushiranna gives him five minas of gold and five of silver and sends him on his way. The priest arrives in Erech; going directly to the stable and sheepfold of the goddess Nidaba, he induces the animals not to produce milk. As a result, the goddess's stables are ruined. With the help of the wise Mother Sagburru, her two shepherds outwit the priest five times before Mother Sagburru kills him for his stupidity and throws him into the Euphrates. When Ensukushiranna learns the fate of his priest, he sends a messenger to Enmerkar saying, "From [the moment of conception], I was not your equal, you are the 'big brother,' / I cannot compare with you ever." (Kramer 1956)

ENMERKAR AND THE LORD OF ARATTA, EPIC OF

The longest extant Sumerian tale, preserved on a tablet almost 4,000 years old, concerns events that may have occurred almost 5,000 years ago. It is a heroic poem of 600 lines about a Sumerian hero named Enmerkar, son of the sun god Utu and ruler of the city-state Erech in South Mesopotamia ca. the third millennium B.C. Erech was located between the Tigris and Euphrates rivers. Beyond seven mountain ranges to the east, in Persia, was Aratta, a prosperous city-state that Enmerkar wants so that he can use its precious metals and stones for building a temple for Enki and other shrines.

The poem's preamble tells of the greatness of Erech and the district of Kullab, and thus the love and war goddess Inanna's preference for it over the inferior Aratta. Enmerkar asks his sister Inanna to aid him. She advises him to find a suitable herald to cross the treacherous mountains and deliver a message demanding that the people send him the materials he requires. Enmerkar selects his herald and sends word that he will destroy Aratta if his demands aren't met. The lord of Aratta, learning that Inanna favors Erech, sends Enmerkar a message that he will submit only if he is first sent large quantities of grain. Although Enmerkar complies, pleasing the people of Aratta, the lord of Aratta refuses to honor his part of the bargain. Instead, he demands carnelian and lapis lazuli from Enmerkar. Enmerkar sends the herald back with no message, only the scepter, the sight of which seems to terrorize the lord of Aratta. Nevertheless, he sends a message suggesting that one of Erech's fighting men engage in single combat with one of Aratta's. Enmerkar accepts the challenge, but demands that the lord of Aratta heap up gold, silver, and jewels for Inanna. He threatens Aratta with total destruction if the people don't comply: "I will make the people of his city flee like the . . . bird from its tree / . . . I will make it desolate . . . / I will make it hold dust like an utterly destroyed city." Although the text becomes fragmented at the end, Enmerkar apparently wins. (Kramer 1956)

ENSUN

Mesopotamian god. *See* Nanna.

ENUMA ELISH, EPIC OF

(Also *War of the Gods*)

In this Babylonian creation epic, ca. 1894–1595 B.C., the opening words are "Enuma elish," which means "When on high." Its hero is the storm god Marduk, son of water and wisdom god Ea and Damika. He is a descendant of the first gods, Apsu (Abzu) and Tiamat, representing fresh, sweet, underground water and salty seawaters; from these two spring Lahmu and Lahamu, who give birth to Anshar and Kishar, who give birth to Anu, the father of Ea.

Other gods come into being who are so active, dancing and disturbing the belly of Tiamat, that Apsu and his counselor Mummu decide to destroy them all. However, Ea drugs them, kills Apsu, and holds Mummu captive with a nose rope. Tiamat, the universal mother, takes a new mate, Kingu. After Marduk is born in the very temple built over Apsu's body, he proves to be such a nuisance with his manipulations of the winds that Tiamat decides to stop him. She creates an army of monsters and, with Kingu as their leader, sends them forth against the gods who befriend Marduk. Although Ea and Anu are defeated, Marduk, armed with thunder and lightning, slays Tiamat and imprisons the army of monsters deep in the earth. He cuts her body into two pieces, forming heaven and earth from the two halves. He places Anu in charge of the region above the firmament, Enlil in charge of the region between firmament and earth, and Ea in charge of the waters underneath the earth. From the body of Kingu, he makes a servant to the gods, man. In gratitude, the gods build him a shining city, Babylon.

Marduk's story is similar to the Greek myth in which the young storm god Zeus battles monsters created by the primal mother, Ge, and imprisons them deep in the earth. (Sproul 1991)

See also Anu; Marduk; Mummu; Tiamat.

EOS

(Also Aurora)

The Greek goddess of the dawn, Eos is the mother of Memnon and is slain by Achilles. She is described by Homer as rosy-fingered and saffron-robed. (Ceram 1972; Graves 1966; Schwab 1974)

EOSTRE

Germanic goddess of spring and of dawn, Eostre is related to the Greek Eos and possibly to the Assyro-Babylonian goddess Ishtar. (Gimbutas 1982)

EPEIUS

(Also Epeus)

In the *Aeneid* (ii) and in the *Epic Cycle* story "The Little Iliad," Epeius is the designer and builder of the wooden horse used to defeat Troy. (Godolphin 1964; Humphries 1951)

EPIC

Typically, an epic is a long narrative poem of grand scope, style, and theme that recounts the fantastic exploits of a legendary or historical figure or figures endowed with superhuman might and, through countless episodes and renderings, epitomizes the character or ideals of a certain race, tribe, or nation at a given time in history. Generally the character traits of the protagonist are stylized ideals of the people. The epic differs from myth in that myths traditionally are concerned with the divine and epics with the deeds of heroes; however, epics often contain mythical elements.

Although there are similarities among folk epics worldwide, and although Western scholars have sometimes taken an ethnocentric view of the elements that make up an epic, the style of epics differs somewhat from culture to culture. The action in European and African epics often turns upon supernatural intervention. European epics often begin with an invocation to the Muse, followed by a declamation of the theme and introduction of characters. These elements may be absent in epics from other parts of the world. Most epics worldwide depend upon the repetition of certain fixed elements, verses, stock epithets, or descriptive tags, unique to the individual bard, that the bard employs to help the listener identify the characters and keep them straight, to fill in between episodes as a signal that an episode has ended, or to drive his message home.

Epics may be classified as folk or literary. Folk epics develop from oral narrations by tribal or family bards and are eventually written down by poets—or, in recent times, recorded and transcribed verbatim by anthropologists during bardic performances. Contrary to general belief, all epics were not gathered centuries ago. An oral-epic tradition oftentimes continues among people even after they have become literate. Oral traditions still exist among 2 million indigenous people speaking 50 languages in the Arctic, 42 million indigenous people speaking 900 languages in the Americas, up to 350 million speaking 2,000 languages in Africa and the Middle East, up to 91 million speaking 700 languages in South Asia, up to 84 million speaking 150 languages in East Asia, up to 55 million speaking 1,950 languages in Southeast Asia, and 3 million speaking 500 languages in Oceania. Many of these people have full-blown epics and others have cycles of poems that have not yet been gathered into epics. It remains to be seen how many epics will develop from these cultures before they either disappear, become assimilated into the dominant culture, or become dominant themselves. In the waning years of the twentieth century, the industrial world has come belatedly to acknowledge the wisdom and values of indigenous cultures, to endeavor to preserve their stories, and, in many cases, to learn from them.

Oral epics occur in many versions, all incorporating a central theme elaborated by different bards inserting their own set of legends. Because of their length, they are usually presented intermittently in an episodic manner. They are frequently performed to a background of music, chanting, or dance. The epic serves a number of functions: as part of feasts, religious festivals, or community gatherings. In each case the epic is not only entertaining, but also reinforces those elements of the group character revered by the audience. Heroic epics were sung before battles to instill courage, and noble warriors had personal bards who went into battle with them in order to give an account of the hero's deeds. Epics were also sung following aggressive actions to justify those actions to the people back home. These epics often had supernatural overtones, suggesting intervention of the gods in tribal affairs.

A literary or written epic is the creation of one poet, often commissioned by a ruler to produce the work. Among the most famous literary epics among Western readers are the *Iliad* and *Odyssey* of Homer (although their oral-formulaic composition suggests generations of accretion); the *Aeneid* of Virgil, which was deliberately conceived; the *Shāh-Nāmah* of Ferdowsi (Firdausi); the *Luciads* of de Camões; *Orlando Innamorato* of Boiardo; *Orlando Furioso* of Ariosto; *Paradise Lost* by Milton; and the *Faerie Queene* of Spenser.

The term *traditional epic* refers to those epics, literary as well as oral, that draw entirely or in great part upon long oral tradition for their content.

EPIC CYCLE

This group of post-Homeric poems (ca. seventh and sixth centuries B.C.), now lost except for a few fragments, concerns figures and actions connected with the Trojan War; they supplement and finish the story of the Trojan War as told in the *Iliad* and *Odyssey.* The contents of these poems were summarized by Photius from an earlier summary outline by Proclus. The various parts of the story are as follows.

"Theogonia" and "Titanomachia," covering the creation and early history of the world.

"Cypria," in 11 books, preceding the action of the Trojan War, which Zeus and Themis plan to bring about. It covers the period from the time of the theft of Helen to the quarrel between Agamemnon and Achilles. During the marriage feast of Peleus, a dispute arises among Hera, Athena, and Aphrodite as to who is the fairest. They go to Mount Ida to ask Paris to settle the dispute. Lured by a promise of marriage to Helen, Paris chooses Aphrodite. She directs him to build his ships, and he sets sail for Sparta. Menelaus welcomes him and then leaves for Crete, instructing Helen to entertain his guests. When he is gone, Paris and Helen steal away to Troy. When Menelaus hears what has happened, he plans an assault on Ilium to get his wife back. He goes on to Nestor, who tells him several stories: of Epopeus and the daughter of Lycus, of Oedipus, of Herakles, and of Theseus and Ariadne. Eventually the two travel around the country gathering leaders for the attack. When Odysseus pretends to be ill to avoid joining them, they seize his son Telemachos for punishment.

They set out for Ilium and land in Teuthrania, sacking it in error. Achilles wounds Telephus, who has come to the rescue. The Greeks leave and are scattered by a storm. Achilles lands at Scyros and marries Deidameia, then heals Telephus, who has been led by an oracle to come there.

As they muster again at Aulis, a boast by Agamemnon angers Artemis, who prevents their sailing by sending stormy winds. To appease her, they try to sacrifice Agamemnon's daughter Iphigeneia, but at the last minute Artemis substitutes a goat and makes the girl immortal.

They sail to Tenedos, where Achilles and Agamemnon quarrel because Achilles has been invited late. They go on to Ilium, but the Trojans prevent them from landing until Achilles kills Poseidon's son Cycnus. The Greeks drive the Trojans back and, as spoils for their first victory, Achilles receives Briseis and Agamemnon takes Chryseis.

"Cypria" has variously been attributed to Stasinos of Cyprus, Hegesias, and Homer.

(The *Iliad,* in 24 books, covers the period from the ire of Achilles to Hektor's burial.)

"Aethiopis," in five books (776–744 B.C.), following the action depicted in the *Iliad,* covers the period from the coming of the Amazons to Aias's suicide. It is attributed to Arktinos of Miletos (Arctinus of Miletus). Achilles kills the Amazon Penthesileia in battle, then kills Thersites for reviling him for his suspected love for the Amazon. Achilles leaves for Lesbos, where Odysseus purifies him for killing Thersites. King Memnon of Ethiopia comes with 10,000 troops to help his uncle Priam. During the battle Memnon kills Nestor's son Antilochus, and Achilles kills Memnon when the latter refuses to fight Nestor because of his age. Achilles is killed by Paris with the help of Apollo. The Achaeans escape with his body, which Thetis transports to White Island. Odysseus and Aias quarrel over Achilles's armor.

"Little Illiad," in four books, covers Achilles's death to the fall of Troy and the Achaeans' departure. It is variously attributed to Lesches of Lesbos, Thestorides, Diodoros, Homer, and Kinaithon. By conspiring with Athena, Odysseus gains Achilles's armor. Aias becomes mad and destroys the Greeks' herds, then kills himself. Philoctetes kills Paris, but the Trojans recover his body and bury it. Helen is then married to Deiphobus. Athena instructs Epeius to build the wooden horse, and Odysseus steals into Troy, where Helen recognizes him and helps him plot how to take the city. The Greeks put their best men into the horse and the rest sail away. The Trojans begin to celebrate and bring the horse into the city.

"Sack of Ilion," in two books (776–774 B.C.), covers the period from the building of the wooden horse to the fall of Ilion and the Achaeans' departure. After much argument about what to do with the horse, including burning it or throwing it off a cliff, the Trojans decide to dedicate it to Athena. During the feasting two serpents appear and kill Laocoon and one of his sons. Sinon raises the torch signal to the Greeks waiting offshore, and those hiding in the horse come out and storm the city. Neoptolemus kills Priam, Menelaus kills Deiphobus and rescues Helen, the Greeks burn the city, Odysseus kills Astyanax, and Neoptolemus takes Andromache as his prize. The Greeks sail away while Athena makes plans to destroy them at sea. "Sack of Ilion" is by Arktinos of Miletos (Arctinus of Miletus).

"The Returns," in five books, covers the return to Greece of various heroes. It is variously attributed to Agias of Troizen, Homer, and an unknown Kolophonian. Athena precipitates a quarrel between Menelaus and Agamemnon; to appease the goddess, Agamemnon stays behind. Diomedes and Nestor sail home. Then Menelaus sets sail with a number of ships, all but five of which are destroyed at sea, and reaches Egypt. As Agamemnon and his troops prepare to leave, the ghost of Achilles appears and warns them against sailing because of a storm at the rocks of Capherides. Many journey overland. Aegisthus and Clytemnestra murder Agamemnon, and Orestes and Pylades take vengeance. Menelaus finally reaches home.

(In the time sequence, the *Odyssey* follows, in 24 books, covering the return of Odysseus.)

"Telegonia," in two books (568 B.C.), covers the period from Odysseus's return to his death. It is attributed to either Eugammon of Kyrene (Cyrene) or Kinaithos of Lakedaimon. Penelope's suitors are buried by their kinsmen. Odysseus sails to Elis to inspect his herds; he is entertained by Polyxenus and gifted with a mixing bowl. He sails to Ithaca, and to Thesprotis, where he marries the queen, Callidice. They have a son, Polypoetes. A war breaks out between the Thesprotians and the Brygi in which Odysseus, leading the Thesprotians, is routed by Ares. After Callidice dies, Polypoetes becomes king and Odysseus returns to Ithaca. Meanwhile, Telegonus, in search of his father, lands on Ithaca and ravages it. Odysseus is killed unwittingly by his son. Telegonus, with Penelope and Telemachos, takes Odysseus's body to his mother Circe's island, where she makes them all immortal. Telegonus marries Penelope, and Telemachos marries Circe. (Godolphin 1964)

EPIMETHEUS

In Greek myth, in *Theogony,* Epimetheus is the son of Titan Iapetus and Clymene; brother of Prometheus, Atlas, and Menoetius; husband of Pandora; and father of Pyrrha, Deucalion's wife. (Lattimore 1959)

ERESHKIGAL

(Also Irkalla)

She is a Sumero-Akkadian goddess, the terrifying queen of the underworld, Kur. In early mythology she was probably a sky goddess who is carried away to Kur; in third-millennium B.C. texts, she is the wife (or mother) of Ninazu. One text describes her as "She who rests, she who rests, the mother of Ninazu, her holy shoulders are not covered with garments, her breast is not covered with linen." In later texts she is the wife of Nergal, who becomes a god of the underworld. She is the sister of Inanna (also Ishtar in Akkadian), the queen of heaven. In the poem *Inanna's Descent to the Underworld,* Ereshkigal makes Inanna undergo tortures and death when she dares to visit her sister. Ereshkigal's son and chief minister is Namtar, symbolizing fate or death. She keeps close guard over the fount of life lest her subjects partake of it and escape. (Kramer 1951; Saggs 1990; Sandars 1972)

See also *Gilgamesh, Epic of.*

ERIDU GENESIS, EPIC OF

In this ancient Sumerian creation epic, after the universe is formed from the sea and the gods are born, they create man of clay so as to have someone to till the soil, care for the flocks, and worship the gods. Man builds cities and kings to rule them. However, as related in the *Epic of Gilgamesh,* the gods are not pleased and determine to destroy man with a flood. The god Enki (Ea), not in agreement about their decision, reveals the plan to the wise and obedient Ziusudra of Shurrupak (Utnapishtim in Akkadian), instructing him to build a boat in which to save himself. Ziusudra follows Enki's instructions and, with his family and "the seed of all living creatures," safely survives the flood in his boat. He is rewarded with eternal life; he lives forever in Dilmun, where the sun rises. (Ceram 1990; Kramer 1956; Sproul 1991)

See also Flood Myths; *Gilgamesh, Epic of;* Utnapishtim; Ziusudra.

ERIKSSON, LEIF

See Leif the Lucky

ERINTSEN MERGEN, EPIC OF

(Also *Erinchin)*

This is a Mongol üliger, or orally transmitted epic story in verse recited by memory. It concerns the career of Erintsen, seventeenth-century jinong, or chief, of the Ordos (Banner of Wang). Warring among the Mongol tribes allows the Manchus to move into eastern Mongolia and take over. Erintsen commands one of these tribes. With the help of the Kharachin and Abagha tribes, he defeats the grand khan of the eastern Mongols, the khan of Chahar, Legdan (Lingdan), in 1627. But this only allows the Manchus under Abakhai to gain a toehold. Erintsen bestows upon Sanang Sechen, of the Jenghiz-khanite and Dayanid family of Ordos of the Ushin Banner, the title of Erke Sechen Khongtaiji, and Sechen begins a history of eastern Mongolia (which he finishes in 1662). However, eastern Mongolia's glory days are over. In the following year, Erintsen must pay homage to Abakhai, head of the Manchus.

In 1649 the Ordos reorganize under six gushu (banners), each under the command of a jasak (prince) descended from the Jenghiz-khanite jinong Gün Bilikt, but the Manchus will remain in power for generations. (Grousset 1970; Preminger 1990)

ERIPHYLE

In the *Odyssey* (xi) and the *Aeneid* (vi), Eriphyle is the wife of Amphiaraus of the Seven against Thebes. Her acceptance of bribes leads to her husband's and son's deaths. (Humphries 1951; Rieu 1961)

ERLIK

In Turkish (Altaic) mythology, Erlik is king of the dead. He is seen as a demiurge, fraudulent cohort of the high god. In the creation myth, he is described as a seabird charged with drawing the earth from the bottom of the primal sea. (Holmberg 1964)

EROS

(Also Amor and Cupid)

Eros, the Greek god of love, appears in the *Aeneid* (i) and *Theogony.* (Graves 1955; Humphries 1951)

ERRA EPIC

In this Assyrian myth ca. 700 B.C., Erra, the god of indiscriminate slaughter, induces the Babylonian god Marduk *(see Enuma Elish, Epic of)* to assign the world to his care while Marduk is having his royal insignia cleaned. While Marduk is occupied, Erra institutes a reign of terror and slaughter. (Pritchard 1973)

ESHU

(Also Elegba)

A benevolent Yoruban (Nigerian) god with dual aspects, Eshu is a protective spirit who also possesses powers of destruction that may be used against enemies. He represents the principle of uncertainty. (Parrinder 1982)

ESTSÁNATLEHI

See Changing Woman.

ESUS

This early Celtic deity is one of the triad of deities mentioned by first-century A.D. Roman poet Lucan: "Esus whose savage shrine makes men shudder." (Chadwick 1976)

ETANA EPIC

This ancient Mesopotamian epic, existing only in fragments, was possibly based on the legendary king of Kish who reigned after the flood, sometime in the first half of the third millennium B.C. In the epic's beginning, the gods set out to find a king to rule on earth. They choose Etana, who rules wisely until he discovers that his pregnant wife is unable to deliver without the aid of the birth plant. Etana must travel to heaven to obtain the plant, so he prays to Shamash, who instructs him to go to a mountain where a wounded eagle has been thrown into a pit. Etana climbs the mountain and rescues the eagle, who then carries him up toward heaven. According to one fragment, Etana becomes dizzy and crashes to earth; however, another fragment indicates that Etana reaches heaven and falls down at the gods' feet. (Pritchard 1973)

ETZEL

In Germanic heroic literature, Etzel is the counterpart of King Attila the Hun, who is called Atli in Old Norse literature. (Hatto 1969; Hollander 1990)

See also *Atli, Lay of; Nibelungenlied.*

EUCHAID OLLATHAIR

Celtic myth. ***See*** *Dagda.*

EURYTUS

In the Argonaut legend, Eurytus is one of the Argonauts. Eurytus is the name of a member of the Calydonian boar hunt. In the Herakles myth, he is the father of Iole and is killed by Herakles when he refuses to allow Iole to marry. Several other men by this name are slain by Herakles as well. (Graves 1955)

See also Argonauts; Herakles.

EVANDER

In Greek mythology, Evander is the founder of a town named Pallantion after his son Pallas, who dies in the war. He entertains Herakles on his return from the conquest of Geryon. In the *Aeneid* (viii), he is a former friend of Anchises, and when Aeneas arrives in Italy, Evander offers him hospitality and assists him in conquering the Rutulians. (Graves 1955; Humphries 1951)

EVE

In Jewish, Christian, and Muslim literature, Eve is the first woman, whose creation from Adam's rib is told in Genesis. Mother of the human race, she is beguiled by the serpent to disobey Yahweh and eat the forbidden fruit of the tree of wisdom or knowledge of good and evil. According to legend, Adam convinces her to stand neck-deep in the Tigris without speaking for 37 days as penance, in hopes that God will forgive them, while Adam fasts for 40 days. Fearing that God will forgive them, Satan disguises himself as an angel and tells Eve to come out of the water at the end of 18 days. Adam recognizes Satan at once and says to Eve, "How canst thou let our adversary seduce thee again? . . ." (Genesis 2:21–3:21; Ginzberg 1992)

EZEMU

Ezemu are epics, still being sung today, of both the old kingdom of Benin and Ubulu, in modern-day Nigeria, West Africa. There are two versions of the same epic. Since the same story appears in two cultures, it is probably based upon a historical incident. According to the Ubulu version, the kings (obas) of Benin are dying of a strange malady as soon as they are crowned. Finally an oba sends an invitation to medicine men throughout the kingdom: Anyone who passes a certain test will have a chance to cure the oba; anyone who fails the test will be beheaded. When the medicine men arrive, the test is announced: "Whoever came with an osuu (sword), / Let him plant it there in the courtyard, / And if it could pierce the ground, then he had won the chance to cure him."

A certain clever man from Ubulu-Ulswu named Ezemu, who has been prepared for the task with some special herbs prepared by his brother Aniobodo, passes the test when his sword pierces a slab of stones. At once he sets about healing the oba, who rewards him with his eldest daughter, the head princess, and a page "for going to market."

The king's jealous high priest and executioner (ezomo) attacks Ezumu's party on their way back to Ubulu and absconds with the princess and the page. Ezemu continues on to Ubulu, where he casts a powerful spell by which the princess and page suddenly appear at his house, "for one never strays far from the yam he's roasting." This angers the ezomo further and ultimately results in a war between the two nations.

Benin, a three days' march away, sends several waves of troops, as well as "witches," against Ubulu. Leading only seven hunters equipped with charmed girdles, Ezemu covers the three-day distance in a twinkling and crushes 500 "Binis" on the very first day. He continues to demolish the troops until the oba must plead for peace. "We beg you . . . / The princess, and everything—take them, take them, / We have abandoned the war." Ezemu establishes a boundary between their two kingdoms at Abudu and warns them never to attack again. During the twentieth-century Nigerian civil war, according to the narration, because "Binis" killed Ubulu people, "their kings began to die" again. In fact, Oba Akensua II of Benin did die a few years after the war.

According to the Benin version of the epic, Ezemu is a powerful chief from "Obolo" who comes to Benin at the invitation of the oba and stays with the ezomo. He becomes enamored of one of the princesses, but she shuns him. When he returns to Obolo, he casts a spell that transports her to him. She continues to refuse his attentions so he digs a pit, fills it with boiling water, and threatens to throw her into it if she does not yield to him. Rather than submit, she chooses to jump into the scalding pit and die.

In retribution, the powerful oba sends his imperial army to Obolo, but it is demolished by Ezemu and his men, aided by magic. The oba sends two more expeditions against Ezemu with the same tragic results. Nothing seems to counteract Ezemu's magic.

However, previously, when he was summoned to Benin to cure a child named Agboghidi, Ezemu completed the cure by making the child impervious to magic charms and even taught him some magic. Now the oba convinces Agboghidi that it is his duty to go to Obolo to destroy the very man who once saved his life. This Agboghidi is able to do, bringing the war to an end. (Okpewho 1992)

See also Ekengbuda.

F

FAEREYINGA SAGA

This early-eleventh-century Norse saga describes the Norwegian invasions of the Faeroe Islands, which lie on the path between the Shetland Islands and Iceland. Although the islands were first settled ca. 700 by Irish monks and colonized by Vikings during the following century, they were Christianized by the king of Norway ca. 1000 and became a Norwegian province in 1035. *Faereyinga Saga* concerns the resistance by island leaders to Norwegian rule. (Jones, G. 1990)

FÁFNIR

In the *Poetic Edda* and other sources for the Sigurth (Siegfried) story, Fáfnir is the brother of Regin and son of Hreithmar, who dies, leaving the gold that Fáfnir takes to the Gnita Heath. There he transforms himself into a dragon and broods over his gold. In "The Lay of Fáfnir," Sigurth slays Regin and Fáfnir and takes the treasure. The story is also found in *Skáldskaparmál* and *Völsunga Saga.* (Hollander *Edda* 1990)

See also *Edda, Poetic;* Siegfried; *Völsunga Saga.*

FAKU

In the epic of *Emperor Shaka the Great,* Faku is the king of the Mpondo nation during the time of Shaka's reign. (Kunene 1979)

See also *Emperor Shaka the Great.*

THE FALL OF AKKAD

This ancient Akkadian epic details the decline of the dynasty of Akkad (ca. 2334–ca. 2154 B.C.) during the reign of Naram-Sin (Naramsin, r. 2254–2218 B.C.). After he subjugates the warlike Lullubi tribes, he pays tribute to his success by causing a great stela to be struck (ca. 2250) upon which he assumes the characteristics of a god. However, the tribes soon rebel and begin to ravage the empire, eventually causing its downfall. The epic blames the fall on the anger of the gods due to Naram-Sin's hubris. (Langer 1980; Pritchard 1973; Wolkstein and Kramer 1983)

See also Naramsin.

FATA MORGANA

Sister of King Arthur, legendary enchantress. *See* Morgan le Fay.

THE FATE OF THE CHILDREN OF LIR

(Oidheadh Chloinne Lir)

See The Fate of the Sons of Usnech.

THE FATE OF THE CHILDREN OF TUIREANN

(Oidheadh Chloinne Tuireann)

See The Fate of the Sons of Usnech.

THE FATE OF THE SONS OF USNECH

(Oidheadh Chloinne Uisneach; also called *The Exile of the Sons of Uisliu)*

Part of the *Ulster Cycle* of early Irish literature, this love story originated in the eighth or ninth century, but has remained in the Scottish oral tradition into the twentieth century. It is preserved in *The Book of Leinster* (ca. 1160). It describes the birth of the fair Deirdre (Derdriu) and the druid Cathub's prophecy to her mother that many men will die on her account: "In the cradle of your womb there cried out / a woman with twisted yellow hair / and beautiful grey green eyes / . . . A woman over whom there will be great slaughter. . . ." The young warriors think the child should be slain, but Conchobar says, "No, I will take her away . . . and I will rear her as I see fit, and she will be my companion." Deirdre, who grows to be the most beautiful of maidens, is reared in seclusion. No one is allowed to see her except her foster parents and a woman named Lebarcham.

One day while her father is slaying a calf in the snow, Deirdre tells Lebarcham, "I could love a man with those three colors: hair like a raven, cheeks like blood and body like snow." Lebarcham tells her that such a man is not far off. His name is Noisiu, the son of Usnech. He has a beautiful singing voice that charms the cows into giving more milk. Although King Conchobar mac Nessa falls in love with Deirdre, once she has heard Noisiu sing, her heart belongs to him. But Noisiu spurns her because of the prophecy. She leaps at him, seizing him by the ears, and demands that he take her with him. His brothers convince him that the only way to escape the prophecy is to take her away to another land. They all leave that night—150 warriors, 150 women, 150 hounds, 150 servants, and Deirdre.

The lovers eventually elope to Albu (Scotland), accompanied by Noisiu's two brothers. There they live an idyllic life, protected by the king of Alba, until the king's stewards bring him word of Deirdre's beauty. The king instructs his servants to go at night and secretly woo her on his behalf, but Deirdre informs her husband, and the brothers begin to do battle with the men of Alba. Conchobar learns of their whereabouts and lures them back to Ulster, guaranteeing their safety. But once they are back in Eriu, the sons of Usnech are slain, and Deirdre is taken to Conchobar with her hands tied behind her back. This act causes riots and bloodshed throughout Ulster, with Conchobar's son Mane and his grandson Fiachnae among the victims. To escape King Conchobar, Deirdre smashes her head against a boulder.

In the fifteenth century the story was combined with two others, *The Fate of the Children of Tuireann* (Oidheadh Chloinne Tuireann) and *The Fate of the Children of Lir* (Oidheadh Chloinne Lir), and the new version was called *The Three Sorrows of Storytelling* (Tri Truaighe Scealaigheachta). In the latter version, Deirdre spends a year living with King Conchobar before killing herself. In this version, she never smiles during that year, and whenever musicians are brought before her, she recites a poem that ends, "I have today no cause for joy / in the assembly of Emuin—throng of chieftains— / no peace, no delight, no comfort, / no great house, no fine adornments."

Whenever Conchobar attempts to comfort her, she tells him, "Break no more my heart today— / I will reach my early grave soon enough. / Sorrow is stronger than the sea. . . ." (Gantz 1988; Kinsella 1969)

See also Deirdre; *Ulster Cycle.*

FAUNA

(Also Bona Mater and Bona Dea)

In Roman mythology, Fauna is the wife of Faunus. She is the goddess of fertility, nature, and animals. After her marriage to Faunus, she never sees another man. She appears in the *Aeneid* (vii). (Humphries 1951)

FAUNUS

(Also Pan)

In Roman mythology, Faunus is the god of fertility, agriculture, and prophecy. He appears in the *Aeneid* (vii). (Humphries 1951)

FENIAN CYCLE

In Gaelic literature, this is a cycle of ballads and tales about the deeds of the legendary hero Finn (or Fionn) Mac Cumhaill (or Mac Cumhail or Mac Cool), his son Oisín (or Ossian), and his band of warriors, the Fianna Éireann. Although this elite corps of warriors gained renown under the reign of Cormac

Mac Art in the third century, and Finn was a popular hero as early as the seventh century, no written records of his exploits have survived older than the twelfth century. Some of the tales were recorded in *The Book of the Dun Cow* (Leabhar na h-Uidhre, ca. 1100) and *The Book of Leinster* (ca. 1160); however, the Fenian myths reached their highest popularity during the thirteenth century with the recording of *Colloquy of the Old Men* (or The Interrogation of the Old Men; Agallamh na Seanorach), a discussion between Oisín (Ossian) and St. Patrick.

As in the earlier *Ulster Cycle*, the chief enemy is Connaught; however, these tales are set in the provinces of Leinster and Munster, instead of Ulster.

One early Fenian tale marks the boy Finn as a hero by assigning him two of the characteristics of so many folk heroes: the states of abandonment and adoption. Finn is a hero even in his boyhood. In "Macgnimartha Finn" (The Boyish Exploits of Finn), after the Fianna chief, Cumhaill, is killed, his posthumous son is secretly reared in the forest, where his boyhood exploits earn him the appellation "the Fair," or Finn. Finn is also descended from a high-ranking druid. As he grows older, he takes vengeance against his father's killer, Goll Mac Morna. He marries the daughter of the great pagan king Cormac Mac Art, and takes over leadership of the Fianna.

Finn acquires wisdom accidentally while he is cooking a "salmon of wisdom" from Fec's Pool in the river Boyne for his druid master, Finegal. A splash of the cooking cauldron's hot liquid lands on his fingers, causing him to put them into his mouth. (A similar event appears in an old British story, in which Kai and the magician Gwyrhyr find a salmon of wisdom in the river Severn.)

Later his son, the poet Oisín (Ossian), joins the band, as does his grandson Oscar. Among the other warriors are the defeated Goll Mac Morna and the handsome young Diarmait (Dermot).

In "The Pursuit of Diarmait and Grainme," Finn, an old man but desiring a new wife, visits the king's court to ask for the hand of his daughter Grainme. But at the banquet, Grainme sees the Fianna warrior Diarmait and falls in love with him. She slips a potion to the other guests, drugging them to sleep, so that she can announce her love to Diarmait. But he refuses her advances because she is promised to Finn, until she lays a geis (spell) upon him. That night Diarmait and Grainme elope, and a furious Finn follows after them. Twice his band finds the couple and surrounds them, but both times friendly gods help the lovers escape. The Fianna are sympathetic to the couple, and eventually the lovers are brought back peacefully into the fold.

But Finn is still angry and plans secret revenge against Diarmait. He dares Diarmait to hunt and kill a wild boar and, knowing that Diarmait's only weakness is in his heel, convinces the warrior to determine the size of the pelt by walking across it barefooted. A boar bristle pierces Diarmait's vulnerable heel, and he is wounded. Finn allows him to die by refusing him water. This story is thought to be the inspiration for *Tristan and Iseult*.

The Fenian cycle gives way to the Oisinic cycle, in which Oisín shares the same mysterious genesis as other heroes. His mother, Sadb, is transformed into a deer, and when he is born, he is named "Fawn," the meaning of Oisín. When

Finn's dog finds the child in the forest, Finn recognizes his son immediately. Oisín becomes a poet and has a son, Oscar, who also joins the Fianna.

The king and the people eventually turn on the aging Finn and the Fianna, but Oisín is not among the warriors as they go into battle. The lovely fairy princess Niamh has seen him and fallen in love with him. She rises from the western sea astride her white horse and entices Oisín to return with her to Tir na n'Og (the Land of Youth). While he is gone, the Fianna are defeated by the Irish king at the Battle of Gabra, and Oisín's son Oscar is among the fatalities.

Even though his father is old and failing, Oisín remains in the Tir na n'Og for 100, or 300 years. Finally, he is overcome with longing to see his old comrades. He persuades Niamh to send him her white steed, but she warns him not to descend from the saddle. She is aware of the dangers awaiting mortals who return to their old world after such a long absence.

Oisín returns to Ireland to discover that those he knew have been dead for hundreds of years, and castles he thought were impregnable are in ruins. In one version, he sees a stone trough that he recognizes as belonging to the Fianna and gets down to examine it. The moment his foot touches the earth, he becomes a withered old man, and Niamh's horse gallops away to Tir na n'Og. In some traditions he tells St. Patrick of the deeds of the Fianna and is converted to Christianity. In others, another of Finn's followers, Caoilte, is said to have been the one to meet St. Patrick.

A Celtic belief in the reawakening of Finn, like the reawakening of Arthur, has persisted.

Another related cycle concerns Cormac Mac Art, his son Cairbre of the Liffey, and his grandfather, "Conn of the Hundred Battles." (Gantz 1988; Rutherford 1987)

See also Fionn Mac Cumhaill; Oisín.

FERONIA

Roman goddess of orchards and woods, Feronia is the mother of Eurulus, a king in Italy, to whom she gives three lives and triple arms at birth. She appears in the *Aeneid* (viii). (Humphries 1951)

FIERY VUK

This cycle of Serbo-Croatian bugarštica (fourteenth century) concerns the hero Vuk, a knight at Kosovo. The bugarštica is the oldest extant South Slavic oral ballad form.

"When Fiery Vuk and Ban Pavo of Srijem Quarreled" concerns an incident when the king of Buda sends his army off to Kosovo. They crush the Turks and capture Hasan-pasha and many Turks. Fiery Vuk, who has led the rear guard where much of the fighting has taken place, tells Pavo, who has led the main army, to take the prisoners back to Buda while he takes his army to Kupjenovac.

When Pavo returns, the king holds a feast, at which he asks, "Who crushed the Turks at Kosovo?" Pavo lies and informs the king that he crushed the Turks while Fiery Vuk betrayed him and fled to the mountains.

The king becomes angry and vows to have Vuk killed. But Mitar steals away to Kupjenovac to tell Vuk about Pavo's lies. Fiery Vuk mounts his unsaddled steed and rides off swiftly to Buda.

He finds the lords feasting at the table, and he sits at the lower end, listening as they toast one another. But they leave out the name of Fiery Vuk. Finally Vuk rises, lays his golden mace upon the table, and drinks a toast to it. He challenges the king to bring the prisoner Hasan-pasha from his cell and question him as to who actually crushed the Turks and captured him.

The king calls for the pasha to be brought before him; he promises to free the Turkish leader if he identifies the man who captured him. The pasha points to Vuk, saying, "Had he not been at Kosovo, / Long would your ladies dress in black." He adds, "Should such a hero serve our Sultan, / He'd surely make him grand vizier." He then identifies Pavo as the one who fled to the mountain.

Vuk's heart seethes with rage, and he leaps up and threatens Pavo with his mace. But the queen of Buda takes hold of his hand and pleads with him not to harm her sister's husband. Vuk complies with the queen's plea, releases Pavo, and leaves the court, taking with him a few good men.

They ride off to Kupjenovac and capture some fierce Turks, whom Vuk marches back to Buda. Some people who see him coming tell the king that Vuk is coming to attack, riding with a party of Turks.

The king rides out to meet Fiery Vuk, asking him, "What have I ever done to you / That you should ride with Turks against me?" But Fiery Vuk directs him to ready some cells because the Turks are his prisoners, whom he has brought to prove to the king which man is true and which man is false.

"When Fiery Vuk Replaced the King of Buda in a Duel and Slew His Opponent" is the story of a request made by the king of Buda to Fiery Vuk. The king, who has spent nine fruitless years besieging the walls of Vienna, sends a letter to Fiery Vuk, telling him that the Viennese Nikola Protopopić has challenged him to a duel. The king asks Fiery Vuk to rush to his aid and to fight the duel in his stead.

Fiery Vuk does not hesitate in his response. He tells his "brother sworn" Mitar Jakšić to fit out their steeds so that the two of them can ride immediately to the Vienna plain. They set out at once and, once they reach the plain, set up camp and await the appearance of Nikola.

Looking down upon the plain from the court's windows, Nikola's sister spies the youthful lords and petitions her brother, "If with God's aid you should prevail, / Do bring me one as my betrothed!"

Nikola strikes her "on her pink, white face" for daring to admire the enemy, and commands her to saddle his steed. The men meet in battle upon the Vienna plain, and Nikola quickly sees that he is outmatched. He flees, but the two Hungarians pursue him, capture him, and take him in chains to Buda's king.

The king orders that Nikola be buried to the waist and shot with arrows. When the lords of Vienna see the awful death that has befallen Nikola, they place the keys to their city upon a golden plate and send them to Buda's king. He leads his army triumphantly into the city and puts "many a lord" to death.

"The Death of Despot Vuk" and "What Fiery Vuk Ordered when He Died" are two bugarštica bearing great similarity as to content. In the former, as the despot lies on his deathbed, his wife, the lady Barbara, asks him, "To whom leave you your lands and towns, / . . . And whose will your rich treasury be, / And whose will your wretched wife? . . ." Vuk tells her that he leaves her to the Lord's care, and his lands and towns will revert to Matijaš, the king. His "brother sworn," the fine young Mitar Jakšić, enters and merrily joshes him to get up. But Vuk tells him that he cannot even turn in his bed. He instructs Mitar to divide his treasury into three parts. The first part is to be given to Mount Athos's monks, that they may pray for his soul. The second part will be the orphans' share ("wretched maidens"), that they will remember him. The third part will be his wife's. He wants his steed adorned in black and led before the king with the message, "They've always said of me, my king, / That I was born of treacherous seed, / . . . And that in battle I'd betray you; / I have, sad despot, now betrayed you, / . . . I've gone to serve a better lord, / A somewhat better lord, my God. . . ." He asks his friend Mitar to lead his other steeds to the stony gorge where there is no grass or water: "May they too know they have no master." He asks Mitar to take his wife south to Croatia, "Whereto the accursed Turks ne'er come . . ." so "that when I die, they shame me not."

In the second bugarštica, "What Fiery Vuk Ordered when He Died," when Vuk locks himself in his bedroom without a word, his wife Barbara informs his mother Vanđelina that she thinks he has brought home a slave girl. She peeks through the keyhole and sees a white fairy washing his wounds and a dragon wiping them. She tells Vanđelina what she has seen, but the fairy and dragon overhear her, and they vanish. Vuk summons his wife and chastises her: "Your poison was not in seeing the fairy, / Your poison was in telling my mother." He orders her to summon his friend Mitar, and to bring a holy monk to relieve him of his sins. Mitar hurries to the bedside of his friend, who instructs him to divide his treasure into three parts: "The first part for my sinful soul" is to go in large part to the priests with a small portion reserved for the poor. The second and third parts are to go to his aged mother and his wife. He asks Mitar to take them far off to the south, "So the accursed Turks may shame me not." He wants his steeds taken to the stony gorge, "So they may know they have no master." He wants to be buried at Mount Athos's church. He sends a message to the king, "I'm off to serve a better lord, / A better lord than you or I." Mitar carries out his wishes. (Miletich 1990)

See also *Kosovo, Battle of.*

FINNABAIR

(Also Findbhair, Findabair, and Guinevere)

In Gaelic literature, in the *Ulster Cycle,* "Cú Chulainn Cycle," *The Cattle Raid of Cooley,* and *Fled Bricrenn,* Finnabair is the daughter of Medb (Medhbh) and

Ailill, who offer her in vain as a prize to the killer of Cú Chulainn. (Gantz 1988; Kinsella 1969)

See also Cú Chulainn; Medb; *Ulster Cycle.*

FINNSBURH, THE FIGHT AT

This Old English fragment of a lost, longer poem recounts another version of the Finnsburh episode found in *Beowulf.* In this version, the young Danish king Hnaef, having already survived a few battles with the Frisians, is attacked by them again while he is inside Finnsburh hall. He calls his noble champions Siegferth and Eaha to guard the door. The Frisians Ordlaf, Gulthlaf, and Hengest try to force the door. Guthere (possibly Gulthlaf's brother) urges Gulthlaf's son Garulf not to join the fray, but the latter ignores the warning. Inside the hall the Danescan hear "the noise of deadly slaughter." The first to die is the young Garulf. Many others die as a raven circles overhead. Lights flash from swords as if all Finnsburh is afire. None of the Danes are killed in their five-day fight to hold the door. (Alexander, M. 1991)

See also *Beowulf.*

FIONN MAC CUMHAILL

(Also Finn Mac Cool and Finn mac Cumhail)

This legendary Irish hero descended from druid aristocracy is believed to have been based on a historical person. According to legend, after he tastes the salmon of knowledge, which has fed on the hazelnuts of wisdom, he possesses great wisdom. In the service of the high Jara king, he organizes the Fianna Éireann, or Fenians. His first wife Sedh is the mother of their son, the poet Oisín (Ossian). His second wife Grainme, with his kinsman Diarmait, betrays him. (Rutherford 1987)

See also *Fenian Cycle.*

FJÖRGYN

(Also Jörd and Hlódyn)

In Old Norse mythology, Fjörgyn is the giantess consort of Óthin (Odin) and mother of Thor. She is also associated with the Lithuanian thunder god Perkūnas, whose thunderclap "unlocks the earth" and makes her fecund. (Jones, G. 1990)

See also Óthin.

FLOIRE ET BLANCHEFLOR

This medieval romance in verse (ca. 1170) is thought to be from an older source, in which the Saracen prince Floire of Spain is in love with Blancheflor, a Christian sold into slavery at the instigation of Floire's parents. He finds her in a tower awaiting service in the sultan's harem. He hides in a basket of flowers to reach and rescue her. (Siepmann 1987)

FLOOD, GREAT
(Also "World Flood")

This oral tale of the Shipibo Incans of Peru is still being sung today about the Ŝhetebo, precursors of the Shipibo in the area of the lower Ucayali River basin. Because of the greed and envy of the Ŝhetebo, and particularly because they have buried the baquē mëraya (child, highest class of shaman) son of the Inca god, they are punished by drowning in the Great Flood, or the World Flood. When they are gone, the Shipibo move into their territory. In reality, the Ŝhetebo were almost entirely wiped out by the introduction of European disease. (Hill 1988)

See also Flood Myths.

FLOOD MYTHS

A widespread theme in traditional epics is the destruction of the world by flood and the survival of one human or family by the grace of a benevolent god. The most well-known flood narrative in the West, that of Noah told in the Old Testament Book of Genesis (chapters 6–9), is based on the Babylonian *Epic of Gilgamesh* tale of Utnapishtim, which itself is taken from the Sumerian legend of Ziusudra, preserved only in part. In China, Nü Kua, a mythical empress and sister to the mythical emperor Fu Hsi (the Chinese equivalent of Adam) is, like the Babylonian Ishtar, opposed to destroying mankind. When the demons of water and fire, aided by rebel generals of her empire, set out to destroy the world, she wages war on them. Her campaign is a success, but not before a giant warrior partially destroys the heavens by bumping his head against one of the four pillars holding it aloft, causing a flood on earth. The empress uses charred reeds to stem the waters, funnels them to the sea, then rebuilds the pillar, and places a tortoise (Atlas) under it. According to Chinese chronology, this flood occurred between 2943 B.C. and 2868 B.C.

In Japan, the story of Nü Kwa becomes the story of Jakwa. The Ainu of Japan also have a deluge myth in which only a few escape by climbing to a mountaintop when waters cover the earth. The Hittite Noah is Ullush. In Greek legend, when Zeus sends the deluge, Deucalion, the king of Phthia, builds a ship, and he and his wife are the only ones saved. The ship comes to rest on Mount Parnassus, and the oracle Themis instructs them to cast the bones of mother earth behind them in order to replenish the race. The two cast stones from the mountain as directed, those thrown by Deucalion becoming men and those thrown by Pyrrha becoming women. The Indian version as told in Shatapatha-Brahmana has Manu being warned by a great fish. The fish counsels Manu that it will save him if he prepares a ship and boards it on a specified date. When the waters come, Manu boards the boat, and the fish appears and ties a rope to the ship's horn. The fish then swims to a mountaintop where

Manu is directed to tie up to a tree. The *Popol Vuh* of the Mayas describes the flood as a method God uses to erase the mistake of his own creation of a race of mortals made of wood who have no minds, souls, or hearts. *The Book of the Hopi* tells how the first world is destroyed by fire, the second by ice. When the third world, Kuskurza, becomes corrupt, Sotuknang tells Spider Woman he will destroy the world with water. She seals the good people inside reeds, to save them. The Vietnamese, in the cycle of *Lac Long Quang and Au Co,* have a story about "A War between Gods," set in the reign of the first royal dynasty of Vietnam. In a confrontation between Son Tinh (Mountain Spirit) and Thuy Tinh (Water Spirit), Son Tinh, a son of the dragon king Lac Long Quang and the fairy queen Au Co, wins the hand of the beautiful princess, My Nuong. His rival, Thuy Tinh, corrals the waters from the sky and the ocean and raises the water level to the mountaintops. But Son Tinh lives on the top of Mount Tan Vien (the Olympus of Vietnamese myth), and so he escapes the devastation. It is said that each year Thuy Tinh again tries to take the princess by causing monsoons.

See also *Atrakhasis, Myth of; Deucalion's Flood;* Flood, Great; Flood of Ogyges; *Lac Long Quang and Au Co;* Nu Kua; *Popol Vuh.*

FLOOD OF DEUCALION

See *Deucalion's Flood.*

FLOOD OF OGYGES

This is one of three floods described by ancient Greeks. The other two are the flood that destroyed Atlantis, described by Plato in the *Timaeus and Critias,* and the flood of Deucalion and Pyrrha, best described in book II of Ovid's *The Metamorphoses.* The flood of Ogyges, as described by the Christian chronicler Julius Africanus, occurs during the time of Ogyges, legendary king of Thebes in Boeotia. According to Julius, "Ogyges . . . who was saved when many perished, lived at the time of the Exodus of the people from Egypt, along with Moses." (Heinberg 1989)

See also Flood Myths.

FOMÓRIANS

(Also Fomóri)

In Gaelic literature, Fomórians are a mysterious and malevolent race of giants led by their chief, Balar, who conquer Partholonian Ireland and then the Nemeds in prehistoric times. From time to time thereafter, the Fomórians come from the sea on raiding parties. The Túatha Dé Danann, like the Partholonians and Nemeds after them, must meet the Fomórians in battle. Scholars believe that the First Battle of Mag Tuireadh may have been a historical occurrence.

When the Túatha bard Coipre visits the Fomórian tyrant Bress and is treated rudely, he leaves, singing the first glam (curse) uttered in Ireland. As a result, the king breaks out in spots and, no longer unblemished, is forced to abdicate. At this time, the handsome god Lugh the Many-Skilled presents himself to the battle-maimed Túatha king Noada.

Meanwhile, Bress is dazzled by a light from the west at dawn and is told by his druid priests that the sun has risen in the west; that it is "the radiance of the face of Lugh." It is Lugh who slaughters 18 Fomórian tax collectors, leaving nine to carry the news back to their leaders. The Second Battle of Mag Tuireadh follows, in which the Fomórians are routed. The Fomórians are also mentioned in the *Destruction of Da Derga's Hostel* and in an anonymous poem, "To the Earl of Argyll before the Battle of Flodden." (Chadwick 1976)

FORNALDAR SAGA

This class of Old Icelandic saga dealing with the adventures of Germanic heroes takes place in Europe before the settlement of Iceland. The sagas are of later date than the Icelandic sagas, but they are thought to be rooted in an earlier oral tradition. The most important is the *Völsunga Saga,* the story of Sigurd, also told in the German epic *Nibelungenlied.* (Jones, G. 1990)

FÓSTBRAEÐA SAGA

(Also *Blood-Brothers' Saga)*

This Icelandic saga (early thirteenth century) contrasts two brothers. One is a ruthless killer; the other, a poet and lover who sets out to find adventure and becomes the favored of the king and his daughter. (Jones, G. 1961)

LE FRESNE

("The Ash Tree")

Lay (ca. late twelfth century) by Marie de France, based by her own account on oral tradition: a Celtic tale originally sung by Breton minstrels. Marie was the first to put her collection of lays into form: the octosyllabic couplet.

"Le Fresne" concerns the fate of a young girl who is abandoned at birth. Her mother slanders the wife of a neighboring knight because the woman has given birth to twin sons (according to popular belief, two children indicate two fathers). When she herself gives birth to twin girls, she realizes that people will believe she is guilty of the same adulterous behavior of which she has accused her neighbor. She decides to murder one of the babies because, "I'd rather make that up to God / than live in shame and dishonor." But one of her attendants volunteers to take the baby to a distant monastery instead.

The baby is wrapped in a fine silk cover from Constantinople, and a gold-and-ruby ring is tied to her finger. The attendant takes her to the monastery gate and places her in the fork of an ash tree for safety. A porter discovers her and gives her to the abbess, who decides to rear the child as her niece. She names her Fresne (Ash) because she has been found in an ash tree.

When Fresne grows up, she is the most beautiful girl in the region. A young lord named Gunrun falls in love with her and becomes a benefactor of the abbey so as to have an excuse to see her regularly. Eventually he persuades her to become his lover, and then he convinces her to come live with him, so that if she becomes pregnant, the abbess will not find out. She takes along her two possessions—the silk cover and the ring—and goes to his castle as his mistress.

At length his knights begin to urge him to get rid of his mistress and marry a noblewoman so that he can produce a suitable heir. They suggest that he marry Codre (Hazel), the daughter of a noble knight of the region. No one knows that Codre is Fresne's twin sister.

Fresne is hidden away while Gunrun prepares to become betrothed to Codre. Fresne does not sulk, but continues to serve him and to be courteous to his knights. When Codre and her mother arrive, the mother is troubled by the presence of a mistress. She wants Fresne expelled at once. However, her attitude changes when she sees how courteously Fresne serves the bride-to-be. The mother even begins to love and admire Fresne.

On the night when the archbishop is coming to bless the newlyweds in bed, Fresne spreads her own silk coverlet on the bed because she thinks the other cover does not look grand enough for the occasion. When the mother sees the coverlet, she recognizes it and calls for an explanation from Fresne. Fresne tells her story of being found at the monastery and produces the gold-and-ruby ring. Full of remorse, the mother faints. Later she sends for her husband so that she can confess to him her terrible sin. He informs Gunrun and the archbishop, who agrees to annul the marriage and to marry Gunrun and Fresne the next day. The father divides his inheritance between his daughters. Later Codre makes a rich marriage as well. (Hanning and Ferrante 1978)

FREYJA

(Also Freya, Frea, Frigg, Frija, Frigg, Frige, Mardoll, Horn, Gefn, and Syr)

Freyja is the Norse goddess of love, fecundity, battle, and death; she is the counterpart of Frey (Freyr), god of peace and fertility. She is the daughter of the fertility god Njörd and the wife of Óthin (Odin), with whom she shares the victims of battle. She may take half of the slain heroes to her great hall in the Folkvangar, while Óthin takes the other half to Valhalla. Her famous necklace, Brisinga men, is stolen by the trickster god Loki, but the watchman Heimdall retrieves it. Freyja rides in a chariot drawn by two cats, or on the back of a boar with golden bristles, or else flies with the wings of a falcon. She teaches witchcraft to the Aesir, which is what the race of gods was called. Because she loves jewelry more than him, Óthin leaves her for Frigga, who in Teutonic mythology is the same as Freyja. Her children are Gersemi and Hnoss. (Jones, G. 1990)

Accompanied by two cats, a lithe Freyja, Norse goddess of love, picks an apple in this 1910 illustration by Arthur Rackham.

FREYR

(Also Frey)

The Scandinavian god of fertility, peace, and rain, Freyr is the son of the fertility god Njörd and counterpart of Freyja. He is the husband of Gerda (Gerd), daughter of the giant Gymir. He was originally one of the tribe of Vanir, but after a war with the Aesir he becomes one of them. He possesses a magic ship, *Skithbathnir,* that can be folded up, a golden helmet, and a famous horse, Bloody Hoof (Blodighofi). (Jones, G. 1990)

FU HSI

(Also Fu Hsia, Fu Hi, Pao Hsi, Mi Hsi, and T'ai Hao)

In Chinese mythology, Fu Hsi is the first emperor, "the Adam of China," born as a divine serpent in 29 B.C. His wife or sister is Nü Kua, who is depicted with him on a stone tablet dated A.D. 160. (Graham 1970; Mackenzie 1990)

See also Hwang Ti; Shen Nung.

FU HSING

In Chinese mythology, Fu Hsing is the Star God of Happiness, sometimes identified historically with the sixth-century mandarin Yang Ch'eng. Star gods and dragons were fathers of many famous Chinese kings. (Mackenzie 1990)

FUTŪḤ IFRĪQIYYA

(The Conquest of North Africa)

This popular folk epic in Tunisia recounts the adventures of a local hero, 'Abd Allāh ibn Ja'far, and the second conquest of Tunis (1054) by the Arab tribes of Banī (Beni) Hilāl and Banī (Beni) Sulaim. Traditionally the epic has been performed in coffeehouses by professional rāwīs (reciters) and shu'arā (poets), as well as at private parties or festivals celebrating a birth or marriage. (Connelly 1986)

See also 'Abd Allāh ibn Ja'far.

G

GAEA

(Also Ge, Gaia, Tellus, and Terra)

In Greek mythology, Gaea is the most ancient divinity, Mother Earth. She appears in the *Aeneid,* the *Homeric Hymns,* and in Hesiod's *Theogony.* After Chaos, Gaea appears and bears Uranus, Father Sky, who covers the earth. She then mates with her son to produce the Titans, the first race, consisting of six males and six females. They also produce the Cyclops, Centimani, and Giants. Gaea has other offspring by other mates. (Humphries 1951; Lattimore 1959)

See also *Aeneid; Theogony.*

GAJAH MADA

He was the prime minister (fourteenth century) of the Javanese Majapahit empire, a national hero given credit for unifying the entire archipelago of Indonesia. He plays a leading role in later sections of the epic *Nāgarakertāgama* (1365) by the poet Prapanca, who describes his military exploits against Bali and Sundra, Sumatra, and Borneo. Although sections of the epic pertain to the reign of Prapanca's religious idol Kertanagara, who lived long before his time and thus whose exploits may have been drawn from oral sources, the poet was a contemporary of Gajah Mada, and those sections of the epic are freer of nonhistoric elements. (Preminger 1990)

GALAHAD, SIR

In later (ca. thirteenth century) Arthurian legend, Sir Galahad is the illegitimate son of Sir Launcelot du Lac and Princess Elaine the Fair of Astolat. As the last descendant of Joseph of Arimathea, he is the purest and noblest knight of the Round Table, able to trace his lineage back to the House of David, and thus the only knight qualified to sit in the Siege Perilous (the Perilous Seat, so called because any but the purest knight who dares sit in it is doomed to death) and to undertake the quest for the Holy Grail. He heals the holy relic's guardian, the Fisher King, of the wound from the same spear that wounded Jesus and restores fertility to the king's realm. When he finally uncovers the chalice in Sarras, he renounces the world and his own life. His story appears in the

This Dogon carving, collected in the West African country of Mali, honors a female ancestor who may represent the oldest of deities, that of Mother Earth, known as Gaea in Greek mythology.

"Queste del Saint Graal," which forms part of the *Prose Launcelot*, or *Vulgate Cycle*, as well as in Malory's *Morte d'Arthur.* (Barber 1961)

See also Arthurian Legend; Lancelot, Sir.

GALATEA
(Also Galathaea)

In the *Aeneid* (ix), Galatea is a daughter of Nereus and Doris, beloved by the Cyclops Polyphemus, whom she spurns for Acis, son of Faunus. The rejected Polyphemus discovers the couple hiding nearby while he sings of his love, and he crushes Acis with a rock.

Galatea is also the name of Pygmalion's statue, with which he falls in love; he asks Aphrodite to give it life. (Humphries 1951)

See also *Aeneid.*

G!!AMAMA
(Also Kwammang-a)

Trickster deity of the G/wi people of the Kalahari in South Africa, G!!amama is less powerful than the creator-god N!adima. G!!amama occasionally initiates malevolent "tricks" against man by sending invisible splinters of magic wood against him. Since N!adima cannot be communicated with and will not change the order he has set up, the G/wi cannot pray for him to intervene against G!!amama's hurtful deeds; however, they can be counteracted by certain methods that N!adima ordained at the time of creation, leaving the people to uncover them with time. Among these methods are herb potions and ceremonial dances. (Radin 1973)

GAMBUSHE

In the Zulu epic *Emperor Shaka the Great,* Gambushe is king of the Mpondos. (Kunene 1979)

See also *Emperor Shaka the Great.*

GAMELYN, THE TALE OF
(Also "The Cook's Tale of Gamelyn")

An anonymous metrical romance of 450 rhymed couplets in Middle English, based on English folklore. Gamelyn, youngest of three sons of Sir John of Boundys, is deprived of his share of the inheritance by his eldest brother. After a number of attempts to reclaim it, he retreats to the forest and becomes the leader of a band of outlaws. His second brother tries to help him but is shackled in chains. Eventually Gamelyn overthrows his wicked brother and all his cohorts, and regains his rightful lands. The poem's similarity to the Robin Hood ballads is apparent. Thomas Lodge adapted the story in his 1590 romance "Rosalynde," as did Chaucer in his unfinished "Cook's Tale" of *The Canterbury*

Tales. It also served as a prime source for Shakespeare's *As You Like It.* (Siepmann 1987)

GANELON

(Also Gan of Mayence and Gano of Maganza)

In *Chanson de Roland,* Ganelon is a traitor among Charlemagne's paladins, responsible for the defeat at Roncesvalles. He appears in both Boiardo's *Orlando Innamorato* and Ariosto's *Orlando Furioso,* as well as Pulci's *Morgante Maggiore.* The archetypical traitor, he is cited by Chaucer in *The Nun's Priest's Tale* and by Dante in *Inferno.* (Harrison 1970; Siepmann 1987)

See also *Chanson de Roland;* Olivier; Roland.

GAṆEŚA

(Also Ganesha and Ganapati)

In Hindu mythology, Gaṇeśa is the elephant-headed god of learning and letters, son of Śiva and Pārvatī. In the epic *Mahābhārata,* he is the scribe to whom the sage Vyāsa dictates the epic. He is inadvertently beheaded at the orders of his jealous father, who mistakes him for a lover of his wife. Śiva promises to restore his son by giving him the head of the first living creature he sees, which happens to be an elephant. Gaṇeśa is displayed in foyers of private homes and in temples as a patron of good fortune. (Buck 1981; O'Flaherty 1975)

GARETH, SIR

In Arthurian legend, Sir Gareth is a knight of the Round Table. In one story, Gareth is killed accidentally by Sir Launcelot during Launcelot's attempt to rescue Queen Guinevere from death at the stake. Gareth's brother attempts to avenge his death and the result is the eventual end of King Arthur's court. (Barber 1961)

See also Arthurian Legend; Guinevere; Lancelot, Sir.

GARUḌA

In the *Ṛg Veda,* Garuḍa, "the devourer," is the bird (eagle) who carries the god Viṣṇu. He is the son of Kaśyapa and Vinatā and the younger brother of Arjuna, charioteer of the sun god Sūrya. He is identified with fire and the sun and is the enemy of serpents. In the *Bhāgavata-Purāṇa,* Vinatā is his wife. When his mother is held prisoner by her co-wife and the wife's serpent-sons, Garuḍa negotiates her release by obtaining for the sons (nagas) the amrta (Soma, or ambrosia), or elixir of immortality, from heaven. On his return, he meets Viṣṇu, who asks to ride on his shoulders. Garuḍa agrees to be his bearer. (O'Flaherty 1981)

See also *Ṛg Veda;* Viṣṇu.

GASSIRE'S LUTE

This is a portion of the longer *Dausi Epic* (ca. 500 B.C.) of the Soninke people, now living in north-central Africa in an area of the Sahel called Faraka.

The epic begins with an explanation about the goddess Wagadu, who "is not of stone, not of wood, not of earth," but is "the strength that lives in the hearts of men." Sometimes she is visible because eyes see her, and "ears hear the clash of swords and ring of shields." However, sometimes she is invisible because "the indomitability of man has overtired her, so that she sleeps." Four times she has appeared: as Dierra, Agada, Ganna, and then Silla. Four times she has slept. Sleep came the first time through vanity, the second through falsehood, the third through greed, and the fourth through dissension. Wagadu sleeps now. If she should ever come again, "She will live so forcefully in the minds of men that she will never be lost again, so forcefully that vanity, falsehood, greed, and dissension will never be able to harm her."

This story takes place while Wagadu is called Dierra. The king, Nganamba Fasa, is growing old. For years the Fasa people have been fighting against the Burdama, a warrior tribe, and the Boroma, whom the Fasa consider their inferiors. Nganamba's son, Gassire, is himself already growing old: He has eight grown sons with children of their own. He is not satisfied just having his deeds praised by heroes; he longs for his father's death so that he can become king. He wants to carry his father's shield and sword. He watches for the death of his father "as a lover watches for the evening star to rise." His rage, discontent, and longing mount daily. He cannot sleep. A jackal gnaws at his heart.

One night he gets out of bed and goes to consult Kiekorro, an old wise man, who informs him, "Nganamba will die, but will not leave you his sword and shield. You will carry a lute. . . . But your lute shall cause the loss of Wagadu." Gassire rages at Kiekorro, but the old man only tells him, ". . . your path will lead you to the partridges in the fields, you will understand what they say. . . ."

Gassire is so frustrated and angry that the next day he orders the other heroes to stay behind so that he can do battle alone against the Burdama. He fights so fiercely that the Burdama drop their spears and flee. Gassire commands the others to gather up the spears, and they all ride triumphantly back to the city, singing of Gassire's great deeds.

Gassire lets the women bathe him and minister to him. As usual, the men gather in a circle to tell war stories, but Gassire does not join them. Instead, he goes to the fields, where he hears partridges singing. One sings, "All creatures must die. . . . Kings and heroes die, are buried and rot. . . . But the *Dausi,* the song of my battles, shall not die. It shall be sung again . . . and outlive all kings and heroes. . . . Wagadu will be lost. But the *Dausi* shall endure. . . ."

Gassire returns to the wise man and tells him, "The partridge boasted that the song of its deeds would live longer than Wagadu. . . . Tell me whether men also know the *Dausi* and whether the *Dausi* can outlive life and death?" The wise man sees that Gassire is driven by vanity. He says, ". . . you are hastening to your end. No one can stop you. . . ." He tells Gassire that he will be a bard.

Still consumed by the desire to be remembered forever, Gassire says, "Wagadu can go to hell!"

He goes to a smith and orders a lute made. The smith says, "I will, but the lute will not sing." As he predicts, when the lute is finished, it does not sing. The smith explains, "This is a piece of wood. It cannot sing if it has no heart." He advises Gassire to carry the lute into battle so that it can absorb blood, breath, pain, fame. "But," he warns, "Wagadu will be lost because of it." Again Gassire says, "Wagadu can go to hell!"

With his lute on his back, Gassire takes his eldest son into battle against the Burdama, explaining, "You and I . . . will . . . live on and endure before all other heroes in the *Dausi.*" The two fight bravely, but the son is killed by a spear. Gassire picks up his body and carries it home on his back. After the son is buried, Gassire strikes the lute, which has caught some of his son's blood. Still it does not sing. Filled with anger, he calls his other sons into battle.

For seven days he rides into battle, each day with a different son. Each day one of his sons is killed, and he carries the bloody body home on his back, with the blood dripping onto the lute.

Finally the men of Dierra tell him they have had enough senseless fighting. They order him to take his slaves (Boroma tribesmen) and his cattle and leave. "The rest of us incline more to life than to fame. . . . We have no wish to die for fame alone." The wise man says, ". . . thus will Wagadu be lost today for the first time."

Gassire takes his last and youngest son, his wives, and his Boroma out into the desert, through the Sahel into the Sahara. One night the lute begins to sing, telling the story of the great deeds of the *Dausi.* Gassire's rage melts and he weeps. At that moment, in the city of Dierra, King Nganamba dies, and at that moment Wagadu disappears.

That was the first time Wagadu disappeared. When she comes for the fifth time, she will be "as enduring as the rain in the south and as the rocks of the Sahara." Every man will have "Wagadu in his heart" and every woman will have "Wagadu in her womb." (Abrahams 1983; Frobenius and Fox 1983)

G//AUNAB

(Also //Gaunab)

Khoikhoi, G//aunab is the deity of death, disease, and calamity. In the Khoikhoi creation cycle, he appears as the adversary of the great creator-god Tsuni-g//oab. (Parrinder 1982; Peires 1982; Sproul 1991)

See also Tsuni-g//oab.

GAWAIN, SIR

(Also Gwalchmei, Walgainus, and Galvaginus)

In earliest Arthurian legend (ca. twelfth century), he is a knight of the Round Table, kinsman of King Arthur, and probable hero of the original stories of the

Grail quest. He is depicted as noble, religious, decent, humble, compassionate, and courteous. He appears in the Welsh *Triads* and in the *Mabinogion* as the solar deity Gwalchmei. Geoffrey of Monmouth's twelfth-century *Historia regum Britanniae* relates that he was King Arthur's ambassador to Rome. Gawain appears in Chrétien de Troyes's twelfth-century verse romances and in the thirteenth-century *Vulgate Cycle.* Two fourteenth-century English works, *The Alliterative Morte d'Arthur* and *Sir Gawain and the Green Knight,* retell the older tale of the beheading challenge. (Barber 1961; Stone, B. 1974)

See also Arthurian Legend; *Sir Gawain and the Green Knight.*

GAYOMART

(Also Gayo Maretan)

In Zoroastrianism, Gayomart is the first man. During the period before the time of man, Gayomart's spirit and that of the primeval ox live for 3,000 years until the evil spirit Ahriman decides to invade creation. Then Ahura Mazda, the supreme god, creates Gayomart as man and places within him and the ox seeds from fire. Ahriman and his devils eventually destroy Gayomart. His body becomes the minerals of the earth, and the seed of his body becomes the gold from which the human race springs. At the time of the resurrection, Gayomart's bones will be the first to rise. (Olmstead 1948; Zaehner 1955)

GEB

(Also Keb and Seb)

In Egyptian religion, Geb is the god of earth who supports the world. With his sister/mate Nut, he is the second generation in Heliopolis's *Ennead.* Egyptian mythology pictures Geb as the third divine pharaoh. (Budge 1969)

GELLERT

In the Welsh tale of "Prince Llewellyn the Great," Gellert is the prince's hound who in 1205 is entrusted with the mission of guarding the prince's infant son. When a wolf attempts to steal the child, Gellert kills the wolf. When the prince returns, he believes that his dog has killed and eaten the child, and he stabs Gellert to death. Later the prince discovers the baby unharmed beneath his cradle, lying beside the corpse of the wolf. He honors Gellert with a burial on Mount Snowdon and names the site Beddgelert, meaning "Grave of Gellert." The same legend appears throughout Europe and the Middle East, and is a late version of the ancient Indian tale that is recounted in the Sanskrit *Pañcatantra.* (Siepmann 1987)

GENDEYANA

(Also Ngendeyana)

In the Zulu epic *Emperor Shaka the Great,* Gendeyana is Shaka's stepfather on the Qwabe side of his family. He is the father of Ngwadi, Shaka's favorite brother. (Kunene 1979)

See also *Emperor Shaka the Great.*

GENGHIS KHAN

(Also Ghenghiz-khan and Jenghiz-khan)

As Jenghiz-khan, he is the hero of the Mongols celebrated in the *Secret History of the Mongols.* (Grousset 1970)

See also *Secret History of the Mongols.*

GESAR'S SAGA

(Also *Kesar Saga* and *Gesser Khan)*

This is a Tibetan epic tale of Gesar, magical king of Ling. As the *Kesar Saga,* it is the national epic of the kingdom of Ladakh as well. The epic can be traced to the eleventh century.

When Gesar is born high in the Amnye Machin mountain kingdom of Ling in Tibet, he lies in the arms of his mother Gogmo, opens his eyes, and says, "Mother, I am Gesar, the Lion King."

Many years before, the old king of Ling vanished while on a pilgrimage, and powerful lords divided the land. Some rule wisely, but one—the evil Lord Trotun—plunders the land and makes the people miserable.

Gogmo knows of an ancient prophecy about a magical child who will become Ling's greatest king. She fears Trotun will hear of her child, so she tries to hide him. But the mischievous Gesar escapes her watchful eye time and again.

One day he encounters Trotun and his men on the road. The wicked lord commands his warriors to throw the child aside, but Gesar's magic holds them fast. The child tells Trotun, "I will be your master and your king."

Trotun, who also remembers the prophecy, plots to get rid of Gesar. He visits a sorcerer, Ratna the Evil, and bribes him to destroy Gesar. But the sorcerer's magic fails. So Trotun tells his nobles that Gesar is possessed of an evil spirit and must be forced to leave the country. The nobles obey, and drive Gesar and his mother from the land.

For many days they travel through treacherous mountains and wild, desolate land. At last they reach the land of the North. During their exile there, Gesar challenges the ghostly monsters who are responsible for storms and rock slides. Eventually he convinces them to work for the good of mankind.

Meanwhile, growing up in Ling is a beautiful girl named Brougmo, of whom even Gesar has heard. He is among the many who hope to make her his bride someday.

He is told in a dream that his time to return to Ling has arrived. He transforms himself into a raven and flies to Trotun's tent, where he informs the wicked lord that a horse race must be held to decide who will be the future ruler of Ling, who will receive the kingdom's treasures, and who will marry Brougmo. Trotun is so sure he will win that he arranges the race.

That night Brougmo has a dream in which a handsome young man introduces himself as King Gesar. The next day one of the nobles, Lord Changpa, tells her that before the race begins, she must travel to the north, find Gesar, and bring him back to contend in the race.

Brougmo travels for two weeks until she comes to Gesar's tent. She becomes irritated when Gesar balks at returning with her and calls him a lazy scoundrel. "I'm pretty enough to find some other prince!" He transforms her beautiful clothes into rags, and immediately she understands the lesson he is teaching her about her pride. Her beauty will one day fade; only her good heart and good deeds will remain untouched.

They set off toward Ling on Brougmo's horse. Soon they see a fine horse, Kyanshay, which Gesar has already tried to tame. When Brougmo calls to the horse, it answers, "Gesar . . . will have to find some other steed. I have been wild too long. . . ." But Brougmo sings a beguiling song to the horse, and it comes docilely to receive a lasso from Gesar's mother Gogmo. Then the horse leaps into the sky and flies away with Gogmo on its back. But Brougmo sweetly calls him back, and gives the horse to Gesar, who does not offer a word of thanks.

They arrive at the race, and Gesar, wearing golden armor, wins it with his magical horse. Gesar receives the homage of the hero, Lord Changpa, and after giving the evil Trotun a jewel, he distributes the rest of the treasure among the people of Ling. He gathers his bride in his arms and the two embark on a long life of adventures together as Gesar brings peace, harmony, and enlightenment to his kingdom. (Gretchen 1990; Schmidt 1927; Wallace 1991)

See also *Kesar Saga.*

GESTE DE HAM-BODEDIO

(Also *Hama le Rouge)*

This is a West African Fula epic about the people of Hambodedjo or Ham-Bodedio. The people of Hamina or Hamana are descendants of Manden Bukari from Sundiata's family.

The Hamana version of the *Epic of Sundiata* differs on certain points; for example, on Soumaoro's end. According to the Hamana version, as Soumaoro is pursued by Sundiata, he evokes his protective jinn, asking them to keep him from being captured by Sundiata. So he is transformed into stone on the mountain of Koulikoro. (Westley *RAL* 1991)

See also *La Guerre entre Ndje Farah Ndje et Hambodedjo; Hambodjo; Sundiata, Epic of.*

LE GESTE DE SEGOU

Mandinkan epic. *See Bambara Epic.*

GHOṢĀ

In the *Ṛg Veda,* in "The Courtship of Ghoṣā" (10.40), Ghoṣā is the hymn's author. She invokes the Aśvins (Horsemen, twin sons of the Sun, physicians) to assist her in finding a husband, not only because they are known to be rescuers of men, the most helpful gods, but also because they appreciate beauty. Ghoṣā reminds the gods of the many people they have helped in the past, including Siñjara, to whom they restored virility. The hymn refers to the wife of an impotent man as a "widow." She describes the ideal marriage, where "plants wafting magic powers have sprouted and flow . . . as rivers flow to a valley." She asks them to bless her future husband: "Grant to the eloquent wealth and strong sons." (O'Flaherty 1981)

See also Ṛg Veda.

GHUL

In ancient Arabic folklore and in pre-Islamic Arabic poetry, particularly in the Bedouin and Berber traditions, the ghul is an evil class of jinn (spirits), usually considered as female, who stalk and eat desert travelers. The word entered the English language as "ghoul," meaning a grave-robber who feeds on corpses. (Bushnaq 1986)

GIKUYU

(Also *Kikuyu)*

This creation cycle of myths of the Gikuyu people of Kenya, East Africa, is still being performed today. In the beginning, the Divider of the Universe makes a great mountain, Keré Nyaga (Mount Kenya), the "mountain of Brightness" or mystery, upon which to rest himself. It is his earthly dwelling place. He cannot be seen, but people pray to him there.

One story says that God has three sons who are the ancestors of the Gikuyu, Masai, and Kamba tribes. He offers his sons the choice of a spear, bow, and digging stick. Masai takes the spear and is instructed to tend herds on the plains. Kamba takes the bow and is sent to hunt game in the forest. Gikuyu takes the digging stick and learns agriculture.

Another story says that God takes Gikuyu to the top of Keré Nyaga and shows him the landscape, pointing out a place in the middle where fig trees grow; he tells Gikuyu that it is his home. When Gikuyu reaches the spot, he discovers a beautiful woman, Moombi (Molder and Creator), who becomes his wife and bears nine daughters. Gikuyu loves his daughters, but he grieves because he has no sons. He goes to Keré Nyaga and asks for God's help. God instructs him to sacrifice a lamb and a kid under a fig tree near his house, pour the fat and blood on the tree's trunk, and offer the meat to God as a burnt offering from all the family. Gikuyu and his family do as they are told, and when they return after the sacrificial offering, they find nine young men there. Gikuyu offers them his daughters in marriage on the condition that they all live under his roof, under a system of matriarchal descent. The young men agree.

All the Gikuyu live together under the family, or tribal, name of the mother, Moombu. When the parents die, each daughter receives a share of the estate. When the number of family members becomes too great, each of the nine daughters makes a clan of her own, named for herself. The women practice polyandry, having several husbands each. The men suffer, and are often jealous and unfaithful. For their infidelities, they are punished and humiliated regularly.

The men begin to plot secretly about revolting against the women, who are very strong and good fighters. The men decide to make all the women pregnant. Only when the women become heavy are the men able to revolt and overcome their pregnant wives. Now men become the heads of the clans. They abolish polyandry and institute polygamy. They change the tribal name from Moombi to Gikuyu. But when they try to change the clan names, the women threaten to kill all the male children, and to refuse to bear any more children. The men yield, so the clans still bear women's names.

As the clans grow, the Gikuyu expand into the forest, but they find it inhabited by Pygmies, who live underground in caves and tunnels they have dug. The Gikuyu think the little people are musicians who can disappear at will. In time they leave the forest, still telling tales of the little people living underground. (Parrinder 1982)

GILGAMESH

Gilgamesh is a hero of five poems in the Sumerian language and of the Babylonian epic entitled *Epic of Gilgamesh.* The works were probably based on the Gilgamesh who ruled at Uruk (Erech) in southern Mesopotamia during the first half of the third millennium B.C., a contemporary of Agga, ruler of Kish. Gilgamesh is a unique figure in traditional epics in that his character changes with events. His is not merely the story of heroic adventures, it is a philosophical journey as well.

As a young ruler of Uruk, Gilgamesh is filled with lust and ambition and is not very popular with his subjects. After his wrestling match with Enkidu, a primal figure, he becomes a more caring ruler. He and his friend undertake many adventures together. He values Enkidu's friendship such that, when Enkidu dies, Gilgamesh tries to bring him back to life. He even traverses the ocean of death in an effort to learn the secret to eternal life. He meets Utnapishtim, who describes to him the great deluge that wipes out civilization but which he and his family escape by building an ark. Now Utnapishtim and his wife have been granted immortality, but it is a gift that can come only from

Gilgamesh, hero of a Babylonian epic dating from about 2000 B.C., holds a lion in his left arm and another by its tail. The epic describes him as "peerless, without an equal among men."

the gods. In the end, Gilgamesh has grown wiser, for he understands that no mortal can escape old age and death. (Kramer 1956; Sandars 1972)

See also *Gilgamesh, Epic of; Gilgamesh, Sumerian Poems.*

GILGAMESH, EPIC OF

A Babylonian poem ca. 2000 B.C., it is based in part on earlier Sumerian poems. It is one of the oldest and most important epics; the cycle from which the epic springs antedates the Homeric epic by at least 1,500 years. The epic consists of many elements of myth and lore that have been linked through a gradual process of accretion, so that tales of early gods appear along with lionized figures probably based on historical characters.

When the epic begins, Gilgamesh, son of King Lugulbanda and the goddess Ninsun, is a grown man, the semidivine king of Uruk (Erech). He is superior to other men in strength and beauty, but he longs for immortality. Gilgamesh has become such a tyrant that "his lust leaves no virgin to her lover," and his weary subjects pray to the god Anu for relief. Anu and the other gods order Aruru, who created him, to create his equal. From clay she molds a wild, hirsute man named Enkidu, who lives with the beasts of the wilderness. When Gilgamesh hears of Enkidu's strength, he sends a harlot to seduce him, knowing that after the seduction the animals will have nothing more to do with him. After the harlot seduces Enkidu, she tells him of Gilgamesh's great strength, and he determines to challenge the king to a wrestling match. The match takes place during the New Year's festival, and after Enkidu defeats Gilgamesh, the two become great friends.

Together, they undertake a journey to the sacred forest to cut down a cedar. The forest is guarded by a fire-breathing monster named Humbaba, who tries to attack them. Humbaba is prevented from killing them when, at the behest of Gilgamesh's mother, Ninsun, the sun god blinds him with hot winds. The two friends behead the monster and fell many cedars before taking the monster's head as an offering to Enlil. But Enlil is enraged, and he curses them.

Gilgamesh washes away the blood of battle and puts on his crown. The goddess Ishtar, seeing his beauty, falls in love with him and offers herself to him. But Gilgamesh reminds her of how her other lovers have fared: She turned them into animals or birds with broken wings. "And if you and I should be lovers," he says, "should not I be served in the same fashion? . . ." Ishtar falls into a rage and tells her parents, Anu and Antum, "Gilgamesh has heaped insults upon me. . . ." She asks her father to give her the Bull of Heaven to destroy Gilgamesh, and Anu obliges.

The Bull's first snort opens cracks in the earth, into which 100 men fall to their deaths. With his second snort, 200 more die. With the Bull's third snort, Enkidu barely escapes falling into the earth, but he manages to grab the beast by the horns, and Gilgamesh is able to slay it with his sword. They cut the Bull's heart out and offer it to the god Shamash, and then they rest. When Ishtar learns of the Bull's fate, she is furious.

Enkidu has a series of dreams revealing that the gods have decreed that he is to die for his part in slaying the Bull of Heaven. He lies alone in his sickness, cursing the various ones who brought him to this place. He tells his friend, "The great goddess cursed me and I must die in shame. I shall not die like a man fallen in battle; I feared to fall, but happy is the man who falls in battle, for I must die in shame."

Gilgamesh is bereft when his friend dies. He wanders over the wilderness, crying, "How can I be at peace? Despair is in my heart. What my brother is now, that shall I be when I am dead. . . ." He admits his fear of death and decides to undertake a long journey to find Utnapishtim, to whom the gods gave everlasting life after the time of the deluge. From Utnapishtim, he hopes to learn the secret to eternal life.

After many adventures, including confrontations with a Man-Scorpion, the god Shamash, and the divine wine-maker and brewess Siduri, he meets Urshanabi (Sursunabu), the ferryman who makes daily trips across the waters of death dividing the garden of the sun from the paradise where Utnapishtim the Faraway dwells. He agrees to take Gilgamesh across the waters to see Utnapishtim.

When he arrives, Gilgamesh asks the old man, "I look at you now . . . and your appearance is no different from mine. . . . Tell me truly, how was it that you came to . . . possess everlasting life?" Utnapishtim tells Gilgamesh how, in the days when "the world bellowed like a wild bull," the gods decided to exterminate all mankind by sending a great flood. In a dream, Ea, the god of wisdom, warned Utnapishtim of the coming flood and instructed him to build an ark in which he and his family, his kin, "the beast of the field both wild and tame, and all the craftsmen" floated for seven days and nights, finally landing on a mountaintop. Utnapishtim sent forth first a dove, then a swallow, and finally a raven to find dry land. When the raven failed to return, the people disembarked and offered thanks to the gods for their safety. At first the god Enlil was furious that some mortals survived the destruction, but Ea calmed him, explaining that Utnapishtim was a wise man and learned of the flood in a dream. So Enlil sent Utnapishtim and his wife to live "in the distance, at the mouth of the rivers," forevermore.

When the old man finishes his story, he asks Gilgamesh, "Who will assemble the gods for your sake, so that you may find that life for which you are searching?" Gilgamesh realizes that immortality is a special dispensation of the gods, and that he will never know the secret of eternal life. The old man banishes the ferryman forever for having brought Gilgamesh to his abode, and the two crestfallen men embark on the journey back to Uruk. As they are leaving, the wife of Utnapishtim takes pity on Gilgamesh, pointing out how weary he is. Utnapishtim decides to reveal a secret to him: "There is a plant that grows under the water, it has a prickle like a thorn . . . but if you succeed in taking it, then your hands will hold that which restores his lost youth to a man."

When Gilgamesh hears this, he heads for the deepest channel of the sea, where he ties stones to his feet and dives overboard. He finds the plant growing on the bottom of the sea, and although it pricks him, he succeeds in taking it. The sea throws him onto the shore, where the ferryman joins him. The two decide to rest for the night, and Gilgamesh goes to a deep pool to bathe. A serpent in the pond smells the flower of the plant and snatches it away, leaving Gilgamesh with nothing but its sloughed skin as it dives back into the water. Gilgamesh weeps and tells Urshanabi, ". . . Is it for this I have wrung out my heart's blood? . . . I found a sign and now I have lost it. . . ." The two break camp and start for Uruk. When they arrive, Gilgamesh is worn out but wiser, and he engraves on a stone the story of his fruitless quest. (Kramer 1956; Sandars 1972)

See also Enkidu; Flood Myths; *Gilgamesh, Sumerian Poems;* Humbaba; Ishtar.

GILGAMESH, SUMERIAN POEMS

These five poems in the Sumerian language, written during the first half of the second millennium B.C., are forerunners of the same stories in the Babylonian *Epic of Gilgamesh.* The poems are entitled "Gilgamesh and the Bull of Heaven," "Gilgamesh and Huwawa" (also entitled "Gilgamesh and the Land of the Living"), "Gilgamesh and the Agga of Kish," "Gilgamesh, Enkidu, and the Nether World," and "The Death of Gilgamesh."

In the fragmentary "Gilgamesh and the Bull of Heaven," the goddess Inanna describes to Gilgamesh the gifts and favors she plans for him, apparently as enticements to accept her proposals of love. A break in the text presumably contains Gilgamesh's rejection of her proposal. Inanna goes to the heaven god An and requests the Bull of Heaven. When he refuses to give it to her, she threatens to call in all the gods, and An relents. Inanna sends the Bull of Heaven down to ravage the city of Erech. Enkidu addresses Gilgamesh and, although the end of the poem is missing, it is presumed that Gilgamesh is victorious over the Bull of Heaven.

"Gilgamesh and Huwawa," a poem pieced together from 14 tablets and fragments, tells the story of Urech king Gilgamesh who, realizing that he must die eventually, determines to "raise up a name" for himself. He plans a trip to the Land of the Living to bring home some cedars from there. His friend Enkidu advises him to inform the sun god Utu of his intention, since Utu is in charge of the cedar land. The god is at first skeptical of Gilgamesh's trip, but at length he decides to help him by neutralizing seven demons who would obstruct his progress. Gilgamesh and 50 companions set off across seven mountains toward the cedars, which are guarded by a ferocious monster, Huwawa. After several attempts to drive off the intruders, Huwawa is overcome by fear when Gilgamesh slaps his cheek. His teeth shake and his hand trembles. Gilgamesh takes pity on the monster and tells his companion Enkidu, "Let the caught man return to the bosom of his mother." But Enkidu advises against leniency: "If the caught man returns to the bosom of his mother, / You will not return to the city of the mother who gave birth to you." Enkidu prevails, and they cut off Huwawa's neck and bring him before the gods Enlil and Ninlil.

"Gilgamesh and the Agga of Kish," a poem of 115 lines, begins with the arrival in King Gilgamesh's kingdom-city of Erech of Agga's envoys bearing the ultimatum that the city of Erech must submit to the house of Kish. Gilgamesh, "the lord of Kullab," calls the elders together with the urgent plea, "Let us not submit to the house of Kish, let us smite it with our weapons." But the elders are of a peaceable mind; they would rather submit than fight. Gilgamesh then assembles the fighting men of the city and puts the same proposition before them. The convened assembly of fighting men agrees with Gilgamesh, "Let us smite it with our weapons." Gilgamesh's heart rejoices and his spirit brightens. Within a few days, Agga attacks Erech, taking its people by surprise. Although the meaning of the remainder of the poem is vague, it appears that in some manner Gilgamesh is able to secure the Agga's friendship without a fight, and the siege is lifted.

In "Gilgamesh, Enkidu, and the Nether World," the huluppu tree, attacked by the South Wind and uprooted by the flooding Euphrates, is rescued by the goddess of Inanna, who plants it in her holy garden in the city of Erech. When it grows big enough, she plans to cut it down and use its wood to make a chair and couch. But after a few years, when the tree has matured, she cannot cut it because, at its base, a snake who "knows no charm" has built its nest; in its limbs the Imdugud-bird has placed her young; and in the middle, Lilith has built her house. Inanna is very tearful over her loss, but Gilgamesh decides to come to her aid. He puts on his armor and slays the snake. When the Imdugud-bird sees this, she flies with her young to the mountain, and Lilith tears down her house and flees to the desolate places. Gilgamesh and his men cut down the tree and present it to Inanna. From the tree's base, instead of furniture, Inanna makes a drum and drumstick, which somehow fall into the nether world. Gilgamesh tries to reach them with his hand and foot, but cannot retrieve them. His servant Enkidu volunteers to descend into the nether world and bring them up, but Gilgamesh warns him, "If now you will descend to the nether world, / . . . Do not put on clean clothes, / Lest like an enemy the stewards will come forth, / . . . In the nether world make no cry" lest the denizens of the underworld be alerted to his presence. However, Enkidu does not heed his master's warnings; he commits the very acts Gilgamesh has warned against. He is seized by the demon Kur and cannot return to the earth. Weeping, Gilgamesh goes before the god Enlil to beg for his help, but Enlil refuses to rescue Enkidu. Gilgamesh then goes to the god Enki, who orders the sun god Utu to open a hole in the nether world so that the shade of Enkidu may appear upon the earth. Utu obeys, and the shade of Enkidu appears before Gilgamesh, who asks him seven questions about treatment in the nether world of fathers of from one to seven sons. Enkidu tells him about treatment of the palace servant, the birth-giving woman, the man who falls in battle, the man whose shade has no one to care for it, and the man whose body lies on the plain unburied.

"The Death of Gilgamesh" exists in fragmentary form. Gilgamesh has been informed that immortality, for which he has been searching, is impossible to attain. He has achieved kingship and victory in battle; he was given "wisdom and a comely face," but "on the bed of fate he lies, he will not rise again." Gilgamesh dies, and "like a hooked fish he lies stretched on the bed." The people of Erech weigh out their offerings to Ereshkigal, the Queen of Death, and to the other gods of the dead. Gilgamesh is laid in the tomb and is praised as "peerless, without an equal among men." (Kramer 1956)

See also Enkidu; Ereshkigal; *Gilgamesh, Epic of;* Inanna.

GISLA SAGA

This Icelandic outlaw saga (ca. early thirteenth century) is considered a masterpiece of artistic skill, incorporating some verses of great beauty said to have been written by the protagonist, Gisla Sursson (d. ca. 980). The story, set in northwestern Iceland and containing rich descriptions of the area, tells of Gisla's loyal attempt to avenge his foster brother, in the process murdering his own brother-in-law. His sister, the dead man's widow, exposes his crime, for which he is outlawed by his enemies. (Jones, G. 1990)

GLOOSCAP

Glooscap is the Algonquin first man, deity, culture hero, demiurge, and trickster, subject of a cycle of tales. Among them are: "Glooscap and the Baby," "Glooscap Grants Three Wishes," and "Glooscap Fights the Water Monster." (Erdoes and Ortiz 1984)

See also "Glooscap Fights the Water Monster."

GLOOSCAP FIGHTS THE WATER MONSTER

This American Indian heroic tale of the Passamaquoddy, Maliseet, and Micmac tribes was recorded from several oral accounts during the nineteenth century.

The story involves Glooscap, who never grows old but occasionally gets tired of ruling the world; he paddles off in his magic white canoe and disappears. But Glooscap knows everything that happens, even before it happens. He sees with his inward eye. He is a medicine man, a shaman, and the spirit who makes all animals, experimenting until he gets them just the right size to fit in with the rest of creation.

The people are happy in their village until the spring runs dry. They send one of their clansmen north to the spring's source to determine the trouble. He finds that the creatures of the north, who have webbed hands and feet, are ruled by a great chief, a monster so huge that he fills the whole valley. The monster has dammed the stream and made himself a large pond. When the clansman asks for water for his people, the monster threatens to eat him. He smacks his lips with a noise like thunder, and the clansman flees for his life, running all the way back to his village.

The villagers are in despair, but Glooscap, who has seen it all with his inward eye, says, "I must set things right. . . ." He girds for war: He paints his body red as blood and draws yellow rings around his eyes. He puts 100 black and 100 white eagle feathers in his scalplock. Dressed for battle, he puts on a ferocious scowl and stamps his feet, making the earth tremble. Now that he looks like a warrior he must have a weapon, so from a flint mountain he makes a knife as sharp as a weasel's teeth. Then he goes north to find the water monster.

When he confronts the monster, it threatens to kill him. Glooscap answers, "Slimy lump of mud! We'll see who will be killed!" They clash, and mountains tremble. Mighty trees are "slivered into splinters." The monster opens his mouth to swallow Glooscap, but the hero makes himself so tall that the monster cannot seize him. With his flint knife, Glooscap slits open the monster's belly. A mighty stream rolls out and flows so strongly that it digs a riverbed past the village and all the way down to the sea. Now that the monster is no longer full of water, Glooscap is able to squeeze it in the palm of his hand until it has shrunk down into a small bullfrog, which he throws into the swamp. Ever since, the bullfrog's skin has been wrinkled because Glooscap squeezed so hard.

Eventually Glooscap leaves to live in his other world in the West, where he fashions arrows to be used in the battle that will take place on the last day. (Erdoes and Ortiz 1984)

THE GODODDIN

This heroic elegy, the oldest extant Scottish poem, is attributed to Aneirin, a sixth-century northern British poet. Gododdin was the name of a kingdom comprised of part of northeastern England and eastern Scotland as far as the Forth River. In the *Mabinogion* story "How Culwch Won Olwen," Gododdin is identified as the territory of the Votadini. Gododdin was apparently ruled by Mynyddawg the Luxurious (ca. sixth century), who is "famous in stress of battle."

The poem tells of men of Gododdin riding forth to Catraeth (probably Catterick in N. Yorkshire) to meet the Angles of Diera (Yorkshire east of the Pennines) and Bernicia (coastal lands extending north to Berwickshire) in battle. Hyfeidd the Tall, who fells "five times fifty" and "a hundred score . . . in a single hour," is in the front rank. The men are renowned; in accordance with the honored custom, they drink wine and mead from gold cups for a year at a feast contrived by Gwlyged of Gododdin, apparently Mynyddawg's steward. But "the pale mead was . . . their poison." Of the 363 men who hasten out after their choice of drink, only three escape "through feats of swordplay—the two war-dogs of Aeron, and stubborn Cynon; and I too, streaming with blood, by grace of my brilliant poetry. . . ." Cynon is identified as the son of an Edinburgh man, living in Aeron (probably Ayrshire). The rest of the men, "drunk over the clarified mead," having "fed together round the wine-bowl in shining array," raise the war cry and sally forth with Rhufawn the Tall, "who gave fold to the altar and gifts and fine presents to the minstrel," in the lead. Although they slay "seven times as many English," the besotted warriors suffer "the agony of death in torment." Those lost include the heroes Caradawn and Madawg, Pyll and Ieuan, Gwgawn and Gwiawn, Gwynn and Cynfan, "Peredur of the steel weapons," Gwawrddur and Aeddan, Rhufawn, and Gwiawn and Gwlyged. (Jackson, K. 1971)

GOFANNON

See Goibniu.

GOG AND MAGOG

According to the Old Testament Book of Ezekiel, Gog is the leader of invading northern people whom God will destroy. An Egyptian inscription of Amenhotep III identifies the northern tribe as Gagi, identified with Gog. Magog is described in Genesis as the son of Japhet, who also appears in Greek mythology as Iapetus, the Titan father of Atlas, Prometheus, and Epimetheus. In Genesis, Magog's grandfather is Noah. In the final onslaught at the end of the age foretold in Revelation, Gog and Magog are described as the anti-God forces.

In ancient Irish tradition, the king of Scythia is Feniusa Farsa, described as a grandson of Magog. Gogmagog is the name of the giant whom Brut the Trojan defeats in Devonshire during his invasion of Britain. (Ezekiel 38 and 39ff.; Genesis 10:2; Graves 1966; Revelation 20:8)

GOIBNIU

(Also Gofannon or Govannon)

This ancient Celtic smith god appears in the Welsh *Mabinogion* as Govannon, son of Don. In the Irish tradition, he is one of a trio of divine craftsmen along with Luchta, the wright, and Credne, the metalworker. In "The Second Battle of Moytura," Goibniu is introduced as the god who can offer the Túatha Dé Danann weapons that never fail. For the other gods he provides the Fled Goibnemm, a feast featuring his ale, which renders those who drink it immortal. Christian folklore named him Gobban the Joiner (Saer), builder of churches. In the Irish tale *The Destruction of Da Derga's Hostel*, one of "three chief warriors" is described by Fer Rogain as being Goibniu, son of Lorgnech. (Gantz 1976)

See also *Destruction of Da Derga's Hostel; Mabinogion.*

GOPI CHAND

This oral epic of the Bengali Hindus of India is still being performed today. (Blackburn et al. 1989)

GORGON

In the *Iliad* (v, xi) Gorgon is a monster of the underworld, produced by Gaea (Ge), Earth goddess, to assist her sons against the gods. In later traditions there are three gorgons, daughters of Ceto and Phorcys (son and daughter of Oceanus and Gaea): Stheno the Mighty and Euryale the Far Springer, both of whom are immortal, and Madusa the Queen, who is mortal. They have brazen claws, hair of serpents, and eyes whose gaze can turn men to stone. They also appear in the *Aeneid* (vi) and *Theogony.* (Graves 1955; Humphries 1951; Lattimore 1959; Lattimore 1976)

See also *Aeneid; Iliad; Theogony.*

GOULBURN ISLAND CYCLE

In this Australian Aboriginal erotic cycle made up of 26 songs, humans engage in sexual activity, in which the significance is that it mimics parallel activity in the rest of nature. (Wilde et al. 1991)

GRAIL

In medieval literature, particularly in Arthurian legend, the Grail is the object of quests by knights of the Round Table. Presumably it is the chalice from which Jesus drank at the Last Supper. The Holy Grail appears in the legend of *Parzival,* in which Parzival, on his way to Arthur's court, encounters the Fisher King, custodian of the Grail, the very presence of which has rendered the king mute. Parzival fails to ask the king what ails him and thus fails to heal him. After long wandering, he returns to the castle, asks the right question, and heals the king. A chair at the Round Table is left vacant, awaiting the one pure knight who is eligible to undertake the Grail quest. Sir Galahad is that knight, and in another tale he becomes the one to heal the Fisher King. (Barber 1961; Matarasso 1984; von Eschenbach 1980)

See also Arthurian Legend; Galahad, Sir; *Parzival.*

GRANI

In Norse epics, Grani (Grane) is Sigurd's extraordinarily swift horse ("Grey-Colored"). (Hatto 1969; Hollander *Edda* 1990)

See also *Edda, Poetic; Nibelungenlied; Thiđrekssaga; Völsunga saga.*

THE GRATEFUL DEAD

In the Old Testament apocryphal book of Tobit, "The Grateful Dead" is a tale about a young man who receives help in winning a bride from a corpse he has helped to bury. The Tobit story is a Judaized version of an older tale. (Ginzburg 1992)

GREAT MOTHER OF THE GODS
(Also Cybele, Ops, Magna Mater, Mater Deum Magna, Dindymene, and Rhea)

This ancient deity, signifying universal motherhood, originated as Cybele in Phrygia in Asia Minor. From there her cult spread to the Greeks, where she became unified with the Titan earth goddess Rhea. As Cybele, she is the daughter of Gaea and the wife of Cronos. She appears in the *Aeneid* (ix). (Ceram 1972; Humphries 1951)

See also *Aeneid;* Rhea.

GRENDEL

In *Beowulf,* Grendel is a giant monster in human form, a descendant of Cain who terrorizes the Danes. With his mother and other loathsome creatures, he lurks in a foul, murky pond from which he and his mother emerge to eat humans for a period of 12 years, until Beowulf slays them. (Hieatt 1968; Raffel 1963)

See also *Beowulf.*

GRETTIS SAGA

This Icelandic outlaw saga (ca. 1320) is considered a masterpiece, the only saga dating from the fourteenth century that can stand with the earlier classics. It tells the story of a headstrong young man of great talents, Grettir the Strong, who at age 14 kills a man during a quarrel and is outlawed for three years. He goes to Norway where he performs many generous deeds. When his banishment is over, he returns to Iceland and learns that the ghost of Glam the shepherd is ravaging the countryside and terrorizing the people. He battles the ghost and saves the people, but a dying friend whom he cannot save curses him with a fear of the dark. Later, as Grettir is performing another altruistic deed, he inadvertently causes a fire in which a chieftain's son is killed. Once again he is outlawed, and a price is placed on his head. He is hounded by bounty hunters and vengeful kinsmen of those he has slain in the past, as well as by trolls and other fantastic entities. His fear of the dark prevents him from remaining in seclusion, and he is eventually killed by his enemies unscrupulously using witchcraft. However, his brother later avenges his death in Byzantium. The story contains several motifs drawn from folklore. (Jones, G. 1990)

GRÍMNISMÁL

"Grímnismál" is an ancient Scandinavian poem of creation described in detail in the *Poetic Edda* entry. Some 20 stanzas of the lay also appear in Sturluson's "Gylfaginning" in the *Prose Edda.*

See also *Edda, Poetic; Edda, Prose.*

GUAHAYONA
(Our Pride)

Hero of the pre-Columbian Taíno creation cycle of the Caribbean Taíno Indians, Guahayona is not superhuman, but an ordinary man who acquires his skills and wisdom through his exploits. He begins as a novice, but on his journey to find a better home, he acquires great skills of leadership. He organizes the migration of his people out of the Cave of the Jagua into civilization. Eventually he overcomes the desire to strive for personal power and learns to resist temptation and gluttony. He overcomes his lust for the Amazon Guabonito as well. By mastering his baser instincts he gains shamanistic powers, which he is careful to preserve. (Stevens-Arroyo 1988)

See also *Cave of the Jagua.*

GUDRUN

In *Völsunga Saga,* Gudrun is Sigurd's wife. In the *Nibelungenlied* she is known as Kriemhild. She is the sister of Gunnar and, after Sigurd's death, the wife of Atli. She is sometimes confused with the heroine of the Middle High German romance *Gudrunlied.* In the *Laxdaela Saga,* Gudrun is the selfish daughter of Queen Grímhild, who marries first Thorwald, then Thord, and finally Bolli. She brings about the death of her lover, Kjartan. (Hatto 1969)

See also Kriemhild; *Kudrun, Epic of; Laxdaela Saga; Nibelungenlied;* Siegfried; *Völsunga Saga.*

GUDRUNLIED

This German epic poem (ca. 1210) in three sections by an unknown author was apparently modeled after the *Nibelungenlied.* The story itself is based on an old legend of the Baltic coast. The first section concerns King Hagen of Ireland; the second, Hertel's courtship of Hilde, King Hagen's daughter; the third, the abduction of Hertel and Hilde's daughter Gudrun. Gudrun is betrothed to Herwig of Seeland but is abducted by Hartmut of Normandy after she refuses to marry him. She is held in captivity for 13 years and forced to do menial chores. Finally Herwig and Gudrun's brother rescue her, and the betrothed lovers are married. (Forster 1957; Siepmann 1987)

LA GUERRE ENTRE NDJE FARAH NDJE ET HAMBODEDJO

This Fula epic of West Africa concerns a clash between two neighboring tribes, one Muslim, one pagan. (Westley *RAL* 1991)

See also *Geste de Ham-Bodedio; Hambodjo.*

GŪGĀ

This epic of the northwestern Indian regions of Rajasthan, Panjab, Harayana, and northwestern Uttar Pradesh is still being sung at village fairs today. The story of Gūgā, a Rajput hero/prince with powers to control snakes, is usually told by Bhagats, ritual specialists of the Jogi caste. Most versions of the epic can be told in one night.

Queen Bachal, barren for ten years, meets the saint Guru Gorakhnāth, who tells her that in order to conceive she must serve his disciples for 12 years, after which she must bring him some curds. The queen serves him for 12 years, but at the end of that time her sister Kachal, also barren, dresses like Bachal and secretly takes curds to the guru. In reward for her service, he gives her two barley seeds that will make her pregnant, then he leaves the village.

Kachal eats the seeds before telling Bachal what she has done. Bachal runs after Guru Gorakhnāth, beseeching him to help her become pregnant also. At the guru's request, the disciple Janamejaya agrees to sacrifice himself for Bachal. (Janamejaya also appears in the *Mahābhārata* as the king to whom the epic is recited and the performer of a great snake sacrifice.) Actually, he knows that Bāsak, the king of snakes, is planning to destroy him anyway as punishment for killing so many snakes. Janamejaya's body is placed in boiling water. After it disintegrates, the guru places his soul in a container and instructs Bachal to mix it with milk and drink it. From this mixture, Bachal becomes pregnant at last.

When she returns home the king, suspicious of her virtue, banishes her to the forest, much as Rāma banishes Sītā in the *Rāmāyaṇa*. In the forest, the snake king Bāsak, who has been cheated out of killing Janamejaya by his sacrifice, attempts to take revenge on Janamejaya by trying to destroy Bachal's baby while he is still in the womb. Finally the baby, named Gūgā, comes out of the womb and threatens to suck all of the poison from Bāsak. The snake king begs for and receives pardon, in exchange for promising to help Gūgā whenever he is in trouble. After 12 more years, Bachal is welcomed back into the palace and gives birth to a son, whom the blind midwife—suddenly receiving her sight—proclaims is a god. At the same time, Kachal gives birth to twins, Arjan and Surjan, whom she cannot nurse, so Bachal nurses them for her.

When Gūgā is 12, the goddess of childbirth, Behmātā, predicts his marriage to a distant Brahmin within the month. Hearing this, Bachal imprisons him to keep him close at home. But he escapes and flees on a magical horse to meet his bride. He is accompanied only by Guru Gorakhnāth and one disciple. Seeing such a small wedding party, the bride's parents refuse to allow the marriage unless the gods attend. The next day the gods arrive, and the marriage takes place.

The twins Arjan and Surjan, in an effort to gain a share of their cousin's kingdom, appeal to the king of Delhi, Prithvīrāj Chauhān, who summons Gūgā to court to discuss the matter. When Gūgā ignores the summons, the king sends 900,000 soldiers to attack his palace. Gūgā, with only 500 soldiers, appeals to Guru Gorakhnāth, who sends 1,400 disciples possessing the power of flight.

King Prithvīrāj sees at once the futility of continuing the attack and proposes negotiations.

However, at the meeting for negotiations, one twin spears Gūgā in the eye, whereupon Gūgā challenges the twins to fight. They flee in terror, but he pursues and beheads them. When Bachal learns of the beheading of the twins, whom she has learned to love as if they were her own, she banishes Gūgā for 12 years. He does not take his wife, Lado Serial, along, but goes alone to live out his banishment with Guru Gorakhnāth.

After 12 years, he secretly visits his wife often but refuses to return openly to the kingdom to live. After 12 more years, Bachal confronts Lado Serial as to Gūgā's whereabouts and learns of his secret visits. When he comes again, Bachal is waiting. She grasps his horse's tail and entreats Gūgā to return to the kingdom. But Gūgā, full of pride because his mother exiled him, and full of anger because his wife betrayed his visits, vows never to show his face again. When he escapes, he persuades Guru Gorakhnāth to open up the earth so that he can perform samādhi (voluntary live burial). The samādhi shrine where Gūgā disappeared still stands 12 miles from Dadrera Khera. (Blackburn et al. 1989)

GUIGEMAR

This medieval heroic/romantic lai by Marie de France is, according to her prologue, a tale she heard from Breton minstrels and put into octosyllabic couplets. It is the second longest of her lais.

At the time when Hoel rules Brittany, a vassal, Lord Oridial of Leonnais, "a worthy and valiant knight," has by his wife a daughter named Noguent and a son Guigemar. There is no handsomer youngster in the kingdom than Guigemar. When the father can bring himself to part with the boy, he sends him to serve King Hoel. "Intelligent and brave," Guigemar makes himself loved by all. When he matures, the king dubs him a knight, and he journeys off to seek his fame in Flanders, where there is "always a war, or a battle raging. . . ."

But Guigemar has one flaw: He gives no thought to love. Although he shows himself to be a superior warrior, he is indifferent to women and to love. At the height of his fame, he returns to visit his family, a hero but psychologically immature, having no desire to show affection, having not even made any romantic dalliances.

While he is on his month-long visit with his family, he organizes a hunting party that sets off in pursuit of a great stag. During the hunt he shoots a hind, but the arrow rebounds, piercing completely through his thigh into the horse's flank. He falls off his horse beside the wounded hind, who speaks to him: ". . . neither physician nor potion / will cure you / . . . until a woman heals you, / . . . And out of love for her, you'll suffer as much. . . ."

Guigemar wants to be healed, but he knows of no woman he has ever wanted to love. He tells his squire to summon his companions. But when the squire rides off, Guigemar bandages his wound with his shirt, mounts his horse, and steals quickly away, anxious that his companions not find him and try to detain him. He rides through the woods and plain until he comes to the sea, where a lone ship with a pure silk sail stands in the harbor. In great pain he boards the ship, but it is deserted. He finds sleeping quarters with a bed inlaid with gold and covered with a quilt of silken cloth woven with gold. Exhausted, he lies down to rest until the pain of his wound subsides.

When he rises to leave, he discovers that the ship is on the high seas. Even if he were not wounded, Guigemar would not know how to sail a ship. He prays that God will bring him back to land safely, then he lies down to sleep.

While he sleeps, the ship sails into the castle harbor of a jealous old man who holds his beautiful young wife captive in her chambers. The ship and its sleeping passenger are discovered by the young wife's attendant, and when he awakens, both women are staring down at him. They spirit him off to the wife's bedchamber.

Guigemar is immediately smitten by the young wife's beauty, and she by his. They fall in love and spend 18 months in their love nest before the lady has a premonition that they will soon be discovered. She ties a knot in his shirt, telling him, "You have my leave to love the woman, / . . . who will be able to undo it." He in turn tightens a belt about her flanks, telling her that whoever can open the buckle is the only one she can love.

As she predicts, the lovers are discovered by a chamberlain sent by the husband to spy through the window. The husband and three of his henchmen break into the bedchamber and attack Guigemar, but he grabs a wooden clothes rod and maims them all before they can strike a blow. In answer to the husband's questions, Guigemar tells his story of arriving on the deserted ship. The husband doesn't believe him, but tells him if he can find the ship, he can board it and leave. They go to the harbor and discover the ship waiting. Guigemar is put aboard, and off it sails. Everyone is sure the ship will be destroyed and Guigemar will drown.

The husband locks his wife in a tower where she pines and wishes to join Guigemar in death. One day she discovers the door unlocked, and she steals away to the shore, where she finds a small boat. She boards the boat, intending to row out to deep waters and drown herself, but suddenly she cannot stand. The boat sets out and sails to Brittany, coming to rest beside a strong castle owned by Meriaduc. He sees the boat arrive and rushes out to board it. He discovers the beautiful lady, whom he immediately adores. He takes her to his castle and assigns his sister to be her attendant.

Meriaduc tries to entice the lady into his bed, but she shows him the belt and tells him that she will never love any man except the one who can open it without breaking it. He tells her, "There's another one like you in this land, / a very worthy knight, / who avoids, in a similar manner, taking a wife. . . ." When he tells her of the knotted shirt, she almost faints. Meriaduc cuts the laces of her tunic but cannot open the belt. He calls every knight in the region, but none can succeed in removing the belt.

Meriaduc plans a tournament against his neighbor, with whom he is at war, and issues a call for knights to enlist, knowing that Guigemar will come. When Guigemar and his entourage arrive, the lady is brought out. Only after she unties the knot in his shirt and he feels the belt about her flanks does he recognize her as his true love. He offers to become Meriaduc's vassal for "two or three years" in exchange for her. However, Meriaduc, who only hopes that he will remove the belt, refuses. Guigemar leaves the lady behind, takes his knights, and rides off to the neighboring castle, where he offers his services to Meriaduc's enemy. The lord of the castle is delighted, and the next day they assault Meriaduc's castle. But its defenses are too strong, and they fail to penetrate them.

Guigemar refuses to give up. He gathers more knights and they surround the castle and cut off its supplies, intent on starving everyone in it. Eventually he captures the castle and kills Meriaduc, then leads his mistress away with great rejoicing. (Hanning and Ferrante 1978)

GUINEVERE

(Also Gwenhwyvar, Finnabair, and Guanhumara)

In Arthurian legend, Guinevere is the wife of King Arthur. In many legends she is the daughter of King Leodegrance, who gives Arthur the Round Table as a wedding gift. According to the *Vita Gildae* (ca. eleventh to twelfth centuries), she was abducted by King Melwas of Aestiva Regio and rescued by Arthur and his knights. In Chrétien de Troyes's *Le Chevalier de la Charette,* she is abducted by Melegant and taken to the land of Gorre, where Launcelot rescues her. In Geoffrey of Monmouth's *History of the Kings of Britain,* she is abducted and seduced by Arthur's nephew Mordred, and this is closely connected with Arthur's death. In most versions, however, she is in love with Launcelot. (Barber 1961)

See also Arthurian Legend; Gareth, Sir; Lancelot, Sir.

GUNTHER

(Also Gunnar)

In *Nibelungenlied,* Gunther, the son of Dancrat and Uote, is the senior Burgundian king who courts Brunhild. But he is king in name and little else. He relies heavily upon his stronger kinsman Hagen. Gunther is weak, spineless, and deceitful, leaving the wooing and taming of Brunhild to Siegfried, promising him the hand of his sister Kriemhild in return for his help. But he forgets his promise until Siegfried reminds him. When Hagan suggests getting rid of Siegfried, Gunther resists at first. The thought makes him sad that, with Siegfried dead, Gunther would rule many kingdoms. When Hagen plots to betray Siegfried, Gunther weakens and follows his advice. However, when Siegfried has been mortally wounded, Gunther laments the act, only to be told by the dying man, "There is no need for the doer of the deed to weep. . . . He should be held up to scorn . . ." and by Hagen, "I don't know what you are grieving for. All our cares and sorrows are over and done with. . . ."

When Hagen proposes taking the widowed Kriemhild's treasure on the grounds that "No man who is firm in his purpose should leave the treasure to a woman . . ." Gunther balks self-righteously: "After all, she is my sister." Later, when all the others are in favor of Kriemhild's marriage to King Etzel, Hagen tells Gunther, "If you have any sense, you will take care not to let it happen. . . ." Gunther disagrees and says with great piety, "We should be glad of any honour that befalls her. My affection bids me stand by her. . . ."

After the matter has been settled, the Burgundians set out for Hungary. At the Danube crossing, Hagen kills the ferryman and pretends to know nothing about him. Then he throws the chaplain overboard and no one, not even Gunther, lifts a hand to save the cleric. However, when the party arrives at Etzel's castle, Gunther defends himself against Dietrich with great courage. When he and Hagen are bound and led before Kriemhild, the queen, Dietrich pleads that she let them live. She puts them in separate dungeons and later visits Hagen to promise, "If you will give me back what you have robbed me of, you may still return to Burgundy alive!" When Hagen refuses to reveal the whereabouts of the treasure, she orders her brother Gunther's head cut off. She carries it to Hagen by the hair, but he still refuses to tell her where the treasure is. She draws Siegfried's sword and cuts off Hagen's head before the eyes of King Etzel. Old Hildebrand avenges Hagen's death by killing Kriemhild. Thus all the Burgundians are dead.

In the *Völsunga Saga,* he is Gunnar, brother of Gudrun. He appears in the Eddaic poem "Atlakviđa," in which Atli (Attila the Hun) slays him and his death is avenged by his sister, Atli's wife. In the eleventh-century Latin poem *Waltharius,* Gunther and his warriors make an unsuccessful attempt upon the life of Walter of Aquitaine in order to steal his treasure. The character may have been based on the historical Burgundian king Gundahar, whom the Huns overthrew in 436. (Hatto 1969; Hollander 1990)

See also Brunhild; *Edda, Poetic;* Gudrun; Hagen; Kriemhild; *Nibelungenlied;* Siegfried; *Völsunga Saga.*

GYLFAGINNING
("The Beguiling of Gylfi")

In the *Prose Edda* (ca. 1220), "Gylfaginning" is a section in which all the major Old Norse gods and their functions are described. In compiling the survey, its author, Snorri Sturluson (1179–1241), drew partly from still-extant Eddaic and scaldic poetry, but also from sources that have since been lost. (Young 1950)

See also *Edda, Prose.*

H

HADUBRAND

In the Old High Germanic heroic fragment *Hildebrandslied,* Hadubrand is the warrior-son of the hero Hildebrand who forces his father into a duel to the death without knowing whom he has challenged. Although the poem breaks off before the outcome is known, indications are that Hildebrand kills his son. (Forster 1957)

See also *Hildebrandslied.*

HAGEN
(Also Hagano and Hogni)

In the *Nibelungenlied,* Hagen is the kinsman and vassal of the Burgundian kings. He is the eldest son of Aldrian, brother of Dancwart, and lord of Troneck. It is Hagen who is responsible for Siegfried's murder and who takes Siegfried's treasure and throws it into the waters. He is taken hostage by Etzel (Atli, Attila), and when he refuses to divulge the treasure's whereabouts to Queen Kriemhild, he is beheaded. The Latin heroic epic *Waltharius* relates of his being held hostage as a youth, his escape, and his pledge of fealty to King Guntharius. In Old Norse poems his name is Hogni, and he is depicted as Gunnar's brother. In the *Lay of Atli,* found in the *Poetic Edda,* both men are killed by Atli (Attila). (Hatto 1969; Hollander *Edda* 1990)

See also Brunhild; *Edda, Poetic;* Gudrun; Gunther; *Nibelungenlied; Völsunga Saga; Waltharius.*

HAINUWELE

In the Ceramese creation myth of the Molucca Islands of Indonesia, Hainuwele is a beautiful girl of magical gift-bestowing powers who grows out of a coconut plant before there are animals or death upon the earth. After she gives the community both the necessities and the luxuries they desire, at the end of the first great annual celebration, she is killed and her body is cut into pieces. Everywhere the pieces are scattered, coconut trees grow. Following her death mankind becomes sexual, able to bring new life into the world for the first time. (Sproul 1991)

HAKON

In Icelandic sagas, Hakon is the name of many characters. In the *Orkneyinga Saga,* Hakon Haraldsson, king of Norway (ca. 935–961) appears; he drives his brother Eirik Blood-Ax out of Norway. In the same saga, there are also Hakon, fostered by Svein Asleifarson, who goes with him on two Viking expeditions; Hakon Ivarsson, an earl in Norway whose daughter marries Earl Paul Thorfinnsson; Hakon Karl, son of Sigurd of Paplay and half brother of St. Magnus, whose sister is made pregnant by Jon Wing; Hakon Paulsson, earl of Orkney, whose escapades are covered in the first section of the saga; Hakon Sigurdson the Broad-Shouldered, king of Norway (1161–1162), killed in a battle against Eindridi the Young and Erling Wry-Neck; and Hakon Sigurdson the Powerful, earl of Norway (ca. 970–995), who sends Thorir Klakka to Orkney.

Hakon Haraldsson (Hakon the Good) appears in *Laxdaela Saga,* in which he makes Hoskuld Dala-Kollsson a member of his court; entertains Hoskuld and presents him with timber, a sword, and a gold bracelet, the latter two of which Hoskuld passes on to Olaf the Peacock; and he accepts as a gift an islandful of oxen. Hakon the Good appears in *Egil's Saga,* in which he becomes the foster son of King Athelstan, then rises to become king of Norway, rejects Egil's offer to serve him and refuses Egil the Berserk's money, demands tribute from Earl Arnvid, leads a campaign to Vermaland, and is killed in battle fighting his nephews.

Hakon Sigurdson, earl of Norway (called the Powerful), also appears in *Njal's Saga,* where he takes Gunnar into his court, befriends Thrain and later is tricked by him, attacks the Njalssons, and is killed by a slave. He also appears in *The Saga of the Jómsvíkings,* about the warrior-Danes whom Earl Hakon defeats in the great naval battle in Hjorunga Bay in 986. He appears in *Laxdaela Saga,* in which he becomes the liege lord of Geirmund the Noisy, and entertains Olaf the Peacock and gives him a gold-inlaid ax. His death is again told. (Hollander *Jómsvíkings* 1990; Magnusson and Pálsson 1960; Pálsson and Edwards 1982; Pálsson and Edwards 1988)

HALDI
(Also Khaldi)

In Urartu religion, ca. ninth to sixth centuries B.C., Haldi is the god of the heavens and of war—the chief god—after whom some authors have referred to the Urartians as Khaldians or Chaldians (not to be confused with the Chaldeans of southern Mesopotamia). His holy city, over which he presided, was Musasir, or Ardini, in eastern Turkey. His consort was Bagmashtu (Bagbartu). He is depicted as standing on a lion, and in some depictions he has wings. He is mentioned in several inscriptions of King Menua, who claims protection of "the dread god Khaldi." (Alexander, D., et al. 1973; Chahin 1987)

HAMBODJO

(Also *Hambodidjo* and *Ham-Bodedio)*

This Fula epic of Mali, West Africa, concerns the eighteenth- and nineteenth-century wars between the Fula and the Bambara. It is told in seven episodes, each by a different performer. (Westley *RAL* 1991)

See also *La Guerre entre Ndje Farah Ndje et Hambodedjo.*

HAMÐISMÁL

("Lay of Hamthir")

In the *Poetic Edda,* "Hamđismál" is probably the oldest of all of the heroic lays. It resembles a story by mid-sixth-century Gothic historian Jordanes, who indicates in his *Getica* that Ostrogothic king Hermanaricus orders a woman named Sunilda bound to wild horses and torn to pieces because of an offense by her husband. In retaliation, her brothers Sarus and Ammimus murder him. In this version, the woman's name is Svanhild, the daughter of Guthrún by Sigurth, and her brothers are Sorli and Hamthir. They are joined by a half brother named Erp. The story breaks off as they reach the castle but the same story continues in the *Völsunga Saga.* (Hollander *Edda* 1990)

See also *Edda, Poetic; Völsunga Saga.*

HAMLET

(Also Amleth)

In Saxo Grammaticus's *Historica Danica* (twelfth century), Hamlet is the prince of Denmark. The account of Hamlet's attempt to avenge his father's murder is the plot of Shakespeare's most famous tragedy. The story may have appeared in the now-lost Icelandic saga of Amlodi, although scholars have noted its similarity to a Persian tale in *Shāh-Nāmah,* to the tale of Amhlaide (killer in 917 of King Niall Glundub, according to the *Irish Annals),* and to Geatish legend in Jutland. (Siepmann 1987)

HANG TUAH

Near-mythical seafaring hero of Malacca (fifteenth century) who, under the bendahara (chief minister) Tun Perak helped conduct an aggressive expansion policy resulting in Malaccan supremacy at sea. His swashbuckling exploits form the basis for the famous Malayan hikayat, or romance, called "Huang Tuah" or "Hang Tuah." (Dixon 1964)

HANGI-OF-DRUM

In the *Mwindo Epic* of the Nyanga of Africa, Hangi is an important deity in the Nyangan pantheon. He is the father of Chief Karisi's principal wife Kahindo. (Biebuyck 1978)

HANISH

In the *Epic of Gilgamesh,* Hanish is a divine herald of storms and other bad weather. (Sandars 1972)

HANUMĀN

In the Hindu epic *Rāmāyaṇa,* Hanumān is the monkey chief who aids Rāma in rescuing his wife Sītā from the demon king Rāvaṇa. Hanumān, the offspring of a nymph and the wind god, sneaks into the demon city of Laṅkā to find Sītā, crossing the strait between India and Ceylon in one leap. He helps to construct a bridge across the water so that Rāma and his troops can march across to rescue Sītā. Later he brings back to life the fallen of Rāma's forces with magic herbs. He is worshiped in some parts of the Hindu world as a deity. (Buck 1976)

See also Rāma; *Rāmāyaṇa;* Rāvaṇa; Sītā.

HARIVAṂŚA

(Also *Genealogy of Hari,* or *Viṣṇu)*

This is a supplement (ca. fifth century) to the Hindu epic *Mahābhārata,* which deals with the legend of the ancestry and exploits of Kṛiṣṇa, friend of the Pāṇḍavas—particularly Arjuna—but later deified and identified as an avatar of the god Viṣṇu. Among the great number of Purānic texts, the *Harivaṃśa* is included among the 18 known as *Great Purāṇas.* (Dimmitt and van Buitenen 1978)

HARPIES

In the *Iliad,* the Harpies (mischievous winds) include one named Podarge (Swiftfoot), who mates with the west wind and becomes the dam of Achilles's horses. In the *Odyssey,* the Harpies are winds that blow ships off their course and carry them away. In the Argonaut saga, Harpies have the faces of women and the bodies of birds; they are malevolent creatures sent to punish Thracian king Phineus for his mistreatment of his children. The episode is repeated in the *Aeneid,* in which the chief Harpy is called Celano (Dark). (Graves 1955; Lattimore 1976; Rouse 1990)

See also *Aeneid;* Argonauts; *Odyssey.*

HÁVAMÁL

("Words of the High One")

A poem in the *Poetic Edda* (Elder Edda) in which the great god, the poetry god Óthin, tells of acquiring the gift of wisdom by hanging on the World Tree for nine nights. Pierced by a spear, he hangs himself and becomes a sacrifice to himself. Thus he becomes also the god of the hanged: "I know that I hung on that windswept tree for nine whole nights pierced by the spear, given to Óthin,

Hanuman, the Monkey King featured in the Hindu *Rāmāyaṇa,* holds a mountain of healing herbs in this late sixteenth-century illustration for a Persian translation of the epic.

myself given to myself on that tree whose roots no man knows. They refreshed me neither with bread nor with drink from the horn. I peered down. I learnt runes, howling I learnt them, and then fell back." (Hollander *Edda* 1990)

See also *Edda, Poetic;* Savior.

HAWK
(Also Kahungu)

In the *Epic of Mwindo* of the Nyanga of Africa, Hawk is a messenger both friendly and antagonistic to the hero. He informs Mwindo where his father has fled and where his aunt Iyangura has gone to be married. But he also tells Mwindo's enemy Kasiyembe about Mwindo's meeting with his aunt. In one version, the Pygmy Shekaruru saves Hawk from being devoured by red ants, and in return, Hawk liberates the Pygmy from a tree where he is hiding from warthogs. In gratitude for his good deed, Mwindo rewards Hawk with chickens. (Biebuyck 1978; Okpewho 1992)

See also *Mwindo, Epic of.*

HEALFDANE

In *Beowulf,* Healfdane is a Danish king, son of Beo, and father of Hergar, Hrothgar, Halga, and Urs. (Hieatt 1967; Raffel 1963)

HEBAT

In ancient Asia Minor, Hebat is the Hurrian queen of the gods, called in another surviving relic the sun goddess Hepatu. She is also identified with the Hittite sun goddess Arinna. She may have been associated with the Hebrew Hawwa (Eve). In Hellenistic times she became Hipta, goddess of Caria and Lydia, and may have been related to the Greek goddess Hecate (Hekate), whom Hesiod depicts as a part-Titan, the daughter of Perses and the nymph Asteria, having dominion over heaven, earth, and ocean. (Gimbutas 1982; Olmstead 1948)

See also Hecate.

HEBE

The daughter of Zeus and Hera, Hebe is depicted by Homer as a cupbearer to the gods. In the Herakles stories, she becomes his bride when he reaches heaven. (Graves 1955)

HECATE
(Also Hekate)

She is the Greek goddess of magic and spells. In Turkey, Hekate (Artemis, Enodia, Zerynthia) was the primary goddess, who could turn herself into a dog. She and her dogs are said to journey over the graves of the dead. (Gimbutas 1982; Olmstead 1948)

See also Hebat.

HECTOR

Trojan hero. ***See*** Hektor.

HECUBA
(Also Hecabe)

In the *Aeneid* (iii) and the *Iliad,* Hecuba is the wife of Trojan king Priam and the mother of the chief warrior, Hektor. When Troy is captured, Hecuba is taken prisoner. (Humphries 1951; Lattimore 1976)

HEIMDALL
(Old Norse: Heimdallr)

In Norse myth, Heimdall is the watchman of the gods, who dwells in Himinbjorg at the entry to the heavenly home, Ásgard. For some reason he has nine mothers, all sisters. Despite being a prodigious partaker of very fine mead, he is the ideal watchman because he can hear grass grow, can see 100 leagues, and needs less sleep than a bird. One story says that he came to the earth in the form of a man, naming himself Rígr, and by three women fathered children from which the serf (thrall), freeman, and nobles arose. A tenth-century scald tells of a struggle between the trickster Loki and Heimdall. At the time of the Ragnarök (end of the world), Heimdall will blow his horn, and he and Loki will slay each other. (Jones, G. 1990; Young 1954)

HEIMSKRINGLA

In Old Norse literature (ca. 1220), *Heimskringla* is a collection of 16 kings' sagas describing the history of the royal house of Norway from legendary times through 1177, attributed to thirteenth-century Icelandic poet and chieftain Snorri Sturluson. The work is taken partly from Icelandic sources, including the work of the poet Tjodolv of Kuin, Ari the Wise, and various accounts Snorri heard during his two trips to Norway and Sweden. Many early narratives were handed down orally by scalds and historians of the Viking age. In his preface he says of the songs of scalds, "We take everything for true which is found in their poems about their journeys or battles. It is the way of scalds, of course, to give most praise to him for whom they composed, but no one would dare tell the king himself such deeds of his as all listeners and the king himself knew to be lies and loose talk; that would be mockery, but not praise."

Although the *Heimskringla* begins with *Ynglinga Saga* and the descent of the Norwegian kings from the god Óthin, the central part of the work is *Olafs Saga,* about the life and 15-year reign of Olaf II Haraldsson, patron saint of Norway.

An earlier twelfth-century version, *Olafs Saga Helga*, survives only in fragments and may have been the inspiration for Snorri's version. (Monsen and Smith 1990)

See also *Ynglinga Saga.*

HEITSI-EIBIB

Prosperity deity of the Khoikhoin, of South Africa, Heitsi-eibib is the hero of a cycle of oral myth. He has been reborn many times throughout history. Because he has the ability to transform his appearance, he is not always recognized. He has died many times, and all of his graves are shrines, to which stones are added by passing visitors. (Frazer 1963; Peires 1982; van der Post 1958)

HEKTOR

(Also Hector)

In the *Iliad,* Hektor is the noblest Trojan warrior; he is the eldest son of King Priam and Queen Hecuba, the husband of Andromache, and a favorite of Apollo. After ten years of fighting, Hektor is slain by Achilles, who lashes him to his chariot and drags his lifeless body three times around the Trojan walls. Eventually Priam convinces Achilles to return his son's corpse so that it may have a proper funeral, with all the honor and ceremony the great hero deserves. Hektor appears in the cyclic epic *Cypria* and is also mentioned in the *Aeneid* (i). (Godolphin 1964; Lattimore 1976)

See also Achilles; *Cypria;* Hecuba; *Iliad;* Priam.

HEL

In Old Norse mythology, Hel is the goddess of death. Originally the name was given to the world of the dead. Hel is the daughter of the trickster god Loki. She presides over Niflheim, the World of Darkness. In the myth of Balder (Baldr), when he is wounded by a shaft of mistletoe thrown by the blind god Hod, the gods send an emissary to ask Hel to spare Balder. She promises to release him if all things will weep for him. (Jones, G. 1990)

See also Baldr.

DAS HELDENBUCH

A book of thirteenth-century heroic romances drawn from two metrical cycles: the Ostrogoth poems, dealing with Dietrich von Bern (Theodoric the Great), Emanaric, and Etzel (Attila the Hun); and the Lombard-Franconian poems dealing with Wolfdietrich, Ortnit, and Hugdietrich. Included in the former cycle are "The Rose Garden" ("Der rosengarten"), "Laurin and the Little Rose Garden" ("Laurin und der kleine rosengarten"), and "Biterolf and Dietlieb." The figure Hugdietrich in the Franconian poems is thought to be Theodoric, son of the Frankish king Clovis, and Wolfdietrich is identified as Theodebert, son of King Theodoric, although these identities have been merged by long accretion. In this cycle, Wolfdietrich, cast out by his own family, lives for some time in exile in the court of Lombard king Ortnit, whose death by dragon he avenges. (Forster 1957)

HELDENLIEDER

Orally transmitted songs in Old High German, heldenlieder are the earliest form of Germanic literature, celebrating the exploits of famous heroes and forming the basis for later heroic epics. (Preminger 1990)

HELEDD

Heledd is the subject of a ninth-century Welsh poem, or narrative prose interspersed with englyn (englynion), concerning one of several Welsh rulers in the Shrewsbury region of Britain who are driven westward into the hills by the English. Heledd fears that her lack of charity has provoked the fates and caused the deaths of her brothers. The term *englyn* refers to eight different terse Welsh meters used in poetry, particularly from the twelfth century. (Preminger 1990)

HELEN

The indirect cause of the Trojan War of Greek epic literature, Helen is the daughter of Zeus and sister of Clytemnestra, Agamemnon's wife. She is the wife of Menelaus, Agamemnon's brother. During her husband's absence, she flees to Troy with Paris (Alexandros), son of the Trojan king Priam. When Paris is killed, she marries his brother Deiphobos, then betrays him when Troy is captured. She then returns to Sparta with Menelaus. At one point in the *Iliad,* grieving over the fallen Trojan Hektor, Helen tells his lifeless corpse, "I should have died before I came with him (Paris)." She says of Hektor, "There was no other in all the wide Troad / who was kind to me, and my friend; all others shrank when they saw me." Helen also appears in *The Cyclic Epics,* the *Cypria,* the *Little Iliad,* and *The Sack of Ilium.* (Godolphin 1964; Lattimore 1976)

See also *Cypria; Epic Cycle; Iliad.*

HELENUS

In the *Iliad* (vi), *The Cyclic Epics,* the *Cypria,* the *Little Iliad,* and the *Aeneid* (iii), Helenus is the son of Trojan king Priam and his wife Hecuba, the brother of Hektor, and twin of Cassandra the prophetess. According to Homer, he is a seer as well as a warrior, and in both the *Cypria* and the *Little Iliad* he foretells the future. It is Helenus who advises building the wooden horse. In later years, he marries Hektor's widow Andromache and rules the land. (Godolphin 1964; Humphries 1951; Lattimore 1976)

HELIAND

(Old Saxon: "Savior")

This Old Saxon epic (ca. 830) based on the life of Christ was written in alliterative verse of almost 6,000 lines by an unknown poet said to be commissioned by Louis the Pious (r. 813–840). The poem portrays Christ as a Germanic king who rewards his warlike followers with arm rings. King Herod's feast is portrayed as a drinking bout. The poem, which survives in four manuscripts, is important because it and a fragment entitled "Genesis" are all that remain of Old Saxon poetry. (Langer 1972)

HENGERDD

(Old Song)

This is an early Welsh collection of short elegies of the sixth-century poet Aneirin about the knights of the sixth-century ruler of Edinburgh, Mynyddawg, and historic odes of Taliesin praising rulers of northern Wales and southern Scotland in the kingdom of Rheged. (Preminger 1990)

See also Aneirin.

HERA

In Greek religion, Hera is queen of the Olympian gods, the jealous sister-wife of Zeus, and a participant in the Trojan War in the *Iliad* and the *Cypria*. (Godolphin 1964; Lattimore 1976)

HERAKLES

(Also Heracles, Hercules)

Herakles is the most famous hero in Greek legend, probably inspired by the life of a real warrior-chieftain of the kingdom of Argos. He is depicted in myth as the son of Zeus and Alcmene, supposed to become the ruler of Greece. But Zeus's jealous wife Hera uses trickery to see that the sickly Eurystheus becomes king instead. Hera begins her vengeful tricks against Herakles while he is still in the cradle, sending two serpents to kill him. However, the baby easily strangles them.

When Herakles has conquered the kingdom of Orchomenus, married its princess, Megara, and fathered children by her, Hera visits madness upon him, causing him to murder his wife and children. As a result, he is forced to become the servant of his half brother Eurystheus. The king imposes a cycle of 12 labors upon him. Accounts of the labors vary, but they usually include: (1) slaying the Nemean lion, (2) slaying the nine-headed Hydra, (3) capturing the hind of Arcadia, (4) capturing the wild boar, (5) cleaning out the stables of King Augeas in one day, (6) shooting the Stymphalian man-eating birds, (7) capturing the

An amphora, from 600 B.C., shows the Greek hero Herakles, left, slaying Nessus, a centaur, who had threatened Deianeira, the hero's wife.

mad bull of Crete, (8) capturing the man-eating mares of King Diomedes, (9) stealing the girdle of the Amazon queen Hippolyte, (10) stealing the cattle of the giant Geryon, (11) traveling to the world's end to capture the golden apples of the Hesperides, and (12) capturing the three-headed dog who guards the gates of the underworld.

After Herakles has completed these labors, he wins the hand of Deianeira in a fight with the river god Achelous. As he is returning with her, he must defend her against the centaur Nessus, whom he kills with a poison arrow. The dying centaur convinces Deianeira that his blood, rubbed on the garment of a man, will result in undying love for her, so she saves his blood. Later, when Herakles falls in love with the Oechalian princess Iole, Deianeira rubs his shirt with the blood. But it proves to be poisonous, and he dies. After his mortal body is consumed on a pyre on Mount Oeta, he is reconciled to Hera and marries Hebe.

He appears in the *Odyssey* (xi), in which Odysseus sees his phantom in the underworld, where he has gone to bring back Cerberus; in the *Homeric Hymns* (1–8); in Euripides's *Heracles,* whose chorus recounts the labors and bewails his remaining in the underworld; in Apollodorus's *The Library* (II), which recounts his labors and names his offspring; in Hyginus's *Myths* (31), which recounts his many deeds; in Theocritus's *Idylls* (13) in which he has been depicted by some as a glutton and buffoon, and by Stoics as a savior; in the *Argonautica* (1), where he takes the youth Hylos on the *Argo* and abandons the Argonautic expedition to search for him after he drowns; and in Virgil's *Aeneid* (viii), in which he is connected to Rome through King Evander, who entertains him on his return from the conquest of Geryon. (When the giant monster Cacus steals some of the oxen of Geryon from Herakles, the hero dislodges a flint rock and shoves it downhill where it breaks open Cacus's den: "That great palace / Under the rock, the chambered vault of shadows." Herakles grabs him and twists him into a knot.) (Bullfinch 1962; Godolphin 1964; Graves 1955)

HERBALD

In *Beowulf,* Herbald is a prince of the Geats, Hrethel's oldest son. He is accidentally killed on a hunting expedition by his brother Hathcyn. His death, which must go unavenged or deprive Hrethel of a heir, causes his father to die of grief. (Hieatt 1967; Raffel 1963)

See also *Beowulf.*

HEREKALI

(Also *Tambuka)*

The oldest Swahili epic extant in manuscript form, dated 1141 Islamic or A.D. 1728, it contains 1,145 stanzas describing Muhammad's legendary campaign against the Byzantine emperor Heraclius. (Westley *RAL* 1991)

HERMES

In Greek religion, Hermes is the son of Zeus and Maia. Although he is associated elsewhere with protection of cattle and sheep, and with patronage of music and eloquence, in the *Odyssey* he is primarily a messenger of the gods who also accompanies the dead to Hades. He is often associated with the Roman god Mercury. (Graves 1955; Rieu 1961)

HERO

According to Hesiod's account of the structure of the cosmos in *Theogony*, the hero is one of four categories of beings—men, heroes, daimons, and gods—indicating that heroes are more than mere men. They are a step above men on the ladder reaching toward God. (Lattimore 1959)

See also *Theogony.*

HERUKA, GREAT

A wrathful deity described in *Bardo Thötröl* (Tibetan Book of the Dead), the Great Heruka is "the space between the five families" of herukas. He creates the energy bequeathed to all the wrathful herukas and their consorts. "Heruka" is the masculine energy principle in a wrathful form. The five herukas are: The Buddha Heruka, Vajra Heruka, Ratna Heruka, Padma Heruka, and Karma Heruka. These wrathful deities represent hope, embodying basic continuous neutral energy, neither good nor bad. (Fremantle and Trungpa 1987)

See also *Bardo Thötröl.*

HIAWATHA

(Also Haion-Hwa-tha, He Makes Rivers)

In Onondaga legend, Hiawatha is the legendary hero/chief and founder of the Iroquois League of Five Nations. He is thought to have been a historical shaman/statesman who lived ca. 1450. Some legends say that he was originally a member of the Mohawk tribe, which rejected his teachings, forcing him to leave and live with the Onondaga. A powerful chief, Wathatotarho, opposed his attempts to unify the five nations of the Iroquois. After Hiawatha defeated him, the chief killed Hiawatha's daughter in revenge.

However, oral tradition gives him divine origin as an incarnation of Ta-ren-ya-wa-gon (Upholder of Heaven). He is able to overcome all the powers of nature that war with mankind. He is said to be the incarnation of progress. At one time he looks down to see his people being terrified by monsters and giants. He descends to earth and leads the people westward, holding a little girl by the hand. He encourages one group to settle on the banks of a beautiful river. He teaches them how to plant corn, beans, squash, and tobacco. He teaches them how to pound corn into grain and how to hunt in the forest with the help of dogs. He gives them bows and arrows and the skill to shoot straight. They are called Mohawk.

He takes a little girl by the hand and continues the journey with the rest of the people. He leads them westward to a fertile valley surrounded by great forests. He leaves a group there, after teaching them how to make weapons and weave baskets. They are named Oneida.

Once more he takes a little girl's hand and heads west, leading the rest of the people. He stops at the foot of a mountain and leaves a group there, giving them knowledge and wisdom to know the will of the Great Creator. They are called Onondaga.

Again he takes a small girl by the hand and wanders westward to the shores of a sparkling lake, where he leaves another group, to whom he gives the canoe and teaches them the skill to maneuver through turbulent waters. They are named Cayuga.

With only a few people left, he goes westward to another lake by a mountain. There he settles the last of the people, giving them swift feet that can outrun a deer. They are called Keepers of the Door. They are the Seneca Nation.

He decides to take the shape of a man and live among the Onondaga. He takes the name of Hiawatha and chooses a wife from the tribe. They have a beautiful and clever daughter, Mni-haha. The tribes live in peace, and Hiawatha travels among the tribes in a magical white birchbark canoe.

But the laws of the universe include sorrow with joy, death with life, adversity with prosperity. From north of the Great Lakes come ferocious marauding tribes who sweep in on horseback and leave devastation in their wake. The Iroquois tribes appeal to Hiawatha for protection from the invaders. He advises them to assemble and wait for his coming.

Just as Hiawatha and his little daughter arrive in the magic canoe, a gigantic bird swoops down, his wings making the sound of a thousand thunderclaps. Mni-haha bids her father farewell, climbs atop the bird, and disappears with it into the sky. Hiawatha sits grieving for several days while the assemblage waits.

After four days of grieving, he comes before them to say, "What is past is past." Turning to the problem of their present trouble, he says, "No tribe alone can withstand our savage enemies, who care nothing of the eternal law. . . . You must have one fire, one pipe, one war club." He convinces the tribes that they must unite for their common good. He appoints the Onondaga, the strongest, as the protectors; the Oneida, the wisest, as counselors; the swift and persuasive Seneca as the spokesmen; the cunning Cayuga as guardians of the rivers; and the farming Mohawk as the nourishers.

The Indians ask him to be the chief, but he declines, telling them that he must leave. He counsels them, "Choose the wisest women in your tribes to be the future clan mothers and peace makers. . . . Let your sachems be wise enough to go to such women for advice when there are disputes. . . ." He bids them farewell and steps into his magic canoe, which rises into the sky and disappears into the clouds. (Erdoes and Ortiz 1984)

HIGLAC

(Also Hygelac, Higelac)

In *Beowulf*, Higlac is a king of the Geats, Hrethel's son, and younger brother of Herbald and Hathcyn. He is Beowulf's uncle as well as his liege lord. (Hieatt 1967; Raffel 1963)

See also *Beowulf.*

HIKAJAT MALÉM DAGANG

This is a northern Sumatran oral epic depicting the Atjehnese War against the invading Dutch (1873). (Siegel 1979)

HIKAJAT PÒTJOET MOEHAMAT

Epic of Atjeh. ***See*** *Pòtjoet Moehamat, Hikajat.*

HIKAJAT PRANG KOMPENI

This Sumatran oral epic exists in manuscript form in the University Library at Leiden. It describes the circumstances of the 1873 Atjehnese War against invading Dutch forces. It contains scenes of the homeless searching for shelter. (Siegel 1979)

HIKAJAT PRANG SABIL

Into this nineteenth-century epic of Atjeh, a florid translation into Atjehnese of the words of the Koran is inserted for the purpose of inspiring warriors to battle. It involves the dreams of a boy of 15, Moeda Bahlia ("handsome youth"), who is going off to war. The "fortunate and clever" youth wakes, weeping, and tells his fantastic dreams of "the expanse of paradise" to Abdoel Wahid. Abdoel Wahid explains, "Those who do not follow the commands of the Lord will get none of these pleasures." He sets the boy on his way by showing him how to implement the Koran's injunction concerning jihad, or holy war: "Marry yourself to the holy war. . . ." Abdoel does not follow Moeda into martyrdom. Instead, he returns home to tell the story of the boy's sacrifice to other listeners, who are dressed in the white shrouds of warriors about to martyr themselves.

The *Hikajat Prang Sabil* was chanted before Sumatran men went off to attack the invading Dutch during the Atjehnese War of 1873. (Siegel 1979)

HIKAYAT BAYAN BUDIMAN

This Malay work contains the story of Ibrahim ibn Adhem. (Jones, R. 1985)

See also *Hikayat Khoja Maimun; Hikayat Sultan Ibrahim ibn Adhem.*

HIKAYAT KHOJA MAIMUN

(Also *Hikayat Bayan Budiman*)

The Malay version of the story of Ibrahim ibn Adhem exists in manuscript form in the collection of the Royal Asiatic Society in London. The legend apparently derives from Persian rather than Arabic sources. (Jones, R. 1985)

See also *Hikayat Sultan Ibrahim ibn Adhem.*

HIKAYAT RAJA-RAPA PASAI

This Malay narrative or essay/poem was composed in the mid-fourteenth to late fifteenth centuries. It contains rhythmical verse, frequent tags, and repetitions to facilitate the performer's recitation, usually signs of a work that has developed by accretion. (Jones, R. 1985)

HIKAYAT SULTAN IBRAHIM IBN ADHEM

This Malay version of an epic narrative of unknown authorship, written down ca. the seventeenth century, concerns a historical figure of the second-century Muslim era, or eighth-century Christian era. Five manuscripts of a long version of the story are known, and five manuscripts of a short version are known, although two other manuscripts of the short version are known to have existed at one time. Although the hikayat contains a great deal of legend, other sources referring to Ibrahim seem to verify that he actually lived. However, the circumstances of his life preclude his ever having been a king of Baghdad, as he becomes in the epic. Earlier legends have him as the son of a king of Khurasan, and in many languages his status has been elevated to king. In the present version, he is king of Irak.

Ibrahim was born ca. A.D. 730 into a wealthy Arab family in Balkh in present-day northern Afghanistan. His name is given as Ibrāhīm ibn Adhem ibn Mansūr. According to the epic, he abdicates to become a mendicant; however, it is more likely that he abandoned his luxurious home as a young man to become a wandering Sufi ascetic, renowned all along the eastern Mediterranean for his wisdom, piety, and generosity. He died ca. 777 on an island during an expedition against the Greeks. He is the subject of the nineteenth-century English sonnet "Abou Ben Adhem" by Leigh Hunt.

The Malay version of the epic refers to "Aulia Ibrahim ibn Adhem, Sultan in Irak." He is known for his asceticism, justice, wisdom, and generosity. At his command, a great new wall of black stone is constructed around the city. When it is finished, he goes forth on his elephant to inspect it. He summons all the people to inspect the wall for flaws, and orders that each person be paid a dinar from the coffers. He is unconcerned about worldly goods but extremely concerned with spiritual matters—for example, abstaining from alcohol.

The sultan's vizier (wazir) and his officers encounter an old man, a new arrival, who claims that there is a flaw in the new city wall. They usher him into the sultan's presence, where he reveals the flaw: Like all things, it will perish in the end. The learned men listen and confirm that this is true, and that only heaven and hell are imperishable. The sultan offers the old man gifts, but he refuses them, fearing that they would alter his status as a fakir. The sultan is enormously impressed by this decision. He muses upon his own status, thinking, "This world is like a dream. . . ."

The next day he announces his intention to abdicate the throne and places his chief vizier as regent with the title of Wazir al-Alam. He assures his people that they have done no wrong to precipitate his leaving; he is going wherever Allah wills. The next morning before dawn, he leaves the city alone and unobserved, taking a staff, a bowl, a knife, and the royal signet ring. As he wanders through the forests, he does not neglect his ritual prayers.

When the people discover that Ibrahim is gone, the vizier, weeping bitterly, orders tens of thousands of people to set off to find him. The vizier follows on the royal elephant. When they find Ibrahim and beseech him to come back to the palace for his own safety, he quotes from the Kuran: "Verily God . . . hears and sees the condition of His servants." But after the people take off their handkerchiefs and prostrate themselves at his feet, he decides to return. ". . . But I refuse to occupy the throne—I will simply reside in the palace and perform devotions to God. . . ."

They return by way of a canal near the beach, where the sultan sees a great blind heron sitting on a log in the sea with its mouth open so that fish jump into it. The sight reminds him of his own lack of faith: "Here is a creature made blind in both eyes . . . but still it is given sustenance by the Lord. . . . How then could he not give sustenance on His earth to me? . . ." He sends all the people away, saying, ". . . it is because of you that I lacked faith in my Lord . . . and wanted to come back. . . ."

After they are gone, he continues on foot until he becomes hungry and thirsty. He comes to a river where he drinks, washes the sand from his trousers and jacket, and lays them out to dry. He sees a ripe pomegranate floating by, and he splits it in two and eats half before he realizes, "This pomegranate . . . must have an owner. In which case I am eating something which belongs to a fellow man." He is filled with remorse for his thoughtlessness.

The story shifts to the home of a learned ascetic named Sharif Hasan, who has a beautiful and sensible 14-year-old daughter named Siti Saliha. On his estate, Hasan has a luxuriant orchard, and in the middle of the orchard is a clear, cool lake with a beautiful pavilion on either bank. The orchard is cared for by two learned sages named Shaikh Miftah al-Arifin and Shaikh Ismail. Sharif Hasan falls ill and, realizing that he will soon die, prophesies the arrival of Ibrahim ibn Adhem, whom he instructs Siti to marry. He leaves her in the care of the two shaikhs and dies.

Eventually Ibrahim arrives at the orchard, where he meets Shaikh Ismail and tells his story of eating the pomegranate, which he sees has come from this orchard. Later he repeats the story to Shaikh Miftah and is conducted in to relate it to Siti. She realizes that he matches her father's description of her future husband, and furthermore she notes that he is very handsome and radiant, with "the mark of piety" on his face. Ibrahim sees that she too is very beautiful and possesses the mark of piety.

Siti will neither sell the pomegranate nor sanction his eating it. She tells him, "Whoever wishes to be exonerated from a charge of eating my pomegranate . . . , his only course is . . . to marry the owner. . . ." So Ibrahim is married to Siti and settles into her home.

Shaikh Miftah comes to Ibrahim for religious instruction and is given six points. First: "If you are minded to disobey God . . . , do not eat of the sustenance which He provides." Second: "If there is no escape from your eating His sustenance, then do not live in His country . . . and then be disobedient to God. . . ." Third: "If you . . . eat His sustenance and live in His country, then when you are to be disobedient, go to some place which God . . . does not see . . . [for] if you are seen by God . . . , how can you think of being disobedient? . . ." Fourth: "When the angel of death comes to take away your soul, say to him, 'Be patient, do not take my soul until I have repented first.'" Fifth: "When [the angels] Munkar and Nakir come to punish you, push them away. . . ." Sixth: "When God . . . commands the angel guardians of hell to take you into hell fire, say to God . . . 'Don't you order them to do that.'" The shaikh is puzzled by the teaching.

Shaikh Ismail comes for instruction as to why his prayers are not answered, and Ibrahim explains ten obstacles: this world, the devil, lust, animal lusts (gluttony), covetousness, doing the forbidden thing, regarding "as true what his wife and children say about loyal service to God . . . being absolutely unnecessary," performing things unnecessary for the service to Allah, paying lip service to the truth while refusing to be loyal to Allah, and holding as right what is wrong.

When it grows late, the married couple go to Siti's bedroom, where he enjoys himself "as is the wont of married men."

After 40 days, Ibrahim announces that he is leaving. He tells his wife not to be upset by partings, "for we . . . are to be likened to (foreign) merchants: When the appropriate season comes we shall return to our proper land. . . . When our allotted span ends . . . we shall return to the eternal land." He likens this world to a woman in fine clothing: "From a distance those who do not know her lust after her . . . But . . . when they . . . get close to her, discover that she is old and ugly. So they detest her. . . ." He prepares to leave, and Siti faints. Her shrieks reach the four layers of heaven. He places her in the care of the two shaikhs and sets off immediately on foot. After long days of travel, he arrives in Mecca, where he performs his devotions night and day without sleeping.

Meanwhile, Siti gives birth to their son, Muhammad Tahir, who is fine and handsome and has a captivating manner. In due time he learns from his playmates that "no one knows who his father is!" They accuse him of being a bastard. When he questions his mother, he learns that his father was the king in Irak before he abdicated to become a fakir. In answer to Muhammad Tahir's pleas, Siti gives her son permission to go to Mecca to find his father.

By the time the boy completes the arduous journey to Mecca, he is 18 (one version says 20) years old. Ibrahim is pleased to see his son, but when he realizes that he has missed performing the tawaf because of his son's arrival, he becomes very angry. He threatens to cut off his son's head if he doesn't leave at once. Muhammad Tahir is distressed to be sent away, destitute, after having traveled for so long and so far; in fact, he does not even remember the way home. But Ibrahim explains that his holy devotions cannot be interrupted for mere family matters. He tells his son the story of Musa (Moses), the moral of which is, "Whoever commits himself to the care of God . . . while he does good . . . is holding fast to a rope which will not break. . . ." He gives his son his signet ring and tells him not to sell it anywhere except in the city of Irak. He adds, "As for your mother, I will be united with her in the hereafter. . . ."

Muhammad Tahir starts out for Irak, coming at last to a fork in the road. One leads home to Kufah, the other to Irak. He feels sorry for his mother, waiting all alone in Kufah, but he decides to go on to Irak.

When he arrives, a merchant in Irak recognizes the ring as belonging to the former sultan. Without the ring, sovereignty is not complete, so Tahir is sent to the regent Wazir al-Alam, to whom he offers to sell the ring. The vizier sees the resemblance of son to father and falls at his feet, weeping. Tahir tells the ministers, "The Sultan is not going to come back again; he has no more desire for the . . . greatness and honours of this world. . . ." He refuses the ministers' offer of the throne.

He instructs them to continue to rule, and to treat the subjects justly. They ask him to define justice (adil), and he tells them: First, the ruler should warn all about the punishment for an offense, and on the third offense, the offender should be punished. Second, the ruler should investigate complaints and punish accordingly. Third, the ruler should not covet the property of the lowly. Furthermore, people should be treated equally regardless of financial circumstances. Finally, the ruler should pay no heed to the class of people.

Tahir gives them advice on how to appoint ministers and enumerates the qualities of a good ruler. The ministers fete him with a feast and offer him fine gifts, but he refuses all but a few precious stones. He also refuses the offer of an escort and sets off for home.

When he arrives, he is greeted by the two shaikhs, and he reports to his mother what has happened, presenting her with the precious stones. Every year thereafter, Wazir al-Alam sends eight camels laden with food and gifts for Siti and Muhammad Tahir. Thus it is narrated by Shaikh Abu Bakar.

Other versions of the story of ibn Adhem appear in *Hikayat Khoja Maimun*, also known as *Hikayat Bayan Budiman*. (Jones, R. 1985)

HILĀLIYYA

This North African Arabian epic is still popular today, particularly in Egypt. (Connelly 1986)

See also Jāziya.

HILDEBRAND

In *Hildebrandslied* (The Song of Hildebrand), extant now only in fragment, Hildebrand is the hero who must slay his son in a duel. Hildebrand also appears as a character in the *Nibelungenlied;* Hildebrand, now old, is tutor and Master-at-Arms to Dietrich of Verona. He is the uncle of the hot-headed Wolfhart, who cannot be restrained from fighting the Burgundians after the murder of Rüdiger. When Hildebrand sees that he cannot hold Wolfhart back, he races him into the fray. After Wolfhart is slain, Hildebrand attempts to wound Hagen but is instead wounded by him. Fearing further hurt, he flees from Hagen. When Kriemhild slays Hagen, however, Hildebrand shouts, "Although he put me in deadly peril, I shall avenge the death of the brave lord of Tranek!" He strikes the queen dead with his sword. (Forster 1957; Hatto 1969)

See also *Hildebrandslied; Nibelungenlied.*

HILDEBRANDSLIED
(Song of Hildebrand)

This Old High German heroic ballad (ca. 800 manuscript; composed ca. 650) remains only as a 67-line fragment. Written in alliterative verse, it is the only extant example of heroic poetry in Old High German. It tells of the duel between the hero, Hildebrand, and a young warrior, Hadubrand, who challenges him, not knowing that Hildebrand is his father. The poem breaks off before the outcome is known, but it is certain that Hildebrand must slay his son. This theme is repeated in the Persian *Shāh-Nāmah* and in the Icelandic *Asmundar Saga Kappabana.* (Forster 1957; Hatto 1969)

HLAMBAMANZI
(Also Jacob Msimbithi)

In the Zulu epic *Emperor Shaka the Great,* Hlambamanzi is a fugitive from white captivity who acts as Shaka's interpreter. (Kunene 1979)

HO HSIEN KU

In Chinese myth, Ho Hsien (also Sien) Ku is the only female among Taoism's Eight Immortals. While she is an adolescent, she is told in a dream that eating mother-of-pearl will make her immortal. She eats some and discovers that she can whisk across the mountaintops in order to collect herbs from exotic places. Each year the Queen Mother of the West, Hsi Wang Mu, is feted at a grand birthday banquet during which the queen serves bear paws, monkey lips, and dragon's liver, and for dessert, p'an-t'ao, "flat peaches" of immortality that ripen every 3,000 years in the royal garden. During one of these celebrations, Ho Hsien Ku and the other Immortals become intoxicated on the royal wine. Ho Hsien Ku has been seen only once since her seventh-century summons from Empress Wu Hou; 50 years after the summons she was sighted floating on a cloud. She is known as the Chinese Artemis. In Japan she is the equivalent of Kasenko. (Mackenzie 1990)

HORAE

In the *Iliad,* the Horae are the Seasons, custodians of the gates of Olympus. In the *Odyssey,* they are responsible for bringing the seasons to earth in their proper order. (Lattimore 1976; Rouse 1990)

HORATII AND CURIATII

In Roman legend, the Horatii and Curiatii are two sets of triplet brothers—one Roman, the other Alban—whose combat with one another is to decide the outcome of the war between Rome and Alba Longa (ca. sixth century B.C.). The contest is won by one of the Horatii brothers, but when his sister mourns the death of a Curiatti to whom she is betrothed, he kills her, saying, "So perish any Roman woman who mourns the enemy." He is condemned to death for his sister's murder but is later pardoned by the people. (Siepmann 1987)

HORATIUS COCLES

A legendary one-eyed hero of Rome (ca. sixth century B.C.), he defends a Roman bridge against the Etruscans and Lars Porsena, then dives into the Tiber as the Romans demolish the bridge. (Bowder 1984; Siepmann 1987)

HORUS
(Hawk, the Avenger)

Horus is one of the triad of gods of the Great Ennead, or state religion of Egypt, as told by the priests of Heliopolis and recounted by Plutarch (ca. A.D. 40–120). Two gods are named Horus. The elder, born on the second epagomenal day (the time of bringing forth), one day after Osiris, is described as a fair god, all but forgotten and overshadowed by the second Horus, born on the vernal equinox to Isis after his father Osiris has died. Horus is born in the reeds of the delta of lower Egypt, where his mother remains all alone. He grows into manhood and sets about avenging the death of his father and punishing his killer, Seth. After he has dealt with Seth, he pursues Seth's helpers. While he is gone, Seth wheedles Isis into freeing him. Returning to find Seth free, Horus cuts off the crown and head of Isis, but Thoth replaces them immediately with the horned head and crown of Hathor, a more ancient goddess. Isis and Horus both pursue Seth, who turns and tears out Horus's eye, that part of his body containing his soul. Horus manages to retrieve it before they chase Seth into the sea. Horus returns to his father's body and, embracing it, transfers to it some of the power of his own ka, or spirit double. He feeds Osiris the eye, and its strength reaches his limbs and makes him a ka-in-harmony. Osiris rises from the dead and lives again.

Osiris ascends the ladder to heaven, and Horus is declared his son and heir on earth. (Budge 1967; Budge 1969; Goodrich 1960)

See also Isis; Osiris.

HOST OF IGOR, THE LAY OF THE

(Also *Slovo o polku Igoreve)*

This Russian lay recounts a historic event that occurred in 1185 in which Russian prince Igor Sviatoslavov of Novgorod-Seversku and his brother Vsevolod, "impetuous buffalo," invade territory held by the Quman (Polovcian, Turkic-speaking people). There is much Slavic myth woven into the poem. It speaks of the shepherd god Voloss, patron of poetry as well as guardian of herds; of Russian ancestor-grandfather Stribog, the wind god; of the thunder god Peroun (also Perkun), who refuses to vanish even after Igor's son Prince Vladimir (St. Vladimir) destroys his statue. It speaks of the Egyptian sun god Horus and the swan-maiden of death who also appears in *Beowulf.* A subplot tells of Russian prince Vseslav, who changes into a wolf at night. It has been suggested that the lay may have been performed at the wedding of Igor's son Vladimir. (Goodrich 1961)

See also *Igor's Host, Lay of; Lay of Igor's Campaign.*

HOTU-MATUA

He is the hero of Easter Island tradition, legendary founder of the culture, whose story was recorded in 1934 from a native, Tepano. Hotu-Matua, originally a chief on a large western island called Marae Renga, is forced to leave because of defeat in war by another chief, Oroi, and because of a conflict with his brother. Among his followers is a "tattooer," Hau-Maka, who dreams of an island to the east upon which he sees six men. Hotu-Matua, considering the dream prophetic, orders a canoe built and sends six men in search of the island. The men land on Easter Island and Hotu-Matua follows close behind, with a canoe of plants and animals to sustain life. As they alight, the wives of both Hotu-Matua and his chief deputy, Tu'u-ko-ihu, give birth to a son and a daughter, respectively. Unbeknownst to the crew, however, Hotu-Matua's enemy Oroi has stowed away in the canoe, and, after dark, Oroi slips ashore. For a long time he hides out and ambushes those who stray from camp. Eventually Hotu-Matua apprehends him and kills him, and peace reigns on Easter Island. As they grow to manhood, each of Hotu-Matua's sons forms a tribe, and Hotu-Matua divides the island between them. When he grows old, he climbs to the rim of the volcano of Rano-Kao and calls across the sea to the gods of his homeland on Marae Renga. The gods hear him and cause a cock to crow as a sign that his time has come to die. He is carried down the mountain to his house, where he dies. (Suggs 1960)

HOU CHI

The Chinese Lord of Millet, Hou Chi is said to be the first ancestor of the Chou royal house. He may have been a cultural hero rather than a tribal chief. He is miraculously conceived when his mother steps on the tracks of a giant or a god. He is abandoned in a desolate spot but is raised in the forest by animals and birds, and grows up to found the house of Chou. (Waley 1960)

See also *Book of Songs.*

HOU T'U

In Chinese mythology, Hou T'u is the Sovereign of the Earth, first worshiped by Han emperor Wu Ti in 113 B.C. and later personified in the hero Kou Lung, who is in turn related to the legendary father of Chinese agriculture, Shen Nung. Fifteen centuries later, Hou T'u became Hou T'u Nai-Nai, earth goddess. (Waley 1960)

HROLFS SAGA KRAKA

This Old Norse heroic saga (ca. fourteenth century) has elements in common with the Old English *Beowulf* and *Widsith.* It is based on the life of Hrolf Kraki, king of the Danes ca. the sixth century, particularly on his clash with Swedish king Athils at the battle of Uppsala. In *Beowulf* he is mentioned as Hrothulf. His death in battle against his brother-in-law Hjorvarthr is the subject of the tenth-century Danish poem *Bjarkamál.* (Jones, G. 1990)

See also *Bjarkamál.*

HROTHGAR

In *Beowulf,* Hrothgar is a Danish king, the second son of Healfdane. He built the mead hall Herot, which the monster Grendel attacks. He is pictured as an old man, wise and courageous. In his younger days, he defended Beowulf's father, which accounts for the hero's desire to help the beleaguered king. (Hieatt 1967; Raffel 1963)

See also *Beowulf;* Grendel; Higlac.

HUAROCHIRÍ MANUSCRIPT

This Quechuan collection (ca. 1598) of the Huaro Cheri people recounts pre-Hispanic Andean myths and legends, probably dating in part to the remote past. The text is comprised of a preface and 31 chapters, much of which relate the mythic cycle of the mountain deity Paria Caca, his human descendants, and other of his contemporary huacas (something embodying a superhuman and sacred being). The work recalls, in the first four chapters, a remote age when cannibal deities harassed a race of immortal humans. Other elements describe ceremonies dedicated to a variety of pantheistic beings, recall Inca rule, and even, in the more recent sections, the invasion of the Spaniards.

The preface indicates that this is the first written record ever made and that it will relate the customs and activities of the people, village by village, from their "dawning age" onward. The author laments, "If the ancestors . . . had known writing in earlier times, then the lives they lived would not have faded from view. . . . But . . . since nothing has been written until now, I set forth here the lives of the ancestors of the Huaro Cheri people. . . ."

Chapter 1 is entitled "Who the Idols of Old Were, and How They Warred among Themselves, and How the Natives Existed at That Time." It relates the defeat of ancient huacas Yana Ñamca and Tuta Ñamca by another huaca, the fire-monster Huallallo Caruincho, who orders the people to bear only two children each, one of which he will eat. In these times, people come back to life on the fifth day after death. Later, another huaca appears named Paria Caca—a sacred mountain, the great deity of the Huaro Cheri people. Two other huacas are introduced: Cuni Raya, a water deity, whose nature almost matches that of the other huaca, the trickster-god Vira Cocha—so much so that the two are combined in the next chapter.

Chapter 2 is titled "How Cuni Raya Vira Coche Acted in His Own Age. The Life of Cuni Raya Vira Coche. How Cavi Llaca Gave Birth to His Child, and What Followed." It relates that Cuni Raya Vira Coche goes around the country posing as a friendless orphan, but he charms local villagers by "performing all kinds of wonders." In one village is a beautiful huaca, a virgin named Cavi Llaca, whom huacas and villagers alike desire. Cuni Raya turns into a bird and puts his semen in a piece of fruit, which he drops to her. When she eats the fruit, she becomes pregnant and bears a child. Later, when she discovers that the father of her child is a "mangy beggar," she leaves in disgrace, determined to disappear into the ocean. Cuni Raya tries to follow her, but he is easily distracted by the two daughters of Urpay Huachac, and he seduces them. When their mother discovers the seduction, she determines to destroy him. She chases after him, pretending only to wish to pick his lice, but secretly intending to push him into an abyss. But Cuni Raya escapes her by saying that he must relieve himself.

Chapter 3 returns to the story of very early people, at a time when "this world wanted to come to an end." A llama warns its owner that in five days the ocean will overflow. The two go to the top of Villca Coto Mountain, where they find a large host of animals already taking refuge. The ocean rises and covers all the rest of the land, killing all the people. "Afterward," the text says, "that man began to multiply once more." No mention is made of a woman in the process.

Chapter 4 describes the sun's disappearance for five days, during which rocks bang against one another, and grinding stones and mortars revolt and begin eating people. This episode ends the section dedicated to remote antiquity.

Chapter 5 begins the mythic cycle of Paria Caca, which comprises the bulk of the text. Paria Caca is born on a mountain named Condor Coto in the form of five eggs. He has a son, a poor man called Huatya Curi, who is apparently born in human form before Paria Caca. Nearby lives a man named Tamta Ñamca who pretends to be a god, demanding that people worship him. However, he falls ill and calls on a number of shamans, none of whom can diagnose his illness. Huatya Curi has a dream in which a fox tells him the nature of and cure for Tamta Ñamca's illness. Huatya Curi goes to the home of the bogus "god" and promises to cure him if he will give him his daughter for a wife.

After he has cured Tamta Ñamca and receives the daughter as his wife, he is challenged to a dance contest by Tamta Ñamca's other son-in-law, who resents having a poor man in the family. For the first time, Huatya Curi goes, with his wife, to Condor Coto Mountain, where Paria Caca dwells in the form of five eggs, to ask his father's advice as to how to win the contest. Paria Caca advises him how to win, but other challenges of drinking, dress, and house building follow. Huatya Curi wins them all, following Paria Caca's advice.

After all of these challenges, Huatya Curi flies into a rage and chases away his rich brother-in-law. Paria Caca flies forth from the five eggs in the shape of five falcons. When he hears that Tamta Ñamca has been saying "I am a god," he goes into a rage as well, rises up as rain, and flushes all the people into the ocean. Then he ascends to the highlands.

Chapter 6 relates that, when Paria Caca has become human, he heads toward the dwelling of Huallallo Caruincho, who eats people. Along the way, he stops at the village of the Yunca, where there is a festival. He sits all day at the end of the banquet table, but no one offers him so much as a drink. Finally, at the end of the day, a woman offers him a gourd of maize beer. He tells her, "It's a lucky thing for you that you offered me this beer. . . . These people have made me damn mad!" He warns her not to be in the village five days hence, as "something awful" is going to happen. The woman heeds his advice and takes her family away. On the fated day Paria Caca brings a torrential rainstorm on the mountain above the village, which causes a mudslide to wash all the villagers into the sea. Then he continues on his way.

At the next village he sees a beautiful woman named Chuqui Suso whom he desires very much. He asks if he may sleep with her, but she makes some conditions concerning changes she wants made in her irrigation system before she will agree. He finally diverts the streams to suit her, and she eventually fulfills her promise, after which she turns herself into a stone so that she may remain precisely where she is at the moment. This explains certain stream flows and rock formation.

Chapter 7 is a diversionary description of a canal-cleaning ritual tied in with the ancient worship of a demon woman named Chuqui Suso, who turned herself into stone in the preceding chapter. Villagers later choose a woman to represent her each year, and have a great feast and dance to celebrate the cleaning of the canals.

In chapter 8 Paria Caca, in the form of five persons, finally reaches the dwelling of Huallallo Caruincho, where he sees a weeping man approaching with a child. The man is going to give his child as a sacrifice to be eaten by Huallallo Caruincho. One of the five men of Paria Caca orders him to take his child and go back to his village, explaining that he is planning to fight Huallallo Caruincho. He tells him to come back in five days to witness his victory. Although the man is fearful of angering Huallallo Caruincho, he obeys.

In five days, the five persons of Paria Caca begin to rain down on Huallallo Caruincho from five directions and flash lightning from five directions as well. All day Huallallo Caruincho flames up in the form of a giant fire, never allowing himself to be extinguished. Finally Paria Caca impounds some of the rainwater into a large lake, which quickly rises and almost submerges the flaming Huallallo Caruincho, so that the villainous god flees toward the lowlands, pursued by Paria Carco, one of Paria Caca's offspring.

Meanwhile, a woman who has been with the flaming god Mana Ñamca appears, also burning in the form of a fire. When Paria Caca attacks her, she shoots at him and hits another of his offspring, Chuqui Huampo, in the foot. After Paria Caca has run the woman off, he goes back to see about his son, who has a broken foot. The boy tells him, "I can't go back. I'll keep watch over that woman Mana Ñamca from right here, just in case she comes back." Paria Caca commands all the villagers to keep his son supplied with food. The coca producers must give him coca first when they harvest before they share with all the others, and when a llama is slaughtered, a young female must be slaughtered in his son's honor and the ear tips must be given to him before the rest may be eaten. The people carry on the custom secretly (after the arrival of the Spaniards) throughout the generations.

In chapter 9, after Huallallo Caruincho flees, defeated, Paria Caca passes sentence on him: "Because he fed on people, let him now eat dogs, and let the Huanca people worship him." The Huanca people inhabiting the upper Mantaro valley of the central Peruvian highlands henceforth sacrifice dogs to Huallallo Caruincho and feed on them themselves.

Paria Caca drives the Yunca Indians from the highlands and ordains that henceforth his children will live on the heights. His law states: "We are all of one birth." In each village he appoints one person, to be called huacsa, to hold an annual celebration reenacting Paria Caca's life and to hold dance festivals three times a year. He gives instructions for all the various ceremonies and rituals to be performed. It is said by the Yunca, banished to the lowlands, "The highlanders are getting along all right. It is because they carry on our old way of life that the people flourish so." This chapter ends the cycle of stories about the life of Paria Caca.

Chapter 10 returns to the story of Chaupi Ñamca, daughter of Tamta Ñamca, who in chapter 5 is given in marriage to the poor man Huatya Curi. She is also known as Mama Ñamca. She claims to be "a maker of people." She travels in human form, trying to satisfy her voracious sexual appetite. Men implore the huacsa Rucano Coto to enlarge their sexual parts so that they might satisfy her. But none is as pleasing to her as Rucano Coto himself, about whom she says, "Only this man . . . is a real man. I'll stay with this one forever." And she turns herself into a stone with five arms, or wings. The people worship her and refer to her as "Mother." Many generations later, when the Spaniards come, the people hide her underground near the Catholic priest's stable, where she remains to this day, inside the earth.

One of the dances the huacsas perform, called Casa Yaco, makes her rejoice immensely because they perform naked. They say, "Chaupi Ñamca enjoys it no end when she sees our private parts!"

Chapter 11 deals with one of Paria Caca's sons, Tutay Quiri, who sets out to conquer the Yunca. When they hear he is coming, the Yunca are "scared stiff," and they flee. However, some of the villagers remain behind in order to pay homage to him. He spares them and tells them to treat the last-born—and thus, lowborn—Checa people as brothers.

The Checa men begin the custom of going on an annual hunt, "following Tutay Quiri's track," and when they return they hold a dance festival called the Chanco.

Chapter 12 continues the story of Paria Caca's offspring, of whom Tutay Quiri is the strongest, excelling beyond the others in every undertaking. He first conquers two river valleys by setting his golden staff on a black mountain as a curse on the Yunca and declaring, "The Yunca will extend to this district." His other brothers climb ahead, hoping to find new lands to conquer, but they find none and, fearing their powerful brother, descend through the Huaro Cheri district, with Tutay Quiri in the lead.

Along the way, one of Chuqui Suso's sisters waits in her field, planning to expose herself to him and therefore beguile him. When he stops at her field, his brothers stop as well, thus ending all thought of conquest.

Chapter 13 shifts to a description of the people of Mama, in a lower region inhabited by Yunca people. They tell a different story about Chaupi Ñamca. According to them, in very early times there is a huaca named Hanan Maclla, wife of the Sun. Their children are Chaupi Ñamca and Paria Caca. Chaupi Ñamca is "a great maker of people, that is, of women, and Paria Caca of men." Before the time of the Spaniards, each June the people hold a five-day dancing and drinking festival to honor Chaupi Ñamca, but later, "for fear of the Spaniards," they confine their festival to Corpus Christi eve.

Chaupi Ñamca is said to be the oldest of several sisters and also to be made up of five persons. The next oldest are Llacsa Huato and Mira Huato. When someone is ill, a priestess of the sisters is consulted. The people pray, "Oh Llacsa Huato, Mira Huato, it is you who make people; / It is you indeed who know my sin, better than Chaupi Ñamca. / Tell me, I beg . . . / For what fault of mine do I live in suffering?" It is said that people consult these two because Chaupi Ñamca is a liar.

Chapter 14 returns to the feats of Cuni Raya Vira Cocha, mentioned in chapter 1. Just before the arrival of the Spaniards, Cuni Raya heads toward Cuzco where he consults with Huayna Capac, last leader of the Incan empire.

They go to Titi Caca, where Cuni Raya tells the ruler to mobilize his people and assemble his shamans. He then instructs the shamans, "Go to the world's lower foundations. Then tell my father, 'Your son sent me here. Send me back bearing one of his sisters.'"

The shamans set out, intent upon returning within five days. The swift's shaman (who acquires his special powers from the fast-flying swift) is the first to arrive and deliver his message. He is given a small chest and warned, "You mustn't open this." The Incan ruler must be the first to open it. But as he nears his destination, the man becomes curious and opens the chest to find a tiny but stately golden-haired lady. The moment he sees her, she vanishes.

When he reports his disobedience to the king, he is sent back to try again. This time he delivers the chest unopened. Before the king opens it, Cuni Raya draws a line across the world and tells the king, "I'll go into this space and you go into this other space with my sister. You and I mustn't see each other anymore!" When the box is opened, the world lights up with lightning. The Inca king sends someone else back to Cuzco to impersonate him while he and his new queen disappear, and so does Cuni Raya.

Chapter 15 relates that before Cuni Raya there was nothing. It is he who first gives shape to mountains, forests, rivers, and fields. He is called Paria Caca's father. It is he who makes and empowers Paria Caca.

Chapter 16 returns to the mystery of the five eggs and the five personages of Paria Caca who develop from them, explaining that the personages are now termed brothers named Paria Caca, Churapa, Puncho, Paria Carco, and Sullca Yllapa.

The tale of Huallallo Caruincho resumes at the point where he is fleeing from Paria Caca. He enters a mountain and hides, but Paria Caca and his brothers shoot lightning bolts into the mountain, almost demolishing it and forcing Huallallo Caruincho to flee again. The demon tries to foil Paria Caca, first with a snake, which Paria Caca turns into a stone, and then with a toucan, whose wing Paria Caca breaks before he turns it into a stone also. Paria Carco stations himself at a pass into the lowlands to prevent Huallallo Caruincho from returning. "Paria Carco remains there today in the form of a heavily snow-capped peak."

Chapter 17 tells of the return of Paria Caca and his brothers to a cliff shelter where they will dwell. Huallallo Caruincho looses one more monster, a hugi, "to bring grief to Paria Caca." But the hugi escapes and roams the land until a man of the Checa captures it. A Quinti man named Choc Payco tells him to cut off the tail as a sign of victory, which the Checa man does. But the Quinti man rushes back to Paria Caca with the carcass, claiming that he himself killed the hugi. Later, when the Checa man delivers the tail, Paria Caca upbraids Choc Payco, "For lying to me, / go fight with the Quinti, / They'll call you a stinker, / and your offspring, too." He rewards the Checa man by making him a yanca, or priest, with the name Ñamca Pariya.

Chapter 18 describes the Incan reverence for Paria Caca. Thirty men take turns offering him food. One day, one of them, a dirty mountain man named

Quita Pariasca, predicts hard times, when Paria Caca will be forgotten. His words anger the others, but only a few days later the Spaniards arrive and demand to know where the eldest huaca's silver and garments are. When the others refuse to tell, the Spaniards pile straw around the eldest huaca and burn him. Although he suffers horribly, he survives; by this time the others have handed over the clothing and silver to the Spaniards. They decide that the mountain man is right: "The world is no longer good." They disband and return to their villages.

When the burned man from Checa has healed, he arrives at a village called Limca carrying a child of Paria Caca named Maca Uisa.

Chapter 19 explains that the Incas have asked Paria Caca for one of his children to help in their conquest of two neighboring provinces. Paria Caca gives them Maca Uisa, and they are able to defeat the provinces quickly after his arrival. But when the Spaniards arrive, they take away the gold and other offerings the people have offered to Paria Caca and Maca Uisa. Don Sebastián, curaca of the Huarochirí province, burns everything that is left. Many years later, another priest asks the burned man, now old, to bring Maca Uisa to him at Llacsa Tambo. The burned man and his six children arrive with the revered Maca Uisa. The people of the village ask Maca Uisa to remain with them, to keep watch over their village from now on. So the old man sacrifices a llama, his children, and himself to fire, having declared, "The world really is very good. There won't ever be temptation or disease anymore." From this time onward, the people serve Maca Uisa.

Chapter 20 deals with a huaca named Llocllay Huancupa, a child of Pacha Camac. While cultivating a field, a woman named Lanti Chumpi digs up the huaca's visible form and, not knowing what it is, throws it back to the ground. But another day, when she finds it again, she thinks, "This might be some kind of huaca!"

She takes it to the village elders. There the huaca reveals himself, saying, "It was my father who sent me here, saying, 'Go and protect that Checa village!'" The people are overjoyed, and for many years they hold festivals for him and serve him. But when their interest wanes he disappears, returning to his father, Pacha Camac.

The people are deeply grieved to lose him. They search for him everywhere, and even build a step-pyramid to him at the site where he was first discovered. Finally they decide to begin worshiping his father again, and so Llocllay Huancupa decides to return. The people continue to serve both father and son until the Spaniards come.

A certain Father Christóbal and the local coraco Don Gerónimo both hate the practices of worshiping the two huacas, so the people stop. Then a great plague of measles comes, and the huaca's house catches fire all by itself, so the people return to their old ways. Much later, just before he dies, Don Gerónimo returns to huaca worship as well.

Don Christóbal, the deceased man's son, is visited nine times in one night by flashing demons. He begins to pray to the Virgin Mary, promising never to worship anyone but her again. When his night of terror is over, he threatens to tell the padre if the other villagers ever go near Llocllay Huancupa's house again. He tells them that Llocllay Huancupa has taken the form of a barn owl. But that night the demon appears to him again in a dream.

Chapter 21 relates his dream of being summoned to the house of Llocllay Huancupa where he asks the demon, "They address you as the animator of humanity and as the World Shaker. People say, 'He is the very one who makes everything!' and all mankind fears you. . . . Shall I not revere this one, the true God? / . . . Or am I mistaken? / . . . Should I believe in you?" At this point someone throws an object at him. He does not know if the demon or God has thrown it. He flees from the house, and then wakes up.

Chapter 22 discusses the people's worship of Pacha Camac, the World Shaker, about whom they say, "When he gets angry, earth trembles. / When he turns his face sideways it quakes. / Lest that happen he holds his face still. / The world would end if he ever rolled over."

Chapter 23 takes place during the time when Tupay Ynga Yupanqui is king of the Incas. A rebellion of three conquered provinces leads the Inca king to mobilize thousands of men. The battle rages for 12 years, but the king's men are exterminated every time he sends a new group. Disheartened, he recalls how he has served all the huacas with his gold and silver all these years. He decides to call them to help him defeat his enemies.

The huacas arrive from near and far, except for Paria Caca, who can't decide what to do. He sends his son Maca Uisa to "Go and find out about it." When the huacas are assembled, the king asks for their help in defeating the rebellious provinces, but no one speaks. The king is enraged and threatens to burn them all. But Pacha Camac explains why he has remained silent: "I am a power who would shake you and the whole world around you. It wouldn't be those enemies alone whom I would destroy, but you as well."

Maca Uisa speaks up and offers to go to the front and speak to the people. While he speaks, a bright greenish-blue color blows from his mouth like smoke. He is borne to the battlefront on a fine litter, and from there he begins to rain on them, eroding great chasms and striking great bolts of lightning. Only a few of the common people are spared. From that time onward, the people revere Paria Caca and Maca Uisa even more.

Chapter 24 discusses the customs of the Checa, the Machua Yunca festival, and its dances.

Chapter 25 takes up the history of the Colli people, who originally reside in the highlands of Yaru Tini. One day Paria Caca arrives in the village during a drinking bout. He takes a seat at the far end of the banquet, but not one single person offers him a drink. Finally one man invites him to drink and to share his coca leaf. Paria Caca tells him, "Brother, when I come back here, you'd better hold on tight to this tree. Don't tell these people anything."

Five days later a violent wind rises up and whirls everyone around, killing some, blowing others away to perish elsewhere. The one man who has clung to a tree has been spared. Paria Caca turns him into stone and promises him that new people will come to provide coca leaf for him to chew in perpetuity.

Chapter 26 repeats the story of Paria Caca being ignored at a banquet, this time as happening to the people on Maca Calla Mountain. In this instance Paria Caca destroys them with rain. Some people escape into a field and there turn into stone. One man begs to be spared, pleading to Maca Calla, who at the time is "just like a man, with a head, feet, and hands." As he weeps, Maca Calla's head falls off. As the man picks it up, it becomes a falcon and flies away: The man has become a mighty shaman. He settles on five mountains in Llantapa and multiplies. The people of his community say, "Here we have Maca Calla's protection."

Chapter 27 explains how in ancient times the dead lie in state for five days. During that time, the dead person's spirit, the size of a fly, darts away, saying, "Sio!" Then it returns to the body and the person will never die again. Therefore, the number of people begins to increase rapidly, and they live in great suffering, scratching for food.

A certain man dies but does not return to life until the sixth day. His elders, brothers, and wife are furious because he has been so slow. When he returns to life, his wife calls him lazy and hurls a maize cob at him. The moment she throws it, he makes a "Sio!" noise and disappears. Since then, not a single dead person has come back.

Chapter 28 explains the Andean customs of feeding the dead during Paria Caca's festival in the days when corpses remained in the open for five days. After the time of the Spaniards, the people take hot dishes to the church on All Saints' Day.

Chapter 29 relates how a constellation called Yacana, which is the animator of llamas, comes from the sky each night to drink water from the ocean. "If the Yacana failed to drink it, the waters would quickly drown the whole world." Other stars are named and their significance described.

Chapter 30 recounts that in ancient times a man named Anchi Cara and a woman named Huayuama have an argument over water rights on their respective properties. The two fall in love and decide to stay together forever, so they turn into stones that remain on their fields to this day.

Chapter 31 gives the history, myths, and laws of the five local lineages. The bulk of the chapter concerns the lineage of Llacsa Misa and his sister Cuno Cuyo, who specialize in water priesthood. He, his sister, and his brothers Pauquir Buxi and Llama Tanya all arrive in a village to take it over. Many residents flee, including the father of a young child named Yasali. Llacsa Misa finds the abandoned boy and, over the objections of his brothers, adopts him and makes him his llamaherd. When Yasali grows older, he marries Cuno Cuyo.

Llacsa Misa acquires the property upon which sits Yanca Lake, in which lives a huaca named Collquiri. Collquiri wants a woman badly and has searched all over the countryside to no avail. Cuni Raya, a deity mentioned in chapters 2 and 14, informs him, "Hey, she's right here, right nearby, your woman!" Collquiri looks out from atop a mountain and sees a woman "dancing very majestically." Her name is Capyama. He sends one of his serving boys to summon the woman by telling her that one of her llamas has given birth. The woman is delighted with the news and hurries up the mountainside. Collquiri turns himself into a callcallo—possibly a grasshopper or lizard—which she catches and puts inside her dress. When he comes out later as a fine, handsome man, she falls in love with him.

Meanwhile, her relatives go in search of her. When they find Collquiri and confront him, he admits that he has taken their daughter. He asks what restitution the family would like. They refuse all restitution, even though Capyama tells her father that she wants to remain with Collquiri. Finally Collquiri offers them the "Goesunder." The family is intrigued, especially the brothers, and they accept, providing Collquiri will deliver the "Goesunder" in five days and providing that he will marry Capyama.

Five days later Collquiri, good as his word, does go under. He heads underground all the way to their village, and where he comes out a spring is formed. (Modern Llambia still draws water from Capyama spring.) The love of Capyama and Collquiri—now called Pedro Batan and pictured as a romantic lover rather than a clownish one—is popular in modern folklore.

The chapter also describes efforts to regulate the flow of water from the spring and from the lake. It relates the descendants of Cuno Cuyo, Yasali, and the other brothers of Paria Caca.

Two supplements describe customs and practices, particularly regarding babies, of the Andean people. (Salomon and Urioste 1991)

HUBRIS

(Also Hybris)

In epic poetry, an excess of self-confidence, overconfidence, or pride, called hubris, is often offensive to the gods and thus the cause of the hero's downfall or that of one of the other characters. In the *Iliad,* Agamemnon's hubris in refusing to return his war prize Chryseis causes Apollo to visit a plague upon the army. Achilles's hubris in refusing to fight after Agamemnon takes his war prise Briseis indirectly brings about the death of his dearest friend, Patroklos. Patroklos himself suffers from hubris and ignores Achilles's command to return to him as soon as he has turned back the Trojans. (Lattimore 1976)

See also Achilles; Agamemnon; *Iliad.*

HUDHUD

This oral epic of the Ifugao people of the Philippines, along with the *Alim Epic,* is still being recited today in performances lasting several days. It is valued because of its pristine state (absence of Western elements). (Preminger 1990)

THE HULUPPU TREE

This Sumerian poem, ca. the third millennium B.C. or before, is part of the cycle of Inanna. It is one of the world's earliest recorded tales of creation. The tree sprouts by the Euphrates River, but the South Wind blows it into the water. Inanna rescues it and replants it in her garden. Later Gilgamesh carves a throne

The Ifugao of Luzon, Philippines, recite the *Hudhud,* their creation cycle that includes a female character called Bugan, to whom women pray.

for her from the tree's trunk, and she makes two emblems of kingship from its bark for Gilgamesh. (Wolkstein and Kramer 1983)

See also Gilgamesh; Inanna.

HUMBABA
(Also Huwawa)

In the *Epic of Gilgamesh,* Humbaba is a guardian of the cedar forest who opposes Gilgamesh and is slain by him and Enkidu. Humbaba is a nature divinity, perhaps originally Anatolian, Syrian, or Elamite. (Sandars 1972)

HUNAB KU

In the *Popol Vuh* of the Maya, Hunab Ku is the supreme god of the Maya, literally "the only god." In the *Books of Chilam Balam,* Hunab Ku is called "the greatest of Gods." (Recinos, Goetz, and Morley 1983; Sawyer-Lauçanno 1987)

HUNAHPÚ

In the *Popol Vuh,* Hunahpú is the name of a god. Literally, it means a "hunter with a blow-gun," a "shooter." He is the twin brother of Xbalanqué, the son of Hun-Hunahpú and Xquic, and the younger brother of Hunbatz and Hunchouén. The twins are born in the forest and make their way to the door of their grandmother, who throws them out because they cry too much. They raise themselves in the forest and elude the venomous deeds of their jealous brothers, eventually avenging themselves on their brothers. They find ball-playing instruments and travel to Xibalda (underground region of evil), where they play ball with the Lords of Xibalda after submitting to preliminary tests. They die in a bonfire but are brought back to life. They perform their dances and slay the Lords of Xibalda, avenging the deaths of their fathers (although they are "twins" they have different fathers). Eventually they visit their dead ancestors and rise up to the sky, to dwell henceforth in heaven. (Recinos, Goetz, and Morley 1983)

HUNAHPÚ-UTIÚ, HUNAHPÚ-VUCH

In the *Popol Vuh,* both are symbolic names given to God. Hunahpú-Utiú, a hunting coyote (a variety of wolf) and god of the night, is the name of the divinity's masculine capacity. Hunahpú-Vuch, a hunting-fox bitch or opossum and god of the dawn, is the divinity in the feminine capacity. Vuch is the moment that precedes dawn. (Recinos, Goetz, and Morley 1983)

HUON DE BORDEAU

See Chansons de Geste.

HURAKÁN

In the *Popol Vuh,* Hurakán is one of the Mayan names of God, a one-legged lightning god. (Recinos, Goetz, and Morley 1983)

HUSENI

This Swahili Islamic epic poem consisting of 1,209 stanzas concerns the life and death of Ḥusayn ibn 'Alī. (Knappert 1979)

HUWAWA

See Humbaba.

HWANG-TI

(Also Huang Ti)

Hwang-Ti was a Chinese emperor and god (ca. 2697 B.C.). (Mackenzie 1990)

See also Ch'i-lin.

HYDRA

In Greek legend, the Hydra is a gigantic monster with nine heads. Destruction of the Hydra is one of the Twelve Labors of Herakles, which he accomplishes with the aid of Iolaus. As one head is severed, two grow in its place, and the Hydra cannot be destroyed until they burn out the roots with firebrands. The blood of the Hydra provides poison for the tips of Herakles's arrows. (Graves 1955; Schwab 1974)

See also Herakles.

HYLAS

In Greek legend, Hylas is Herakles's favorite companion on the Argonautic expedition. At Cios, Hylas goes ashore for spring water and is captured by the nymphs of the spring. When Herakles cannot find his friend, he threatens to destroy the land. Each year the inhabitants set aside a day to call for Hylas. (Graves 1955)

HYMN TO ISTANU

("Istanui")

This verse epic of the New Kingdom of the Hittites (ca. 1400–1200 B.C.) is addressed to the sun god Istanu, who is described as "lord of judgment." (Preminger 1990)

HYPSIPYLE

In Greek legend, Hypsipyle is the queen of Lemnos, who becomes the lover of the Argonaut Jason and bears him two sons. Soon after, pirates capture her and sell her to the king of Nemea, whose son Opheltes she nurses. While she is aiding the Seven against Thebes, the child in her charge dies from a poisonous snakebite. Dionysus sends her own sons to rescue her from being punished. (Schwab 1974)

I

IALDABAOTH

In Sethian Gnostic cosmology, Ialdabaoth is an evil and imperfect demiurge, a son of the thirtieth aeon, Sophia ("wisdom"). He is usually described as the God (Yahweh) of the Old Testament, who either alone or with the angels makes the world. In the Gnostic view, since the universe is imperfect, it could not have been produced by the supreme unknown power, which is perfect and good. According to Sethian Gnostics, when Ialdabaoth, "becoming arrogant in spirit, boasted himself over all those below him, and explained, 'I am father and God, and above me there is no one,' his mother . . . cried out against him, 'Do not lie, Ialdabaoth; for the father of all, the primal Anthropos, is above you; and so is . . . the son of Anthropos.'" (Pagels 1979)

IAPETUS

In Greek mythology, Iapetus is one of the Titans, son of Uranus and Ge (heaven and earth), the husband of Themis, and the father of Atlas, Epimetheus, Prometheus, Menoetius, and all mankind. According to the *Iliad,* he is banished to Tartarus, the lowest region of the underworld, for revolting against Zeus. He also appears in Hesiod's *Theogony.* (Lattimore 1959; Lattimore 1976)

IAPIS

In the *Aeneid* (iv), Iapis is a Trojan favored by Apollo, who gives him knowledge of the use of medicinal herbs. (Humphries 1951)

IARBAS

In the *Aeneid* (iv), Iarbas is a suitor of Dido, from whom she buys the land upon which to build Carthage. When Aeneas arrives and becomes the center of Dido's attention, Iarbas prays to his father Zeus to send his rival away. According to some accounts, Dido then kills herself rather than marry Iarbas. (Humphries 1951)

See also Aeneas; Dido.

IASION

(Also Isaius)

In the *Aeneid* (iii) and in *Theogony,* Iasion is a son of Zeus and Electra, husband of the goddess Rhea, and father, by Demeter, of Plutus. The Arcadians of the Peloponnesian Peninsula consider him one of the gods; his chief interest is agriculture. (Humphries 1951; Lattimore 1959)

IBE OHAFIA ZHIA BIA

This migration legend of the Ohafia people of Nigeria, West Africa, is still being recited today. It tells of the travels of the founding fathers from Benin through Idon (perhaps Adoni on the Niger River) and Ibeku to their present homeland. (Azuonye *RAL* 1990)

ICARIUS

In the *Odyssey* (xvi), Icarius is the father of Odysseus's wife Penelope and the grandfather of Telemachos. (Rouse 1990)

See also Penelope; Telemachos.

IDOMENEUS

In Greek legend Idomeneus is the king of Crete, a suitor of Helen, and a participant in the Trojan War, where he becomes renowned for his valor. In the *Odyssey* he returns home safely following the war, although in later versions he promises Poseidon that if he escapes a violent tempest he will sacrifice the first thing he sees upon reaching home. His son is the first person to greet him. Some accounts say he kept his word to Poseidon; others say that the sacrifice was interrupted by the appearance of a pestilence. (Rouse 1990; Schwab 1974)

See also Helen; *Odyssey.*

IDUN

(Also Ithun and Iounn)

In Old Norse mythology, Idun is the wife of the god of poetry, Bragi, and the goddess who guards the apples of youth. When the giant Thiazi captures her and her apples, the gods begin to age. She appears in "The Flyting of Loki" in the *Poetic Edda.* (Hollander *Edda* 1990)

See also *Edda, Poetic.*

IGOR'S HOST, LAY OF

(Also *Song of Igor's Campaign* or *Slovo O Polku Igoreve)*

This Kievan heroic poem recounts the unsuccessful campaign of Prince Igor Svyatoslavich against the Kipchak forces in 1185. The anonymous poem, probably written ca. 1185–1187 by a participant in the campaign, has become a Russian classic. It was preserved in a single manuscript discovered by Count A. I. Musin-Pushkin in 1795 and published in 1800. In the first part, Igor, driven by his fierce nationalistic pride, enters into combat greatly outnumbered, but initially he is successful. However, ultimately he is captured because, according to his cousin Svyatoslav III, the prince of Kiev, he has tried to accomplish the victory without the aid of the other Russian princes. Svyatoslav entreats these princes to come to Igor's rescue. In the last section, Igor's wife prays to the powers of nature to deliver her husband. Eventually Igor escapes and returns to his people. (Goodrich 1961)

See also *Host of Igor, The Lay of the.*

IGRAINE, QUEEN

In Arthurian legend, Igraine is the mother of King Arthur. In some versions, she is the wife of Duke Gorlois of Tintagel and is unwittingly seduced by King Uther Pendragon, to whom Merlin has magically given the appearance of her husband. In other versions, Gorlois is slain in a battle with Uther, who then forces Igraine to become his wife. Nine months later, Arthur is born on the day that Uther dies. (Barber 1961)

See also Arthurian Legend; Merlin.

IJEOMA EBULU

This heroic legend of the Ohafia people of Nigeria, West Africa, is still being recited today. It concerns a prosperous Ohafia merchant whose wife and her greedy relatives murder him and steal his wealth. (Azuonye *RAL* 1990)

IKUTA

This ancient Japanese legend was recorded in the tenth-century *Tales of Yamato* by an anonymous scribe. It concerns a maiden, Unai, living by the Ikuta River in Settsu province, who is courted by two youths alike in looks, age, and social standing. She cannot decide whom to marry, so her mother suggests that she wed the one who shoots a waterfowl floating on the river. Both men strike the bird, and the maiden Unai feels great guilt over the death of the innocent bird for naught. Furthermore, she has caused great strife between the two young men. Grief-stricken, she drowns herself. Her suitors are heartbroken, and they kill each other beside her tomb. Now her restless soul is doomed to suffer forever in hell, where the waterbird will peck at her skull and foul fiends will pursue her. (Tahara 1980)

IKWOGHO

This heroic legend of the Ohafia people of Nigeria, West Agrica, is still being recited today. It concerns a great warrior who makes a long race to and from a distant waterfront to inform those at home of the good news concerning the deeds of the Ohafia warriors. Having performed his task, he collapses and dies from the exertion. (Azuonye *RAL* 1990)

ILIA

(Also Rhea)

In the *Aeneid* (i, vi), Ilia is a daughter of Numitor who is raped by Mars and becomes the mother of Romulus and Remus. (Humphries 1951)

See also Romulus and Remus.

ILIAD

This Greek epic poem (ca. ninth century B.C.) by Homer is set during the closing days of the Trojan War, a conflict that was apparently an actual historical event. The poem is composed of 15,693 lines, written in dactylic hexameter and, like the *Odyssey*, has been divided into 24 books. Experts believe that this division was made somewhere around the third century B.C., long after the first written version of the story appeared. Although the war provides the backdrop for the story, the epic, with its many passages pertaining to the activities of the gods, is not the story of the war. Neither the beginning nor the end of the war is depicted. The poem begins during the tenth year and covers events of four days during that year, ending before the city of Troy has been taken.

The primary story line, as the opening lines of the epic attest, concerns the anger of Achilles (Achilleus), and covers the time from his quarrel with Agamemnon to the death and burial of the Trojan warrior Hektor. Although the epic is labeled "Greek," the people who fought on the side of Troy were Ionians and Aiolians, while those fighting on the "Greek" side were pre-Greeks who called themselves Hellenes, but whom Homer called Achaians, Argives, and Danaans. The *Iliad* and the *Odyssey* have long been regarded by Greeks as symbols of heroism and national unity and a source of ethical standards.

In book I, the Achaian (Greek) commander Agamemnon is blamed for a pestilence that occurs when he refuses to restore Chryseis, whom he has held as a prize of war, to her father Chryses, the Apollonian priest. When a plague is blamed on Chryseis's captivity, the people rise up in protest against Agamemnon, and he is forced to release Chryseis, replacing her with Briseis, who had been Achilles's war prize. When this act is proposed, it infuriates "powerful Achilles," and "within / his shaggy breast his heart was divided two ways," whether to stab Agamemnon or to "check the spleen within" and swallow his anger. He is stayed from killing the commander by the goddess "grey-eyed Athene," who counsels him that "some day three times over such shining gifts shall be given you / by reason of this outrage. Hold your hand, then, and obey us." But although Achilles relinquishes Briseis to Agamemnon without a fight, he cannot let go of his anger, and he announces that he and his troops will no longer fight. He wanders along the seashore in shame and pours out his sorrow to his mother Thetis, a sea nymph. He asks her to convince Zeus

A gold funeral mask found in 1876 by Heinrich Schliemann at the fortress city of Mycenea has come to represent Agamemnon, Greek hero of the *Iliad*.

to help the Trojans defeat the Achaians so that his honor and worth will be restored.

When Zeus's wife Hera learns that Zeus and Thetis are plotting against the Achaians, she chides him, saying, "Always it is dear to your heart in my absence to think of / secret things and decide upon them. Never have you patience / frankly to speak forth to me the thing that you purpose."

But Zeus is quick to put her in her place with a threat, ". . . Go then, sit down in silence, and do as I tell you, / for fear all the gods . . . can do nothing / if I come close and lay my unconquerable hands upon you."

In book II, Zeus visits a dream upon Agamemnon that says if he goes into battle now, he can take the city of Troy. He assembles the weary troops and, in a challenge designed to stir up their passion, suggests that they abandon the fight and return home. To his dismay, the troops stir up the dust in their haste to leave with their ships, and it is only with the intervention of Athene, acting on Hera's suggestion, who touches Odysseus's heart, that the ships are detained. Odysseus reminds them of their duty: "Always it is disgraceful / to wait long and at the end go home empty-handed." When one man, Thersites, "of the endless speech," scolds Agamemnon for keeping the women all to himself and exhorts the troops to "leave this man here / by himself in Troy to mull his prizes of honour / that he may find out whether or not we others are helping him," Odysseus attacks him, both verbally and physically.

In book III, Alexandros, also known as Paris, the Trojan prince who kidnapped Agamemnon's brother Menelaos's wife Helen and precipitated the war, challenges any Argive to a battle. But when Menelaos steps forward, "the heart was shaken within him." Alexandros withdraws and attempts to hide, but his brother, the Trojan warrior Hektor, rebukes him: "Evil Paris, beautiful, woman-crazy, cajoling, / better had you never been born, or killed unwedded." Wounded by these bitter words, Alexandros duels with Menelaos, with the understanding that the winner will get Helen. Menelaos bests Alexandros easily. But as he is about to be killed, Aphrodite, Helen's protectress, spirits him away to his own room.

In book IV, Zeus calls a council and decrees that, since Menelaos has won, he should take Helen away and the matter should be at an end. But Athene and Hera mutter, "devising evil for the Trojans," and although Athene only sulks, Hera asks him how he can "make wasted" all her efforts to destroy the city of Troy. She says of his proposed truce, "Do it then; but not all the rest of us gods will approve you." Wanting no more bitterness between himself and Hera, Zeus gives in and says, "Do as you please then."

Athene, a supporter of the Achaians, causes the Trojan Pandaros to shoot and wound Menelaos. This attack precipitates a movement of troops on both sides, and the war begins again. The killing of some favorite sons on both sides causes fervor for war to mount even higher.

In book V, when the Achaian Diomedes is wounded by Pandaros during the resumed battle, he appeals to Athene for help. She gives him the courage to continue, and he kills Pandaros, the one who had wounded Menelaos. Still filled with the gift of courage, he lays waste to a number of Trojans, wounding Aineis (Aeneas), son of the goddess Aphrodite. When she comes to her son's aid, Diomedes wounds her as well, sending her screaming back to Olympus. Apollo rescues Aineis, while Ares joins the fray at the Trojan Hektor's side. Hera and Athene receive permission to join the Achaians, to counteract Ares's ferocity. Athene, who had exacted from Diomedes a promise to fight no god except Aphrodite, removes that injunction and sets him against Ares; he drives a spear into the depths of the war god's belly.

In book VI, the Trojan commander-in-chief Hektor returns to the palace of Priam at Troy to ask his mother and the other women to go to the temple of Athene and offer sacrifices "if only she will have pity / on the town of Troy." However, these entreaties by the good women of Troy do not move Athene. Hektor also goes to find his brother Alexandros (Paris), who has not returned to battle but is still at home with Helen. Hektor shames him into returning to the battle: "Up then, to keep our town from burning at once in the hot fire." Being a devoted family man, albeit with a deep sense of his patriotic duty, he visits his wife Andromache "of the white arms" and their son, but finds them gone to the battlements, where she hopes to help. He finds them there, bids them a heartfelt farewell, and tells her, "Go . . . back to our house, and take up your own work, / the loom and the distaff . . . but the men must see to the fighting." Soon Alexandros rejoins his brother Hektor on the way back to the battlefront.

In book VII, when the tide appears to be turning against the Achaians, the gods confer, and Athene and Apollo decide that the war should be settled by a battle between Hektor and some Achaian warrior. The decision as to who will go up against the fierce Hektor is such a difficult one that in the end it is decided by lots. "Glorious Aias" (Ajax) draws the lot and faces Hektor in a duel so bloody that messengers from both sides intervene to end the conflict in a draw. At this point, both sides are exhausted and faced with burying scores of victims. The Trojans pressure Alexandros to give up Helen and allow her to return to her husband Menelaos. He refuses but offers instead monetary restitution, which the "flowing-haired Achaians" refuse in outrage. This act only embues them with a new will to fight, and they fortify their ships with a strong wall. Zeus tells Apollo, "earth-shaker of the wide strength," that once the Achaians have returned to their own land, he can "break their wall to pieces and scatter it into the salt sea."

In book VIII, the battle resumes, and Zeus, who is tired of the endless war, orders the gods not to intervene further. However, he does consent when Athene requests permission to advise the Achaians. With only Zeus on high to decide the outcome, the day's battle goes to Hektor's Trojans. When the tide turns against Agamemnon, he retreats behind the wall and might have sailed for home, but Hektor orders a thousand fires built to prevent Agamemnon from sailing away under cover of darkness.

In book XIX, Agamemnon faces a demoralized army and tells them that all is lost. But wise old Nestor speaks his mind and tells him that his trouble all started when he took the girl Briseis from Achilles, "against the will of the rest of us, since I for my part / urged you strongly not to, but you, giving way to your proud heart's / anger, dishonoured a great man, one whom the immortals / honour. . . ." Agamemnon acknowledges his error and says that he will offer Achilles gold, horses, seven women of Lesbos, and even the girl Briseis, "And to all this I will swear a great oath / that I never entered into her bed and never lay with her. . . ." And further, if Achilles will rejoin him to prevail over Troy, he can load his ship with gold and bronze, "and let him choose for himself twenty of the Trojan women . . ." as well as take his pick of Agamemnon's own daughters. He sends Odysseus, Aias, and others to deliver his message to Achilles. But the proud Achilles is unmoved by Agamemnon's offer, saying, "let him try me no more. I know him well. He will not persuade me." When the Achaians return with the discouraging message for Agamemnon, Diomedes "of the great war cry" tells him, "I wish you had not supplicated the blameless son of Peleus [Achilles] / with innumerable gifts offered. He is a proud man without this, / and now you have driven him far deeper into his pride. Rather / we shall pay him no more attention, whether he comes in with us / or stays away. . . ."

In book X, Diomedes and Odysseus slip behind enemy lines to spy on the Trojans. They capture Dolon and discover Hektor's whereabouts, then they kill Dolon. They ambush Rhesos, the king of Thrace, and make off with his fine horses and gold chariot. There is much rejoicing back in camp when they return.

In book XI, Agamemnon launches a new attack. After some initial success, he, Odysseus, Diomedes, and many others are wounded and forced to retreat, with Hektor in furious pursuit. Achilles sees Nestor being carried away on one of the horses along with the healer Machaon, and he calls his own companion in arms, Patroklos, to go to Nestor to ask if it was really Machaon whom he has seen retreating. Nestor urges Patroklos to beg Achilles to come to their aid and, if unsuccessful, suggests that Patroklos put on his friend's armor himself to fool the Trojans into believing that Achilles has rejoined the battle.

In book XII, the Trojans under Hektor break through a gate in the wall, despite the omen of an eagle with a serpent in its talons that flies overhead.

In book XIII, while Zeus is distracted, Poseidon, "angered about the heart at his grandson's / slaying in the bitter hostility," disguises himself as Kalchas, the bird-interpreter of the gods. He flies to the discouraged Achaians and revitalizes them, encouraging them to fight on.

In book XIV, old Nestor leaves the wounded Machaon to his bath and goes out to confer with the wounded warriors Agamemnon, Odysseus, and Diomedes. He finds Agamemnon convinced of the futility of their cause, sure that the gods have willed their defeat. His only thought is to retreat by sea. But Odysseus is convinced that at this point retreat is not even possible. Meanwhile, Hera borrows Aphrodite's magic girdle and seduces Zeus, casting a spell that puts him to sleep while Poseidon comes to the aid of the Achaians. Aias strikes Hektor in the throat with a huge rock. The tide of the battle has turned once again.

When Zeus awakes, in book XV, Poseidon must withdraw. Apollo resuscitates Hektor, who then leads the Trojans in an attempt to burn up the Achaian fleet. Patroklos returns to Achilles and offers Nestor's suggestion: that he be allowed to wear his friend's armor into battle to convince the Trojans that the mighty Achilles has returned to the battle.

In book XVI, when he sees the flames from the burning ships, Achilles gives Patroklos his armor and tells him to return as soon as he has repelled the Trojan advance. The Trojans are terrified when they see a warrior whom they believe to be Achilles entering the battle. Patroklos kills nine Trojans in a single charge, including one of the strongest, Sarpedon, who is lord of the Lykians, a son of Zeus, and Hektor's charioteer. But Apollo strikes Patroklos so hard that Hektor is able to recover and run a spear through him.

In book XVII, Hektor strips Achilles's armor from Patroklos's corpse. He intends to cut off Patroklos's head, haul off the body, and give it to the dogs at Troy, which would mean that Patroklos would wander forever before the gates of the Land of the Dead without gaining entry. But Menelaos, Aias, and the Achaians engage the Trojans in a battle to rescue Patroklos's corpse, for it is important that he be given a proper burial. Apollo and Athene also join the battle, while Hektor turns his attention to the magnificent horses of Achilles. However, the horses escape and the Achaians manage to rescue Patroklos's body and carry it back to camp.

In book XVIII, Achilles, bereft to the point of weeping when he learns of his friend's death, determines to avenge it despite his mother Thetis cautioning him that he will himself be killed if he tries. But Achilles tells her, ". . . then I will accept my own death, at whatever / time Zeus wishes to bring it about. . . ." She asks him to wait until dawn, when she will return from Olympos with new armor made by the smith Hephaistos. She flies to Olympos, where Hephaistos fashions the finest armor ever, then "like a hawk" she comes "sweeping down from the snows of Olympos" carrying the shining armor to her son.

In book XIX, while Achilles dons the elaborate armor, Thetis distills ambrosia and red nectar through the nostrils of Patroklos so that his flesh will not spoil. Achilles calls the troops together and proclaims his feud with Agamemnon to be over. Agamemnon offers to return Briseis to him but Achilles, eager to confront Hektor in battle, tells him, "Let us remember our joy in warcraft. . . ." However, Odysseus advises him to allow the men to rest and "to take food and wine, since these make fighting fury and warcraft." Achilles vows not to eat until Patroklos's death is avenged, but Athene distills nectar and ambrosia inside his chest "so the weakness of hunger will not come upon him." While the men are refreshing themselves, Achilles reproaches his horses, Xanthus and Balius, for allowing Patroklos to be killed, but they explain that Apollo intervened. They tell him that if he goes into battle, he too will die. Nevertheless, Achilles is determined; a clash comes "from the grinding of his teeth" and his eyes glow as if they are "the stare of a fire." He says, "I will not stop till the Trojans have had enough of my fighting."

In book XX, Zeus gives the gods permission to take sides and join in the war. Hera, Hermes, Athene, Poseidon, and Hephaistos join the Achaians, while

Apollo, Artemis, Ares, Aphrodite, and Leto join the Trojans. Achilles almost kills Ainais, but Poseidon rescues him, while Apollo saves Hektor.

In book XXI, the battle continues. Achilles fights like a man possessed, and the terrified Trojans flee. Only Apollo's intervention saves the Trojans from total annihilation.

In book XXII, while the Trojans, "who had run like fawns," dry the sweat from their bodies and slake their thirst, Hektor waits outside the gates of Troy to confront Achilles, despite his parents' frantic entreaties to seek safety inside the walls. When Achilles arrives, he pursues Hektor around the walls three times. Then Athene tricks Hektor into believing that he will have assistance, and Hektor turns to face Achilles and fight. Achilles kills him with a spear thrust to the throat. As Hektor dies, he begs that his body be returned to his family. Instead, Achilles drags the corpse behind his chariot all the way back to the ships. Hektor, embodiment of family principles, is defeated by Achilles, embodiment of barbarism.

In book XXIII, as is the custom, Achilles holds a large funeral feast, after which Patroklos appears in a dream and asks that his funeral be held at once so that he can rest in peace. The Achaians build a large pyre and burn Patroklos's body as well as those of 12 Trojans and several animals. Funeral games are held in Patroklos's honor, while Hektor's forgotten corpse is guarded by Apollo and Aphrodite.

For nine days, in book XXIV, Achilles continues to drag Hektor's corpse behind his chariot, but the gods continue to preserve the body so that it will not deteriorate. On the twelfth morning after Hektor's death, the gods assemble and decide that Hektor should be given a proper burial. Thetis is instructed to inform her son of their decision, and Iris is dispatched to tell the old Trojan king Priam to go offer ransom gifts to Achilles for the return of his son's body. When Priam's wife hears of the plan, she berates him for even considering dealing with Achilles: "I wish I could set teeth / in the middle of his liver and eat it. That would be vengeance / for what he did to my son. . . ." But "aged Priam the godlike" will not disobey a command from the gods. Hermes guides King Priam to Achilles's camp to beg for the return of Hektor's body, then returns to Olympos rather than accompany him inside, "for it would make others angry / for an immortal god so to face mortal men with favor." Priam grovels before Achilles, asking him to "take pity on me," reminding him of his own father, "on the door-sill of sorrowful old age." He offers him "gifts beyond number" and says, "I put my lips to the hands of the man who has killed my children." For the first time Achilles shows compassion. He is moved to tears of grief for his own father and for Patroklos, while Priam weeps for Hektor. Achilles returns Hektor's body to his father and grants the Trojans a 12-day truce so that a proper funeral can be conducted for the fallen Trojan warrior.

When the body of Hektor is returned to Troy, both Hektor's wife and mother tear their hair and lament their sorrow. Finally, Helen, whose abduction by Alexandros precipitated all that has befallen them, grieves over Hektor's body, telling him, "I should have died before I came with him." She continues, "There was no other in all the wide Troad / who was kind to me, and my friend; all others shrank when they saw me." The *Iliad* ends, following the building of the pyre and the burning of the body, with a funeral banquet in Priam's palace. (Lattimore 1976)

See also Achilles; Agamemnon; Briseis; Chryseis; Hektor; Paris; Patroklos.

ILMARINEN

In Finnish cosmology, Ilmarinen is one of the chief deities, the dependable smithy god and creator of the universe who forges the pillar, or sampo, that supports the sky, and fashions the firmament, using his knee as an anvil. Ilmarinen is also the weather god and is related to the Lapp god of bad weather, Ilmaris. He is one of the three heroes, along with his boon companions Väinämöinen and Lemminkäinen, of the *Kalevala,* in which he appears as an ordinary man and not a god. His duties as a weather god are assumed by Ukko. (Lönnrot 1963)

See also *Kalevala;* Lemminkäinen; Väinämöinen.

ILUS

In Greek mythology Ilus, the fourth king, is the founder of Ilion, which he renames Troy after his father Tros. His grandson is Priam. Ilus is also the alternate name of Aeneas and Creusa's son Ascanius. He appears in the *Aeneid* (i). (Graves 1955)

ILYA OF MUROM

(Also Ilya Muromets)

Ilya is the hero of the oldest known Russian byliny (or bylina), a tenth-century bogatyr, or knight-errant, in the Kievan court of Vladimir I. The son of a peasant, Ilya cannot walk for the first 30 years of his life. He lives the life of a shut-in atop the stove in his parents' peasant dwelling until some pilgrims arrive and offer him a miraculous formula that enables him to walk. He is also given a magical horse, upon which he rides off to join Vladimir's court, where he performs untold feats of daring and strength. He slays Nightingale the Robber, a monster that has terrorized the area, and he drives out the threatening Tatars. On one occasion Vladimir gives a feast to which Ilya is not invited, and the enraged bogatyr tumbles all the steeples in Kiev. However, he immediately forgets his pique when Vladimir sends for him. In the typical byliny of the period, Vladimir is the King Arthur of Russian epic tradition, playing a secondary role while the main action involves some member of his court. (Preminger 1990)

IMDUGUD

(Mighty Wind)

Imdugud is an earlier name of Ninurta, Mesopotamian god of thunder and rainstorms. (Saggs 1990)

IMRAN

In Old Irish Gaelic literature, an imran is a tale about an adventurous voyage, such as *The Voyage of Brân* (Imram Brain), which describes a voyage to the Land of Women. Other famous imrans are *The Voyage of Mael Dúin's Boat, The Voyage of O'Corra's Boat, The Voyage of Snédgus and Mac Riagl,* and *Ossian's Voyage.* (Chadwick 1976; Evans-Wentz 1990; Meyer 1987)

See also Journey; *The Voyage of Brân, Son of Febal.*

INANNA

(Also Ishtar in Akkadian)

In Mesopotamian religion, Inanna is the Queen of Heaven, Sumerian tutelary goddess of Erech (Uruk) and Zabalam in the grassland region, and the goddess of erotic love and of war. However, since her name means Lady of the Date Clusters, she appears to have originally personified the powers of the date storehouse. Her marriage to Dumuzi-Amaushumgalana (both Dumuzi the Shepherd and the Wild Bull Dumuzi) takes place in the House of the Date Cluster. She is the heroine of the Sumerian myths *Inanna and Bilulu, Inanna and Shukallituda,* and *Inanna's Descent to the Nether World.* (Kramer 1956; Perera 1980; Wolkstein and Kramer 1983)

INANNA AND BILULU

In this ancient Sumerian myth, Inanna leaves her home in Uruk to visit her shepherd-husband Dumuzi on the desert where he is tending his flock. She discovers that he has been slain by two sheep-raiders, Bilulu and her son Girgire. In a rage, Inanna enters the alehouse where Bilulu, Girgire, and their clan have gathered, and pronounces a curse upon them. Bilulu is changed into a waterskin, and both she and her son become jinns of the desert, who must notify Dumuzi each time a desert traveler offers them a drink. Inanna and Dumuzi's sister Geshtinanna then offer a lament for the slain shepherd. (Kramer 1956; Wolkstein and Kramer 1983)

INANNA AND SHUKALLITUDA

In this ancient Sumerian myth, a gardener named Shukallituda has met with nothing but withered crops, despite his best efforts. He lifts up his eyes to the heavens, observes, and learns the divine laws before attempting to replant. This time, filled with new wisdom, he grows a successful garden. One day the

A modern impression from an Akkadian-period (about 2371–2255 B.C.) cylinder seal shows a worshipper, arms raised, with the winged goddess Inanna, whose foot rests on a lion's back.

goddess Inanna, who has traveled the heaven and earth, lies down to rest near his garden. He takes advantage of her extreme weariness and lies with her. When Inanna awakens, she determines to find out who has so shamelessly defiled her, so she sends three plagues against the land. She fills all the wells with blood, and she sends destructive winds and storms. The nature of the third plague is unclear because of the fragmentary condition of the tablet upon which the myth is preserved. Despite the three plagues, Inanna is unable to discover who has abused her, for after each plague Shukallituda goes to his father's house for advice, and the father advises him to go to the city and remain: "Son, stay close to your brothers' cities, / Direct your step and go to your brothers, the blackheaded people, / The woman [Inanna] will not find you in the midst of the lands." As a result, Inanna cannot find him. She therefore decides to go to the city of Eridu, to the house of the Sumerian god of wisdom, Enki, to seek his help. The poem breaks off at this point. (Kramer 1956; Wolkstein and Kramer 1983)

INANNA'S DESCENT TO THE NETHER WORLD

In this ancient Sumerian myth Inanna, Queen of Heaven, longs for greater power and decides to descend to the nether world, ruled by her older sister and bitter enemy, Ereshkigal. Fearing that her sister might kill her, she instructs her vizier Ninshubur on a course of action if she has not returned in three days. She then descends to the nether world and approaches Ereshkigal's temple of lapis lazuli. The gatekeeper leads her through seven gates, at each of which she must give up some of her garments and jewelry. When she has passed through the last gate, she is brought to kneel naked into the presence of Ereshkigal and the Anunnaki, the seven judges of the underworld. They fasten upon her the eyes of death; she becomes a corpse and is hung from a stake.

When she does not return, Ninshubur follows her instructions. He goes to Nippur, the city of Enlil, to plead with him to intervene. When Enlil refuses to help, he goes to Up, the city of the moon god Nanna, and repeats his plea. When Nanna refuses, he goes to Enki, who devises a plan to restore Inanna to life. He fashions two sexless creatures, called the kurgarru and the kalatruur, and gives them the food and water of life to sprinkle upon Inanna's corpse. They proceed into the nether world and bring Inanna back to life.

But Inanna is still unable to return to earth unless she provides another deity to take her place in the "land of no return." Accompanied by a number of ghoulish demons, she first goes to the two Sumerian cities Umma and Bad-tibira, where the protecting gods grovel before her in terror. She is so touched that she refuses to allow the demons to carry off either of them in her stead. She proceeds to the Sumerian city of Kullab, where her husband Dumuzi is the guardian deity. Dumuzi does not grovel before her; instead, he dresses in festive finery and sits haughtily upon his throne. Inanna is so enraged that she casts the eye of death upon him, and the demons carry him away. Dumuzi weeps, and his face turns green as he pleads to the sun god Utu to save him:

"I am one who brings cream to your mother's house, / . . . Turn my hand into the hand of a snake, / . . . Let me escape my demons, let them not seize me." The poem breaks off at this point. (Kramer 1956; Perera 1980)

INARI

In Japanese mythology, Inari is a god of vegetation protecting rice cultivation; he is also a god of prosperity revered by merchants and tradesmen. In some Shinto traditions Inari is identified with the goddess of food, Uke-mochi-no-kami, and with Uka-no-mitama-no-kami, the August Spirit of Food. (Mayer 1948)

INCWALA
(National Ceremony)

In Swazi religion, the Incwala is the most sacred of all ceremonies, in which the king is depicted as the source not only of power and unity, but of fertility as well. The festival, held in December or January, lasts for six days and consists of folklore, dance, and song, as well as a highly ritualized martial display. (Parrinder 1982)

INDRA

In Vedic literature, Indra is the Hindu chief of the gods, son of Adití and Kaśyapa, warrior of the gods, and god of rain, whose cycle of myths are alluded to in the *Ṛg Veda*. He is father to Arjuna, hero of the *Mahābhārata*. In typical warrior fashion, he vanquishes numerous human enemies, and demons as well. In order to learn the myths of Indra, it is first necessary to read later writings and reworkings concerning the myths, then to read the Vedic hymns that allude to him. For example, the story of Indra beheading Dadhyañc, who reveals Tvaṣṭṛ's mead (the intoxicating Soma juice drunk by priests) to the Aśvins (who have the heads of stallions) is alluded to in the *Ṛg Veda* and the *Satapatha Brāhmana*. The story of Indra's using Dadhyañc's bones to slay 99 Vṛtras is explained in a fourteenth-century Vedic commentary by Sāyaṇa, and the link between the two stories is explained in the fifth-century B.C. *Bṛhaddevatā* of Śaunaka. (O'Flaherty 1975; O'Flaherty 1981)

INTERROGATION OF THE OLD MEN
(Also *Dialogue or Colloquy of the Ancients* and *Agallamh na Senórach*)

In the Old Irish *Fenian Cycle* of Gaelic literature, this is the most important tale. It was probably compiled ca. 1200 from oral tradition and older texts. In prose interspersed with verse passages, it is preserved in the sixteenth-century *Book of the Dean of Lismore*. The tale begins as the poets Oisín (Ossian) and Caoilte (Caeilte), having survived the Battle of Gabhra, return to Ireland from Tir na n'Og (the Land of Youth) and discover that they have been gone for 300 years. They encounter St. Patrick, who questions them about the heroic deeds of Finn and his contemporaries. Oisín returns to his mother, who is living in a fairy mound. Caoilte accompanies Patrick on a tour of Ireland, recounting for Patrick's scribe Brogan legends and myths about each town they visit. (Evans-Wentz 1990)

INTI

(Also Apu-punchau and Inca-Yupanqui or Cápac)

In Inca religion, Inti is the sun god, believed to be the father of all Incans. His sister/consort is the moon goddess Mama-Kilya, or Quilla, or Mama Curi-Illpay. (Garcilaso 1987)

INYAM OLUGU

This heroic legend—one of the few with a female protagonist—of the Ohafia people of Nigeria, West Africa, is still being recited today. It is the story, recounted in many versions, of a brave woman who kills four men during a raid on palm trees in enemy territory. She gives their heads to her cowardly husband so that he can take them back to his village as proof of his heroism and prowess in single combat. (Azuonye *RAL* 1990)

INYIMA KAALU

Inyima is the central character of a tale of the Ohafia people of West Africa still being recited today. It is the oral legend of *Egbe Nri Adighi,* in which the newborn baby of Inyima, a famous hunter, is killed by an unloaded gun that discharges by itself. (Azuonye *RAL* 1990)

IOLAUS

(Also Iolas)

In the legends of Herakles, Iolaus is a Greek hero, son of Iphicles, king of Thessaly. Iolaus assists Herakles in his second labor of slaying the Hydra and its ally the crab. Iolaus cauterizes the place where the Hydra's head has been cut off. He also goes with Herakles on his tenth labor to capture the cattle belonging to the giant Geryon. At Herakles's request, Iolaus restores Hebe's youth and innocence. (Graves 1955; Schwab 1974)

See also Herakles; Hydra.

IPHIGENEIA

In Greek mythology, Iphigeneia is the eldest daughter of Agamemnon and Clytemnestra, and sister of Orestes and Electra. Her father, who angered Artemis when he killed her favorite stag, has to sacrifice Iphigeneia in order to

A wall painting from the Roman town of Pompeii shows the Greek hero Agamemnon, right, sacrificing his daughter Iphigeneia, center. He needed to appease Artemis, goddess of the hunt, upper center, whose favorite stag he killed. Iphigeneia appears as a character in the *Aeneid* and as Chrysothemis in the *Iliad*.

appease the goddess, so that the Achaean fleet can be delivered from the calm that prevents it from sailing on to Troy. In the *Iliad* (ix), Iphigeneia is called Chrysothemis. She also appears in the *Aeneid* (ii). (Humphries 1951; Lattimore 1976)

See also Agamemnon; Clytemnestra; *Iliad.*

ISAACS, N.

In the Zulu epic *Emperor Shaka the Great,* Isaacs is one of the early white traders, who is kindly received and sheltered by Prince Myaka of the Mthethwas. (Kunene 1979)

See also *Emperor Shaka the Great.*

ISEULT

In the medieval cycle of *Tristan and Iseult,* Iseult is the legendary Irish princess whom Tristan woos in the name of his uncle, King Mark of Cornwall. (Heer 1961)

See also *Tristan and Iseult.*

ISHTAR

(Also Astarte, Ashtoreth, and Athtar)

Ishtar is the Babylonian goddess of love and war who developed from the Sumerian goddess Inanna. Canaanites knew her as Astarte; Israelites, as Ashtoreth; and Arabs, as the god Athtar. In the *Epic of Gilgamesh,* when Gilgamesh spurns her advances, Ishtar flies into a rage and has her father Anu, the lord of heaven, send down the Bull of Heaven against Gilgamesh. He and Enkidu kill the bull, but Enkidu dies as punishment. (Saggs 1990; Sandars 1972)

See also Enkidu; *Gilgamesh, Epic of;* Inanna.

ISIS

Isis is one of the Triad of Abydos, the three maid gods of the Great Ennead, or state religion of Egypt, as told by priests of Heliopolis. Isis is the wife and sister of Osiris, and lady of heaven. She is born on the fourth epagomenal day (the time of bringing forth), and her name means "chamber of the birth of a god." Isis and Osiris even embrace in the mother's womb, and after they are born, they marry and rule Egypt together, "making it a land of music and delight." But the evil Seth murders Osiris, and Isis wanders the banks of the Nile weeping and searching for her husband's corpse. Among the reeds she finds a baby, Anubis, the son of Osiris and Isis's sister Nephthys, who has left the baby there to die because of her fear of her husband Seth. Isis loves the baby, who

A palm wood statuette made between 332 and 320 B.C. represents Isis, a goddess of ancient Egypt, who was wife and sister of Osiris, god of the underworld. She wears a headdress topped by cow horns holding a sun disc, symbols associated with Hathor, goddess of joy and motherhood.

has a dog's head and a spotted coat, and she rears him to be watchdog to the gods.

Eventually Isis finds Osiris's casket, which has washed ashore and become embedded in a huge tamarisk tree. When the king of Syria, Melkarth, orders the tree to be cut down for a pillar in his palace, Isis follows to Syria, where she sits daily beside the pillar, stroking it. The queen of Syria, Ishtar, not knowing that Isis is a goddess, commands her to remain at the palace at Byblos as a nurse to her oldest son. Concealing her identity, Isis tends the child and allows it to suckle her fingers. She holds him over a flame in order to singe away the mortal parts and render him immortal. When everyone is asleep, she takes the form of a black swallow and flies down to the tamarisk pillar, shrieking loudly with longing for her dead husband.

One night Ishtar finds Isis holding her son over the flame. She screams, thus breaking the spell so that her son cannot become immortal. Isis reveals herself as the Lady of the Sunrise and tells her story to Ishtar, who prostrates herself before the goddess and gladly gives her the pillar. Isis removes the casket from the pillar and sails back to the delta of Egypt, where her sister Nephthys will help her to revive Osiris. They hide the casket so that Seth will not find it, but Seth hears of it and drags Isis away to prison. She escapes with the help of Anubis and retreats to the reeds of the river, where she settles on a stool and gives birth unaided to Osiris's son, Horus.

Meanwhile, Seth discovers the casket and cuts Osiris's corpse into 14 pieces, which he tosses into the Nile. When Isis discovers the empty casket, she quickly makes a frail boat of papyrus reeds and embarks to recapture the 14 pieces of her husband's body. She gathers all she can find and takes them to Abydos, where Nephthys and Horus wait. Horus reassembles the body and discovers that the phallus is missing, having been eaten by three fishes. Isis fashions an artificial phallus, and hereafter priestesses must carry them in all ceremonies.

Horus sets off after Seth, and after a three-day struggle, he brings Seth to Isis in chains. After Horus leaves again in pursuit of Seth's infernal legions, Seth convinces Isis to release him. When Horus discovers that his mother has freed Seth, he becomes so angry that he cuts off her head. Thoth quickly replaces it with the horned head of Hathor, the more ancient female god. Together, Horus and Isis pursue Seth, who tears out Horus's eye. Later Horus retrieves his eye and feeds it to Osiris, who is revived by it. Horus makes a ladder up to heaven, and Isis, Nephthys, Thoth, and Osiris—with Horus's help—ascend to heaven. (Budge 1969; Goodrich 1960)

See also Horus; Moses; Osiris.

ITZAMNA

(Iguana House)

In pre-Columbian Mayan religion, recorded in the *Popol Vuh,* Itzamna is the principal deity. It is Itzamna who gives mankind writing and the calendar. He is also the patron god of medicine. (Recinos, Goetz, and Morley 1983; Sawyer-Lauçanno 1987; Schell and Freidel 1990)

See also Itzananohk'u.

ITZANANOHK'U

(Also Itzamaku, Great God Itzana and Itzamna)

This modern Mayan deity of the Lacandon people of Mexico is a recent form of Itzamna, "He who makes hail." (Toor 1947)

See also Itzamna.

IXCHEL

(Also Ix Chebel Yax and Ix Chel)

Ixchel is the Mayan goddess of the moon, patroness of womanly crafts, sometime wife of Itzamna, and sometimes possibly a female manifestation of Itzamna. Ixchel is often depicted as an evil old woman. (Schell and Freidel 1990)

IYANGURA

In the *Mwindo Epic* of the Nyanga of Africa, Iyangura is the sister of Chief Shemwindo and the paternal aunt of Mwindo. She is married to Mukiti, the Water Serpent. When his father rejects him, Mwindo sets off to find Iyangura, whom he transforms into his faithful adviser. In another version of the epic, Iyangura is the wife of Chief Shemwindo and the mother of Mwindo and his sister Nyamitondo Mwindo. (Biebuyck 1978)

See also *Mwindo, Epic of;* Shemwindo.

IZANAGI AND IZANAMI

In the Japanese creation myth as depicted in the *Nihongi*, Izanagi no Mikoto and Izanami no Mikoto are the eighth pair of brother and sister deities to appear after heaven and earth separate out of chaos. They stand on the floating bridge of Heaven and thrust down the jewel-spear of Heaven, and "groping about therewith," find the ocean. The brine that drips from the point of the spear coagulates and becomes the first land, an island named Ono-goro-jima, which also appears in *Kojiki*. It is identified with a small island near Ahaji. The two deities descend and dwell upon this island. They wish "to become husband and wife together, and to produce countries." They travel in opposite directions around the island, and when they meet, the female speaks first: "How delightful! I have met a lovely youth." The male deity is displeased and says, "I am a man, and by right should have spoken first. . . . This is unlucky. Let us go round again." They retreat and, meeting again, the male deity speaks first, saying, "How delightful! I have met a lovely maiden." The two unite and produce a number of islands. Finally they consult and say, "We have now produced the Great-eight-island country, with the mountains, rivers, herbs, and trees. Why

The Japanese creation myth is shown in a nineteenth-century scroll. Izanami, left, watches her brother and husband Izanagi create the first land by letting ocean brine drip from his spear.

should we not produce someone who shall be lord of the universe?" They then produce the sun goddess Ama-terasu no Oho-kami. (Aston 1972)

See also Ama-terasu no Oho-kami; *Nihongi.*

J

JACOB

In the Old Testament, Jacob is the grandson of Abraham, who is father of the nation. Jacob is the son of Isaac and the younger brother of Esau, from whom he steals the birthright. He wrestles all night with a strange man, perhaps an angel or messenger of God, telling him, "I will not let you go unless you bless me." The man tells him, "Your name shall no longer be Jacob, but Israel." Jacob is reconciled with his brother Esau. He becomes the father of the 12 tribes of Israel. (Genesis 24–49ff.)

JAHANGIR
(Also Janggar)

Jahangir is a Tatar villain, the subject of a üliger, an orally transmitted Mongolian epic story in verse. He is the eldest son of the slaughtering Islamic Turk Tamerlane (Timur), who conquers the entire area from Mongolia to the Mediterranean between the 1360s and 1390s. Jahangir dies ca. 1375 or 1376 in Samarkand fighting the forces of Qamar al-Din. His death is celebrated by the Mongols in this üliger. (Grousset 1970)

See also Genghis Khan; *Secret History of the Mongols; Timurid Epic.*

JAMA

Jama is the king of the Zulus and grandfather of Shaka the Great. In the epic *Emperor Shaka the Great,* Shaka's temperament is said to resemble strongly that of Jama. (Kunene 1979)

See also *Emperor Shaka the Great.*

JANKO THE DUKE

Central character in a Serbo-Croatian cycle of traditional bugarštica and decasyllabic poems. Bugarštica are oral traditional narratives, the oldest extant South Slavic ballad form. It is a long-line narrative song, balladic in structure, that deals with heroic matters, often tragic, and frequently set within the melee of the feudal court. The form flourished from the end of the fifteenth century to the eighteenth century. According to Slavic scholar John S. Miletich, history suggests that the bugarštica originated in medieval Serbia and were brought to Hungary during the Serbian migration. New songs were added to the old in the lower Danube region of Srem. When Srem fell to the Turks in the sixteenth century, singers fled to the coast, where bugarštica were preserved until recorded.

In "When Janko the Duke Married Mihailo Svilojevic's Sister," Mihailo informs his beautiful sister—whose name is not given—that two suitors are riding across the plain to ask for her hand. One is Duke Janko, accompanied by his nephew Sekula. The other is young and handsome Ban Stjepan. He tells her to choose Janko. She does as she is told, but when her dark eyes catch sight of Stjepan's face, the tears flow down her cheeks. Janko sees this but ignores it. They go off to feast at the brother's table, and afterward Janko tells Mihailo that he is off to Sibiu and wants Mihailo's blessing to take his sister along. Mihailo gives his blessing, and the couple leaves for Sibiu, where the people welcome them with festivities. The bride bears Janko two sons: Laus and Matijas.

In "When Durad the Despot Imprisoned Janko the Duke," after the Hungarian duke Janko is wounded at Kosovo *(see Kosovo, Battle of)*, he reaches one end of Smederevo, where the despot Durad has proclaimed that no Hungarian may cross. When Janko disregards this proclamation, he is seized and thrown into prison. Janko calls for paper and pen so that he can write to his wife. He asks her to bring his sons, "the falcons twain," so that they can deceive the traitor Durad and Janko can escape.

His wife obeys, and on her way to see Durad she meets her brother Svilojevic, who warns her that her sons will be killed in this endeavor. Besides, she is foolish to take both of her sons: "A fool alone gives two for one!" But she replies, "More sons will my spouse beget with me, / But ne'er will sons beget my spouse!"

When she arrives at Smederevo, the guard tells Durad, "There never was a lady here / Like this Hungarian noblewoman, / Two lordly children at her side." The despot receives her politely, and she asks him to accept her two sons in place of her husband. He honors her request, casts the children into prison, and sets Janko free.

The despot's son Lazar comes to play dice with Janko's sons. One of the boys, Matijas, wins 300 ducats, but Lazar refuses to pay; instead he strikes Matijas, who retaliates by stabbing Lazar, who falls dead across his cot.

Outside, Janko tells the guard to inform Durad, "Unless my sons are home for supper, / Three hundred Hungarians I'll gather swift, / With them I'll come to Smederevo; / And stone by stone I'll topple it." When the traitor hears this, he frees the boys. As they are leaving they tell the guard to inform the despot's wife, "We've left behind a golden apple, / Oh send it to us in Sibiu." The woman hurries to the cell to get the golden apple and finds her son dead upon the cot. Durad gathers some men to pursue the boys, but they escape. Sadly, Durad returns to Smederevo.

The action of "When Janko the Duke Struck Durad the Despot with His Mace" takes place at the wedding of Buda's king to a Krusevo bride. Janko, the Hungarian duke, is his marriage witness. Janko shows his displeasure because the guest of honor is "the faithless Despot Durad," of whom he tells the king, "I've a mind to take my sword to him." The king suggests that Janko wait until the next day when the party will pass the ramparts of Smederevo, where among the ladies will be Durad's wife Jerino. "Then of his hoary beard take hold, / And strike him with the golden mace: / Thus shame for shame you will repay."

In the rituals to claim the bride, the challenges, meant to be performed by Durad, are instead performed by Janko: shooting a golden apple, leaping over 12 horses, and picking the betrothed from among 12 maidens. As the triumphal party rides past Smederevo, Janko takes Durad by the beard and strikes him with his mace. But Jerino calls out for mercy, and Janko delivers Durad, "scarce alive," to her servants. The party continues on to Buda, where there is great feasting.

"Duke Janko and Sekula Race Their Steeds" is a short poem in which, while Janko and his nephew are riding toward Kosovo, Janko proposes a race. But Sekula tells his uncle, "Fine steeds so many have you ridden, / You'll leave me behind in Kosovo." He adds, "The Turks so fierce will catch up with me, / They'll send me to a wretched death." But Janko proposes an oath between them: "Since I do have the better steed, / . . . Let's never part no matter what!" As it happens, Sekula has the fastest steed, and he leaves Janko behind. Janko asks Sekula if he will exchange steeds, but Sekula refuses an exchange; instead, he gives Janko his steed, named Sustica. Sustica will be responsible for Janko slaying 300 Turks.

"Ban Milos and Sekula's Sister" are lovers, but Sekula finds out and asks his uncle Janko's advice, saying he will slay the Transylvanian Ban Milos. Janko tells him that because Milos is the king's friend, they mustn't slay him. Instead, he suggests they put him in a dungeon and let him starve. This they do, but Sekula's sister, Janka, visits Milos, bringing him bread and wine. She asks him what he wants. He tells her he has had his fill of heroes' wine and bread and "of riding hard." He expresses his desire for Janka. The following day, Sunday, while her mother is in church and her uncle Janko is hunting with her brother Sekula, Janka steals the dungeon's keys and frees Milos. She leads him to her brother's court, where he takes the weapon of his choice: Sekula's dagger. She saddles two steeds, and the two of them flee to Ohrid.

"Duke Janko Shoots a Serpent in the Air and Thus Strikes Sekula in the Heart" tells of the time when Sekula asks his uncle, "Oh give me leave to fight the Turks!" Janko discourages him because he is young and gentle: "You've not yet learned to fight the Turks, / . . . [They] will slay you." Nevertheless, Sekula rides to the sultan's tent and looses a winged serpent from his shirt. He also looses a falcon, and the two lock and rise into the air. As Duke Janko and his men sit in his tent drinking wine, the falcon and the serpent strike his tent. Janko asks his men which he should shoot, and they warn him not to shoot the serpent, but to shoot the falcon. However, he elects to shoot the serpent. Later in the day, Sekula arrives looking ill-tempered. When Janko asks him if he drank too much at Kosovo, or loved too many maidens, or became afraid of battle, Sekula tells him that the reason for his ill-temper is that Janko's arrow struck his heart. "And from this wound I'll not recover." Janko says he will get healing herbs from pirate knights, but Sekula breathes his last upon the saddle. He rides away saying, "There is no time for talk!"

"The Death of Sekula's Mother" tells of Janko's sister Rude, a "fair widow," who writes Janko to ask him to send her son Sekula home to Sibiu. She has a maiden picked out for him to marry. But Janko sends word to her that Sekula is already married off, and that Janko has built the boy a white court, and before it, a fine white tomb. The widow Rude is cheered, and she assembles fine gifts, cakes, vassals, and even drums and trumpets, and sets out for Kosovo. There her vassals tell her to look across the level field and try to see her son's white court. She sees something white rising high, so she quickly spurs her steed toward it. She comes to the white monastery of Mount Athos. When the monks come out of vespers, she asks them, "Who is it built this white retreat?" The monks answer, "Duke Janko built this white retreat, / And fine, white tomb in front as well, / . . . He buried Sekula within." The widow asks them to open the tomb, and she falls within it and breathes her last.

In "Duke Janko Predicts Buda's Fall to the Turks and the Death of King Vladisav from a Maiden's Dream," a maiden calls King Vladisav of Buda, "if you're at love, don't love too long! / If counting cards, don't count them long, / . . . If you're asleep, don't sleep too long! / For I have dreamt a dream so strange . . ." that even the moon turns dark. No one can divine her dream except the aged Duke Janko, who curses her because her dream means that the Turks will slay the Hungarians and King Vladisav will die. No sooner has he spoken the words than "the accursed Turks" climb Buda's walls and "cut off the glorious king's fair head. . . ."

"King Vladisav's Hand" tells of a young mountain maid who strolls before Buda calling for the king, asking why the gates are closed, the courts are decked in black, and instead of song, only sobbing and moaning are heard. She asks why the fine ladies do not dance the kolo. From Kosovo a wounded hero comes to announce that the despot Vuk has marshaled the troops "and knew not how." He has sent the Hungarians against the Anatolian pasha and all the nobles have perished. As soon as Janko hears this, he rises from his sickbed, mounts his fine steed, and rides off to Kosovo. There he finds "many Hungarians sorely wounded." With his lance he turns 20 heads, looking for the head of Vladisav. He finds nothing but the king's right hand, which he recognizes by the gold ring. He wraps it in his silk handkerchief and takes it to the king's mother and wife. They kiss the hand as bitter tears flow down white faces. (Miletich 1990)

JASHAR, BOOK OF

This legendary Jewish history from Adam to Joshua was composed presumably in Italy during the ninth century. (Ginzberg 1991)

JASON

In Greek mythology, Jason is the leader of the Argonauts in the quest for the Golden Fleece. He is the son of Aeson, king of Iolcos in Thessaly. He is educated by the wise centaur Chiron, who protects Jason when Aeson's half brother Pelias seizes the throne. He returns as a young man to claim his inheritance, which Pelias promises in exchange for the Golden Fleece. Many heroes of renown accompany him to Colchis on the *Argo,* including Herakles, Admetus, Meleager, Orpheus, and Pelias. With the help of Medea, Jason obtains the Fleece. She murders Pelias when he fails to live up to his bargain, but Pelias's son drives Medea and Jason away to Corinth. There they are sheltered by King Creon, whose daughter wins Jason's heart. He deserts Medea for Glauce (Creusa), but Medea sends a gown covered with poison to Glauce. The poison causes a fire that kills Glauce, King Creon, and everyone in the palace. Jason's story appears in Apollonius of Rhodes's four-book epic *Argonautica,* written ca. 260 B.C. (Graves 1955)

See also Argonauts.

JĀZIYA

Heroine of the North African Arab epic *Hilāliyya,* Jāziya dons male battle garb and leads her Arab troops into battle. (Connelly 1986)

See also *Hilāliyya.*

JENGHIZ-KHAN

(Also Genghis Khan)

Hero of the Mongols celebrated in the *Secret History of the Mongols.* (Grousset 1970)

JEPHTHAH

(Also Jephte)

Jephthah is a Jewish hero/judge whose story in the Old Testament bears great similarity to the classical legend of Idomeneus of Crete, who rashly promises Poseidon that if he escapes a dangerous storm on his way home, upon his arrival he will sacrifice the first living thing he sees, which turns out to be his own son. In the Jewish version, on his way into battle to defend the Gileads against the oppressive Ammons, Jephthah promises God, "If thou shalt without fail deliver the children of Ammon into mine hands, / Then it shall be, that whatsoever cometh forth of the doors of my house to meet me, . . . shall surely be the Lord's, and I will offer it up for a burnt offering." When the battle is won and his only child, his daughter, comes out to greet him, he rends his clothes and says, ". . . I have opened my mouth unto the Lord, and I cannot go back." She asks him for two months, during which she goes into the mountains to bewail her virginity. After two months' time she returns, and he sacrifices her. (Judges 10:6–11:40; Schwab 1974)

JIMMU TENNŌ
(Also Kamu-yamato-ipare-biko-no-mikoto and Kami-Yamato Ihare-biko Hohodemi)

In the *Nihongi* and the *Kojiki*, Jimmu Tennō is the legendary first emperor of the Yamato line and founder of the imperial dynasty of Japan. He is the fourth child of Hiko-nagisa-take-u-gaya-fuki-ahezu no Mikoto. His mother, Tama-yori-hime, is said to be the daughter of the sea god. He is descended from the sun goddess Ama-terasu through Ninigi, whom she sends down as governor of the earth. From birth, Jimmu is "of clear intelligence and resolute will." He is made heir to the throne at age 15. He marries Ahira-tsu-hime of the district of Ata and has two children. His consort is a descendant of the storm god Susanowo. When he reaches the age of 45, the world is "given over to widespread desolation." It is a time of darkness and disorder. He consults his imperial princes and decides to make an expedition along the inland sea (607 B.C.), bringing the tribes along the way under his subjugation. When he arrives at Yamato, he makes it his capital and names his wife empress. The lively account of his expedition makes up book III of the *Nihongi* book I. According to the *Nihongi*, he is 127 years old when he dies; the *Kojiki* records his age as 137. (Aston 1972; Philippi 1968)

See also Ama-terasu no Oho-kami; Susanowo.

JINGŌ KŌGU
(Also Okinaga-tarishi-hime no Mikoto)

In the *Nihongi* and the *Kojiki*, Jingō Kōgu is the semilegendary empress of Emperor Chuai (reigned 192–200) and regent for her son Ōjin. She is the daughter of Prince Okinaga no Sukune and Katsuraki no Taka-nuka-hime. When her husband dies in his ninth year of reign, she believes that he died prematurely because he had not followed the divine instructions. She immediately sets about finding out which god has sent the curse. After seven days and nights of prayer, she receives her answer: "I am the Deity who dwells in the Shrine of split-bell Isuzu." Other deities identify themselves as well, and she institutes worship of them according to their instructions so as to gain their assistance. She then embarks upon a conquest of the Land of Treasure, Silla (Korea). During this time, according to one version given in the *Nihongi*, her unborn son remains in her womb until she has time to complete the conquest and return home. Her followers want to put the king of Silla to death, but she says, "When I first received the Divine instructions, promising to bestow on me the Land of Gold and Silver, I gave orders to the three divisions of the army, saying:—'Slay not the submissive.' Now that we have taken the Land of Treasure, and its people have freely offered submission, it would be unlucky to slay them." Another version, also offered in the *Nihongi,* says, "She took the Prince of Silla, and going to the sea-side, plucked out his knee-caps, and causing him to crawl on the rocks, suddenly slew him and buried him in the sand." She goes on to conquer Pèkché and Koryö. Later she becomes known as the Grand Empress. She dies at age 100. Her story makes up book IX of the *Nihongi* book I. (Aston 1972; Philippi 1968)

JOBE

In the Zulu epic *Emperor Shaka the Great,* Jobe is the father of Dingiswayo and king of the Mthethwas. (Kunene 1979)

See also Dingiswayo; *Emperor Shaka the Great.*

JÓMSVÍKINGS, THE SAGA OF THE

This Icelandic heroic saga (twelfth century) tells about the famed members of a warrior community involved in the victory (A.D. 986) of Norse king Earl Hákon over invading Danes in the naval battle of Hjórunga Bay. Although it is generally classed as a historical saga, the story has been layered with accretions of legend. Practically all the characters are historic, but their deeds and speech are either deliberate fiction or folk traditions that have developed through many tellings.

The story begins with the origin of Knút, born from the incestuous union of a brother and sister. He is abandoned under a tree, found, and adopted by the king. King Gorm has three dreams that hard times will befall Denmark. The dreams are interpreted by his new queen, Thýra, who advises him how to forestall them. Gorm invites Earl Harold, his father-in-law, to his Yule feast, but Harold has visions three years in a row that convince him not to go. Thýra convinces Gorm not to take these absences as insults, and when Gorm is told the reason for the missed visits, he pardons Harold, who soon gives all his dominion to Knút and leaves the country for good.

During the reign of King AEthelstan in England, Gorm, Knút, and Gorm's son Harold raid Northumberland and subdue a great realm to their rule. Later, while Gorm is in Jutland, AEthelstan retaliates. During the fighting, Knút is slain, and the Danes return to Denmark. Harold reports the death to his mother, but when Gorm returns and hears the news, he falls ill and dies, having been king for 100 years. Harold Gormsson becomes king.

Knút is survived by a son also named Harold, called Gold-Harold, who returns from a raid to live at Harold's court. Another Harold, called Grayfur, and his mother Grunnhild rule over Norway. Earl Hákon flees Norway with ten ships and comes to Denmark seeking the friendship of King Harold Gormsson. The three plot against the king of Norway and his mother, and in the spring, they fall upon Harold Grayfur; Gold-Harold slays him. Later Earl Hákon has Gold-Harold led to the gallows and assumes the rule of all of Norway.

On the Danish island of Funen west of Zealand live three brothers, Áki, Palnir, and their bastard half brother Fiolnir, to whom the other two deny a portion of their inherited land. Fiolnir leaves and joins King Harold, becoming his retainer and counselor. He is a clever man, and he sets out to malign his brother Áki to the king. The king orders an ambush of Áki as he returns from a visit with Earl Óttar of Gotland, and all the party is killed and the booty taken.

Palnir falls ill, seeing no chance of revenge against the king. Another man, Sigurd, is a foster brother of Áki and Palnir. Sigurd is a wise and wealthy man, whom Palnir seeks out for advice. Sigurd suggests arranging a marriage with Ingeborg, daughter of Earl Óttar of Gotland. Although Palnir fears he may not win the woman, Sigurd sets out on a journey to Gotland on Palnir's behalf and is able to convince Óttar of the advantages of the marriage. On the appointed day, the earl arrives with Ingeborg, the marriage is celebrated with much magnificence, and the newlyweds are led to their marriage bed.

Ingeborg relates to Palnir a dream in which she sees Harold Gormsson's head as a weight on a loom. The couple become very fond of one another, and Ingeborg bears a son called Palnatóki, who greatly resembles his late uncle Áki.

Palnatóki grows up and goes on a raid against Stefnir in Wales. But he becomes attracted to Stefnir's daughter Álof and, after marrying her, receives half of the earl's land. Upon Stefnir's death, he is to have the rest. He appoints Bjorn the Welshman to rule in his stead so that he can return to Denmark, where he is considered the most important man next to the king.

Palnatóki discovers that the king has fathered a child, Svein, by a waiting-woman named Aesa. The king refuses to acknowledge the child, but Palnatóki vows to care for him and become his foster father. There is little love lost between the two men afterward.

When Svein becomes 15, his foster father sends him to his father the king to demand his assistance. Harold reluctantly admits that Svein is his son. He gives Svein three ships and a hundred men, and Palnatóki provides the boy with three more. Svein harries the realm of his father all summer, causing much grumbling among the farmers. Svein returns to the king to get six more ships, and Palnatóki gives him six more as well. Again he harries the kingdom of his father, killing many people. The farmers go to see the king, but he lets their complaints pass unheeded. Svein comes to the king a third time, demanding 12 ships, threatening to fight him if he does not get the ships. The king finally agrees, and Svein goes to his foster father with 30 ships. Palnatóki is proud of Svein's accomplishments; he reveals his own plans to return to Wales for good, so Svein is free to lay waste to Denmark, killing, robbing, and burning the countryside. When King Harold comes after Svein, Palnatóki comes to his foster son's aid unbeknownst to Svein, slays the king, and proclaims Svein the king over all Denmark.

Palnatóki's father-in-law dies, leaving all his Wales kingdom to him. Svein invites his foster father to a feast honoring the late king. Palnatóki arrives with Bjorn the Welshman, three ships, and a hundred men. During the feast, Svein learns that his foster father is the slayer of his father, and he orders the whole company killed. But Palnatóki and his company escape, with the exception of one Welshman, whose body Bjorn bears back home.

The following summer, Álof, Palnatóki's wife, dies. Palnatóki leaves Bjorn to rule Wales and sets out with 30 ships to harry in Scotland and Ireland. After three years of acquiring much wealth, he sails east to Wendland (present-day Mecklenburg and Pomerania in the Baltics). The king there offers him friendship and even a district of land to rule, called Jóm, in exchange for protection. Palnatóki accepts his offer and builds a large fort called Jómsborg. He establishes laws and codes of conduct to which the warriors must adhere. Each summer they go on Viking expeditions and win great renown. They are considered the greatest of warriors and are called Jómsvíkings.

Meanwhile, Palnatóki and Álof's son Áki marries Thorgunn, daughter of the ruler of Bornholm. The couple has a son named Vagn, who soon becomes a problem child. No one can control him except his maternal uncle Búi. He is a strong, handsome lad with great accomplishments.

A feud develops when Earl Strút-Harold's sons Sigvaldi and Thorkel plunder the land of Véseti, ruler of Bornholm and Vagn's grandfather. The brothers ask to join the Jómsvíkings and are accepted; meanwhile, Véseti appeals to King Svein to intervene because of the damage to his land. The king calls Earl Strút-Harold to court to inform him of what his sons have done and bids him to make good the losses. When Harold refuses on the grounds that he has not received any of the booty, the stage is set for a fight. King Svein arbitrates the feud and war is averted. Sigurd, brother of Búi and Thorgunn, is married to Tova, uniting the families.

Now Búi is anxious to join the Jómsvíkings and win fame. Sigurd wants to go too, even though he is newly married. They set sail at once with 120 men and are admitted into the company once they have proven their worthiness. Meanwhile, the ungovernable Vagn, who killed three men by the time he was nine, has reached age 12. He too sails to Jómsborg, but his bad reputation precedes him, and no one will allow him to enter. Vagn challenges Sigvaldi to a fight on open waters, and when Sigvaldi begins to lose ground, Palnatóki commands the fighting to cease, and he orders Sigvaldi to take Vagn and his crew into their company.

When Palnatóki nears old age and death, he gives Vagn half of his kingdom in Wales and appoints Sigvaldi to take over leadership of the Jómsvíkings. The king of Wendland, Burisleif, has three daughters. Sigvaldi wants the oldest, Ástrid, as his wife. But she lays two conditions on the union: first, that he relieve the country of having to pay tribute to Denmark and second, that he lure King Svein to Wendland so as to get him in Burisleif's power. Sigvaldi tricks Svein into coming, offering him the hand of the second daughter, Gunnhild, whom he claims is the most beautiful. He also convinces him to suspend Burisleif's paying of tribute, which will thus enable him to marry Ástrid. Svein agrees, and the couples are married in a double ceremony, each bride wearing a heavy veil. When Svein sees his bride, he does not think she is the most beautiful of the three daughters at all. But he makes the best of a bad bargain; after feasting, he returns home with his bride and a number of new ships.

When Earl Strút-Harold dies, Svein sends word to Sigvaldi and Thorkel that they should return to Denmark to inherit their father's Zealand estate. Svein is there when the Jómsvíkings arrive. He serves the party a feast and makes certain that everyone has plenty to drink. Then he asks each to make a vow as to what he will accomplish during the next three years. Sigvaldi boasts that he will drive Earl Hákon from his land or kill him. The others all make vows to accompany him. By morning, the men realize that they have been tricked into undertaking this difficult task. Svein offers to provide some of the ships for the mission. They begin with a raid on the town of Túnsberg, taking it by surprise and laying it to waste. A magistrate named Geirmund escapes and flees to warn Earl Hákon. Since he is warned, Hákon is able to amass a large fleet to meet the Jómsvíkings. A storm blows up, further hampering the invaders. Sigvaldi decides to flee; Vagn tries to prevent it by hurling a spear at him, but he misses. Búi jumps overboard, and Sigurd and Thorkel abandon the fight when Sigvaldi flees. Twenty-four ships sail back to Denmark. Vagn remains with Bjorn the Welshman. So many men fall that scarcely 80 are left, ten of whom die of their wounds during the night.

The rest are taken prisoner, and Thorkel is chosen to deal the prisoners the death blow. Each man comes forward in turn and is killed. A young man with golden-yellow hair ducks his blow and is allowed to live when it is learned that he is Svein, son of Búi. Another, Vagn, comes forth and with much arrogance says that he plans to sleep with Thorkel's daughter and kill Thorkel. Thorkel lifts his sword in both hands, but Bjorn rushes forward and pushes Vagn out of the way. The blade cuts Vagn's rope so that he is free. He leaps up and grabs the sword, dealing Thorkel a death blow. Earl Hákon, who has been watching the slaughter, orders that Vagn be killed at once, but his deputy, Earl Eric, refuses to allow the killing, saying that he wants Vagn in his band. Vagn refuses unless the rest of the men are released, and they are freed.

Vagn marries Ingeborg of Víken and returns to Funen to manage his possessions. Bjorn goes home to Wales to rule, and Sigvaldi returns to his wife Ástrid and rules over Zealand with great shrewdness. Sigurd takes over his paternal inheritance on the island of Bornholm, where he and his wife Tova produce a long line of heirs. Some say that Búi, who jumped overboard, has become a dragon who inhabits Hjórunga Bay. Earl Hákon rules Norway for a long time before he is murdered, and then King Ólaf rules Norway, converting it to Christianity. (Hollander *Jómsvíkings* 1990)

JORD

(Also Joro, Fjorgyn, and Hlodyn)

In Old Norse mythology, Jord is Earth, the giantess mistress of the god Óthin and mother of Thor. She is also identified with the Lithuanian thunder god Perkūn and the Bulgarian thunder god Perun. (Georgieva 1985; Greimas 1992; Young 1954)

JOSHUA

Joshua is the Old Testament leader of Israel, successor to Moses, who leads the tribe into the promised land. He crosses the Jordan and encircles the Canaanite city of Jericho. The Israelites fight a war of nerves, circling the walls and blowing their horns for seven days before attacking. After the fall of Jericho, the war widens, but the Israelites prevail. In all, including those previously defeated by Moses, 31 Canaanite kings are defeated. (Deuteronomy 31; 34:9ff.; Exodus 17:9ff., 24:13, 33:11; Joshua 4, 6, 13ff., 23–24; Numbers 13, 14, 27)

JOURNEY

A popular motif in heroic literature, the journey is often part of a quest in search of treasure, a land in which to settle, a sanctuary from danger, or a loved one. The journey may also be to right a wrong or to avenge a death. The *Odyssey* is the story of a journey home. The *Aeneid* is the story of a journey to a new land. Sundiata's journey is a search for asylum. Shaka's journey is a flight from home, as is his mother Nandi's and Mwindo's. Mwindo's story is one journey after another. He also journeys to the underground and wakes up all his maternal uncles. But Shemwindo flees and gets lost in the palace of the god Muisa, where "fire is unknown . . . in that dark place," so later Mwindo must journey to find him. In the *Rāmāyaṇa*, Rāma journeys to find Sītā. Isis journeys to Syria to obtain Osiris's casket. Gilgamesh's journey searching for the key to immortality epitomizes the ultimate journey to find some meaning for existence.

The traveler not only traverses space and time but encounters obstacles and adventures along the way that often result in new knowledge gained; thus time is both quantitative, measuring years of life, and qualitative, measuring changes wrought in the traveler. The journey becomes a rite of passage, testing the traveler's mettle—leading from trial to purification, from experience to wisdom, from death of the old to birth of the new.

The song of the journey springs from man's awareness that he is borne along in a reality not of his making or liking. The journey originates from the desire to be more than that reality, to escape from it. The journey song expresses the universal dream of no longer being what one is. Preliterate people may escape through myth, but they remain closer to the organic realities of the human condition than people in a technological society. Regardless of the degree of sophistication, all share the same yearning: At the heart of the human condition is the desire to rise above it. This yearning is realized only as a dream conveyed in myth or song. Man's secret desire to escape his destiny proves its own futility in most journey myths, for man knows only too well his destiny. As Pierre Clastres says of the Guarani Indians of Peru, the journey toward death is the one road he knows how to travel. (Clastres 1987)

See also *Aeneid; Emperor Shaka the Great; Gilgamesh, Epic of;* Isis; *Mwindo, Epic of; Rāmāyaṇa; Sundiata, Epic of; The Voyage of Brân, Son of Febal.*

Epics often recount wanderings and desperate challenges and battles against demons and nature. Here, in a detail from a sixteenth-century painting, Greek argonauts led by Jason sail aboard the *Argo* during their quest for a ram's golden fleece.

JUDITH

In this Old English poem, of which only a fragment remains, apparently Judith and her handmaiden have entered the camp of Assyrian chief Holofernes in order to persuade him not to attack the Hebrew town of Bethulia. On the fourth day of her confinement at his camp, Holofernes orders a great drinking feast, after which Judith is to be brought to his bedchamber, where he plans to "defile" her. However, he becomes so drunk that his men have to drag him unconscious to his bed. Judith takes a sword and, in two swipes, severs Holofernes's head from his body. She places it in a bag, which her handmaiden carries, and the two of them return to Bethulia, where their people rejoice at her safe return. She tells them to arm for battle, and the Hebrews march forth with Holofernes's head on a stake to drive the Assyrians out of the land. They return triumphant with Holofernes's sword, helmet, and gold-encrusted mail as gifts for Judith.

Judith is also the name of an apocryphal work included in the *Septuagint* (Greek Bible), which recounts the same story. Judith, a widow, asks the Hebrews to delay capitulating to Holofernes for five days while she goes to his camp. After the Assyrians are routed, they do not threaten the Hebrews again during Judith's 105-year lifetime. The earliest extant version of the book is a Greek translation, but scholars believe it was originally written in Hebrew during Persian times. Judith's name also appears in the Old Testament, where she is the Gentile wife of Esau.

Judith is also the name of a Croatian epic by Peter Hektorovic. (Dvornik 1962; Genesis 26:34; Hieatt 1967)

JUNO

In Roman religion, Juno is the chief goddess, the equivalent of the Greek queen of the gods, Hera, and the consort of Jupiter. (Graves 1966)

JUPITER

In Roman religion, Jupiter is the chief god, equivalent of the Greek Zeus, ruler of heaven and earth, gods and men. (Graves 1966)

K

KAALU EZE NWA MGBO

This heroic legend of the Ohafia people in present-day Nigeria, West Africa, is still being sung today. It concerns a great wrestler who is cursed by the gods with infertility until one day, during a wrestling match, his back touches the ground. This union with the earth makes him virile. (Azuonye *RAL* 1990)

KAHINDO

In the *Mwindo Epic* of the Nyanga of Zaire, Kahindo is an important deity. In some versions of the epic she is the daughter of Muisa, bringer-of-death. On his journey to the underworld, Mwindo meets her at the wading place and heals her yaws. In exchange, she advises him on how to overcome his father's trickery. She becomes his lover, but when Muisa proposes her for Mwindo's wife, the hero rejects the offer, postponing any marriage until "later."

In other versions, she is the daughter of Nyamurairi, god of fire. Mwindo meets her at the underworld wading place and heals her of scurvy, in exchange for which she offers her love and advice. In other versions, she leads the hero into a dark forest by changing into a wild boar, then into the daughter of a blacksmith, then into a woman harvesting bananas. She exposes the hero to tests prepared by her father. Later she marries Mwindo and bears Ndurumo and Kanyironge.

Kahindo is also the name of the daughter of Hangi-of-Drum and principal wife of Chief Karisi in some versions of the *Mwindo Epic.* Her husband rejects her because of barrenness, but she bears a son, Little-one-just-born-he-walked, without conceiving. Later she has a son, Mwindo, born normally. (Biebuyck 1978)

See also *Mwindo, Epic of.*

KAIDARA

This mythical epic of the Fula-speaking people of West Africa tells about a fantastic adventure involving mythical creatures. (Westley *RAL* 1991)

K'AI LU SHEN

(Spirit Who Clears the Road; also Hsien Tao Shen, Spirit of Dangerous Roads)

It is the duty of this Chinese deity of funeral processions and travel to sweep away evil before funeral processions or before travelers take to the road. (Mackenzie 1990)

KĀLAKĀCĀRYAKATHĀ

(The Story of the Teacher Kālaka; also *Kālakācārya)*

This cycle of legends of the Śvetāmbara ("white robed") sect of the Indian religion of Jainism in western India made its appearance in the twelfth century or earlier. The stories revolve around a renowned Jaina teacher of the first century B.C. called the "black teacher." Versions written in Sanskrit, Prākrit, and other languages vary, and some of the historical events described point to the probability that the stories do not all relate to the same person. Some legends concern his invitation to the Śakas, a Scythian tribe, to help him overthrow King Gandabhilla of Ujjayinī (modern-day Ujjain), who has abducted his sister, the Jaina nun Sarasvatī. Kālaka is said to have traveled to Southeast Asia, perhaps to present-day Vietnam; to have written the original texts of the *Mūlaprathamanuyoga;* and espoused the Nigoda Doctrine (the existence of tiny groups of invisible souls packed into every element of the world: earth, air, fire, and water) before Indra (Sakra), chief of the gods. He is said to have chastised the arrogant monk Sagaracandra, a follower of Kālaka's disciple. He is said to be responsible for moving the date of the Parysana festival forward by one day. Since the historical events coinciding with these stories range over many years, scholars speculate that they relate to as many as three different teachers, possibly all bearing the same name. (Embree 1988)

KALEVALA

The Finnish national epic, *Kalevala* was compiled from the oral tradition by poet and scholar Elias Lönnrot in 1835 and revised in 1849. The work, presented in more than 12,000 nonrhyming, alliterative, octosyllabic, trochaic verses, contains 50 cantos in its final 1849 version. Kalevala is the poetic name for Finland and means Land of Heroes. This epic enjoys a unique position, standing at the juncture of the traditional and the literary epic; its uniqueness is derived from the fact that its author made use of a large number of oral epic songs, mostly from Russian Karelia, which he recorded, then wove together, to produce a work that has not only preserved its myths but also fostered Finnish national spirit and pride. Many shorter "charms" are included within the 50 cantos.

The first poem describes the creation of the world: In the beginning, a beautiful teal is searching for a place to nest, but there are only chaotic waters. A virgin of the air descends to the sea and becomes the Mother of Waters. She

An incident in the *Kalevala*, the Finnish national epic, is represented by nineteenth-century artist Akseli Gallén-Kallela. Lemminkäinen, a hero, is being restored to life by his mother. He was poisoned after accepting a challenge to kill a swan in Death's domain; Death's son found the body and chopped it into five pieces.

raises herself from the waters far enough that a goldeneye, mistaking her knee for a hillock, can make its nest and lay its seven eggs upon her knee. Six of the eggs are of gold, and one is of iron. When the virgin's knee grows hot, she moves, causing the eggs to roll out and break. The pieces are transformed into earth, heaven, sun, moon, stars, and clouds.

The hero Väinämöinen is born and drifts upon the waves until he is washed ashore. He is destined to become a master of the Kantele, the Finnish stringed instrument similar to a harp.

Poem 2 concerns Väinämöinen's sowing of the primeval wilderness. A sower's charm is included. Poem 3 describes how Väinämöinen grows in years, fame, and wisdom. Joukahainen, a "young scrawny Lappish lad," sets out to defeat him in a test of wisdom. When Väinämöinen bests him, Joukahainen offers him his own sister, Aino, as a wife. Although his mother is delighted with the arrangement, Aino is heartbroken. In Poem 4, Väinämöinen tries to woo Aino, but she only weeps continuously, saying she does not want to marry such an old man. She runs to an unfamiliar seashore and drowns herself. Väinämöinen attempts, in poem 5, to retrieve her on a line, but she changes into a fish on his hook and flips away.

Väinämöinen's dead mother speaks to him, advising him to woo instead the maid of North Farm. In poem 6, Joukahainen, who harbors a grudge against Väinämöinen, attempts to shoot him but hits only his horse. Väinämöinen falls into the water and is carried out to sea. In poem 7, he floats for several days and is eventually rescued by an eagle, who carries him to his destination, North Farm. The mistress there, Louhi, promises him her daughter if he will first forge her a Sampo (a three-sided mill that grinds grain, salt, and gold). He promises to send her the great craftsman Ilmarinen, a forger of the "lids of heaven" at the time of the world's creation, to make the Sampo. She provides him with a horse and sleigh for his return home. On the way, he meets the maiden of North Farm and proposes to her. She agrees to marry him only if he is able to make a boat from a bit of a distaff and get it into the water without touching it. As he is making the boat, he injures his knee with his ax and is unable to stanch the blood. In poem 9, he finds an old man who doctors his knee and tells him the origin of iron, as well as how the craftsman Ilmarinen was born and how he learned to forge iron. The poem contains Origin Charms of Iron, Charms against Abuses by Iron, Charms for Stanching Blood, an Ointment Charm, Protective Charms, and even a Bandage Charm. In poem 10 Ilmarinen forges the Sampo. As payment for his labor he asks for the girl, but she refuses, saying that she cannot yet leave home.

The scene shifts, in poem 11, to Lemminkäinen, "that handsome man with the far-roving mind," the reckless son of Lempi. He is described as "the very finest of men." He sets out to woo Kyllikki, of the island, who, like himself, has grown up in a very fine home. Hers is, in fact, much better than his. His mother warns him that the women of the island will laugh at him, but he vows to stop the women's laughter: "I will knock a boy into their wombs. . . . / There is an end to even good ridicule." When Kyllikki spurns his advances, he drags her away and ties her to the slatted bottom of his sleigh. She quickly succumbs and tells him that she will marry him if he promises not to go to war. He in turn makes her promise not to gad about dancing.

In poem 12, Kyllikki forgets her promise and goes gadding, so Lemminkäinen decides to go to war against North Farm, "to fight the children of Lapland" and incidentally to woo a maiden there. Once at North Farm, he uses magic to bewitch every man except an old cattle herder named Soppy Hat. In poem 13, Lemminkäinen asks the dame of North Farm, Louhi, for her tallest daughter. When Louhi points out that he already has a wife, he boasts that he will tie up his wife at a stranger's gates. Louhi assigns him the first task of skiing down the Demon's elk (meaning pursuing the elk until it drops of exhaustion: an ambitious undertaking). He sets out confidently, but soon sees that he has taken on a nearly impossible task. In poem 14, following some Huntsmen's Charms, Lemminkäinen manages to capture the Demon's elk and bring it back to North Farm, only to be assigned another task: bridling the Demon's fire-eating gelding. After he accomplishes this second chore, he is challenged to shoot a swan in the river of Death's Domain. But the cattle herder Soppy Hat, whom he has previously insulted, is waiting for him. He shoots a poison tube into Lemminkäinen's heart and throws his corpse into the river's whirlpool. Lemminkäinen bumps down the rapids to Death's Domain, where the son of Death chops him into five pieces.

In poem 15, Lemminkäinen's death is announced at his home when blood oozes from his brush. His mother rushes to his rescue, using a rake to retrieve the pieces of his body, which she puts back together with the help of charms. She restores him to life, and sets out for home with her "Reckless Lemminkäinen."

In poem 16, Väinämöinen directs the lad Sampsa, the Spirit of Arable, to find the timbers he needs to build a boat, but he cannot locate the three charms he needs to complete the job. He goes to Death's Domain, where they want to prevent him from leaving. He escapes by using magic to change himself into several forms, including a snake. In poem 17 he sets out to get the needed charms from Antero Vipunen, a man "richly stocked with them." He wakes Antero Vipunen from a long sleep underground by slipping into his mouth and torturing his belly. He eventually gets the charms he requires and returns to finish the ship.

In poem 18, Väinämöinen sails in his new boat toward North Farm to woo the beautiful maid. Along the way, Ilmarinen's sister Annikki calls to him from the shore and, learning of his mission, rushes to warn her brother, who is now engaged to marry the maid. Ilmarinen hurries to North Farm also, to argue his own case. North Farm's mistress, Louhi, urges her daughter to marry the wise old Väinämöinen, but the maiden insists that she will marry Ilmarinen, forger of the Sampo.

Ilmarinen arrives at North Farm in poem 19, asks for the daughter's hand in marriage, and is assigned three tasks: He must plow an adder-infested field and turn over a snake-ridden one, capture Death's bear and bridle the wolf of the Abode of the Dead, and snare the great scaly pike from the river of Death's Domain. The maiden instructs him to fashion two plows—one of gold, one of silver—to accomplish the first task. She tells him to make the bits out of steel and the bridles of iron to accomplish the second task, and to forge a fiery eagle, a flaming griffin, to catch the pike. Following her instructions, he succeeds in completing the tasks, and the mistress gives her daughter to him. Väinämöinen returns home, downcast, lamenting the inequality of having to compete with a younger man: "Woe is me, decrepit man, / . . . that I did not know enough / to marry at a youthful age. . . ." He quotes a saying, "A man regrets everything he has done. . . ."

In poem 20, a bullock is slaughtered, food and beer are prepared, and invitations are sent for the wedding at North Farm. Only Lemminkäinen is not invited. In poem 21, the bridegroom and his company arrive, and the festivities begin. Väinämöinen sings and plays far into the night, much to the delight of the guests. Poem 22 contains the "Lay of the Handing Over of a Bride." The bride becomes reluctant to leave home and is both scolded and comforted by a "Cheering-Up Lay." In poem 23 the bride hears an "Instruction Lay" as to her myriad duties, and then an old woman recounts her own experiences as a new bride in "A Daughter-in-Law's Lay." In poem 24, the bridegroom is told not to "instruct her with slave whips" or "flog her with whip thongs," but if, during the fourth year of marriage, she still does not obey, he should "instruct her with a birch branch" (but only inside the house, where the neighbors won't hear). The bride sings a "Lay of Going Away," and Ilmarinen snatches her into his sleigh and begins the three-day journey home.

Poem 25 contains "Lays of The Reception of a Bride" and "The Return of a Bridegroom." Väinämöinen sings toasts of praise all around. On his way home, Väinämöinen breaks a sleigh runner and must stop to repair it. In poem 26, Reckless Lemminkäinen learns of the wedding to which he was not invited and decides to go anyway. He sings a Charm to Calm Down Snakes that he meets on the way. He arrives at North Farm in poem 27. The wedding feast is still in progress. He behaves boorishly, and the master of North Farm challenges him to a sword fight. When Lemminkäinen strikes off the master's head and flees, the dame of North Farm calls up a thousand swordsmen to go after him.

In poem 28, he flees for home where his mother, after reproaching him for his reckless behavior, advises him to sail for a far island where his father once hid out. She makes him swear that for ten summers he will not go to war for love of silver or gold. In poem 29 he sails for the island, where he sings his way into the hearts and beds of a thousand brides and a hundred widows. After three years, only one is left unsatisfied, "one wretched old virgin." She tells him, "If you will not notice me, / I will, when you go from here, / . . . let your ship run into a rock." The menfolk decide to kill him, so he sets sail but is soon shipwrecked by a storm. He builds a new boat and sails for his homeland, only to find that his home has been destroyed by fire. He finds his mother living in the backwoods, where she had to flee when the North Farm people came and burned down all the buildings. Lemminkäinen vows to rebuild their home and exact revenge upon the people of North Farm.

In poem 30, he and his dearest friend, Snowfoot, set out to North Farm to avenge the destruction of their village. The dame of North Farm learns that he is on the way and sends Jack Frost ("my own lovely foster child!") to "freeze the rascal's boat at sea." He retaliates with a Charm against Jack Frost, walks ashore on the ice, and eventually reaches his mother's home again.

In poem 31, Untamo, the owner of some wolves, lays fish traps in his brother Kalervo's waters, and from that act a feud erupts. Untamo and his men slay everyone in Kalervo's clan except one "pregnant virgin," whom they take home to be a servant. Her child is born, and she names him Kullervo, while Untamo calls him "War-Hero." At the age of three months the boy reflects, "If I should get bigger, / . . . become sturdier of body, / I would avenge the blows my father received, / . . . repay my mother's tears." Hearing this, Untamo vows to kill him. He tries many times but cannot succeed, so he gives Kullervo the task of a slave: looking after a little child. But Kullervo proves to be inept at babysitting. He breaks off a hand, gouges out an eye, and finally kills the child. When he fails at other tasks as well, Untamo sells him to Ilmarinen.

In poem 32, Ilmarinen's lady sends Kullervo to tend the cattle, sending for his lunch a loaf into which she has mischievously baked a stone. In poem 33, while tending the herd, Kullervo breaks his cherished knife trying to cut the loaf. Vowing revenge, he drives the herd into a fen and replaces them with a pack of wolves and bears, which he herds into the corral in the evening. The mistress goes out to milk the cows and is torn to pieces by the wild animals.

In poem 34, Kullervo flees before Ilmarinen learns of his wife's death. In a thicket he meets an old woman who tells him that his mother, brother, and sister are still alive on the headland of Lapland. He hurries there and finds his mother, who tells him that his sister went out to pick berries and never came back. In poem 35, we learn that Kalervo has not died, either. He puts Kullervo to work and discovers that he is no good at anything, so he sends him on an errand to deliver the taxes. On his way home from this errand, Kullervo meets and seduces a girl whom he later discovers to be his sister. She jumps into the river of Death's Domain and kills herself, while Kullervo rushes home to confess his sin to his mother. He considers suicide, but decides to go back and take vengeance on Untamo first. In poem 36, he travels to Untamo's farm and burns it to the ground. He returns home only to find the place deserted. Despondent, he roams in the forest until he comes to the spot of the infamous seduction, and there he falls upon his sword and dies.

In poem 37 Ilmarinen, still grieving for his wife, fashions a new one out of silver and gold, but finds that she is cold. He offers her to Väinämöinen, who refuses her and advises him to throw her away. In poem 38 Ilmarinen sets out to North Farm to woo his late wife's younger sister, but he is met with rebuke by the family. So he kidnaps the girl and takes her away in his sleigh. But she so reviles him during the journey that he finally sings her into a sea gull and leaves her behind.

In poem 39, Väinämöinen urges Ilmarinen to return with him to North Farm to capture the Sampo. As they begin their journey, Lemminkäinen hears where they are going and offers to go along. In poem 40, the three sailors become stuck on the back of a large pike, which they kill and cook. From the pike's jawbone, Väinämöinen fashions a harp, but for some reason no one can play it, not even the great musician Väinämöinen himself. In poem 41, Väinämöinen finally plays the harp, drawing every living creature they meet to listen to the music. Everyone is moved to tears by his music. His own tears flow into the water, where they are changed into blue pearls.

In poem 42, the three heroes arrive at North Farm, where the mistress assembles a force to prevent them from taking the Sampo. Väinämöinen plays his harp, lulling the crowd to sleep, and the men are able to capture the Sampo and set sail for home. On the third day, the mistress of North Farm awakes and creates a deep fog, wind, and storm to stop the boat. During the storm, the harp vanishes. In poem 43, the mistress of North Farm sets out in a warship to regain the Sampo. The two forces meet in a sea battle. Although the Kaleva people win, Louhi, mistress of North Farm, gets the Sampo out of their boat, where it sinks into the sea in pieces. Small bits are washed to shore, where Väinämöinen hopes they will provide the seeds of a new fortune. Louhi threatens to destroy the whole Kaleva district: "I will kill the nation by plagues, / . . . slay your whole clan, / so that it will never, never / . . . in the world be mentioned." But Väinämöinen scoffs at her: "No Lapp will enchant me. . . ." She returns to North Farm with only a small bit of the Sampo on her ring finger. Väinämöinen goes ashore and gathers the pieces of the Sampo.

In poem 44, Väinämöinen sets out to look for his harp at sea. When he cannot retrieve it, he makes a new one from birchwood and delights everyone with his music. In poem 45, Louhi, hearing that the Kaleva district is prospering, prepares a disease with which to inflict them, but Väinämöinen cures the people with charms. In poem 46, she conjures a bear to destroy the Kaleva cattle, but Väinämöinen sings a Bear Charm and then prepares a banquet for the whole district, to whom he serves bear meat. In poem 47, he continues to play his harp and sing, and even the sun and moon come down to listen. Louhi captures them and hides them inside a hill, then steals the fire from the Kaleva hearths. Ukko, the god on high, looks for the sun and moon; not finding them, he strikes fire and makes a new sun and moon. The fire drops to earth, and Väinämöinen and Ilmarinen set out to find it. A virgin of the air tells them that a fish in Lake Alue has swallowed it. The men attempt to net the fish but fail. In poem 48, Väinämöinen weaves a flax-cord net, and the two men are able to get the fish and find the fire in its belly. But it breaks loose and burns Ilmarinen's hands and cheeks. The fire travels into the forest but is finally tamed and brought to Kavela's hearths. Ilmarinen recovers from the burns. In poem 49 Ilmarinen forges a new sun and moon but can't get them to shine. Väinämöinen learns the whereabouts of the original sun and moon, and sets out to retrieve them. After battling the people at North Farm, he goes to the hill but cannot gain entrance. He returns home, and Ilmarinen begins to forge tools with which to tear open the hill. Meanwhile, Louhi, "gat-toothed dame of North Farm," senses disaster coming and releases the sun and moon. Väinämöinen sees them in the heavens and salutes them.

In poem 50, the virgin shepherdess Marjatta eats a magic whortleberry from which a boy is born. Her family turns her out, calling her a whore. An old man is called to determine whether or not the child should be allowed to live. Väinämöinen comes to investigate and decides the boy should be put to death. But the two-week-old child berates him, reminding him that as a young man, he had given away his mother's child to ransom himself, and had drowned young girls. The child is quickly baptized king of Karelia, guardian of the whole realm. Väinämöinen is put to shame and leaves forever, leaving his harp behind. The poem ends with an epilogue from the epic singer. (Lönnrot 1963)

KALEVIS

In the Baltic region, Kalevis is the Heavenly Smith and Dragon Killer. Every morning he forges a new sun for Aušrinẹ, maid of the dawn, and golden stirrups and a silver belt for the morning and evening stars. (Greimas 1992)

See also Aušrinẹ.

KĀLĪ

In Indian tradition, Kālī is a malevolent, destructive ogress goddess, called by some a "Tooth Mother," as opposed to the benevolent "Breast Mother" goddesses. Her name is the Sanskrit word for "black"; as an aspect of Devī, the universal goddess, she is called the Dark Goddess of Destruction in the *Purāṇas.* In her Pārvatī aspect, she is sometimes associated with Śiva and is possibly even a counterpart of the Ugaritic goddess Anath. As a wet nurse of Skanda in the *Mahābhārata,* she is the mother "born of anger, drinker of blood," who tries to kill him. She is the goddess of great anger, which connotes great passion as well. In the *Saura Purāṇa,* in which Śiva destroys Kāma, god of desire, Hara (another form or name of Śiva, "eternal savior of those who follow dharma," the Giver of Boons) grants Kālī a boon, and she says, "Great god, let Kāma live and heat the world. My lord, without Kāma, I do not request anything at all." So Hara restores the god of desire. Earlier, Pārvatī has informed Śiva, "Without Kāma there can be between a man and a woman no emotion which is like ten million suns. When emotion is destroyed, how can happiness be attained?" In the *Ḍholā Epic,* Durgā and Kālī take opposite sides in Nal's battle with his enemy Phūl Siṃh Panjābī. (Blackburn et al. 1989; Buck 1981; Dimmitt and van Buitenen 1978; O'Flaherty 1975)

KĀMA

In Indian mythology, Kāma is the god of love, sometimes depicted as a cupidlike figure who shoots love-producing arrows. One story involves his rousing Śiva from his meditation to impassion him for Pārvatī, making the great god so angry that he burns Kāma to cinders with the heat from his third eye. (O'Flaherty 1975)

KĀMAMMA KATHA

This medieval Telugu sacrificial folk epic of southern India is still being sung today. In a sacrificial epic, the main character is a woman who in the end immolates herself and is deified as a goddess. Unlike some other folk epics of the area, no palm-leaf manuscripts exist linking the epic to any author. The main characters are of the Besta caste, whose men are tradesmen, fishermen, and mercenary soldiers, and whose women enjoy a relatively high position. However, widows practice self-immolation to elevate their caste status.

Kāmamma is a Besta girl whose parents both die in a famine. She is raised by her fisherman uncle, who treats her kindly. She is married to a kinsman, Marayya, who leaves her behind as he goes to Madras to serve as a mercenary for the British East India Company. After seven years he starts for home, but falls ill and dies. When his body is returned to her, Kāmamma locks it in a room and informs her family that she is going to Kakinada to gain permission from the district collector to perform sati, a ritual whereby the widow kills herself on the funeral pyre.

On the way to Kakinada, she and her party come to a deep canal that they must cross. As a sibling of the river goddess Ganga, Kāmamma has the power to command the waters to become shallow enough for her to cross. But the men in her party are unable to follow, so she fashions boats to ferry them. When she reaches Kakinada, the officer explains to her that widows of the Besta caste have the option of marrying again. He urges her not to perform sati, but she rages that he is insulting her caste. The officer decides to force her to prove her status as a "woman of truth." He orders her to prison with no food rations for seven days and challenges her not to suffer. Meanwhile, he orders that Marayya be cremated.

While her body is locked away in prison, Kāmamma projects her soul to Madras, where she enters an official's dream and asks for help. The official challenges her to perform some miracles before he will believe her or consider her case. She performs the miracles and returns to Kakinada with the Madras official's permission to perform sati. The district collector orders a funeral pyre built and Kāmamma invites all her friends and relatives to attend the ceremony, where she mounts the pyre and perishes proudly in the flames. (Blackburn and Ramanujan 1986; Blackburn et al. 1989)

KAMBILI, EPIC OF

(Also *Kambili Sanarfila)*

This epic of a hunter/hero of the Mande people of Mali, West Africa, is still being sung today. One version, related by Seydou Camara, contains 2,727 lines.

In the beginning of the epic, several soothsayers are invited to predict which of the king's nine wives will give birth to the he-child Kambili, who is to be "born for a reason." Several prophets fail to predict correctly and are executed. Then "the holyman of the Koran" comes forward and correctly predicts the child as being Dugo's. The child is born and knows that his mission is to destroy the lion-man Cekura, who has been ravaging the community of Jimini.

Kambili grows to manhood. One day an old woman, even though she is warned not to go out alone, goes to pick leaves. Cekura sneaks up, grabs her by the jaw, and breaks her into two pieces, one of which he eats. Kambili, who has been having a love affair with Cekura's wife Kumba, climbs a tree and waits for the lion-man to appear again. He does not fear death because he knows that his reputation will live after him. He lures Cekura to the waiting Kumba, who has set a trap for her husband. After Cekura is killed, Kambili and Kumba are married. (Bird et al. 1974; Okpewho 1992; Westley *RAL* 1991)

KAN PÜDEI

This hero tale of the Altai Turks parallels portions of the story "Segrek Son of Ushun Koja" in *The Book of Dede Korkut*. The hero Kan Püdei is born after his father has been killed, but when he asks his mother, "Where is my father?" she does not answer. When Kan Püdei and some other boys are playing, a fight breaks out in which Kan Püdei beats the others and takes away their skins. The boys chide him, "If you're such a hero, why don't you go after your father?" He returns to his mother to learn the truth about his father, then sets out to avenge his father's death. (Lewis 1974)

KANTETELAR

This Finnish collection of legends and ballads, some with historical basis, was published in 1840 by Elias Lönnrot, who had published the *Kalevala* five years earlier. (Lönnrot 1963)

KANYAKĀ AMMAVĀRI KATHA

This is a medieval Telugu sacrificial folk epic of southern India. In a sacrificial epic, the main character is a woman who in the end immolates herself and is deified as a goddess. Later literary versions of the epic in Sanskrit and Telugu are ascribed to the Brahmin sage Bhāskarācārya and are called *Śrī Vāsavi Kanyakā Purāṇamu*, whereas the Mailāru folk priests who perform the epic refer to it as *Kanyakā Ammavāri Katha.*

The main figures in the epic are of the Kōmaṭi caste, whose members engage in trade and commerce. The men are not warriors; in fact, according to Telugu scholar Velcheru Narayana Rao, "Kōmaṭis were viewed as timid, miserly, cunning, untrustworthy, secretive, and even physically ugly" people who, rather than fight, would attempt to avoid conflict by trying to please all factions. A Kōmaṭi man is "ugly, dark, lethargic with a fat belly." A stereotypical Kōmaṭi woman is similarly unattractive. Women are held in relatively high esteem, although widows are not permitted to remarry.

Kōmaṭis have taken the epic of Kanyaka and the deity Kanyaka with them wherever they have migrated. An annual ritual and performance of the epic occurs in the West Godavari town of Penugonda, setting of the epic, to honor the goddess Kanyakā. Kanyakā temples abound all along the east coast of southern India.

Although later generations of Kōmaṭis have aspired to Vaiśya status requiring Brahmin legitimization and thus have adopted the literary Sanskrit version of the epic, the rejected Mailāru priests, who no longer perform in the public ritual at Penugonda, still do so in private households, where, according to Rao, "they are received in the back of the house by the women."

The epic tells of the wealthy Kōmaṭi leader Kusumaśrēṣṭi, who lives in Penugonda with his daughter Kanyakā, the most beautiful maiden in the land. When the king comes to town, he sees Kanyakā, who welcomes him with a flame offering. Smitten by her beauty, the king sends a message to her father that he wants to marry her, and that he will invade the city and take her by force if necessary.

The Kōmaṭi elders meet to decide how to avoid conflict with the king, even if they have to surrender the city to him. Kanyakā sends a message to the king that her father has agreed to the marriage but requests time to prepare for the wedding. The king is asked to wait beyond the hills that surround the city. Then she confides to the town elders that, rather than marry, she will immolate herself among the flames. She arranges for the adult men of her caste to die with her, and their wives volunteer to die as well. Of over 100 families who volunteer, she chooses only mature parents, leaving the young women and men to carry on the caste line. All others are ordered out of the caste. Then she orders a large, deep pit dug and a fire built in it.

Meanwhile, the king becomes impatient and sends a group of soldiers to determine what is taking so long. When the soldiers learn of Kanyakā's noble plan, they are filled with admiration and decide to remain in the city to serve her.

Kanyakā pronounces some decrees for the young Kōmaṭis who will remain, designed to strengthen the caste: Cross-cousin marriage is sanctioned, even if one member is ill, deformed, or poor; Kōmaṭi girls are henceforth to be born ugly so that no man will lust after them, and they are to be named after her; Penugonda will become the Kōmaṭis' pilgrimage site, where a celebration ritual will be conducted in her honor annually. She further decrees that if the king enters the city, he is to die at once.

When the soldiers of the king fail to report back, he suspects foul play and invades the city. He arrives too late: Kanyakā and the Kōmaṭi elders have perished in the fire. But the king is doomed, for the younger Kōmaṭi survivors fulfill Kanyakā's wishes. (Blackburn and Ramanujan 1986; Blackburn et al. 1989)

KAPEPE

(The Little Feather)

This epiclike narrative of the Bene-Mukuni of East Africa is still being recited today. It concerns a hero who makes a journey to Nkuba's celestial region. (Westley *RAL* 1991)

KAPILA

Kapila was a Vedic sage (ca. 550 B.C.) and founder of the Sāṃkhya school of Vedic philosophy. Although Buddhist teachings show him as a scholar/philosopher whose teachings resemble those of Buddha, Hindu mythology has attached itself to his origins, ascribing to him descendance from Manu, the mythological lawgiver, and deifying him as a son of Brahmā. He appears in the *Bhagavadgītā* as a recluse. (Bhakitvedanta 1981; Mascaró 1962)

KARAGÖZ
(Gypsy, Black Eyes)

Karagöz is a Turkish hero in shadow puppet plays, which are also called Karagöz for their hero. The Karagöz play, which is still extant although not as popular as in former centuries, dates from at least Turkey's sixteenth century. It later spread to Greece and Northern Africa. Karagöz is a good-natured if bumbling character who is accompanied on various misadventures by his pompous friend Hacivot. A related figure, the Turkish karaconcolos, is a nighttime bogey who appears from 25 December to 6 January or from 10 January to 16 January, mounts people, and lures them away. It is akin to the Bulgarian karakondjo, wild man or wolf, who appears 12 days after Christmas. (Georgieva 1985)

KARHUHAS

Ancient Hittite (ca. 1400–ca. 1190 B.C.) and Luwian (ca. 900 B.C.) god, Karhuhas is the protector of nature's forces, mentioned particularly in the texts from the Syrian city of Carchemish. (Ceram 1990)

See also Kubaba.

KARṆA

In the *Mahābhārata,* Karṇa is the son of Princess Kuntī and the Sun, and thus he is the half brother of the five Pāṇḍavas. He becomes the rival of Arjuna, but for a long while he does not realize that Arjuna is his half brother. During the great war between the two sets of cousins, Karṇa eventually takes command of the Kaurava forces, even though his death has been predicted if he does so. He confronts Arjuna in a climactic battle, but at a crucial moment, an earthquake causes his death. (Buck 1981)

KĀṬAMARĀJU KATHA

This medieval Telugu martial folk epic of southern India is still being performed orally today. A written version has been attributed to Śrīnātha, a fifteenth-century Brahmin poet. Tangorāla Venkaṭa Subbā Rāo collected and edited palm-leaf and paper manuscripts of the long and complex narrative and published them in 1976–1978 in two volumes.

The epic is of the martial genre, which means that the heroes are warriors. In this case, they are Yādavas, a caste called Gollas, or cattle herders. The Yādavas are a proud people who trace their lineage back to the god Kṛiṣṇa. In fact, the epic traces the Yādavas from Kṛiṣṇa down to Yadu, who appears in the *Mahābhārata.*

The Gollas hire Untouchable Madiga singers called Kommulavāḷḷu to perform the epic during their Gaṅgā Jātra festival. Because the Gollas are interested in the land only for cattle grazing and are therefore not landowners but merely lessors, their main concern is having enough water to produce lush grassland. Their caste deity, therefore, is Gangamma, a water goddess.

In the epic, a great Yādava cattleman, Kāṭamarāju, enters into a contract with the king of the Cōḻa dynasty, Nallasiddhi, whereby "All the grass that is born out of the water is yours [Kāṭamarāju's] and all the male calves that are born from the cattle are ours [Nallasiddhi's]." The agreement means that Kāṭamarāju has permission to use the king's grassland, but when a drought causes the grass to wither, Kāṭamarāju puts a literal interpretation upon the contract. Since rice is another grass "born out of the water," he moves his cattle into the king's rice fields to graze. In addition, the Yādavas, while shooting arrows at wild animals that threaten their cattle, accidentally kill a pet parrot belonging to the king's mistress, Kundavā Dēvi. In retaliation, she incites the local hunters, who consider the wild animals their private game, to kill Yādava cattle. Kāṭamarāju is so angry that he refuses to pay rent.

During the battle that inevitably follows, a Brahmin soldier named Tikkana loses his courage when he rides out and sees the ferocious enemy forces, and he returns home, where his people deride him as a coward. His wife insults him by pouring him a hot bath behind a cot-screen, as if he were a woman. She also puts out a ball of turmeric, a feminine symbol. His own mother serves him curdled milk because, she claims, the cows, seeing him break and run from battle, gave "broken" milk. Tikkana cannot abide the derision, so he returns to the battlefield, only to be mortally wounded. He is brought home for cremation, and his wife, as would any well-valued female in a matriarchal epic, joins her husband on the funeral pyre. (Blackburn and Ramanujan 1986; Blackburn et al. 1989)

KATARI-BE

These families of professional oral reciters in ancient Japan (prior to fourth century A.D.) handed down myths and legends, reciting them at official occasions. A katarimono is a story recited to musical accompaniment. (Mayer 1948)

KAUNDINYA

A legendary Brahmin founder of the state of Funan in Cambodia, Kaundinya arrived from India in the first century A.D.; subdued a local woman, Willow Leaf, whom he later married; and gave rise to the state of Funan. (Reischauer and Fairbank 1960)

KAURAVA

In the *Mahābhārata,* Kaurava is the surname of the 100 cousins of the Pāṇḍava brothers. The Kauravas, not wishing to share the Bhārata kingdom with their cousins, eventually wage a bloody war against them and are defeated. (Buck 1981)

KAY, SIR

In the Welsh *Mabinogion* tale "Culhwch (Kulwch) and Olwen" (ca. 1100), Sir Kay is the heroic steward of King Arthur. Later tales depict him as a rogue. (Gantz 1976)

KAYARWAR EPIC

This epic of the Kanuri people of northwestern Africa commemorates the ninth-century victory of the Islamic hero Ali at the Battle of Haiwara. Various versions of the epic exist. One performance of 90 minutes has been recorded, but other versions require several days to recite. (Westley *RAL* 1991)

KAYOR, EPIC OF

This is a West African Mandé epic of the seventeenth- to nineteenth-century Wolof kingdom of Kayor, in present-day Senegal. It contains many stories covering the expedition of the Geedj sons against their half brother Mawa, who is competing for the crown of Kayor; the public disgrace of King Daoud Demba, whose excesses have become intolerable to the elders; the rise of Ndiadiane Ndiaye; the career of Lat Dyor Diop (ca. 1842–1886); and the Lamane (chief of the land) Diamatil Kotche Barma.

In the story of King Demba, at the pintch (public square), the elders wait to confront the flamboyant king. When he arrives, they rise without a word and leave him alone, forcing him to resign.

In the story of Ndiadiane Ndiaye, the hero, humiliated when his mother marries a war captive, flees his royal family in Tékrour and goes into exile. While he sleeps at the river's edge, a Walo fisherman appears in his dream. He is protected by the spirits of the river, and he makes a pact with them. He appears in the form of an amphibious spirit and eventually claims the throne as a pacifist. He carries the peace emblem.

Lat Dyor Diop, whose mother is of royal blood, is eligible for kingship. In 1862 he is chosen to serve, but after a conflict with the French, he is forced to flee to Saloum. There he takes refuge with the Muslim leader Maba Diakhou Ba and is converted to Islam. Ba is killed in 1867, and Lat Dyor eventually makes peace with the French and returns to Kayor (1871), where he is reinstated as king. Four years later he joins the French in a war against Ahmadu ibn 'Umar Tal, who is struggling to maintain his Tukolor empire against encroachment by the French.

Lat Dyor, enjoying the patronage of the French, decides to take over the neighboring state of Baol (1877) and convert it to Islam. He continues to thrive until the French decide to build a railroad through Kayor. Then he must go to war against his former allies. He receives a gris-gris of protection, which is so large that, dressed in it, he weighs almost double his normal weight. Although he holds out for a while, eventually he is killed by the French. (Azuonye *RAL* 1990; Lipschutz and Rasmussen 1989; Wright 1980)

KERESĀSPA

Keresāspa is an Iranian hero, son of Sama, representing good. According to some traditions, he battles the evil dragon Azhdahak (Azhi Dahaka), who has broken loose from his fetters on the Mountain of Demavend and brings devastation across the land until Keresāspa slays him with his mace. This battle, the final confrontation between good and evil, is referred to as the Great War in both Zoroastrianism and Manichaeanism, but in some traditions its hero is Thraētaona (Feridun). Keresāspa also avenges the murder of his brother Urvakhshaya, a judge, by killing Hitaspa and carrying the corpse home in his own chariot. He battles several monsters, once unwittingly cooking his meal on the back of one. (Olmstead 1948)

KERET EPIC

This Ugaritic epic fragment (ca. fourteenth century B.C.) concerns King Keret, whose sons have all died, leaving him with no heir. In a dream, El advises him to launch a military expedition either to rescue an abducted woman or to obtain a new wife. Keret makes elaborate preparations and invades the city of Udum, forcing its king, Pabel, to give him his daughter Hurriya. Keret brings her home, and Hurriya has many children. Later, when Keret falls ill, El saves him. (Pritchard 1973)

KERTANAGARA

A Javanese king (fl. thirteenth century) of the Tumapeli, he is the hero of *Nāgarakertāgama,* the epic of Majapahit. He is still venerated in Java as a great ruler and the unifier of all of Java. (Preminger 1990)

KESAR SAGA

(Also *Gesar's Saga* and *Tales of Kesar)*

This is the national epic of Tibet and the mountain kingdom of Ladakh, which is bordered by Tibet, China, and India. It is a collection of myths surrounding the story of creation and the development of civilization through the courage of 18 heroes. A king, son of an Ur-god, rules the land of Ling and has many exploits subduing evil giants. Along with his heroine, Cho-cho-dogur-ma

(Brougmo in the Tibetan version), he participates in many adventures, which continue to be serialized on Ladakhi radio. Bards from the villages recite the *Tales of Kesar,* and daughters of each household learn the tales and recite them at home in the evenings.

Although the saga tells the fantastic adventures of the future king of Ling, some reference may be made to historical rulers such as Lang Darma, a ninth-century ruler in central Tibet, who drives the monks from the region because of the tremendous secular and religious power they hold. The historical Lang was assassinated in A.D. 842 by a monk, and his death is celebrated with the dismembering of a tsampa doll at the end of the mystery play that describes the event. His descendant, Ny-magon, is said to be the father of the first independent Ladaki dynasty. He gives his eldest son, Pal-gyi-gon, the western part of the kingdom and divides the rest of the kingdom among his other sons. His descendants establish the Lha-Chen dynasty, which is said to last to the fifteenth century, when a minor branch, the Namgyal kings, establish a new dynasty.

During the reign of the Namgyals, King Tashi wards off occupation attempts by Islamic forces, while King Jamyang, by his marriage to the Balti princess Gyal Khatun, daughter of Ali Mir, ruler of Skardu, unites Buddhist and Islamic forces. According to legend, he converts to Islam to win her love, and she is proclaimed the White Tara, the Buddhist female deity. When Gyal becomes pregnant, her father has a vision of a lion leaping into her womb, which foretells the birth of the legendary hero Sengge (lion) Namgyal. Sengge consolidates the kingdom by subduing the eastern kingdoms of Zanskar and Guje, but when his son Delegs intervenes in a religious dispute between Tibet and Bhutan, Tibet makes an arrangement with the Mongols to attack Delegs, and Tibet gains permanent influence over Ladakh. (Gretchen 1990; Rao 1989; Schmidt 1927; Wallace 1991)

See also *Gesar's Saga.*

KGODUMODUMO

This Sosotho myth of the Basotho tribe of Africa concerns a fabulous monster, Kgodumodumo, who appears without warning and swallows every living thing in every village in his path. In one village a pregnant woman avoids being eaten by lying perfectly still and pretending to be an inanimate object. When Kgodumodumo leaves, she delivers a son, Senkatana, who grows up to attack the monster and free the people from his belly. (Kunene 1979)

AL-KHADIR

(Also al-Qadir)

He is a legendary Islamic hero who gains eternal life, the hero of a cycle of myths and legends. He is the patron saint of wayfarers who has gained immortality by drinking from the fountain of life. (Nicholson 1962)

KIGUMA

This epic of the Lega-speaking people of West-Central Africa is still being performed today. (Westley *RAL* 1991)

KIHO

The Tuamotu god of creation, Kiho is the subject of the creation myth called *The Dwelling Places of Kiho.* The Tuamotu Islands are 76 atolls south of the Marquesas in the South Pacific. According to the epic, Kiho is the "source of sources," who dwells in the void before or outside creation in "Black-gleamless-realm-of-Havaiki." First he produces chaos, the dark teeming waters "through the potency of his eloquence." He floats to the top of the waters and creates the foundation of night (not-being), and of light (being). As he gradually turns over and stands, the various realms of heaven and earth come into being. Finally he produces the yang principle Atea-ragi and the yin principle Fakahotu-henua. He sets apart sea, soil, and sand, then looks upon his astral-self stretched out below him, makes a shape out of red sand, and exhales his vitalizing breath into it. His astral-self enters into it and it becomes a sentient being. He names him Atea and commands him to produce progeny. He tells Atea, "Thou shalt embark upon wars of reprisal, / . . . Thou shalt be the instigator of disaster, / . . . Thou shalt evoke thy Activating-self. . . ." He gives Atea his girdle and returns to his realm of Black-gleamless-realm-of-Havaiki. (Sproul 1991)

KIJA
(Also Chi-Tzu in Chinese)

Kija is a legendary king of Korea who in 1122 B.C. came from China bringing 5,000 refugees who refused to serve the Chou (Zhou) ruler who had overthrown Kija's Shang relatives. However, historians date the end of the Shang and the beginning of Chou as 1050 B.C. Kija migrated to southern Manchuria and founded the state of Chosôn. Some legends ascribe to him shamanistic powers. Other more credible stories credit him with bringing the art of writing to Korea. His story was recorded in the first century B.C. in the *Historical Records of Ssu-ma Ch'ien.* (Reischauer and Fairbank 1960)

KING, J. S.

In the Zulu epic *Emperor Shaka the Great,* J. S. King is the only white trader who can be "trusted," but he too grabs as much land as he can. (Kunene 1979)

See also *Emperor Shaka the Great.*

KING OF THE BATTLE

This epic tale of the Akkad dynasty (third millennium B.C.) describes the exploits of the Mesopotamian ruler Sargon the Great (ca. 2360–2305 B.C.) into Anatolia and even across the Mediterranean to Crete. (Langer 1980)

KINGS, CYCLE OF

Charlemagne plays the major role in this significant cycle within the body of French chansons de geste. (Harrison 1970)

See also Chansons de Geste.

KINGU

In the Babylonian creation story *Enuma Elish,* Kingu is the consort of the sea goddess Tiamat; she raises an army of monsters to destroy the gods who are churning up waves and disturbing her rest. She places Kingu, who holds the tablets of fate, at the army's head, but on his first encounter with the hero Marduk, Kingu loses courage and is easily defeated and taken captive. Marduk takes the tablets of fate from Kingu and parades all his prisoners before the leaders. Kingu is made the scapegoat, being charged and convicted as the instigator of the rebellion. He is executed, and from his blood the great god Ea creates man. (Sproul 1991)

See also Enuma Elish, Epic of; Marduk; Tiamat.

KINTU

In the creation cycle of Buganda, Uganda, Kintu is the first man and ancestor. There are many legends concerning Kintu. The first concerns his arrival on earth.

When he first arrives, he dwells by himself with only one cow. Then a woman, Nambi, comes, but she soon returns to her father, Gulu, king of heaven. Nambi's relatives object to her marrying Kintu because he knows no food but milk. Gulu tests Kintu by stealing his cow so that Kintu must live on leaves and seeds. But Nambi sees the cow in heaven and reports to Kintu where it is so that he can retrieve it.

When Kintu arrives in heaven, he is surprised to find livestock, fowls, and houses. Gulu orders a feast large enough to feed 100 men and tells Kintu that if he doesn't eat it all, he will be executed. Kintu is shut into a house with the food. When he has eaten all he can, he hides the rest in a hole in the floor.

Gulu is not satisfied and orders a new test. He orders Kintu to cut firewood from a rock. Kintu finds a rock with cracks, which he is able to break with an ax, so Gulu orders another trial. He tells Kintu to fetch water, which can only be dew. Kintu leaves his pot in a field and is surprised when the next day it is full of dew. Gulu is so impressed that he agrees to the marriage.

Gulu tells Kintu to pick out his own cow from the herd, but Kintu cannot tell the cows apart. A bee promises to light on his cow's horns, but when the herd is brought in, the bee remains in a tree. Kintu tells Gulu that his cow is not in the herd. Gulu is pleased, and says that nobody can deceive Kintu. The marriage of Nambi and Kintu takes place. Kintu and Nambi have a son.

When Kintu goes old, he wanders out on the plains and disappears. It is taboo to say that he has died, so the chiefs say that he has vanished. His body is wrapped in cowhide and placed in an open grave so that later his jawbone (a sacred bone because it moves by itself) can be removed. Kintu's son, who succeeds him, also disappears, and his son Kimera becomes king.

Kimera is the product of an adulterous relationship between his mother, daughter of a neighboring king, and a visiting prince. When he is born, he is thrown into a clay pit, where a potter finds him. Later when Buganda needs a new king, they call upon him to rule. It is the custom for the mother to come along with the king, but his mother has to remain outside the capital.

After many years Kimera sends his own son on an expedition, during which the son dies, leaving a son named Tembo. When Tembo grows up, his mother tells him that his father was killed by his grandfather, Kimera. Tembo decides to avenge his father's death, so he watches for his chance and one day kills the king while he is on a hunting trip. He tells the people that the king met with an accident. Tembo becomes king, while Kimera's jawbone is enshrined upon a hill.

Later Tembo sends his son and daughter to be servants to one of the gods, but the two become lovers along the way, and a river springs up on the spot. The daughter gives birth to twins at another spot, and another river springs up. Tembo eventually becomes insane until a human sacrifice cures him.

The stories of 30 kings follow. Kintu's ghost summons the twenty-second king to the throne, but as the king and his wife arrive at the temple, another chief comes up, and Kintu's ghost flees. The greatest king is the thirtieth, Mutesa, who builds a large army, introduces guns, and trades slaves and ivory for cotton. (Parrinder 1982)

KLINGSOR

Klingsor is an evil magician appearing in German *Parzival* legends. (Eschenbach 1980)

See also *Parzival.*

KNIGHT OF THE SWAN

See Lohengrin.

KOJIKI

(Also *Koji-ki,* Record of Ancient Things)

Along with the *Nihongi,* the *Kojiki* is the earliest remaining written record of Japan. It consists of myths and historical and pseudohistorical narratives as well as legends, anecdotes, songs, and genealogies. It was compiled ca. 712 from oral tradition and from documents no longer extant by Opo nö Yasumarö. In the preface he states that Emperor Temmu (r. 673–686) deplored the errors and falsehoods that appeared in family historical and genealogical documents. Deciding to emend these records, the emperor commanded a toneri (court attendant), 28-year-old Piyeda nö Are, to "learn" the texts of a genealogy,

Imperial Sun-Lineage, and a collection of myths and legends of the forebears of the Yamatö family, also *Imperial Sun-Lineage.* Some scholars, notably Hirata Atsutane, believe that Are was a woman whose specialty was memorizing oral literature. However, the work was not completed during Temmu's reign and was abandoned at his death. Twenty-five years later, in the fourth year of the reign of Empress Gemmei, in the process of moving the palace to the new capital of Nara, the empress became aware of the historical errors and commanded Yasumarö to complete the project by rewriting the documents "learned" by Are.

The work consists of a preface and three books. The "Preface" is actually a document presenting the work to Empress Gemmei. Book 1 consists of mythological tales from anecdotal sources; because of its rhyming and descriptive qualities, it is particularly suitable for oral recitation. Its 46 chapters are as follows. 1, The Five Separate Heavenly Deities come into existence. 2, The Seven Generations of the Age of the Gods come into existence. 3, Izanagi and Izanami are commanded to solidify the land. They create Onögörö Island. 4, Izanagi and Izanami marry and bear their first offspring, whom they abandon because he is a leech-child. 5, Izanagi and Izanami, learning the reason for their failure, repeat the marriage ritual ("Because the woman spoke first, [the child] was not good."). 6, Izanagi and Izanami give birth to numerous islands. 7, Izanagi and Izanami give birth to numerous deities. Izanami dies after bearing the Fire-Deity. 8, Izanagi kills the Fire-Deity. Various other deities come into existence. 9, Izanagi visits Izanami in the Land of Yömï. Breaking the taboo, he looks upon her corpse. 10, Izanagi flees and eludes his pursuers. Izanagi and Izanami break their troth. 11, Izanagi purifies himself, giving birth to many deities, including Ama-terasu-opo-mi-kami and Susa-nö-wo. 12, Izanagi entrusts their missions to the Three Noble Children. 13, Susa-nö-wo disobeys his divine trust and is expelled by Izanagi. 14, Susa-nö-wo ascends to take his leave of Ama-terasu-opo-mi-kami. 15, Ama-terasu and Susa bear offspring to test the sincerity of Susa's motives. He is victorious. 16, Susa rages with victory. (He breaks down ridges between rice paddies, defecates, and strews feces around the dining hall.) 17, Ama-terasu conceals herself. The other deities lure her out. Susa is expelled. 18, Opo-gë-tu-pime produces food and is killed by Susa. 19, Susa slays the Eight-Tailed Dragon. 20, Susa dwells in the palace of Suga and marries Kusi-nada-pime. 21, Opo-kuni-nusi cures the rabbit and wins Ya-gami-pime. 22, Opo is killed by his evil brothers and is revived twice. To save his life he is sent away. 23, Opo arrives at the land of Susa and is protected by Suseri-bime. A mouse saves him from the fire on the plain. 24, Opo returns the arrow. Outwitting Susa, he escapes with Suseri-bime. Susa follows and gives them a blessing. Opo subdues his 80 brothers. 25, Opo woos Nunakapa-pime in song. 26, Nunakapa replies in song. 27, Opo bids farewell to his jealous wife Suseri in song. 28, Suseri replies in song and dissuades Opo from leaving. 29, Genealogy of the descendants of Opo. 30, The deity Sukuna-biko-na appears and assists in creating the land. After his departure, the deity of Mount Mi-mörö appears. 31, Genealogy of the descendants of Opo. 32 through 37 deal with the process by which Japan is ceded to the offspring of the deities. 38,

Piko-po-nö-ninigi-nö-mikötö is commanded to descend from the heavens and rule the land. Saruta-biko meets him to serve as his guide. 39, accompanied by various deities, Piko descends from the heavens bearing the Three Items of the Sacred Regalia. He establishes his palace at Taka-ti-po. 40, Saruta returns and is caught by a shellfish. Amë-nö-uzume punishes the sea slug for failing to swear loyalty. 42, Piko marries Kö-nö-pana-nö-saku-ya-bime but rejects her elder sister Ipa-naga-pime. Their father curses him with a mortal life. Kö-nö bears triplet sons in a fiery ordeal to prove her innocence. 42, Po-wori loses his elder brother Po-deri's fishing hook. He tries to make compensation, but Po-deri insists on having the original hook. 43, Following the advice of Sipo-tuti-nö-kamī, Po-wori goes to the palace of the Sea Deity, is warmly welcomed, and marries Töyö-tama-bime, the Sea Deity's daughter. 44, Po-wori tells the Sea Deity of his quarrel with his elder brother. The Sea Deity gives him the means to subdue his elder brother and sends him home on the back of a crocodile. He brings his elder brother to "abject submission." The brother becomes poorer and poorer until he becomes violent. Po-wori takes out the tide-raising jewel given to him by the Sea Deity, causing him to drown. Then he takes out the tide-ebbing jewel and saves him. 45, Toyo emerges from the sea to give birth. Her husband Po, breaking the taboo, looks upon her during the delivery and sees her transformed into a crocodile. Shamed, she returns to the sea. She exchanges songs of yearning with her husband. 46, Offspring of U-gaya-puki-apëzu-nö-mikötö are named.

Books 2 and 3 are largely genealogical, and their source was probably a work originating in the fifth or sixth centuries, with redactions occurring up until the time of the actual writing. There are 62 chapters in book 2, beginning with the reign of Emperor Jimmu and ending with the death of Emperor Ǫjin. There are 40 chapters in book 3, beginning with the reign of Emperor Nintoku and ending with the reign of Empress Suiko. (Philippi 1968)

KOJORURI

Kojoruri are Japanese puppet plays dating from the sixteenth century. (Sansom 1958)

KÖNIG ROTHER

This medieval German romance contains lighter elements of heroic literature and tales from the Crusades. The story was told by wandering minstrels ca. 1160. Rother is a young king who sends envoys to Constantinople asking the emperor for his daughter in marriage. Before they depart, Rother plays three songs for them, for which they are to listen in case of peril. After the emperor of Constantinople imprisons the envoys, Rother and his man Berchter set out with a large force to rescue the prisoners, seven of whom are Berchter's sons. Rother introduces himself to the emperor as "Dietrich" and claims to be an enemy of King Rother. When he meets the princess and learns that she plans to remain true to Rother, he reveals his real identity. She convinces her father to give the prisoners three days' parole so that they may eat, and while they are at liberty Rother signals to them by playing the songs. He rescues them and escapes with the princess, but the emperor, with the help of a trickster, gets her to return. Rother engages in a new campaign to retrieve her. (Siepmann 1987)

KORDABBU

This an epic, or pāḍdana, of the Tulu-speaking people of Karnataka on the southwestern coast of India. The pāḍdanas are now written down and must be sung. The Tulu speakers have no writing system and no written language. The form may be derived from various ancient Dravidian poetry forms, but as it has developed, it is unique to the Tulu-speakers. The pāḍdana of Kordabbu, who is a hero of low caste, is sung by both women and men. Versions of the epic differ in length. The men's versions are generally longer.

The epic begins with the hero's mother Malvedi, who is orphaned at a young age and raised in Kaccura Manor, where the lady treats her as her own. She is called Kaccura Malvedi. At puberty, she undergoes cleansing rites, then discovers she is pregnant. Rumormongers point to the manor's lord, Kodange Bannaya, as the father. The two are brought before the king, but deny that they have had intercourse. Nothing is done to the lord, but Malvedi must prove her truthfulness by being immersed three times in boiling oil. Even after she emerges unharmed, she is forced to undergo two more trials before she is believed.

Shortly thereafter, she gives birth to a son, Kordabbu, but dies in childbirth. So Kordabbu, too, is raised by the lady of the manor.

He grows extremely fast and is performing miracles by the age of one month. Often his miracles do not please people, particularly his foster mother, and he must undo them. After a Brahmin complains to the king about his "tricks," his foster mother scolds him soundly, and Kordabbu runs away from home.

Along his sojourn, he continues to live by his wits, performing miracles and learning more tricks, including astrology. At one point he steals some coins from the mint of a neighboring region. His escapades are reported to the king, who decides that Kordabbu must be stopped. He summons him to court to do some important divination work. Kordabbu realizes it is a trick, but he cannot honorably refuse the king.

The king sends him to the bottom of a very deep well to see why no water flows. As soon as Kordabbu descends into the well, the king orders a large boulder placed over the opening, sealing the hero inside.

Kordabbu calls for help to passersby, including the Billaca heroes Koti and Chennaya. They use their magic swords on the rock to no avail. Later, the Mugeru heroes Deyu and Perne pass by, but they cannot lift the rock. Tani Maniga, Perne's wife and Deyu's sister, brings food for the hunters and hears Kordabbu calling. She touches the rock with her silver blade, praying to the sky above and the earth below. Then, after she draws 16 lines in the earth, the rock breaks open.

But Kordabbu has no way to climb to the top, so Tani, admonishing him not to look at her, unwinds her sari and hangs it into the well for him to climb on. He ignores her warning and looks at her, smiling with pleasure. They learn they are of compatible clans and decide to become brother and sister, thus preserving her virtue. They go other places together, performing magical deeds, for which they are honored and worshiped. (Blackburn et al. 1989)

KÖROĜLU

This legendary robber/hero appears in many Turkish and Iranian folk epics. He was a noble warrior, probably a real person, whose legendary character shares many aspects with Robin Hood. He may have been based on the Uiger Körgü (1235–1242), who, as an official of the Mongol regime in Persia under the Grand Khan Ogödäi, put an end to corrupt practices of tax collectors and became a champion of the local people. A Buddhist, he became the protector of the Persian Muslims against the Mongol officials who previously had the power to seize property without cause and behead citizens at their whim. (Grousset 1970)

KOSALA

In the *Rāmāyaṇa,* Kosala is a large kingdom in India ruled by the sun-descendants, of whom Rāma is one. His son Kuśa founds and rules a southern kingdom called Great Kosala. (Buck 1976)

KOSOVO, BATTLE OF

(Also *Kossovo)*

See *The Battle of Kosovo.*

KOTAN UTUNNAI, THE EPIC OF

This Ainu epic was first recorded in writing sometime prior to 1889. Before massive acculturation, the Ainu regarded eloquence (pawetok) as one of the chief manly virtues. Epic material of the Ainu includes mythic narratives of up to 1,000 lines and sung with burdens, dealing with deities or the culture hero (the sacred ancestor of the human race); heroic narratives as long as 15,000 lines and sung without burdens, dealing with exploits of a single hero, usually either Poiyaunpe or Otasam-un-kur; novelistic narratives involving the lives of persons other than these two heroes, some sung with burdens, others without; and Parodies, often referred to as "dream epics," embodying the paranormal or fantastic.

As with other oral poetry, Ainu epic poetry contains many traditional patterns and formulas, which the reciter repeats often to express ideas or depict frequently occurring situations.

The best reciters were frequently women, who also functioned as shamans (tusu). The reciter accompanied her/himself only by tapping a wooden stick (repni) against the hearth frame or even against her/his own stomach. In some cases the listeners, too, would each hold a repni and beat the time, from time to time interjecting exclamations of "het! het!" at rhythmical intervals. Some recitations lasted throughout the night.

The Ainu epic poetry reflects the traditional society as it existed prior to Japanese subjugation between 1669 and 1672. According to specialists in the poetry, it appears to have reached back many centuries.

The *Epic of Kotan Utannai* is sung in first person. The hero, Poiyaunpe (whose name means "little mainlander"), is reared by a repunkur (the Okhotsk culture or people of the sea) woman whom he refers to as an elder sister. He grows up in an out-of-the-way place called Kotan Utannai. During that time, he says, "sounds of some gods fighting / could be heard rumbling / throughout the land." As he grows older, coming from atop his grass hut he recognizes the rumblings of spirits of the yaunkur (people of the land); his companion spirits send forth their own rumblings, and the two mingle together. This makes him wonder about his origins, so he questions his elder sister, Chiwashpet-un-mat.

She tells him that his warrior father, elder brother Kamui-otopush, and mother, with the baby Poiyaunpe strapped on her back, set out on a trading expedition. They were lured ashore on the island of Karapto (Sakhalin) and plied with "poison drink." When the besotted father proposed to buy the treasure of Karapto, fighting broke out. The father and mother were killed, and the elder brother has been fighting ever since against the people of the sea. The foster sister took the baby and has raised it as her own.

Learning that he has been reared by the enemy, Poiyaunpe comes "very near to killing her," but manages to calm himself. He asks her for his parents' belongings. He dresses in six robes and, taking his father's sword and helmet, goes flying up the smokehole of the grass hut with Chiwashpet-un-mat in pursuit, entreating him not to put himself in danger. But he travels on, first into the land of the Pa-hor-kamui (Pestilence Deities), who cause such diseases as smallpox and cholera. In black, red, and blue-green robes in turn, he battles and vanquishes the gods while Chiwashpet-un-mat battles and vanquishes their corresponding goddesses.

They travel on, into a forest of metal trees, where they encounter six stone-armored chieftains from Shirapet (Stone River) with six ugly women. Sitting across the campfire from these 12 are six metal-armored men from Kanepet (Metal River), accompanied by six women. At the head of the campfire is an ugly monster who looks like "a small mountain / with arms growing out of it." His face is like "a cliff after a landslide," with a nose like "a steep mountain spur." His name is Etu-rachichi, which means "Nose Dangles" or "Dangling Nose." In some versions his name is Eton-rachichi, meaning "Dangling Snot" or "Snot Dangles."

Overhead, tied in a tree, hangs Poiyaunpe's mortally wounded brother, whom the chieftains say they are planning to take to the leader Shipish-un-kur as a trophy. Poiyaunpe begins to fight the chieftains and the women, and manages to slay half of them. Meanwhile, his foster sister unties his brother and spirits him off to his other brother and sister, who are able to revive him. The foster sister then returns to help him fight. Eventually only Etu-rachichi remains, and he and Poiyaunpe engage in a hand-to-hand struggle in which the hero finally prevails.

He decides that he must see for himself this person Shipish-un-kur, whose name the chieftains mentioned to frighten him. He flies along until he comes to Shipish-un-kur's palace. He peers into the window and sees a very young boy with a maiden even more beautiful than his own sister, Chiwashpet-un-mat. He eavesdrops and learns that she is the king's sister, a shamaness named Shipish-un-mat, and that she has seen the defeat of the warriors Shirapet and Kanepet and the monster Etu-rachichi. She predicts a battle between Poiyaunpe and Shipish-un-kur in which the latter loses. But Shipish-un-kur calls her a false prophetess and angrily denies that he would even fight Poiyaunpe if he were to appear: "Even if he comes / some time, / I intend / to greet him / in peace / and with kindness."

Poiyaunpe appears, challenges Shipish-un-kur to fight, and quickly absconds with the sister-shaman, who immediately forgives him for capturing her and turns against her own brother, who has called her a false prophetess. Poiyaunpe's restored elder brother Kamui-otopush appears to help him do battle against Shipish-un-kur, so he allows the brother to finish the fight while he hurries on toward a distant land called Chirinnai (Trickling Stream), where his elder sister is in grave danger.

On the way, in the land called Terke-santa, Hopuni-santa, he and Shipish-un-mat encounter a man and woman whom, just for "a little fun," they trick and slice to pieces. They continue on to Chirinnai, where Poiyaunpe finds his elder sister Chiwashpet-un-mat clinging to life, still slashing her sword even though her entrails are hanging out. He slices her into several bits and swings her heavenward with the prayer that the gods will restore her to life.

After he and Shipish-un-mat have completely ravaged the land of Chirinnai, a black mist arises. Out of it come black birdlike monsters that attack Poiyaunpe. He fights valiantly and is barely alive when they fly away. Shipish-un-mat heals his wounds with puffs of her breath.

Again, dark clouds descend, this time bringing the storm demon and his sister, who launch a vicious attack. But after vanquishing him once, Poiyaunpe discovers that he is a mere child. The child grabs a sword and fights all the more ferociously, but to no avail. After Poiyaunpe slices the bad-weather demon to pieces, he turns to help Shipish-un-mat, who has been battling the demon's sister. They defeat her by removing her armor.

Poiyaunpe and Shipish-un-mat return to his native land, where he learns that his foster sister Chiwashpet-un-mat has been restored to life by the gods. His elder brother Kamui-otopush has finished his battles and returned. His eldest brother, Yai-pirka, proposes that Kamui-otopush and Chiwashpet-un-mat marry, and that Poiyaunpe marry Shipish-un-mat as well. The two couples marry, and they "all lived on and on, uneventfully and peacefully." (Philippi 1979)

KOTHAR

(Also Khasis and Khayin)

An ancient Semitic god of crafts ca. the second millennium B.C., Kothar was charged with supplying weapons for the gods. Phoenician tradition attributed him with the gifts of poetry and magic. (Pritchard 1973)

See also *Aqhat Epic.*

KOUMBI SALEH, SNAKE OF

(Also Snake of Wagadugu)

In a Soninke epic of the great ancient empire of Ghana in West Africa, the subject is the great snake of Koumbi Saleh, capital of Wagadugu. The snake lives in a pit and expects to receive a yearly sacrifice of a young virgin. One year the lover of the chosen maiden jumps into the pit and, after cutting off the snake's head nine times, finally manages to kill it and save his beloved maiden. But before it dies, the snake curses the land and dooms it to suffer a drought for nine years, nine months, and nine days. As a result, the people of Wagadugu are forced to disperse to other areas. (Sisòkò 1992)

KPELLE

Kpelle are the people of the West African countries of Liberia and Guinea about whom the epic *Woi-meni-pele* (Dried Millet Breaking) is told. (Stone, R. 1988)

See also *Woi-meni-pele.*

KRIEMHILD

(Also Gudrun in Norse *Völsunga Saga* and Gutrone in Wagner's *Ring des Nibelungen)*

In Germanic heroic tradition, Kriemhild is the sister of the Burgundian kings Gunther, Gernot, and Giselher. She is the central character in the *Nibelungenlied,* the princess whom Siegfried woos and wins while also wooing Brunhild for Gunther. After Siegfried is slain, she marries the Hunnish king Etzel (Attila) and avenges her husband's death by having her brothers killed. The warrior Hildebrand then kills her. In the *Lay of Atli,* in which Kriemhild is called Gudrun, she murders Attila to avenge his murder of her brothers Gunnar and Hogni. The legend of Kriemhild may have originated with the redaction and fusion of tales of two historical events, the Hunnish decimation of Burgundian king Gundahar's forces in A.D. 437, and the 453 death, in his bridal bed with his German bride Hildico, of Attila. (Hatto 1969)

See also *Atli, Lay of;* Gudrun; Gunnar; Hagen; *Nibelungenlied;* Siegfried; *Völsunga Saga.*

KṚṢṆA
(Also Krishna and Kṛiṣṇa)

An important Hindu deity, most of his myths appear in the *Mahābhārata* and its appendix, *Harivaṃśa* (fifth century), as well as the *Purāṇas.* He takes the shape of the eighth incarnation of Viṣṇu, the son of Yadavan Vasudeva and Mathurān Devakī. His uncle, King Kaṃsa of Mathurā, having heard a prophecy that he will be killed by his sister's son, attempts to destroy Devakī's children, but Kṛṣṇa is taken away and reared by the cowherd Nanda and his wife Yásodā. He becomes a remarkable child who performs miracles. As he grows older, his flute-playing lures the women from their homes to dance for him. When he is grown, Kṛṣṇa and his brother Balarāma return to Mathurā, slay their uncle, and lead the Yādava clan to Dvāraka. There he marries several princesses, among them Rukmiṇī.

In the *Mahābhārata,* he becomes Arjuna's best friend, but he refuses to bear arms for either side in the conflict between the Pāṇḍavas and the Kauravas. However, he offers his personal services to one side and his army to the other. Arjuna elects to have Kṛṣṇa as his charioteer. On the eve of the great battle, when Arjuna is filled with misgivings about the morality of killing his own kinsmen, he seeks Kṛṣṇa's advice. Lord Kṛṣṇa's answer and his dialogue with Arjuna form the most beautiful poem in Indian literature, the *Bhagavadgītā,* in which Kṛṣṇa, although addressing Arjuna's present dilemma, also addresses the larger question of the struggle of the human soul. In the 18 books of the *Bhagavadgītā,* Kṛṣṇa instructs him in taking a detached commitment to right action, dharma, without becoming attached to the outcome, whether good or evil. (Buck 1981)

See also Arjuna; *Mahābhārata.*

KUAN TI

Kuan Ti, a popular Chinese god of war and of literature, is based on the historical Kuan Yü (third century). Kuan Yü lived during the era of the Three Kingdoms, and his chivalrous exploits were romanticized in legend and in the Ming novel *San Kuo yen-i.* According to legend, Kuan Yü rescues a young girl from her abductor by killing him. While fleeing the guards, he changes the color of his face and passes them unrecognized. He was actually captured and executed in A.D. 219, but the event only served to augment his legend. In 1594 he was canonized by the Ming dynasty emperor as Kuan Ti, protector of China. Belief in his power is so great that actors who portray him temporarily derive

A twentieth-century painting shows the principal character of the Indian epic *Bhagavadgītā,* the Lord Kṛṣṇa, right, driving a chariot into battle with his friend, the archer Arjuna.

power over demons from him. Worship of Kuan Ti spread to Korea in the seventeenth century, thus protecting that nation from Japanese invasion, according to his adherents. (Bloodworth and Bloodworth 1977; Mackenzie 1990)

KUAN-YIN

The Chinese version of the bodhisattva Avalokiteśvara, the Kuan-yin has the power to assume various forms in order to relieve suffering. Although there is some difference of opinion as to whether she is a goddess, a cult assigning her the qualities of a maternal goddess has existed since at least the twelfth century. She has been ascribed the power to grant children. Some believe that the Kuan-yin is neither male nor female. (Mackenzie 1990)

KUBABA

(Also Küpapa)

In Hittite religion (ca. 1400–1190 B.C.), Kubaba was originally a minor goddess. After the fall of the Hittite empire, she became a more important figure in the neo-Hittite cultures (ca. 1180–700 B.C.), being elevated to chief mother goddess. Phrygians also adopted her ca. the eighth century B.C. in the form of Cybele (or Cybebe), but the Luwians called her Kubaba, the "queen of Carchemish." (Ceram 1990)

KUBERA

(Also Jambhala and Vaisravana)

In Hindu mythology, Kubera is the god of prosperity and king of the yaksas (nature spirits). Most legends say that his half brother Rāvaṇa stole his Lanka (Ceylon) palace, so he fled to a new home on Mount Kailāsa, near Śiva. He appears in several folktales, such as "The Prince and the Painted Fairy," and "Gomukla's Escapade." He also appears in Buddhist and Jaina mythology. (Dimmitt and van Buitenen 1978; van Buitenen 1969)

KUDRUN, EPIC OF

(Also *Gudrunlied*)

Middle High German romance of the Baltic Coast, unrelated to the Old Norse legends, about the abduction of a maiden Kudrun, who is eventually rescued by her lover, who must kill the father who pursues her. (Hatto 1969)

KULWCH AND OLWEN

See "Culhwch and Olwen."

KUMA
(Word)

Among the Malinke people of Hamana of West Africa, *Kuma* is the history of the Almany Samari Touré (1830–1900) and the heroes who have lived since. It is the newest of the oral tradition of the people of Mali. (Laye 1984)

KUMA KORO
(Ancient Word)

Among the Malinke people of the Hamana of West Africa, *Kuma Koro,* one of four categories of "Words," is the "history of the men before our era." (Laye 1984)

KUMA KOROTOLA
(Aging Word)

Among the Malinke people of the Hamana of West Africa, *Kuma Korotola* is the genealogy of the various tribes of the upper Niger River area. (Laye 1984)

KUMA LAFOLO KUMA
(History of the First Word)

One of four categories of "Words" of the Malinke people of the Hamana of West Africa, it is the history of the great Sundiata, first emperor of Mali, "Son of the buffalo-panther woman and of the lion." (Laye 1984)

See also *Sundiata, Epic of.*

KUMĀRA VYĀSA

This is the Kannada translation (ca. fifteenth century) of ten cantos of the *Mahābhārata,* the work of Gadugu. (Blackburn and Ramanujan 1986)

KUMARBI

This ancient Hittite myth resembles the Uranus myth. (Saggs 1990)

KUMARLI

In *Bardo Thötröl* (Tibetan Book of the Dead), Kumarli is the virgin yoginī of the east, described as "red, with the head of a yellow bear, holding a short spear in her hand." (Fremantle and Trungpa 1987)

KUMULIPO

Hawaiian creation chant celebrating the Polynesian seven stages of the primordial night: "The intense darkness, the deep darkness / . . . Nothing but night. / The night gave birth." Kumulipo, a male, and Po'ele, a female, are born. The chant names many living sea creatures that are born, first shellfish in verse 1, then fish in verse 2. "Born was man for the narrow stream, the woman for the broad stream." Plants are born, and "Earth and water are the foot of the plant / The god enters, man cannot enter." Various birds are born in verse 3, and turtles, lobsters, "sluggish-moving geckos" and "sleek-skinned geckos" are born in verse 4. The pig child is born in verse 5, and many kinds of men follow. "The children of Lo'iloa multiplied. / The virgin land sprang into bloom / The gourd of desire was loosened / With desire to extend the family line. . . ." Rats are born in verse 6, as food grows "plentiful and heaped up." And still it is night. Fear comes in verse 7, "Fear of the receding night / Awe of the night approaching. . . ." But still it is night. Verse 8 tells of the birth of "men by the hundreds." The time when men come is tranquil. It is called Calmness (La'ila'i), which is also the name of a woman. A man named Ki'i is also born, as is a god, Kane. Then the girls Groping-One (Hahapo'ele) and Dim-Sighted (Ha-popo) are born. Maila (Beautiful), also called Clothed-in-Leaves (Lopala-pala), is born. Naked ('Olohe), another female, lives in the land of Lua (pit). Others are born: a female, Expected-Day (Kapopo); Midnight (Po'ele-i); First-Light (Po'ele-a); and the youngest, Opening-Wide (Weki-loa). Man spreads abroad and is here. It is day. (Sproul 1991)

KUN

Kun is a mythic hero of ancient China who, ordered to control the great deluge, steals from heaven a piece of magic soil with which to build a dam. The gods are so angry at the theft that the harder Kun works to control the flood, the higher the waters rise. Shang Ti orders Kun to be executed for his crime. Three years after the execution, when his corpse is slit open, his son Yu the Great emerges. With the help of dragons who drag their tails across the best paths, Yu is able to dredge outlets to the sea to drain away the floodwaters.

Kun (Qun) was also the name used in Hungary for the Turko-Mongol people from the eastern steppes of Asia known as Kipchaks. (Campbell *Oriental* 1976; Grousset 1970; Kramer 1956)

KUNAPIPI

This Australian Aboriginal song-cycle contains 129 sacred and 49 secular songs of the Northern Territory and the Yirrkalla area. Kunapipi is one of the sacred names of the Great Mother, responsible for fertility and reproduction in all living things. She is also responsible for the coming of the northwest monsoon. (Wilde 1991)

K'UNG-CHÜEH TUNG-NAN FEI

("A Peacock Flew," or "Southeast the Peacock Flies")

A Chinese folk ballad of the era of the Han dynasty, it probably originated ca. A.D. 200, growing by accretion and oral transmission until its written version ca. 550. At 353 lines, it is the longest poem of the period in China. It concerns a young married couple who suffer from the cruelty of the husband's mother, "the Great One," who is discontented with her son's choice. She tells him, "Our neighbor to eastward has a steadfast daughter; / . . . The loveliest limbs that ever yet you saw! / Let mother get her for you to be your wife. . . ." When the son refuses, the mother bangs the bed and flies into a great rage. The spineless son, who is a lowly prefect's clerk, sends his wife Lan-chih back to her father's house, "just for a little while." The wife leaves behind all her precious possessions and returns to her parents' home.

Her mother quickly finds her another suitable mate, a magistrate's son. But Lan-chih refuses. Now her brother and her parents begin to pressure her to marry. A son of the Lord Prefect is proposed, and Lan-chih, deciding that she and her husband will never meet again, sorrowfully accepts. But the day before the marriage, the young clerk hears of it and comes to see his wife. They realize the hopelessness of their situation. The clerk goes home to tell his mother of his great grief, indicating that he will die. She is adamant, still wanting to bring in a new wife: "I'll be quick about it; you shall have her between dawn and dusk."

Meanwhile, Lan-chih takes off her silk shoes, lifts her skirt, walks into the lake, and drowns herself. Hearing of her death, her husband hangs himself from a courtyard tree. The two families bury them in the same grave. (Waley 1982)

KUNG KUNG

This mythic Chinese villain accidentally falls against one of the pillars of heaven during an attempt to overthrow Shang Ti, causing the destruction of Mount Pu-chou and leaving heaven slightly tilted from then on. (Campbell *Oriental* 1976; Kramer 1956)

KUNI NO SA-TSUCHI NÖ MIKOTO

(Land of Right Soil of Augustness)

In the *Nihongi* of Japan, Kuni no sa-tsuchi is the second kami (god or power) mentioned, following Kuni toko-tachi no Mikoto. (Aston 1972)

See also Kuni no Toko-tachi nö Mikoto.

KUNI NO TOKO-TACHI NÖ MIKOTO

(Also Kuni toko-tachi no Mikoto, Eternal Spirit of the Land)

He is the Japanese deity of creation and the ancestor of Izanagi and Izanami, who create all lands, deities, and things upon the earth. In one account in the

Nihongi, Kuni is the second kami (the first being Umashi-ashi-kabi-hiko-ji nö Mikoto) mentioned in the creation story; in another account in the same work, he is the first. Before heaven and earth separated, "there was something which might be compared to a cloud floating over the sea. It had no place of attachment for its root. In the midst of this a thing was generated which resembled a reed-shoot when it is first produced in the mud. This became straightaway transformed into human shape and was called Kuni no toko-tachi nö Mikoto." (Aston 1972)

See also Izanagi and Izanami; *Nihongi.*

KUO-TZU-I

The Chinese god of happiness and prosperity, his historical counterpart was an eighth-century T'ang general who saved his country from the threat of the An Lu-shan Rebellion. As a reward for his service, Emperor Tai Tsung gave his daughter in marriage to Kuo's son. He was deified as legends built around his deeds. According to legend, on the night of the festival for Chih Nu (goddess of weaving), he is visited by the heavenly maid, and he asks for the boon of happiness and wealth. She grants his wishes, naming him the god of happiness and promising him long life and riches. (Reischauer and Fairbank 1960)

KURELDEI THE MARKSMAN

Named Kureldei Mirgan, he is the hero of the Tatar oral heroic lay entitled *Blood Marksman and Kureldei the Marksman* (recorded in Siberia in the nineteenth century) in which Kureldei rescues his people from imprisonment in a stone. (Finnegan 1978)

See also *Blood Marksman and Kureldei the Marksman.*

KURUKULLĀ

(Also Ku-ru-ku-le)

Kurukullā is the Tibetan and Mongolian counterpart of Tārā, the Buddhist goddess of love and prosperity. Her male counterpart is Kormuzda, father of the gods, whose youngest son is reborn on earth as Gesar, hero of the Tibetan national epic *Gesar's Saga.* (Schmidt 1927)

See also *Gesar's Saga; Kesar Saga.*

KURUT SZÉKELY

These poems or ballads, usually anonymous, celebrate the adventures of the Hungarian Kuruts (or Kurucs), who opposed the Habsburgs in the late seventeenth and early eighteenth centuries, and particularly recount the deeds of Transylvanian prince Ferenc Rákóczi II (Rakoczy), who led the last uprising in 1703–1711. (Dvornik 1962; Preminger 1990)

KUSANAGI

In Japanese mythology, as found in the *Nihongi* and *Kojiki,* Kusanagi is the miraculous sword that Ama-terasu presents to her grandson Ninigi when he descends to earth to rule Japan. The sword, along with the jeweled necklace and the mirror, are still part of the imperial treasures of Japan. It is in the shrine at Atsuta in Nahoya. (Aston 1972; Philippi 1968)

KUTI

Kuti was a Javanese rebel who revolted against Majapahit king Jayangara in 1319 and seized the capital. Prime Minister Gajah Mada escorted the king to safety and spread the rumor that the king had been killed. Then he secretly organized an insurrection in which Kuti was killed. Kuti plays a villainous role in the Majapahit epic *Nāgarakertāgama.* (Preminger 1990)

See also *Nāgarakertāgama.*

KUTUNE SHIRKA

The longest epic (6,000 lines) of the Ainu people of Japan, it is about a man raised in a castle who hears of a golden sea otter. He leaves the castle for the first time to search for the golden otter. He captures it, angering his brother. The people of Ishkar try to recover the otter during an unsuccessful battle. (Finnegan 1978)

KUYUNJIK

(Also Kouyunjik and Koindsjug)

Among the documents of this library collection of some 2,000 texts dating from the seventh century of the Old Assyrian and Middle Assyrian periods found at Kuyunjik (ancient Nineva) are several fragmentary copies of the Sumerian and Babylonian epics of Gilgamesh. The collection also includes most of the other epics known from Babylonia as well as two epics composed in Assyria. (Saggs 1990)

See also *Adad-narari, Epic of; Tukulti-Ninurta Epic.*

KVASIR

In Norse mythology, Kvasir is a poet and sage. His murder by the dwarfs is recounted in "Braga Raedur" (Conversations of Bragi) in the *Prose Edda.* The "sacred mead," or poetry, is brewed from a mixture of Kvasir's blood and honey. All who drink it become wise and filled with the gift of poetry. The giant Suttung makes the brew, but it is stolen by Odin, who flies in the form of an eagle carrying the magic brew in his craw until he can spit it into the gods' dwelling. (Young 1954)

KWATAY-NAMAK
(Book of Kings)

This Persian legendary history was compiled in the sixth century A.D. by ibn al-Muqaffa. This may have been one of the sources from which Ferdowsi drew his *Shāh-Nāmah,* also called the *Book of Kings.* (Levy 1967)

KWOTH

Kwoth is the high god of the Nuer people of southern Sudan. In one story of olden times, when Nuer people grew old they could climb a rope to Heaven, become rejuvenated, and return to earth. After Hyena and Weaver-Bird climb the rope, God attempts to keep them so they won't cause any more trouble. But they escape and cut the rope behind them. Thereafter, old people cannot reach Heaven to become rejuvenated.

Another story tells how Kwoth, after creating humans, throws a gourd into the water. It floats, signifying that people will never die. He sends a woman to earth to demonstrate the fact, but she uses a clay pot instead of a gourd. It sinks, and thus the people can no longer live forever. (Parrinder 1982)

KYA-GUD-PA

This Ladakh school of oral tradition, based on the *Bardo Thötröl (Tibetan Book of the Dead),* was handed down by Tilo-pa, who incorporated yoga into Buddhism. (Rao 1989)

L

LABARNAS I

(Also Labernash)

This Hittite ruler (r. ca. 1680–ca. 1650 B.C.) is given credit as the founder of the first Hittite empire, or Old Kingdom (ca. 1700–ca. 1500 B.C.), in Anatolia. Just as the name Caesar gave rise to the titles of Czar and Kaiser, so the name Labarnas came to mean "king." Although there were at least three Pitkhanas (elected kings) of the House of Kussara before Labarnas, it is he who united city-states into a federal government. "Wherever he took the field, his strong arm overcame the enemy." His story appears in a record left by King Telipinus, who lived some 150 years later. This work on clay tablets, by no means the only record of the kingdom's beginnings, is commonly known as the *Edict of Telipinus.* (Ceram 1990)

LAC LONG QUANG AND AU CO

(Also *Lac Long Quan and Au Co)*

This ancient legend of Vietnam received its literary form only after A.D. 1200. Prior to that time, the stories were told and retold countless times; each time, the teller reworked his material artistically and adapted it to the circumstances of his listeners. However, the stories remained faithful in general content to the originals from the mountain tribes, lowland farmers, and fishing people. The legends supply a sense of cultural identity, and they go a long way toward explaining the inexplicable. They impart wisdom and insight, convey spiritual truths, provide models for behavior, and offer light relief from the harsh realities of life. The cycles generally begin with the storyteller's words, "Hoi xua" (One time in the past) or "Ngay xua" (A long time ago). The historical epics then begin with "Duoi thoi vua" (Under the reign of King ____).

According to this cycle of legends, King De Minh, a descendant of a divine Chinese ruler and the father of Chinese agriculture, mates with an immortal mountain fairy and produces Kinh Duong Vuong, ruler of the Land of Red Demons. He in turn marries the daughter of the Dragon Lord of the Sea and they produce a son, Lac Long Quang, called Dragon Lord of the Lac. He becomes the first king of the Vietnamese, and thus the people of Vietnam claim to be "children of a dragon and grandchildren of a fairy."

In order to placate Lai, the Chinese invader from the north, Lac Long Quang captures and marries Au Co, Lai's daughter (some versions say Lai's wife), an immortal. From this union of the king of the race of dragons and the queen of the race of fairies, 100 eggs come forth, yielding 100 sons. Later the couple separates, and Lac Long returns to the lowland Kingdom of the Waters with 50 sons, while Au Co moves to the mountains with her 50. The same division of mortal and immortal is found in legends across all of Indonesia. The legend shows the immortals as mountain dwellers, while the people along the sea, the dragon people, are the mortals.

Lac Long continues to rule over the lowlands, and when his sons reach manhood, one is chosen king and named Hung Vuong (meaning King Hung), the first of the Hong Bang dynasty. Hung Vuong is regarded as the true founder of the Vietnamese nation. The dynasty continues through the reign of 18 kings, each of whom has a rule of 150 years. Their country was called Van Lang, meaning "Land of the Tattooed Men."

Other tales in the legendary cycle concerning the descendants of Lac Long Quang and Au Co include: *The Magic Crossbow, How the Dao People Came To Be,* and *A War between Gods.* (Terada 1989)

See also *The Magic Crossbow; A War between Gods.*

LADY FROM THE NORTH/OMAN

(Also *Utenzi wa Mwana Manga)*

This 52-verse Swahili epic poem is attributed to Fumo Liyongo. (Westley *RAL* 1991)

See also Liyongo.

LAERTES

In Greek mythology, in the Argonaut legend, and in the *Odyssey,* Laertes is one of the Argonauts and the father of Odysseus by Anticleia. (Graves 1955; Rouse 1990)

See also Argonauts; *Odyssey.*

LAHAMU AND LAHMU

In the Mesopotamian creation epic *Enuma Elish,* Lahamu and Lahmu are twin gods, firstborn of Apsu and Tiamat. (Sproul 1991)

LAIMĖ

(Also Laima-Dalia)

Laimė is the Lithuanian goddess of Fate who, with Dievas (the sky) and Saulė (the sun), predestines the length of human life and fortunes. Stories abound in which three laimės, or fates, wander about the countryside and are present at the birth of a child; however, in other stories one laimė, a goddess, appears. At times she appears as an anthropomorphic being; at others, she wears a sash-rainbow. The dwelling of Laimė is often a lighted cottage deep in the thick forest. She is a mythological being confirmed as much by historical sources as by folklore. While in some sources she is called "Goddess of Birth," she participates in birth only by pronouncing her words of destiny. However, more importantly, she guides the birth of all mankind. Her mission on earth is temporary, because her permanent dwelling is "in the sky." She often appears with her sister Giltinė, the "Goddess of Death," who looks after the ailing, deciding whom to keep and whom to kill. Laimė, whose name means "happiness," also oversees other human rites such as marriages and field-planting, when she may even dress in farmers' clothes and accompany the farmer during sowing. She has the power to determine the life span of plants and animals as well. She is akin to the Bulgarian lamia and the Greek lamai. (Greimas 1992)

See also Lamai; Lamia; Saulė.

LAKṢMAṆA
(Endowed with Lucky Signs)

In Hindu mythology, Lakṣmaṇa is the younger half brother of Rāma and one of the avatars of Viṣṇu. In the *Rāmāyaṇa* he loyally accompanies Rāma into exile and fights at his side against Rāvaṇa's forces to rescue Sītā. (Lattimore 1976)

See also *Rāmāyaṇa.*

LAKṢMĪ
(Also Lakshmi)

In Hindu mythology, Lakṣmī is the goddess of wealth and beauty and the wife of Viṣṇu. In the *Rāmāyaṇa,* she is said, like Aphrodite, to have sprung from the sea's foam. (Lattimore 1976)

See also *Rāmāyaṇa.*

LALITAVISTARA
(Also *The Detailed Narration of the Sport of the Buddha)*

This legendary Indian Sanskrit/vernacular biography covers the early years of Gautama Buddha up to the time of his first discourse. Although it is claimed that accounts of his life were recited within a year of his death, no date can be placed on this work, which is the result of continual growth and alteration. Although the work has evolved over a long period of time, it does contain some ancient material; an early version was translated into Chinese in A.D. 308. (Preminger 1990)

LAMAI

In classical mythology, Lamai is variously the name of a daughter of Poseidon, a female demon who eats children, a daughter of Egyptian king Belus and herself a queen of Libya whom Zeus loves (causing the jealous Hera to deform Lamai and rob her of all but one of her children; in retaliation Lamai kills strangers); in Latin, Lamai is a witch whom Apollonius destroys. (Graves 1966)

See also Laimė; Lamia.

LAMANG

This epic of the Ilocano people of the Philippines, still being performed today, is noted for the absence of Western influence. (Preminger 1990)

LAMASHTU

(Also Lamme or Lamar)

In Mesopotamian religion, Lamashtu is the daughter of Anu, god of heaven. She is the most fearsome of goddesses, having seven names and sometimes referred to as "seven witches." She brings sickness and death to men and vegetation. (Saggs 1978)

LAMIA

In Bulgarian mythology, the lamia is a female spirit believed to have come from a serpent's head that had fallen on an ox or buffalo horn and formed a new being. It looks like a huge flying lizard with a dog's head. It lives in caves and guards treasure troves. It may withhold water and not release it until it receives a human sacrifice. It can change form, appearing as a fog or strong wind, and destroy everything. The lamia is the sworn enemy of heroes, particularly St. George, and of dragons and twins.

A popular Bulgarian legend is the one in which St. George slays the lamia and frees the king's daughter. Another legend, from the village of Eles in Greece, tells of an old man who loads a donkey with tinder, ignites the tinder, and sends the donkey out. The lamia gulps down the donkey, tinder and all, and she is set ablaze. She tears through a hill, from which water begins to gush out. (Georgieva 1985)

See also Laimė; Lamai.

LANCELOT, SIR

(Also Launcelot, Lancelot du Lac, and Lancelot of the Lake)

In later Arthurian tales, Lancelot is the most famous knight of the Round Table. He is the son of King Ban of Benwick, the favorite knight of King Arthur, the lover of Queen Guinevere, and the father, by Elaine, of Sir Galahad. He does not appear in the early Welsh legends, but makes his first appearance in Chrétien de Troyes's *Erec* (twelfth century) and later in the same author's *Le Chevalier de la charette* (The Knight of the Cart), which recasts an existing legend about Guinevere's abduction in which Lancelot rescues the queen and becomes her lover. In the thirteenth-century *Vulgate Cycle,* or Prose Lancelot, at the time of King Ban's death, Lancelot is spirited away by Vivien, the Lady of the Lake, who educates him and prepares him for life as a knight. In Malory's *Morte d'Arthur* (ca. 1469), Lancelot is deceived into believing that Elaine the Fair of Astolat, daughter of the Grail keeper, King Pellas, is Guinevere, and he fathers a child by her—the pure knight Galahad. Guinevere's jealousy drives him to madness for a while. His adulterous love for Guinevere causes him to fail in his Grail quest. King Arthur finally exiles him, and they eventually meet in battle at Benwick. Lancelot mortally wounds Sir Gawain during combat, and when he returns to England he finds King Arthur dead as well. The Round Table has been abandoned, and Guinevere has become a nun. Lancelot also plays a major role in Tennyson's *Idylls of the King* (1859–1885). The Celtic name for Lancelot is Lanval, which is also the name of a lay recounting his adventures by Marie de France. (Barber 1961)

See also Arthurian Legend; *Lanval.*

LANVAL

Lanval is the Celtic name for Lancelot, and the title of a twelfth-century romantic lai by Marie de France. Little is known about Marie de France outside of her work and her position as the first major woman writer in medieval Europe. She claimed no literary source for her lays, which are written in octosyllabic couplets. They were Celtic tales that she had heard, and she made it clear that she was the first person to put the stories into rhyme. She composed the lais sometime between 1160 and 1199.

About Lanval she says, "For his valor, for his generosity, / for his beauty and his bravery, / most men envied him," and he is mistreated at Arthur's court. Lanval retreats within himself and imagines or discovers a lover who comes to him whenever he needs her, but she remains invisible to everyone else. Love gives Lanval the means to win attention at court, but it also ends his interest in receiving the court's attention. Out of loyalty to his secret love he must reject the queen, thus offending her. Lanval is brought to trial after the queen accuses him of trying to make love to her. Ultimately, Lanval's mysterious lady appears at court, making herself visible to all, and justice prevails. She tells the king, ". . . the queen was in the wrong. / He never made advances to her. . . ." When the trial is over, the girl leaves the hall. Outside stands a great marble stone, which Lanval climbs, and when the girl comes through the gate, he leaps onto the palfrey behind her. The two ride off to Avalon, "to a very beautiful island," and "no man heard of him again." (Hanning 1978)

See also Lancelot, Sir.

EL LANZÓN
(Also Smiling God or Great Image)

This early Andean deity, thought to be the chief god of the pre-Incan peoples, is depicted in a carving at Chavin, Peru. Although archaeologists believed for some time that the chief object of worship was a cat, probably a jaguar, El Lanzón is a human figure armed with thunderbolts carved upon a slab of white granite 15 feet high. (Alexander, H. 1964)

LAOCOON

In the *Aeneid* (ii), Laocoon is a son of Priam and Hecuba and a priest of Apollo. He warns the Trojans against accepting the wooden horse and is killed, along with his twin sons, by two sea serpents. He has offended Apollo by breaking his vow of celibacy and fathering children. Another legend has him as the son of Agenor of Troy; another, the brother of Anchises and thus Aeneas's uncle. (Humphries 1951)

See also *Aeneid;* Hecuba; Priam.

LAOMEDON

In Greek legend Laomedon, son of Ilus and Eurydice, is the king of Troy. He is the father of Priam and Hesione. Zeus punishes Apollo and Poseidon by sending them to build the walls of Troy, but Laomedon refuses to pay them their wages when they have finished. The gods send a sea monster to ravage Troy, which can be redeemed only by the sacrifice of his daughter Hesione. Herakles intervenes, kills the monster, and rescues Hesione with the understanding that Laomedon will give him his magnificent horses. When Laomedon refuses to honor his bargain, Herakles brings a band of warriors to take Troy and kill everyone in Laomedon's line except Priam. Laomedon appears in both the *Aeneid* (ii) and the *Iliad* (xxi). (Graves 1955)

LAPITHAE
(Also Lapiths)

The Lapithae are a semilegendary people of Thessaly, mentioned by Homer, who are ruled by Theseus's friend Pirithous. Through their king, they are related to the Centaurs, whose father is Ixion. However, the Lapithae continually fight the Centaurs. At the wedding of the king to Hippodamia, daughter of King Adrastus of Argos, Lapithae threaten the bride, and in the ensuing conflict many Centaurs lose their lives. The Lapithae appear in the *Aeneid* (vi). (Graves 1966; Humphries 1951)

LARENTALIA

A festival for the Roman goddess Acca Larentia, Larentalia is celebrated on 23 December. One tradition makes the goddess the wife of the shepherd Faustulus, who adopted Romulus and Remus; another makes her a prostitute of great means who wills her wealth to the Roman people. (Frazer 1963)

See also Romulus and Remus.

AL-LĀT
(Also Alilat)

This pre-Islamic goddess of northern Arabia is associated with two other goddesses, al-'Uzzā ("Strong") and Manāt ("Fate"). The three were called daughters of Allah (earlier, El or Ilah). Al-Lāt ("the Goddess") may have been consort or daughter of El, but she was also a city goddess for various places. Herodotus (ca. fifth century B.C.) mentions her along with another goddess, Ruda, as the principal goddesses of the Arabs. (Olmstead 1948; Selincourt 1988)

LAT DYOR DIOP

Ruler of the Wolof kingdom of Kayor. *See Kayor, Epic of.*

LATINUS

In Roman legend, Latinus is a son of Odysseus and Circe, king of Latium, husband of Amata, and father of Lavinia. According to the *Aeneid* (ix), Aeneas lands at the mouth of the Tiber and is welcomed by Latinus, who has been advised by an oracle that his daughter must not marry Amata's choice, Turnus, but must wait to become the wife of a foreign prince. Aeneas ultimately marries Lavinia. Another legend makes Latinus the son of the god Faunus and the nymph Marica. (Humphries 1951)

LATONA

See Leto.

LAUNCELOT, SIR

See Lancelot, Sir.

LAXDAELA SAGA

This Icelandic saga of the Middle Ages (thirteenth century) encompasses several generations of a hero-family from the ninth to the eleventh centuries. The saga opens in Norway, where one of King Harald Fine-Hair's chieftains, Ketil Flat-Nose, decides to move to Scotland. But his sons emigrate to the newly discovered Iceland, and his daughter, Unn the Deep-Minded, eventually joins them. From Unn and from Ketil's son Bjorn the Easterner, the two main threads of the family descend.

The first 31 chapters of the saga follow Unn's descendants. Unn is a forceful matriarch who marries her granddaughters to carefully chosen suitors in Scotland, Orkney, and the Faroes. She leaves her estate of Hvamm to her grandson Olaf Feilan, whose great-grandson Thorkel Eyjolfsson later marries the main heroine, Gudrun.

The saga then follows the line of another of Unn's grandchildren, Thorgerd, who marries Dala-Koll and gains access to her dowry of the whole of Laxriverdale. Thorgerd's great-grandsons are Bolli and Kjartan, both of whom play large roles in the central plot of the saga.

The second section, chapters 32–56, opens with the other main dynastic line from Ketil Flat-Nose, the descendants of Bjorn the Easterner: Osvif Helgason and his daughter Gudrun. She is a beautiful, self-confident teenager who describes to a seer, Gest Oddleifsson, four strange dreams she has had. Gest predicts that she will have four husbands. Later, when he sees the two cousins Kjartan and Bolli together, he predicts with tears in his eyes that one day Bolli will stand over Kjartan's body and earn his own death in the bargain.

The central plot is a love triangle wherein the jealous heroine, Gudrun, brings about the death of her true love, Kjartan. It is a classic case of misunderstanding and misinformation such as occurs in the stories of Antony and Cleopatra or Romeo and Juliet. At age 15 Gudrun marries, against her will, a wealthy old man named Thorcald Halldorsson, whom she divorces after only two years. She next marries Thord Ingunnarson, who must divorce his fiery-tempered first wife in order to marry Gudrun. Thord is drowned by a family of sorcerers, leaving Gudrun a young widow. She meets Kjartan and the two fall in love. But while Kjartan is away at King Olaf's court, his cousin Bolli, who also desires Gudrun, tells her that Kjartan is romantically involved with the king's sister, Ingebjorg. Out of spite, Gudrun marries Bolli, and when Kjartan returns to Iceland and learns of the marriage, he too acts out of spite. He marries Hrefna, conferring upon her an ornate headdress that the king's sister had sent for Gudrun. Gudrun arranges to have the headdress stolen, and in retaliation Kjartan besieges Gudrun and Bolli's home for three days, denying them access to the outdoor privy. At last Gudrun goads her husband and brothers to make an attempt on Kjartan's life. When Kjartan sees Bolli, he throws down his weapons rather than fight him, and Bolli kills him with his sword "Leg Biter."

Kjartan's brothers eventually kill Bolli. Gudrun is pregnant, but one of Bolli's killers prophesies that her unborn son will cause his own death in revenge.

In the last section, chapters 57–78, Gudrun lays plans to avenge Bolli's death. She marries Thorkel Eyjolfsson, who becomes a great chieftain. However, Thorkel drowns while on a trip to purchase Hjardarholt. Gudrun's son Bolli Bollason grows up to be a man of great pomp and chivalry. Her son Gellir Thorkelsson, by her fourth husband Thorkel, also becomes a man of great influence, but he dies at age 64 on a return trip from Rome. Gudrun becomes a nun. Before she dies, her son Bolli Bollason comes to see her and asks, "Which man did you love most?" She answers, "I was worst to the one I loved the most." (Magnusson and Pálsson 1969)

See also Bard; Bardi Gundmundsson; Beinir the Strong; Bjorn; Bolli Bollason.

LAY OF IGOR'S CAMPAIGN

Russian byliny. *See Host of Igor, The Lay of the.*

LAYAMON

Layamon was an Early Middle English poet and author of the *Brut* (ca. 1200), the first work in English to detail the legends of King Arthur and the Round Table. Layamon, a priest at Arley Kings in Worchester, used as his source his own translation of Wace's *Roman de Brut,* which was itself an Anglo-Norman adaptation in verse form of Geoffrey of Monmouth's Latin *History of the Kings of Britain.* The poet tells, in some 16,000 alliterative lines, of the landing in Britain of Brutus, great-grandson of Aeneas, the Trojan hero. He carries the history forward to the Saxon defeat of the Britons in 689. Fully one-third of the poem deals with Arthurian legend, and details of the lives of Merlin, Lear, and Cymbeline appear in the *Brut* for the first time. Prior to Layamon's time, no work of English literature had appeared since the Norman conquest. (Jones, G. 1990; Rutherford 1987)

LAZAR

(Also Hrebeljanovic)

Serbian national hero, and prince from 1371 to 1389, Lazar was renowned for his leadership against the Ottoman Turks. He originally repulsed the Turks, but ultimately succumbed to them in the Battle of Kosovo, as recounted in the epic of that name. He was captured in 1389 and put to death by the Turks. (Matthias and Vučković 1987)

See also The Battle of Kosovo.

LEAR

(Also Llyr)

Lear is a legendary king of Britain whose story of his division of his kingdom among his daughters appears in Geoffrey of Monmouth's *History of the Kings of Britain* (twelfth century). King Lear is the subject of Shakespeare's play by the same name, in which the weary old king, wishing to divest himself of his responsibilities, expresses his intention to divide his kingdom among his daughters, Goneril, Regan, and Cordelia. When his youngest, Cordelia, refuses to make eloquent professions of her love for him, he divides her share of the kingdom between his other two daughters. But he soon realizes that his other two daughters are greedy, and that their conduct belies their professions of devotion. Their conduct eventually drives him mad, and Cordelia raises an army to try to regain her inheritance and restore her father. She and Lear are reunited, but they are defeated by Goneril and Regan, whom Goneril soon poisons. Goneril stabs herself, Cordelia is executed, and Lear dies of a broken heart. Lear also appears in Edmund Spenser's heroic poem *The Faerie Queene.* (Graves 1966; Siepmann 1987)

LEDA

In Greek mythology, Leda is, by some accounts, the daughter of Thespius; by other accounts she is the daughter of Thestius. She is the wife of King Tyndareus of Sparta. Zeus, in the form of a swan, seduces her and, according to some accounts, she bears quadruplets. From one egg come Polydeuces (Pollux) and Helen, and from the other (fathered by Tyndareus) come Castor and Clytemnestra, who becomes the wife of King Agamemnon. Leda appears in many myths and legends, including the *Odyssey* (xvi). (Graves 1955; Lattimore 1967)

LEI KUNG
(Also Lei Shen)

A Chinese Taoist deity, Lei Kung is the Duke of Thunder, or Thunder God, whose duty is retribution for the commission of sin. He carries out Heaven's edicts to punish both mortals and evil spirits who use Taoist wisdom for ill purposes. With help from Tien Mu (the Mother of Lightning), Yu-tzu (the Rain Master), and Feng P'o (Madame Wind), he causes terrible electrical storms, downpours, and wind storms. (Mackenzie 1990; Waley 1949)

LEIB-OLMAI
(Alder-Man)

Leib-olmai is a forest deity of Lapland, god of hunters, and guardian of forest creatures, particularly the bear. Hunters made offerings to him to ensure success at the hunt, from which women were barred because Leib-olmai despised women. Similarly, menstruating women were forbidden from walking near the shore where fishermen laid out their catch. According to some traditions, it is said that women were prohibited from having weapons of any kind because it would displease Leib-olmai; however, Olaus Magnus depicts Lapp women on skis hunting with men, and the Byzantine historian Procopius claimed that Lapp women did not suckle their babies but instead gave them the marrow from the bones of beasts they slew. In celebration of a successful bear hunt, hunters were splashed with a red "blood" made from alder bark.

The corresponding deity in the *Kalevala* is Tapio. (Frazer 1963; Jones, G. 1990; Lönnrot 1963)

LEIF THE LUCKY
(Leif Eriksson)

Norse explorer of the eleventh century, Leif is the subject of the Icelandic *Eiriks Saga* and a hero of the *Groenlendinga Saga.* According to *Eiriks Saga,* he was the second son of Erik the Red, the first European colonizer of Greenland. He sailed in 1000 from Greenland to Norway, where he was converted to Christianity by King Olaf I Tryggvason, who then commissioned the new convert to Christianize his fellow Greenlanders. However, Leif sailed off-course and landed in a place he called Vinland, possibly Nova Scotia. Returning to Greenland, he converted his mother, who built the first church at Brattahild.

According to the *Groenlendinga Saga,* Leif sailed to Vinland after hearing of it from the Icelander Bjarni Herjulfsson, who had been there 14 years earlier. In addition to Vinland, Leif traveled to Helluland and Markland, possibly Labrador and Newfoundland. (Jones, G. 1990)

LEMMINKÄINEN

In the Finnish epic cycle, *Kalevala,* Lemminkäinen is one of the three heroes. The name presumably means "lover boy," an appropriate appellation. He is referred to repeatedly as "reckless" and "the handsome man with the far-roving mind." When he sets out to woo the high-born maiden of the Island, his mother warns, "you may not be tolerated in the great clan of the Island." She further warns, "the maidens will ridicule you, the women laugh at you." But Lemminkäinen answers, "I will certainly stay the women's laughter . . . I will knock a boy into their wombs . . ." (Lönnrot 1963)

LESHY
(Also ljeschi)

In Slavic mythology, the leshy is a forest spirit who regulates hunting, assigning certain prey to hunters and protecting other wild animals. The leshy is as tall as the trees, but as soon as he leaves the woods he shrinks to the size of a blade of grass. In later times the leshy became the protector of herds and flocks. In twentieth-century peasant Russia, offerings of eggs and bran are made to the leshy for the safe return of a missing herdsman or cow. The Russian ljeschi are partly human, with the legs, horns, and ears of goats. (Frazer 1963)

Leif Eriksson, Norse hero of the *Groenlendinga Saga,* sails on a voyage of discovery to Vinland in the tenth century in this 1893 painting by Christian Krohg.

LETO

(Also Latona)

In Greek mythology, Leto is the daughter of Titans Coeus and Phoebe and the mother of Apollo and Artemus. She appears in the *Iliad* (xxi) and *Theogony.* (Lattimore 1959; Lattimore 1976)

LEUCOSIA

In Greek mythology Leucosia is one of the three Sirens (the others are Ligeia and Parthenope), daughters of the river god Achelous and the Muse Calliope. They live on the rocky coast and, with their sweet songs, lure sailors to their deaths. As Odysseus returns from Troy *(Odyssey,* xii), he stuffs his sailors' ears with wax and lashes himself to his mast so that the boat can safely pass the Sirens. When they fail to lure Odysseus and his men, they throw themselves into the sea. (Rouse 1990)

See also *Odyssey.*

LEZA

Leza is the supreme being of the Ba-ila people of Zambia. Oral traditions associate him with the sky. His counterpart is Bulongo (meaning clay), who is associated with the earth. The union of the two deities produces grain and all other things. A popular legend concerns a woman against whose family Leza, "the besetting One," stretches out his hand. She loses her children and the children of her children. She becomes withered with age, and it seems to her that she herself is at last to be taken. Instead, a change comes over her: She grows younger. Her heart is filled with desire to find God and ask the meaning of it all. She tries to climb to heaven by building a structure to reach heaven. When the structure rots, she travels the earth, thinking, "I shall come to where the earth ends, and there where earth and sky touch, I shall find a road to God, and I shall ask Him: 'What have I done to Thee that Thou afflictest me in this manner?'" She never finds where earth ends, but wherever she goes, she tells her brothers, "I am seeking Leza," and explains why. The people she meets answer her, "In what do you differ from others? [Leza] sits on the back of every one of us, and we cannot shake Him off!" She never obtains her desire, and she dies of a broken heart. (Smith 1968)

LHA-MO

A Tibetan goddess, city goddess of Lhasa, and one of the "Eight Terrible Ones," defenders of the Buddhist faith, Lha-mo is the only female among the eight and one of the most ferocious. She is associated with the Sanskrit Kāli-Devī and the Mongol Ökin Tengri. Lha-mo is also the name of present-day female healers in Ladakh, where their religious text is based on the *Bardo Thötröl* (Tibetan Book of the Dead), and where an active body of folklore and oral epic exists. (Male healers are Lha-bas.) Lha-mos are living oracles of the Spirit of Mercy, Pal-den Lha-mo. They acquire their occult powers through years of rigorous training. (Rao 1989)

See also *Kesar Saga; Lha-ringa.*

LHA-RINGA

This cycle of 360 festival songs is the most important musical form of the Himalayan country of Ladakh. Parts of the *Lha-ringa* are performed at all important occasions, particularly when there is a ceremonial feast for incarnate llamas. Just as this cycle of festival songs is evidence of Ladakh's oral poetic tradition, the *Kesar Saga* (the national epic) combines songs, proverbs, and myths that vary from village to village. (Rao 1989)

See also *Kesar Saga.*

LI CHI
(Collection of Rituals)

This ancient Chinese literature, ca. 500 B.C., is said to have been compiled by Confucius. It is one of the Five Classics (Wu Ching) of Confucian literature. (Creel 1960)

LI HO

Li Ho was a Chinese poet (791–817) of great genius about whom much legend has grown. It is said that he began to compose verse at the age of seven. Legend says that he composed lines on small slips of paper while horseback riding, dropping the slips into an embroidered black bag that he would empty each evening, arranging the slips into poems of great beauty and originality. He was excluded from the examination that would have afforded him a career as court poet, and the disappointment was said to have shortened his life. (Graham 1970)

LIANJA

This national epic of the Nkundo Mongo of Zaire in south-central Africa was recorded by Nsong. The epic is composed of many versions that have been collated by several different researchers to form a single written narrative. In one version, the narrative has been divided into two parts. Premiere Nuit tells the story of Lianja's ancestors. Second Nuit recounts the adventures of the Mongo hero Lianja. (Westley *RAL* 1991)

LICHAS

In Greek mythology, Lichas is the herald of Herakles. Deianeira assigns Lichas to deliver the poisoned tunic of Nessus to Herakles. The garment sticks to Herakles's flesh, and when he tries to pull himself free, large pieces of his flesh are torn away. Mortally wounded, Herakles hurls Lichas into the air, where he turns into stone and falls into the sea. (Graves 1955)

See also Herakles.

LIF AND LIFTHRASIR
(Also Lif and Lifprasir)

In Norse mythology, Lif and Lifthrasir are a human couple, corresponding to the biblical Noah and his wife, who survive the chaos at the end of the world and become the progenitors of the new race of mortals. Their names mean Life and Vitality. (Jones, G. 1990)

LILITH

In Jewish folklore, Lilith is a demon said to roam during stormy weather and to be particularly dangerous to pregnant women and to children. The person of Lilith is probably of Babylonian-Assyrian origin, a variation of the demon Lilu or Lilit. In Hebrew legend she is created simultaneously with Adam and is his first wife. When she refuses to take an inferior role, she is expelled from Eden to a region in the air. Three angels try in vain to induce her to return. She is also depicted as the mother of Adam's demonic offspring conceived following his separation from Eve. In Arabic mythology, Lilith marries the Devil and bears evil spirits as her children. The King James Version of the Bible refers to her as "the screech owl," and the Revised Standard Version calls her "the night hag." The fearsome screech-owl witch of the Indians of northern Mexico is possibly a variation of the Lilith myth. (Ginzberg 1992; Graves 1966; Isaiah 34:14)

LIONGO FUMO
(Also *Hadithi ya Liongo,* The Story of Liongo; *Mashairi Ya Liongo* or *Utendi wa Liongo,* The Poem of Liongo)

This Bantu Swahili cycle, no longer extant, concerns a hero, Liongo Fumo, or Fumo Liongo, whose family is said to have included Persian shahs, and who supposedly lived as early as the twelfth or thirteenth century. His brother is the usurping ruler and the enemy who throws him into a dungeon. While he is imprisoned, Liongo sings "Song of Saada" to his slave girl, asking her to implore his mother to bake a loaf of bread containing a file. He composes "Takhmia Ya Liongo" (The Song of Liongo) to distract the populace while he makes his escape using the file. He reveals to his brother that only a bronze nail pierced through his belly can kill him, and this is the weapon the brother uses to put him to death. The hero is most certainly the same as Liyongo, a poet-hero said to have lived as late as the seventeenth century. (Westley *RAL* 1991)

See also Liyongo.

LIR

(Also Manannán mac Lir)

This ancient Irish sea god is generally connected with stories of rebirth. He is not associated with the Dagda, but is said to have come to Ireland from across an ocean or a lake. He is generally also identified with the Welsh Manawydan fab Llŷr of the *Mabinogion,* although the myths about the two differ. (Graves 1966)

See also Lear; Llŷr, Children of; *Mabinogion.*

LITTLE WAR GODS

(Also the Hero Twins)

A pair of culture heroes of many of the Indians of the southwestern United States, they help stabilize the surface of the earth and teach the Indians the ceremonies and traditions of their culture. The Twin Gods of the Pueblo are a combination of trickster and helpful god. Twin gods also appear in various Mayan traditions, as well as other traditions around the world. (Schell and Freidel 1990)

LIYONGO

(Also Fumo Liyongo wa Baury or al-Baury of Liyongo Fumo)

Liyongo is a Swahili poet-hero to whom is attributed an impressive body of oral poetry, including the 52-verse epic *Utenzi wa Manga* (Lady from the North/Oman). A large body of strong oral tradition and epic material about his life exists, including the *Wajiwaji wa Liyongo* (or *Takhmisa ya Liyongo)* by Sayyid Abdallah bin Ali bin Nasir (ca. 1730–1820). The so-called *Liongo Epic* is considered a "lost epic," of which only a fragment remains. Some scholars place his life as having been sometime between the ninth and thirteenth centuries. A second group of scholars believes that Liyongo lived in more recent times, having died as late as 1690. (Westley *RAL* 1991)

See also *Liongo Fumo.*

LLŶR, CHILDREN OF

In Celtic mythology, the Children of Llŷr (Lir), a sea god, are a family in frequent conflict with the Children of Don (Dana, Danu, Túatha Dé Danann), but the myths differ from Welsh to Irish. In the Welsh tradition, the Children of Llŷr are found in the *Mabinogion,* which was written down in the thirteenth century. Llŷr's children are Manawydan; King Brân of Britain, god of poets and poetry; Branwen, wife of Ireland's sun god King Mallolwch; and Creidylad. Earlier myths make Ludd the father of Creidylad. In the *Mabinogion* story "Branwen Daughter of Llŷr," Brân and Manawydan receive a message tied to a starling's leg that indicates Branwen is being disgraced and mistreated by Mallolwch. They set sail for Ireland to avenge their sister, leaving behind seven men as leaders. Brân is captured and decapitated, and Branwen dies of a broken heart. There are only seven survivors, among them Manawydan and Pryderi, son of Pwyll. The story of Pryderi and Manawydan, who marries Rhiannon, Pryderi's mother, is found in the *Mabinogion* story "Manawydan Son of Llŷr."

The Irish Lir, a sea god who dwells on the cliffs of County Antrim with his four offspring, the Children of Lir (three sons and a daughter), appears in a fifteenth-century Irish saga, *Fate of the Children of Lir.* (Gantz 1976; Graves 1966)

See also Lear; Lir; *Mabinogion.*

LLYWARCH HEN
(Also Llywarch the Aged)

This Welsh poet/hero, whom tradition says lived in the sixth century, is the subject of several ninth-century sagas that are preserved in the *Red Book of Hergest* (ca. 1400). Llywarch was the cousin of Urien (Urbgen) of Rheged, sixth-century patron of Taliesin, and Llywarch's patron as well. Llywarch was involved in the vain struggle of the Welsh of Powys to withstand invasion by the Anglo-Saxons of Mercia. In the poems about the Battle of Chester (ca. 616) in which Edwin cuts off the ancient Britons, "Men of the North," from the Welsh of Wales, Llywarch is supposedly the speaker or observer of the action. However, the poems actually date from ca. 850 and the conflicts around Shrewsbury between the English and Welsh. Although no sixth-century poems written by Llywarch survive, he is (erroneously, it is generally agreed by scholars) named as author of a number of ninth-century poems such as "Senility," which is actually the lament of Llywarch as an old man. The poet speaks of his 24 sons, naming two, Llawr and Gwen, who have been slain, and "The four things I have most hated ever have met together / in one place; coughing and old age, sickness and sorrow." (Chadwick 1976; Jackson, K. 1971)

LO-FU HSING
(The Song of Lo-fu; also Me shang sang, Roadside Mulberry Tree)

This ancient Chinese ballad (ca. the first century A.D.), consisting of 53 lines in the yeuh-fu, or five-syllable meter, tells the story of a lovely young woman of the house of Ch'in, Lady Lo-fu, who "loves her silk-worms and mulberry-trees." She is admired by all passersby as she plucks leaves from the walls outside the house of Ch'in. The Lord Prefect sees her, slows his coach, and sends his officer to learn her name and age. The officer reports, "A score of years she has not yet filled; / To 15 she has added somewhat more." Pleased by this report, the Lord Prefect approaches Lady Lo-fu and asks her to ride in his coach, but "she gives him answer straight: / 'My Lord Prefect has not ready wits. / Has he not guessed that just as he has a wife / So I too have my husband dear?" She points to the east where more than a thousand horsemen are riding, "and my love is at their head." She describes her husband as "a wholesome man, fair, white and fine; / Very hairy . . . the finest man of them all." (Waley 1982)

LOFOKEFOKE EPIC

This is a Congo oral epic of the Mbole, or Mbuli, in which a magical hero who has superhuman powers at birth undergoes a series of tests as soon as he is born. There are brief accounts of the deeds of other heroes of the Mbole (Bambuli) as well. (Westley *RAL* 1991)

LOHENGRIN

In German legend, Lohengrin is the Knight of the Swan, hero of a tale in which a mysterious craft, drawn by a swan, arrives in Antwerp carrying the knight who has come to help a princess regain her rightful heritage. They fall in love and marry, but not until he has exacted a promise from her that she will never question him as to his identity. When she breaks her promise, he must leave, never to return. Many versions of the story exist; in the first German version, *Parzival* (ca. 1210), by Wolfram von Eschenbach, the Knight of the Swan's name is Loherangrin. He is the son of the Grail hero Parzival (Perceval) and Brobarz queen Condwiramurs, and the twin brother of Kardeiz. The princess whom he marries is Elsa, duchess of Brabant, and the swan is Elsa's brother Gottfried, who has been placed under a spell by the sorceress Ortrud. (Ruland n.d.; von Eschenbach 1980)

LOKAPALAS

(Also 'jig-rten-skyong, shitenno, and t'ien-wang)

In Hindu and Buddhist mythology, the lokapalas are the four guardians of the four cardinal directions. The gods of the four quarters, from whom influences flow, are: the Blue (or Green) Dragon of the East, the Red Bird of the South, the White Tiger of the West, and the Black Tortoise of the North. They are first mentioned in ancient Buddhist texts. They receive Buddha at birth, accompany him when he renounces the world, and feed him under the Bo tree. Their identity is different in various traditions, although Kubera, god of wealth and protector of the north, is common to both Hindu and Buddhist traditions. (Mackenzie 1990)

LOKI

In Scandinavian mythology, Loki is the satanic trickster god, son of the giant Farbauti (Cruel Striker), father of the giantess Angerboda (Distress Bringer), by whom he then fathers three monsters: the Midgard serpent Jormungand, the wolf Fenriswolf (Fenrisulfr), and the goddess of death, Hel. In the legend *Baldr's Death,* Loki is the god who contrives the hero's death. He is finally punished by being bound to a rock with ten chains and tortured by falling drops of serpent's venom. One legend says that he is loosed at Ragnarök, where he and Heimdall slay each other; another version keeps him in chains until the Twilight of the Gods, when he will break free. (Jones, G. 1990; Young 1954)

LORD LO
("Pra Lo")

This Siamese poem of tragic romance is attributed to King Narai (ca. seventeenth century). It is the final version of a much older poem that had been sung for generations. (Preminger 1990)

LOTUS EATERS
(Lotophagi)

In the *Odyssey* (ix), the Lotus Eaters are people on the coast of Africa whom Odysseus and his men encounter during their journey home from the Trojan War. The people feed on sweet lotus fruit, which they offer to Odysseus's men. Those who eat the lotus forget their home and family, and desire only to remain with the Lotus Eaters. (Rouse 1990)

See also Odysseus; *Odyssey.*

LU HSING

In Chinese mythology, Lu Hsing is the god of prosperity. Historically, he was a second-century B.C. scholar named Shih Fen in the court of Emperor Ching whose family was made wealthy because of the emperor's patronage. Lu Hsing is honored as the third of a triumvirate of stellar gods of personal success, Fu-Shou-Lu. Fu Hsing is a god of happiness, and Shou Hsing is a god of longevity. Lu Hsing is particularly important because he can influence promotions and raises in salaries. (Mackenzie 1990)

LU TUNG-PIN
(Also Lu Yen and Lu Tsu)

In Chinese mythology, Lu Tung-pin is the most renowned of the Eight Immortals of Taoism. In the Taoist text "The Dream of the Yellow Sorghum," the student Lu, after meeting with one of the Immortals, falls asleep and dreams that a terrible disaster interrupts his life. When he wakes, he renounces the world. Legends abound concerning his good deeds: He once rewards an old woman for her honesty by turning her well water into wine. (Creel 1960)

LUBANGO NKUNDUNGULA

In this epic of the Kaonde-speaking people of Central Africa is an oral history of the migration of the Kaonde people. It contains no elements of the mythical or fantastic. (Westley *RAL* 1991)

LUCRETIA

(Also Lucrece and Lucresse)

The legendary heroine Lucretia is a noblewoman of Rome, the wife of Lucius Tarquinius Collatinus. She is ravished by Sextus Tarquinius, son of the Etruscan king of Rome. She tells her husband of the rape, exacting a vow from him that the deed will be avenged, then stabs herself with a dagger. The rebellion that follows (509 B.C.) marks the beginning of the Roman Republic. Her legend is told in Shakespeare's "The Rape of Lucrece." (Graves 1966)

LUDMILA, ST.

Ludmila was a Slavic patroness of Bohemia (ca. 860–921) about whom an oral tradition arose after her death, making her a martyr. She was the wife of Prince Borivoj, the first Czech ruler to adopt Christianity, and mother of Ratislav, who married a pagan, Drahomira. Upon Ratislav's death, Ludmila brought up her grandson Wenceslas as a Christian, angering Drahomira, who is given "credit" for having Ludmila strangled. Many legends arose following her murder, the best known being a tenth-century account of the life of Wenceslas and Ludmila, "Christian," attributed to a monk. (Dvornik 1962)

LUDUL BEL NEMEQI

("Let Me Praise the Expert" or the "Poem of the Righteous Sufferer")

This ancient Mesopotamian composition is similar to the biblical Book of Job in which a man bemoans his fate of having been forsaken by the gods. (Preminger 1990; Pritchard 1973)

LUG

(Also Lugus, Lug Lamfota, Lug of the Long Arm)

In Gaelic mythology, Lug, the only survivor of triplets all named Lugus, is a hero of the Túatha Dé Danann (people of the goddess Dana).

Later he becomes one of the most important Celtic gods, the deity for the Sons of Mil, the first Celts in Ireland. He is all things: warrior, craftsman, musician, poet, sorcerer; thus his name in Irish tradition, Samildanach ("Skilled in All the Arts"). His son is the great Ulster hero Cú Chulainn. (Chadwick 1976; Rutherford 1987)

LUGALBANDA AND ENMERKAR

This ancient Sumerian epic, ca. 2500 B.C., is one of two epic tales having as their central character a man who, from another poem, "Gilgamesh and the Land of the Living," we learn is the father of Gilgamesh and the husband of Ninsun. The surviving poem contains more than 400 lines.

The epic opens with Lugalbanda in the distant land of Zano, apparently against his will, longing to return to his home city of Erech in southern Mesopotamia. The journey to Erech is a terrible one that no one survives. To bring his journey to a successful conclusion, he decides first to gain the good graces of the Imdugud-Bird who decides fates and issues the decrees that none is allowed to transgress. In the bird's absence, he goes to its nest and gives its young gifts of honey, bread, and fat. He paints their faces and places the godly crown of honor, the shugurra, upon their heads. The Imdugud-Bird is pleased when she returns to find her fledglings thus honored, and she announces that she wishes to bestow favor upon the benefactor.

Lugalbanda acknowledges that he is the birds' benefactor, and the Imdugud-Bird showers him with blessings. When Lugalbanda tells her of his desire to travel to Erech, the bird decrees him a favorable journey. She also gives Lugalbanda some counsel, which he is to share with no one, not even his closest friends.

When Lugalbanda announces his intention to make the treacherous journey to Erech, his friends try to dissuade him, for no one has survived the passage across the high mountains or the dangerous river of Kur. However, Lugalbanda is confident because of the Imdugud-Bird's blessings and advice, and he makes the journey successfully.

In Erech, he finds that his lord Enmerkar, son of the sun god Utu, has been besieged by a Semitic nomadic tribe called Martu, which has been raiding both Akkad and Sumer for years. To withstand the assault, Enmerkar needs the aid of his sister, the goddess Inanna of Aratta. Until Lugalbanda's return, he has been unable to find anyone courageous enough to undertake the dangerous journey to deliver his message to Inanna. Lugalbanda bravely volunteers for the task, and when Enmerkar gives him the message and insists on absolute secrecy, Lugalbanda vows to make the journey alone. Again, his friends try to dissuade him from making the trip, but he takes up his weapons and sets out alone. He travels across seven mountains to reach Aratta, where he is greeted warmly by Inanna.

When Lugalbanda repeats Enmerkar's secret message to her, she answers with a symbolic magical formula of tasks that Enmerkar is to perform. The first has to do with a river containing unusual fish, which Enmerkar is to catch; the second, with water vessels that he is to fashion in a special way; the third, with workers of metal and stone whom he is to import and settle in Erech. Although the outcome of Enmerkar's struggle with the Martu is not told, since the epic ends with words of praise for Aratta, it can be presumed that the outcome is successful. (Kramer 1956)

See also *Gilgamesh, Sumerian Poems.*

LUGALBANDA AND MOUNT HURRUM

This is an ancient Sumerian epic, ca. 2500 B.C., that exists in fragmentary form on clay tablets unearthed in 1952. According to Sumerian scholar Samuel Kramer, the tale probably runs well over 400 lines in its entirety; there are now some 350 lines, with the beginning and ending both missing. Of the extant text, only about half is in excellent condition. From these fragments, the following story emerges.

Lugalbanda and his followers are on a journey from their homeland of Erech to distant Aratta, which we have learned from the epic *Lugalbanda and Enmerkar* involves traversing seven treacherous mountains that reach from one end of Anshan to the other. When they arrive at Mount Hurrum, Lugalbanda falls ill, and his companions, believing that he will soon be dead, decide to continue without him. They plan to continue onward to Aratta and return to Erech by the same route, at which time they will retrieve his remains and take them home for burial. They leave him a large store of provisions: food, water, weapons, and strong drink, which is meant to last him for the rest of his days. Ill and forsaken, Lugalbanda prays to the sun god Utu, father of Enmerkar, the king of Erech. Utu answers his prayer and restores him to health with the "food of life" and the "water of life."

For a great length of time, Lugalbanda wanders across the steppe, surviving on game and plant life. Following the directions he receives in a dream, he kills a wild ox and offers its fat to the rising sun, the god Utu. Also following directions from the dream, he slaughters a kid, empties its blood into a ditch, and lays out its fat upon the plain. For the deities An, Enlil, Enki, and Ninhursag, he prepares a feast with food and strong drink.

Following this is apparently a eulogy of seven heavenly lights that, with Nanna, the moon god Utu, and Inanna, the Venus goddess, light the heavens. The end of the poem has been lost. (Kramer 1956)

LYBED

In *Tale of Bygone Years* (Povest vremennykh let), or the *Russian Primary Chronicle,* Lybed is the sister of the founders of the Ukrainian city of Kiev, for whom they name a stream the Lybed. According to this legendary work, three brothers of the Slavic Polyane tribe—Kiy, Shchek, and Khoriv—establish separate settlements that collectively become known as Kiev for the oldest brother, Kiy. Kiev is thought by archaeologists to have been founded ca. the sixth or seventh century A.D. (Dvornik 1962; Jones, G. 1990)

See also *Russian Primary Chronicle.*

M

MAAHISET

(Also maa-alused in Estonia)

In Finnish folk religion, the maahiset are elf spirits who dwell in the middle earth. Their home is said to be the source of various human skin disorders, also called maahiset. (Frazer 1963)

MABINOGION

This collection of 11 anonymous medieval Welsh prose tales, rooted in ancient Celtic history, myth, and legend, evolved from storyteller to storyteller over centuries. The work derives its name from four of the stories, which are known as "The Four Branches of Mabinogi." The name was given to the complete collection by the first person to translate them into English, Lady Charlotte Guest (1812–1895). The earliest manuscript to preserve even parts of the tales is called *Peniarth 6* and dates ca. 1225, although scholars argue that their language suggests that they probably were written ca. 1055–1063. Most of the tales were apparently committed to paper long before the writing of the earliest extant—albeit fragmentary—version, the *White Book of Rhyderch* (ca. 1325), a no longer complete work. All are found in their entirety in the *Red Book of Hergest* (ca. 1375–1400). However, the oral tradition from which these works sprang is in some cases as much as 300 years older.

The tales fall into three categories, the first being "The Four Branches of the Mabinogi," considered the finest stories in the collection. They are: "Pwyll Lord of Dyved," "Branwen Daughter of Llyr," "Manawydan Son of Llyr," and "Math Son of Mathonwy."

The second category, referred to as "The Four Independent Native Tales," includes "The Dream of Maxen" (Macsen Wledig), "Lludd and Llefelys," "How Culhwch Won Olwen" (the earliest Arthurian tale in Welsh), and "The Dream of Rhonabury."

The third category consists of later Arthurian tales: "Owein," or "The Countess of the Fountain," "Peredur Son of Evrawg," and "Gereint and Enid." Many later epics and legends have their roots in these works. The final three stories, for example, parallel Chrétien de Troyes's romances "Yvain," "Perceval," and "Erec." (Gantz 1976)

MACAIRE

In this medieval chanson de geste, or epic poem, Charlemagne's wife Blanchefleur is pursued by Macaire, accused of infidelity, and exiled. When her faithful attendant Auberi de Mondidier is slain by Macaire, his dog avenges his master's death by attacking the murderer and killing him. Blanchefleur, who has given birth to Louis, the emperor's son, has gone for solace to the court of her father, the emperor of Constantinople. He raises an army to defend his daughter's honor against Charlemagne's insult. In a confrontation between Charlemagne's warrior, Ogier the Dane, and Blanchflor's defender, Varocher, the latter prevails, thus clearing the queen's name. Charlemagne begs his wife's forgiveness and they are reunited. The same theme appears in another chanson de geste, *La Reine Sebile.* (Harrison 1970; Heer 1962; Preminger 1990)

See also Chansons de Geste.

MACHA

In Celtic religion, Macha is the goddess of Emhaine Mhacha, capital of the kingdom of Ulster. Macha is the name of three deities in Irish tradition. The first is the wife of Nemhed mac Agnomain, leader of the second invasion by the gods as described in *Lebor Gabala* (The book of invasions). The second is the sole ruler of Ireland until she marries Cimbaeth. This Macha forces five sons of her chief rival to build the royal fortress that becomes known as Emhaine Mhacha. The third is the wife of Crunnchu mac Agnomain, who is so proud and boastful of his wife's supernatural strength and speed that she is required by King Conchobar mac Nessa to race against his team of horses while she is in labor. Nevertheless, she wins the race and gives birth to twins before the horses arrive. However, the strain of childbirth kills her, and she invokes a curse upon the men of Ulaid (Ulster), so that in times of crisis they will suffer the pains of childbirth. The story is told in the *Ulster Cycle* and is called "The Labor Pains of the Ulaid and the Twins of Macha." (Gantz 1988; Kinsella 1969)

See also *Ulster Cycle.*

MACINGWANE

Macingwane is king of the Chunus in the epic *Emperor Shaka the Great.* He is a great and able warrior, but is finally defeated by Shaka. (Kunene 1979)

MADAR-AHKKU

(Also Madderakka)

She is the Lapp goddess of childbirth whose daughters oversee the child from conception through babyhood. The daughters are: Sarakka, the cleaving woman; Uksakka, the door woman; and Juksakka, the bow woman. Madar-ahkku, who receives the child's soul from the god Radien, places it in the mother's womb. (Weyer n.d.)

MADLEBE AND MADLISA

Madlebe and Madlisa are sons of an early Swazi ruler. In the oral history of the Swazi people of northeast South Africa, rulers' names go back 30 generations, although only the last eight can be accurately dated. Madlebe, the son of a junior queen, is an unusual child, said to have been born wearing a magical bracelet. He cries tears of blood, and his bracelet cries "Tsi, tsi!" in sympathy. One day the king calls his people together and announces that the son who can spit the farthest will be crowned Little Chief. He strikes each child with a hippo whip to make him spit, but Madlisa can only dribble. Madlebe, however, spits a long way. Then the sky roars, Madlebe cries tears of blood, and the bracelet cries "Tsi, tsi!"

The king gives Madlebe a pot, gourd, and spoon. He instructs the boy to place the pot high on a shelf so that it can never be broken. One day Madlisa gets hungry and talks his brother into reaching for the pot. The pot falls to the ground, and Madlebe flees in terror to the forest, for he knows that the king will kill him for disobeying. The king's soldiers follow him, but when they lift their weapons to strike him, thunder roars and lightning strikes the earth. Fearing for their own lives, the soldiers send Madlebe to a far country. People believe that he is dead.

When the old king dies, Madlebe returns to his mother's house. There he meets a beautiful girl to whom he makes love. When she weeps for joy, she weeps blood. When he asks, "Do you weep blood too?" the girl tells her mother, who then recognizes her son. When the other warriors learn that he has returned, Madlebe is made king. (Parrinder 1982)

THE MAGIC CROSSBOW

This ancient Vietnamese legendary epic received its literary form ca. A.D. 1200. The story has both historical and legendary sources. It explains the defeat in 207 B.C. of An Duong Vuong, ruler of Au Lac, by Chinese general Trieu Da. Au Lac was a large kingdom prior to Vietnam's consolidation as a nation. Its ruler was one of the sons of Lac Long Quang and Au Co, whose story makes up the first sequence of the legends.

This story commences as An Duong begins his reign. He decides to protect his kingdom against enemy invasions by building a walled citadel. However, each night the day's work is undone by spirits led by a thousand-year-old chicken from a nearby mountain. At length, Kim Quy, a golden turtle from the sea, defeats the chicken and remains on guard until the citadel is completed. As a parting gift, the turtle gives the king one of his toenails to use as a trigger for his crossbow. He promises that the toenail will enable a single arrow from his crossbow to kill thousands of the enemy.

An Duong Vuong fashions a bow according to Kim Quy's instructions and prizes it almost as much as he treasures his beloved daughter Mi Chau. Thereafter, whenever his Chinese enemy Trieu Da attacks, the victory goes easily to An Duong Vuong. Eventually Trieu Da realizes that if he is to defeat An Duong Vuong, it will be only through great patience and cunning.

When Trieu Da's most personable son, Trong Thuy, is old enough, he is sent as his father's emissary to Au Lac, ostensibly to sue for peace, but in reality to ferret out the king's weakness. The young prince makes many missions to Au Lac and soon falls in love with the king's beautiful daughter, Mi Chau. Both kings favor a match between the two young people; An Duong Vuong, because it will give him a claim to new lands, and Trieu Da, because with free access for his son to every room in the palace, he is sure to discover the king's weakness. His son has sworn to remain faithful to his father's wishes, even though he will be joining the household of his beloved bride.

The couple marries and lives in the Au Lac palace. Although they are very happy, Trong Thuy has not forgotten his vow to his father. One night he questions his bride concerning her father's invincibility. She shows him the magical crossbow, which he quickly sketches. He takes the drawing to his father so that he can make a duplicate bow.

Trong Thuy returns to Au Lac, concealing the fake crossbow in his robes, and is able to switch it for the magical one while the rest of the household sleeps. The next day he makes an excuse to his wife and leaves again for his own kingdom. Before he goes, sensing danger, she promises him that if, during his absence, anything should happen that forces her to leave the palace, she will take her embroidered silk robe of goose down and make a trail of feathers for him to follow.

As soon as Trong Thuy is safely home, his father gives orders to his forces to attack Au Lac. When An Duong Vuong sees them coming, he climbs the ramparts and with great confidence aims his bow and shoots. When the arrow fells only one of the enemy instead of a thousand, he knows that he has been duped. He knows also that he is doomed unless he escapes. He puts his daughter behind him on his horse and gallops away with the enemy in close pursuit.

When he reaches the sea, there is no ship on hand to take them away from Trieu Da's approaching forces. He prays aloud for help from Kim Quy, the golden turtle who has helped him in the past. Kim Quy appears from out of the sea, but he tells him, "Your enemy is behind you on your own horse. I cannot help you."

An Duong Vuong looks back and sees his daughter and the trail of feathers that she has dropped. With no remorse, he cuts off her head, and then he follows Kim Quy down into the sea. Mi Chau's blood flows into the ocean, where it enters oysters and forms pearls.

Meanwhile, Trong Thuy, traveling with his father's soldiers, has reached the palace and discovered that his wife is gone. He follows her trail of feathers and finds her decapitated body on the shore. Heartbroken, he carries her back to the palace and gives her a fine burial. Then he wanders, inconsolable, through the rooms of the palace.

Day after day he wanders the palace in deep grief, unable to find solace in anything. One day he goes to the well where Mi Chau used to take her baths and throws himself into its depths, ending his anguish.

The historical defeat in 207 B.C. of An Duong Vuong by Trieu Da (Chao T'o in Chinese) marked its incorporation into the kingdom of Nam Viet and, in the next century, the beginning of more than a thousand years of Vietnamese subjugation to China.

Other tales of the cycle include *Lac Long Quang and Au Co* and *A War between Gods.* (Terada 1989)

See also *Lac Long Quang and Au Co; A War between Gods.*

MAGNUS SAGA

Only a fragment remains of this biography of Norwegian king Magnus VI Lawmender by Sturla Thordarson (1277–1278). Magnus was the last Norwegian king whose biography appears in the Icelandic sagas. (Jones, G. 1990)

MAHĀ MĀYĀ

Mahā Māyā was the mother of Gautama Buddha and wife of Rāja Śuddhodana. She is said to have dreamed that a white elephant with six tusks entered her right side, meaning that she would give birth to a leader, or great soul. Ten months later, she gave birth to Gautama through her right hip, while standing erect, holding onto a branch of a tree. After seven days she died and was reborn in Tāvatiṃsa (Heaven).

Mahā Māyā is also the name of a Tibetan tutelary deity. (Dimmitt and van Buitenen 1978)

MAHĀBHĀRATA

This epic of ancient India, ca. the second century B.C. to the second century A.D., reached its present form in its original Sanskrit about A.D. 400. It is the longest epic ever composed. Its almost 100,000 couplets makes it nearly eight times as long as the *Iliad* and *Odyssey* together. As is typical of Sanskrit poetry, each two successive lines use the same meter. It consists of 18 books, or parvans, plus a supplement, *Harivaṃśa,* which is the "Genealogy of Hari" or Viṣṇu.

The *Mahābhārata,* the story of a dynastic struggle, is believed to have a historic source. When the epic was composed, the Bhārata war was already legendary. This struggle for succession, which comprises the central theme of the epic, probably occurred between 1400 and 1000 B.C., according to Indian scholar B. A. van Nooten. The formation of the epic was an evolutionary process. When in the course of its growth the ballad-cycle concerning the war was being transformed into an early version of the epic, the Kṛiṣṇa teachings and actual syncretization of the Kṛiṣṇa personality from non-Vedic god to avatar of Viṣṇu were incorporated. The epic was added to as late as A.D. 600. The tale of the feud, which decries war but makes the point that war is sometimes a religious or moral duty, makes up only about one-fifth of the total work. There are the *Bhagavadgītā,* the "Lord's Song," the most important religious text in Hindu, which makes up book VI; the legend of Sāvitrī's constancy to her dead husband, which so impressed the god of death, Yama, that he returned him to her in the *Anugītā,* book XIV; the romance of Nala and Damayantī the *Nārāyanīya,* in book XIII, to name but a few of the many myths and legends which are included. The story of the war itself should be understood as a reenactment of a cosmic moral confrontation. The epic is a great compendium of Hindu life, legend, and thought, and within its pages is said, "What is not in the *Mahābhārata* is not to be found anywhere else in the world." Therefore, it would be a mistake to think of it exclusively as an epic of India; versions of the *Mahābhārata,* both written and oral, are found throughout Kashmir and South and Southeast Asia. In Indonesia, it is dramatized in shadow-puppet versions and in musical dramatizations. Versions throughout the Tamil-speaking world had begun to appear at a very early time. In the tenth century three poets—Pampa, Ponna, and Ranna—brought the epic into Kannada. Three poets over three centuries—Nannayya in the eleventh, Tikkana in the thirteenth, and Yerrapragada in the fourteenth—produced a Telegu version of the epic. Sarala Das fashioned an Oriya version in the fourteenth century. The fifteenth-century Malayalam poet Tunchattu Ezhuttacchan produced, among his many accomplishments, a version of the *Mahābhārata.* Sixteenth-century Marathi poet Mukteshvar brought the epic to the masses by rendering it in Marathi, and Kasirama produced a version for the Bengali in the seventeenth century.

The epic begins with the old poet Vyāsa, supposedly the author of the epic, who meets a boy and offers to tell him the history of his race. Ganeśa, the god with the elephant head, appears and offers to be his scribe. Vyāsa tells of his own birth: He is the second son of King Śaṇtanu, whose first wife is a river goddess who gives birth to a son Bhīṣma. Bhīṣma renounces women and vows never to have a child, thus spurning marriage to Amba, who promises vengeance for life. Śaṇtanu has a third son who becomes king but dies. Only Vyāsa can keep the line going, so he is asked to sleep with two princesses. He is not a desirable lover. One princess shuts her eyes rather than look upon him, so he declares that her son will be blind. The other princess blanches at his touch, so he declares that her son will be pale. The two sons are Dhṛitarāṣṭra, the blind (Dritharashtra), and Pāṇḍu, the pale.

King Pāṇḍu is under a curse; he will die if he sleeps with either of his wives, Kuntī and Madri. But each wife invokes a god so as to have a child. Kuntī has three sons: Yudhiṣṭhira (Yudhishthira), who is sired by Dharma, god of earthly harmony, duty, or right conduct; Bhīma, sired by Vayu, god of the wind; and Arjuna, sired by the king of the gods, Indra. Madri gives birth to twins, Nakula and Sahadeva, sired by the twin gods, the Ashwins (Aśvins). The epic has many heroes, but if only one were cited, it would be Yudhiṣṭhira, who has no enemy.

The blind Dhṛitarāṣṭra becomes king and marries Gāndhārī. Out of respect for her husband, she perpetually wears a blindfold so that she can't see, either. She gives birth to 100 sons at once, called the Kauravas, the firstborn of whom, Duryodhana, is driven by a passion to rule the earth. Pāṇḍu succumbs to the temptation to make love and dies.

In the household of Bhīṣma, the celibate uncle, all the cousins are reared in constant conflict. It is clear that each side aspires to the throne, but the rights of succession are unclear. A master of martial arts, Droṇa, is employed to instruct the brothers. He recognizes Arjuna's potential to become a great warrior. During an archery contest, a newcomer arrives named Karṇa, who is also a great warrior. No one knows that he is the firstborn son of Kuntī, sired by the sun god, so he is really a Pāṇḍava, but he joins with the Kauravas.

Because Kuntī has told Arjuna that he must share everything with his brothers, when he brings back the beautiful Draupadī for a wife, the other four (known) brothers also marry her. She bears each brother a son.

As the conflict between the two sides of the family deepens, Kṛiṣṇa (possibly also the incarnation of Viṣṇu) appears, come to make peace. Kṛiṣṇa is a friend of Arjuna, whom he remembers from past incarnations. He advises the Pāṇḍavas to go before the blind king and negotiate an end to the strife in order to avert open bloodshed. At first Yudhiṣṭhira is willing to accept an inferior part of the kingdom as the Pāṇḍavas' share, but Dhṛitarāṣṭra is jealous of his wisdom and cannot let the matter rest there. On the advice of his uncle Shakuni, he challenges Yudhiṣṭhira to a game of dice, in which Yudhiṣṭhira, who cannot resist gambling, wagers everything: his kingdom, his brothers, even Draupadī. He loses it all.

When Draupadī is ordered to strip naked before the court, Kṛiṣṇa performs a miracle, so that each layer of clothing that she removes reveals yet another layer beneath it.

The Pāṇḍavas, having lost everything, are condemned to exile for 13 years, after which they may come and claim their share of the kingdom. They retreat to the forest, where they meet Amba, the woman Bhīṣma spurned. She is still intent on vengeance, still looking for someone to kill him.

Draupadī and her husband number two, Bhīma, urge her husband number one, Yudhiṣṭhira, to fight back against the Kauravas, who have stolen the kingdom. But he has given his word and will not retaliate before the specified time of 13 years is over. Twelve years will be spent in the wilderness and a thirteenth year will be spent incognito in a populated place.

During their exile, Arjuna goes into the mountains in search of a divine weapon with which to regain their lands someday.

While the others sleep, a magical creature appears to Bhīma. He sires a son by her named Ghatotkacha, who is also magical and who promises to come to his father's aid whenever he is needed.

The Kauravas, who have lived in fear back at the palace, make a raid into the forest with the idea of surprising the Pāṇḍavas and killing them. But the Pāṇḍavas are saved by a warning from Vyāsa. The Kauravas, in order to learn the whereabouts of Arjuna, invoke a vision and see the god Śiva giving Arjuna the ultimate weapon of destruction, called Pasupata. Afterward, Arjuna spurns the attentions of a seductive woman who in turn puts a curse on him, saying that one day he will lose his virility.

When the Pāṇḍavas, because they have ignored the voice in the lake, drink poisonous lake water and die, Yudhiṣṭhira brings them to life by wisely answering a series of questions posed by the voice of the lake. For example, "What is swifter than the wind?" the voice asks. "The mind," he answers. "What is the greatest marvel?" "Each day death strikes, and we live as though we were immortal." "What is the most valuable possession?" "Knowledge." "What is not thought of until it departs?" "Health." The voice is discovered to be the voice of his father, Dharma.

The Pāṇḍavas go into hiding, and Vyāsa tells them to choose the disguise of their secret desire. Disguised, they can move about more freely, unfettered by their promise to remain in exile for 13 years.

Meanwhile, Karṇa asks an old hermit for a weapon as powerful as Arjuna's. At first the hermit grants his wish, but when he discovers that Karṇa is not a man of peace, he calls forth a curse such that, when Karṇa calls for the weapon, he will forget its formula and so will die.

The Pāṇḍavas, in various disguises, find asylum at King Virāṭa's court in the kingdom of Matsya. Arjuna is disguised as a transvestite named Vrihannala. A Matsyan general who takes a liking to Draupadī steals off to her bed, only to find Bhīma waiting to batter him.

The Kauravas have invaded Virāṭa's territory and taken all the cattle, and the king makes ready to give chase. When the commander of Virāṭa's troops, his son Uttara, calls for a charioteer, Draupadī points to Vrihannala (Arjuna in disguise) as the best driver on earth. Arjuna cannot refuse to help. He drives the chariot to victory, but must reveal his true identity to Uttarah.

In gratitude for their service to him, the king offers the Pāṇḍavas his own kingdom, but they refuse. Next he offers Arjuna his daughter, Uttarah, as a bride, and Arjuna accepts. King Virāṭa hosts a fine wedding celebration and feast in the couple's honor.

Now that their true identity is known, the brothers must leave. But before the Pāṇḍavas leave the kingdom of Matsya, Vyāsa repeats the legend of the destruction of the world and its rebirth in a child's belly.

Because the Pāṇḍavas have revealed their true identity before the end of the thirteenth year, as proscribed by the terms of the wager, the Kauravas refuse to restore their cousins' kingdom to them. A conflict is inevitable. Both sides of the approaching battle ask Kṛiṣṇa for his support. The Kauravas take Kṛiṣṇa's armies, but Kṛiṣṇa offers to drive his friend Arjuna's chariot into battle himself.

In the Kauravas' palace, the old blind king asks the elderly Bhīṣma to take command of his forces. Bhīṣma agrees, on the condition that Karṇa refrain from joining the battle. Kṛiṣṇa attempts to dissuade the Kauravas from fighting. He reminds Karṇa that he is a long-lost elder brother of the Pāṇḍavas. Karṇa, abandoned at birth by his mother Kuntī, asks Kṛiṣṇa not to reveal his identity to the Pāṇḍavas. He chooses to remain with the Kauravas, even though he foresees his own death if he joins the fight.

As Arjuna prepares to go into battle against his cousins, he is assailed by doubts about the morality of killing his own kin. In the 18 books of the sublime poem *Bhagavadgītā,* Kṛiṣṇa attempts to resolve Arjuna's doubts, arguing for a detached commitment to action without attachment to its outcome, its good or evil consequences. He draws on the Sāṅkhya, a Hindu teaching counseling salvation through knowledge; on Yoga, which seeks salvation through ascetic practice; and on the doctrine of Bhakti, or love of God, which permits the entrance of Viṣṇu's divine grace to those who surrender to him. He teaches the art of "acting and yet not acting," or acting without becoming personally involved in the action or even its consequences.

An example of this moderate teaching that Kṛiṣṇa espouses is: "Religion is not his who too much fasts / Or too much feasts, nor his who sleeps away / An idle mind; nor his who wears to waste / His strength in vigils. Nay, Arjuna! call / that the true piety which most removes / Earth-aches and ills, where one is moderate / In eating and in resting, and in sport; / Measured in wish and act; sleeping betimes, / Waking betimes for duty." (book VI)

Again, he stresses dharma when he says, "Better one's own dharma, though done imperfectly, than another's well performed. Better is death in the fulfillment of one's own dharma. To adopt the dharma of another is perilous. . . ." (book III)

Arjuna resolves to fight, and the war begins. During the war, for the first time the Pāṇḍavas will employ, under the direction of Lord Kṛiṣṇa, ruses that have not previously been in strict accordance with the rules of righteous warfare. The ghost of Amba visits Bhīṣma, explaining that she has taken her own life and has been reborn as a man named Sikhandin, son of King Drupadi, father also of Draupadī. The Pāṇḍavas tell Bhīṣma that, unless he sacrifices himself, the world ultimately will be destroyed by the terrible war to come. Bhīṣma tells the generals to put Sikhandin, formerly Amba, on the front line of battle so that she can fulfill her vow. They do so, but Amba does not strike him because she has forgotten her bitterness and her vow to kill him for spurning her so many years before. Instead, it is Arjuna who strikes him with an arrow, and the wounded Bhīṣma lies maimed for the rest of the war.

Karṇa is relieved of his promise not to fight. His mother Kuntī begs him not to do battle against his brothers, but he refuses to listen. However, he promises to kill only Arjuna.

Arjuna's young son is charged with the task of breaking through the Kauravas' "iron disk" formation, which he does with great cleverness. However, no one else can follow him through the breach, because of Jayadratha's magic, and so he is trapped and killed. Arjuna vows to avenge his son's death, and to kill Jayadratha by sunset the following day. If he cannot succeed, he vows to throw himself into the fire. When Arjuna is unable to get to Jayadratha, Kṛiṣṇa causes an eclipse of the sun. In the darkness, Arjuna is able to reach Jayadratha and kill him.

Karṇa has a lance that can be used only once. Kṛiṣṇa invokes the magical creature Ghatotkacha, son of Bhīma. The creature fights with Karṇa and is killed with the spear, which is henceforth useless. The leader of the Kaurava army is killed, and Karṇa assumes command, but he dies when he is unable to remember the words invoking the absolute weapon.

At last the Kauravas are defeated. The war, in which all of the Indian dynasties and tribes eventually have taken sides, has lasted 18 days. Only seven warriors, including the Pāṇḍavas, remain alive. It has been a terrible, bloody waste of manhood, and this is the great message of the *Mahābhārata.* Yudhiṣṭhira, the wise Pāṇḍava brother, announces his decision to reign henceforth.

Ironically, Kṛiṣṇa, mistaken for a deer, has been mortally wounded by a hunter's arrow. Before he dies, he saves a child, Parikshita, who has been hit by a fragment in the womb of his mother, Uttarah. It is this child to whom Vyāsa is telling the story.

Thirty-six years later, the blind king and his wife and Kuntī are talking about the war. The old king orders his wife to remove her blindfold just once before she dies. She tells him that she has removed it, but in truth she has not. They and Gāndhārī walk into a forest where a fire rages, where they die.

Yudhiṣṭhira arrives in Indra's paradise. His brothers and wife, who have come with him, have fallen into the abyss. The gatekeeper tells him that he must leave behind the dog that he carries. He refuses to do so but is admitted anyway. There are further tests of his faithfulness along the way. The essence of the teachings of the epic are spoken: "With uplifted arms I cry, none heeds; from dharma, from dharma, material gain and pleasure flow; then, why is not dharma pursued? Neither for the sake of pleasure, nor out of fear or avarice, no, not even for the sake of one's life should one give up dharma; dharma stands alone for all time; pleasure and pain are transitory." He is surprised to find that his former enemies are in paradise, while his own family is in hades. But the gatekeeper explains, "This is the last illusion," whereupon his family appears, smiling. Yudhiṣṭhira is at peace, knowing that all is illusion, even hades and paradise.

The *Mahābhārata* was published in India in 11 volumes consisting of about 5,000 pages. (Brooks [film] 1989; Buck 1981; Embree 1988)

See also Arjuna; *Bhagavadgītā;* Draupadī; *Harivaṃśa;* Kaurava; Kṛṣṇa; Yudhiṣṭhira.

MAHĀCINATĀRĀ

(Also Eka jeta, Ekajaṭā, Ugra-Tara, and Ral-gcic-ma)

She is a ferocious form of the Buddhist goddess Tara. The name means "the Tara of Great China," or Tibet. She is depicted wearing snakes and severed heads. (Rao 1989)

MAHĀDEVA

Hindu god. ***See also*** Śiva. (Dimmitt and van Buitenen 1978)

MAHAJATI

(The Great Jākata)

This Thai epic poem (ca. 1475) is one of the first written in the Siamese language, although it is based on Sanskrit models. The *Jākata* is a collection of folktales retold in Pali incorporating Buddhist themes. The *Mahajati* is heavily religious, stressing ethical values. Because the Siamese language is tonal, the poem uses an elaborate rhyme scheme. (Preminger 1990)

MAHĀKĀLA

(Also Mgon-po, Yeke qara, and Ta-hei-wang)

A protective aspect of the Hindu god Śiva, Mahākāla means "the great black one" in Sanskrit. She appears in the *Bardo Thötröl* (Tibetan Book of the Dead). In Japan, Mahākāla is identified with Daikoku, one of the seven gods of luck. (Fremantle and Trungpa 1987)

MAHĀKĀVYA

The Mahākāvya, meaning "great poem," is a genre of Sanskrit epic poems. Widely used until the thirteenth century, the form is similar to the epyllion, or short epic, used by Greek poets ca. the third to first centuries B.C. (Preminger 1990)

MAHĀPURUṢA

(Also Śalākāpuruṣa, great man or great soul)

A common belief that great leaders or great souls are born into the world bearing identifying birthmarks or physical peculiarities is held by Buddhists, Hindus, and Jains. The latter, particularly, developed a body of epic literature, such as the ninth-century *Mahapurana* (The Great Legend) by Jinasena, around the lives of their "great souls." (Embree 1988; Sproul 1991)

MAHĀVAṂSA

(Great Chronicle)

This historical Pali chronicle (ca. the fifth or sixth century) of Ceylon (Sri Lanka) deals with the period from the sixth century B.C. to the early fourth century A.D. It is thought to draw on an earlier fourth-century work, *Dīpavamsa,* as well as upon oral tradition, since it contains much mythical material. (Embree 1988)

MAHĀVASTU
(Great Story or Great Event)

This legendary life of Buddha was written ca. the second century B.C., with material added as late as the fourth century A.D. (Embree 1988)

MAHĀYOGINĪ

Hindu goddess. *See* Kālī. (Dimmitt and van Buitenen 1978)

MAHUIKE

Mahuike is the earth goddess of Polynesia and Micronesia, keeper of the flame of fire and, in the cycle of *Maui-tiki-tiki*, mother of the trickster god Maui. (Dixon 1964)

See also Maui.

MAID MARIAN

In the English ballad cycle of Robin Hood, Maid Marian is the sweetheart of Robin Hood. In one version, when the earl of Huntington is outlawed for nonpayment of debts, Marian follows him into Sherwood Forest in the disguise of a page and lives among his men. Some of the Robin Hood ballads date from at least the fourteenth century, but Maid Marian did not make an appearance until the postmedieval period, ca. the sixteenth century. (Graves 1966; Siepmann 1987)

MAÍRA

In the Tupian "Twin Myth" of eastern Brazil, Maíra is the deity-father of the principal twin. Having impregnated his wife, Maíra sets out to travel, planning never to return. Maíra's child speaks from the womb and suggests that his mother go to look for Maíra. She follows his instructions, but after she gets stung by a wasp and slaps it on her belly, the child in the womb becomes angry and refuses to give her any more directions. She becomes lost and arrives at Opossum's house, where she spends the night. During the night Opossum impregnates her.

The next day she continues her journey, but is killed by the hunting dogs belonging to a jaguar. They open her stomach and find the twins, whom the jaguar woman decides to raise. But the twins escape from her and plan to avenge the death of their mother by killing all of the jaguar people. They make magical piranhas and place them in the river, then overturn the bridge where the people stand fishing. They begin their search for their father, and when they find Maíra, they must convince him that they are his sons. When he is convinced, all three withdraw to the "Village of the Gods," where they live to this day. The myth bears a resemblance to the Venezuelan and Colombian Guajiro epic verse *Maleiwa*. (Bierhorst 1988)

See also Little War Gods; *Maleiwa*.

MALDON, THE BATTLE OF

This heroic poem (late tenth century) in alliterative verse is extant only in a fragment consisting of 325 lines. Both the beginning and ending have been lost. It relates the confrontation between the Viking leader Anlaf (possibly Olaf Tryggvason, later king of Norway) with his 93 ships and Bryhtnoth, ealdorman of Essex, stationed with his fyrd (local band of men) on the mainland across the causeway from Northey Island. The poem describes an attack by Vikings that occurred in 991 against the forces defending "Ethelred's realm."

The poem picks up with Offa's kinsman letting his beloved hawk fly away into the woods while he goes forth to battle. Likewise, Eadric wants to help his lord, and his spirit is undaunted as long as he can hold his shield and broadsword. Fresh from ravaging raids at Folkestone, Sandwich, and Ipswich, the Vikings beach at Northey Island and send the Saxons a demand for tribute. A Viking messenger calls out from the riverbank (the river Blackwater, in Essex) that the British must send their treasure: "It will be far better for you all to avoid the flight of spears by giving precious treasure rather than clashing in hard battle with us." When the ealdorman refuses to pay, saying, "Spears shall be all the tribute they send you, / viper-stained spears and the swords of forebears, / such a haul of harness shall hardly profit you," the Vikings try to cross to the mainland at low tide. The Saxons can easily cut them down, and Bryhtnoth, the elderly "war-hard" earl, strides toward his enemy, "earl to churl." He raises his shield, shakes his spear, and promises, "Heathens are about to fall in battle." However, East Saxons and Vikings cannot reach one another because the flood tide makes it impossible for either side to cross.

When the tide goes out, Wulfstan is ordered to hold the causeway. By his side stand Alfhere and Maccus. When the Danes see that their way is barred, they ask for access, which Bryhtnoth, in the interest of sportsmanship, grants them: "Come quickly to us, men prepared for war." The battle cry is raised. The British form a wall of shields against the fierce attackers. Bryhtnoth is wounded, but Wulfmar sends the spear back to kill the thrower of the spear. Another attacker advances, planning to take the wounded man's treasures—armor, rings, and sword. Bryhtnoth draws his sword and tries to fight back, but his arm is soon maimed. He looks to heaven and gives thanks for all the joys he has seen in this life, and then the heathen warriors cut him down. Both Alfnoth and Wulfmar are also killed.

An undisciplined retreat now ensues, with Offa's son Godric being the first to flee. Both his brothers, Godwin and Godwig, join him in flight. But most of the leaderless men press forward, eager either to lose their lives or avenge their lord. Alfwin, the young son of Alfric, reminds them of their vows and rushes forward to stab one of the seamen. Offa speaks up and encourages the others, then advances angrily into battle. Dunnere shakes his spear and says, "None may turn away who wishes to avenge his lord . . . nor may he worry about saving his own life!"

Still at the forefront stands Edward the Tall, vowing never to turn back. He slays many seamen before he is cut down. Ethelric fights in grim earnest. Offa cuts down an attacker before he too is felled. Wistan kills three among a throng of attackers before he is slaughtered.

An old retainer, Bryhtwold, lifts his shield and shakes his spear and says, "I am far advanced in years and I shall not leave. I intend to lie by the side of my dear lord."

Another Godric, Ethelgar's son, fights in the forefront until he is struck down. The final words remaining inform the reader that this is not the Godric who fled from battle.

Although many desert, the earl and his personal retinue fight on. He says, "Courage shall grow keener, clearer the will, / the heart fiercer, as our force faileth." He vows, "Though I am white with winters I will not away. . . ."

The poem breaks off, but the entry for the year 991 in the *Anglo-Saxon Chronicle* says, "They killed the Ealdorman and the battlefield was theirs. . . ." (Alexander, H. 1964; Hieatt 1967)

MALEIWA

This Guajiro Indian oral verse tale in 423 lines was recorded in Kasusain, Venezuela, in 1969. Maleiwa is "he who made us . . . grandfather of all the Guajiro," according to another poem, who "is born of a woman but is devoured by Jaguar." There are similarities to the Maíra myth of the Brazilian Tupians *(see* Maíra). When Maleiwa's mother becomes pregnant, no one knows who made her so. She tells her father, "No man has ever come to see me. / It took shape by itself in my womb." The unborn baby soon begins to speak, instructing her, "Make me some arrows, / I want to go hunting." She wonders, "How could he go hunting, / since he is still in my womb?"

One day she is accidentally blinded and loses her way home, but the child in her womb refuses to tell her which way to go. She comes to a house where Jaguar's mother lives. The old woman feeds and hides her, but when Jaguar (Kulirapata) comes, he finds and kills her. He begins to eat her, but the scraps that remain between his teeth begin to move. They drop to the ground and weep. The Jaguar mother picks them up and feeds them, and they become three boys. The Jaguar mother raises them, and even Kulirapata becomes fond of them.

The youngest, Maleiwa, is the only one with supernatural powers. He and his brothers begin to steal melons from Old Dove, who discovers the theft and insults them, calling them, "Leftover from death! Remains of food!" Thus it is that the boys learn that Jaguar killed their mother. Maleiwa is furious; he burns Dove's eyelashes with a wisp of burning cotton wool and then decides to kill Jaguar's mother. He shoots her with an arrow, and the boys cut her into pieces and cook them, hiding the head. Maleiwa disguises himself as Jaguar's mother, wearing cotton wool for hair, and feeds Jaguar the flesh of his mother. But Jaguar's teeth speak out, "It's your mother!" and he spits the meat to the ground. He grabs his arrows and tries to kill Maleiwa. The two shoot many arrows but fail to hit each other. Finally Jaguar flees, with Maleiwa in pursuit. Maleiwa magically builds many fires behind and in front of Jaguar.

Exhausted, Jaguar arrives at the dwelling of the snail Julera and begs him, "Help me, grandfather! / Give me something to drink! I'm dying of thirst!" Jaguar has black burn marks on his skin that are visible to this day. Julera promises to give him a drink only if he may enter Jaguar's anus. When Jaguar finally consents to the homosexual act, Julera enters him but immediately afterward hides in a Brazil tree without giving him the water. Jaguar claws the tree's bark, causing scratches, which the Brazil tree still has in its bark, but he cannot find Julera.

Jaguar starts running again until he meets Armadillo, who also promises to give him water, "if you give me your arse." Jaguar reluctantly agrees, but after Armadillo "skewers him," he refuses to give Jaguar a drink. Jaguar claws Armadillo's body and cuts off his head, then he runs on.

Maleiwa finds Armadillo's body and gives him the head of a bird. He sets off in pursuit of Jaguar again. Meanwhile, Jaguar has gone to an abode in the trees. When Maleiwa reaches him, he assumes the form of a woman and lures Jaguar up into a tree. Then he makes the tree grow so high that when he shakes it, Jaguar falls all the way into a desolate region, where he has remained ever since.

Maleiwa leaves the Jaguar's abode and meets a woman to whom he wants to make love. But the woman is really the sea, and she does not want his advances. She chases after him, trying to drown him. He flees from the advancing waves and climbs to the very top of the highest mountain. The sea finally comes to a halt, but it has covered the whole earth.

Maleiwa builds a hot fire and places stones into the blaze. When they are hot, he takes a sling and sends them in every direction. The sea flees the hot stones and dries up, so that the earth reappears.

Maleiwa says, "What can I do now?" He descends to the shore and begins to make living beings out of clay. He distributes the people into clans and gives them animals and food. But there is a serious defect with the women's vulvas: They have teeth, and the men are frightened of mating. Maleiwa goes swimming with a girl named Tonkolu and, seeing the large teeth of her vulva grinding together in the water, he shoots them with his bow and arrow. At once her teeth turn into stones covered with blood. She gets out of the water and is transformed into a large stone, which can still be seen at Wotkasainru. It is surrounded by smaller red stones—her teeth. (Perrin 1987)

See also Little War Gods; Maíra.

MANANNÁN MAC LIR

(Also Manadán son of Ler or Manawydan in the *Mabinogion*)

Manannán, son of the sea, is an Irish sea god who supposedly came from the Isle of Man. He is a benevolent god who protects seamen and oversees the crops. His father Lir is an Irish god who dwells on the cliffs of County Antrim. Among the oldest stories of Irish gods are those having to do with rebirth, in which Manannán mac Lir plays a key role. He presides over Tir na n-Oc, the land of the "ever young," where people "do not die, but live from generation to generation." The dweller in this paradise loses all track of time and, upon leaving, would find that epochs had passed on earth. An anonymous eleventh-century poem, "A Storm at Sea," calls the sea his wife. His Welsh equivalent, Manawydan Son of Llŷr, is the brother of Brân and the second husband of Rhiannon. He is the subject of the third of the "Four Branches" tales in the *Mabinogion.* Both Manannán and Manawydan were apparently derived from an earlier Celtic deity. (Gantz 1976; Rutherford 1987)

See also Lear; Lir; *Mabinogion;* Manawydan Fab Llŷr.

MANASĀ-MAṄGALS

These are poems concerning Manasā, the Bengali folk goddess of snakes and childbirth. The poem cycle of Manasā is still recited in Bengal villages, although it has existed in written form, taken from older oral tradition, since the sixteenth or seventeenth century. In one version, Dharma, missing his three sons, produces Manasā from a sigh and mates with her, then regrets it and has Śiva agree to marry her. She throws herself on a pyre and is reborn as Parvati, who becomes Śiva's wife.

A second group of poems concerns Śiva's daughter, who is Manasā. Śiva lusts after her but fears the jealousy of his wife Candī. He hides Manasā in a basket where Candī finds her and berates her. In still other versions Manasā, who wants to be worshiped by men, alternately bribes and punishes worshipers of Śiva, Kṛiṣṇa, and others, offering them wealth or turning snakes on them if they do not worship her. When the merchant Cando refuses to turn from his worship of her father, she destroys his crops and ships; turns snakes on his seven sons, killing them; and finally turns snakes on Cando himself. His wife floats his corpse downstream in an effort to persuade Manasā to revive him, a practice that still survives among Bengali village people. Manasā promises the wife that, if she will convince Cando to worship her, she will revive him. In the seventeenth century, the poet Ketakadas drew from oral tradition to produce a 12,000-line Manasā-maṅgal. (O'Flaherty *Śiva* 1981)

MANAWYDAN FAB LLŶR

Welsh god of the sea. *See* Manannán mac Lir.

MANCO CAPAC

(Also Manqo Qhapaq)

According to native writer Salcamayhua and Incan historian Garcilaso, Manco Capac was the founder of the Incan dynasty, ca. A.D. 1200. Other sources, however, designate Rocca as the founder.

Legend gives Manco Capac a mythical beginning. With his three brothers and four sisters, he emerges from the middle cave of three at Paqari-tampu, about 15 miles south of Cuzco. Ten groups of people emerge from the caves on either side, and Manco and his family lead them on a ten-year nomadic trek in search of arable land, which they finally find near Cuzco. During that time, Manco Capac does away with his brothers and marries his sister, Mama Ocllo, who bears a son, Zinchi Roq'a (Sinchi Roca). The Incas drive the indigenous people from the land and begin exacting tribute from neighboring tribes. Manco establishes his firstborn, Zinchi, a peace-loving man, on the throne and charges him with the responsibility of protecting all his other children and their offspring. (Garcilaso 1987)

MAṄGAL-KĀVYA

These are Bengali "auspicious poems," sometimes running to thousands of lines, eulogizing a particular god or goddess and performed at festival times. Although each performer incorporates his own favorite legends into the poems so that they are never the same, they are considered historically valuable. (Preminger 1990)

MANIK CHANDRA, EPIC OF

This Bengali Hindu oral folk epic is still being recited today. (Blackburn et al. 1989)

MAṆIKKUṞAVAṈ

This Tamil oral tale, commonly sung in the Madurai area of India, was recorded in 1977. The last verse tells the reader that "Happy Ibrahim Sahib put this song in writing."

The story is not usually used as part of a ritual. Each verse is performed by the main singer, then repeated by his accompanists, although it is not a word-for-word repetition. Like most Tamil folk narratives, it alternates between songs and dialogue. The meter, which has been used in Tamil literature for at least 2,000 years, breaks each line into two parts of three measures each of either one long sound or two short sounds.

The first verse, or Introduction, explains that this will be the story of how King Maṇikkuṟavaṉ dies. He is called "king of kings." There is no one who laughs as loudly and boisterously as he.

As is often the case with narratives from this area, the last is told first, or at least the narrative does not progress in a linear fashion. In the prose section, Maṇikkuṟavaṉ is introduced as a man who has committed 62 murders and hasn't been caught. As he is strutting like a hero, the police come and arrest him. He is sentenced to seven years in prison. Without a lawyer, Maṇikkuṟavaṉ argues his own sentence: "I'm just a boy, a little boy; let me go." But he is ignored and pushed into jail. Of the judge, he vows, "When I get out next, . . . Our next murder is going to be him!"

When his seven years are finished, he goes to the judge's house, climbs over the wall, and kills the judge. He also kills the judge's wife, then jumps over the wall and escapes. A reward of a thousand rupees is offered for his capture, dead or alive. The people who try to capture him over the next nine years—a total of 61—are all murdered.

Maṇikkuṟavaṉ is hired by Tēvar, the distiller, to help distill the arrak. Fearful of having a murderer in their town, the village people march with knives and spears to Tēvar's house, where Maṇikkuṟavaṉ is lying drunk. Tēvar's nice young brother is among the crowd. He stabs Maṇikkuṟavaṉ, and the hero's intestines come out. Maṇikkuṟavaṉ jumps up, grabs his intestines with one hand, takes up his knife with the other, and kills Tēvar. Holding a towel over his intestines, he runs out onto the road. He runs for a long way before, "just like a dead tree," he falls in the middle of the road.

Again at the end, we are reminded that he is "supreme king of kings." (Blackburn and Ramanujan 1986)

MANIMEKHALAÏ

(Also *Manimekalai, The Dancer with the Magic Bowl,* or *The Girdle of Gems)*

This Tamil verse epic (ca. A.D. 171) was written by Merchant-Prince Shattan (Catanar), a friend of Prince Ilango Adigal, author of *Shilappadikaram,* or *Cilappatikāram* (The Ankle Bracelet), of which this work is a continuation. It is considered both a verse epic and a didactic novel; however, the work contains traditional and legendary elements as well as a historical context. The story is set in three South Indian kingdoms—Chera, Chola, and Pandya—whose dynasties fade into prehistory.

The work consists of a prologue and 30 cantos. The prologue sets the scene in the city of Puhâr. In canto I, the annual festival of the god Indra is proclaimed in the city of Puhâr to honor the god who has accomplished 100 sacrifices in his former existences. The kings of all neighboring countries are summoned. It is said that "if the festival were not celebrated, Puhâr's guardian genie would be consumed with wrath and molest all inhabitants."

In canto II, Chitrâpati, Mâdhavi's mother, learns that her beautiful granddaughter Manimekhalâ and her daughter refuse to take part in the dances in Indra's honor and have decided to abandon the profession of dancer and prostitute to join the monastic life. Vasantamâlâ, Mâdhavi's faithful companion, tries to convince her: "For a girl destined by birth for art and pleasure to become an ascetic and mortify herself is an impious act. . . . The entire population of the city condemns Mâdhavi without pity." Mâdhavi explains that her former lover Kovalan has died and his legitimate wife Kannaki has also immolated herself upon his pyre, so for Kovalan's daughter Manimekhalaï, "the monastic life seems to me more fitting than the vicious commerce of her charms and the base acts which are the courtesan's life."

In canto III Manimekhalâ, who for the first time has heard the terrible fate of her father and his virtuous wife, retreats to one of the city's gardens and sheds bitter tears.

In canto IV, when the Chola prince Udayakumâra passes by in his chariot and learns that Manimekhalâ has entered the garden, he follows her. She hears the chariot's approach and says to her monastic companion Sutâmati, "Prince Udayakumâra seems to be infatuated with me." Sutâmati leads Manimekhalâ, "beautiful as a doll," to the garden's crystal pavilion and locks her inside.

In canto V, the Chola prince sees the girl's "charming body" through the transparent walls of the pavilion and is consumed with desire. After he leaves, Manimekhalâ rejoins Sutâmati, and soon appearing before them is the goddess of the ocean, also named Manimekhalâ. She has come to Puhâr "to amuse herself with the joyful din of the festival. . . ."

In canto VI the goddess, who has adopted "the simple form of a towns-woman," removes Manimekhalâ through the air and takes her to "the isle of Manipallavam in the midst of the sea."

In canto VII the goddess returns to Puhâr and appears to the Chola prince, advising him to "cast far from you this blameworthy desire which draws you to Manimekhalâ, since she is destined for the monastic life." Then she returns to the garden and awakens Sutâmati, who has fallen asleep. The goddess instructs her, "Run and tell Mâdhavi of my arrival here and of the spotless path for which her daughter has been chosen." Then she rises to the sky and disappears.

Meanwhile, in canto VIII, Manimekhalâ awakens on the island, frightened at being alone, and begins to weep and call for Sutâmati. She sees a vision of the Buddha on a divine pedestal and no longer feels abandoned.

In canto IX, at the sight of the jewel-encrusted pedestal, Manimekhalâ suddenly recalls her past life and is aggrieved.

In canto X, while she wanders, burdened with sadness at her memories, the goddess appears and explains that Prince Udayakumâra is the reincarnation of her former husband Rahul in her past life, in which she was called Lakshmi. The goddess then teaches her some magic formulas.

In canto XI, when the goddess departs, Tivatilakaï, the divine protectress of the island, appears and presents Manimekhalâ with a marvelous magic bowl with which she must feed the destitute. The goddess tells her, "This magic bowl will only be filled in the hands of those whose charity, the fruit of their past virtues, is sincere."

In canto XII, with her magic bowl Manimekhalâ returns to her mother and companion. They all go to visit the sage Aravana Adigal, who tells her, "You now possess the magic bowl, Cow of Abundance, which contains the substance of life. You must now go about the world to put an end to the pains of hunger suffered by living beings. There exists no more meritorious act towards gods or men than to assuage the pangs of hunger."

Cantos XIII and XIV are the story, as told by Arvana Adigal, of Apurta, the first possessor of the bowl, Cow of Abundance, and how he had received it from Chintâ, the goddess of knowledge.

In canto XV, when the three women have heard the tale of the bowl, they return to the city. As Manimekhalâ carries the bowl through the streets, the young people of the town, "stupid and loud-mouthed," ask, "How is it possible that Manimekhalâ . . . now roams the streets of Puhâr with a beggar's bowl in her hand?"

In canto XVI, the matron Atiraï, whose husband Shaduvan was once presumed lost at sea but has now returned, in gratitude pours into the bowl alms for Manimekhalâ to distribute to the poor.

In canto XVII the food placed in the magic bowl by Atiraï multiplies without ever running out; thus its possessor can feed a mass of poor people. One woman, Kayashandikaï, approaches and tells her that she has an insatiable hunger. Manimekhalâ satisfies her hunger and then leaves for the travelers' hospice called Ulaka-aravi.

When, in canto XVIII, Prince Udayakumâra learns of Manimekhalâ's whereabouts, he visits the hospice. She thinks, "In my former life, this man was my husband, my dear Rahul. . . . It is therefore proper for me to greet him humble." She bows before him. But the prince prostrates himself before her, saying, "My fate is in your hands."

In canto XIX, to escape the prince, Manimekhalâ, still carrying her begging bowl, takes the form of Kayashandikaï, the wife of a genie magician who had placed the insatiable hunger upon her. She arrives at the city's prison and has it transformed into a monastery.

In canto XX, Kanchana, Kayashandikaï's genie-husband, approaches Manimekhalâ, who is still disguised as Kayashandikaï. When she is indifferent to him, he is dismayed, even outraged. He sees the prince approaching, lusting after the woman who looks like his wife, and he kills the prince with his sword.

In canto XXI, Manimekhalâ, waking to discover the prince's body, wails and laments. A statue possessed by a genie begins to speak and explains that the prince's death is due to an action in his past life. The statue warns her that the king will throw her in prison and the queen will order her release in order to torture her, but Mâdhavi will seek Adigal's help in obtaining her release, after which she will go to the city of Vanji in the disguise of a monk.

In canto XXII, as the statue has predicted, the bereft king has Manimekhalâ thrown into prison for causing his son's death. But at the queen's insistence, she is released into the queen's custody.

In canto XXIII, on Manimekhalâ's advice the king transforms the prison into a hospice. The queen plans to drive Manimekhalâ insane as revenge for her son's death, but Manimekhalâ explains that the prince's death was due to "the grave fault committed by your son in his former life."

In canto XXIV, as predicted, Mâdhavi comes with Aravana Adigal to rescue Manimekhalâ. He teaches the queen and the women of the court the nature of the dharma and instructs Manimekhalâ to leave for Apurta's kingdom.

In canto XXV, Manimekhalaï accompanies Apurta to the isle of Manipallavan, where she learns details of her own former life.

In canto XXVI, Manimekhalâ takes the form of an ascetic and flies to Vanji, where, in canto XXVII, she studies religious dogmas with the teachers of various sects.

In canto XXVIII, still disguised as a monk, she visits Kanchi and finds her mother and other women with Aravana Adigal.

In canto XXIX, she puts aside her disguise and prostrates herself before Aravana Adigal, who instructs her in the Buddhist dharma. She adopts the monastic life.

In canto XXX, Manimekhalâ practices austere self-denial and is freed from the cycle of births and deaths. (Shattan 1989)

See also *Cilappatikāram;* Murugan.

MANNA-HEIM

In Norse mythology, Manna-heim is Midgard, the world of men. (Jones, G. 1990)

MANQO QHAPAQ

See Manco Capac.

MANSA MOUSSA
(Also Musa)

Mansa Moussa was the emperor of the West African empire of Mali (r. 1307–1332) at the height of its power. "Mansa" is a title equivalent to "King." Moussa was a son or grandson of Sundiata, the legendary founder of Mali whose story is told in the *Epic of Sundiata* (or Sonjara). Of Moussa the griot says, "Hajji Mansa Moussa, of illustrious memory, beloved of God, built houses at Mecca for pilgrims coming from Mali, but the towns which he founded have all disappeared. . . ." Under Moussa, Timbuktu grew to be an important city. (Niane 1989; Sisòkò 1992)

See also *Sundiata, Epic of.*

MANTANTISI

In the Zulu epic *Emperor Shaka the Great,* Mantantisi is queen of the ba Tlokwa, who leads her own armies into battle. She is called "a fierce woman." The narrator of the epic says, "She raided and terrorized the Mabiti nations of the Sothos. / She chased the Fukengs and the Kwenas." Shaka says of her, "I always marvel at how men could be terrorized by a woman. / Perhaps there is something in her of which I am ignorant! / She may yet possess magic herbs unknown to us." The narrator goes on to explain that Shaka was only "making fun of men who flee from a woman in battle." (Kunene 1979)

See also *Emperor Shaka the Great.*

MANU

In Hindu legend, Manu is the progenitor of the human race, called m̲anava (human) after him. It is said there have been 14 Manus, or primal kings, one in each new era or period of 306,720,000 years (Manvantara) of Indian mythical life, mentioned first in the major *Purāṇas* (ancient lore) in the *Amarakosa* (ca. fifth or sixth century A.D.). The seventh Manu, Manu Vaivasvata, is the progenitor of the present race of mankind.

Manu is also author of the *Manu-smṛti,* Sanskrit code of law. The legend of the *Four Heads of Brahmā* tells that when Brahmā sees his daughter Śatarūpā, made from his own body, he becomes smitten with her beauty. He is ashamed of his desire to stare at her in the presence of his sons, so a face appears on each side of his head. As she springs into the air, a face appears on the top of his head. He tells his sons, "From now on you must produce all the creatures. . . ." When they leave in order to create, the universal soul marries Śatarūpā, "lost in love" and making love to her for 100 years "Just like an ordinary man." After a long time, she bears a son, a Manu called Svāyambhuva, "said to be the Primal Person because he shares the qualities of Brahmā."

In the *Śatapatha Brāhmana,* Manu is warned by a fish, to whom he has been kind, that a flood is coming that will destroy humankind. The fish, identified in the *Purāṇas* as an incarnation of Viṣṇu, and in the *Mahābhārata* as an incarnation of Brahmā, instructs Manu to build a boat. When the flood comes, Manu ties the boat to the fish's horn and is led safely to a mountaintop. When the waters recede, Manu offers a sacrifice of butter and sour milk upon the waters. From the waters a woman is born who tells him that she is "the daughter of Manu." These two repopulate the earth. (Dimmitt and van Buitenen 1978; O'Flaherty 1975)

MAN'YŌSHŪ
(Collection of Ten Thousand Leaves)

One of the world's great collections of poems, it is the oldest anthology of Japanese verse, compiled in the mid-eighth century but containing some material of a much earlier date. It consists of 4,500 poems employing a wide variety of form and subject matter and evincing relatively little Chinese influence. The work was compiled in the Nara Period, the golden age of court poetry, during which both the older *Kojiki* (712) and *Nihongi* (720) also appeared. Prior to that time, the popular form was the tanka. The longer choka or naga-uta are able to bring powerful imagery and more comprehensive experience to the poems than the tanka could provide.

A titleless example, written by a warrior called to duty, describes his leave-taking from wife and mother, ending with, "Sorely do I grieve that with my sobs / I shake the war arrows I carry / Till they rattle in my ears."

The poems, written in first person on a wide range of subjects, carry an immediacy and a spontaneity that are missing in the more polished work of later centuries. One long poem, written by a grieving widower, tells of walking with his late wife among the elm trees "thick with spring leaves. Abundant as their greenery / Was my love. On her leaned my soul."

In "A Dialogue on Poverty," the poet confesses to putting up a brave front, saying, "There's none worthy, save I!" But he admits, "I shiver still with cold. . . . We moan like the night thrush. . . ." (Keene 1960)

MARDAN

Mardan is a legendary culture hero of the Yelabuga (Russia) Votyak Finns. He is honored in seven villages with annual ceremonies commemorating his role in leading the Finno-Ugric peoples from the north to establish the villages. He has been given semidivine status, and sacrifices are offered during the ceremonies. (Holmberg 1964)

MARDUK
(Also Bel and Baal)

In Mesopotamian religion, Marduk is the supreme god of the Babylonians who may originally have been a storm god. The creation epic *Enuma Elish* (ca. twenty-second century B.C.) relates that, in the beginning, the monster Tiamat rules primeval chaos until Marduk leads the gods from Heaven to wage war against her. He cuts Tiamat's body into two parts, from which he forms the sky and earth. Man is created last of all, and Marduk becomes "lord (or Bel) of the gods of heaven and earth." His consort is Zarpanit. (Sproul 1991)

See also Anu; *Enuma Elish, Epic of;* Tiamat.

MARGAWSE, QUEEN

In Arthurian legend, Margawse is the wife of King Lot of the Orkneys (although in *Orkneyinga Saga,* Lot is married to Ragnhild). Arthurian legend names her as the mother of the knights Gareth, Gaheris, Gawain, and Agravain (Aggravaine), although other sources name Arthur's half sister Anna (or Belisent or Bellicent, in Tennyson's *Idylls of the King)* as the mother of Gawain and Agravain. In Malory's *Morte d'Arthur,* Margawse is also the mother, by Arthur, of Mordred. She is beheaded by her son Gaheris when he finds her with her lover Lamerok, whom Gawain slays. (Siepmann 1987)

See also Arthurian Legend.

MARĪCĪ
(Also Marishi-ten and 'Od-zer-can-ma)

In the tradition of Mahāyāna Buddhism, Marīcī is the goddess of the dawn. In Hindu mythology, Marīcī is born from the shoulder of the Creator and is referred to as "shining mote," one of the seven sages and father of Kaśyapa, another of the seven sages. (O'Flaherty 1975; van Buitenen 1969)

MARK, KING

(Also March ap Merichion, March son of Meirchyawn, and March son of Meirchyon)

In the medieval legend of *Tristan and Iseult,* "How Trystan Won Esyllt," Mark is king of Cornwall, husband of Iseult, uncle of Tristan, and cousin to Arthur. He is the unsuspecting cuckold of his wife and favorite nephew. He appears in the *Mabinogion,* in "The Dream of Rhonabwy," as March son of Meirchyon, Arthur's first cousin. He leads the men of Norway and acts as one of Arthur's advisers at the Battle of Camlann. (Gantz 1976; von Strassburg 1960)

See also *Mabinogion; Tristan and Iseult.*

MARKO KRAL

This king of Prilep is the subject of both Bulgarian and Serbian epics. (Matthias and Vučković 1987; Miletich 1990)

See also *The Battle of Kosovo; Marko Kraljević.*

MARKO KRALJEVIĆ

This Serbo-Croatian cycle of bugarštica (oral traditional narratives) and decasyllabic poems relates to Marko the Prince. The earliest Marko ballad (1556) is clearly an oral traditional text; however, of the Marko poems, it is only in "Marko and the Mina of Kostur" that he emerges in a traditional epic as a heroic figure—the great South Slavic hero who had a famous horse, Sarac. The horse, however, does not appear in the poem.

"Marko the Prince and His Dear Brother Andrijaš" tells of two young Turkish brothers, knights who fight side by side and always divide the booty. But once when they take three fine, heroic steeds, they argue over who is to get the third horse. Marko, knight and prince, draws his bright gilt sword and strikes his brother in the heart. Andrijaš, his dear brother, asks him to leave the sword within his heart until he has said his last few words. He asks Marko to be sure to give his share of the booty to his mother, and to tell her that he, Marko, bloodied his sword killing a deer. He asks Marko to tell her, when she asks, "Where is your brother Andrijaš?" that Andrijaš has stayed abroad, "enamored of a maiden fair" who has bewitched him with strange herbs. He tells Marko that when he is attacked in the dark woods alone, he should call out for Andrijaš, which will cause the attackers to flee, just as they always have at the sound of his name. Then he adds, "May your retainers find you out, / Who killed your brother without cause!"

"Marko the Prince and Minja of Kostur" tells of three messages that Marko receives. The first is from the king of Hungary, who invites him to witness his marriage; the second is from the Hungarian duke Janko, who invites him to his son's christening; the third is from the honored sultan, who wants him to come to Araby and be his standard-bearer. Although Marko wants to go fight in Araby for the sultan, his mother advises him first to attend St. Petka's church and witness the king's marriage, then to go and christen Duke Janko's son, and finally, to go to the Imperial City to serve the sultan.

The Turkish knights battle in Araby for three years. At the end of that time, a message reaches Prince Marko that Minja of Kostur has looted his white court, set it aflame, and carried off his wife and mother. The sultan promises him that if he will fight for one more year, he will give him his knights to fight Minja. But Prince Marko says, "My own right hand will vengeance take!" He rides off to Mount Athos disguised as a monk. When he reaches the ducal court, his wife greets him but does not recognize him. He asks if he may spend the night. She asks her lord, who agrees. Prince Marko invites her into the court, where she serves him wine. She sees his sheepskin coat under the monk's robe and recognizes it as belonging to her husband. He tells her that Prince Marko came to his monastery ill and died, leaving him the coat and a horse. She weeps so hard that the duke strikes her on the face, whereupon "the fine hero" draws his sword and cuts off the head of the Hungarian duke, gathers up his treasure, and burns down the court before he rides safely out of Hungary.

In "Prince Marko and the Moorish Maiden," his mother asks him, "How did you leave that Moorish prison, / My Prince? Was it some ransom that you paid, / Or was it a sharp, Damascus sword, / Oh handsome hero?"

Marko answers that a pretty little Moorish maiden came to him asking, if she were to free him, would he take her as a wife. He promised to marry her, but after he was freed, he cut off the maiden's head. His mother tells him that he has greatly sinned. She informs him that she would have kept the Moorish maiden all of her life.

"The Betrothed of Prince Marko" tells of young Marko pitching his silken tent in Buda's field. Buda's maids rise early and stroll past his tent on the way to the spring each morning, wishing him good morning as they pass. But the youngest and fairest of the maids does not speak to him nor even look at him. He asks her the name of her family and clan, and wants to know why she has not wished him good morning.

She calls him a rogue and identifies herself as sister to Pavle Ban and cousin to the Buda king. She tells him that she is the betrothed of Prince Marko and therefore is not interested in telling him good morning. Marko leaves his tent, grips her by the hand, and pulls her into his tent, where he kisses her. Incensed, she tells him to come to Buda town and she will ask the king to hang him. But Marko releases her, and sends her brother and the king his greetings by her.

The maiden rushes back to town and asks her brother, "Who is that rogue in Buda field / who 'neath his tent leads Buda's maids? . . ." The brother answers, "That is no rogue beneath the tent, / But your betrothed, the hero Marko!" The maiden blushes and casts her gaze downward. (Miletich 1990)

See also *The Battle of Kosovo.*

MARS

Roman god of war, Mars is the counterpart of the Greek Ares. While Ares appears in the *Iliad* and the *Odyssey,* Mars makes his appearance in the *Aeneid.*

The Roman god of war, Mars, rides triumphantly in a chariot drawn by lions in this detail from a sixteenth-century Belgian tapestry.

In early times Mars may have been a god of vegetation. (Graves 1955; Humphries 1951)

MARUTS
(Also Māruts)

In the Indian *Ṛg Veda,* Maruts are wind gods, the heroic warrior sons of the storm god Rudra, who is the embodiment of wildness and unpredictability. The Maruts are companions to Indra, the king of gods. The *Ṛg Veda* refers to the Maruts as "workers of marvels" who "adorned themselves like women." (O'Flaherty *Veda* 1981)

MASHOBANA

In the Zulu epic *Emperor Shaka the Great,* Mashobana is Zwide's son-in-law, the father of Mzilikazi. (Kunene 1979)

MAS̄NAVĪ
(Also Mathnavī or Mathnawī, The Doubled One)

Mas̄navīs are narrative or didactic mystical poems of rhyming couplets, the favorite form of the Persians in the tenth century. Using the mas̄navī, Islamic poets strung together verses to form romantic and heroic narratives or long didactic allegories. Although epic poetry per se was foreign to the Arabs, the Persians perfected the rhyming couplet and employed it in extensive compositions; narrative mas̄navīs often ran into hundreds of couplets. The *Shāh-Nāmah* employs some 60,000 verses to tell its story. Mas̄navī narratives were popular in northern India, where they were recited in public places. The mas̄navī is also used by some Hindu Sūfis. (Preminger 1990)

MATIWANE

In the Zulu epic *Emperor Shaka the Great,* Matiwane is the roving ruler of the Ngwanes, who were feared and hated by many nations of the western and southern regions of Central Africa because of their sneak attacks. (Kunene 1979)

MATSYA THE FISH

In the *Purāṇas,* Matsya is the first of the "ten descents," or avatars, of the Hindu god Viṣṇu. He is rescuer of the Earth and the *Vedas.* He inhabits the cosmic ocean between creations. In the story of the great flood, Manu catches a small fish who begs to be saved, so Manu places the fish in a well. But it grows so large that he places it in the Ganges. Still it grows until it has reached a gigantic size, and Manu realizes the fish, Matsya, is a god. Matsya instructs Manu to build a boat so as to avoid the impending deluge. "Then you must take the seeds of life from everywhere," he says. When the flood comes, Manu saves himself by tying his boat to the fish's horn.

In the *Bhāgavata-Purāṇa* there is an account of the demon Hayagrīva snatching the *Vedas* from Brahmā's mouth. Viṣṇu, taking the form of a fish, returns the *Vedas* to Brahmā and slays Hayagrīva. (Dimmitt and van Buitenen 1978)

See also Flood Myths.

MATSYENDRANĀTHA

(Also Mīna-nātha, Fish Lord)

He is the legendary founder of the Natha Yogis of India, a wandering Hindu sect that also incorporates Buddhism and Hatha Yoga into its beliefs. A body of oral tradition surrounds him. According to one legend, Matsyendranātha fathers two sons, Pārosenāth and Nīmnāth, by queens of Ceylon, and these sons become leaders of the Jaina sect. According to another legend, he rescues the sacred texts from the belly of a fish. Another legend has him receiving instruction from Śiva while in the form of a fish. His disciple Gorakhnāth is credited as founder of a Hatha sect, the Kānphata Yogis. (Keith 1964)

MAUI

(Also Maui-tiki-tiki)

Polynesian, Melanesian, and Micronesian trickster god of many attributes, Maui is the hero of a cycle of myths that vary from island to island. He is usually depicted as having been abandoned as a baby, raised by sea gods, and instructed by the sky god. When he returns to earth, he tricks his brothers into revealing who his parents are. His mother is the earth goddess Mahuike, who returns to the underground at dawn. His father is the creator god. The Maoris tell how he discovers fire in the belly of the earth, where his ancestress Mahuike keeps it hidden. He steals the fire, much as Prometheus, and places it into a tree. Thereafter it has been possible to obtain fire from a tree's wood. According to an old Tahitian chant, when Ru and Hina discover the earth in the bottom of the primordial ocean, Maui sets sail in his canoes and visits each island, going all the way to the north "to flaming Hawaii." As fisherman god, he is able to fish the land from the sea and to hook the sun and regulate its movement. He is also god of the first yam harvest, having first separated earth from sky. However, in attempting to overcome death, he loses his life.

A Rarotongan legend tells of an expedition led by Maui Marumamao from the island of Raiatea in the Society Islands to the east, past Easter Island to a "land of ridges"—possibly Peru. After remaining for some time in Peru, Maui Marumamao dies and his son Kiu leads the expedition back to Polynesia. (Dixon 1964)

See also Mahuike.

MAWGOON

Mawgoon is a type of Burmese epic-ode (ca. fifteenth century) evolving from marching songs in praise of a leader. (Preminger 1990)

MBENGI

In the Zulu epic *Emperor Shaka the Great,* Mbengi is the ruler of the Abasema Langini and a relative of Shaka's mother Nandi. (Kunene 1979)

See also Nandi.

MBIKWANE

In the Zulu epic *Emperor Shaka the Great,* Mbikwane is the paternal uncle of King Dingiswayo, in the Mthethwa empire where Shaka grows to manhood. He is a highly respected political figure whom Shaka names as governor over the white coastal settlement. (Kunene 1979)

See also Dingiswayo.

MBIRE

(Also Nembire)

Hero of a local oral epic in Zimbabwe, Mbire is the founder of the realm later known as the empire of the Munhumtapa (Monomatapa), or the Mwene Matapa. According to legend, in 1325 Mbire leads his people from Lake Tanganyika to the banks of the Zambezi River. There he, or his son Mbire II, found a city called Zimbabwe, for which the modern country is named. Mbire's great-great-grandson Nyatsimba is credited historically as the first mambo, or ruler, to hold the title of Mwene Matapa (Lord of the Plundered Lands). Under him the seat of power was moved to Mount Fura on the Zambezi River. Another stage begins about 1425 when Mutoto, king of the Karanga, and his son Matope overrun the area and establish their own rule. (Davidson 1991)

See also Mwene Matapa.

MBOPHANA

In the Zulu epic *Emperor Shaka the Great,* Mbophana is the learned counselor of whom Shaka's mother Nandi says, "I fear him as I fear a snake. / Often I feel he shall bring great tears to our house / . . . He has killed the very child I loved. / Such a man is dangerous! / He kills today; he shall always thirst for more blood." Mbophana is the instrument by which Shaka is assassinated, providing a diversion by suddenly appearing to disrupt the assembly. He pretends to rebuke the northern expedition for its late return, allowing the other assassins to enter unnoticed. He is the first to stab Shaka, but in the end the brothers make him the scapegoat and order him killed. (Kunene 1979)

See also *Emperor Shaka the Great;* Nandi.

MBURU
(Monkey)

In the Nyangan *Epic of Mwindo* of the Banyanga of Zaire, Chief Mburu is one of the monkey people, who rebels against Mwindo. In another episode, Chief Mburu, of the Banamburu group (a monkey group), is caught in the snares set by one of Mwindo's trappers. In the battle of Mwindo against the Banamburu, Mwindo's dogs and his scepter defeat the Banamburu. (Biebuyck 1978)

MEDB
(Drunken Woman)

Medb is the legendary Celtic queen of Connacht (Connaught), a warrior woman and daughter of the king of all Ireland; she is depicted as a harridan. In the eighth-century Irish epic tale *Taín Bó Cúailnge* from the *Ulster Cycle,* Queen Medb is in the forefront of the battle against the men of Ulster. In the famous "pillow talk" scene of Medb and her husband Ailill, the couple argues about whose wealth is greater, and this leads to her decision to obtain the Brown Bull of Cúailnge at all cost. She asks Dare, son of Fiachna, to give her the bull in exchange for land, a chariot, and her own favors in bed. After her negotiations fail, she decides to steal the bull. She needs the help of the mighty hero Fergus, so she grants him special favors, which Ailill overlooks until he can ignore them no longer. One day, finding her bathing in Fergus's presence, Ailill orders his man to throw the javelin, killing Fergus.

In the tale of *Bricriu's Feast,* Queen Medb is asked to judge which is the best warrior, Cú Chulainn, Conall, or Lóegure. She declares that Cú Chulainn is the best, but when he beats her during the battles for the Brown Bull, she initiates the children of Calatin into her service. They slay him on her behalf.

In the story of "The Drunkenness of the Ulstermen," she entertains the Ulstermen while sitting between Ailill and her lover Curoi mac Deare; the latter convinces her to kill her guests. Only Ailill and Cú Chulainn's help allows the Ulstermen to escape annihilation. (Gantz 1976; Jackson, K. 1971; Kinsella 1969; Rutherford 1987)

See also *The Cattle Raid of Cooley;* Cú Chulainn; *Ulster Cycle.*

MEDEA

In Greek mythology, in the legend of the Argonauts, Medea is the enchantress, a daughter of King Aeetes of Colchis and niece of Circe, who helps Jason obtain the Golden Fleece from her father. She has magical powers and the gift of prophecy. She causes the death of Jason's betrothed, Glauce, and marries him herself. She restores Jason's aged father, Aeson, to health. When Jason abandons her, she kills their two children, Mermerus and Pheres, then flees to Athens, where she marries King Aegeus. Later she leaves him and returns home. (Graves 1955)

See also Argonauts; Jason.

MELEAGER

In Greek mythology, in the legend of the Argonauts, Meleager is the son of Calydon's King Oeneus and Queen Althea, an Argonaut, and the main hero in the Calydonian boar hunt. In the *Iliad,* it is related that Meleager's father neglects to sacrifice to Artemis, who in retaliation sends a wild boar to ravage the country. Meleager gathers a band of men including the Curetes, warriors from a neighboring country, and hunts the creature down. Meleager kills the animal with his own hands and gives the head to Atalanta, with whom he is in love. This causes an argument over the spoils, which Meleager finally wins, after repulsing the Curetes and killing his own uncles, Plexippus and Toxeus, Althea's brothers. Althea then burns the log whose span of life is the same as Meleager's, thus bringing about her son's death. This episode does not appear in the *Iliad,* which only relates that Meleager has died before the Trojan War begins. (Graves 1955)

See also Argonauts.

MELQART

(Also Malku, Melkarth, Melkart, and Tyrian Baal)

Melqart was a Phoenician deity of Tyre and its colonies Carthage and Cádiz (Spain). He was identified also with the Babylonian god of the underworld, Nergal, as well as with the Carthaginian god Baal Hammon (Baal Amon). (Ben Khader and Soren 1987)

MELUSINE

In French folklore, Melusine is the daughter of Albanian king Elinas and the fairy Pressine; she is the wife of Raymondin of Poitiers and chatelaine of the castle of Lusignan. She imprisons her cruel father in a mountain, and as punishment she is transformed into a half-serpent each Saturday. She exacts a promise from Raymondin that he will never look at her on Saturday. When he breaks his promise, she disappears forever. (Siepmann 1987)

MEMNON

In Greek mythology, Memnon is the king of the Ethiopians, son of Tithonus and Eos, the grandson of Laomedon, and legendary king of Troy. After the death of Trojan warrior Hektor, he takes 10,000 troops to Troy to assist his uncle Priam. After he slays Nestor's son Antilochus, Nestor challenges him to single combat, but Memnon refuses in deference to Nestor's age. Achilles takes up the challenge in Nestor's place and kills Memnon. (Graves 1955)

See also Achilles; Hektor; Menelaus; Nestor; Priam.

THE MEMORIAL FEAST FOR KÖKÖTÖY KHAN

This is a medieval Kirghiz epic from Central Asia. (Hatto 1964)

MENELAUS

In Greek mythology, Menelaus is the king of Sparta, brother of Agamemnon, and the husband of Helen, whose abduction by Paris causes the Trojan War. After the war, according to Euripides, Menelaus must travel to Egypt to find Helen, who has been held there. He returns with her to Sparta. He appears in the *Iliad* and the *Aeneid.* (Graves 1955)

See also Agamemnon; Helen; *Iliad.*

MĒNESS

(Also Mẹnuo and Messechina)

In Baltic religion, Mēness is the Latvian god of the moon. In Lithuanian religion, the god is Menulis (Mẹnuo), a provider of health, beauty, and youth. It is believed that "a man born on the new moon will remain his entire life of youthful appearance, be handsome, not age quickly. . . ." However, he will be "weak and anxious, fearful of the 'evil eye.'"

In Bulgaria, the moon is Messechina and is generally feminine. Wet-nurse witches (a combination of mother and daughter or mother-in-law and daughter-in-law) can bring down the moon, which comes in the form of a cow. The witches milk it, using the milk for witchcraft, and a blood-red stain appears in the sky. Usually this occurs in March. When the moon returns to Heaven, it bellows like a cow. The myth is preserved in a folk song: "They pulled the moon down, / Turned it into a white cow / And got fresh milk from it." (Georgieva 1985; Greimas 1992)

MENTOR

In Greek legend, Mentor is a loyal old Ithacan friend and adviser of Odysseus. In the *Odyssey* (xvii), Odysseus makes him guardian of his household and Telemachos's teacher. Earlier in the *Odyssey* (iii), Mentor is a steward whose identity Athena assumes in order to act as Telemachos's guide. Mentor is also the name of a son of Herakles. (Lattimore 1967)

See also Odysseus; *Odyssey;* Telemachos.

MERLIN

In Arthurian legend, Merlin is the magician, enchanter, and prophet who plays an important role throughout the cycle. His character is probably based on the sixth-century Celtic bard Myrrdn (Myrddin). The first full-blown treatment of Merlin is found in Geoffrey of Monomouth's *Libellus Merlini* (Little Red Book of Merlin, ca. 1135), in which, in the capacity of a druid, he moves the stones of Stonehenge from Ireland to England's Salisbury Plain. Monmouth is also responsible for bringing to light the most important of Merlin's legends, in which Merlin arranges for Uther Pendragon to go to Igraine disguised as her husband. The result of that encounter is Arthur's conception. Merlin's capacities as a magician are explored in Wace's *Roman de Brut* (1155), and he plays a major role in Arthur's attaining the throne in Malory's *Morte d'Arthur.* (Barber 1961)

See also Arthurian Legend.

MICTLANTECUHTLI

He is the Aztec god of the dead, located in the Underworld. "Mictlan" is the Aztec name for underworld. (Bierhorst 1989)

MILITSA, TSARITSA

In the Yugoslavian epic cycle *The Battle of Kosovo,* Tsaritsa Militsa is the wife of Tsar Lazar, who is killed fighting the Turks. She plays a leading role in the poems "Tsar Lazar and Tsaritsa Militsa" and "Tsaritsa Militsa and Vladeta the Voyvoda." (Matthias and Vučković 1987; Miletich 1990)

See also *The Battle of Kosovo.*

MILOSH OBILICH, CAPTAIN

Milosh is the Serbian hero of the Yugoslavian epic cycle *The Battle of Kosovo,* in which the Serbs are soundly defeated by the Turks and the heroes are slain. He is the subject of one of the longest bugarštica in the cycle, in which he gains access to the Turkish camp by pretending to be a deserter. He manages to stab Sultan Murad, but the sultan's son quickly rallies the Turks and demolishes the Serbian forces. (Matthias and Vučković 1987; Miletich 1990)

See also *The Battle of Kosovo.*

MIMAMEIĐR

In an Old Norse myth in the *Poetic Edda,* Mimameiđr is used in "The Lay of Svipdag" as another name for Yggdrasill, the world tree. (Hollander *Edda* 1990)

See also *Edda, Poetic.*

MÍMIR

In Old Norse mythology, Mímir is the smith god, wisest of the gods of Aesir and the mentor of Siegfried, who instructs him in his craft. He appears chiefly in the "Lay of Sigrdrífa" in the *Poetic Edda.* (Hollander *Edda* 1990)

See also *Edda, Poetic.*

MINERVA

Minerva is the Roman goddess of handicrafts. (Graves 1955)
See also Athena.

MIORITA

("The Lambkin")

This Rumanian poem is probably a fragment of a much longer, ancient epic, now lost. The poet Vasile Alecsandri recorded it from the performances of street minstrels and included it in a collection of ballads published in 1853. The ancestral poem depicts three shepherds wandering the Rumanian pastures when they encounter one another. One of them, a Moldavian, not only has a fine flock of sheep, but trained dogs and horses as well. The other two, a Vrancean and a Transylvanian, plot to kill the wealthy shepherd and divide his stock between them. But the Moldavian has one other thing the others do not: a magical talking lamb with golden fleece, Miorita, which warns its master to turn his flock toward the safety of the dark wood. However, the shepherd, sensing the inevitability of his death, asks the lambkin to tell his murderers that he wishes to be buried among his flock. (Preminger 1990)

MITRA-VARUṆA

Mitra-Varuṇa is an Indian Hindu composite god, combining the worldly Mitra ("the friend") and the spiritual Varuṇa ("All-enveloping"), a Vedic god who despises falsehood and inflicts disease, particularly dropsy, on sinners. Together they represent the dualities of fire/water and earthly/spiritual power. Later, Mitra is a sage, son of Vasiṣṭha, and Varuṇa is the god of the waters and guardian of the western quarter. (O'Flaherty 1975)

MIZHIMO

(Also the Great Mizhimo)

Among the Ila-speaking peoples of what is now Zambia in west-central Africa, Mizhimo is above all the individual, family, and village chief's divinities. It is the mizhimo's function to care for the common interests of the communes to which they belong. Within the family the ghosts of one's remote ancestors eventually cease to be worshiped or regarded, but the respect to the communal divinity continues. The communal divinities, unlike other divinities, are never reincarnated, but remain in the spirit world forever. The Ba-ila people also honor the mizhimo, but they have three categories of mizhimos: genii, divinities, and demigods. (Smith and Dale 1968)

MKHABAYI

In the Zulu epic *Emperor Shaka the Great,* Mkhabayi is the daughter of King Jama and the sister of King Senzangakhona. She is a priestess, the most influential figure in Zululand. When Jama dies, she acts as regent until her brother comes of age. She is Shaka's paternal aunt. Eventually she acts in collusion with Shaka's brothers to assassinate him. (Kunene 1979)

See also *Emperor Shaka the Great;* Senzangakhona.

MKHABI

In the Zulu epic *Emperor Shaka the Great,* Mkhabi is the main and favorite wife of Shaka's father, Senzangakhona. She convinces her husband to turn out Nandi and her children so that her own son will inherit the throne. (Kunene 1979)

See also *Emperor Shaka the Great.*

MOCEDADES DE RODRIGO

This thirteenth-century Spanish epic depicts the Cid, hero of *Poema del Cid,* as a rash, fiery youth. This depiction of the hero Rodrigo Díaz de Vivar (Bivar) is the one that captured the romantic imagination of later balladeers and playwrights. (Merwin 1962)

MOELO

Among the Bushongo and related tribes of the African Congo, Moelo is one of twin grandsons of two very old people who lived at the very beginning of the tribal history. This old couple had never had children, but one day the sky opens up and a man of white color comes toward them, calling himself Bomazi, the Lord, and promises them the birth of a child. In spite of their ages, a daughter is born to them. Bomazi takes the girl for his wife, and the couple has five children, all of whom become chiefs of their own tribes. The first two born are the twins Woto and Moelo. When they are grown, Woto has three wives, but when he comes home one day, he finds Moelo's son with one of his wives. The boy begs his uncle's forgiveness for committing incest, but soon Woto finds the boy with his other two wives. Woto becomes so distraught that he leaves and wanders in the forest, becoming in time the father of all the Bushongo. (Parrinder 1982)

MOKE MUSSA AND MOKE DANTUNAM

This Malinke folk epic of West Africa dating from the Middle Ages was recounted from the griot Babu Conde by the Guinean Camara Laye in 1974.

Moke is the name of the mother of the two characters. Even today, the Malinke continue the custom of placing the mother's name first. Moke Mussa and Moke Dantunam are two hunters from Damissa Ulambama who hear of a buffalo that is terrorizing the kingdom of Do, and they decide to kill it.

The adventurers do not yet know that the buffalo is the ancestral totem (tana) of the king's sister, Do-Kamissa. When her father died, her brother Do-Samo, the new king, deprived her of her rightful inheritance because she is a woman. Although she left Dafolo, the capital city, and founded a new village some kilometers away, she has been bent on revenge ever since. Her only inheritance is the magical powers of her ancestor, so she uses these to transform herself into a buffalo, ravaging the rice fields and scouring the 12 villages of Do.

Before setting out on their adventure, Mussa and Dantunam consult a soothsayer, who assures them of victory provided they follow his advice. They are to pay no heed to calls people make to them along the way, they are to win the good graces of an old woman whom they encounter, and after their victory, they are to choose the ugliest wife they are offered.

The warriors have many adventures along the way until one day they come upon a ragged old woman. Mussa instructs his younger brother to tend to her while he goes on into Dafolo to announce their arrival. After Dantunam feeds her, the old woman reveals herself as Do-Kamissa and admits to being the buffalo of Do as well. She has a protégée in the city, an ugly girl named Sogolon Conde, whom she wants Dantunam to marry. After Dantunam promises to marry the girl, she gives him three talismans: a distaff, a flat stone, and an egg. With these, she tells him, he will be able to kill the buffalo.

Dantunam and Mussa meet again and continue on their way. After a few more encounters, they finally meet the buffalo, who is so ferocious that Mussa runs away. Dantunam tries to kill it with his bow and arrows, but when that fails he throws his magic distaff at the advancing beast. Immediately a forest of bamboo springs up, shielding him temporarily from the buffalo so that he can escape.

Meanwhile, Mussa has climbed a tree. He feels shame for his cowardice, but he continues to watch the drama in safety. As the buffalo again gains on Dantunam, he throws his flat rock, which transforms the plain into a labyrinth of stones through which the buffalo must walk slowly. Dantunam continues to run, "hurtling along like a meteor." As the buffalo again approaches, he throws the egg, and a vast marsh appears, in which the buffalo gets mired. Dantunam is able to slay the bull with his bow and arrows. After the kill, he blows a victory signal on his hunter's whistle, and Mussa appears. They cut off the buffalo's tail and stride off to Dafolo to present it to the king. A great celebration is held, and the king offers Moke Dantunam his choice of beautiful girls as a reward.

Dantunam walks down the line of girls all vying for his attention, but a hawk dives three times into the back of the crowd. Dantunam knows this is a sign. He parts the crowd and finds a very ugly, hunchbacked girl named Sologon; remembering his promise to Do-Kamissa, he chooses her. When he shows the king the girl he has chosen, he is met with peals of laughter, "crackling like a prairie conflagration." Insulted, the three leave.

They travel until nightfall, at which time Dantunam offers Mussa, as the elder brother, the first chance at Sologon. But when Sologon feels Mussa's hands upon her, she calls up her double, a porcupine, which protects her even from Mussa's double, which he calls up as well. At dawn, "unstrung by his desire," he angrily returns to Dantunam and tells him, "It is up to you. . . ." That night Dantunam thinks, "I shall tell her that she no longer belongs to herself. . . ." But when he tries to enter Sologon's hut, a blackness descends and he is struck motionless. He falls into a deep sleep that lasts until morning. The two brothers realize that by listening to Do-Kamissa, they have made a great mistake that they will have to live with. (Laye 1984)

MOKṢADHARMA

This chapter (book 12) in the *Mahābhārata* is a philosophical synthesis of older beliefs with newer Aryan beliefs. Four philosophical schools are mentioned: Sāṃkhya-Yoga, Pāñcarātra, the Vedas, and Pāśupata. (Buck 1981)

MOON BONE

This song cycle of the Mandjikai and Wanguri Sandfly clan of Australian Aborigines is made up of 13 songs that form a nonsecret but sacred cycle celebrating the death and rebirth of the moon, seen as a reflection of the cyclical process of all things. Moon is an ancestral man who lives near the clay-pan of the Moonlight at the Place of the Dugong by Arnhem Bay. After his death, he descends into the sea, where his bones become nautilus shell. Ever since, Moon repeats his death, casting away his bone and being reborn. (Finnegan 1978; Wilde et al. 1991)

MOPUS

In Greek mythology, Mopus is the name of two soothsayers. Mopus is the name of an Argonaut, a Lapith (a northern mountain people) from Thessaly, who participates in the Calydonian boar hunt and takes part in the battle of the centaurs and the Lapithae. He dies in Libya of snakebite. Mopus is also the name of the son of Carian King Rhacues and Queen Manto, daughter of the famous prophet Tiresias. This Mopus, who may have been a historical person, is associated with the founding of oracles in Asia Minor. (Graves 1955)

MORDRED, SIR

(Also Medrawd and Medraut)

One of the knights of the Round Table in Arthurian legend, Mordred is the betrayer of Arthur. The *Annales Cambriae* (ca. 955) mentions that in the Battle of Camlan (537) a historical Arthur and Medraut lost their lives. In the thirteenth-century *Mabinogion* story entitled "The Dream of Rhonabwy," Mordred appears as Medrawd and is named as Arthur's nephew. In Malory's *Morte d'Arthur,* Mordred is the bastard son of King Arthur and Queen Margawse. He usurps the throne during his father's absence and tries to seduce Guinevere to be his wife. Arthur returns to defend his throne, and each man deals the other a fatal blow. (Barber 1961)

See also Arthurian Legend.

MORGAN LE FAY

(Also Fata Morgana and Mórrígan)

Sorceress, enchantress, and antagonist of Arthurian legend, she is sometimes portrayed as King Arthur's sister, and other times as his half sister. Geoffrey of Monmouth's *Vita Merlini* (ca. 1150) calls her the ruler of the island of Avalon, where Arthur is sent to be healed from near-fatal wounds. She acquired her magic skills from Merlin and from books. In the *Vulgate Cycle* (thirteenth century), she is responsible for stirring up trouble between Arthur and Guinevere. (Barber 1961; Stone, B. 1974)

See also Arthurian Legend; Mórrígan; *Sir Gawain and the Green Knight.*

MORKINSKINNA

This Icelandic saga (ca. 1220) relates a number of tales involving poets and adventurers who visit the courts of Scandinavia. It deals particularly with the kings of Norway for a period of 130 years, beginning in 1147. (Jones, G. 1990)

MORNA

Morna ia a melancholy form of story/song and dance, based on the Portuguese fado, that is performed by the inhabitants of the Cape Verde Islands off the coast of West Africa. The natives are considered among the most poetic of all Africa, and their stoic but nostalgic poetry reflects their geographical, tropical isolation: "The demand at every hour / To go away is brought to us by the sea. / The despairing hope for the long journey / And yet to be always forced to stay." (Dathorne 1975)

MÓRRÍGAN

(Also Morgan le Fay)

Mórrígan is one of three Celtic war goddesses, queen of demons. With Badb and Macha, the raven and frenzy, she can influence the outcome of a battle. She is the consort of the Irish god Dagda. (Markdale 1986)

See also Morgan le Fay.

MORTE D'ARTHUR

This is the first prose account (1470) in modern English of the Arthurian legend, by Thomas Malory, who based his version on French tales. (Siepmann 1987)

See also Arthurian Legend.

MOSES

Old Testament leader and lawgiver, Moses is born of a Hebrew woman who places him in a basket of reeds in the Nile when the pharaoh decrees that all Hebrew boy babies must be killed. He is found by a daughter of the pharaoh and reared in the harem. From a burning bush the voice of God calls Moses to lead his people out of bondage in Egypt. According to Jewish legend, when Moses balks at doing God's bidding, the Lord first gives him a leprous hand, then heals it. He turns his rod into a serpent; He makes blood flow from a rock. For seven days He tries to persuade Moses. Moses tells God to send a great scholar instead, but finally he is convinced that scholars of the future will depend on him for interpreting the Torah. But for his long hesitation to do God's bidding, God punishes him: "It was appointed that thou should be priest and Aaron should be Levite. Because thou hast refused to execute My will, thou shalt be the Levite and Aaron shall be priest." Moses is not made a Levite, but his descendants are. He is hard of hearing, but as punishment, God does not heal him. Moses goes to the pharaoh to receive permission to take the children of Israel out of Egypt. When the pharaoh refuses Moses's request to leave, nine plagues are visited upon the land. Eventually the people of Egypt are anxious for the Israelites to leave, and a new feast is celebrated: the Feast of the Passover (ca. 1290 B.C.). According to the Book of Exodus, some 600,000 men (not including women and children) begin the trip. At the Red Sea, now pursued by the pharaoh's forces, the people are momentarily stopped until God parts the Red Sea, allowing them to cross safely. Moses escorts the people of Israel to Sinai and through 40 years of desert wandering. At Mount Sinai, God establishes his covenant with the people and gives Moses his law-code for Israel: the Ten Commandments. (Exodus 2 to Deuteronomy 34; Ginzberg 1992)

See also Aaron; Abandonment; Sargon of Akkad.

MOT

Ancient West Semitic god of the dead and sterility, Mot is the master of barren places. He is the favorite son of El and the natural enemy of Baal, the god of fertility, spring, and harvest. Mot and Baal engage in a yearly battle in which Baal is inevitably slain. However, Mot is also killed annually by Baal's sister Anath, which brings about Baal's resurrection. (Pritchard 1973)

See also *Baal Epic.*

MPANE

In the Zulu epic *Emperor Shaka the Great,* Mpane is Shaka's brother, who later becomes king after the death of Dingane. The present Zulu royal house is composed mainly of his descendants. (Kunene 1979)

See also Dingane; *Emperor Shaka the Great.*

MSHWESHWE
(Also Moshoeshoe)

In the Zulu epic *Emperor Shaka the Great,* Mshweshwe is king of the Basothos. He is a great nation-builder, the founder of the Sotho nation, and the subject of local epics celebrating him. In book 10 of the Shaka epic, Mshweshwe, whose people have been terrorized by the guerrilla raids of Matiwane, asks Shaka for help. Shaka dispatches an army led by General Mdlaka, which destroys Matiwane once and for all. Mshweshwe is one of Shaka's staunchest allies. (Kunene 1979)

See also *Emperor Shaka the Great.*

MSIRE

See *Mwindo Epic.*

MTHANIYA

In the Zulu epic *Emperor Shaka the Great,* Mthaniya is Shaka's paternal grandmother and the wife of King Jama. (Kunene 1979)

See also *Emperor Shaka the Great.*

MTORO BIN MWINYI BAKARI, BWANA

In the late nineteenth century, with the help of some other scribes, this Swahili master of prose, a Zaramo of Bagamoyo, wrote down the ancient oral traditions, customs, and wisdom of his people in a document called the *Desturi za Waswahili* (Customs of the Swahili People). (Allen 1981)

See also *Desturi za Waswahili.*

MUBILA
(Also *Mubela)*

Mubila is an epic of the Lega-speaking people of central Africa. Mubila is a typical epic hero, able to speak from his mother's womb. When he is born, he possesses many fantastic powers, enabling him to triumph in battle over the supernatural enemies of his village. (Westley *RAL* 1991)

MUCIUS

***See** Scaevola, Gaius Mucius.*

MUDANG

Mudang is the Korean word for shamaness. Mudangs are priestesses who use magic to heal, assist in childbirth, foretell the future, repel bad spirits, or assist the dead in making the transition. Mudangs often dance and sing during a ritual designed to produce a specific end. Their male counterparts become singers of p'ansori, which is an opera or epic performed by a single singer. (Reischauer and Fairbank 1960)

MUDLI

In the Zulu epic *Emperor Shaka the Great,* Mudli is Shaka's granduncle, who saves the child Shaka from death by his father.

See also Abandonment; *Emperor Shaka the Great.*

MUGODO

In the Bantu Lovedu myth of *Mujaji the Rain Queen,* Mugodo is the son of a great king of the Transvaal who treats his son like an outcast in public while secretly instructing him in the magic of rain charms. When it is time for Mugodo to assume the throne, the people have no respect for him because of his public treatment, and an era of rule by queens begins. Mugodo goes to one of his daughters, Mujaji, and convinces her to give birth to an heir to the throne. She understands that Mugodo intends to be the father, and she accepts his will. Mujaji becomes the first queen and learns the secrets of rainmaking from her father. Her daughter, Mujaji II, inherits the throne from her mother. (Parrinder 1982)

See also Muhale; *Mujaji the Rain Queen.*

MUHALE

In the Bantu Lovedu myth of *Mujaji the Rain Queen,* Muhale is the illegitimate son of Zimbabwe king Mambo's unnamed daughter. To avoid having to reveal Muhale's father, his daughter steals the rain charms and the secret beads and flees south with her son, where they found the Lovedu tribe. Muhale becomes the first king; he invites his northern relatives down to help clear the timber and teaches his people the use of fire. (Parrinder 1982)

See also Mugodo; *Mujaji the Rain Queen.*

MUHAMADI

A Swahili epic cycle of 6,280 four-line stanzas, *Muhamadi* recounts the life of Muḥammad for the Bantu people. It is the longest written epic that has been preserved in any African language. (Westley *RAL* 1991)

MUJAJI THE RAIN QUEEN

Semimythical queen of the Bantu Lovedu tribe of Zimbabwe, Mujaji is the subject of an oral tradition. The first Mujaji, the daughter of Mugodo, becomes the first ruling queen of the tribe and is revered by other tribes as the queen of the rainmakers. By her father, she has a daughter, Mujaji II, who is not so successful as a ruler. Her land is invaded by both Zulus and Europeans. She goes into hiding and presents a distant half sister as "She Who Must Be Obeyed." Eventually she takes her own life by swallowing poison. She is replaced by Mujaji III and then by Mujaji IV (the present queen; considered more of a rainmaker than a monarch). She is called "Transformer of Clouds," and works with a rain-doctor who tries to find the cause of drought. She can only control rain by agreement with her ancestors, whose skins are believed to be the most important ingredient in her rain pots. (Parrinder 1982)

See also Mugodo; Muhale.

MUMMU

In the Babylonian creation epic *Enuma Elish* (ca. 1894 B.C.–ca. 1595 B.C.), Mummu is one of the offspring of Apsu, fresh underground water, and Tiamat, seawater. As the "original form," Mummu acts as Apsu's page and encourages Apsu in his plan to do away with all the gods when their dancing begins to disturb Tiamat's insides. When Apsu's plan fails and Ea kills Apsu, Ea places Mummu in captivity, held by a nose rope. (Sproul 1991)

See also Apsu; *Enuma Elish, Epic of;* Tiamat.

MUONG

The Muong are a people of North Vietnam whose legendary ancestors are thought to be Au Co and her 50 sons who returned to the mountains to live. (Terada 1989)

See also *Lac Long Quang and Au Co.*

MURAD I

Murad I (ca. 1326–1389) was an Ottoman sultan from 1360 to 1389 who figures in the Serbian epic *The Battle of Kosovo.* He first expanded the Ottoman empire into the Balkans and Anatolia, and in the 1380s he expanded westward again, conducting offenses into Albania, Bosnia, and Eperus. In 1388 a coalition of Bosnians and Serbians held the Ottomans back at Plocnick, but in 1389 Murad defeated them at the Battle of Kosovo. However, he was mortally wounded and died on the battlefield. Another version of his death is celebrated in a bugarštica about Captain Milosh. (Matthias and Vučković 1987; Miletich 1990)

See also *The Battle of Kosovo;* Milosh Obilich, Captain.

MURUGAṈ

Murugaṉ is the chief Dravidian deity of the ancient Tamils of southern India. Originally a fertility god, he is the god of youth and beauty, the son of Koṟṟavai, and later associated with the northern Indian war god Skanda. He appears in the *Manimekhalaï.* (Shattan 1989)

MUSICH STEFAN

Musich is a Serbian hero killed by Turks in *The Battle of Kosovo* and the subject of a poem that bears his name in the epic cycle. When the Turks come, Musich's wife begs his servant Vaistina not to wake him, fearing that he will be killed if he joins in the battle, but Vaistina quotes his master: "Whoever is a Serb, of Serbian blood, / Whoever shares with me this heritage, / And he comes not to fight at Kosovo, / May he never have the progeny / His heart desires. . . ." (Matthias and Vučković 1987; Miletich 1990)

See also *The Battle of Kosovo.*

MUSOKA

In the Nyanga epic *Mwindo,* Musoka is a snake, junior sister of the water serpent Mukiti, so long that people ride on her back to cross rivers. She blocks Mwindo's road to Iyangura. (Biebuyck 1978)

See also *Mwindo, Epic of.*

MVET

(Also *Le Mvett)*

This is the best-known Cameroon epic of the Fang. The mvet, an idiochord zither, is essential to epic performances in Gabon, Cameroon, and Guinea. This mvet epic describes a battle between the Oku Oveng Ndouma Obame and the Engong Engouang Ondo. (Abrahams 1983; Tala 1984; Westley *RAL* 1991)

MWENE MATAPA

(Also Monomotapa and Munhumtapa)

A title meaning Ravager of the Lands, it was used by kings of the Matapa empire of Great Zimbabwe. Oral tradition names Mbire as the fourteenth-century founder of the empire, although his great-great-grandson Nyatsimba was the first to unite the tribe and use the name. (Davidson 1991)

See also Mbire.

MWINDO, EPIC OF

(Also *Mwendo* and *Msire)*

This Nyanga oral epic of the Banyanga of eastern Zaire concerns one of the most successful nation-builders in central Africa. Many versions of the epic exist, with the following central features.

Long ago, a chief named Shemwindo builds a village called Tubondo in the state of Ihimbi. He has one sister named Iyangura. Shemwindo marries two (in some versions, seven) wives, one of whom is Iyangura. After he marries, he calls all his people together and proclaims that the wife who bears a male child will be killed. He commands his wives to give birth only to females. Then he "throws himself hurriedly into the houses of the wives / then launches the sperm where his wives are." Among his wives is a beloved one and a despised one. The despised one has her house built on the garbage heap, while his other wife or wives are in the clearing.

The beloved wife Iyangura gives birth to a son through the palm of her hand. The baby has special physical attributes at birth that set him apart from the rest of the people: He speaks and walks from the moment of birth. He carries a set of magic objects. Among them are a shoulder bag that contains a rope or a magic medicine, a conga-scepter, a billhook, an adze, and an ax. The bag permits him to store people, trees, and tools. The rope is a means by which he can communicate with his paternal aunt. The conga-scepter destroys enemies, restores people to life, and allows him to fly. The billhook clears the forest and keeps enemies in check, while the ax fells trees and the adze harvests honey. Mwindo himself is small and never destined to be a powerful fighter; he must depend upon his magical objects. Mwindo's mother also bears a daughter, Nyamitondo Mwindo.

The despised wife also bears a son and daughter. The king orders that his son Mwindo be thrown into a grave, but during the night, the boy emerges and sleeps on his father's hearth. The people are astounded, and the king decrees that his son will not be buried again.

Mwindo's sister Nyamitondo is given in marriage to Lightning, who takes her to his village in the air and teaches her to cultivate. She returns to earth for a visit and shows Mwindo how to cultivate bananas. Before she leaves to rejoin her husband, the two find an egg, which they place in a hen's nest.

A bird hatches from the egg, and Mwindo cares for it. As the bird grows, it begins to devour goats and chickens, making the people very angry. Mwindo climbs up to the sky through a hollow tree to ask Lightning's advice. His sister returns to earth with him bearing weapons supplied by Lightning, but they discover that the bird has eaten all the people. The bird even swallows Nyamitondo, but she cuts her way out. Mwindo and his sister cut the bird's heart open, and all the people of the village pour out, including a young man, Beautiful-One, who dances for the crowd. In gratitude for Lightning's help, King Shemwindo gives his daughter two maidens for her husband, who comes to take her back into the air.

The king decrees that all people will hereafter dance with buffalo tails as scepters, so Mwindo sets out to get buffalo tails for his people from his friend, the chief of Buffalo. While he is obtaining the tails, he also buys two hunting dogs, Ndorobiro and Ngonde, for his Pygmy, Shekaruru. Upon his return, dances are held in honor of the dogs.

The Pygmy sets out on a hunting trip with the dogs and meets Hawk, who is being eaten by red ants. He saves Hawk, who promises to help him in return. The Pygmy kills a wild pig and takes it back home where, as first kill of the dogs, it is eaten ceremoniously by Mwindo, Shekaruru, and the dogs.

The next day the Pygmy leaves for his second hunt. He meets a herd of warthogs, who chase him up a tree. Hawk rescues him and flies him back to his village, where Mwindo rewards Hawk with chickens.

The other chiefs grow jealous of Mwindo, even though he has provided them with buffalo tails. Chief Itewa plots war against Mwindo, who learns of the plan and warns his people to be ready. At the first encounter, Mwindo confronts Itewa with his scepter, but his people, who have no weapons, are annihilated. Itewa holds a celebration, while Mwindo plots revenge. He goes to Itewa's village, throws his scepter on the ground, and destroys the whole village.

When he returns to his own destroyed village, Mwindo provides food for his dogs with his scepter. He throws his scepter to the ground, and immediately his people come to life and the houses rebuild themselves.

Mwindo tells his people he has decided to visit God. He takes his scepter and billhook knife and enters the underground through a kikoka fern. At a wading place, he meets Kahindo, daughter of the fire god Nyamurairi. Her body is covered with scabs, which she asks him to clean. Mwindo heals her, then faints; when he is revived, she warns him against the trickery of her father.

He enters the fire god's village and refuses the god's invitation to bathe in the water, which is in fact beer. He refuses to eat banana paste with frogs, which are really the fire god's counselors. Mwindo spends each night with Kahindo, and each day he goes forth and is tested with a new trick by her father. At length, he returns home through the fern, having given Kahindo a maidservant as a farewell gift. In honor of his return home, his father provides all the bachelors with wives and gives Mwindo nine women.

Meanwhile, a young man goes into the forest to check on his traps and arrives at the village of the dragon-ogre Kirimu, where he meets Kirimu's daughter Ukano. Kirimu orders the young man to sing and play the zanza all night as the price for his daughter. But the young man falls asleep during the night, and Kirimu kills him.

The young man's brother comes in search of him, taking along Mwindo's dogs. He meets Ukano and decides to play the zanza all night without falling asleep. In the morning, Kirimu is still sleeping, so the brother lets the dogs loose, and they kill Kirimu. The brother forces Ukano to tell him where his brother's body has been thrown. He finds his brother's skull and heats a grub from it on a potsherd. The young man returns to life, arising from the grub.

The brother sets up animal snares in which the mburu monkey chief becomes trapped. The brother carries the mburu back to the village. When the other mburus arrive in the village, the brother, who is revealed as Mwindo, and his dogs kill the mburus. Mwindo points his scepter to the sky and destroys the mburu village.

The Pygmy asks Mwindo's permission to hunt with the dogs. While he is hunting, he meets Nyamwanda, wife of the god Muisa. "She carries a pregnancy the size of a house." When he strikes her on the belly, stones pour forth, and she changes into a beautiful woman. She gives him a bark cloth and a whistle that will make him famous. The Pygmy continues on to a village where the chief's son has just died. Shekaruru awakens the dead youth, heals him, and brings him outside. The chief rewards him with presents and a maiden, and the Pygmy gives the chief his own son in return.

The Pygmy returns to Mwindo's village, where his kinsmen demand that he share his gifts. He gives them the whistle, thus giving away his power to bring people back to life. Mwindo takes the maiden for himself.

Shekaruru the Pygmy goes to set traps, arriving at the village of the specter Mpaca while she is gone. He places glue on Mpaca's drying rack and dozes off. When Mpaca arrives home, she plants nails in the Pygmy but gets stuck by the glue, and the Pygmy is able to escape back to Mwindo's village. He goes hunting with Mwindo's dogs again, arriving at the village of Shakwece, who is angry because one of his wives has burned his dog Ringe. He plans a test to determine the guilty one. He places a vine across the pool and demands that each wife walk it. The despised wife crosses the pool easily, but the beloved wife, carrying his child, drowns. Shakwece refuses to save the child. The Pygmy leaves. The dogs kill 25 baboons, and they all return to Mwindo's village.

The Pygmy presents the baboons to Mwindo, who gives him a wife in exchange. Mwindo's father calls the people together and proclaims that henceforth Mwindo will be their king. He gives his son seven wives and the robes of office. The village drums beat in celebration, and Mwindo lives in glory from that time onward. (Abrahams 1983; Biebuyck 1978; Biebuyck and Mateene 1969; Okpewho 1992)

See also Bisheria; Buriru; Hawk; Kahindo; Musoka.

MYTH

A myth is a traditional legend involving figures on the supernatural, or divine, plane. It serves to explain a group's beliefs, social practices, or the origin of the world order in general. Mythological themes often have to do with the origin of the universe and the creation of man, conflicts between supernatural forces of good and evil, and the resultant social order established on earth.

MYTHICAL CYCLE

This series of sagas in Old Gaelic are extant in medieval Irish manuscripts, but date from much earlier times and originally were possibly recited entirely in verse. The stories include *The Wooing of Étaín, The Nurture of the Houses of the Two Milk-Vessels, The Battle of Moytura,* and others, tales of heroes of the race called Túatha Dé Danann. (Evans-Wentz 1990; Gantz 1976)

See also Túatha Dé Danann; *The Wooing of Étaín.*

MZILIKAZI

(Also Moselekatse, Umziligazi, and Silkoats)

Mzilikazi is the subject of an oral tradition among the Kumalos of East Africa. Mzilikazi grew up in the Swaziland court of his maternal grandfather, Nguni king Zwide. The king mistrusted Mzilikazi's father and had him killed, making Mzilikazi chief in his stead. During a Nguni war with Shaka, Mzilikazi defected and took his army with him. But in a few years, he broke away from Shaka's army to found the Ndebele, or Matabele, kingdom in Zimbabwe. He took 300 followers and left Zululand for the Transvaal (ca. 1821–1823), naming his people the Ndebele or Matabele. In the next 12 years, his empire increased to 15,000 or 20,000 people. He organized a caste system, making his original Nguni followers the upper caste, the Sotho the middle class, and the Shona the lowest caste. He was able to repel Boer incursions and conclude a peace treaty with the Transvaal in 1852, but the discovery of gold 15 years later brought in such an influx of foreigners that his kingdom was overwhelmed. (Lipschutz and Rasmussen 1989)

See also *Emperor Shaka the Great.*

N

NA' VAHINE

In Hawaiian cosmology, Na' Vahine is a goddess, member of Teave's royal family, the wife of Lord Tane (Tani), and the mother of three sons: Tanaroa (southern Pacific), Rono (east), and Tu (north), who, with their father (west), are the "Four Major Male Pillars of Creation." Na' Vahine is also the mother of three daughters who married their brothers: Rata (sun), Tapo (South Pacific), and Hina (agriculture and chief justice). (Melville 1990)

See also Tani; Teave.

NABIBANGSA

This oral Muslim folk epic of Bengal is still being performed. (Blackburn et al. 1989)

NĀGARAKERTĀGAMA

This epic of Majapahit was composed in 1365 by a Buddhist priest about the Javanese kingdom founded and ruled by Kertangara (1268–1292). The epic traces the history down to 1364 and is in large part in praise of Gajah Mada, chief minister of Majapahit from 1330 to 1364, portraying him as a master administrator and reformer. The historical Gajah Mada was commander of the royal bodyguards who suppressed a rebellion against King Jayanagara in 1328. Thereafter, the king stole his wife, and in retaliation, Gajah Mada convinced the royal surgeon to allow his knife to "slip" during an operation on the king. The king's heir was his daughter Tribhuvana, under whose rule Gajah Mada became prime minister, a post he held for a quarter of a century. (Garraty and Gay 1981; Jackson, G. 1990)

See also Kertanagara; Kuti.

NAISADHACARITA

This Sanskrit poem (twelfth century) honoring the life of Nala, king of Niṣhadha, was written by Śrīharsa. Nala appears in the *Mahābhārata.* Nal is the hero of the *Ḍholā Epic.* (Blackburn et al. 1989; Buck 1981; Preminger 1990)

NALA

(Also Nal)

Nala, the king of Niṣhadha, who appears in the *Mahābhārata.* The princess Damayantī falls in love with Nala before she has met him, but four gods want her for themselves. They send the unsuspecting Nala to speak for them, and after she professes her love for him, the gods come to her disguised as Nala. However, she chooses the correct man and is to be married. When Nala loses everything in a gambling match, he becomes an outcast, and Damayantī returns to the court of her father. Many years and adventures later, the lovers are reunited. As Nal of Navargarh, he is also hero of the *Ḍholā Epic.* (Blackburn et al. 1989; Buck 1981; Narayan 1993)

See also Damayantī; *Ḍholā Epic; Mahābhārata.*

NAM VIET

(Also Nan Yueh)

Nam Viet was an ancient kingdom formed in 207 B.C. in what is now North Vietnam. In the legendary history of *Lac Long Quang and Au Co,* Lac Long Quang's older son Hung Vuong succeeds his father and heads the Hong Bang dynasty, which lasts for 150 years. It ends with the invasion of Van Lang, who rules the new state, Au Lac, under the name An Duong Vuong. Au Lac is incorporated in 208 by the former Chinese general Trieu Da into the kingdom of Nam Viet. The end of Au Lac in 207 B.C. marks the end of the legendary history and the beginning of recorded history. (Garraty and Gay 1981; Terada 1989)

See also *Lac Long Quang and Au Co.*

NAMBI

In the creation mythology of Buganda, Uganda, the first woman is Nambi, daughter of Gulu, king of heaven, who comes to the first man, Kintu. Her relatives despise Kintu because he knows of no food except milk. To test Kintu, Gulu steals his cow so that he is forced to eat herbs and leaves. Nambi sees the cow in heaven and invites Kintu up to retrieve it. Kintu goes to heaven and performs a number of tests, proving that he is a worthy husband for Nambi.

As the couple leaves heaven, Gulu warns them to hurry, or Nambi's brother Death will want to go with them. He cautions them that if they have forgotten anything, they must not come back for it. They set out with cows, a goat, a sheep, a fowl, and a plantain tree. On the way Nambi remembers grain for the fowl and returns to heaven for it. She tries to steal away, but Death follows her, angering Kintu. The three continue to earth, where Nambi lives happily, bearing many children.

One day Death asks Kintu for one of his children to be his cook. When Kintu refuses to give his child for such menial work, Death promises to kill the child. Kintu does not know the meaning of "kill," but the child soon grows sick and dies. Other children begin to die, so Kintu returns to heaven to complain to Gulu about Death. Gulu decides to send Death's brother Kaizuki to stop Death from killing any more children.

Kaizuki comes to earth and tries to catch Death, but he fails. He tells Kintu that he is tired of hunting Death, and he returns to heaven. Since then Death has lived on earth, and it is all Nambi's fault. (Parrinder 1982)

NAN YUEH

Ancient kingdom. ***See*** Nam Viet.

NANA BULUKU

She is the primordial mother of the West African Fon who gives birth to the supreme god Mawu and her/his partner Lisa. According to the Fon creation myth, Nana Buluku creates the world and then retires, leaving the twins to become parents of all the other gods, of which there are seven pairs. (Sproul 1991)

NANDI

Nandi is a Zulu princess (d. 1827) who figures prominently in the epic *Emperor Shaka the Great* as the mother of Chief Shaka. She is a great political force behind his achievements, and is recognized as a strong and intelligent leader in her own right.

Nandī is also the name of the bull of the Hindu god Śiva, originally a form of the deity, later one of his chief attendants. (Kunene 1979; O'Flaherty *Śiva* 1981)

See also Bhuza; *Emperor Shaka the Great;* Senzangakhona; Śiva.

NANG SHEK, NANG TALUNG, NANG YAI
(Also Wayang, Wayang Kulit, and Wayang Topeng)

These are shadow-puppet theaters of Southeast Asia through which epics are conveyed. They are called Nang Shek in Cambodia, and shadow play is called Nang Talung in Southern Thailand. Nang Yai is a type of shadow play using masked mime, popular throughout the region. (Grosvenor and Grosvenor *Ntl Geo* 1969)

See also Wayang.

NAÑHAITHYA
(Also Haurvatat and Ameretat)

In the *Avesta,* sacred book of Zoroastrianism, Nañhaithya is an Indo-Iranian god, the counterpart of Nāsatya of the Vedas. Nañhaithya is associated with

This granite sculpture from India, carved in about the tenth century, represents Nandi, a Hindu deity who became chief attendant to Śiva.

Anahita (Nanaca), "the Immaculate," the goddess of fertility; the twin aspects of the gods were health and immortality. (Olmstead 1948)

NANNA

In Mesopotamian religion, Nanna is the Sumero-Akkadian god of the moon, son of Enlil and Ninlil, husband of Ningal. (Kramer 1956)

See also *Gilgamesh, Epic of.*

NANSHE

In Mesopotamian religion, Nanshe is the daughter of Enki (Ea), sister of Inanna (Ishtar), wife of the tax-gatherer of the sea Nindara, and the Sumerian city goddess of Nina in the Lagash region. Her father placed her in charge of fishes and fishing. Sumerian hymns mention her as being devoted to truth, justice, and mercy, "who knows the orphan, who knows the widow, / Knows the oppression of man over man, is the orphan's mother, / . . . the queen brings the refugees to her lap, / Finds shelter for the weak. . . ." She judges mankind on New Year's Day. On several monuments she is depicted with the god Sucellos. She holds a cornucopia. (Kramer 1956)

NANTOSUELTA

A Gaulish Celtic goddess, her name means "She of the Winding River." She has been associated with the Irish queen of demons, Mórrígan. (Chadwick 1976)

See also Mórrígan.

NAPI
(Oldman)

In Blackfoot Indian oral tradition, Creator Sun puts Oldman, Napi, on Mother Earth to steal in among the people and take charge, teaching them the ways to better living and setting a good example for them. Napi is "just a good-looking man." He has a prominent, proud look about him, leading the people to believe that he is probably one of the chiefs. His power is almost as great as Creator Sun's. He goes from camp to camp, teaching, at times using magic power to heal the sick or revive the dead.

As time goes on, Napi's power gets the better of him, and he begins to use more power for himself. While Creator Sun is busy elsewhere, Napi begins to get into mischief and eventually breaks away from Creator Sun and Mother Earth entirely. Some become his followers, while others continue to follow Creator Sun and Mother Earth. He comes to be called My-stu-bun, Crowfeather Arrow, for a while. At least 24 tales of Napi and Crowfeather Arrow's adventures exist. (Bullchild 1985)

NARAMSIN
(Naram-Sin)

Fourth (r. ca. 2254–ca. 2218 B.C.) of the five kings of the Akkadian empire, whose story is told in the Akkadian epic *The Fall of Akkad*. The king's pride is blamed for the gods' retaliation against his kingdom, which results in its eventual downfall. He discards the title of King of Kish, by which his predecessors have been known, and insists upon being known as "king of the four quarters of the earth." He subjugates the troublesome Lullubi tribes and commemorates his victory with the famous Naram-Sin Stele. His use of the title "god of Akkad" angers the gods and causes him to fall out of favor, and the Lullubi rise up and begin their harassment anew. Naramsin is the key figure in another tale in which his pride and invasions by the barbarous Lullubi tribes play parts. (Saggs 1984; Wolkstein and Kramer 1990)

NARESUAN
(Also Phra Naret)

Called the "Black Prince," this king of Siam is revered in local oral epic as a national hero for liberating his country from Burma in 1584. (Allen *Art in America* 1991)

NARTS

In the Iranian mythology of the Ossetes of the Caucasus region, Narts are heroic men of the otherworld who represent various aspects of nature. Batradz, for example, represents lightning and Sozryko, the sun; Syrdon is a trickster and hero of many adventures. The dead must first face an interrogation before they can cross a river bridge to reach the world of the Narts. (Keith and Carnoy 1964)

NAṬARĀJA

Naṭarāja is the Lord of the Dance, source of all cosmic movement, the Hindu god Śiva in his role as cosmic dancer. Śiva visits the forest of Tāraka, where the inhabitants set a tiger upon him. After he flays the tiger with his fingernail and dons it as a robe, they send the serpent Śeṣa against him. He uses it as a garland and begins to dance. They send the dwarf Muyalaka against him, but he breaks Muyalaka's back with his toe and continues the dance. The most famous sculptures of Śiva show him in his Naṭarāja form. (Coomaraswamy 1985)

NAUPLIUS

An Argonaut, knowledgeable in seafaring and astronomy, Nauplius is the builder of Nauplia. Nauplius is also the name of the father of Oeax and Palamedes, sacrificed by the Greeks because of Odysseus's animosity. (Graves 1955)

An Akkadian stele from Mesopotamia, carved in 2270 B.C., represents the conquest of King Naramsin over a nearby tribe. His story is told in the epic *The Fall of Akkad*.

NAUSICAA

In the *Odyssey* (vi), Nausicaa is the daughter of King Alcinous of the Phaeacians. When Odysseus is shipwrecked off the coast, she befriends him and persuades her father to be kind to him. By some accounts she later marries Odysseus's son Telemachos. (Lattimore 1967)

See also Odysseus; *Odyssey;* Telemachos.

NDIADIANE NDIAYE
(Also Njajan Ndiaye)

Ndiadiane Ndiaye is a hero of the West African Wolof (Jolof) *Epic of Kayor.* (Lipschutz and Rasmussen 1989; Wright 1980)

See also *Kayor, Epic of.*

NEMAIN

See Mórrígan.

NEOPTOLEMUS
(Also Pyrrhus the Fair)

In the *Iliad* (xix), the *Odyssey* (xiii), and the *Aeneid* (ii, iii), Neoptolemus is the son of Achilles and Deidameia, daughter of Scyros king Lycomedes. After the death of his father, Odysseus and Diomedes bring Neoptolemus to Troy when the Trojan seer predicts that Troy cannot be taken without Neoptolemus's help. He fights bravely but cruelly kills Priam at an altar and hurls Astyanax from the walls of Troy. He takes Andromache captive and fathers a son, Molossus, by her. Later he marries Hermione, who has been promised to Orestes. He is murdered at Delphi soon after. (Humphries 1951; Lattimore 1976; Rouse 1990)

NEREIDS
(Also Nereides)

In Greek mythology, the Nereids are the 50 daughters of the sea god Nereus and Doris, and attendants of Poseidon. Among the best known are Amphitrite, Galatea, Thetis (mother of Achilles), and Clymene. They appear in the *Iliad* (xviii) and *Theogony.* (Humphries 1951; Lattimore 1976)

NEREUS

In Greek mythology, Nereus is the sea god son of Oceanus, or Pontus (Sea), and Gaea (Earth), and father by Doris of the Nereids. He appears in the *Iliad* (xviii), *Theogony,* and the Herakles tales. Homer calls him "Old Man of the Sea." During his eleventh labor for the golden apples of the Garden of the Hesperides, Herakles wrestles with Nereus in several forms before obtaining directions to the garden. (Graves 1955; Lattimore 1959; Lattimore 1976)

NERGAL

In Mesopotamian religion, Nergal is king of the underworld, husband of Ereshkigal. He appears in the *Epic of Gilgamesh* and in *Inanna's Descent to the Nether World.* (Kramer 1956; Saggs 1990; Sandars 1972)

NERTHUS

(Also Terra Mater, Mother Earth)

Nerthus is an ancient Germanic goddess of the Baltic region, identified with the Old Norse sea god Njord. (Jones, G. 1990)

NESTOR

In the *Iliad* (i), *Odyssey* (iii), and the Herakles tales, Nestor is the son of Neleus and Chloris, and is the king of Pylos. He is the only one of 12 brothers who is not killed by Herakles. He attends the wedding of Peirithous and Hippodamia, when the Centaurs and Lapiths engage in a bloody confrontation. He participates in the Trojan War as an old sage of 70. He encourages men into battle by relating stories of his own exploits. (Graves 1955; Lattimore 1976; Rouse 1990)

See also Herakles; *Iliad; Odyssey.*

NGASAUNGGYAN, BATTLE OF

This battle of the Mongol defeat of the Pagan dynasty of Burma under the command of the Pagan king Narathihapate (1277) is celebrated in local oral epic. The event is recorded in a book called *The Glass Palace Chronicle of the Kings of Burma,* collected and authorized by King Bagyidaw in 1829. (Garrett 1971)

NGOLO DIARA

Oral epic of the kingdom of Segu of the Bambara people, Ngolo Diara is also the name of the hero of the epic and one of the kings of Segu. The story concerns the village chief Yiriba, whose younger brother Diara Dja is sickly and cannot find a wife. Finally some traders suggest a girl in the next village who has a crippled foot. The two marry and have a son and a daughter. The son is named Ngolo Diara. When Ngolo is four years old, a filelikela (diviner) of Niolla predicts that Ngolo will someday become king of all of Segu. Yiriba is troubled when he learns this, for he has four healthy sons of his own who would like to be king. He decides to get rid of Ngolo.

When tax time comes, Yiriba convinces his brother that, since he has no money, he must send his son to the king in lieu of taxes. Yiriba himself volunteers to take Ngolo to Segu with him. All along the way to Segu, Yiriba and Ngolo encounter village chiefs who berate the chief for taking his brother's son as a tax payment. When they reach Segu, the king, Biton Mamari, accepts the boy, although he thinks it is a highly irregular arrangement. His wife Baniaba asks the king for Ngolo, so the boy serves the queen, and she treats him like a son.

However, when word reaches the king concerning the prophecy, he decides to test the boy. He orders a dish prepared containing a gold nugget, and he invites all the boys of the kingdom to eat. The boy who finds the nugget is meant to be king. When Ngolo finds the nugget, the king, hoping he will lose it so that he can punish him, asks Ngolo to keep it for him. Ngolo sews the nugget into his clothing so that he won't lose it.

The king's sons suggest that he kill Ngolo, but the king cannot kill the boy without a reason. He tells his sons where the gold is hidden, and while Ngolo sleeps, they slip in and steal it. The next day when the king asks Ngolo to return the nugget, he can't produce it. The king now has an excuse to order his execution. Ngolo runs to tell the queen, who hurries to a diviner for advice. The diviner tells her, "Go to the river and tend to your laundry." The queen and Ngolo go to the riverbank, where a fisherman gives them a large carp for the king's dinner. When Ngolo cuts the fish open, he finds the king's gold. He hurries back to court to give it to the king.

The king asks his wife to give Ngolo back to him, and she cannot refuse. He then sends the boy to Timbuktu as a gift to the great morike Seku Mochtar Kadiri. When the emissary Suma Buare arrives in Timbuktu with Ngolo, the great morike is suspicious. He pretends to accept the gift, but while Ngolo sleeps, he sees a light radiating from the boy's body and knows the truth. He tells Suma Buare to take the child back to court, and he asks Ngolo to make him the paramount morike when he becomes king of Segu. When Suma Buare returns to court with Ngolo, the king can do nothing but return the boy to the queen.

When Ngolo grows to be a man, the king decides to send him into the bush as a tax collector, in hopes that he will be killed as his other tax collectors have been. Ngolo goes to live at his tax station, and nothing bad happens to him. He makes a new friend, Sumana Djire, to whom he confides that he is lonely. He wants a wife, but he has no family to speak for him, as is the custom in obtaining a wife. Sumana Djire offers his own father to speak for him. Many women are suggested as possible wives, but Ngolo has his heart set on Nakurni, the daughter of King Biton Mamari. Sumana Djire's father travels to Segu City to ask for the king's daughter. Surprisingly, the king, at last resigned to the outcome of fate, agrees to the marriage. He says, "I know now that there is no magic strong enough to deflect destiny."

Ngolo and Nakurni are married, and they take their place in the life of Segu City. They have three children. Ngolo is accepted into the Tonjon, the army of nobles. At last the king grows old and dies, but no change occurs in the line of succession. The king's eldest son, Chekoro, is placed in power. When he dies, the second son, Dankoro, a leper, comes to power. But Dankoro is cruel and ruthless. One day he executes 440 Tonjon officers whom he thinks are not loyal enough. The rest of the Tonjon officers decide that Dankoro must be killed, so he is strangled during the night while he sleeps.

The officers decide to abandon the line of succession and place one of their own officers, Ton Mansa, on the throne. He is a good ruler with many wives, but he has no children. He announces that he wants to be immortal and threatens death to the morikes if they do not find a way to make him immortal.

The morikes travel to Timbuktu to consult with the great Seku Mochtar Kadiri, who tells them, "You morikes have studied the mysteries of the Koran. . . . That is good. But to be great in your profession you must also study the mysteries of a man's mind." He explains that Ton Mansa does not actually want to live forever; he wants his name to be remembered forever. The morikes return to Segu City and employ workers to dig a large well, into which they place 100 frogs who have been taught to sing the praises of Ton Mansa every night. The king is satisfied: "Yes, this is what I want."

When the king dies, the Tonjons elect another king, and then another. Finally Ngolo is the most senior member of the group, and he demands his turn as king. The officers agree to elect him king with the stipulation, "You will not do harm to anyone, and no one will do harm to you."

But Ngolo's grown son Bamudje is angered when he learns of the stipulation. He tells his father, "The Tonjon gives and the Tonjon takes, according to its urges. . . . I will see to it that the proper pledges are given by the Tonjon."

While the people are gathered for a feast, Bamudje rides in at the head of an army he has recruited from another town. He encircles the Tonjons with his army and asks, "How dare you say to him, 'Do nothing bad to us and we will do nothing bad to you? . . . Whoever created you equal to the king of Segu? . . . " He orders his soldiers to open fire, and many Tonjons are killed. The rest cry out, ". . . You are right. . . . Ngolo is our king, and we are his club of slaves. . . . Whatever he wants us to do, we will do it. . . . It is he alone who will appoint his heir."

In this way the power of the Tonjon ends. Ngolo rules and Segu remains strong for many years. When he dies, his son becomes king, and the Diara line rules for a long time to come. (Courlander 1982)

NGOMANE

In the Zulu epic *Emperor Shaka the Great,* Ngomane is commander-in-chief of the Mthethwa armies and close adviser to Shaka. (Kunene 1979)

NGOZA

In the Zulu epic *Emperor Shaka the Great,* Ngoza is the famous king of Thembus, the enemy of Shaka. (Kunene 1979)

NGQENGELELE

In the Zulu epic *Emperor Shaka the Great,* Ngqengelele is Shaka's close companion and one of the most outstanding political minds of the Shaka era. His position is equivalent to that of prime minister. (Kunene 1979)

See also *Emperor Shaka the Great.*

NGUNZA

Ngunza is the hero of a tale of the Mbundu tribe of Angola. While Ngunza is away from home, he dreams that his brother has died. He rushes home and demands to know who has killed his brother. His mother answers that Death has killed him. Ngunza vows to fight Death, and he commissions a blacksmith to make an iron trap. He places the trap in the bush and snares Death in it. Death pleads to be released, but Ngunza refuses, claiming that Death is always killing people. Death denies the allegation, explaining that people die through their own or other people's fault. He convinces Ngunza to release him so that he can take Ngunza to the land of the dead to see for himself.

Four days later they arrive in the underworld, where Ngunza questions new arrivals. Each has died through the fault of some human being. Ngunza searches out his brother and finds him living much as he had on earth. When Ngunza proposes that his brother come home with him, the brother refuses, saying he is much happier where he is. As Ngunza prepares to return home alone, Death gives him the seeds of all the plants now cultivated in Angola.

Later Death comes back to earth to look for Ngunza. He stalks Ngunza from place to place until Ngunza confronts him, pointing out that he has done no harm, and reminding Death that he has told him that he does not kill anyone. But Death throws an ax at Ngunza, who turns into a spirit at once. (Parrinder 1982)

NIBELUNGENLIED

More is known of the evolution of this Middle High German epic poem (ca. 1191–1204) than any other heroic epic. Among the other sources of corroboration are Latin chronicles dating from the sixth century, the Latin epic *Waltharius* (ca. ninth or tenth century), lays in the *Poetic Edda* (thirteenth century), the *Völsunga Saga* (thirteenth century), the prose *Thiđrekssaga* (Thidrik's Saga), a reference to an oral version of the story in the writings of a Latin author, references in Old English poetry, and many medieval German, Danish, and Faroese poems dating from the thirteenth century onward. Composed of four-line stanzas, the poem was probably written for performance at court in Austria by an unknown poet from the Danube region.

In one early-fourteenth-century manuscript, the epic is called the *Book of Kriemhild,* an appropriate title since the story begins with her and ends with her death. In the first part of the poem, Nibelung is apparently the name of

Siegfried's lands, peoples, and treasure, but in the second part, it is used as an alternate name for the Burgundians.

The first two cantos of the epic introduce the main characters: Kriemhild; her brothers, the Burgundian princes of Worms; and Siegfried, prince from the Lower Rhine. Kriemhild, a beautiful princess in the land of the Burgundians, is in the care of three great kings—her brothers Gunther, Gernot, and Giselher. Kriemhild dreams that she rears a falcon that is torn apart by two eagles as she looks on. Her mother Uote interprets the dream, "The falcon you are rearing is a noble man who, unless God preserves him, will soon be taken from you." But Kriemhild assures her mother, "I intend to stay free of a warrior's love all my life . . . and never be made wretched by the love of any man."

Down the Rhine, in the Netherlands city of Xanten, a young knight, Siegfried, for whom his father the king holds a festival when he comes of age, assures his father that he does not wish to wear the crown so long as both his parents are alive. He has heard of Kriemhild's rare beauty, and he sets out to win her, despite his parents' warnings. When Siegfried arrives in Worms, he is recognized by Hagen, King Gunther's retainer, who recounts Siegfried's heroic deeds, including the manner by which he gained his treasure: He has slain the Nibelung kings and a large number of men who had just brought the Nibelung treasure of gold from a cavern. After subduing hundreds of warriors, Siegfried had commanded that the treasure be returned to the cave; confiscated their cloak of darkness, which makes the wearer invisible; and had slain a dragon and bathed in its blood, rendering his skin impervious except for one spot, which a fallen leaf covered.

Siegfried wins the three brothers' friendship by helping them fight off the Saxons. He promises to help Gunther win the hand of the mighty Queen Brunhild of Iceland on the condition that he be allowed to marry Kriemhild. Gunther agrees to the arrangement.

Brunhild has set three tasks that her suitor must perform in order to win her favor: He must cast a weight, follow through with a leap, and then throw a javelin in a contest. Siegfried dons his magic cloak and performs the tasks for Gunther while invisible, and both men win their chosen wives.

But Brunhild is troubled about Siegfried's suitability as a mate for Kriemhild because he has been introduced as Gunther's vassal. When Gunther comes to her bed, she binds him with her girdle and hangs him up in her room, saying that he will not be allowed to consummate their marriage until she learns the truth about Siegfried. Again Siegfried dons his cloak and comes to the rescue, wrestling the mighty Brunhild for hours until he subdues her; then Gunther quickly slips into his place. Once Brunhild sleeps with her husband, she loses her great strength.

Siegfried has taken Brunhild's girdle and ring during the encounter, and he presents these items to his bride as gifts. Later Gunther invites Siegfried to attend a festival in Burgundy; after they arrive, the two queens argue over whose husband is the more important. Finally Kriemhild shows Brunhild the ring and girdle Siegfried has given her, claiming that her husband slept with Brunhild before Gunther.

Siegfried apologizes to Brunhild for any discomfort Kriemhild's boast has caused; in fact, he punishes his wife by beating her. But Hagen, Gunther's retainer, is not satisfied and vows to get even for the insult. He tricks Kriemhild into sewing a spot on Siegfried's clothing to indicate his vulnerable area, saying he wants to know where it is so that he can protect it. Then Gunther and Hagen plan a hunting party, and while Siegfried is bent over the brook for a drink, Hagen drives a spear into Siegfried's heart.

Siegfried's father Siegmund comes to get his son's body, but Kriemhild refuses to return to the Netherlands with him; instead, she plans to remain near her family. Hagen convinces Gunther and his brothers to have Kriemhild bring her treasure (Siegfried's gold) from Nibelungland. Later he takes it from her and sinks it into the Rhine with the intention of retrieving it later.

Kriemhild grieves for Siegfried and for her lost treasure, and when King Etzel (Attila the Hun) proposes, she accepts, provided that he help her take revenge for her losses. After the wedding, they invite her brothers, Hagen, and the other knights to Hungary for a visit, and they confront the Burgundians in the mead hall. The Burgundians meet their attacks time and again and hold out with great success. The epic gives a lively account of their battles.

Eventually Queen Kriemhild burns the hall, killing many more men. But it is not until they receive the aid of Hildebrand and Dietrich of Bern that the tide is turned. When Hagen refuses to restore Kriemhild's treasure, she has her brother Gunther's head cut off, then cuts off Hagen's head herself. Hildebrand is so horrified that he kills her and cuts her to pieces, shouting, "She shall not go scot-free for having dared to kill him, whatever becomes of me!" (Hatto 1969)

See also Brunhild; *Edda, Poetic;* Etzel; Gunther; Hagen; Kriemhild; Siegfried; *Thiđrekssaga; Völsunga Saga; Waltharius.*

NIDHOGG

(Also Nidhād and Níthoth)

In Norse mythology, Nidhogg is an evil serpent or dragon who lives in the world of the dead, Niflheim, and guards at the roots of Yggdrasill, the world tree. In the "Völuspá" of the Elder or *Poetic Edda,* Sibyl prophesies that at the end of the world, Nidhogg will suck the blood of the dead. (Hollander *Edda* 1990)

See also *Edda, Poetic.*

NIFLHEIM

In Norse mythology, Niflheim is the world of the dead below the roots of the world tree, Yggdrasill. It is ruled by the goddess Hel. (Jones, G. 1990; Young 1954)

NIFLUNGS

(Also Nibelung)

In the first part of the epic poem *Nibelungenlied,* Niflungs is the dynasty of the Nibelung and their followers. In the second part of the poem, it is an alternate name for the Burgundians. (Hatto 1969)

See also *Nibelungenlied.*

NIHONGI

(Also *Nihon shoki)*

These chronicles of Japan from earliest mythological times to A.D. 697 consist of 30 books compiled by court order and laid before the empress Gemmiō in A.D. 720 by Prince Toneri and Yasumaro Futo no Ason. Up until recent times, its preeminence as a source of information on Japanese antiquity has not been contested.

Nihongi refers to Nihon, or Nippon, and *Nihongi,* or the *Chronicles of Japan,* is the original name. Later writers introduced the syllable "sho," (writing) and called it Nihon-sho(ki), or "Shoki," for short. It is not the earliest Japanese work of its kind. An earlier book, the *Kiujiki,* or *Kujiki* (Chronicle of Old Matters of Former Ages), was largely destroyed by fire in A.D. 645. Other historical works, particularly *Kana Nihongi,* are said to have been in existence before the date of the *Nihongi.* The only extant work comparable to the *Nihongi* is the *Kojiki* (Records of Ancient Matters), compiled for the imperial household in A.D. 712. The two books, which were planned and finished approximately the same time, often complement and elucidate each other. The *Kojiki* is both mythical—beginning, as does the *Nihongi,* with the creation myths—and historical. But the larger *Nihongi,* although often fictitious, provides positive dates of royal events, from invasions to the annual moves to the summer palace; names of family members; and facts concerning many aspects of the reign of each ruler, including the periodic, kingdomwide, royal forgiving of debts. Too, although the *Kojiki* closes, for all practical purposes, with the end of the fifth century, the *Nihongi* continues the narrative 200 more years. Originally, a book of genealogies of the emperors was included that is no longer extant.

Although it is mainly concerned with the Asuka period (552–645), the first two books of volume I of the *Nihongi,* "The Age of the Gods," contain the myths that form the basis of Shinto religion. Various accounts are given of each myth, and a genealogy of gods is given. Following that, a section, or book, is devoted to each ruler, beginning with Jimmu Tennō (ca. 660 B.C.) and ending with Muretsu Tennō (A.D. 499). Volume II begins with the reign of Keidai Tennō (A.D. 507) and carries the history through the reign of Jitō Tennō (A.D. 687). (Aston 1972)

NINIGI

(Also Piko-po-nö-ninigi-nö-mikötö)

In the Japanese *Kojiki* and the *Nihongi,* Ninigi is the grandson of the sun goddess Ama-terasu. He establishes the Yamato clan, the imperial house of Japan. Ninigi is said to have been the great-grandfather of Jimmu Tennō, the first emperor in the *Nihongi.* When Ama-terasu charges her grandson with overseeing the central land of the reed plains (Japan), she presents him with three symbols of office: a jewel (for benevolence), a mirror (for purity), and a sword, Kusanagi (for courage). These remain the symbols of imperial Japan to this day.

Ninigi arrives on the island of Kyushu, where Okuni-nushi is already ruling. However, he agrees to relinquish his throne if he is allowed to maintain power over religious matters. (Aston 1972; Philippi 1968)

See also Ama-terasu no Oho-kami; *Kojiki; Nihongi.*

NINLIL

In Mesopotamian religion, Ninlil is the Sumero-Akkadian goddess of the air, grain, and harvest; the wife of the storm god, Enlil; and the daughter of Nundarshegunn. Her mother instructs her in the ways to please Enlil, enticing him to appear in three forms to mate. Their children include Nergal, king of the underworld, and Ninazu, another god of the underworld. (Saggs 1990; Sandars 1972)

See also *Gilgamesh, Epic of.*

NINSUN

Ninsun is the mother of Gilgamesh and "well-beloved wife" of Lugulbanda. (Sandars 1972)

See also *Gilgamesh, Epic of.*

NINTU

(Also Ninhursag and Ninmah)

Nintu, a Sumerian goddess, may be a later version of the earth goddess Ki. The water god Enki is unable to create man, so Nintu molds six kinds of humans from clay. She and Enki have a daughter, Ninsar, who mates with Enki and has a daughter, Ninkur, who mates with Enki and has a daughter, Uttu, the goddess of plants. When Enki begins to eat the plants, Nintu puts a curse upon him. (Sproul 1991)

NINURTA

(Also Ningirsu)

Ninurta is the Sumerian and Babylonian god of war, the south wind, and irrigation; he is the son of Enlil. Ninurta is the hero of a fragmentary epic poem relating his battles with the dragon Kur of the underworld. Ninurta has a magic weapon, Sharur, that eventually guides him to kill Kur. However, the death of the dragon affects the irrigation water, and Ninurta channels the overflowing waters into the Tigris so that the fields can flourish again. He blesses all the stones he throws to slay the dragon and curses those hurled at him. (Ceram 1972; Saggs 1990; Sandars 1972)

See also Gilgamesh, Epic of.

NISUS

In the *Aeneid* (ix), Nisus is a Trojan, son of Hyrtacus, and a friend of Euryalus the Argonaut. While participating in the games after the fall of Troy, he slips and falls in a footrace. He trips the leader, enabling his friend Euryalus to win. Later, on a night raid against the Rutulians, he is killed while trying in vain to rescue Euryalus. (Humphries 1951)

NJÁL'S SAGA

This Icelandic epic prose narrative (ca. 1289) is the mightiest and most popular of the classical sagas. Its author is unknown, and the original manuscript has not survived. The earliest extant version is from ca. 1300. It is broadly based on authentic historical events—the Burning of Bergthorsknoll is referred to in the twelfth-century history *Landnámabók.* Its material is drawn from written records and oral tradition.

The saga begins ca. 960 with the betrothal of Hrut and Unn. Reference is made to Hrut's niece Hallgerd and her "thief's eyes." Hrut travels to Norway before the wedding to claim an inheritance. Gunnhild, the Queen Mother of Norway, seduces him before she helps him to regain his inheritance. When he prepares to return to Iceland, she tells him, "The spell I now lay on you will prevent your ever enjoying the woman in Iceland on whom you have set your heart. . . ."

Hrut and Unn marry, but he is unable to consummate their union, so after two years she divorces him. He is so outraged that he refuses to return the dowry. Meanwhile, Hallgerd has married twice, in 956 and 959, but both husbands have been killed by Thjostolf, her jealous stepfather.

Unn persuades her cousin Gunnar to pursue her dowry claim against Hrut. Gunnar goes to his friend Njál (Njáll) for advice. Njál tells him to trick Hrut into believing that he is too stupid to press the claim. The scheme works; Hrut agrees to meet Gunnar in court and eventually is forced to pay the dowry.

Unn soon forgets Gunnar's good deeds on her account. She marries a man named Valgard and has a son, Mord, who grows up to hate Gunnar.

After the lawsuit Gunnar goes abroad to make his fortune. When he returns in 974, he marries the beautiful but ruthless Hallgerd, much to his friend Njál's dismay. Njál's wife Bergthora and Hallgerd do not get along. During a feast at Njál's house, they argue when Hallgerd refuses Bergthora's demand that she move from the dais to make room for Thorkalla. Gunnar takes Hallgerd home, and the two friends, Njál and Gunnar, refuse to get involved in the feud.

The men own a piece of property together, and the wives squabble over the land, directing their employees in violence against one another until seven men are killed, including Njál's foster father. Hallgerd begins the feud anew by stealing food from a farmer, Otkel, on Njál's land. When Gunnar offers to repay Otkel, his offer is refused. Njál helps Gunnar out of several antagonistic episodes, but finally Gunnar is ambushed by Otkel's son Thorgeir, forcing Gunnar to kill him. Gunnar is prosecuted for the killing and outlawed, but he refuses to leave Iceland. Eventually, in 990, he is attacked at his home and killed while defending it.

Njál's oldest son, Skarp-Hedin, helps Gunnar's son Hogni avenge Gunnar's death by killing four men. Njál's two younger sons, Helgi and Grim, travel to Norway and are befriended during a fight with the Vikings by Kári, who then goes to Iceland and marries their sister Helga. The three men eventually confront and kill Thrain, who was present at the killing of Njál's foster father.

In an effort to bring about peace, Njál decides to adopt Thrain's son Hoskuld. Hoskuld marries Hildigunn, Chief Flosi's daughter, and becomes a chieftain. But Mord becomes jealous of the new chieftain and convinces the Njálssons that Hoskild is betraying them. In 1011 they waylay Hoskuld in a cornfield and kill him.

Njál persuades Flosi to take a wergild (financial settlement) for the killing of his son-in-law. But Flosi brings 100 men to attack Njál's house, Bergthorsknoll, and old Njál insists that his sons try to defend the house from the inside. All are burned to death except Kári.

Kári and Flosi continue the feud both in and out of court. But as Flosi's supporters are killed off one by one, he quits fighting. Flosi begins a pilgrimage, sailing across the channel and walking all the way to Rome, where he receives absolution from the Pope before returning to settle in Norway. Kári then takes a pilgrimage to Norway. To show good faith, Flosi gives the widowed Hildigunn to Kári. The couple has three sons, the youngest of whom (also named Flosi) becomes the father of Kolbein, "one of the most outstanding men of that line." When the elder Flosi is very old, he sets sail from Norway in a very old boat and is never seen again. (Magnusson and Pálsson 1960)

See also Bergthora; Bjarni Brodd-Helgason of Hof; Bjorn; Bork Starkadarson; Burnt Njal.

NJÖRD

In Norse mythology, Njörd is the god of the sea, father of Freyr and Freyja, and a divine ruler of the Swedes. The Vanir, the tribe of gods of whom he is a member, give him as a hostage to their rivals, the Aesir, a tribe of giant gods. The giantess Skadi chooses him for her husband, but the couple is unable to agree on a dwelling place, and the marriage fails. (Jones, G. 1990)

NNE MGBAAFO, EPIC OF

This West African oral epic, one of few epics featuring a woman, is still performed in Nigeria. However, Nne Mgbaafo is pictured as having "masculine" traits. In one version, she is of Aru-Oke-Igbo, a patronymic praise name of the people of Aro Chukwu, south of Ohafia in West Africa. She is of the matriclan of Okwuru-Egbu-Enyi. After her first husband dies in her native community of Arochukwu, she behaves "very much like a man." She buys a matchet, a war cap, and a dane-gun. She sharpens her matchet, catches it in the air, and announces that she is going in search of another husband. After she searches through many villages without luck, she arrives at Nde-Ana-m-Ele-m-Ulu-Uma, where she meets and marries a man named Uduma.

According to Ohafia heroic standards, a man who has not won a human head in battle is despised by his age-mates as a coward (onye-ujo), and Uduma has not yet been named a ufiem (honorable warrior) because he has not won a head. Nne Mgbaafo cooks him a special meal and prods him to go off to Ibibioland, where a war has just broken out. Uduma goes into battle, but he is slain.

When Nne Mgbaafo hears the news, she hurries to the people of Ama Achara, who started the battle. They provide her with escorts to the battlefield, where she finds her husband's beheaded body among a pile of slain warriors. She buries the body beneath a tree and sacrifices a goat on the grave. Three market-weeks later, at Usukpam, she comes upon a young man wandering alone. She beheads and buries him beside her husband "to wash his right hand and his left."

In another version of the epic, Nne Mgbaafo appears as a member of the matriclan of Eleghe Ofoka, born in the patriclan of Asaga. In this version, her husband Ndukwe Emea goes into battle of his own volition, despite her "womanish pleas" that he remain at home. He is captured in Ibibioland, but Nne Mgbaafo boldly confronts the enemy people of Ikpe Mmaku and demands that they either kill her or release her husband. The Ikpe Mmaku marvel at her courage, saying, "She is truly full of valor! / . . . Let her not be killed!" Ndukwe Emea is set free and returns home with Nne Mgbaafo. (Azuonye *RAL* 1990)

NOAH

Noah is the hero of the flood myth of the Old Testament. Because mankind has become so corrupt, God plans to destroy life on earth. But because Noah is an upright man, God instructs him to build an ark for himself and his family, and to collect two of every species of animal so that they will be saved from the flood that covers the earth for 40 days and nights. According to Jewish legend, only animals who have maintained sexual purity (mating with their own kind) are saved. As the rains come, people storm the ark, trying to get aboard. Noah can't make room for the reëm, a giant animal, so he ties it behind the ark. He also can't make room for the giant Og, the king of Bashan, so Og sits on top of the ark, and Noah doles out food through a hole. Og has promised that if he is saved, he and his descendants will serve as slaves in perpetuity. Falsehood begs to be allowed to come, but Noah says he can accept only pairs. So Falsehood goes to seek a partner. He meets Misfortune, who says she will come if she can henceforth appropriate whatever Falsehood earns. Falsehood agrees, and Noah takes them aboard.

After the rain stops, the ark comes to rest on Mount Ararat. Noah and his sons Shem, Ham, and Japeth repopulate the earth, and God sends the rainbow as a sign of his promise never to flood the earth again. (Genesis 6:5–9:17; Ginzberg 1992)

See also Flood Myths; *Gilgamesh, Epic of;* Utnapishtim; Ziusudra.

NOMAHLANJANA

In the Zulu epic *Emperor Shaka the Great,* Nomahlanjana is King Zwide's heir; he is killed at the battle of Ookli. (Kunene 1979)

See also *Emperor Shaka the Great;* Zwide.

NOMCHOBA

In the Zulu epic *Emperor Shaka the Great,* Nomchoba is Shaka's sister. (Kunene 1979)

NOMNXAMAMA

Nomnxamama was the great Zulu national poet of Shaka's era who committed suicide at Shaka's death. (Kunene 1979)

See also *Emperor Shaka the Great.*

NORGES KONUGA SOGÜR

Norwegian kings saga. ***See*** *Heimskringla.*

NSONG' A TOOT

This epic of the Kuba-speaking Bushongo people of Africa was recorded in 1953 at Mushonge during a performance by the Nyim, or king of the tribe. The epic is a reminder that the Bushong rulers are descended from divine kings. It is usually performed at coronation ceremonies. (Westley *RAL* 1991)

NTOMBAZI

In the Zulu epic *Emperor Shaka the Great,* Ntombazi is one of the most politically influential women. She is queen mother of Ndwandwe king Zwide and his great supporter. (Kunene 1979)

See also *Emperor Shaka the Great;* Zwide.

NÜ KUA
(Also Nua Kwa and Nu Kwa)

In Chinese legends of antiquity, Nü and Kua are the first humans, brother and sister, who appear at the moment of creation on the Kunlun Mountains. They offer a sacrifice to the gods, asking to know if they are to become husband and wife. When the smoke from the sacrifice becomes stationary, they know they have received an affirmative answer.

In Chinese mythology, Nü Kua is the patroness of matchmakers who establishes the standards of conduct between sexes. She is the wife of Emperor Fu Hsi. When the rebel Kung Kung destroys the pillars of Heaven in a fit of anger, Nü Kua repairs them, using the feet of a tortoise. (Mackenzie 1990)

NUHIÑO
(Earth Story)

This creation epic of the Jivaros of Ecuador tells of several generations of sacred powers, beginning with Kumpara the Creator and his wife Chingaso, who fight and mate, producing fantastic creatures by various means. Kumpara and Chingaso have a son, Etsa, the Sun. While Etsa sleeps, Kumpara takes a piece of mud into his mouth and blows it onto Etsa. It becomes a daughter, Nantu, the Moon, supposed to be Etsa's mate. But the two fight and Nantu goes off by herself to produce a son out of dirt, whom she names Nuhi. She is so fond of Nuhi that the bird Auhu becomes jealous and breaks Nuhi, who dies and becomes the Earth. Now Nantu is lonely, and she consents to become Etsa's wife. They have a son, Unushi, the sloth, the first of the Jivaro. Nantu and Etsa fashion a canoe and launch it on the river, where their second son is born. He is Apopa, the manatee. The couple goes to the mountains, where a third son, Huangani, the peccary, is born. In a forest clearing, their daughter, Nijamanche, the manioc plant, is born.

Unushi marries Mika, a woman who is hatched from an egg. The two have a son, Ahimbi, the water serpent. Ahimbi travels far away and meets a white man, Apachi, who is traveling in an iron canoe. Apachi teaches Ahimbi how to construct a canoe from iron but tells him, "Now you know these things but they are not for you. On the water you are to use canoes and balsas." Apachi leaves, and Ahimbi travels on. He has many adventures before he starts for home.

On the way, he comes upon his mother Mika in the forest and sleeps with her. But he oversleeps, and when Etsa comes at dawn, he is angry to find the two sleeping together. Etsa banishes them, and they wander into the wilderness. They have many children, but they are unable to find a place to settle because the birds and animals are offended by their unnatural union.

Meanwhile, Unushi has learned of their conduct and vows to take revenge. When Nantu arrives to visit her offspring, he accuses her of consenting to the union, beats her violently, throws her into a hole, and covers her with earth. Nantu eventually escapes, returns to the sky, and tells the others what has happened. The sons of Mika and Ahimbi go in search of Unushi and cut off his head.

When Mika learns what has happened, she beats her sons born of Ahimbi until they are dead. Ahimbi fights Mika, causing a great tempest with torrential rains and terrific thunder and lightning.

At the height of the hurricane, Masata, the embodiment of war, appears with a thunderbolt. He encourages both sides in the fight, which has now widened to include a number of fighters on each side. When Etsa and Nantu look down on the turmoil, they descend to earth and accuse Ahimbi of being responsible for the fight. They change him into Pangi, the boa.

Ahimbi thrashes his tail and sprays water into the air, forming a rainbow as a sign to Etsa that he wants to restore peace. But Matasa sees the rainbow first and places clouds to obscure it from Etsa's view. Each time Ahimbi tries to signal, Matasa thwarts his efforts to bring about peace. (Sproul 1991)

NUMMO

(Also Nommo)

In the creation myth of the Dogon tribe of Mali in West Africa, Nummo is the name of primal twins, creations of the god Amma, who are spirits of light and water. They make earth ready for habitation and decree the creation of the eight ancestors. (Sproul 1991)

NXAZONKE

In the Zulu epic *Emperor Shaka the Great,* Nxazonke is Shaka's maternal uncle and leader of the delegation that goes to the north in search of iron, a pivotal event near the end of the epic. (Kunene 1979)

See also *Emperor Shaka the Great.*

NYAMBI

Nyambi is the creator god, the sun, of the Barotze, or Lozi, people of Zaire. In the beginning he lives on earth with his wife Nasilele, the moon. A creature Nyambi has created, Kamonu, begins to imitate everything Nyambi does. One day Kamonu forges a spear and begins killing antelope and other things. Nyambi sends Kamonu to another land, but Kamonu returns. He continues to kill animals, but soon his dog and his child die and his pot breaks. When Kamonu goes to tell Nyambi what has happened, he finds his dog, his child, and his pot at Nyambi's house. Nyambi tries to escape Kamonu by moving his court across the river, but Nyambi makes a raft of reeds and floats across. Nyambi continues in vain to try to escape Kamonu, and all the time men are multiplying. Finally a diviner tells him, "Your life depends on Spider." Spider finds an abode for Nyambi in the sky and spins a thread upon which Nyambi can climb. Kamonu tries to build a tower to reach Nyambi, but the tower

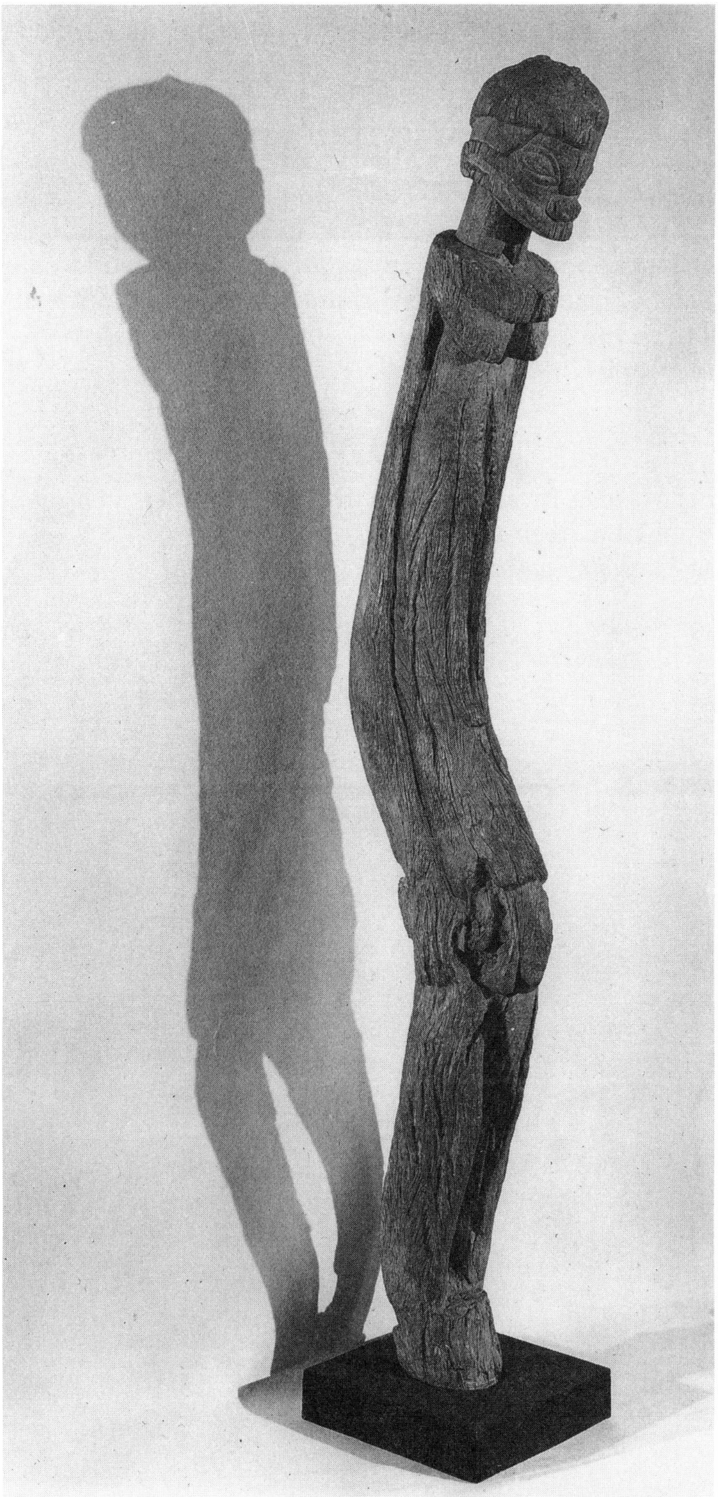

A character carved from wood and collected in the West African nation of Mali, represents Nommo, primal man of the Dogon people.

collapses. Kamonu and the other men can only worship the sun and moon from a distance. (Lipschutz and Rasmussen 1989; Sproul 1991)

NYAMURAIRI

In several versions of the *Mwindo Epic,* Nyamurairi is the god of fire and chief of the underworld who exposes Mwindo to various tests. In one version he marries his daughter to Mwindo. In another version, Mwindo dies and then does battle with Nyamurairi. Later Nyamurairi's servant returns Mwindo to earth. (Biebuyck 1978)

See also Journey; *Mwindo, Epic of.*

NYAMWINDO

In the *Epic of Mwindo,* Nyamwindo is the hero's mother, who remains a great influence upon him. (Biebuyck 1978)

See also *Mwindo, Epic of.*

O

OBERON

In medieval legends of western Europe, Oberon is king of the fairies, possibly a later development of Alberich, king of the elves. He appears in the French medieval romance *Huon de Bordeaux* (thirteenth century) as the son of Morgan le Fay and Julius Caesar. (Siepmann 1987)

See also Chansons de Geste.

ODUDUWA

Oduduwa is the semimythical first leader (ca. fourteenth century) of the original West African Yoruba kingdoms, from which came the Oyo empire in present-day Nigeria. Tradition states that he descended from heaven to become the ruler of Ife, the first kingdom. His progeny founded other kingdoms. (Lipschutz and Rasmussen 1989; Parrinder 1982)

See also Oranyan; Oyo Empire.

ODYSSEY

This Greek epic poem (ca. ninth century B.C.) is attributed by ancient Greeks to Homer. It spread by way of reciters called rhapsodoi throughout Asia Minor before it was introduced in written form ca. 535 B.C. The poem tells, in over 12,000 lines divided into 24 books, of the adventures of Odysseus on his way home to Ithaca after the Trojan War. Although it is written in heroic verse in dactylic hexameter, the epic has been called the world's first novel because of its gripping narrative, told beginning in the tenth year of the story's main action, when events are nearing their climax, and because of the masterful use of flashbacks, particularly Odysseus's account of his Great Wanderings. Greek scholar W. H. D. Rouse has called it "the best story ever written."

Modern scholars believe that, for the most part, the epic is Homer's work, but it appears to be a later composition than the *Iliad.* With the exception of the very beginning, known locations do not figure in the narrative, nor do traditional characters, except in book X: Odysseus's visit to the Land of the Dead. The *Iliad* is a collection of material attaching itself to an event, the Trojan War, that in all probability actually occurred toward the end of the Mycenean era; however, the *Odyssey* appears to be the weaving together of a number of folktales from a variety of unrelated traditions, made more homogeneous by attributing them all to the same hero. The techniques of Homer set the standard for epic poetry of later writers, and his work was viewed as the final authority on history, ethics, and theology in ancient Aegia.

The 24 books are divided by Greek scholar Richmond Lattimore into four broad categories: Books I–IV concern the adventures of Telemachos, Odysseus's son; books V–VIII and part of book XIII concern Odysseus's homecoming; books IX–XII tell of Odysseus's wanderings; books XIII.187–XXIV describe Odysseus's activities on his return to Ithaca.

Book I opens with an invocation to Muse to tell what happened to "the man of many ways." The answer comes that the king of Ithaca, Odysseus, who is first identified as "godlike" and then "wise," has been on Ogygia, the far western island of the sea nymph Kalypso, "bright among goddesses," who has kept him imprisoned for seven years, tempting him with immortality if he will remain with her. But Odysseus is anxious to return home to Ithaca and his beautiful and clever wife Penelope, who is now, unbeknownst to him, sought after by a bevy of young suitors who have ensconced themselves in Odysseus's palace.

The story shifts to Odysseus's son Telemachos, back from Ithaca, where Penelope's suitors have literally taken over. Under the guidance of Athena, "the grey-eyed goddess," in book II, Telemachos resolves to set out to find his father. In book III, with Athene, he first consults Nestor in Pylos, who entertains him with a high feast. Nestor's son Peisistratos accompanies him to Sparta where, in book IV, Menelaos and Helen entertain them. Menelaos tells Telemachos of his own wanderings and reports that he has learned of Odysseus's captivity on Ogygia. Back in Ithaca, Penelope's suitors learn of Telemachos's quest and set out to ambush him. Meanwhile, in book V, on Zeus's orders, Hermes commands Kalypso to release Odysseus. The hero sails away on a raft but is shipwrecked on the Phaeacian island of Scherie by Poseidon, who has become his enemy for a reason that is revealed in book IX. In book VI, protecting his identity, he is befriended first by the young princess Nausikaa, then, in book VII, by her parents, King Alcinous and Queen Arete. In book VIII, during a palace feast, Demodakos sings of the feats of Odysseus of Troy, while Odysseus, described as "great-hearted," covers his head and cries. Games are held to console him, but he declines to compete. Angered when Euryalos tells him, "You do not resemble an athlete," Odysseus takes the discus and excels in the art of throwing. He spends some time boasting about his athletic prowess and eventually reveals his identity. In book IX he begins to describe his wanderings to the assemblage. After leaving Troy and making a raid on the Kiconians, he tells them, he landed in the land of the Lotus Eaters. Some of his men ate the lotus, which made them forget their past and their homes, and they had to be forcefully carried away. Next, Odysseus tells them, they landed on the island where the Cyclops lived. Polyphemos trapped them in his cave, and those who were not eaten alive escaped by trickery after blinding the Cyclops. This is the

Odysseus, the principal character in the Greek epic the *Odyssey,* draws his bow to slay suitors of Penelope, his wife, who remained faithful during his 20-year absence. This vessel, a *skyphos,* was made between 450–440 B.C. and was found at Tarquinia, an Etruscan city on the west coast of the Italian peninsula.

act that so angered Poseidon, for Polyphemos is his son. In book X, Odysseus continues his story. On reaching the island of Aiolos, he was presented the unfavorable winds tied up in a leather bag so that he could sail directly toward Ithaca with only good winds. However, thinking that the bag contained treasure, Odysseus's men opened the bag just as they reached Ithaca, and the ship was blown all the way back to Aiolos's island, where the god would have nothing more to do with them. A cannibal, Laistrygonians, then destroyed all but one of Odysseus's ships. He and the crew escaped to Aeaea, where the enchantress Circe awaited. She transformed most of the crew into swine; however, Hermes gave Odysseus an herb called moly that saved him, and he frightened Circe into changing his men back. In book XI, Odysseus tells of descending into the Land of the Dead, where the ghost of the Theban seer Teiresias told him how to reach home. In book XII, following Circe's advice, Odysseus sailed past the Sirens by stopping the ears of his crew with wax so that they would not become enchanted by the sweetness of the Sirens' singing, and by commanding his rowers Perimedes and Eurylochos to lash him to the mast until they were safely out of earshot. He tells how he avoided the whirlpool monster Charybdis and the man-eating monster Skylla, who snatched six of his men and ate them alive. The hungry crew overrode the advice of Odysseus and landed on Thrinakia, the island of Helios, where his sacred cattle and fat sheep grazed. After they ate some of Helios's oxen, Zeus punished them by destroying their ship with a thunderbolt, and only Odysseus escaped to the island of Ogygia on a keel and mast he had lashed together. There he was rescued by Kalypso, who kept him captive for so long. So ends his account to the Phaeacians of his wanderings.

In book XIII, the Phaeacians provide Odysseus with a ship, laden with treasures, to take him home to Ithaca. Once he has arrived, Poseidon, called "the Earthshaker," takes vengeance on his rescuers, the Phaeacians, by turning the ship into stone. Odysseus wakes on his own shore with his memory and even his identity clouded by Pallas Athene, until she can explain to him "all the details" of what has transpired in his absence, so that he can punish the suitors for their "overbearing oppression." After she reveals herself to him, he is transformed into an old tramp, a disguise that will afford him safe entry into his palace. Then she goes off to Lakedaimon to fetch Telemachos.

In book XIV, Odysseus finds Eumaios, the swineherd, to whom he tells a fictitious story of his life, claiming that he is a veteran of Troy who was waylaid in Egypt. He claims to have heard that Odysseus is still alive. Although Eumaios is skeptical, he offers the old tramp hospitality. Meantime, in book XV, Telemachos, at Pallas Athene's urging, leaves Menelaos's court. Helen prophesies that Odysseus will return to Ithaca. "The thoughtful Telemachos" returns to Pylos, avoiding Nestor but taking a fugitive prophet, Theoklymenos, as a passenger. Meantime, Eumaios tells Odysseus his own life story and reveals that he was once the son of a king.

Telemachos arrives in Ithaca and, in book XVI, visits Eumaios and dispatches him to tell Penelope of his whereabouts. When Athene gives him the signal, Odysseus reveals his true identity to his son. After Odysseus learns of the conduct of Penelope's suitors, father and son make plans to deal with them. Meanwhile, Penelope's suitors plot another ambush of Telemachos.

In book XVII, father and son decide to return to the palace separately. Telemachos arrives first, and immediately sends for his prophet-passenger Theoklymenos to join him. Telemachos tells his mother that the "ever-truthful Old Man of the Sea" has told him that Odysseus has been held captive by Kalypso for all these years. Theoklymenos tells her that he has interpreted a bird sign that indicates her husband is already here in Ithaca. Eumaios arrives next, accompanied by the "much-enduring great Odysseus," still disguised as a beggar. His faithful old dog recognizes "patient-hearted Odysseus," but dies before he can reveal his master's identity. Odysseus is invited by Telemachos to go begging among the suitors, the chief of whom, Antinoos, hits him with a footstool. After reporting to Penelope that he has brought a beggar who has news of her husband's whereabouts, Eumaios returns to his home, leaving Odysseus to his own devices.

In book XVIII, a public beggar named Iros arrives. Egged on by the suitors, Iros challenges Odysseus to a fight. Odysseus is obliged, with his son's help, to break Iros's jaw. Penelope appears to suggest to the suitors that, since her son is now grown, the suitor who gives her the finest gifts might possibly win her. During the feast and dance that follow, Odysseus steps forward boldly and orders the maids who are keeping the fires burning to return to the house; he himself will provide the light for the dancing. One maid scolds him for his arrogance, and he answers, "I think I will go to Telemachos, you bitch, and tell him / how you are talking, so that he will cut you to pieces." This speech sends the women fluttering to the house, "and the knees of each one / went loose with fear." When Odysseus speaks equally boldly to the men, Eurymachos, one of the leading suitors, also throws a footstool at him, but misses.

In book XIX, Odysseus and Telemachos remain in the hall after the others have retired and remove the suitors' armor. Penelope calls for him to tell her what he knows about her husband. Odysseus pretends to have come from Crete where, he tells her, he entertained Odysseus. He claims that her husband is even now on his way home. In gratitude for his news, she offers him hospitality and calls for his old nurse, Eurykleia, to wash his feet. But the old woman finds a scar and recognizes him as her master. She would announce the news to Penelope except that Athene has momentarily "turned aside her perception." Odysseus silences the old nurse by telling her that if she reveals his identity, "I will not spare you / when I kill the rest of the serving maids in my palace." Odysseus suggests to Penelope that she hold a contest using his bow, wherein each man first strings it, then sends an arrow through 12 axes.

In book XX, after a sleepless night, during which he is comforted by Athene, he joins all the other principals who have assembled for the contest. In book XXI, Penelope fetches Odysseus's bow and explains that she will marry the winner of the contest. After all the suitors have failed even to string the bow, Odysseus, who has come as Telemachos's guest, reveals himself to Eumaios and asks for a try at stringing the bow. When the suitors object, "circumspect Penelope" shames them into giving him a chance. But "thoughtful Telemachos" sends his mother to the back of the house with a tongue-lashing, telling her, "mine is the power in this household." After Penelope retires in tears, Odysseus easily strings the bow and shoots through the 12 axes that Telemachos has set up.

At that point, in book XXII, Odysseus strips off his rags and reveals his identity, and the battle begins. Odysseus and his men lock the suitors in the great hall of the palace, where he shoots them down with his bow. In book XXIII, the old nurse informs Penelope that her husband is in the house. Penelope is at first unable to recognize her husband, who tells her, "No other woman, with spirit as stubborn as yours, would keep back / as you are doing from her husband who, after much suffering, came at last in the twentieth year back to his own country." He tells his nurse to make him a bed in another chamber, "for this woman has a heart of iron within her." At length she recognizes him and he invites her to "come, my wife, let us go to bed, so that at long last / we can enjoy the sweetness of slumber, sleeping together." He is reestablished as the king of Ithaca and is also reunited with his aged father, while Athene calms the resentment of the suitors' families.

In book XXIV, the leaders of Troy hear the story from the suitors' ghosts, and eventually Odysseus must fight the kinsmen as well. Athene comes "in a flash of speed down the pinnacles of Olympus" and commands Odysseus to "hold hard, stop this quarrel in closing combat, for fear / Zeus of the wide brows, son of Kronos, may be angry with you." "With happy heart," Odysseus obeys her, and peace settles upon the land. (Lattimore 1967; Rieu 1961; Rouse 1990)

OEDIPUS

Son of Laius, king of Thebes, and Jocasta. He murders his father and, after destroying the Sphinx and ascending to the throne of Thebes, unwittingly marries his own mother. They have four children: Eteocles, Polynices, Antigone, and Ismene. When his sin is revealed, he puts out his eyes and leaves Thebes, led by Antigone. He retires to Colonus, near Athens, where he disappears into an opening in the earth. Oedipus appears in the *Odyssey* (xi). (Graves 1955; Rieu 1961)

OENEUS

In the *Iliad* (ix), Oeneus is king of Calydon, father by Althea of Meleager and Deianeira, and by Periboea of Tydeus. When he forgets to sacrifice to Artemis, she sends a boar to ravage his kingdom. Many heroes participate in the Calydonian boar hunt, but the boar is killed by Meleager. (Lattimore 1976)

ÓENGUS, THE DREAM OF

(Also *Oenghus)*

In this Old Celtic tale, Óengus (Angus) mac Oc becomes enamored of a beautiful maiden who appears in his dreams but vanishes when he attempts to hold her. When he falls into a "wasting sickness," his physician, Finghin, seeks the help of Óengus's father, Dagda (Daghdhae, "the Good God," chief of the Irish gods), who orders a search for the elusive maiden. The search lasts for one year before Óengus is summoned to examine a line-up ("thrice 50") of young maidens. From among them he picks Caer, the woman of his dreams. But she is a swan-woman who, at the time of Samain's Feast (31 October), will revert to her other form. When she becomes a swan, Óengus goes down to the lakeside and proclaims his love for her. Caer agrees to become his mate if he will agree to become a swan. He does so, and the two fly away to Óengus's castle, singing the Noble Strain, which lulls the populace to sleep. (Jackson, K. 1971; Rutherford 1987)

OFFA OF ANGEL

Offa is the Anglican ruler (fourth century A.D.) from whom the royal house of Anglo-Saxon Mercia claimed descent. He is thought to be the Offa mentioned in *Beowulf.* In the Old English poem *Widsith,* he saves the throne of his father, King Wermund, by meeting a Saxon prince in combat. Later Offa ruled the kingdom of Angel on the continent of Europe. An eighth-century Mercian ruler, also named Offa, built an earthen wall between Mercia and Wales, naming it Offa's Dyke after his predecessor Offa of Angel. (Alexander, H. 1964; Raffel 1963)

See also *Beowulf; Widsith.*

OGBABA OKORIE

This is an oral heroic legend of the Igbo community of Ohafia in Imo State, southeastern Nigeria, West Africa. Performances of the legend, which is several hundred years old, by the griot Kaalu Igirigiri were recorded in the 1970s. The legend tells the story of a famous Ohafia dancer of the Ekpe dance who is killed, his knees shattered by gunfire from jealous rivals in a neighboring clan. (Azuonye *RAL* 1990)

OGIER THE DANE

Ogier is the hero of a cycle of French chansons de geste dealing with several wars against Charlemagne, *Geste de Doon de Mayence.* He is also the central character in *La Chevalerie Ogier de Danemarche, Les Enfances Ogier,* and various tales in Iceland, Spain, and Italy. His character is based on the historical Autcharius, liege of Carloman, the younger brother of Charlemagne. After Carloman died in 771, Charlemagne invaded and overtook Autcharius's kingdom. Ogier is celebrated in Danish song as a national hero, although the area of his kingdom may have been the Ardennes instead of Denmark. The twelfth-century *La Chevalerie Ogier de Danemarche* tells of his military adventures in Italy and his reconciliation with Charlemagne. In *Les Enfances Ogier,* he is a member of Charlemagne's court who confronts the emperor over his son's slaying of

Ogier's son and is put into prison. When the Saracens hear a rumor that Ogier is dead, they invade the kingdom. Ogier offers to lead the Frankish warriors against the Saracens in exchange for Charlot, Charlemagne's son. Ogier does not kill Charlot, but merely slaps his face. He goes on to victory against the Saracens and is rewarded by Charlemagne. (Harrison 1970)

See also Doon de Mayence.

OGMIOS

(Also Ogma and Ogmae)

Ogmios is a Celtic god of Gaul, identified with Herakles. In Irish legend, Ogmae is the inventor of writing. Ogma is a god of the clan of Túatha Dé Danann. (Gantz 1988; Hubert 1980)

OGUN

God of war of the Yoruba people of Nigeria and Benin, Ogun figures in a creation epic cycle. In the beginning a huge gulf exists between the gods and mankind. Ogun rises in council and offers to end the separation. After he clears a path through the jungle to the world of men, the gods try to crown him king of the gods, but he refuses. He withdraws in solitude until the people of Ire persuade him to lead them in war against their enemies. But Ogun, who loves palm wine, becomes so drunk that he kills friend and foe alike. When he becomes sober, he retires again to the hills until the Ire convince him to become their king. Ogun is also the god of smithery, hunting, wood-cutting and carving, and, more recently, of driving motor vehicles. (Parrinder 1982)

OĞUZNÂME

Oğuznâme is a major Turkish epic composed in the Uiger tongue of Turfan ca. 1300. The Oğuz tribes moved into Anatolia ca. the ninth to mid-eleventh centuries, bringing a highly developed popular literature formed before the influence of Islamic Arabic/Persian cultures. This epic names the grey wolf Kök-böri as the mythical ancestor of the Turks: "From a beam of light came a great dog-wolf with a gray coat and mane." It tells the illustrious migratory history of the Turkish tribes. The argument for identifying the Oğuz tribe with the Uiger is supported in part by a statement in the *Oğuznâme* in which Oğuz-Khan, the eponymous hero of the epic, says, "I am the khagan of the Uiger."

The epic contains the story of Dabaku, "ugly and loathsome," with a single eye on the top of his head (Goggle-Eye), whose mother is an ocean demon and whose father is so large that his bonnet is made of the skins of ten rams. He ravages the lands of the Turks and slays many of the great men before he is slain. (Lewis 1974)

See also *Dede Korkut, The Book of.*

OGYGES, FLOOD OF
(Also "Ogygus")

This is the account of a flood in which the legendary king of Thebes in Boeotia is spared. According to early Christian chronicler Julius Africanus, Ogyges "was saved when many perished" and he "lived at the time of the Exodus of the people from Egypt, along with Moses." (Heinberg 1989)

See also Flood Myths.

OHO-KUNI-NUSHI NO KAMI

See Opo-kuni-nusi-nö-kamï.

OISÍN

Oisín is a legendary Irish warrior-poet of the *Fenian Cycle.* (Rutherford 1987)

See also Ossian.

ŌJIN TENNŌ
(Also the Emperor Homuda, Homuda wake, or Pomuda-wake-no-mikoto)

According to the *Kojiki,* Ōjin Tennō was the fifteenth emperor of Japan, who ruled ca. 362–394. He was the son of Emperor Chuai by Empress Jingu. During his reign the Yamato kingdom increased its suzerainty on the Korean peninsula. He was deified as Hachiman, god of war. (Philippi 1968)

OKUNI-NUSHI

Land-creator in Japanese mythology. **See** Opo-kuni-nusi-nö-kamï.

OLAF GUTHFRITHSON

King of Northumbria and Dublin, his invasion of England (937) is the subject of the Old English poem "The Battle of Brunanburh." (Alexander, M. 1991; Hieatt 1967)

See also "Brunanburh, The Battle of."

ÓLAFS SAGA HELGA
(Also "The History of St. Olav")

In the *Heimskringla* (ca. 1220), Icelandic poet Snorri Sturluson tells the story of Olav's birth in Norway in 995 to Harald the Grenlander and Asta, of his adoption by King Sigurd, and of his leaving Norway at the age of 12 to go on Viking raids, attacking Canterbury and Hampshire two years later. Olav and Thorkel the High make peace with King Ethelred in 1012, and the next year he helps Richard II, duke of Normandy, conquer Brittany. He is baptized in France and returns to England with Edward (the Confessor) the following year.

After joining with the English in fighting the Danes, he leaves for Norway where, after the Battle of Nesjar, he is elected king of Norway. He marries Astrid, daughter of the Swedish king. He establishes the Church of Norway in 1024. But his kingdom is soon threatened by King Canute of England and Denmark, who subjugates Norway in 1028 and forces Olav to flee in 1029 to Kiev, Russia, to stay with his wife's relatives. He returns to Norway the following year and attempts to reconquer the land. He meets the Danes at the Battle of Stiklastader and is mortally wounded by three blows of the ax and the spear.

Thereafter the king's legend begins to grow. Many pray to him and their prayers are answered. After 12 months and five nights, the king's coffin is dug up, and the king's body is found to be intact: His cheeks are red as if he has just fallen asleep. His hair has grown; the bishop cuts a lock and casts it into the fire, but it does not burn. The king is canonized. His body is borne to St. Clement's Church and placed over the high altar, where many kinds of miracles occur. Olav was the last Western saint of the Eastern churches. (Monsen and Smith 1990)

ÓLAFS SAGA TRYGGVASONAR
(Also "The History of Olav Trygvason")

Saga of the Viking king of Norway (ca. 964–ca. 1000) as told by Snorri Sturluson in *Heimskringla.* Olaf flees with his mother Astrid first to Sweden and finally to the court of the king of Gardarik (Russia) to escape Harald II Greyskin, the murderer of his father, King Trygvi Olavson. Astrid's brother Sigurd is already there and has a reputation of great honor. One day Olaf is in the marketplace and recognizes Klerkon, the murderer of his foster father. He drives an ax into Klerkon's head and then runs to tell Sigurd what he has done. Sigurd takes him to Queen Allogia, who looks at the boy and says that no man should kill so fine a boy. She takes Olaf under her protection and pays his fine.

When Olaf grows older, King Valdemar makes him chief of the army in Gardarik, but many warriors are jealous of him because he is a foreigner. So Olaf decides to sail to the Baltic and join the Vikings. During rough weather, he lays over in Vendland, where he meets Queen Geira, the daughter of King Burislav (Boreslav I of Poland). Geira owns the land where Olaf lands. She invites the men to spend the winter, and before the spring comes, Olaf and Geira marry.

He stays in Vendland for three years until Geira becomes ill and dies. He then mans his warships and goes back to fighting. In 991 he sails to England and then Scotland, where "the battle-glad wolf feeder / Wasted the Scots widely / With the sword. . . ." He meets Queen Gyda, daughter of an Irish king and widow of a mighty jarl in England, who is now ruling his lands. She is allowed to choose another husband, and she chooses Olaf. Before they can marry, Olaf must fight his rival, Alvini. After they marry, he lives with Gyda in both England and Ireland.

When Olaf learns of the growing unpopularity of Norwegian king Hakon the Great, he returns to Norway. When Hakon dies in 995, Olaf becomes king. In the summer of 1000 he sets sail down the western coast of Norway, collecting ships along the way until he has a fleet of 60 warships. He sails to see Burislav the Pole, ruler of Wendland, father of Geira, and also briefly the husband of Olaf's current wife Thyri (Thóra). He goes ostensibly to recover his wife's dowry, which she left when she fled Burislav. Burislav repays the dowry in full and the two men form an alliance. As Olaf returns to Norway, he engages in a sea-fight with the Danes headed by Eirik. After heroic resistance against great odds, he dies during the Battle of Svolder, and loses his kingdom as well. (Monsen and Smith 1990)

OLEG

In the *Russian Primary Chronicle* (twelfth century), Oleg is the semilegendary Varangian (Viking) warrior-ruler of Novgorod who sails down the Dneiper River ca. 879 to capture Smolensk and, in 882, Kiev. He is given credit for founding the state of Kiev and for uniting a number of Slavic and Finnish peoples under his domain. He later defeats the Khazars and even instigates raids against the Byzantine capital of Constantinople, which results in the Byzantine payment of a substantial indemnity and an agreement to establish trade relations between Novgorod-Kiev and Byzantium. (Dvornik 1962; Vernadsky 1959)

See also *Russian Primary Chronicle.*

OLIVIER
(Also Oliver)

In the Old French epic poems, or chansons de geste, Olivier is a close friend of Roland, a paladin of Charlemagne. He has the prudence and common sense that his friend lacks, for Roland is too preoccupied with winning glory for himself. Roland and Olivier meet in a long and arduous duel during a war between Olivier's family and Charlemagne. The battle is ended by divine intervention, and the two become fast friends. Roland is betrothed to Olivier's sister Aude. The *Chanson de Roland* describes how Roland's stepfather Ganelon plots with the Saracens to bring about Roland's downfall. The poem deals with the historic Battle of Roncesvalles in 778, when Roland refuses to follow Olivier's advice to blow his horn and summon help from Charlemagne until it is too late. Olivier, who has been blinded, accidentally strikes Roland, and they both die. When Aude learns of their deaths, she falls dead at the feet of Charlemagne.

Olivier appears in Pulci's comic Florentine poem "Il Morgante Maggiore," and as Rinaldo in the Italian Renaissance epics, Boiardo's *Orlando Innamorato* and Ariosto's *Orlando Furioso.* (Harrison 1970)

See also *Chanson de Roland;* Ganelon; Roland.

OLORUN

Olorun is the Supreme Being, Owner of the Sky in Yoruba (Nigeria, West Africa) religion. (Abrahams 1983; Parrinder 1982)

See also Orisha Nla.

OMETÉOTL
(Spirit of Duality)

This Aztec deity of creation is sometimes divided into two: Ometecuhtli (Lord of Duality, also Tonacatecuhtli) and Omecihuatl (Lady of Duality, also Tonacacihuatl). The two dwell in the Thirteenth Heaven, the highest.

Ometéotl is synonymous with the heroic deity Quetzalcóatl in the myth of *Quetzalcóatl.* (Bierhorst 1974)

See also *Quetzalcóatl, Topiltzin.*

OMPHALE

In Greek mythology, Omphale is a queen of Lydia who desires to see Herakles. Hermes sells Herakles to her as a slave, and Herakles spends three years in her service, ridding Lydia of robbers and other threats. The couple has several children, and after three years she releases him to return to Tiryns. Ovid and other later writers embroidered the story with accounts that the couple exchange clothing, Omphale wearing the lion's skin and Herakles a woman's dress. (Graves 1955)

See also Herakles.

OPO-KUNI-NUSI-NÖ-KAMÏ
(Also Oho-kuni-nushi no kami, Oho-na-mochi, or Ō-kuni-nushi)

In the *Nihongi* and the *Kojiki,* Opo-kuni-nusi is the land-creator and culture hero of the "Idumo," or "Idzumo," cycle of Japanese mythology. In the *Kojiki* he is the sixth-generation descendant of the storm god Sosa-no-wo, but the *Nihongi* also includes one account in which he is the son of Sosa-no-wo. Before he becomes "Great-country-master," he undergoes a series of ordeals, including being killed twice by his 80 evil brothers.

In the *Kojiki*, while he is carrying the bags of his 80 brothers to Inaba, where they are going to marry Princess Ya-gami-pime, he encounters a naked rabbit who has been skinned of his fur by a crocodile. The 80 evil brothers instruct him to bathe in saltwater, causing his whole body to blister. Opo-kuni-nusi advises him to bathe in the river, then cover his skin with the pollen of the kama grass. The rabbit is healed by following this advice, and he repays Opo-kuni-nusi by using his magic: "These 80 deities will certainly never gain Ya-gami-pime. Although you carry their bags, you shall gain her." However, the marriage is unsuccessful because of the princess's fear of the chief wife, Suseri-bime.

The story of his wooing of Suseri-bime, daughter of Sosa-no-wo, is told in another *Kojiki* tale, in which he travels to the nether world and the two fall in love at first sight. She protects him from snakebite with a snake-repelling scarf. Sosa-no-wo, the storm god, sets fire to the plain, but a mouse saves Opo-kuni-nusi from burning. The couple elopes, making their escape from the palace after Opo-kuni-nusi ties Sosa-no-wo's hair to the rafters while he sleeps and takes his sword of life, his bow and arrows of life, and his heavenly cither (Kötö, also cittern, having a long neck and five or six strings). As they flee, the cither brushes against a tree, waking Sosa-no-wo, who pursues them to the place where the land of darkness meets the land of light. Then he gives the couple his blessing.

In one story, Opo-kuni-nusi is sitting by the sea when he hears a voice coming from the surface of the water. He sees nothing at first, then spies a dwarf riding in a boat made of the rind of a kagami (gourd) and wearing clothing made of wren feathers. He takes the dwarf into the palm of his hand and plays with him until the dwarf jumps up and bites him on the cheek. Opo-kuni-nusi sends a message to the Gods of Heaven, and Taka-mi-musubi nö Mikoto answers that he himself has produced 1,500 children. "Amongst them one was very wicked, and would not yield compliance to my instructions. He slipped (or dripped) through my fingers and fell. This must be that child, let him be loved and nurtured." The dwarf is named Sukuna-bikona nö Mikoto, who is still a popular god to this day. He is glorified as the inventor of medicine and of the art of brewing sake.

Opo-kuni-nusi and Sukuna-bikona, "with united strength and one heart," begin to build the world. They determine the method of healing diseases and controlling calamities caused by birds, beasts, creeping things, and things coming from the unseen world.

Opo-kuni-nusi marries many times and has many children. Having subdued his 80 brothers, he continues to rule Idumo until Take-mika-duti-nö-kamï is sent to demand that he surrender the Central Land of the Reed Plain. After his sons are defeated in a contest of strength, Opo-kuni-nusi agrees to surrender his land, after which he is worshiped at his shrine in Idumo. (Aston 1972; Philippi 1968)

See also *Kojiki; Nihongi.*

ORACLES OF HYSTASPES

This Greek text (ca. first century B.C.) introduced the Zoroastrian and Manichaean myths of Mithras to the West. According to the text, God will save the righteous by sending the Great King from heaven to vanquish the powers of evil with fire and sword. The Great King is the incarnated Mithras, ancient Persian sun god, embodiment of wisdom, goodness, and light, and agent, through the sacred bull, of the creation of all living things. (Olmstead 1948)

ORANYAN

Oranyan is the great warrior son of Oduduwa, first Ifé king of Oyo, in present-day Nigeria, West Africa, celebrated in oral tradition. (Lipschutz and Rasmussen 1989; Parrinder 1982)

See also Oduduwa; Oyo Empire.

ORESTES

In Greek mythology, Orestes is the son of Agamemnon and Clytemnestra and brother of Electra, Iphigeneia, and Chrysothemis. According to Homer, when Orestes grows to manhood, he and Pylades go to Mycenae and, with Electra's help, avenge Agamemnon's death at the hands of Clytemnestra's lover Aegisthus by murdering the two lovers. (Graves 1955)

See also Agamemnon; Clytemnestra.

ORISHA NLA

(Also Orisha Oko, or Great God)

He is the chief god of the Yoruba people of Nigeria in West Africa, celebrated in the creation cycle. He is instructed by Olorun, the Supreme Being, Owner of the Sky, to create firm ground. Later he is given part of the task of creating human beings, whom he forms out of earth. But the Creator reserves for himself the task of bringing the beings to life. Jealous of this life-giving work, Orisha decides to spy to learn how it is done. But the Creator knows he is hiding nearby and sends him into a deep sleep. When he awakens, the humans have come to life. Orisha still makes the bodies of human beings, but he leaves marks on them, some showing his displeasure. (Parrinder 1982)

See also Olorun.

ORKNEYINGA SAGA

Written ca. 1200 by an Icelander, this saga gives the Norse history of the earls of Orkney from ca. 900 to 1200. It is the only Norse saga concerned with an area that is now part of the British Isles. The Orkneys consist of about 70 islands off the northern coast of Scotland, 20 of which are inhabited. The saga, which is a prose account interspersed with poetry, relates the ninth-century conquest of the islands by the Viking kings of Norway and the establishment of the earldom (from the Norwegian jarl) of Orkney, beginning with Sigurd Eysteinsson the Powerful, the first to hold the title of earl. Sigurd is given Shetland and Orkney by his brother Rognvald, and is granted the title of earl by Norwegian king Harald Fine-Hair, the original conqueror of those islands and the Hebrides.

Sigurd, one of the three most powerful earls of Orkney, joins with Thorstein the Red and travels to Caithness, Argyll, Moray, and Ross to conquer and plunder. The saga includes the stories of the 28 men who hold the title of earl from the late ninth century to 1206.

Among the later earls, the most famous—still revered today—is St. Magnus the Martyr, who is joint ruler of Orkney with Earl Hakon and granted the title of earl by King Eystein. Later he and Earl Hakon have a falling-out over their joint rule, and Hakon takes him prisoner. Magnus suspects treachery but refuses to run away. Hakon orders his cook Lifolf to kill Magnus (1117), and the rocky ground where he dies becomes a green field. His body is taken to Mainland and buried at Christ Church, where a heavenly light is often seen over his grave. Some sense a heavenly fragrance at his grave, and many go in secret to receive miracles of healing there. But so long as Earl Hakon lives, no one dares make the miracles public. After a visiting bishop, William, becomes blind and has his sight restored at the grave site, he orders the body disinterred. When the bones will not burn, Magnus is declared a saint. (Pálsson and Edwards 1982)

See also Bard; Botolf the Stubborn; Brian.

THE ORPHAN

This Chinese ballad (ca. first century A.D.) of the yeuh-fu category consists of lines that vary in length to suggest the sobbing voice of the singer. The poem is written in first-person by a young boy whose parents have died and whose brother and sister-in-law send him south and east to be a merchant. After a year he comes home ragged and covered with lice and vermin, and is treated as a servant in his brother's home. Once, he is sent out with the melon cart, which turns over. Few people help him right it, but many steal his melons and eat them. He says, "I want to write a letter and send it / To my mother and father under the earth, / And tell them I can't go on any longer. . . ." (Waley 1982)

ORPHEUS

Orpheus is a legendary Greek musician and poet, son of Apollo and Calliope, and husband of Eurydice. He is a master of the lyre, and accompanies the Argonauts on their expedition to gain the Golden Fleece. His music is so beautiful that when he plays, rivers cease to flow, mountains are moved, and wild beasts become tame. He saves the Argonauts from the witchery of the Sirens by playing music even more beautiful than theirs. (Graves 1955)

See also Argonauts.

ORT

In Finno-Ugric mythology, the ort is a free soul or shadow that can detach itself while the person is still alive and wander far distances beyond the body. After death the ort is said to hover over the spot where the body is buried. (Holmberg 1964)

OSAI TUTU

Osai Tutu is the fourth king (eighteenth century) of the Ashanti people in West Africa (Ghana), celebrated in oral tradition. It is for Osai Tutu that a medicine man, banished from a neighboring tribe, brings down from the Supreme Being Nyame in the sky the Golden Stool, symbol of the soul of the Ashanti people. The stool becomes so precious that when the British invade in 1896, the Ashanti surrender for fear that the stool will be damaged. When a second war breaks out, the Ashanti hide the stool, and it is not discovered again until 1921. (Parrinder 1982)

OSIRIS

(Also Serapis)

Osiris is the Egyptian god of the underworld and judge of the dead. He is the son of Zeus and Niobe, brother and husband of Isis, and brother of Typhon, who murders him. Osiris is one of three main gods, the Triad of Abydos, incorporated into the Great Ennead, or state religion of Egypt, by the priests of Heleopolis. The three are Osiris, Isis, and Horus the Hawk, the Avenger. (Budge 1967; Budge 1969)

See also Horus; Isis.

OSSIAN

(Also Oisín)

Ossian is the legendary Irish son of Fionn Mac Cumhail, who becomes a bard in his old age (ca. late third century A.D.) As such, he is the chief bard of the *Fenian Cycle* of sagas. (Rutherford 1987)

See also *Fenian Cycle; Ossianic Ballads.*

OSSIANIC BALLADS

These Irish Gaelic narrative poems and lyrics named for the Irish warrior-poet Oisín deal with the legends of Fionn Mac Cumhail, but were composed at a much later date than the *Fenian Cycle.* The Ossianic ballads consist of over 80,000 lines and actually took shape over a period of seven centuries, beginning with the eleventh century, although some of the themes go back as early as the third century. They were collected in the sixteenth century by Sir James MacGregor and published in *The Book of the Dean of Lismore.* (Siepmann 1987)

See also *Fenian Cycle.*

ÓTHIN

(Also Odin, Ódinn, Wodan, and Woden)

In Norse mythology, throughout the *Poetic Edda,* Óthin is one of the principal gods, appearing in heroic literature as a war god and protector of heroes. Óthin is the Scandinavian name of the Anglo-Saxon god Woden. He dwells in Valhalla, heavenly home of fallen warriors. He is also the god of poets who steals the poets' mead, and the god of magic, inventor of the runes. (Hollander *Edda* 1990; Jones, G. 1990)

See also *Edda, Poetic.*

OUKALEGON

(Also Ucalegon)

In the *Iliad* (iii), Oukalegon is a Trojan counselor of Priam. In the *Aeneid* (ii), he is Anchises's friend. (Humphries 1951; Lattimore 1976)

OXLAHUNTIKU

In Mayan cosmology, Oxlahuntiku is the composite name given to the 13 gods who preside over the heavens. (Bierhorst 1974)

OYA

In the Yoruba mythology in Nigeria, West Africa, Oya is the goddess of tornadoes and one of the three wives of Sango, or Shango, the storm god. Once when Sango is beset by powerful enemies, he sends her to a nearby king—one version says the king of Bariba, others say the king of Esu—for medicine with which to make thunderbolts. She is to bring it back to him hidden under her tongue. But before she gives it to him, she appropriates some for herself, thus acquiring prior rights to make thunderbolts.

According to another version, Shango is a Koptic king, worshiped as god of thunder and destruction all over Guinea, whose surname is Obbato Kousa, Shango, but who is also known as Iakouta or Kheviosa. He is born at Ife, and his three wives are Oya, Osoun, and Oba. (Diop 1974; Gleason 1987; Parrinder 1987)

OYO EMPIRE

The Oyo empire, extant from the sixteenth to the nineteenth centuries, is an old kingdom of the Yoruba people in present-day Nigeria. Oral tradition attributes the name Oyo to a great hero, Oduduwa, who comes from the east to settle at Ife-Ife, which the Yoruba regard as their place of origin (Orisha Nla). One version of the Yoruba creation story says that when Orisha is sent to earth, he becomes very thirsty, drinks palm wine, and lies down to sleep. He is away such a long time that the Creator sends his brother Oduduwa to continue the work of creation. Oduduwa is regarded as the first king of Ife and the founder of the race. His son is Oranyan, a great warrior, who in old age retires to a grove where he remains unless his people are attacked, at which time he emerges and disperses them single-handedly. However, one day during a festival, someone calls to him, and he rides out in full attack until someone begs him to stop destroying his own people. He is so dismayed that he drives his staff into the ground and vows never to fight again. He and his wife, as well as the staff, are turned to stone. Another myth of the kingdom of Benin is that in the beginning, the people of Benin, having no ruler of their own, ask the king of Ife, Oduduwa, to send one of his sons to rule them. He sends Oranyan, who after some years renounces the throne in favor of his son and returns to Ife. (Parrinder 1982)

See also Oduduwa; Oranyan; Orisha Nla.

OZIDI SAGA

This oral legend of the Ijo (Ijaw) people of Nigeria, West Africa, was collected by Nigerian poet John Pepper Clark in 1963. The plot has six stages or acts, which may involve as many as 80 scenes requiring seven nights to sing, dance, mime, and enact with ritual. Clark's version, encompassing all of these elements and employing audience participation, is told over the seven-day period of a festival among the Tarakiri-Orua subgroup of Ijo. The storyteller assumes the roles of the hero Ozidi, his brother, and his father, Ozidi Senior. During the dancing, chanting, and singing, girls volunteer from the audience.

It is the story of a political coup in which corrupt officials are ousted and the new breed takes over. Ozidi is the posthumously born child who avenges his father's death by killing his murderers, then destroys all the other evil forces in his community and ultimately takes supreme control. Ozidi engages and destroys one opponent after another, beginning with the assassins of his father: Ofe, Agbogdedi, Azezabife, Ogueren, and Fingrifin. Then he meets the various monsters in the community: Odogu the Ugly, the Scrotum King, the head-walking Tebekawene, the seven-headed ogre Tebesanon, and finally Engradon, the Smallpox King, and his retinue.

Each encounter goes through approximately the same five stages: (1) the opponent makes light of Ozidi's strength and sets out to kill him; (2) the rivals, locked in deadly combat, come to realize that they have underestimated the strength of their opponent; (3) his grandmother Oreame uses magic to help Ozidi neutralize his opponent's magic (in one case she transforms herself into a young girl to attract his opponent); (4) Ozidi kills his opponent and dumps him or his head into his shrine-house; and (5) he rages around, bragging about his great ability.

In his confrontation with Fingrifin, Oreame brings out a big bag, throws Fingrifin's head into it, slings it over her shoulder, and says, "My son, on with it to the house. Let's be off. Let's continue our walk." His longest fight is with Azemaroti. In his fight with Azeza, the latter, upon crushing a medicinal gourd under his foot, regains his power. When Ozidi tries to provoke a fight with Odogu the Ugly by making love to Odogu's wife in his own home, Odogu bursts in and says, "How sweet that an animal has walked of its own accord into my house today for me to kill and eat!" At one point, Oreame and Ozidi are about to kill the monster Tebesonoma's sister and her little baby, and Ozidi balks. Oreame thinks Ozidi's tenderheartedness is a sign of weakness. She says, "Are you dilly-dallying here? I say do the job quickly." Ozidi answers, "Oh mother, I'm horrified." She darts away, telling the audience, "So this boy has eyes running with tears! . . ." The fight against the Smallpox King is the final test of the hero. When he wins that, he is the undisputed king. (Clark 1964; Okpewko 1992)

OZOLUA

(Also Okpame the Conqueror)

In the oral tradition of the ancient West African kingdom of Benin, called Kingdom of the Leopard, Ozolua (d. 1504) is the greatest warrior oba of the kingdom of Benin in West Africa. He was born Okpame, the youngest son of King Ewuare the Great, and was named oba, or king, in 1481. The stories of the Benin obas have only recently been collected into a written epic cycle by Nigerian poet Chi Chi Layor. The Nigerian State of Benin is not to be confused with the country of Benin. (Layor 1994)

P

PĀBŪJĪ, EPIC OF

This Indian oral epic is performed in Rajasthan in northwestern India. Pābūjī's parents are the Rajput Dhā̃hal Rāṭhoṛ and a nymph (pari) who disappears shortly after his birth but promises to return as a mare when he is 12 years old.

While he is still a young boy, Pābūjī's older half brother Būṛo quarrels with the Khīcī brothers over the spoils of a hunt. In the resulting battle, the Khīcīs' father is killed. To make peace, Pābūjī and Būṛo offer J̄idrāv Khīcī their sister Pemā̃ in marriage. Although Khīcī accepts their offer, he remains hostile to them.

Pābūjī and his men visit the Cāraṇ lady Deval, an incarnation of the goddess, to ask for the mare Kesar Kāḷamī. Although Khīcī has threatened to plunder her cattle if she gives the mare to anyone but him, she finally gives it to Pābūjī when he promises to protect her. The mare, who is actually Pābūjī's mother, recognizes her son and takes him for a ride in the sky.

Pābūjī is saved from drowning while bathing by Goga (Gūgā) Cauhāṇ, the snake god, and as a reward, he offers the god Būṛo's daughter Kelam as a wife. During the wedding, Pābūjī makes the boast that he will steal she-camels from the demon king Rāvaṇa for a wedding present. Later, when he must fulfill his promise, he and his men travel to Lanka. Pābūjī kills Rāvaṇa and brings back the she-camels to Kelam. On their way home, they pass through the city of Umarkot, where the Princess Phulvantī sees Pābūjī and falls in love with him.

When he reaches home, Pābūjī receives a marriage proposal from Phulvantī's parents. He accepts the offer and returns to Umarkot for the wedding. But while he is there, he receives word that Khīcī has stolen the lady Deval's cattle. Remembering his promise to her, Pābūjī returns home to try to recapture the cattle, but he decides to leave behind his good friend and constant companion, Ḍhẽbo.

But the lady Deval sends Ḍhẽbo out as well. Ḍhẽbo recaptures the cattle and defeats Khīcī's forces, but he is killed in the process. Sadly, Pābūjī returns Deval's cattle. But Khīcī is able to enlist the aid of his uncle, who launches his own attack against Pābūjī. This time Pābūjī is killed, and the rest of his men die as well.

Būṛo's wife Gahlotaṇ and Pābūjī's wife Phulvantī decide to become satī, but Gahlotaṇ, who is pregnant, cuts open her belly and takes out her child before she enters the flames. She names him Rūpnāth.

Rūpnāth grows up a wayward child, ignorant of his origins until he meets the lady Deval, who tells him the history of his family. He avenges his father's death by killing Khīcī, then he retreats from the world as a holy man. (Blackburn et al. 1989)

PACHACUTEC INCA YUPANQUI

(Also Pachacuti)

This Inca emperor (r. 1438–1471) in northwestern South America extended his empire from southern Peru to Quito, Ecuador, and planned the capital city of Cuzco. According to myth in the community of Sonqo and elsewhere in the Andean highlands, the Incas will return to power during a pachakuti, or cataclysm. (Garcilaso 1987; Salomon and Urioste 1991)

PACHAMAMA

Pachamama is the Central Andean Inca earth mother. No creation myths have been recorded about her. She appears in the lore of the modern Tacana, who speak of her as the old woman of the forest. Modern Quechua in the Cuzco area say that Pachamama lives inside the earth and is in charge of agriculture. Quechua women consider her their special deity, referring to her as "companion." (Garcilaso 1987; Salomon and Urioste 1991)

PAEKCHE

(Also Pèkché)

Paekche is one of three kingdoms of ancient Korea (Corea) mentioned in the *Nihongi.* The other two are Koguryŏ (Koryö) and Silla. Paekche is said to have been founded in 18 B.C. by a legendary leader named Onjo. Although an epic tradition survives from Koguryŏ *(see Samguk sagi* and *Samguk yusa),* only one song from Paekche—"Chongupsa," still performed today—remains as evidence of the kingdom's former rich literature. However, Paekche's influence on Japanese culture is still evident. (Aston 1972)

See also *Samguk sagi and Samguk yusa.*

PAGHAT

(Also Paqhat)

In the Canaanite poem *Aqhat Epic,* Paghat is the sister of the hero. She avenges her brother's death by tracking down his killer, much as Baal's sister Anath does in the *Baal Epic.* (Siepmann 1987)

See also Anath; *Aqhat Epic; Baal Epic.*

PALAMEDES

In Greek myth, Palamedes is the son of Nauplius and Clymene. Prior to the Trojan War, he is sent to fetch Odysseus to serve, but Odysseus pretends madness. *Cypria,* one of the Cyclic epics, tells that at Palamedes's suggestion, the Achaeans seize Odysseus's son Telemachos for punishment. Palamedes is one of the heroes who fights against Troy, alternating between Odysseus and Diomedes in commanding the army. Odysseus and Diomedes become jealous and drown him. Known for his wisdom, Palamedes is said to have invented scales, measures, the discus, dice, coins, and several letters of Cadmus's alphabet. (Graves 1955; Hammond 1986)

See also *Cypria.*

PALAVĒCAMCĒRVAIKKĀRAR CĀMI KATAI

This is a Tamil bow song tradition from southern India. It was recorded in 1978 in a performance lasting over five hours. Narratives of this type are usually performed by a group of men with accompaniments such as mime, props, dance, and instruments. The lead singer may be male or female, but all other performers are male. This story type, whose pattern is violation-death-deification-revenge, is widespread throughout India. It is found in cults of hero worship. Its ritualistic performance is usually part of a festival in a temple dedicated to a now-deified human. This story, which is still performed, also exists on a palm-leaf manuscript. It differs from the normal pattern in that the heroes exact revenge before they are deified instead of afterward.

Although a cult to Palavēcam (a deified robber-hero) flourished among the Nāṭārs (low-caste agricultural laborers and toddy tappers) in the adjacent Tinnevelly district during the middle of the last century, the story is now sung at a few temples near Kanya Kumari. These temples are managed by Nāṭār families who migrated to the region in the early nineteenth century.

The story concerns a family of the Maṟavar caste who are forced out of their ancestral village during a land dispute. The family settles in a village a hundred miles away. The eldest son, Irulappan, marries but remains childless until his wife makes a pilgrimage to several temples to worship. She eventually gives birth to a son. A diviner predicts the birth of a second son and the death of both boys when the elder is 22. The brothers are called Palavēcam (or "many guises").

The boys grow up and are trained in the martial arts. When the older boy, Big Palavēcam, marries and learns that his hereditary land rights have been taken from him, he and his brother vow that they will go back to their ancestral village and secure their rights. Older family members try to dissuade them, but they will not listen. They return to the village and, when no one will even sell them land or building materials, they determine to steal them. Their enemies pretend to have a change of heart and invite the boys to a wedding. The brothers attend, but they show their contempt by refusing to participate. This precipitates a battle in which the brothers kill or wound a large number of the villagers. The older brother has a powerful sword that makes the two almost invincible.

Thereafter the brothers continue to raid the enemy and to engage in open battles until finally the villagers petition the British government for permission to kill them. Taking a hoard of food, the brothers retreat to a temple. They arrange with a toddy tapper to bring them liquor, but he informs the villagers where the brothers are hiding. Fearing the might of Big Palavēcam's sword, the villagers bribe a Muslim friend of the boys to get the sword by trickery. Despite the younger brother's objections, the older brother relinquishes the sword to his Muslim friend. The villagers immediately swarm in and capture the two boys, hacking the older one to pieces. As they prepare a funeral pyre for the brothers, the younger one breaks his bonds and, rather than suffer an ignoble death at the hands of his enemies, impales himself on a stake. The villagers cut off his head, burn the bodies, and parade toward town with the two heads.

On the way, the younger brother's spirit appears in the middle of the road. The villagers panic and attmept to flee, but he kills them all. Then he seeks out both the toddy tapper and the Muslim and slays them as well.

When the rest of the village learns what has happened, they consult an astrologer, who tells them to build a temple to the brothers and dedicate a festival to them. The villagers hurry to comply. The story ends as the two brothers, now gods, enjoy a feast of offerings in their own temple. (Blackburn et al. 1989)

PALNĀḌU, THE EPIC OF

(Also *Palnāṭi Katha* or *Palnāṭi Virula Katha)*

This medieval Telugu martial folk epic of southern India is still being recited today. Portions of the epic have been attributed to Śrīnātha, a fifteenth-century Brahmin poet-scholar; however, the epic is much older than the fifteenth century. A literary version, written by Mudigonda Virabhadrakavi in campu form, is called *Palnāṭi Vīrula Bhāgavatamu.*

According to Telegu scholar Akkirāju Umākānatam, the legendary author of the epic lost his health "because of his sexual excesses" and moved to Palnāḍu in order to regain his strength. There, in a dream, the god Cennakēśava commanded him to write the story of the heroes of Palnāḍu. He was too weak to accomplish it unaided, so he dictated the story to seven scribes over a period of two months. Although he eventually regained his health, he soon returned to his old excesses and was cursed in a dream by the god, who told him that his work would fall into the hands of two Untouchables, Mālas and Mādigas. Although Śrīnātha subsequently threw the manuscript into the river, the Untouchables retrieved portions of the text. This legend is also told with a different conclusion, where the scribes belonged to a tribe, the Lambadis, rather than a caste. A similar legend of lost sacred knowledge and its recovery appears often in Sanskrit texts, including the legend of the *Kātamarāju Katha,* where the text is also thrown into the river. The Vedas were stolen by demons and brought back from underground to Viṣṇu. (*See* the *Mahābhārata*: 12.334.21–65.)

The *Palnāṭi,* as one of the martial epics, describes men of the land-owning castes who aspire to the status of warrior-hero. These castes—Telaga, Velama, and Kamma—equate women with the land and keep them under strict control. Women's chastity is associated with soil fertility. The least respected figure in a martial epic is one who submits to the power of a woman, and a woman behaving like a man who plays a leading role in an epic is the most despised character. Such a player appears in *Palnāṭi.* She is Nāyakurālu, a childless widow and the villain of the story.

The epic singer, as a priest, represents in the *Palnāṭi* the voice of the goddess Aṅkalammā. The ritual performance singers are usually Untouchable Mālas, and the participants, or "actors," in the performance are from the land-owning castes.

The epic has elements reminiscent of the *Mahābhārata,* with its warring factions of half brothers. The story begins with a North Indian monarch, Alugu Rāju, who learns that his ancestors were guilty of slaying Brahmins. He decides to embark on a pilgrimage to the south to absolve his sins. He is accompanied by his patron god, his Velama-caste minister named Doḍḍa Nāyuḍa, and his family, consisting of three sons by one wife and five by another. At Amaravati a son of Doḍḍa Nāyuḍa kills a local overlord during a quarrel, and in order to make peace, Alugu Rāju adopts the slain man's son, Uttarēśvaruḍa. When Uttarēśvaruḍa grows to manhood, he vows to avenge his father's death, and he assembles an army to fight Doḍḍa Nāyuḍa's son. But another of the minister's sons, Brahmāa Nāyuḍa, is an incarnation of Viṣṇu. He obtains a weapon from the son of Lord Śiva with which to win a battle against Uttarēśvaruḍa.

A shrewd widow, Nāyakurālu, entertains Alugu Rāju's party, and in exchange for her hospitality is granted the boon of sitting on his throne for seven hours. The king is so impressed by her performance that he makes her a minister, and he also makes Brahmā Nāyuḍa his minister, replacing his father. When Brahmā Nāyuḍa bows to Alugu Rāju, the latter, unable to accept obeisance from an incarnation of Viṣṇu, dies.

At the point of death, King Alugu Rāju entrusts all of his sons to Brahmā Nāyuḍa. Brahmā Nāyuḍa, described as "a warrior of great power and divine virtue," appoints Alugu Rāju's eldest son, Nalagāma Rāju, to succeed his father.

But the new king soon becomes the least respected player in the drama because he allows the widow Nāyakurālu to exert too much influence over the kingdom's affairs. When she effects an estrangement between the king and his young half brother Pedda Malidēva Rāju, the wise Brahmā Nāyuḍa divides the kingdom in two, awarding the boy Pedda Malidēva the Macerla half and assuming a regency until the boy reaches majority. This action effectively puts Brahmā Nāyuḍa directly at odds with the widow Nāyakurālu, who with the weak son Nalagāma Rāju controls the half of the kingdom that has its capital in Gorajala.

The opposition between the two factions culminates in a cockfight on which both wager, the loser going into exile for seven years and the winner ruling the whole kingdom during that period. Brahmā Nāyuḍa's side loses and honors the terms of the wager. But when the seven years have ended, King Nalagāma Rāju—at Nāyakurālu's prodding—refuses to relinquish Malidēva's half of the kingdom. War is inevitable between the two factions. At the last minute, Nāyakurālu, fearing for her life, sends a message saying that Nalagāma Rāju has had a change of heart and is ready to share the kingdom with his half brother.

But Brahmā Nāyuḍa's young son, Bālacandruḍu, whose friend has been slain and who wishes to prove his own prowess as a warrior, defies his father and rides out to initiate the battle. The Māla warrior Kannamadāsu, although not of his master's caste, enters the fray and fights with great bravery. During the long battle many brave men are slain, including the boy-warrior Bālacandruḍu. Nāyakurālu, whose meddling, cunning, and treachery have led to the destruction of an entire noble family, flees in terror. (Blackburn and Ramanujan 1986; Blackburn et al. 1989)

PALNĀṬI KATHA

***See** Palnāḍu, The Epic of.*

P'AN KU

In Chinese Taoist creation mythology, P'an Ku is the first man, born from an egg of chaos. Using his understanding of yin-yang, he forms the mountains and valleys of earth. According to other legends, the universe formed from his corpse: His sweat and blood form rivers, and his eyes become the sun and moon. (Mackenzie 1990; Sproul 1991)

P'AN T'AO

In Chinese Taoist creation mythology, found in the garden of Queen Mother of the Immortals Si (Hsi) Wang Mu is p'an t'ao, the peach of immortality, which ripens every 3,000 years, occasioning a feast for the Eight Immortals. Legend says that while Wu Ti is emperor, Si Wang Mu appears riding on a white dragon, followed by a dwarf carrying seven peaches on a tray. She offers one to Wu Ti, and after eating it, he becomes immortal. (Mackenzie 1990)

PAÑCATANTRA

In this ancient Indian Sanskrit collection of animal tales (ca. 100 B.C. and A.D. 500) is one upon which is based the story of Gellert, the beloved hound of Prince Llewellyn. The collection appears in Europe as *The Fables of Bidpai.* It was translated into Persian in the sixth century. Hebrew and Buddhist versions exist as well. (Siepmann 1987)

See also *Bidpai, The Fables of;* Gellert.

PANDARUS

(Also Pandareus)

In the *Iliad* (ii) and the *Aeneid* (v), Pandarus is the son of Lycaon, a Lycian. He breaks the truce between the Trojans and Greeks by wounding Diomedes and Menelaus, but is killed by Diomedes. (Humphries 1951; Lattimore 1976)

PĀṆḌAVAS

In the *Mahābhārata,* the Pāṇḍavas are the five sons of the hero Pāṇḍu, the victors in the great war against their cousins, the Kauravas. (Buck 1981)

See also *Mahābhārata.*

PANYASSIS

Panyassis is a Greek epic poet (ca. fifth century B.C.) whose chief poems, of which only fragments remain, are the *Heracleia,* recounting the adventures of Herakles, and the *Ionica,* relating the founding of the Ionic colonies in Asia Minor. (Preminger 1990)

See also Herakles.

PARAŚURĀMA

In Hindu tradition, Paraśurāma is the sixth of the avatars of Viṣṇu. In the *Mahābhārata* and in the *Purāṇas,* Paraśurāma is said to have been born to the Brahmin sage Jamadagni to rid the world of the oppressive warrior-caste Kṣatriyas. He slaughters all the male Kṣatriyas 21 times. (Buck 1981; Dimmitt and van Buitenen 1978)

PARIS

(Also Alexandros)

In the *Iliad* (iii), Paris is the son of Trojan king Priam and his queen Hecuba and husband of Oenone, a nymph of Mount Ida. As a result of a dream about his birth, he is abandoned by his family as an infant and left for dead. He is raised by shepherds, and as a young man enters a boxing contest against Priam's other sons. When his true identity is uncovered, the family receives him into the fold.

Zeus appoints him to judge a contest among the goddesses for the golden apple labeled "For the Fairest." In exchange for the prize, Hera offers him power and all the kingdoms in Asia; Athena offers him beauty, wisdom, and victory in battle; and Aphrodite offers him the most beautiful woman in the world. He awards the apple to Aphrodite and as a result abducts Helen, "the most beautiful woman in the world," precipitating the Trojan War. During the war, he fights with little courage, finally going home to Helen to hide. When he returns, he shoots the arrow that, with Aphrodite's help, causes Achilles's death. Paris is finally killed by a poisoned arrow from Philoctetes. (Lattimore 1976)

See also Achilles; Hecuba; Helen; *Iliad;* Priam; Zeus.

PARŚVANĀTHA
(Lord Serpent)

In Jaina religion of India, Parśvanātha is the twenty-third saint, or Tirthaṅkara, of the present age. He is the first saint for whom there is historical evidence, although accounts of his life are embedded with myth and legend. His mother is said to have seen a black serpent before his birth, and he has been associated with serpents ever since. He once rescues a family of serpents from a fire and later is protected from a demon's storm by Dharaṇa, lord of the underworld of snakes. (Embree 1988)

PĀRVATĪ

In Hindu religion, in the *Purāṇas,* Pārvatī is "she from the mountain," daughter of Himālaya and Menā and wife of Śiva, whom she wins only after strict ascetic discipline. She is called by several names: Umā ("Oh don't!" or "mother"), Gaurī ("white"), and Satī ("virtuous"). In one incarnation in which she is married to Śiva, her father insults her husband, and she immolates herself in fire, becoming the original satī, or virtuous woman. As Satī, she is the daughter of Dakṣa, son of Brahmā and one of the seven sages.

In one story, wishing to be the perfect wife and mother, Pārvatī must use various subterfuges to seduce the reluctant Śiva into fatherhood. She becomes the mother of Ganeśa, the elephant-headed god, and Skanda, the six-headed god. Pārvatī is a benevolent aspect of the Mother Goddess Devī. (Dimmitt and van Buitenen 1978)

See also Śiva.

PARZIVAL

This German verse epic (early thirteenth century) by Wolfram von Eschenbach (fl. ca. 1195–1225) was adapted from the unfinished *Perceval* by Chrétien de Troyes. The hero of the main action is Parzival, member of the Gral family through his mother Herzeloyde, and of the House of Anjou through his father Gahmuket. He is the husband of Condwiramurs, queen in her own right of Brobanz, and the father of twin boys, Loherangrin and Kardeiz. Described as a guileless fool, Parzival leaves his wife to visit his mother. Along the way, he chances upon the castle of the Holy Gral, where the Gral king Anfortas, his mother's brother, suffers from a festering wound that will not heal. Anfortas has been told that only the sympathy of a guileless fool can heal the wound,

A medieval manuscript shows events from *Parsifal,* an early thirteenth-century German epic.

which was caused by Lucifer because of Anfortas's pride. Parzival ignores his compassionate and humanitarian impulses and does not ask the cause of his uncle's suffering. He thus must leave the castle and later the court of King Arthur as well.

He now becomes determined to win the Gral but cannot find the key to success until me meets his hermit uncle Trevrizent, Anfortas's brother. Parzival admits to him that he "saw all the marks of suffering [upon Anfortas] yet failed to ask his host, 'Sire, what ails you?'" The hermit advises that, "If [one] asks his Question in season he shall have the Kingdom. . . . Thereby Anfortas will be healed. . . ."

Parzival's successful quests allow him to be received at the Round Table, and he asks the question that will heal Anfortas: "Sire, what ails you?" Anforth is healed and Parzival becomes king of the Gral and is reunited with his wife.

A subplot concerns Gawan, a distant cousin of Parzival and the son of King Lot of Norway and Sangive. He is the paragon of knighthood at King Arthur's court. Gral king Anfortas loves Orgeluse, duchess of Logroys, but Gawan woos and wins her.

Wagner's *Parsifal* is largely based on this version. (Eschenbach 1980)

See also Gawain, Sir; Percival.

PASCON CIGAN ARLUTH
(The Passion of Our Lord)

This Cornish narrative poem of 2,072 lines in 259 stanzas concerns the passion and temptation of Christ. The earliest extant version is fifteenth century. (Preminger 1990)

PATINEṆ-KĪKKANAKKU
(Eighteen Ethical Works)

This Tamil poetry collection, written ca. the fourth through seventh centuries, contains at least one selection, "Tirukkuṟal," of 1,330 hemistichs, attributed to Tiruvaḷḷuvar, that is a product of long accretion. (Preminger 1990)

PATROKLOS

In the *Iliad* (ix, xi, xvi, xvii, xviii), Patroklos is Achilles's loyal friend and constant companion. When Achilles, angry at Agamemnon, refuses to fight, Patroklos begs to be permitted to wear his friend's armor and enter the battle. Leading the Myrmidons into battle, Patroklos, with Apollo's intervention, is killed by Hektor. Grieved at the loss of his friend, Achilles reenters the war and slays Hektor to avenge Patroklos's death. (Lattimore 1976)

See also Achilles; Agamemnon; Hektor; *Iliad.*

PE-HAR

Pe-har is a protective deity worshiped by Tibetan Buddhists of the Yellow Hat sect. He derives from a pre-Buddhist god worshiped by adherents of Bon. (Grousset 1970)

PELE

The Hawaiian goddess of fire, Pele resides with other fire deities in the volcano Kilauea. Originally Pele lives in the western Pacific until her sister, the evil sea goddess Na-maka-o-ka-hai, floods her home repeatedly. Pele first travels to Kauai, where she uses her magic digging tool, the pa-oa, to make fire pits in which to dwell. But water puts out the new fires again and again, so she goes from island to island trying to find a home, always settling near the sea. Finally she finds Kilauea, where she can live in safety with her family. Occasionally Pele creates new land with lava; sometimes she destroys dwellings of her kinsmen. When she is angry, she stamps her foot, causing an earthquake. (Dixon 1964)

PELEUS

In the *Iliad* (ix), Peleus is the father, by Thetis, of Achilles: the only instance where a goddess marries a mortal. Peleus is an Argonaut and participates in the Calydonian boar hunt. He helps Herakles conquer Troy during the period when it is ruled by Laomedon, King Priam's father. Peleus is too old to participate in the Trojan War, but he gives his armor to Achilles. (Lattimore 1976)

See also Achilles; Argonauts; *Iliad;* Thetis.

PELIAS

In the Greek Argonaut legend, Pelias is a son of Poseidon by Tyro and the king of Thessaly. He imposes upon his nephew Jason the task of bearing off the Golden Fleece. He promises Jason the crown if he will go to Colchis to avenge the murder of Phrixus, who was slain by Aeetes. When Jason returns with Medea, she tricks the four daughters of Pelias into murdering their father. (Graves 1955)

See also Argonauts.

PENDRAGON

This ancient British title of chief or king was given to a chief at times of great danger when he required supreme power. The title is particularly associated with Uther Pendragon, father of King Arthur. (Barber 1961)

See also Arthurian Legend.

PENELOPE

In Greek mythology, in the *Odyssey* (xvi, xvii) and the *Iliad,* Penelope is the daughter of Icarus and Periboea, the wife of Odysseus, and the mother of Telemachos. During her husband's long absence, she is besieged by 108 suitors, whom she, described as a model of virtue and chastity, puts off with disdain. She tells them that she will decide whom to marry when she has finished weaving a shroud for her father-in-law Laertes. Each night for three years she unravels what she has woven that day, until a maid reveals the ruse to the suitors. The most persistent suitors are Amphinomus, Antinous, and Eurmachus. After an absence of 20 years, Odysseus returns to rescue her, with their son's help. (Rouse 1990)

See also Odysseus; *Odyssey;* Telemachos.

PERCIVAL

In Arthurian legend, Percival is one of the most famous knights of the Round Table. Percival first appears in the twelfth-century French poem *Perceval* (Le conte du Graal), by Chrétien de Troyes, and in the medieval Welsh tale *Peredur, Son of Efrawg,* found in the *Mabinogion.* He appears in Malory's *Morte d'Arthur* as Sir Percival and as Parzival in the tale of the same name by Wolfram von Eschenbach. The story in each instance is roughly the same: He spends his boyhood in the forest, unschooled in chivalry or courtly manners. When he is grown, he goes to King Arthur's court where, because of his naïveté, he commits many courtly faux pas. However, he trains as a knight and is granted, during his quest for the Grail, a sight of it. (Siepmann 1987)

See also *Parzival.*

PERSA PEN

This Gond folk epic is still being sung in India today. (Blackburn et al. 1989)

PERSEUS

In Greek mythology, Perseus, called by Homer the "most renowned of all men," is the son of Zeus and Danae and husband of Andromeda, to whom he remains faithful throughout his life. The two found the family of the Perseids, from whom Herakles is descended.

Before Perseus is born, a Delphic oracle predicts that Danae will have a son who will kill his grandfather, King Acrisius. So when Zeus appears to Danae in a shower of gold, causing her to become pregnant and bear a son, Acrisius casts her and the babe Perseus adrift in a chest. Zeus causes waves to carry them to the island of Seriphus. They are rescued by Dictys, the fisherman brother of King Polydectes, who desires Danae and would have ravished her but for Dictys's opposition. When Perseus is grown, Polydectes, in an attempt to remove the young man from the picture, tricks him into agreeing to obtain the head of the Gorgon Medusa as a gift. But with the assistance of Athena and Hermes, Perseus is able to kill Medusa and take her head, which turns all who look upon it into stone. Perseus punishes Atlas for interfering by turning him into a mountain. He rescues the beautiful maiden Andromeda from a rock and wins her for his wife. He returns to Seriphus and rescues his mother from Polydectes by turning the king and his friends into stone. He then gives the throne to the kind fisherman Dictys. Later, while taking part in the games in Larissa, he accidentally strikes his grandfather Acrisius with a discus, killing him. He becomes king of Argos and Tiryns and founds Mycenae. (Ceram 1972; Graves 1955)

PHAKATHWAYO

In the Zulu epic *Emperor Shaka the Great*, Phakathwayo is king of the Qwabes, cousins of Shaka, with whom he is exiled during his childhood. Phakathwayo is a member of the senior branch of the House of Malandela. (Kunene 1979)

See also Abandonment; *Emperor Shaka the Great.*

PHARSALIA, EPIC OF

This Latin historical epic by Lucan (A.D. 39–65) depicts an event that occurred a century earlier: the decisive Battle of Parsalus (48 B.C.) during the Roman civil war between Julius Caesar and Pompey, which led to Pompey's flight to Larissa. (Preminger 1990)

PHILOCTETES

In Greek legend and in the *Iliad* (ii), Philoctetes is a hero who plays a key role in the final moments of the Trojan War. He is a friend of Herakles, present at his death, who has been bequeathed Herakles's bow and arrows, which have been dipped in the poison of the Hydra. He is also one of the suitors of Helen; en route to Troy to avenge her abduction, he is bitten by a snake. When his wound will not heal, the Greeks leave him on the island of Lemnos, where he remains for nine years. After Achilles' death, the oracle Helenus reveals that the war will never be won without the poison arrows, so Odysseus and Diomedes are sent to Lemnos to fetch Philoctetes. But he is so angry with them for deserting him that he refuses to accompany them until a shade of Herakles appears and convinces him of his duty, promising him that his wound will be healed at Troy. He agrees to go, and after his wound is healed, he goes into battle and kills Paris, Helen's abductor. After the war, he refuses to return to Greece; instead, he goes to Italy where he founds two cities. Ultimately he dies in battle in Italy. (Graves 1955; Lattimore 1976)

P'HRA LO-THU
(Also P'hra Lo, Lord Lo)

This long Thai poem probably originated ca. the sixteenth century. It concerns a tragic romance in which the hero, Lord Lo, is lost at sea. His lover evokes the stars and "thou wind which whirls through space, seek our prince, / Go to him, waft him to us!" During the seventeenth-century reign of P'hra Narai, called "the Golden Age of Thai Literature," the king, a poet himself, wrote the final version of the poem, using the lilit verse form. (Preminger 1990)

PHUNGASHE

In the Zulu epic *Emperor Shaka the Great,* Phungashe is king of the powerful Buthelezi nation whom Shaka defeats in battle. (Kunene 1979)

PILLARS OF HERCULES

These are the rocks binding the entrance to the Mediterranean until Herakles tears them apart to reach Gades (Cádiz). They are also mentioned in *Bricriu's Feast.* (Gantz 1988; Graves 1955)

See also Herakles; *Bricriu's Feast.*

POEM OF AQHAT

Caananite epic. ***See*** *Aqhat Epic.*

POEM OF BAAL

Caananite epic. ***See*** *Baal Epic.*

PÕHJANAEL
(Nail of the North)

Põhjanael is the Estonian name for the North Star. In Baltic folklore, the sky is an overturned cauldron with a nail affixed, upon which the cauldron revolves. Finns refer to it as the Nail Star (naulatahtl), and Lapps call it the Nail of Heaven (alme-navle). According to a Lapp myth, on the last day, the hunter Favtna, who is chasing the elk Sarva (the Big Dipper), will shoot and strike the Nail of the North, and the heavens will fall. In the Finnish epic *Kalevala,* the Maid of North Farm is called Pohjan, or Pohjolan neiti, and the Master of North Farm is Pohjolan isäntä. (Lönnrot 1963)

See also *Kalevala.*

POHJOLA

(Also Manala and Tuonela)

In Finnish mythology, Pohjola is the realm of the dead. In the Finnish epic *Kalevala,* North Farm is called Pohjola. (Lönnrot 1963)

See also *Kalevala.*

POLEVOY

In Slavic mythology, polevoy is the male spirit of the fields who appears in the fields only rarely during the noon hour. He is related to the poludnitsa, the female spirit of the fields. (Holmberg 1964)

See also Poludnitsa.

POLUDNITSA

In Slavic mythology, poludnitsa is the female spirit of the fields, who appears at noon while the workers are resting. She is related to the polevoy, the male spirit of the fields, who appears less frequently. In Bulgaria, and in northern Slavic countries, the poludnitsa is a variation of the water nymph—a tall, beautiful girl dressed in white. At high noon during harvest time, she walks about the fields and punishes with a headache anyone found working. She is also known to western Slavs and to the Slovenes among the southern Slavs. (Georgieva 1985)

See also Polevoy.

POLYDAMAS

(Also Polydamus)

In the *Iliad* (xii, xiii), Polydamas is a Trojan, the son of Panthous, born on the same night as Hektor. A valiant warrior, he slays many Greeks before he is killed by Ajax. Also in the *Iliad,* Polydamas is the Trojan son of Antenor and Theano, and the husband of Lycaste, Priam's daughter. (Lattimore 1976)

POLYDORUS

In the *Iliad* (xx) and the *Aeneid* (iii), Polydorus is the son of Priam and Hecuba. In the *Iliad,* he fights at Troy and is killed by Achilles. In the *Aeneid,* he is too young to fight and is sent with much treasure to stay with King Polymnestor of Thrace, who steals the treasure and kills Polydorus. (Humphries 1951; Lattimore 1976)

POLYPHEMUS

In the *Odyssey* (ix) and the *Aeneid* (iii), Polyphemus is the son of Poseidon and chief of the Cyclops. On the way home from the Trojan War, Odysseus and his men stop at the island of Sicily where Polyphemus lives. They enter a cave and are imprisoned inside. After Polyphemus devours some of his men, Odysseus manages to get him drunk, then while he is asleep blinds him by driving a burning brand into his eye. Odysseus ties himself and his six remaining men under the bodies of Polyphemus's sheep in order to escape. But Polyphemus appeals to his father, Poseidon, and the god's enmity causes Odysseus many delays.

Polyphemus is also the name of one of the Argonauts in the *Argonautica.* He is the son of Elatus of Arcadia and engages in the fight against the Lapithae. (Rouse 1990)

See also Cyclops; Odysseus; *Odyssey.*

POLYXENA

In the *Aeneid* (iii) and other Greek myth—although Homer does not mention her—Polyxena is the beautiful daughter of Trojan king Priam and Queen Hecuba who is courted by Achilles. She accompanies her father to claim the body of Hektor. After the fall of Troy, she is claimed by Achilles's spirit as spoils of war and is therefore sacrificed on his tomb. Other accounts say that when Achilles is killed, she willingly sacrifices herself at his tomb. (Graves 1955; Humphries 1951)

POPOL VUH
(Sacred Book or Book of Community)

This epic cycle of the ancient Quiché Maya was committed to writing ca. 1554 to 1558 from the oral tradition by educated Quiché Indians. That version, now lost, was copied in the seventeenth century, again in Quiché using Latin script, by a Guatemalan priest, Father Francisco Ximénez, who borrowed the original manuscript from one of his parishioners in the village of Santo Tomás Chichicastenango. In the nineteenth century, two European travelers, Carl Scherzer and Abbe Charles Etienne Brasseur de Bourbourg, each separately "discovered" the *Popol Vuh* in Guatemala and published Spanish and French versions. The work is of high literary quality, suggesting that it must have been transcribed by a member of the royal family. De Bourbourg, describing it as the most valuable record of the origins of Central America, writes, "This manuscript . . . is written in a Quiché of great elegance, and the author must have been one of the princes . . . who composed it in a few years after the arrival of the Spaniards, when all their ancient books were disappearing."

Following a preamble, the *Popol Vuh* is divided into four parts, which are further divided into chapters. The preamble explains that the book will deal with Quiché origins written "now under the Law of God and Christianity," but that an original book, "written long ago," is now "hidden to the searcher and the thinker."

Part I, chapter 1, describes the beginning of life, before which there is "only the calm sea and the great expanse of the sky" and "immobility and silence in the darkness." In the water, the Creators Tepeu and Gucumatz, called the

A Mayan ocarina from about 750 was found in the El Petén region of what is now Guatemala. It represents the goddess Ixchel, a figure in the *Popol Vuh*, as Xquic, mother of hero twins Hunanhpú and Xbalanqué.

Forefathers, come together and talk, and the idea of creating man is born. They plan the creating of the earth and of other life, and also create the "Heart of Heaven": gods who manifest as thunder and lightning.

In chapter 2, after making the small animals, the guardians of the woods, the spirits of the mountains, and the guardians of the thickets, the Forefathers ask, "Shall there be only silence and calm under the trees? . . . It is well that hereafter there be someone to guard them." They assign various animals areas to inhabit. Then they discover that "It is impossible for them to say our names, . . . their Creators. . . . This is not well." They make a new species out of mud, but the creature has no strength. It is limp, and it cannot look behind. The Forefathers destroy this creation and consult Xpiyacoc and Xmucané, grandparents and soothsayers, who advise them to make figures of wood. These first creatures are more serviceable than the mud figures; they speak and multiply, but they do not have souls, nor minds, and they no longer remember their creators.

In chapter 3, the Heart of Heaven causes a flood that destroys the wooden creatures "to punish them because they had not thought of their mother, nor their father, the Heart of Heaven, called Huracan." Small and large animals also attack them, saying the wooden men have mistreated them. The men try to escape, and those that do become ancestors of the monkeys of the forest. (According to Bishop Las Casas in *Apologetica Historia, The Indians of Guatemala,* the flood myth preceded the introduction by the Spaniards of the biblical account.)

In chapter 4, the sky and earth exist, but the faces of the sun and moon are covered. A being named Vucub-Caquix, who may have survived the flood, declares, "I shall now be great above all the beings created. . . . I am the sun, the light, the moon. . . . Because of me men shall walk and conquer." But he is "only vainglorious of his feathers and his riches." He claims that he can see very far, but he can see only as far as the horizon.

In chapter 5, two youths, Hunahpú and Xbalanqué, who are really gods, decide to destroy the arrogant Vucub-Caquix. But Vucub-Caquix also has a wife, Chimalmat, and two sons, Zipacná, who claims to have made the earth, and Cabracán, who claims to shake the sky and make the earth tremble. Hunahpú and Xbalanqué decide that the sons must also be destroyed.

In chapter 6, when Vucub-Caquix makes his daily climb to the top of a nantze tree to eat its fruit, the youths hide at the foot of the tree. Hunahpú strikes him in the jaw with a pellet from his blowgun, then rushes to overpower him when he falls to earth. But Vucub-Caquix tears off Hunahpú's arm and escapes, taking the arm and nursing his sore jaw. He goes home and tells his wife to hang the arm over the fire, for he is sure the youths will come looking for it and he plans to trap them. Meanwhile, Hunahpú and Xbalanqué consult the wise old Creator-couple who are called Zaqui-Nim-Ac and Zaqui-Nima-Tzus. The youths convince the old couple to come with them to retrieve the arm and to tell Vucub-Caquix that they are healers who only know how to set hands, cure eyes, and cure toothaches by removing the worm that causes the pain. The four reach Vucub-Caquix's house, and he is in so much pain that he allows the old couple to pull all his teeth. They promise to replace the teeth with ground bone, but instead they use grains of white corn, which are of no use as teeth. Then they pierce his eyes and take all his riches. The wife also perishes, and Hunahpú recovers his arm.

In chapter 7, Vucub-Caquix's son Zipacná is befriended by 400 boys, who ask him to carry an enormous log they have been dragging along, intending to use it as a ridge-pole to support their house. When they see how strong Zipacná is, able to carry the pole all by himself, they decide he must be destroyed. They tell him, "We like you very much" and ask him to dig a pit for them. They plan to drop a large log into the bottom of the pit and kill him, but he is aware of the plot. He digs a side passage at the bottom and hides there while the log is dropped into the pit. He cuts his hair and gnaws off his nails, giving them to ants to carry out of the pit as proof to the boys of his death. While the 400 boys celebrate his murder in a drunken orgy, Zipacná causes their house to fall on them, killing them all.

In chapter 8, the youths Hunahpú and Xbalanqué hear of the deaths of the 400 boys and decide to destroy Zipacná. They fashion a huge mock crab and put it at the bottom of a cave. When the ravenous Zipacná enters the cave to get the crab for his supper, the hill slides in and crushes him to death.

In chapter 9, because Cabracán has also been exalting his glory, grandeur, and power, Huracán tells the two youths Hunahpú and Xbalanqué, "Let the second son of Vucub-Caquix also be defeated. . . . Lure him to where the sun rises." The youths find Cabracán and tell him about an eastern mountain that he can demolish. They even offer to go along with him to show him the way. Along the way, the three stop to eat birds, which the youths have shot. But one bird has been rubbed with lime, and after Cabracán eats it, he becomes weak. The two youths tie him up and bury him. Thus the evil hubris-filled family of Vucub-Caquix has been eliminated from the earth.

Part II, chapter 1, returns to a time "during the night," before there was sun or moon or man. Xpiyacoc and Xmucané are the parents of two sons, Hun-Hunahpú and Vucub-Hunahpú. The latter never marries, but Hun-Hunahpú takes a wife, Xbaquiyalo, and has two sons, Hunbatz and Hunchouén. By nature these sons are wise, "soothsayers of good disposition and good habits." They are taught all the arts, all the crafts. Soon their mother dies. Their father and uncle do nothing but roll dice and play ball all day. Sometimes the two young boys play ball against the two men. The lords of Xibalba (the underworld), Hun-Camé and Vucub-Camé, covet the playing gear of the men—leather pads, rings, gloves, and crowns. They call a council to discuss how they can wound and torment the men and thus possess the playing gear.

In chapter 2, four owls, messengers of Xibalba, arrive at the ball court where Hun-Hunahpú and Vucub-Hunahpú are playing, and summon them to come quickly and bring their playing gear along. The two bid their mother Xmucané good-bye, leaving their ball as a pledge that they will return. They instruct the boys Hunbatz and Hunchouén to "Keep on playing . . . and singing . . . and warm the heart of your grandmother." She bursts into tears as the men leave for the land of the dead, but they comfort her, "We have not died yet."

The messengers lead them through ravines and across rivers, one made of blood. They arrive at Xibalba and are instructed to sit on a bench, but the bench is a hot stone and they refuse. They are then directed to spend the night in the House of Gloom, one of the Houses of Punishments in Xibalba, where there is only darkness. They are given lighted cigars and pine sticks to brighten the house, but are told that they must return them whole the next morning. The following morning, the two report to their hosts that they have burned up all the pine sticks and smoked all the cigars, so the hosts decree that as punishment they must die. They kill both men and cut off the head of Hun-Hunahpú before they bury the bodies together. The lords of Xibalba order the head placed in the branches of a barren calabash tree, which immediately produces fruit for the first time, fruit so abundant that the head cannot be seen.

In chapter 3, a maiden named Xquic, daughter of Lord Cuchumaquic, hears about the tree covered with fruit and goes to see it for herself. The head of Hun-Hunahpú spits in her palm, explaining that great men "do not lose their substance when they go, but they bequeath it . . . to the daughters and . . . the sons. . . . I have done the same with you." She goes home, "having immediately conceived the sons in her belly by virtue of the spittle only." These babies are Hunahpú and Xbalanqué, who appeared in part I. The maiden's angry father appears before Hun-Camé and Vucub-Camé to confess that his daughter is pregnant. The gods tell him that if she refuses to speak the truth concerning the babies' father, she should be sacrificed. When Xquic insists that she has never known a man, the father commands his owl messengers to sacrifice her in the forest and bring back her heart in a gourd. When they arrive at the place of sacrifice, the girl convinces the messengers to spare her and to use the red sap from the cochineal tree with which to fashion a heart. She flees up to earth while the messengers return to the lords of Xibalba with the gourd containing the bogus heart. The lords order the heart burned, and the fragrance from the burning is very sweet. While the lords draw near the fire to smell it, the four messengers fly from the abyss upward toward earth, where they become the maiden Xquic's servants.

In chapter 4, while Hunbatz and Hunchouén are with their grandmother, Xquic arrives, introducing herself as her daughter-in-law. She brings the news, "Hun-Hunahpú and Vucub-Hunahpú are not dead. . . . You shall soon see their image in what I bring to you." The old grandmother thinks she is an impostor and decides to test her. She tells her to go gather a netful of corn for supper. Xquic takes the net to the field, where only one stalk stands, bearing a single ear of corn. She prays to Chahal, guardian of cornfields; Xtoh, goddess of rain; Xcanil, goddess of grain; and Xcacau, goddess of cacao. Then she removes some cornsilk and arranges it in the net, where it changes into ears of corn. She returns the net, completely filled, to the grandmother, who is now convinced that the girl speaks the truth. The grandmother predicts, "I shall now see your little ones, . . . who also are to be soothsayers."

In chapter 5, Xquic goes to the forest to give birth, then brings her sons back to the house. But soon the old woman demands that they be thrown out because "Truly they cry very much." Hunahpú and Xbalanqué are placed on an anthill, where the jealous older half brothers Hunbatz and Hunchouén hope they will die. But they sleep peacefully, not bothered by the ants. Next the babies are put into the thistles, but they still thrive. The older brothers refuse to let the babies into the house, so they are brought up in the fields and allowed to eat only the scraps that are left after the others have eaten. Later the two young boys even provide the birds for the family meals, but they are denied food. The two older brothers never hunt; they spend their days playing and singing.

Hunahpú and Xbalanqué decide to teach their stingy older brothers a lesson. They complain that they have shot some birds, which are stuck in the top of a tree, and they are too small to get them down. The two older brothers grudgingly agree to climb the tree and fetch the birds, but after they climb the tree, it grows and swells so that they cannot get down. They are changed into monkeys by their little brothers, who then return to their grandmother, claiming their brothers have gone away into the forest. Four times the monkey-brothers try to come home, but the grandmother laughs them away, so they return to the woods for good.

In chapter 6, Hunahpú and Xbalanqué go to the forest to clear a field for planting corn so that their grandmother will think well of them. They let their magic ax chop the trees and their magic pick clear the brambles, but the next day the forest has been restored. They put their magic tools to work again while they hide to catch the forest animals responsible for undoing their work. They are unable to catch any of the animals except a rat who, to save his life, tells them that their dead father's playing gear is hanging in their grandmother's attic. They take the rat home with them, and while they divert the two women, the rat climbs into the attic and gnaws the ropes holding the playing gear.

In chapter 7, with their newly acquired gear Hunahpú and Xbalanqué begin to spend their time playing ball. The lords of Xibalba hear the racket overhead and send messengers up to command them to come in seven days to play ball with the lords of Xibalba. The two young boys are not at home when the messengers arrive, so the grandmother promises to send the message to them. She entrusts it to a louse, who is swallowed by a toad, who is eaten by a snake, who is devoured by a hawk, who flies to where the boys are playing. One by one the creatures are regurgitated, and the louse delivers the message. The two boys return to their grandmother's house and plant two reeds in her dirt floor. If the reeds dry, it will be a sign that the boys are dead. If the reeds sprout, it means the boys are alive.

In chapter 8, Hunahpú and Xbalanqué descend to the underworld and send a mosquito to sting the men so that they can learn their names ahead of time. The mosquito gets no response from the first two, who are wooden, but after the third is stung and cries out, his companions say, "What is the matter, Hun-Camé?" And so around the room the mosquito goes until it has stung 11 lords whose names have been called out. Hunahpú and Xbalanqué then make their presence known and are not fooled by the two wooden figures placed in front. They confound the lords by calling them by name. The lords try to get the boys to sit on the hot stone, but they refuse, so the lords direct them to the House of Gloom.

In chapter 9, the two boys are given lighted pine sticks and cigars and told to bring them back whole the next morning. The boys attach fireflies to the cigars to convince the night watchmen that they are obeying orders. At dawn they are able to return the sticks and cigars whole, so the nonplussed lords must consent to playing the ball game. When the boys easily defeat them, the lords direct them to pass the next night in the House of Knives and to return at dawn with four gourds full of flowers. The lords intend that the constantly moving knives in the house will kill them, but the boys promise the knives, "Yours shall be the flesh of all the animals." Immediately the knives become still. The lords intend that, if the knives do not kill the boys, the flower guards will. The boys send cutting ants to cut flowers during the night, thus avoiding the guards the lords have set over the flowers. When they present the cut flowers to the lords the following morning, the lords must consent to play ball again. Several games end in a tie, so they agree to a match the next day.

In chapter 10, the boys are sent to the House of Cold, which is full of hail, but they do not freeze because they build a fire. They are then sent to the House of Jaguars, but escape by throwing bones to the animals. They are taken to the House of Fire, but are not burned. They are put in the House of Bats, where lives Camazotz, the Death Bat, a vampire god. The boys climb inside their blowguns to sleep, but at dawn, when Hunahpú looks out, he is decapitated by Camazotz. The lords of Xibalba hang Hunahpú's head in the ball court and rejoice.

In chapter 11 Xbalanqué calls on the animals and soothsayers from heaven for help in fashioning a new head for Hunahpú. The new head is made from a turtle who climbs atop the decapitated body. The two boys return to the ball court to play, instructing a rabbit to mislead the lords when Xbalanqué knocks the ball out of the court. As the lords run off after the ball, Xbalanqué retrieves Hunahpu's head and hangs the turtle up in its place. He restores the head to Hunahpú's body.

In chapter 12 the boys, having the presentiment that they are to be burned to death, call the diviners Xulú and Pacam and instruct them to dispose of their bones by grinding them into a powder and throwing the powder into the river. The boys agree to a game of jumping over a pit of fire, and to the lords' surprise, they simply jump in. The diviners advise the lords about how to dispose of the bones so that the boys will not come back to life. But once the bones are in the river, they reassemble themselves and the boys are restored to life.

In chapter 13 the boys disguise themselves as vagabond magicians who slice people up and restore them to life. The lords of Xibalba are fascinated by this trick and demand that they perform it on them. But when the boys chop up Hun-Camé and Vucub-Camé, they refuse to restore them to life. The other lords flee in fear, but ants drive them back, and they give themselves up.

In chapter 14, the two boys mete out punishment to the people of Xibalba, lowering the class or estate. Meanwhile, the grandmother worships before the reeds, which have withered and now resprouted. The boys search out the buried bodies of their fathers and promise them that they will be remembered by all the people. Then they rise into the sky to become the sun and moon. The 400 boys killed by Zipacná (part I, chapter 7) also ascend and are changed into stars.

Part III, chapter 1, begins with the history of mankind. The Creators, Tepeu and Gucumatz, hold a council to decide which material to use to form the flesh of man this time. They decide on ground white and yellow corn. From its dough they form the body, and from nine corn drinks they form the body's liquids.

In chapter 2 four wonderful ancestors are formed: Balam-Quitzé (jaguar of sweet laughter), Balam-Acab (jaguar of the night), Mahucutah (not brushed), and Iqui-Balam (jaguar of moon or black jaguar). These men can see everything in the world and they know everything there is to know. But the Creator and the Maker are not pleased that their creations are so much like gods. They call a council, where it is decided that the creatures must be changed. The Heart of Heaven blows mist into their eyes, clouding their sight so that they can see only what is close and know only in part.

In chapter 3 God himself carefully makes them four wives of great beauty: Cahá-Paluna (vertical water falling from above), Chomihá (beautiful, chosen water), Tzununihá (water of hummingbirds), and Caquixahá (water of the macaw). (Another document, *Título de los Señores de Totonicapán,* says that Iqui-Balam is single.) The first three couples become founders of the principal tribes of the Quiché. They are country people who wander through the woodlands. Their speech is "all the same," although they are black and white and speak many tongues. In other words, they can understand each other. They do not worship idols, but are loving and obedient to their god.

In chapter 4, the first four men travel to the city of Tulán in search of their tribal symbols, or gods. Balam-Quitzé finds Tohil and carries him on his back; Balam-Acab finds the god Avilix; Mahucutah carries the god Hacavitz; and Iqui-Balam carries Nicahtacah, who is not mentioned again since Iqui-Balam does not have descendants. The people of the tribes arrive in Tulán, but they can no longer understand one another's languages. Their clothing is only animal skins, and they are very poor, but they have "the nature of extraordinary men."

In chapter 5 the people do not have fire and are freezing. Only Tohil possesses fire. Balam-Quitzé and Balam-Acab ask Tohil for fire, and he instantly makes fire by "turning about in his shoe." Other people come to ask the four ancestors for fire, but their languages can no longer be understood. Beggars come, offering the ancestors money in exchange for fire. Balam-Quitzé and Balam-Acab refuse, but they agree to ask Tohil what he wants in exchange for more fire. Tohil answers, "Are they willing to give their waist and their armpits?" (meaning physical sacrifice of the human heart). The people agree to human sacrifice and are given fire.

In chapter 6 the bat tribe, Cakchiquel, does not want to have to sacrifice, so they steal the fire. The Quiché subdue and subject whole tribes, offering Tohil the blood, substance, breasts, and sides of all the men. Tohil commands the four ancestors to leave Tulán and travel to the west. They weep and mourn, "Pity us! We shall not see the dawn here, when the sun rises and lights the face of the earth." They revere the Morning Star, whom Quetzalcóatl becomes after his death.

In chapter 7 the four ancestors, with their gods and their tribes, have crossed a sea as if there were no sea: "They crossed on stones placed in a row. . . ." They reunite on a mountaintop and await the dawn and Morning Star. But their hearts are troubled, for they have nothing to eat. They fast into the darkness.

In chapter 8 the gods tell the ancestors, "Take us to a secret place. Already dawn draws near. Would it not be a disgrace for you if we were imprisoned by our enemies? . . ." So the ancestors carry the gods on their backs, hiding Avilix in a ravine, Hacavitz on a large red pyramid on the mountain called Hacavitz, Muhucutah in a similar place, and Tohil in a ravine. The four ancestors await the dawn on the mountain, while a short distance away other tribes, with other gods, also await the dawn. The four cannot sleep; they remain standing, "overcome with great sorrow, great suffering . . . oppressed with pain." They lament, "If we lived in harmony in our country, why did we leave it?"

In chapter 9 the Morning Star rises and the four ancestors offer incense and dance, weeping for joy. Then the sun comes up "like a man," and instantly the surface of the earth is dried. The heat is unbearable; it turns the gods Tohil, Avilix, and Hacavitz to stone.

In chapter 10 the ancestors mourn for their gods, whom they have hidden. They go to sacrifice and give thanks for the dawn. The gods warn them not to show the other tribes the real gods, but instead to use deerskins to replace them.

In part IV, chapter 1, the whereabouts of the four ancestors are not known. But when they see the tribes that pass below them on the road, they begin screaming like the coyote, the mountain cat, the puma, and the jaguar. The tribes know that they are the voices of the ancestors. The people take blood from their own ears and arms and offer it as sacrifice to the stone gods.

In chapter 2 the four ancestors begin abducting and killing men of the enemy tribe, Vuc Amag, leaving only tracks behind. The enemy tribe members decide that the gods Tohil, Avilix, and Hacavitz must be overcome in order to defeat the Quiché. The Vuc Amag chiefs send two maidens, Xtah and Xpuh *(Título de los Señores de Totonicapán* adds a third maiden, Quibatzunah), to wash in the river while the gods, transformed into youths, are bathing. The maidens are instructed to remove their clothing and seduce the gods. "And if you do not give yourselves to them, we shall kill you." The maidens are to ask of each god a token "as proof that you have seen their faces." The maidens do as they are told, but they cannot tempt the gods. When the girls explain to the gods why they have been sent, the gods retire and consult with the ancestors, who paint three capes, one with the image of a jaguar, one with an eagle, and one with bees and wasps. The capes are sent home with the maidens as proof to the Vuc Amag chiefs that they have seen the gods' faces. The main chief tries on all three cloaks, but when he wears the third, the bees and wasps sting his flesh.

In chapter 3 the enemy tribes assemble, dressed in rich battle gear, intent upon storming Hacavitz Mountain to overcome the Quiché and capture their gods. But the ancestors, Balam-Quitzé, Balam-Acab, and Mahucutah, hear all their plans, as does the god Tohil. While the enemy warriors sleep, the ancestors slip down, pull out their beards, and take the metal ornaments from their crowns and necklaces and from the handles of their spears. They return to the mountain and build a wall around their town, enclosing themselves with boards and thorns and even a moat. They make wooden figures, adorning them with the metal they have taken from the warriors, and place the figures atop the walls. Then Tohil instructs them to gather bumblebees and wasps and shut them inside four large gourds. The enemy spies, seeing the wooden figures on the wall, report to their chiefs that there are not many men to overcome.

In chapter 4, while Balam-Quitzé, Balam-Acab, Mahucutah, and Iqui-Balam wait on the mountain with their wives and children, more than 24,000 men surround the town, "crying out loudly, armed with arrors and shields, beating drums, giving war whoops, whistling, shouting, inciting them to fight. . . ." At that moment the gourds are opened and the bees and wasps pour out "like a great cloud of smoke." They sting the eyes of the warriors and fasten themselves to their noses, mouths, legs, and arms. When the men fall, the Quiché set upon them with arrows and axes. Balam-Quitzé and Balam-Acab use only blunt sticks. Even their wives take part in the killing. The enemy tribes surrender and are made vassals of the Quiché.

In chapter 5 the four ancestors, having a presentiment of their death, bid their sons and wives farewell. Balam-Quitzé leaves two sons, Qocaib and Qocavib. Balam-Acab also leaves two: Qoacul and Qoacutec. Mahucutah leaves Qoahau. Iqui-Balam has none. Balam-Quitzé leaves them a Bundle of Greatness, which will be for them a symbol of authority and sovereignty, and which they must not unwrap. The ancestors take their leave and disappear.

In chapter 6 three of the sons—Qocaib, Qoacutec, and Qoahau—set out on a journey across the sea to the East, to receive the investiture of the kingdom from the king of the East, or the Orient (the Yucatán), Lord Nacxit (the famous Toltec king Topiltzin Acxitl Quetzalcóatl, who emigrated to the Yucatán at the end of the tenth century and repopulated Chichén Itzá). The king gives them the insignia of royalty and they return to rule the tribes of Hacavitz. The wives of the ancestors die, and later the people move on to found another capital, Chi-Quix. The people spread across the country, but the old tribe members do not become accustomed to the new places; they suffer many hardships.

Chapter 7 tells of the new town where they settle, Chi-Izmachí, the last capital of the Quiché. There, under the fourth generation of kings, they develop their power and construct buildings of mortar and stone. The three great houses founded by the original ancestors live in peace without envy and with no thought of grandeur. They are ruled by King Cotuhá and Lord Iztayul. Then the people of Ilocab, wanting a chief of their own, begin a revolution. They attack the town but are defeated, and the king orders them sacrificed before the gods. The tribes, large and small, are filled with fear of the great kings. The three clans begin the custom of having feasts and orgies for their daughters when suitors come to ask for them in marriage.

In chapter 8 the three clans leave Chi-Izmachí and come to the town of Gumarcaah, and the fifth generation begins. Their empire grows, but they no longer drink together, and jealousies arise over the price for their sisters and daughters. They divide into nine families and turn against one another. They throw the skulls of the dead at one another. Later they end their dispute over the women and agree to divide the kingdom into 24 great families, which are named in the text.

In chapter 9 the town is constructed of stone and mortar by vassals. The lords are beloved by the vassals, as is the great King Gucumatz. For seven days, he mounts to the skies, and for seven days he goes down into Xibalba, for seven days he becomes a snake, for seven days he becomes an eagle, for seven days he is a jaguar, and for seven days he changes himself into clotted blood, "only motionless blood." The lords are filled with terror before him. "Tidings of the wonderful nature of the King . . . spread," and this is the beginning of the grandeur of the Quiché. Gucumatz is succeeded by Tepepul and Iztayul.

In chapter 10 two great kings, Gag-Quicab and Cavizimah, perform heroic deeds, destroying neighboring towns and dividing their fields. When one or two tribes do not bring tribute to Quicab, he falls upon them and makes them slaves. Some he wounds, some are tied to trees and killed with arrows. The conquered people are filled with terror "like a flash of lightning which strikes and shatters the rock." The enemy towns are abandoned, but the Quiché lords assemble and decide to man positions around the towns "just in case by chance the tribes might return. . . . These shall be like our forts . . . here shall our valor and manhood be proved." They set out across the mountains, "the sentinels of war." They make war and take captives. Some are heroes and receive rewards when they deliver their prisoners. It is decided that there should be ranks of distinction, promotions and titles, thrones and seats.

Chapter 11 describes the building of the temples of Tohil, Avilix, and Hacavitz, and rituals and prayers. Chapter 12 names all the generations of lords of the Quiché. The author says, "No longer can be seen [the book of the *Popol Vuh*] which the kings had in olden times, for it has disappeared." (Recinos, Goetz, and Morley 1983)

See also Hunab Ku; Hunahpú; Xbalanqué.

POSEIDON
(Also Neptune)

In ancient Greek religion, Poseidon is the chief sea god, son of Cronos and Rhea, and brother of Zeus, Hades, Demeter, Hera, and Hestia. He is one of the 12 great Olympians and also god of the horse. After Poseidon and Apollo build the walls of Troy, Laomedon refuses to pay them, and this causes Poseidon to side with the Greeks in the Trojan War. It is Poseidon who, angry at Odysseus

Poseidon, god of the sea and of horses, holds a trident in this copy of a fourth-century B.C. Greek sculpture.

for blinding his son Polyphemus, delays Odysseus's return to Ithaca. Poseidon also appears in the *Homeric Hymns.* (Graves 1955)

PÒTJOET MOEHAMAT, HIKAJAT

This is an epic of Atjeh, ca. the eighteenth century. The two million people of Atjeh, a kingdom on the northern tip of Sumatra, have a view of historical events that differs from official accounts. Their version, as expressed in their epic poetry, is based on a flow of words that is immune to or above the past. Composers and enumerators of the epics actually use not only the aspects of music—tempo, rhythm, melody, and rhyme—but also dream interpretation and even braggadocio to create their own version of historical events. They take into account nuances of belief and custom that go far beyond cold historical "fact" as it would be described in a Westerner's account. The historical narrative epics of Malay and other languages are circulated orally until someone writes them down, usually in verse form.

During the recitation, which is from memory, a copy of the epic is placed before the reciter. The reciters—there are usually two who alternate, due to the length of the recitation—will usually vary from the written text, but the older listeners and perhaps the performers as well are usually illiterate and are more interested in rhythm, tempo, and melody than in strict content. The alternate reciter, in addition to relieving the first speaker from time to time, offers "color" for the recitation with sound effects or visual representation such as acting out.

Each line of an Atjeh epic contains four pairs of feet, with the accent on the last syllable of each foot. The final syllable of the middle two pairs of feet rhymes, as do the final syllables in each line. Thus it is easy to see, particularly in a performance where the speaker is diverging from the written text, where sound and rhythm would take precedence over strict meaning or adherence to "facts" in some cases. The epics are composed to be chanted. The recitation can take a whole night and sometimes two or three nights, during which time the audience and even the reciters may wander in and out.

Hikajat Pòtjoet Moehamat was recorded by Trungkoe Tam Roekam from an oral account of a civil war. Pòtjoet Moehamat, who in one place is described as a very small man but a true champion, and in another as not very impressive, is the youngest brother of Radja Moeda, one of two kings ruling Atjeh.

Pòtjoet has a dream that convinces him that the situation of two rulers for the country is untenable. He goes to the neighboring region of Pidië to recruit warriors to help him overthrow the other king, Djeumalōj Alam. This is a daring idea, because Djeumalōj Alam claims descendancy from the Prophet and is therefore a rightful ruler, as is Moeda.

Although Pòtjoet is not very impressive to look at, sometimes when he speaks he is very persuasive. The people respond to the sound of his words and to his radiance, and are anxious to join him in overthrowing Djeumalōj.

In the region of Pidië, King Djeumalōj has an adopted son, Béntara Keumangan, a warrior both brave and handsome. This description is the listener's clue that Béntara Keumangan is the more important hero of the epic. Pòtjoet knows that Béntara Keumangan's support is necessary for either side to win, so he sends a letter to Béntara attempting to persuade him to join his side of the conflict. When the two men meet face to face, Pòtjoet's flattering words and costly gifts compel Béntara to change sides.

When Béntara informs his mother that he plans to go to war against his adopted father the king, she reminds him of the good things the king has done for him and begs her son not to do battle against him. Béntara answers with a somewhat classic example of the Islamic attitude at that time regarding the shame involved in refusing to do battle and regarding women in general: "One cannot listen to what women say; we must throw it out; it is of no use. / Like water in a plowed rice paddy, their fluent mouths always moving, / Making a breeze, raising waves across the entire field of rice, / [Their] only knife is [their] mouth; [their] only strength is cursing. / You do not think of shame; you fight only with your moving mouth."

Béntara Keumangan joins the troops of Pòtjoet Moehamat and they journey to the battle site. After a long and bloody battle, which Pòtjoet and Béntara are not winning, the sultan Djeumalōj, learning that the young man whom he befriended and adopted as his own is fighting against him, confronts Béntara. He reminds Béntara of all the circumstances surrounding his adoption and all the gifts and largesse that have since been bestowed upon him, even though the king has other, natural-born sons. Now, Béntara's betrayal has negated his sonship. The price of forgetting what one has been given is death. The king takes out his gun and aims it at a tree branch over Béntara's head. The branch snaps off, and the "shadow" kills Béntara. The people are mystified as to how he died, because there are no marks on his body.

Béntara's funeral is described in great length and detail, for the warrior is greatly revered. His body is returned to his mother's house, where mourners are amazed to see figures on the walls: pictures of the moon and a scorpion, signifying both passage of time and death. The natives' frenzied expressions of grief are excessive and violent in and of themselves. The mourners beat themselves and thrash around, throwing themselves against the walls, to be forced back again and again to the center of the room where the coffin stands. They cannot but acknowledge their hero's death.

But Béntara's death has galvanized the people into action. When at length the mighty battle resumes, despite the fact that Béntara is dead, Pòtjoet Moehamat defeats Djeumalōj Alam. Even though he is descended from the Prophet, the people chase him across the land to the sea, and finally to the mountains, where they leave him among the thorny rattan. Radja Moeda, who has avoided becoming involved in the fight, is left the undisputed ruler of the land. An early scene where the king Radja Moeda begs to be excused from joining his brother in battle and actually scurries back to his palace makes it clear that he, also, is not the hero of the epic.

As a sign that the war is over and that all the people should return to their homes, the sun and moon are eclipsed and the earth quakes for seven days and nights.

A year after the war, Pòtjoet Moehamat marries the daughter of a chieftain of Gampōng Lambhoe', a prosperous section of the Atjehnese capital, and, as is the custom, lives in a house provided by his in-laws in his wife's village. He prospers collecting taxes from incoming ships, dividing the revenues half for himself and half for his brother the king.

Thus it is through the death of the handsome warrior that the battle is won, even though the warrior was not killed in battle. (Siegel 1979)

PRADYUMNA

In Hindu mythology, Pradyumna is the son of the god Kṛiṣṇa and Rukmiṇī. He also appears in an old Indian folktale, "Destiny Conquered." (Shattan 1989; van Buitenen 1969)

See also *Manimekhalaï.*

PRAJĀPATI
(Lord of Creatures)

In the *Vedas,* Prajāpati is one of the creators, formed from primal waters. After undertaking ascetic practices (tapas), and with the help of his female counterpart, Vāc (the word), Prajāpati produces the universe and all its creatures. In other accounts, his counterpart/daughter is the dawn, Uṣas. (O'Flaherty 1975)

PRAJÑĀPĀRAMITĀ
(Perfect Wisdom)

Goddess of Mahāyāna Buddhism, she is called the goddess of all Buddhas. (Allen *Art in America* 1991)

PRIAM

In Greek mythology, Priam is the last king of Troy, the son of Laomedon, and husband of Hecuba. According to the *Iliad* (vi), he is the father of 50 legitimate sons—the most famous being Hektor and Paris—and 12 legitimate daughters, as well as 42 children by concubines. When Herakles slays Laomedon, he places Priam on the throne. At the end of his life, he sees 13 of his sons slain by Achilles. After Hektor is slain, Priam travels to Achilles's tent to ransom his son's corpse so as to give it a proper burial. After the Greeks from the wooden horse throw open the gates of Troy, Achilles's son Neoptolemus slays the old king on an altar. (Lattimore 1976)

See also Achilles; Hektor; *Iliad;* Paris.

PRINCE LORD SKY

("Ezen tengger khaan")

This brief oral epic found in Khovd Province of western Mongolia was still sung by shepherds as recently as the late 1960s. (Finnegan 1978)

PROETUS

In Greek mythology, Proteus is the son of Abas and twin of Acrisius, with whom he fights over the kingdom of Argos. His attempts to kill Bellerophon, slayer of the Chimera, are related in the *Iliad* (vi). (Lattimore 1976)

PROTESILAUS

In Greek mythology, Protesilaus is a king of Thessaly and uncle of Jason. In the *Odyssey* (ii), he is the first Greek arriving on Trojan soil and the first to be killed in the Trojan War, even though he has been warned by an oracle of the death of the first Greek to land. (Rouse 1990)

PROTEUS

In Greek mythology, Proteus is a sea god, son of Oceanus and Tethys, to whom Poseidon gives the gifts of prophecy and transformation. Menelaus encounters him in the *Odyssey* (iv). (Rouse 1990)

PTE CYCLE

This mythology of the Oglala Sioux (Lakota) concerns the Pte, or buffalo people, who live on a level of the cosmos below the level of humans. The cycle begins with the arrival in the land of Pte of Tate, whom the sky god Škan (the source of movement but unmoving) has commanded, "Assume the form of manhood and go abide with the Pte. When you have learned how they fare, resume your godly estate." The Pte try to decide his role or position among them.

Tate soon becomes enamored of Ite, daughter of a Pte leader, Wa. Because he must set aside his godly attributes in order to experience romantic love, his name becomes Kola. The oldest and wisest chief, Ate, tells the Pte, "When an alien seeks your hospitality, he is your guest and should be so treated while he remains inoffensive among you. In this manner you shall do service for the Gods."

Ate recognizes Kola as a superior man who could replace him as chief if he would take a Pte wife and beget an offspring. But Kola tells him, "I am of the Gods. . . ." He suggests that, if there is to be a change in leadership, Wa's wife Kan, a seer, should give the tribe advice. Kola says he will gladly give up his godly estate in order to marry Ite, if Kan thinks it is wise. The people approve of the match, and even Wa, who has been jealous, agrees to welcome Kola as a son.

Assuming his true identity as Tate, Kola returns to Škan to tell him what has happened. Škan gives him permission to return to the Pte and remain with them until he has offspring old enough to leave home.

The demon Gnaski comes to the Pte disguised as Ksabela. He tells his demon-mother Unk, "I have extended your hold into the regions under the world. I will make for like authority in the domain of Maka (Earth)." Unk answers, "You, my son, shall make my hate effective."

Gnaski, who is very handsome, convinces Ksa (Wisdom), who is dissatisfied with his own appearance, to assume an appearance identical to Gnaski's. But when Ksa is caught participating in Gnaski's evil schemes, he is punished by being transformed into Iktomi, the trickster, who must forever manipulate the weaknesses of others throughout eternity. Škan tells the Pte people, "The God of Wisdom and the demon of folly are so alike that they can be distinguished only by careful examination. . . . As you listen to Ksa or to Gnaski, so shall be the welfare of . . . your people." By the end of the cycle, Iktomi has lost his identity as Ksa altogether.

Tate and Ite marry and have five sons. But Ite dies and Tate is left to raise his sons by himself. He waits for a message from Škan, who sends his daughter Wohpe as mediator. She informs him that she will help the sons, but only if they will always view her as a sister. But three of the sons lust after her, and so are destined to journey all around the world, founding the directions of the world. The fourth son, Okaga, wins her as a wife by being kind and helpful.

As the brothers travel the world, Iktomi imitates a whippoorwill to divert Okaga from his mission by tricking him into believing that Wohpe needs him at home.

When the directions of the world have been founded, a great feast is held, and the Lakota history begins on the present level of existence. Their first leader, Tokahe, teaches the people rituals and knowledge to help them survive. At last he proclaims that he is from another world and must return. (Walker 1983)

PULURU
(Also Puluri)

Puluru is one of a pair of heroes (Silamaka is the other) who are subjects of an oral epic of the West African Fulani people of Pankshin, Nigeria. (Okpewho 1992; Westley *RAL* 1991)

See also Silamaka and Puluru.

PURSUIT OF DIARMAID AND GRÁINNE

One of the tales in the Irish *Fenian Cycle*, it is a variation of the story of Deirdre and the *Tristan and Iseult* legend. Diarmaid (also Diarmuid or Diarmait), a nephew of Fionn MacCumhail, abducts Fionn's wife Gráinne. The lovers flee to the wilderness to escape Fionn's men but are finally captured. (Jackson, K. 1971; Rutherford 1987)

See also Deirdre; *Tristan and Iseult.*

PURUṢA-SŪKTA

In the *Ṛg Veda,* Puruṣa-sūkta is the Hymn of Man. The gods create the world by dismembering the primeval male, the cosmic giant Peruṣa. From him all other things spring. From him the active female creative principle, Virāj, is born, and from Virāj comes Man. Later Virāj is replaced by Prakṛti, or material nature, the mate of Puruṣa in Sānkhya philosophy. (O'Flaherty *Veda* 1981)

PWYLL
(Also Pelles)

In Celtic mythology, in the *Mabinogion,* Pwyll (meaning sense or judgment) is the prince of Dyved, land of the cauldron of plenty. To earn the friendship of King Arawn of Annwvyn, king of the underworld, he swaps kingdoms with him, becoming Pwyll Pen Annwvyn, so that he can rid Arawn of the oppression of a neighbor, Havgan of Annwvyn. Pwyll is ultimately able to win the hand of Rhiannon, daughter of Heveyedd the Old, from his rival Gwawl, although in the beginning, Gwawl outwits him so badly that Rhiannon tells him, "I have never seen such a feeble-witted performance." They have a son, Pryderi, whom Gwawl abducts, but who later returns and becomes king of Dyved and Annwvyn. In Arthurian legend, the cauldron of plenty is the Holy Grail, and Pwyll becomes Pelles, Keeper of the Grail. (Gantz 1976)

See also Arthurian Legend; *Mabinogion.*

PYGMALION

In the *Aeneid* (i), Pygmalion is a son of King Belus of Tyre, brother of Dido, and murderer of Dido's husband Sichaeus, whom he kills for his treasure. But Dido flees to Africa with the treasure and establishes the city of Carthage. Pygmalion is also the name of the sculptor-king of Cyprus who, disappointed in women, falls in love with a statue. He prays to Aphrodite to give the statue life, and she changes it into a woman, Galatea, whom Pygmalion marries. The two have a daughter, Paphos. (Ben Khader and Soren 1987; Humphries 1951)

See also *Aeneid;* Dido; Elissa.

Q

QAṢĪDAH

In Arabian poetry from the sixth century forward, qaṣīdah is a formal ode of up to 100 couplets, all using the same rhyme, which might be boasting, panegyric, satire, or warlike. Usually it is an account of the poet's journey. The name means "Purpose Poem." The poem is composed extemporaneously one verse, or bait, at a time, and sung to some familiar tune. The audience takes up the verse, clapping and adding body movements to fill in until the poet adds another verse, gradually developing, from a medley of stories or themes, a single poem. The Persian qasida, after the Arabian model, has been popular throughout Persian literary history. (Levy 1990; Preminger 1990)

QAT

Qat is the legendary hero of many cycles in the Banks Islands near Java. He has 11 brothers all named Tagaro, one being Tagaro the Wise and another, Tagaro the Foolish. On the island of Mota, all the brothers conspire against Qat and his friend Marawa the Spider, but on the island of Santa Maria, Marawa is the enemy. According to one tale, when Qat finishes creation, he cuts down a great tree and proposes to his brothers that they make a canoe. But each morning he discovers that his work of hollowing out the trunk has been undone overnight. One night he shrinks to a very small size and hides to watch. He spies an old man who emerges from the ground to put the wood chips back into the trunk. He springs out, growing to his normal size in an instant, and swings his ax. But the old man, who is Marawa in disguise, begs Qat to spare his life. Qat does so and uses his nails to finish hollowing out the canoe. When all the brothers' boats have been finished, Qat tells his brothers to launch them. Each boat slips into the water and, as Qat raises his hand, each boat sinks. Then Qat and Marawa paddle about in their canoe.

The brothers decide to destroy Qat so they can have his wife and canoe. They entice him into a hole to dig for a crab, and then they tip a stone over the hole, believing they have crushed him to death. But Qat calls to Marawa, "Marawa! Take me round about to Ro Lei." By the time his brothers reach the village, they discover Qat there, sitting beside his wife. The brothers try many schemes to kill Qat, but he is always victorious. (Dixon 1964)

QIṬ'AH

From pre-Islam forward, this is an Arabian poetic form based on a single theme, perhaps developed from the original qaṣīdah. It deals with less serious subjects, such as everyday happenings. (Preminger 1990; Turco 1986)

QUEST

The quest is a metaphor for the soul's yearning for immortality that appears in epics as old as the *Aqhat, Baal,* and *Gilgamesh.* Often the nebulous yearning is embodied in a symbolic item. In medieval literature, the epitomization is often the Grail, the sacred cup used by Jesus at the Last Supper. According to tradition, the cup was preserved by Joseph of Arimathea, who used it to collect the blood from the crucified Savior. The Grail had miraculous powers to heal and nourish the pure in heart, and to strike dumb the sinful (as it did the Fisher King). Tradition further says that Joseph's descendants in Britain continued to preserve the Grail, and thus it became the object of desire of many knights of King Arthur's Round Table. The quest was undertaken by Percival *(Parzival)* and later by Sir Galahad.

Other quests, always characterized by the noblest of intentions, include those undertaken by *Mwindo* to find his relatives in the underworld; by *Bakaridjan Kone* to get cattle; by Hamunān, in the *Rāmāyaṇa,* to find Sītā; and by Hunahpú and Xbalanqué to find their fathers.

See also *Aqhat Epic;* Arthurian Legend; *Baal Epic; Bakaridjan Kone, a Hero of Segu, Epic of;* Hunahpú; *Mwindo, Epic of; Parzival;* Percival; *Popol Vuh; Rāmāyaṇa;* Xbalanqué.

QUETZALCÓATL, TOPILTZIN
(Plumed Serpent)

Quetzalcóatl is the major deity of ancient Mexico, from the third century onward. His myths survive in five fragments, in the *Annals of Cuauhtitlan* and the so-called *Florentine Codex* and *Codex Vaticanus 3738,* primarily. He represents not only the hero-child (the power of doing) of Mother Earth and Father Sky (the powers of being), but the generative halves as well: He is synomymous with the omnipotent Spirit of Duality. Originally he was probably a vegetation god, closely associated with the rain god Tlaloc.

According to Aztec belief of the fifteenth century, Quetzalcóatl came to earth during the Toltec period (A.D. 600–1000) as a princely ruler and reformer. He is driven away and becomes the god of the morning and evening star with a temple in Tollan (Tula), the Toltec capital, but he promises to return someday to reestablish his kingdom on earth.

In Aztec times (fourteenth to sixteenth centuries), he was patron of the priests, protector of craftsmen, and inventor of learning and of calendars. Accounts of a historical Toltec king, Topiltzin Huemac, have occasionally been woven into the myths of *Quetzalcóatl,* whom historians consider entirely mythical.

As the morning and evening star, *Quetzalcóatl* is also the symbol of death and resurrection. In fragment A, called "The Restoration of Life," accompanied by the dog-headed deity Xolotl he descends to the underground ruled by Mictlan to collect the bones of the dead. He brings them to paradise and places them within the womb of Earth Mother. He inseminates them with his own blood, fathering the race of men who now inhabit the earth. Next, he discovers maize and also brings it to paradise, where the gods "laid it upon our lips so that we were made strong." But the lightning god Nanahuatl splits open the cache of maize so as to make it available to the earth people as well. Then quickly the rain gods come and steal all the maize.

In fragment B, "The Ceremonial Fire," Ce Acatl (the planet Venus) discovers that his father, the sun, has been murdered by his uncles Apanecatl, Zolton, and Cuilton (the stars) and covered up in the western sea. He retrieves the corpse and buries it in a sacred earth mountain. He calls upon his uncles, the moles, to dig for him a passage through the mountain and to the summit. He crawls through the passage and lights a fire at the top of the mountain, thus outwitting his uncles, the stars, who attempt to put it out. Thus he brings his father back to life. Having rescued the sun, he proceeds to renew himself, traveling eastward. He reaches the shore, where he dies, and is transformed by fire into the morning star.

Fragment C, "A Cycle of Transformation," weaves at least four separate myths pertaining to the savior and the symbol of light. The hero Quetzalcóatl is born to a mother named Chimalma, who swallows an emerald that becomes the child. He is a bringer of culture to the people, and as the discoverer of plants, gems, and metals is the originator of crafts and fine arts. Among the gems is the sun, which he hides beneath the earth as his death nears. He is also a priest, a religious reformer, pure and penitent, whom the jealous god Tezcatlipoca (Titlacahuan, god of night and diviner of secret thoughts) contrives to make drunk and incestuous with his sister Quetzalpetlatl. Two other antagonists are involved, the Aztec war god Huitzilopochtli, and the "human log," Tlacahuipan, the embodiment of human guilt. Tezcatlipoca is also called by an alternate name, Titlacahuan, "he to whom we are slaves." Again, as in fragment B, the personified Venus inters the corpse of his murdered father-sun, then proceeds eastward, dies, and is reborn as the morning star. Another episode identifies the hero as Tlahuizcalpanteuctli, "Lord of the House of Dawn," the warlike Venus whose arrows strike humankind with vengeance.

Fragment D, "The Fall of Tollan," part I, shows Quetzalcóatl as both priest and patron of crops. He succumbs to the tricks of the jealous Titlacahuan, who again makes him drunk and sends him away. In part II, Titlacahuan impersonates a peddler of chili peppers named Toueyo, who appears nude before the beautiful daughter of Huemac, making her ill. Huemac sends for Tuoeyo and demands that he cure his daughter. But first he is trimmed, bathed, and clothed. Then he appears before the daughter and "knows" her. She is cured, and she marries him. But the Toltecs are scornful of the marriage of Huemac's daughter to a common Toueyo, and they set out to drive him away. But he marshals the dwarfs, the hunchbacks, so as to attack and kill them all. When the king hears of this, he is most uneasy. He summons the Toltecs and says, "We must go to greet / this cherished son-in-law of yours." They meet him in full regalia, dancing and singing, appeasing him. Huemac speaks to Toueyo: "You have done well. Be received on this soil." But as the Toltecs step and dance, the man appears as a sorcerer and begins to lead them closer and closer to the crags in the gorge, until they fall in and are destroyed. Again, the same enchanter appears as a warrior and slays more of the Toltec. Another time, he seats himself at the center of the market square, where he causes a manikin to dance. The people crowd in to watch, and many are killed in the crush. Others turn upon the sorcerer and stone him to death. After a while, the corpse reeks, and the people begin to die of the stench. They try to drag the body away, but it is too heavy. They tie ropes to it, but they fail to move it. Suddenly the dead man moves and causes a log to roll over them, crushing them. Those who are left finally throw the body away. Again, the sorcerer causes the food to become bitter. An old woman (the sorcerer in disguise) begins to roast maize in the square, and its smell spreads across the land. The hungry Toltecs come from far and wide, but the woman kills them all.

Because of all the suffering of the Toltecs, Quetzalcóatl grieves. He leaves Tollan and goes to Tlapallan, after burying his treasures in a mountain or in chasms. On the way, he marks a rock with his hands at the place where he rests. He meets a sorcerer who entices him to drink strong wine. As his hunchback subjects (rain spirits) travel the snowy pass between Iztactepetl and Popocatepetl, they are chilled and freeze to death. Quetzalcóatl is shaken by their death. He gazes eastward and sees the mountain home of rain, toward which he heads. At last he arrives at the seashore. There he constructs a litter of serpents, which he uses as a boat. It carries him out to sea.

Fragment E, "A Song of Survival," begins in the form of a dialogue between Cintéotl (variegated maize) and a chorus, which explains the birth of Cintéotl as a result of the death of Topiltzin Quetzalcóatl. The first section of this brief fragment laments his death. The second segment describes the birth of the ear of maize. The third section, in which the poet speaks with his own voice, asserts that the poem will live on in the hearts and minds of the people. He describes his poem as a sprig of divine inspiration that will take root and flower like the peyote or cacao. (Bierhorst 1974; León-Portilla 1982)

R

RĀDHĀ

In Hindu mythology, in the *Purāṇas,* Rādhā appears as the consort of the youthful Kṛiṣṇa while he dwells among the cowherds of Vṛndāvana. In one place he is pictured as a child whom she comforts during a thunderstorm. She takes him to the woods where she sees a beautiful dark man lying on a couch. The child becomes that man. He leaves the dancing cowherd women to steal away to the woods with Rādhā, with whom he makes passionate love. Kṛiṣṇa plays out "the eight ways of love as a master of the Kāmaśāstra." He robs her of her wits; she steals his heart in the dance. Later, after lovemaking, he becomes a child again. Kṛiṣṇa the man has gone to kill his uncle Kaṃsa. While he is gone, she misses him terribly. She weeps and falls to the ground, but a disembodied voice says, "Remember Kṛiṣṇa's lotus feet! As long as the circle of the Dance exists, he will return to it and you shall have all the love play you wish. . . ." She returns the baby, wet and sticky, to his mother, Yaśoda. But every night she makes love with the man. (Dimmitt and van Buitenen 1978)

See also Kṛiṣṇa.

RAGANA

In Lithuanian folklore, Ragana is a prophetess. The name is sometimes used in connection with the woodland fairy, lauma (laumę), as lauma-ragana, indicating that the fairy may have been a prophetess as well. In Lithuanian tales, the fates (laimės) predestine the newborn's life. In some tales Ragana appears as an old woman or a beggar. She is a goddess of the forest, afraid of water. One of the most important activities of her servants, the women-witches (raganas), is the spoiling of cow's milk. According to one story, she kidnaps a child and prepares to eat him, but first fattens him up with nuts and boiled milk so that his flesh will be tender. Ragana lives in the forest, a nonhuman world where ancient mythic beings such as Ragana, Laumę, Vęjas, and even the Senelis Dievas (Old Man God) can appear. (Greimas 1992)

RAGNAR LOTHBROK
(Also Lothrocus Hairybreeks)

Ragnar is the Danish Viking legendary hero (fl. ninth century) of several twelfth-century Icelandic works: *Ragnars saga lodbrokar, Thattr of Ragnarssonum,* and a twelfth-century poem, *Krakumal.* He appears first in the ninth-century *Anglo-Saxon Chronicle* and in the later poem *Hattalykill* from the Orkney Islands. He is confused with the historical Danish Viking leader Ragnar, or Reginherus, who in March of 845 led a raid up the Seine to plunder Paris. The authenticity of Ragnar Lothbrok of legend is in question. The *Anglo-Saxon Chronicle* names three sons—Ivar the Boneless (Yngvarr), Ubbi, and Halfdane—who come from Scandinavia and Ireland to England in 865 to avenge the death of their father. According to Danish historian Saxo Grammaticus (twelfth century), Ragnar had come to England where King Ella of Northumbria defeated him and had him thrown in a snakepit to be bitten to death. The two Icelandic sagas are accounts of the same incident. The *Krakumal* has him married to a daughter of Sigurd and Brynhild of the *Nibelungenlied.* (Jones, G. 1990)

RAGNARÖK
(Doom of the Gods)

In the tenth-century Icelandic poem "Völuspá" found in the *Poetic Edda,* and in the thirteenth-century *Prose Edda,* Ragnarök is the term for doomsday, or the end of life for men and gods. One version of the myth says that the world tree will not be destroyed, and two humans, Lif and Lifthrasir, will emerge from the tree to repopulate the world. (Hollander *Edda* 1990; Young 1954)

See also *Edda, Poetic.*

RA'I RA'I

Divine progenitress of the Hawaiian people, whose story is told in the ancient chant of the *Tumuripo* and also in the legend of *Ra'i Ra'i and Te Ari'i Vahi Rani.* Although the *Tumuripo* was composed thousands of years before the arrival of the first Christian Bible in Hawaii, the story of Ra'i Ra'i bears a resemblance to the tale of Adam and Eve. Ra'i Ra'i, spirit of joy and sunshine, is born of the mind of her father Tane and her mother Uri in the highest heaven. Lady Ra, goddess of the sun, sends her to earth to deliver into life human beings who were to spring from the Tree of Life in Po. She is to clothe the souls in earthly skin suitable for life on earth. In the Garden of Sunshine, she is visited by the king who comes from heaven, Te Ari'i Vahi Rani, or Tane, God. She gives birth to her first son, the handsome Mure, who will someday rule the Land of Rua. At daylight she gives birth to her second child, the beautiful Ta Rua. As the day progresses, Ha'i and Haria, two daughters, are born, followed by her second son, Hatea. Ta Rua becomes curious and plucks a forbidden fruit, the ape, which is traditionally planted at the gate to ward off evil powers. She discovers for the first time the masculine beauty of her brothers, who are clothed only in sunlight. She shares her secret with her sisters, but only Ha'i tries the forbidden fruit. The two girls set out to seduce their brothers into trying the fruit, and when they do, their eyes are opened to their sisters' beauty. The boys invent the game of sex, but they tire of it before the girls because they have to work harder. The girls discover that they are pregnant and, fearing the wrath of Ra'i Ra'i, run away to live in the forest. They bear their children in secret and deny to their mother and brothers that they exist. But when the children grow old enough, the sisters feed ape to their children and then sleep with them.

Tane observes this misbehavior from his throne in the sky and hurls stones upon them. The people run for cover but continue their behavior. They pick up the stones and, making weapons with them, battle one another. Ra'i Ra'i is killed while trying to bring about peace among her descendants, and her spirit floats away to the heavens. Tane gives Mure to his beloved child Haria, who is still a virgin. Thus Ta Rua, the world's first temptress, loses her claim to become the first lady of the Land of Rua. (Melville 1990)

RĀKṢASA

In Hindu mythology, rākṣasa is the name of a class of flesh-eating demons having the power to change their appearance, known from the time of the *Ṛg Vega.* They are ruled by a king, Rāvaṇa of the ten heads. An account in the *Purāṇas* tells of a female rākṣasa, Pūtanā the Child-Killer, who steals into the home of Vāsudeva, picks up the sleeping infant Kṛiṣṇa, and offers her breast of poison milk. But the god grabs her by the nipple, squeezes tightly with both hands, and "furiously" sucks her to death. Rākṣasas appear in paintings depicting scenes from the *Rāmāyaṇa.* They appear in *Manimekhalaï* and in *Bardo Thötröl* (Tibetan Book of the Dead), as well. (Fremantle and Trungpa 1987; O'Flaherty *Veda* 1981; Shattan 1989)

RAM DEVRA

This oral folk epic in Rajasthan is based on the *Rāmāyaṇa,* which is still being performed in India today. (Blackburn et al. 1989)

***See also** Rāmāyaṇa.*

RĀMA

(Charming; also Rāmacandra or Prince Rāma of Ayodhyā)

In the Hindu *Purāṇas,* Rāma is the heroic seventh avatar of Lord Viṣṇu and the god epitomizing chivalry and virtue. He is the hero of Vālmīki's Sanskrit epic, the *Rāmāyaṇa,* and he also appears in the *Mahābhārata.* He may have been a historical figure of heroic exploits who was transformed by legend into a deity, then later absorbed by Viṣṇu. He is born a prince in line for the throne of Ayodhyā, but his stepmother's meddling forces him to abdicate his claim in favor of one of his half brothers, Bhārata. With his wife Sītā and his devoted half brother Lakṣmaṇa, Rāma withdraws to the forest for 13 years, where they encounter both demons and sages. Rāma and Lakṣmaṇa protect them all from harm from the mischievous demons until the demon king kidnaps Sītā. Rāma and Lakṣmaṇa form an alliance with the monkey-king Hanumān, who travels to Laṅkā to discover Sītā being held prisoner there. With the help of the monkeys, Rāma and Lakṣmaṇa set about rescuing Sītā by force. A tremendous battle ensues in which Rāma is victorious. It is then that he learns that he is an incarnation of Viṣṇu. Rāma and Sītā return home, and he is crowned king. He reigns for many years before he is overcome by doubts as to Sītā's purity after her long incarceration at the hands of Rāvaṇa. He expells her to the forest, where she gives birth to his two sons, Kuśa and Lava. They are cared for by the poet Vālmīki, who teaches them the story of their father's great exploits. Rāma is the subject of a number of epics in the vernacular. (Buck 1976)

See also Hanumān; Lakṣmaṇa; *Rāmāyaṇa;* Rāvaṇa; Sītā.

RĀMACARIĪTMĀNAS

(Also *Ramcaritmanas)*

This is the medieval (sixteenth century) Hindi vernacular version of the *Rāmāyaṇa* by the poet Tulsīdās. The title means "Sacred Lake of the Acts of Rama." This version is preferred over the Sanskrit original in the Hindi-speaking area of India. (Embree 1988)

RAMAKIEN

This is the Thai version of the Hindu epic *Rāmāyaṇa,* celebrated in classical dance. (McDowell 1982)

See also *Rāmāyaṇa.*

RAMAKIRTI

These are Thai versions of the *Rāmāyaṇa,* some of the earliest works of Thai poetry. However, the only extant versions date from the sixteenth century or later. (Preminger 1990)

See also *Rāmāyaṇa.*

RĀMĀYAṆA

(Romance of Rāma; literally, Rāma's Way)

This great Sanskrit epic of ancient India was composed ca. 200 B.C. to A.D. 200 (some parts date to ca. 500 B.C.) by the poet Vālmīki. In its present form it consists of some 24,000 couplets divided into seven books. Along with the *Mahābhārata,* the poem epitomizes the spirit of ancient Hindu tradition. The poet doubtless drew upon a number of popular Rāma folktales, to which he added a number of fabulous incidents and tales from the supernatural. Historians have always speculated as to whether the battle depicted in the epic is based on an actual historical event. The first and last books are considered by scholars to be later additions, agreeing with the *Purāṇas* as identifying Rāma as the seventh incarnation (avatar) of the god Viṣṇu. But the remainder of the poem depicts him as the perfect, reasonable, and wise man and the perfect king; Sītā as the ideal wife; and Lakṣmaṇa as the ideal brother.

The *Rāmāyaṇa* spread widely over Southeast Asia, where it has been assimilated into local cultures, including those in Burma, Indonesia, Thailand, and the Philippines. Changes have occurred in the various local versions; often the local court singer would portray his patron as the hero Rāma. Among others, the *Rāmāyaṇa* appears in the Tamil version of Kambar, the Bengali version of Krttibas, and the Hindu version of Tulsīdās. (*See also Rāmacariītmānas.*)

As in the *Mahābhārata*, the *Iliad*, the *Odyssey*, and many other early works, gods frequently interact with mortals, but they are far from infallible. They are powerful and immortal, but not omnipotent.

Book I, the "Book of the Boyhood of Rāma," describes the royal birth of Prince Rāma, the son of King Daśaratha and his first wife, Queen Kausalyā, in the kingdom of Ayodhyā (Oudh). On the same day, his brother Bhārata is born of the king's youngest wife, Kaikeyī, and later that same day, his brothers Lakṣmaṇa and Śatrugha are born to the king's second wife, Sumitrā. As the boys grow older, Lakṣmaṇa attaches himself to Rāma, while Śatrugha accompanies Bhārata wherever he goes. When the four princes reach the age of 16, the Brahmin Viśvāmitra comes to court and tells the king that there is no more safety for him in the forest from the demon king Rāvaṇa, ruler of Laṅkā. He has come to ask for Rāma to go to the forest and rid it of the demon menace. The king reluctantly sends Rāma and Lakṣmaṇa to the forest, where they remain for 13 years, fighting demons and learning from the sage Viśvāmitra. They meet the Videha king Janaka, who possesses a gift from Śiva, a bow, now the dowry of his beautiful daughter, the half-divine Sītā, whose mother is the goddess Earth, Prithivi. At the bridegroom tournament set up to choose Sītā's mate, Rāma succeeds in bending the mighty bow and wins Sītā as his bride. At the time of their marriage, his three brothers are married to Sītā's sisters. Little by little, King Daśaratha turns over the work of the kingdom to Rāma, who ennobles whatever he does.

As book II, the "Ayodhyā Book," begins, Rāma and Sītā have been married for 12 years. Old King Daśaratha decides that it is time to make Rāma the king. But Kaikeyī, Bhārata's mother, to whom the king once granted two wishes, asks now that those wishes be granted: "Make Bhārata king and not Rāma. Send Rāma to the forest for 14 years." The king reluctantly grants her wishes and, amid much lamenting from the people, Rāma, Sītā, and the faithful Lakṣmaṇa depart for the forest—Lakṣmaṇa even placing his loyalty to his brother above that to his wife. At the last minute the king relents and runs out to stop them, but he is too late.

The three exiles are befriended first by Guha, the hunter king, who adorns Sītā, the perfect wife, with a necklace of pink seashells and adopts her into his family. As hermits do, Rāma and Lakṣmaṇa mat their hair with a sticky paste made from banyan bark, and they put on deerskins, gifts from Guha. Guha gives Sītā a fine feather cloak, and the exiles go on their way.

Meanwhile, Sumantra, the charioteer who had driven them from the kingdom to the edge of the forest, returns to find that the old king has been struck blind. The king says that his sight has followed Rāma and does not return. He begs the charioteer, "If I have ever done any good thing, drive me to Rāma!" But Sumantra answers, "I cannot. I don't look back. I don't know where he is." Later, alone with Queen Kausalyā, the king tells her that he remembers what he did so long ago to cause all this misfortune: "I have cut down sweet fruit trees for being slow-growing. In their place I've faithfully watered the rampant gay-colored trees bitter of fruit. . . . I looked forward to happiness but all the while I coveted delusion." During the night, the old king dies, heartbroken.

Bhārata is summoned home and learns that his mother is responsible for Rāma's exile and indirectly for the old king's death from grief. He vows that he will not be king under the circumstances, but instead will take Rāma's place in the forest. He starts out to find Rāma, followed by the three queens, 9,000 elephants, 6,000 chariots carrying bowmen, then scores of horsemen, foot soldiers, wives, children, and pack animals. When Bhārata finds his brother Rāma, he kneels before him and begs him to come home to rule, saying, "Our father who enjoyed the world is dead." But Rāma tells him, "A man's unbroken word is like a bowl of clear glass; once shattered, no one can put it back as it was by any art. I must do what I said I would do, stay here for 14 years. . . . Death does not change a promise made." Bhārata begrudgingly agrees to rule until Rāma returns, but he asks for Rāma's sandals, which he will place on the throne. "If I do not see you on the first day after those 14 years, I'll walk into a fire and die." Thereafter the ministers and noblemen of Kosala bow to Rāma's shoes sitting on the throne as to a king. A barefoot Rāma and his companions continue their forest exile, staying eight months or so in one place before moving on to the next. In this way they pass 13 years. Book II ends late in the fourteenth and last springtime.

Book III, the "Forest Book," again introduces a woman as the troublemaker. The demon king Rāvaṇa's sister, Śūrpaṇakhā, described as misshapen, with yellowy skin rutted "like a bad road," and "a pot belly and ears like flat baskets, claws on her fingers and toes, squinty eyes and messy hair," comes across the three wanderers. She sees the handsome Rāma and desires him, so she tells him bluntly, "I have chosen you for my husband." When Rāma politely refuses, she cracks her knuckles and rushes at Sītā with "her claws curved like elephant hooks." But Lakṣmaṇa intervenes, lops off her ears, and sends her on her way.

She rushes back to the Rakṣasa camp and tells the troops, "I've been attacked!" The entire garrison of 14,000 assembles and marches off to avenge her. But Rāma, after hiding Sītā and Lakṣmaṇa in a cave, kills the entire army with his golden arrows. No one escapes except Śūrpaṇakhā, who flies to tell her brother Rāvaṇa of the massacre, and to goad him into kidnapping Sītā for himself. Rāvaṇa, easily swayed, goes to his demon uncle Mārīca for help in stealing Sītā and threatens to kill him if he refuses. That being the case, Mārīca decides to assist Rāvaṇa, even though Rāma will probably kill him, because "it is better to be killed by the better person."

He transforms himself into a golden deer and lures Rāma far away from his companions during the hunt. After Rāma shoots him, he lets out such a cry that Lakṣmaṇa, fearing that Rāma is hurt, starts to rush off in rescue and leave Sītā unguarded. She begs him not to go, but he says, "Wrong words are nothing new for a woman." He draws a circle around her and commands her not to step out of it. As soon as he leaves her, Rāvaṇa swoops in and kidnaps her. As they fly away on his chariot, she calls in her mind to the tree gods and to the vulture king Jaṭāyu, "Tell Rāma."

The vulture king tries to save her, but is mortally wounded. Her jewels are spilled on the forest floor. Only two monkeys are left behind to bear witness, and it is they who retrieve the jewels.

Rāvaṇa takes her to his palace and imprisons her with the promise, "When winter comes . . . if you haven't come into my bed, I'll eat you minced for breakfast!"

Meantime, on his high heaven, Lord Brahmā summons Indra and says, "Sītā must not die nor end her life in Laṅkā." Indra goes down with a bowl of heavenly wheat and butter and tells her, "Eat this and never will you hunger nor thirst for a year." While Indra comforts Sītā, Rāma and Lakṣmaṇa return to discover she is missing. The dying vulture Jaṭāyu tells them what has happened. They build a funeral pyre for Jaṭāyu and then begin their hopeless search for Sītā. They come across an old hermit woman Sāvarī, who tells them that the search for Sītā is now in the hands of the white monkey Hanumān. They climb onto Rishyamuka Hill in search of the monkeys, while Sugrīva and Hanumān, the two monkeys, watch them coming closer.

In book IV, the "Book of Kishkindhya" (the land of the monkeys), Rāma and Lakṣmaṇa meet Sugrīva and Hanumān and learn that they too are in exile, placed there by Sugrīva's brother, King Vālin, who wrongly believes that his brother is guilty of treason and who is holding Sugrīva's wife Ruma as a hostage. The four agree to help one another.

Inside the monkey palace, Queen Tara tells Vālin that Sugrīva is approaching. She warns him, "Don't go out. Be kind to your brother, and return him his wife, she is so sad here." But Vālin gives her a pat and tells her, "The only reason to consult a woman is to find out what not to do." Then he adds, "And it is actually wrong for wives to command their husbands." He rushes out to attack his brother, and Rāma shoots him with an arrow. Tara follows and, seeing her husband lying dead, removes the arrow and plunges it into her own heart. Sugrīva is reunited with his comely wife just as the rains begin to fall. The two humans withdraw to the forest with a promise from the soon-to-be-king Sugrīva that as soon as the rainy season ends, they will find Sītā.

True to his promise, when the rains end, the monkeys and vultures team up with Hambavān, the lord of bears, for the purpose of finding Sītā. Hanumān volunteers to leap into Laṅkā to spy on the palace and learn Sītā's whereabouts.

Book V, the "Sundara Kanda," the Book Beautiful, begins with Hanumān's journey to Laṅkā Island. He slips past watchmen, and peers into windows and doors before sneaking into the palace. He finds Rāvaṇa's bedroom, where the demon king lies sleeping surrounded by a pile of beautiful, naked women, "the love-skilled Queens of Laṅkā." He sees one beautiful queen sleeping apart in her own bed and thinks at first, "She is Sītā!" But he quickly rebukes himself, "That's not her. What a shameful apish idea. Where would Sītā have any place in this bedroom?" Finding no trace of her, he leaves the palace and climbs an aśoka tree to spend the night, hoping that Sītā will take a morning walk in the garden.

When she appears the next day, he approaches and tells her that he has been sent by Rāma. He offers to fly her home on his back, but she says she wants to be rescued by Rāma. He leaves her, promising to return soon with Rāma, but on his way out he cannot resist a little devilment. After he has turned up the palace grounds and created havoc on all sides, he is captured and brought before Rāvaṇa. When the demon king asks him how he got to Laṅkā, Hanumān says, "I crossed the ocean, as a person without attachment to worldly desire easily crosses the ocean of existence." Rāvaṇa orders the monkey's head cut off, but the king's brother, Vibhīṣaṇa, countermands the order: "You can brand or shame a messenger but not kill him." Hanumān eventually escapes and flies back to the mainland, where he reports to Rāma, "She lives!" He asks Rāma to make him one promise: "Kill Rāvaṇa!"

Book VI, the "War Book," begins with plans for the invasion of Laṅkā by Rāma, Lakṣmaṇa, the bears, vultures, and monkeys. Among their number is the monkey Nala, son of the heavenly architect Viśvakarman. Nala constructs a bridge 10 leagues wide and 100 leagues long over which the motley army marches to Laṅkā. The demon king watches their advance and begins amassing his own forces. A terrible battle ensues, during which Rāvaṇa's brother Vibhīṣaṇa, unable to stop his brother, goes over to the other side.

But Rāvaṇa has another brother, the giant Kumbitakarna, who sleeps for six months at a time. He wakes the giant and commands him to "Scatter my enemies like a strong wind!" The giant strides forth and, one by one, Rāma severs his arms, legs, and head before the giant stops advancing. Later Rāma must also slay Rāvaṇa's son before the demon king and Rāma confront one another. Rāma shoots an arrow all the way through Rāvaṇa, and the demon king dies. Hanumān and Vibhīṣaṇa, now the new king, bring Sītā back to Rāma.

When Sītā is led before Rāma, he haughtily rebuffs her as being defiled by Rāvaṇa and thus no longer fit to be queen. She requests that Lakṣmaṇa build a fire so that she can immolate herself, but Agni, the god of fire, rises from the flames and refuses to burn her, since she is unblemished. He chides Rāma for questioning her chastity, and the two are reunited.

Meanwhile, Vibhīṣaṇa shares a secret with Hanumān: He takes him to a chamber that no one outside of Laṅkā has ever seen before. On the wall in gold letters is the message, "Please yourself. Tell the truth and be tranquil." Vibhiṣana tells Hanumān that he is sharing this secret room because the monkey is his friend. "People meet in this life and pass by each other like pieces of driftwood afloat on the wild and stormy sea, touching seldom, and once meeting, gone and parted again. Therefore a friend is also a treasure." He opens a dusty book for Hanumān to read. It contains the Mantras of Compassion, which will enable him to bring back to life all the dead animals. Hanumān returns to the battlefield and restores the animals to life. Then, the 14-year exile having come to an end, the whole party flies back to Ayodhyā in the giant chariot of a thousand wheels, Puṣpaka.

People line the streets to welcome them. Bhārata kneels and ties Rāma's sandals back on his feet. The palace trembles with noise as the first festival in 14 years begins. The next day Rāma is crowned king, and his wife is crowned queen. So begins the first day of Rāma's reign of 11,000 years. While he is king, men are long in life and the old never have to hold funerals for the young. There is rain, the earth is fertile, and peace and good fortune prevail.

The "Uttara Kanda," book VII, begins a month later as all Rāma's animal and demon friends prepare to return to their own homes. After they have gone, the action shifts quickly to 10,000 years later, when Sītā, who is with child, announces to Rāma that she wants to go again to the retreats along the Ganges. He gives his permission because he knows the strange longings of pregnant women. Rāma learns that the people still question her suitability to be queen, fearing that she has been defiled by Rāvaṇa. So he instructs Lakṣmaṇa that, when he takes Sītā for her sojourn to the Ganges, he is to abandon her there. With reluctance, Lakṣmaṇa does as he is told.

Sītā wanders in the forest where she meets the sage and poet Vālmīki, the author of the epic, who gives her shelter in his hut. There she gives birth to Rāma's sons, Kuśa and Lava. The three live with Vālmīki for 12 years while he composes the *Rāmāyaṇa* and teaches it to the boys.

Rāma decides to have a festival, over which he presides with a golden image of Sītā. The whole country, even the monkeys, attends the festival, at which Kuśa and Lava recite the *Rāmāyaṇa.* Afterward, Sītā comes forward, as does her father Janaka, who so long ago had given Śiva's bow to Rāma as a dowry. Janaka offers Rāma ten million pieces of gold to relinquish his throne. When Rāma refuses, he offers him less, then still less. Rāma puzzles, "In the world of men one offers more and more of money for what he cannot get at first, but you have swiftly lowered the price." Janaka explains, "So quickly does your life pass by . . . hurry to do right while you can, before it's too late." Then Sītā asks permission to prove her innocence, and she calls to her own mother, Mother Earth, "If I have been faithful to Rāma, take me home, hide me." Mother Earth, ever patient and enduring, rises on her throne from underground and takes her only child Sītā on her lap, then sinks back beneath the ground. All the living creatures in the world rejoice and are exceedingly happy. (Blackburn et al. 1989; Buck 1976)

See also Hanumān; Lakṣmaṇa; Ṛavaṇa; Sītā.

RĀMLILA

This Indian ballet or dance drama is performed in celebration of the victory of the widely worshiped Hindu god Rāma over the forces of the demon king

Rāvaṇa. It is also performed in Cambodia by the Royal Ballet. (Abercrombie 1964)

See also *Rāmāyaṇa.*

RAOUL DE CAMBRAI

In this chanson de geste of the twelfth century, on Good Friday, the hero burns down a convent filled with nuns. He returns to his castle and orders meat for supper. His knights remind him of the sin of eating meat on Good Friday and ask him, "Do you want to slay our souls?" (Harrison 1970)

See also Chansons de Geste.

RASHNU

In a yasht of the Zoroastrian *Avesta,* Rashnu, god of justice, the "Truest True, god of the ordeal," is praised as one of a triad of deities (along with Mithra, god of truth, and Sraosha, god of obedience) who determine the future of dead souls. He stands on the Bridge of Requiter and weighs the deeds of the dead to determine their fate. (Olmstead 1948)

RĀVAṆA

In the *Rāmāyaṇa,* Rāvaṇa is a ten-headed, 20-armed rākṣasa (demon). In Hindu myth, Śiva's leg holds him captive between heaven and earth for 10,000 years because of his attempt to move the hill of heaven to his kingdom of Laṅkā. In the *Rāmāyaṇa,* he kidnaps Prince Rāma's wife Sītā and takes her to his kingdom in Laṅkā. He is defeated in a bloody battle with Rāma, Lakṣmaṇa, and Hanumān. (Buck 1976)

See also Rākṣasa; *Rāmāyaṇa;* Rāmlila.

RAWIS

In pre-Islamic Arabian society, rawis were professional reciters of the poetry who preserved the oral tradition until it was recorded in the eighth century. (Dawood 1973)

THE REDISCOVERY OF WAGADU

This is a Soninke oral legend of the western Sahel area of West Africa, a strip of grassland bounded on the north by the Sahara, on the south by the steppes of Sudan, on the west by the Senegal, and on the east by the Nile. At one time, possibly as early as 500 B.C., this area was a land of the troubadours. Wagadu is the name of the legendary city of the aristocratic Fasa people that is mentioned often in the fragmentary Soninke epic *Dausi,* of which "Gassire's Lute" is a portion. "The Rediscovery of Wagadu" does not have the epic quality of

"Gassire's Lute," but rather shows a Semitic influence and a striking resemblance to the biblical story of Jacob and Esau. In the story, Wagadu has disappeared and the great war drum, Tabele, has been stolen by jinns (devils) who have tied it to the sky. King Mama Dinga decrees, "If the great war drum, Tabele, is beaten, Wagadu will be found again."

King Mama Dinga, who is blind, has an old bondsman with whom he has been raised. The king's six eldest sons treat the old man very badly, often playing cruel tricks on him. Only the youngest son, Lagarre, is kind to him. Mama Dinga recognizes his oldest son by feeling his arm, which is hairy and decorated with an iron arm ring, and by sniffing his gown. The old bondsman, knowing that he will be treated even more cruelly once the old king dies, suggests to Lagarre that he borrow his brother's gown and arm ring, and that he skin a goat so that he can wear the hide over his arm.

At midnight Lagarre goes to his father disguised as his brother. The old king instructs him as to the whereabouts of nine jars, telling him that if he follows a certain ritual and then washes himself in the contents of the jars, he will be able to understand the language of the jinns and of the animals and birds as well. Then he will be able to discover the whereabouts of the great drum and thus of the lost city of Wagadu.

The next morning the king discovers the deception, but the bondsman explains, ". . . if your eldest son found Wagadu he would quickly destroy it. So now, if you must slay, slay me—for the blame is mine." But the king tells the eldest son that it is not possible for him to become king, for the secrets of the kingdom have been given to his youngest brother. He tells his son that he can become a wizard and learn how to ask god for rain, and then he will have great influence.

Meanwhile, Lagarre, having followed his father's instructions as regards the jars, sets out on a quest for the drum. He meets several jinns, each of whom passes him on to an older jinn. At last he meets the oldest jinn, Koliko, who instructs him to bring him the hearts and livers of a young horse and a young donkey every day for seven days, and in exchange, he will fly to heaven and bring back the Tabele. Lagarre does as he is told, but at the end of seven days, Koliko says that he is not yet strong enough for the trip. Lagarre must bring him hearts and livers for three more days. After that time, Koliko flies to the sky and returns with the Tabele, which he instructs Lagarre not to beat for two days. Lagarre takes the Tabele home; on the third day, he beats the drum, and Wagadu materializes before his eyes. (Frobenius and Fox 1983)

LA REINE SEBILE

Chanson de geste. *See* Macaire.

RENAUD DE MONTAUBAN

See Chansons de Geste.

RESHEPH

(Ravager; also Resup-Mekal)

This ancient West Semitic god of the underworld and of war is the equivalent of the Babylonian god Nergal. His companion is Anath, and thus he may be a form of Baal. It is believed that he is related to Mot, god of death, as he is also god of the plague. (Olmstead 1948)

REYNARD THE FOX

Reynard is the hero of several tenth- to thirteenth-century satirical, antiestablishment French, German, and Flemish beast fables, or animal tales, told in verse form about a sly rascal who uses his cunning to survive, usually against the stupid but brutal wolf Isengrim (Ysengrimus). Other adversaries of Reynard are Sir Bruin the bear, King Noble the lion, Chanticleer the rooster, and Tibert the cat. Portions of the cycle are of the Greek and Roman tradition, while others are similar to folktales found around the world. Reynard first appears in Latin epics derived during the tenth century from tales common to the area southeast of Flanders. In 1152 Nivard of Ghent made him the hero of his Latin poem "Ysengrimus," and in 1180 Heinrich der Glichesaere adopted a no-longer-extant French poem into a 2,000-line poem in Middle High German, "Fuchs Reinhard." (Terry 1992)

See also *Roman de Renart*.

ṚG VEDA

(Also *Rig Veda)*

This Sanskrit collection (ca. 1200–900 B.C.) of 1,028 hymns in ten books details early Indian daily life and mythology. The hymns were transmitted orally for several hundred years before they were recorded. The name means "The Veda of Praise." The hymns refer to many different theories of creation. Several of these indicate that creation is a byproduct of a cosmic battle or a part of the separating of heaven and earth. In addition to Creation, its hymns deal with Death, the Elements of Sacrifice, the Horse Sacrifice, Agni, Soma, Indra, Gods of the Storm (the Maruts), Solar Gods, Sky and Earth, Varuṇa, Rudra and Viṣṇu, Realia, Women, and Incantations and Spells. (O'Flaherty *Veda* 1981)

See also Puruṣa-Sūkta.

RHEA

(Also Cybele, Magna Mater, Bona Dea, Terra, Opis, Tellus)

In Greek religion, Rhea is the "mother of the gods" or "great mother goddess," daughter of Uranus and Gaea, wife of Cronus, and mother of Zeus, Poseidon, Hades, Demeter, Hestia, and Hera. Cronus swallows all of his children except Zeus because he has been warned that they will replace him. Rhea substitutes

Reynard the Fox is an example of fables whose characters are animals. Here the clever Reynard flatters Chanticleer, a rooster, in a thirteenth-century illustrated manuscript of *Roman de Renart*.

a stone for Zeus and hides the baby in a cave. Later Zeus overthrows Cronus, forcing him to spit up his brothers and sisters. (Ceram 1972)

RHIANNON

In Celtic religion, Rhiannon, daughter of Heveydd the Old, is the Welsh equivalent of the Irish goddess Macha. In the *Mabinogion* story of "Pwyll Lord of Dyved," Rhiannon appears "dressed in shining gold brocade and riding a pale horse." When Pwyll's man cannot catch her, Pwyll himself tries and fails. He finally calls to her, "Lady, for the sake of the man you love best, stop for me!" She answers, "I will, gladly, and it would have been better for your horse had you asked me that earlier." She marries Pwyll, but later she is wrongly accused of killing her own child and sentenced to carry visitors to court on her back, like a horse. (Gantz 1976)

See also *Mabinogion.*

ROBIN HOOD

This legendary folk hero of England is best known through a cycle of medieval ballads, some dating from the fourteenth century or earlier. The most important ballad, near-epic in size, is "A Lytell Geste of Robyn Hode" (1510), consisting of 456 four-line stanzas. He is said to have been born ca. 1160 at Locksley, Nottinghamshire. One tradition identifies him as the earl of Huntington, Robert Fitzooth, disinherited and outlawed unjustly. During the reign of Henry III, many landowners who supported the king's brother-in-law, Simon de Montfort, leader of the loyal opposition, were deprived of their lands following the Baron's War (1264–1265), and they took to the forests to fight back. The dissatisfaction continued and escalated for over a century to encompass an ever-widening segment of the population, culminating in the Peasants' Revolt of 1381. During this tumultuous time, the ballads of Robin Hood were born, although the first mention of him by name is in William Langland's allegory *Piers Plowman* (1377): "I can't say my Paternoster perfectly as the priest sings it, / But I know rhymes of Robin Hood. . . ." In most of the ballads he lives in Sherwood Forest, robs from the rich, and gives to the poor. He dies at the hands of the prioress of Kirkley, who allows him to bleed to death. (Langland 1990; Siepmann 1987)

ROCA, INCA

(Also Rocca)

In Incan oral tradition, a woman, Siyu-Yacu, "of noble birth and high ambition," spreads the rumor that her son, Inca Roca, has been carried off by the Sun. A few days later Prince Inca Roca appears wearing garments of gold; he tells the people that corruption of their ancient religion caused their downfall, but that he can lead them back to their original splendor. Thus Inca Roca becomes the first of the new Incas, Cuzco is restored as the capital (ca. 1200),

Legends arose in fourteenth-century England about a Robert Fitzooth of Nottinghamshire, who came to be known as Robin Hood. American illustrator N. C. Wyeth portrayed him with his band of fellow outlaws for the cover of *Robin Hood* published in 1917.

and a new empire begins that exceeds the ancient empire in grandeur. By other accounts, Inca Roca is the eldest son of Inca Cápac Yupanqui by Coya Mama Curi-Illpay, his wife and sister. (Alexander, H. 1964; Garcilaso 1987)

RODRIGO, DON

(Also Roderick and Roderigo)

Roderigo is the name of a Spanish hero (d. 711), the last Visigothic king of Spain and the subject of a number of legends.

Rodrigo is also the name of the popular military leader Rodrigo Díaz de Bivar (or Vivar) (d. 1099), called affectionately El Cid, whose exploits have been embroidered by legend; he is the hero of the great Spanish epic *Poema del Cid.* (Merwin 1962)

See also *Cid, Poema del.*

ROLAND

(Also Orlando)

In the medieval romances, Roland is the most famous of Charlemagne's paladins. Roland has been linked to the historical leader of Charlemagne's rear guard at Roncesvalles, Hroutland of Brittany, and as such, he is the hero of the famous epic *Chanson de Roland.* Tradition assigns to Roland the position of son of Charlemagne's sister. He is a loyal and courteous, if somewhat naive, knight whose pride is his ultimate downfall. Other episodes involving Roland appear in other chansons de geste, in which he battles giants. Several accounts exist as to how he acquires his sword Durendal and his horn Olivant. Two Latin versions of his story are the *Chronicle of Charlemagne* (twelfth century) and the twelfth-century poem *De Proditione Guenonis* (Ganelon's Betrayal). Italian bards called him Orlando, and from the fifteenth century onward he began appearing in works such as *Morgante Maggiore* by Pulci, *Orlando Innamorato* by Boiardo, and *Orlando Furioso* by Ariosto. (Harrison 1970)

See also *Chanson de Roland; Roland, Chanson de.*

ROLAND, CHANSON DE

This French epic poem (chanson de geste) first entered the tradition as a French ballad, said to have been sung by Taillefer in 1066. The chanson was written ca. 1050 concerning the Battle of Roncesvalles in 778. The poem, consisting of 4,002 decasyllabic lines, is attributed in the last line to Turold, a Norman poet. The historical battle was a minor one against the Basques, but the poem elevates it to a major encounter with the Saracens. The poem begins with a message to Charlemagne, who in seven years has conquered all of Spain except Sargossa, from the Saracen king Marsile, indicating that he wishes to negotiate a settlement. The paladin Roland urges the emperor to send his stepfather, Ganelon, as his representative. Angered at his stepson for his interference, Ganelon plots with the Saracens to betray Roland, whom he makes sure will be commanding the 20,000-man rear guard of the army as it enters the narrow pass of Roncesvalles. Headstrong and proud, Roland refuses the advice of his more prudent friend Olivier that he blow his horn to summon help until it is too late. Olivier and Roland are both slain during the ambush by the 400,000 Saracens, the latter by his blinded friend in error. Charlemagne must bear the sad news home to Olivier's sister Aude, who is betrothed to Roland. When she hears the news, she falls dead of grief. For his part in the perfidy, Ganelon is tried and executed by quartering.

See also *Chanson de Roland;* Chansons de Geste; Ganelon; Olivier; Roland.

ROMAN D'ALEXANDRE, LE

These French poetry cycles, based on old Celtic material, employed the alexandrine, or 12-syllable line, which thereafter became the standard French line. (Previté-Orton 1982)

ROMAN DE BRUT

This French verse narrative (1155) is by the Norman poet Wace, who adapted Geoffrey of Monmouth's *History of the Kings of Britain* into his own interpretation, particularly of the Arthurian legend. In this work, the Round Table motif appears for the first time. (Mason 1962)

See also *Brut the Trojan;* Wace.

ROMAN DE RENART

This loosely organized collection of some 30 French "branches," or verse tales, consists of nearly 40,000 lines of verse, to which the title *Roman de Renart* was applied in the late twelfth century. Approximately 15 were written between 1174 and 1205. All branches derive directly or indirectly from the work of Pierre de Saint-Cloud, whose renditions of the adventures of the wily fox Reynard and his wolf-adversary Ysengrin and his wife Hersent, were the first in French. (Terry 1992)

See also Reynard the Fox.

ROMI KUMU
(Woman Shaman)

She is the female creator-god of the Barasana Indians of the northwestern Amazon River region. According to the creation cycle, in the beginning, before life, the world is rock. Romi Kumu fashions a clay griddle (the sky) and places on it three pot supports (mountains). In other stories she creates the underworld and causes the earth to be covered with floodwaters, after which she continues to rule, or manipulate, the inhabitants, beginning each day as a young woman but growing old with each night.

The neighboring Makuna Indians also revere Romi Kumu as ruler of the air, earth, night, and forest, although two thunders named Adyawa and Adya are actually creators of the earth and the air. (Alexander, H. 1964)

ROMULUS AND REMUS

Legendary founders of Rome, ca. 875 B.C., Romulus and Remus appear in the *Aeneid* (ii, vi). They are twin sons of Mars and Rhea Silvis, who as infants are thrown into the Tiber by Rhea's uncle Amulius, who has usurped the throne of his brother Numitor. But the crate containing the twins does not sink; it is washed ashore near the present site of Rome, where a she-wolf protects the children and feeds them her milk. Later, a shepherd, Faustulus, finds them and takes them home to be reared by his wife Acca. When the boys are grown they build a city on the spot where they washed ashore, but they get into an argument, and when Remus jumps over a wall Romulus has built around the town, Romulus kills him. Romulus and his men need women to populate their new city, so he invites Titus Tatius, king of the Sabines, to bring his people to a festival. The Romans rape the women, and Tatius vowes revenge. He bribes Tarpeia, daughter of the Roman governor, to open the gates of the citadel so that his warriors can enter. Romulus's forces are overcome, and Titus Tatius becomes co-king for a brief time until he dies. Romulus rules for 39 years before he vanishes in 714 B.C. Believing that he has been transformed into a minor god of war, the Romans name him Quirinus, which is also a Roman name for Ares. (Frazer 1963)

See also Abandonment; Larentalia; Titus Tatius.

ROSTAM
(Also Rustam)

Rostam is a hero of the Persian epic *Shāh-Nāmah.* According to legend, he is born during the 120-year reign of Manuchehr and he lives through the 100-year reign of Kai-Kobad, the 150-year reign of Key Kāvus, the 60-year reign of Key Khosrow (Kai-Khosrau), the 120-year reign of Key Lohrāsp (Kai-Lohrasp) of Balkh, and he dies during the 120-year reign of Key Goshtāsp (Kai-Gustasp). Like many heroes, his birth involves magic. His father, the albino Persian hero Zāl, has been abandoned at birth and raised by an Indian bird, a Simurgh, who gives him a feather to burn if he should ever need her help. When Rostam's mother, Princess Rudāba, goes into labor and cannot deliver, Zāl burns the feather. The Simurgh appears and says of the unborn baby: "The Creator has not made him like ordinary mortals, / He is an elephant for size, / and a lion for courage."

The bird gives instructions for cutting Rudāba's side and drawing the baby out, and for instantly healing Rudāba's wound. The child is so large that he requires the milk of 20 nurses. Word is sent to his grandfather, the great warrior

Sām Suwar, who comes as soon as he is able to leave his current war. The baby has grown so quickly that he is placed on a golden throne atop an elephant and sent out to meet his grandfather. To the amazement of the crowd, he speaks: "Greetings, great Paladin! / May I draw my courage from my grandfather Sām, / a lion among men."

Rostam gains renown as the bravest man who ever walked the earth. He goes alone into the White Demon's cave to rescue the shah and his men. He defeats three kings in Arabia and makes them bow in the dust. The stories of his deeds reach the Semitic princess Tahmina, who comes to his bedchamber while he is a guest of her father after his horse has been stolen. She offers herself to him saying, ". . . you wander lonely through the world, / living only to defend mankind from danger, / able to bear wounds without a cry / and cold and hunger without blanching." She wants to bear him a son. She tells him he is the only man she can ever love: "The wary eagle wheels high overhead when you are near. / The fiercest lion fears the sting of your lasso / Whole armies fly in terror at the mention of your name." Rostam, a man of great honor, summons Tahmina's father and asks permission to marry her that very night. He is not, however, so devoted that he does not leave her as soon as his horse is returned.

A man of superhuman strength, he sires a son, Sohrāb, of the same ilk, whom he meets unknowingly in conflict many years later and eventually mortally wounds. As Sohrāb lies dying, he reveals his identity to Rostam. An old warrior standing nearby remembers the wonderful elixir of the shah that will stanch the blood of any wound. But with little show of fatherly love, Rostam refuses to send for the elixir because his son has threatened to hang him. The youth dies; Rostam builds him a magnificent grave and lives on alone for more than 300 years. (Levy 1967)

See also *Shāh-Nāmah.*

ROZWI

The Rozwi are mythical Shona heroes of Central Africa. According to oral tradition, fire is unknown to the Shona's ancestors until the Rozwi, rulers of a large, faraway kingdom, bring it to them. The Rozwi also bring grains and other seeds. They dwell in zimbabwe, residences or burial places of leading chiefs. Many of the zimbabwes still stand, and they were occupied by Rozwi (supposedly descendants of the ancient Rozwi) until fairly recent times. (Davidson 1991; Parrinder 1982)

RUDRA

In the hymns and verses of the *Vedas,* and in the Sanskrit *Purāṇas,* Rudra is a minor Hindu god, divine archer, who must be appeased lest he shoot arrows of disease and death. He is also a god of healing and the bestower of 1,000 remedies. He is the father of the storm gods, Rudras (or sometimes Maruts). His name later evolved into Śiva, who shares his unpredictable temperament.

(Dimmitt and van Buitenen 1978; Fremantle and Trungpa 1987; O'Flaherty 1975; O'Flaherty *Śiva* 1981)

See also *Bardo Thötröl; Ṛg Veda;* Śiva.

RURIK

(Also Rorik, Ryurik, and Hrorekr)

In the *Russian Primary Chronicle* (early twelfth century), Rurik is the Scandinavian prince (Varangian or Viking) who is invited by the people of Novgorod to come and bring about an orderly reign to their country. Rurik and two of his brothers arrive with a large retinue ca. 862 and take command of the city of Novgorod, establishing the Rurik dynasty. Modern historians consider the account legendary; however, some believe that Rurik came from Jutland or Scandinavia ca. 855, invaded and captured Ladoga, then moved on to invade Novgorod. Rurik's successor Oleg conquered Kiev ca. 882, and upon his death was succeeded by Igor, who was, according to legend, Rurik's son. It was Igor's wife, Saint Olga, who became regent from 965 to 969, until her son Svyatoslav came of age. The Rurik dynasty lasted until 1598. (Dvornik 1962; Jones, G. 1990; Vernadsky 1959)

See also *Russian Primary Chronicle.*

RUSSIAN PRIMARY CHRONICLE

(Also *Nachalnaya Letopis, Stepennaja Kniga, Chronicle of Kiev, Chronicle of Nestor, Povest Vremennykj Let,* or *Povest-Vremennykh,* Tale of Bygone Years)

This medieval chronicle, compiled ca. 1112, contains oral sagas, legends, folktales, and historical events in Russia from 852 to early in the twelfth century. For years the chronicle was attributed to Nestor, a monk in the monastery at Kiev, because it includes the legendary account of the founding of the Russian capital of Kiev; however, scholars now doubt his authorship and believe that it was instead a compilation from various sources, including extant Slavonic literature, Byzantine annals, and oral tradition. According to the *Chronicle* account, between A.D. 860 and 862, the inhabitants of central European Russia invited some men known as *Rus* to bring order to the area. Three brothers came: the oldest, Rurik, settled in Novgorod. "On account of these Varangians (Scandinavians), the district of Novgorod became known as the land of the Rus." Elsewhere in the *Chronicle* is the account of three brothers—Kiy, Shchek, and Khoriv, chiefs from the eastern Slavic Polyane tribe—who arrive upon the banks of a stream that they name Lybed for their sister, and each man establishes a settlement on a nearby hill. These become the city of Kiev (ca. sixth century), named for the oldest brother. (Dvornik 1962; Wilson 1975)

See also Lybed; Rurik.

S

SAANE, KELEFA

This Mandinkan hero of the nineteenth century is the subject of an epic, *Kelefa Saane,* still performed in the area around Senegal in West Africa. (Westley *RAL* 1991)

SAGA

A saga is a long narrative epic indigenous to medieval Iceland. Its prose form differentiates it from the poetic epic. The century dating from 930 is designated as the saga age, or Iceland's heroic age, about which the thirteenth-century family sagas were written. (Jones, G. 1990)

ST. ILIYA

In Bulgarian oral tradition, in Christian times, St. Iliya became the substitute for the god of thunder, Zeus. Official Christianity considered St. Iliya the bringer of rain, but the popular belief was that St. Iliya was a thunder-wielder who rode the skies chasing away the lamia that fed on the grain.

On St. Iliya's feast day, the oldest cock, worshiped by the Slavs as a solar symbol and called father, is sacrificed, and divinations concerning good health and fertility are made from it. If a thunderstorm comes on St. Iliya's Day, the shells of hazelnuts and walnuts will be empty. One song says, "Thunder-wielder St. Iliya fell ill lying in bed for nine years. No cooling wind blew . . . nor did fresh dew fall. When he had a drink of doe's milk, he got well. He unlocked the Black Sea. A cool breeze began to blow and drizzle set in." (Georgieva 1985)

ŚAKAṬ, THE KATHĀ OF

This Hindu folk narrative of North India was recorded in the 1920s in the village of Karimpur. A Kathā is a myth evolving primarily to instruct in proper ritual form. Kathās differ from other narrative forms in that they are performed as part of the ritual of vrat, which requires fasting and worship as well as telling the Kathā. Kathās are primarily part of the nonpublic tradition maintained by women in purdah. Kathās such as this one are told by older women to their daughters and daughters-in-law. Śakaṭ is a woman's fast and festival, and most men do not even know *The Kathā of Śakaṭ*. The ritual of Gaṇeś cauth (another name for the Kathā of Śakaṭ) is performed annually by them for their families' welfare, honoring the elephant-headed Ganesha (Gaṇeś), son of Śiva and Pārvatī.

The story concerns two sisters-in-law—a younger, poor woman and an older, wealthy one. In order to receive a daily handout of food and drink, the younger woman works in the older one's kitchen. The day of Śakaṭ, or the fast of Gaṇeś, arrives, and the younger woman asks the older woman to give her something with which she can prepare suitable offerings for Śakaṭ. But the older woman gives her only a handful of bad rice. The poor woman grinds and pounds the rice as best she can to prepare a proper offering.

During the night, Panīś Śakaṭ, or Gaṇeśjī, comes and says, "O mother, I am hungry." The poor woman answers, apparently without knowing the identity of her visitor, "I am hungry, so what can I give you? There is nothing in my house; I am poor. . . ." She explains that the rich woman has given her only a handful of rice, but she offers it to him, and he eats heartily. She offers him hospitality for the night, and he repays her with wealth.

The next day when she does not make her usual trip to work for food at the house of her sister-in-law, the older woman comes to see why. When she learns the details of the younger woman's good fortune, she thinks, "I too will fast."

The following year on the day of Śakaṭ, the wealthy woman prepares only bad rice and waits for the god to arrive. The god's visit progresses as had his visit to the poor woman's during the year before, but he sees her true intention. When he leaves without bestowing wealth on her, she says, "To those who act out of poverty, to those God gives. And to those who turn away from [faith], to those God does not give." (Blackburn and Ramanujan 1986)

SALMĀN AL-FĀRISĪ

Salmān is a national hero of Iran (seventh century). According to Muslim legend, during a long religious quest to find the prophet who will revive the religion of Abraham, he is sold into slavery. He meets Muḥammad in Medina, and with his help is able to obtain his freedom. According to tradition, it is Salmān who in 627 suggests to Muḥammad that a ditch be dug around the entrances to Medina to protect it from a siege by Meccans, a tactic that results in Muḥammad's victory in the so-called Battle of the Ditch. History relates that the Meccans marched on Medina with 10,000 men, but the Muslims shut themselves up in the town. After a three-week blockade, the Meccans grew bored and rode away in search of adventure. (Glubb 1988)

SAMBA GANA

This Sudanese legend of the Soninke people of Africa tells how a prince named Samba Gana wins the favor of a beautiful and wise princess, Annallja Tu Bari. Her father loses everything in a duel, and it is such a blow to his pride that he dies. Annallja loses all joy in life. She is very beautiful, but she announces that she will marry only if her suitor wins back the town her father has lost, plus 80 more villages.

Samba Gana, who has already been conquering towns, hears of Annallja's beauty and her sadness. He decides to conquer the 80 towns and make her laugh. After he has won them, he goes to her and says, "All that you wished for is now yours." She says, "You have done your work well. Now take me." But Samba Gana answers, "Why don't you laugh? I will not marry you until you laugh." She tells him that she cannot laugh because of her father's pain. She tells him to conquer the serpent of the Issa Beer.

Samba Gana travels to Faraka, to Koriume, to Bamba, even farther upstream, until he finds the serpent. He struggles with the monster for eight long years, splintering 800 lances and breaking 80 swords. He gives the bloody lance to his bard-companion Tararafe, and tells him to deliver it to Annallja. "See if she laughs now."

When Tararafe delivers the bloody lance, Annallje tells him that only when she sees Samba Gana with the dead serpent will she laugh. But when Tararafe returns with the message, Samba Gana says, "She asks too much." He plunges the sword into his breast and dies.

Annallja orders a fine tomb built for him. Eight times 800 people dig a deep burial chamber, and with the dirt build a high pyramid. Every evening, accompanied by knights and bards, the princess climbs to the top of the pyramid, where the bards sing songs about the hero. Annallja will not allow the digging to stop until the mountain is so high that she can see the town of Wagana from its peak. After eight years, Tararafe tells her, "Today I can see Wagana." Annallja says, "Samba Gana's tomb is at last as great as his name deserves." She laughs. She commands the others to go away, and she laughs once more and dies. She is placed beside Samba Gana in his tomb, while eight times 800 princes ride away in different directions, each to become a great hero. (Frobenius and Fox 1983)

SAMGUK SAGI AND SAMGUK YUSA

(Also *History of the Three Kingdoms* and *Memorabilia of the Three Kingdoms)*

These two collections of Korean myths, legends, folktales, and epics, compiled during the Koryo dynasty, preserve stories from prehistoric times of the three kingdoms Koguryŏ, Paèkché, and Silla. The *Samguk sagi,* compiled by a Buddhist priest, contains the epic of the founding of Korea by King Tongmyŏng. Among the most important myths are another account of the founding of Korea by Tan'gun, the myths of the sun and moon, and tales of the lives of ancient kings. One poem found in the *Samguk yusa,* "Ke-chi-Ka," is related to the myth of the founding of the early Korean Karak tribe. (Reischauer and Fairbank 1960)

SAMHAIN
(Also Samh'in and Samain)

The Druid God of the Dead, Samhain is honored, along with the sun god, on 1 November, the Druidic New Year. Samh'in, meaning "fire of peace," is still observed in the Highlands of Scotland. Samhain marked the beginning of winter in Wales, Ireland, the Scottish Highlands, and Brittany. Druids believed that the dead returned during the festival to mingle with the living. On the evening before, now called Halloween, old fires were allowed to go out, and a new one kindled from the sacred fire, which was never allowed to go out. The fire gave the dying sun new life and kept evil spirits at bay. In the eighth century, Pope Gregory III moved All Hallows Day from 31 May to 1 November in an attempt to discourage the practice of Druidic festivals. (Bullfinch 1962; Rutherford 1987)

SAMSON

Israelite hero of an epic narrative in the Old Testament, he is the possessor of remarkable strength, which he uses to slay a lion, move the gates of Gaza, and repeatedly repulse assaults by the Philistines. However, he disregards his religious principles by eating with a Philistine woman and visiting harlots. When he falls in love with Delilah, she entices him into revealing the source of his strength: his long, flowing hair. While he sleeps, she cuts his hair, rendering him helpless before the Philistines. He is captured and enslaved, after being blinded. However, he eventually regains his strength and destroys the temple of Dagon, where the Philistines worship. In the process he destroys himself as well, returning to his former purity. (Judges 13–16ff.)

ŚANTI PARVAN
("Book of Consolation")

In the *Mahābhārata,* the twelfth book, detailing proper conduct and statesmanship, is entitled "Śanti Parvan." (Buck 1981)

SANYĀSAMMA KATHA

This medieval Telugu sacrificial folk epic of southern India is still being sung today. In a sacrificial epic, the main player is a woman who in the end immolates herself and is deified as a goddess. Unlike some other folk epics of the area, no palm-leaf texts exist linking it to any author. It is an epic belonging to the Gazula and Kāpu castes, tradesmen aspiring to land-owning peasant status. The men are frequently mercenary soldiers for higher castes. The women, by legend illegitimate descendants of the Pāṇḍavas of the *Mahābhārata*, enjoy a relatively high status, but practice self-immolation for the purpose of elevating their caste status.

The epic begins with the birth into a family of Gazula Kāpus (bangle sellers) of the girl Sanyāsamma, described as a satyavatī (woman of truth), a term used only to denote powerful virgins. When her mother dies, her father Dālnāyuḍa, a weak man who watches impassively when Sanyāsamma is mistreated by others of the household, eventually abandons her to marry another woman. Her older brother Rāmināyuḍa and his wife Pāpamma take her to raise, but it is her brother who performs the motherly chores of bathing and feeding her, of braiding her hair and adorning her eyes with kāṭika (mascara).

While still a child, she is given in marriage to her father's sister Dālamma's son, Cencanna, who is being educated in English. She remains in her brother's home until she matures, but her brother, a landowner, must leave home to attend to his lands some distance away. He is so fond of his sister that he "cries like a woman" when he has to be parted from her. He asks his wife to care for his sister in his absence, but she refuses, claiming that she is too busy managing the servants.

While Rāmināyuḍa is gone, Sanyāsamma and her young stepbrother go out one day to watch a show of dancing bulls. Her stepmother rushes out and hits her with a broomstick, accusing her of taking the boy without permission. Sanyāsamma pronounces a curse on the woman: If the stepmother is in the wrong, the pain from the broomstick blows will be visited instead upon the stepmother. The woman soon begins to bleed from the painful wounds.

Sanyāsamma leaves her brother's house and goes to live in her mother-in-law Dālamma's house with her husband Cencanna, his older brother and wife, and his younger brother Appanna. But Cencanna leaves her behind to seek work with the British East India Company. While Cencanna is gone for a period of seven years, Sanyāsamma is at the mercy of her cruel mother-in-law and older sister-in-law. The two women starve her and assign her impossible tasks that can be accomplished only because she is a satyavatī.

The younger brother Appanna takes pity on her and steals into her room to take her a glass of milk. Sanyāsamma fears that her mother-in-law will think that Appanna and she are engaged in an illicit affair, but he finally convinces her to drink at least part of the milk. She drinks half, and he drinks the rest—an unusual act, since a woman only drinks after a man, her husband. As Appanna leaves her room, he is spotted by his mother Dālamma, who accuses Sanyāsamma of being a harlot.

Sanyāsamma remains in her room, but projects her soul out in search of her husband, who is stationed in Madras. When she finds him, she pleads for him to come and deliver her from her persecution, and he agrees to do so. Once home, he learns of her hardships at the hands of the other women and decides that he must set up a separate household for Sanyāsamma. He asks his older brother for his share of the inheritance, but the brother refuses and even belittles Cencanna. Humiliated, Cencanna takes the "feminine" way out of his dilemma and kills himself.

When Sanyāsamma learns of her husband's death, she decides that she must perform satī, a ritual whereby the widow kills herself on the funeral pyre. Appanna accompanies her to Madras to ask permission from authorities at the British East India Company to perform satī. Unable to dissuade her from her chosen course, the British official imprisons her. But using her powers as a satyavatī, she escapes and convinces the official by her magic that he must acquiesce to her wishes. Before she burns herself, she gives Appanna turmeric and kumkum, both traditionally feminine symbols. Then she disappears into the flames. (Blackburn and Ramanujan 1986)

SAOSHYANS

In Zoroastrianism, Saoshyans, a posthumous son of Zoroaster, is the last and most important of the saviors of the world, who will appear on Judgment Day and wipe out evil. His two brothers are the other saviors who precede him: Ōshētar and Ōshētarmāh. "Saoshyanto" means Savior. (Olmstead 1948)

SARASVATĪ

In the Hindu *Purāṇas,* Sarasvatī is the goddess of learning and the arts, credited in legend with having invented the language of Sanskrit. She also appears in Jaina and Buddhist mythology. In one tale in the *Purāṇas,* King Navaratha, pursued by the ferocious rākṣasa (demon) Duryodhana, races to the sanctuary of Sarasvatī and begs her to protect him. When Duryodhana appears with upraised spear, "a mighty creature that blazed like the sun at the end of the Age" appears and splits open the demon's breast. The creature tells the king, "Leave quickly, great king; there is nothing more to fear in this place." Elsewhere in the *Purāṇas,* Sarasvatī is referred to as a river, but also as "the mother of all the worlds." (Dimmitt and van Buitenen 1978; O'Flaherty 1975)

SARDANPALUS

An Assyrian tale of a despot, its "hero" is a combination of two Assyrian kings: Ashur-nasir-apad (885–860 B.C.) and Ashur-bani-apal (669–633 B.C.). (Olmstead 1948)

SARGON OF AKKAD

Ancient Mesopotamian ruler (r. ca. 2334–2279 B. C.), founder of the first known empire and the subject of several epic tales. One, similar to the Moses account in the Bible, involves his abandonment as a baby boy by his priestess-mother, who places him in a casket in the river. He is found by an orchard gardener who rears him. Another narrative called "The King of Battle," which was still being recited 1,000 years after his death, describes his defeat of Lugalzaggisi of

Erech and his territorial expansion throughout southern Mesopotamia to northern Syria and southern Anatolia. Eventually his empire extended from the Mediterranean Sea to the Persian Gulf. One story credits him with an expedition to protect the merchants in Asia Minor with whom he traded. (Garraty and Gay 1972)

SARPEDON

In the *Iliad* (xvi), Sarpedon is the king of Lydia and the son of Zeus and Laodameia. In the Trojan War, he fights with the Trojans. When Zeus learns that Sarpedon will die at the hands of Patroklos, he weeps. Sarpedon is also the name of a son of Europa and brother of Minos and Rhadamanthus, whom Minos drives from Crete when he takes the throne. (Lattimore 1976)

See also *Iliad.*

SASUNTZI DAVITH
(Epic of David of Sassoun)

This Armenian folk epic (ninth century), now lost, deals with the exploits of King David of Sasun (or Sasoun) and his son Mher the Younger, who are Christians, in their battles against the invasions of Arabian Muslims from Persia and Egypt. Despite the Christian flavor of the epic, numerous fantastic creatures, good and evil, influence the action. In 1873 the poet Thoumanian finally wrote down *Sasuntzi Davith* from the surviving oral tradition still popular among street bards. (Preminger 1990)

See also *David of Sassoun.*

SAULĖ

In Lithuanian mythology, in such tales as *Saulė and Vęjų Motina* (The Sun and the Mother of the Winds), Saulė is the Sun Maiden, the central deity in Baltic religion. She is confused with her daughter, Saulės Meita (sometimes plural). Her chief rival is Aušrinę (Morning Star). Saulė is first the wife of Mėnulis, or Meness, the Moon, by whom she bears the earth and stars. But Mėnulis falls in love with Aušrinę. Perkūnas, God of Thunder, "greatly enraged," smites him in half and asks, "Why did you leave Saulė? / Fall in love with Aušrinę? / Walk alone at night?" He answers, "Because . . . there was born such a beautiful maiden as has never, anywhere, been born. I became so transfixed I did not rise." Saulė is also the wife of Dievas (God, the Sky), and as such, she rides across the sky each day in a chariot drawn by horses who never tire. In one legend Saulė explains why she descends in the evening: "Because there is in the sea another maiden who is more powerful than I. When she in the evening rises from the sea, then I must descend." *See also* Aušrinę for the story of *Saulė and Vęjų Motina.* (Greimas 1992)

SAVIOR

A central figure in major world religions and in many epics, the savior brings renewal and new life. Originally a figure from the planter cultures, the savior, a vegetation god, sacrifices himself or is sacrificed, and is reborn as a symbol of the new season of growth. In later myths he is given other attributes: He may bring healing; salvation from sins, death, or enslavement; reconciliation with God; or integration of the personal soul with the divine soul. The term has been associated with Jesus, Buddha and the bodhisattvas, Dumuzi of Sumeria, Mithra of Persia, and the Saoshyan of Zoroastrianism, but there are many examples of saviors in secular works. Sundiata, the hero of Mali, saves his and the neighboring countries from the tyrant Sumanguru, who has overrun their lands. Senkatana, the hero of the Sesothos, saves his people, who have been eaten by the Kgodumodumo monster. Son of Light, hero of the Hopi, saves his wife and others who have been carried off by Man-Eagle. (Campbell 1982; Campbell *Myths* 1988)

See also Dumuzi; Saoshyans; Senkatana; *Son of Light; Sundiata, Epic of.*

SAWOYE

Sawoye is a hero of the Chaga people of Kenya, husband of the heroine Marwe. Marwe and her brother are sent to the bean field to guard it from the monkeys, but in the afternoon they become hot and leave to drink from a nearby pool. When they return, the monkeys have stripped the field bare. Fearing her parents' wrath, Marwe throws herself into the pool to drown. She sinks down until she arrives at the hut of an old woman, who takes her in as a helper. After she has stayed underground for a long time, she asks permission to return to her parents. The woman grants her permission, but before Marwe leaves she is given a choice between "the hot" and "the cold." Marwe chooses "the cold" and must dip her arms and legs in a pot of cold water. When she takes them out, they are covered with rich bangles. The old woman gives her a beautiful beaded petticoat and prophesies that her husband will be named Sawoye. Marwe returns to the bank of the pool and sits down. Soon word spreads that a beautiful rich girl is sitting on the bank. Many men, from the chief on down, come to ask her to marry them, but Marwe waits for Sawoye to come. People do not understand her choice, because he has an ugly skin disease, but as soon as they marry, the disease disappears. They use the bangles to buy a great castle, but the neighbors are jealous, and they kill Sawoye. Marwe uses magic to bring him back to life, and she hides him in the castle. When the neighbors come to the castle to divide the spoils, Sawoye kills them all. Thereafter, the couple lives happily and peacefully. (Parrinder 1982)

SBORNIK

This medieval Russian manuscript containing the story-poem "Prince Igor" was discovered late in the eighteenth century by Count Pushkin when he purchased it from a monk. In 1800 he printed it for the first time in Russia. The original was burned in 1812 during Napoleon's invasion of Moscow. (Goodrich 1961)

See also *Igor's Host, Lay of.*

SCAEVOLA, GAIUS MUCIUS

This legendary Roman hero is credited with saving Rome from falling to Etruscan king Lars Porsena ca. 509. He is captured when his attempt to assassinate Porsena goes awry, but he convinces the Etruscan king—by holding his right hand in the altar flames until it is consumed—that he is telling the truth when he claims that he is only one of 300 who plan to attempt to assassinate him. Rather than face another attempt on his life, the king orders Mucius released and immediately withdraws from Roman territory. In appreciation for saving Rome, Mucius is given a large holding of land and the title Scaevola ("left-handed"). (Bowder 1984)

SCÉL

In Irish Gaelic literature, scél is the name of verse or prose legends of gods and heroes, most originating ca. the eleventh century or earlier. The scéls have been collected into three main cycles: the mythological; the *Ulster Cycle,* having to do with the first-century B.C. Ulster heroes in the kingdom of Conchobar mac Nessa; and the *Fenian Cycle,* having to do with Finn Mac Cumhaill and his band during the third-century reign of King Cormac Mac Art. (Rutherford 1987)

See also *Fenian Cycle; Ulster Cycle.*

SCYLLA

In Greek myth, the sea nymph Scylla is changed into a frightful monster by Circe, who is jealous of the sea god Glaucus's attentions to Scylla. When Odysseus's ship passes her cave, she reaches out and devours six of his men. (Graves 1955; Rouse 1990)

See also *Odyssey.*

SECOND BATTLE OF MOYTURA

In this Old Irish saga, the poet Carpre has the power to turn the tide of battle by satirizing the enemy. When King Lugh asks the poet, "What power can you wield in battle?" Carpre answers, "I will satirize [the enemy], so that through the spell of my art they will not resist warriors." (Rutherford 1987)

SECRET HISTORY OF THE MONGOLS

(Manghal un Niuca Tobca'an)

This combination saga and epic chronicle dating from the thirteenth century (compiled ca. 1240 in Uigar writing) relates the origins and exploits of the

Mongols from their beginnings to the time of the death of Jenghiz-khan. Embedded in the work are fragments of much older oral poetry. The work precedes the appearance of the first heroic epic, whose origins can be traced to the period.

The Mongolian empire of Jenghiz-khan has its roots in the Turkish empire of Tu'-chüeh, Uigur, and Khitan. The Tu'-chüeh gave themselves the name "Blue Turks," just as the Mongols would later refer to themselves as Kökä Mongol, or Blue Mongols. The blue is derived from Tängri, the sky, of which the grand khans proclaimed themselves to be agents on earth.

Legend holds that even prior to the twelfth century a Mongol chief named Qaidu gains prominence by defeating the rival Jelair tribe. He begins to count among his followers families from a number of different tribes. It is the first early attempt at Mongol unity. Qaidu's great-grandson, Qabul-khan (posthumously Qabul-khagan), a vassal of the Kin Jurchid rulers of northern China, visits the Kin emperor in Peking and behaves like a barbarian, eating and drinking to excess and even pulling the emperor's beard. The emperor forgives him and even bestows lavish parting gifts upon him. But Qabul continues to irritate the emperor openly and is soon imprisoned. He easily escapes and slays the officers who pursue him. This legendary incident may have a historical counterpart in the historical battles of the Kin against the nomadic Mongols during the years 1135 to 1139.

Another legendary hero, Qutula-khagan, is described as having a voice that "resounded like thunder; his hands were like the paws of a bear and could snap a man in two as they would snap an arrow." Qutula sleeps naked in the open air even in winter, lying beside a great fire that spits huge sparks on him that he doesn't even feel. When he awakens, he mistakes the burns for insect bites.

His brother Okin-barqaq and his cousin Abbaqai are captured by Tatars and delivered to the Kin, who nail them to a wooden donkey, "a torture reserved for rebel nomads." Qutula takes revenge by plundering Kin territory. Chinese annals report that in 1161 the Kin empire was forced to send an expedition to quell a Mongol uprising, while the Mongol tradition recounts a battle near Bor Nor against the combined Kin and Tatar forces. This battle has the effect of destroying the first royal dynasty; neither of Qutula's sons, Jöchi or Atlan, receives the title khagan, indicating that a khanate no longer exists. The people revert to the ancient order of individual tribes and clans.

Meanwhile, a minor chieftain of the Kiyat clan named Yesugei helps Kerayit pretender Togrul to triumph over a rival kinsman, Gur-khan. In the process of the fight, Yesugei abducts Oelun, the wife of a Märkit chief, and marries her. In ca. 1167 she gives birth to Temüjin, whom Yesugei immediately betroths to Börte, the daughter of a Qongiral chief. Shortly thereafter, the Tatars poison him at a meal on the steppe.

Temüjin is left an orphan; at about the age of 12 (ca. 1179), the Borjigin clans refuse to recognize him as leader and refuse to obey him. One by one the clans leave with their herds until there is no one left but his brothers, stepbrothers, and his mother. They are forced to hunt and fish in the mountains in order to survive. The new leaders from a rival clan, Targhutai Kiriltuq and his brother Tödöyän-Girte, think that Temüjin is dead until he and his brother Qasar get in a fight with their half brother Bekter and slay him. When Taraghutai Kiriltuq learns they are still alive, he sets out to capture Temüjin. But with the help of the Suldu chief, Temüjin escapes. He enlists the support of his skillful brother Qasar, and the two begin to accumulate wealth: horses. When he has sufficient wealth, he goes to the Qongirat chief Dai-Sechen to collect his promised wife, Börte. Dai-Sechen gives her a cloak of black sables as a dowry.

In ca. 1175 Temüjin makes friends with the Kerayit ruler Togrul, who will be his ally in coming confrontations. Shortly afterward, a band of Markit attacks, and only by leaving his wife Börte behind can Temüjin escape. He asks for Togrul's help, as well as that of another young Mongol chief of the Jairat tribe, Jamuqa. The three attack the Markit and rescue Börte, who is pregnant. She bears a son, Jöchi, whom Temüjin takes as his eldest son; however, there is some question that he may be the son of one of the abductors, Chilgerbökö.

Temüjin and Jamuqa become great friends; they wander together for one year. But both have ambitions to revive the Mongol khanate. Temüjin is encouraged by the Jelair Muqali, who reminds him of all the bad days the Mongols have suffered since the time of the last khan, Qutula: "A hero should rise among the Mongols, to be a dreaded khan and avenge their wrongs. . . ."

Temüjin and Jamuqa camp on the spot where Qutula had been elected. Temüjin camps in the mountains, while Jamuqa camps by the river. Jamuqa says, "On the slopes of the mountains, the tents of the horse breeders; beside the river, the pastureland of the shepherds." Jamuqa is said to enjoy novelty and despise tradition; thus, historians conclude that he represents the populists while Temüjin represents the nobility.

Temüjin also has the support of the spiritual leaders. Sometime earlier the Ba'arin chief Qorchi tells the clans, "Tangri (heaven) has ordained that Temüjin should be our khan. This is what the Spirit has revealed to me. . . ."

The Mongol aristocracy rallies behind Temüjin and elects him king of the Mongols (1196), giving him the name Chinggis-khan (Jenghiz-khan), the meaning of which is still in question among scholars.

During the next ten years, serving as second in command, he accompanies the Wang-khan to defeat the Naimans (a Turko-Mongol people, perhaps Mongolized Turks, who inhabited the present district of Kobdo and the vicinity of Ubsa Nor). Shamans enjoy great influence among the Naimans. In war they are able to invoke storms and the elements to influence the outcome of battles, but the Mongols are able to withstand the magic. They go on to defeat the Tayichi'uts and their leader Targhutai Kuriltuq.

Meanwhile, Jamuqa forms a counterleague and has himself proclaimed gur-khan, or emperor of Mongolia (1201). He urges Wang-khan to support him in a confrontation with Jenghiz-khan, saying, "I am the lark living ever in the same place in the good season and the bad. Jenghiz-khan is the wild goose which in winter flies away." But Wang-khan remains faithful to Jenghiz-khan. The two sides meet in a bloody battle at Köyitän. Oirat and Naiman magicians cause a great storm, but despite the magic, Jenghiz-khan and Wang-khan defeat Jamuqa.

Then Jenghiz-khan must again confront the Tayichi'ut, who has succeeded in wounding him. But his faithful attendant Jelme sucks the clotted blood from his wound. Jenghiz-khan pardons the young warrior who has shot his horse and, renaming him Jebe, makes him one of his own captains.

Jenghiz-khan now takes on his father's assassins; he massacres the Tatars but forbids private looting by his forces, although he takes two Tatar women, Yesui and Yesugän, for himself. Almost immediately he must beat back an attack by Toqto'a, king of the Markit.

All this time he has remained a loyal vassal of Wang-khan, but when Wang-khan refuses to give him the hand of Princess Cha'ur-bäki in marriage, he is deeply wounded. The two come to a parting of the ways that eventually leads to war.

The Kerayit outnumber him greatly, and at the first clash his third son, Ogödäi (Ögedei), is wounded in the neck by an arrow. The sight causes the great warrior to shed tears. He retreats to shore up his diminished forces, and the following fall, he returns to defeat the Kerayit army (1203). Togrul and his son flee, but Togrul is beheaded by a Naiman officer who fails to recognize him.

After Jenghiz-khan has subjugated the Kerayit, only one independent power remains: the Naiman. He gives his definition of supreme joy or success: "To cut my enemies to pieces . . . seize their possessions . . . and embrace their wives and daughters." He goes after the Naiman the following year, hammering away for several years until he defeats them.

However, even before their fall he has himself proclaimed supreme khan by all the Mongol and Turkic tribes, "of all those who live in felt tents" (1206).

Having unified Mongolia, he embarks on the conquest of northern China, taking first Hsi-Hsia, then the Jurchid kingdom or Kin empire (1211). The war is to continue even after his death in 1227. While this is taking place, his enemy Küchlüg, son of the last Naiman king, has conquered the Central Asian empire of the Kara-Khitai, gur-khans. Jenghiz-khan cannot allow his old enemy to remain in power, so in 1218 he orders Jebe to attack with a force of 20,000 men. Thus the whole of eastern Turkestan comes into the Mongol empire, making it and the Khwarizmian empire of Muhammad next-door neighbors. Jenghiz-khan cannot tolerate that.

With his youngest son Tolui, he marches into Bukhara (1220) and destroys the town. From there, joined by his sons Jagatai and Ogödäi, he marches on Samarkand and loots it, deporting the skilled craftsmen of the town to Mongolia and massacring everyone else, even the Turkic garrison that rallied to their side.

The following year they take the capital, Gurganj, and submerge it under the waters of the Amu Darya. Then Jenghiz-khan begins the conquest of Afghanistan. During the siege of Bamian, his favorite grandson, Mütügen, is killed. Jenghiz-khan curses the city and orders everything destroyed and every living creature massacred.

While he is in Afghanistan, a Taoist monk arrives (1222) whom Jenghiz-khan had summoned from China two years before. Jenghiz-khan is eager to learn of the Taoist drugs of immortality.

He returns to Mongolia three years later to learn that the king of Hsi-Hsia has not sent his obligatory company of men to participate in the war against Khwarizm (Turks). An aide named Asha-gambu explains on behalf of his king that if Jenghiz-khan does not have troops enough, he does not deserve to wield supreme power. Infuriated, Jenghiz-khan launches a siege against the Hsi-Hsia capital while the inhabitants scramble in vain to the mountains. The Mongols show no mercy: "The fields were covered with human bones."

While the siege is going on, Jenghiz-khan dies of a heart attack at age 60, having experienced little of the grandeur and ease of most rulers of great empires. He says of his progeny that they "will wear garments of gold; they will eat sweet, greasy food, ride splendid coursers, and hold in their arms the loveliest of women, and they will forget that they owe these things to us. . . ." (Finnegan 1978; Grousset 1970)

SÉGOU EPIC

(Also *Segu Epic)*

This epic cycle concerns the heroes of the West African kingdom of Segu. (Courlander 1982)

See also *Bakaridjan Kone, a Hero of Segu, Epic of; Bassadjalan Zambele, Epic of; Da Monzon, Epic of.*

SELA

In the creation story of the Luyia people of Kenya, Sela is the first woman, whom God creates as a companion to the first man, Mwambu. God instructs them in which animals they may eat and which are forbidden. They are not allowed to eat crawling beasts like snails and lizards, or carrion birds like hawks or buzzards. Mwambu and Sela build a house on stilts because they are afraid to live on the ground. Although their children live on the ground, treehouses are still seen in the forest, and houses on piles are still seen on the banks of lakes. (Parrinder 1982)

SENKATANA

Senkatana is the hero of the African Basotho legend of the Dragon-Killer Wonder-Child. It tells of a ferocious monster, the Kgodumodumo, which appears mysteriously and eats everything in its path, devastating whole villages. One pregnant woman pretends to be a lifeless object and is passed over unnoticed by the monster. When he is gone, she gives birth to Senkatana, who immediately grows into a young warrior ready for combat, even with weapons. He uses his skill to perform a number of socially beneficial deeds, particularly to deliver the people from the Kgodumodumo's belly. (Kunene 1979)

SENZANGAKHONA

In the Zulu epic *Emperor Shaka the Great,* Senzangakhona is the playboy king of the Zulus, father of Shaka. When he is warned in a dream that a great hero is to be born, he attempts to eliminate Shaka and is cruel to Princess Nandi, Shaka's mother and a member of the Langeni. A battle between the clans ensues, which Senzangakhona wins. But he does not reclaim Nandi and her children under his roof and only reluctantly stages Shaka's manhood ceremony, as any good father must.

As Shaka's reputation as a fighting youth grows, Senzangakhona becomes more jealous, and the conflict between the Zulus and the Langenis continues. Finally Nandi and her children are expelled and begin a journey of many miles to seek asylum among their cousins, the Qwabes.

Senzangakhona continues to grieve over the long-past loss of a son, Bhokuza, during a battle between the Mthethwas and the Buthelezis. He is mocked by his aunt, Princess Michabayi, who says, "The King is courting disaster by mourning a hero. / Perhaps as he grows older he forgets our customs. / Was it not always a heinous crime to mourn the heroes of battle?"

Nevertheless, the still grieving king travels to visit Dingiswayo, the new Mthethwa leader, unaware that Shaka is now Dingiswayo's chief warrior. At a feast in his honor, Senzangakhona is treated to a dance by a young man of great grace and skill. He asks, "Who was the young man who danced like a spirit?" Dingiswayo answers, ". . . There are singers and great composers. / Some boast their skills in battle; / Some boast their power of poetry. / Our fame spreads to all parts of the earth, / Yet there are still others who possess all gifts. / The young man of great dancing skill is Shaka himself; / This Shaka who fears nothing is your son."

Shaka asks Senzangakhona if he can come home, and the king claims that "Nothing would fill me with greater joy." But he repeats the advice of their forefathers: "Two bulls cannot live in one fold." He explains that Shaka's stepbrother, Prince Sigujana, is now grown and has become powerful at home. Two such powerful men in Zululand would be too many.

Later Shaka approaches his father again while the king is bathing. He asks for the gift of the spear Senzangakhona had carried at the festival. Senzangakhona claims that the spear is not really his; he promised it to Sigujana when he reached manhood. Shaka tells his father that he is hurt to be denied his only request. When Senzangakhona shakes Shaka's hand in farewell, he can feel his son's hand trembling, and his own power is drained out of him from the contact. Even Dingiswayo notices the weakening of Senzangakhona's movements. It is the beginning of the end for Senzangakhona. (Kunene 1979)

See also Bhuza; Chaka; Dingiswayo; *Emperor Shaka the Great;* Shaka.

SERGLIGE CONCULAINN OCUS AENÉT EMINE

(Cú Chulainn's Sickbed and Emer's One Jealousy)

This tale from the *Ulster Cycle* is not directly related to the *Taín Bó Cúailnge.* It concerns the love of the goddess Fann for Cú Chulainn and how she lures him to the underworld. (Kinsella 1969)

See also *Ulster Cycle.*

SEVEN SLEEPERS OF EPHESUS

They are the heroes of a legendary fifth-century tale popular among Christians during the Middle Ages and preserved in the Koran. The men are soldiers who serve during the third-century reign of Roman emperor Decius 7 or 8. To protect themselves from having to perform pagan rituals, they hide in a cave near Ephesus, Turkey. The cave is sealed off for two centuries, but is reopened during the reign of Emperor Theodosius II of the eastern Roman empire. The men emerge unharmed, having been in a deep sleep for 200 years. As soon as they have related their experience and interpreted its profound implications, proving the truth of the doctrine of the Resurrection, they die. The emperor has them enshrined, and absolves from guilt all bishops hitherto punished for preaching the Resurrection.

SEVEN VIZIERS

(Also Seven Wise Masters, Seven Sages, and Sinbadnameh)

The oldest recorded account of Seven Viziers occurs in the *Epic of Gilgamesh.* They are named as wise men who brought civilization to the seven oldest cities in Mesopotamia.

Seven Sages, or *Seven Viziers,* is also the name of a cycle of stories originating in India but entering Western legend through Persia ca. the late sixth century. They are built around the situation of a king who hires a wise tutor, Sindbad the Wise (not to be confused with Sindbad the Sailor), for his son. To teach the prince self-discipline, Sindbad orders him not to speak for one week. During that time, his stepmother tries to seduce him but fails. Out of spite, she goes to the king with tales of how the prince tried to seduce her. In all, she tells seven different stories, but each is refuted by seven sages, who in turn tell a story exemplifying the perfidy of women. At last the prince is allowed to speak, and he tells his father the truth. (Sandars 1972)

SHĀH-NĀMAH

(Also *Shah Nameh,* or Book of Kings)

It is the national literary epic of Persia, containing elements of folk epic that were on the verge of oblivion, and covering almost 4,000 years. In scope it

A page from a fourteenth-century manuscript from the Persian epic *Shāh-Nāmah* shows a hero battling the winged and horned Habash monster.

outranks all Western epics. It is the retelling (ca. 1000), in part, by a brilliant poet whose title was Abo'l-Qāsem Mansur (Abu'l-Qasin Mnsur), called Firdausi or Ferdowsi, of a much older history, *Khvatay-namak,* which reached back into mythical times. It took Firdausi 35 years to compile the epic, whose nearly 60,000 couplets cover a period from 3223 B.C. to A.D. 651. He incorporated 1,000 verses of the earlier poet Daqtat, used other written sources now lost, and relied on the dying oral tradition. A large portion of the work is very ancient.

The epic covers the reign of Keyumars, ruler of the world; the reign of Hūshang, during which fire is discovered; the reign of the primal priest-king Jamshīd, whose hubris precipitates his fall and the world's thousand-year subjection to the grotesque tyrant Ẕaḥḥāk; the birth of the hero Farīdūn and his successful war against Ẕaḥḥāk; the birth and accession of the hero Zāl; the long career of the hero Rostam; the reign of Sīyāvosh; the reign of Key Khosrow; the reigns of Lohrāsp and Goshtāsp; the appearance of Zardosht (Zoroaster); the reign of Bahman; the story of King Dārāb, left by his mother Homāy in a casket on the Euphrates; the reign of Dārā; the reign and adventures of Sekandar; the rule of the Ashkāni (Arsacid or Parthian) kings; the Sāsā dynasty; the story of King Haftvād and the worm; the reign of Ardashir; the reign of Ahāpur and his war with the Romans; the reign of Shāpur Zu'l Aktāf; the life of Babrām, son of Yazdegerd the Sinner; the story of the famine during the reign of Piruz; the reign of Qobād; the reign of Kasrā Nishirvān, in which the wise Vazir Bozorgmehr comes to the palace; the reign of Hormazd; the reign of Khosrow Parviz; the reign of Bahrām Chibina, including his trip to China; Firdausi's lament for the death of his son; the story of Gordiya, Bahrām's sister; the romance of Khosrow Parviz and Shirin; the story of Shiruy and Shirin, wife of Khosrow Parviz; the reign of Ardashir; the reign and murder of the evil Gorāz, known as Farāyin; the reign of Purān Dokht; the reign of Farrokh-Zād; the reign of Yazdegerd, last of the Sāsānian shahs, whom Māhuy commissions the miller Khosrow to assassinate; the ascension of Māhuy to the throne; the conclusion of the *Shāh-Nāmah,* in which the poet calls his work "fame-worthy" and boasts, "The whole surface of the world will re-echo with reports of me." He cannot die, he says, "for I live, having broadcast the seeds of my verses." His last statement is, "Anyone of good sense . . . will after my death offer up praise for me."

The most well-known episode in the West, in which the hero Rostam (Rustam) unknowingly meets and kills his own son in battle, was popularized by British poet Matthew Arnold in his 1853 poem "Sohrab and Rustam."

Shāh-Nāmah takes up Persian legendary history with the third wave of Aryans who, under King Kavimers, moves into the land that is now Iran. His reign is followed by that of Husheng and of Tahumers, who makes war against evil magic.

The fourth king, Jamshīd (Jemshid), the Emperor of the Golden Age, corresponds with the first king, whom historians recognize as Yama. The king, who reigns for 700 years, builds a large underground palace to protect against a flood that will cover the earth. He constructs a magnificent throne upon which, in subsequent reigns, palaces are built. But people see Jamshīd sitting on his magnificent throne and begin to worship him instead of their Creator. Jamshīd, intoxicated by their adulation, begins to believe in his own grandeur, and thus he provokes the wrath of Heaven. He loses his power and is killed by conquerors whose Semitic three-headed king, Ẕaḥḥāk, rules cruelly for a thousand years.

Then a savior, the dragon king Farīdūn (Feridun), heeding the advice of a blacksmith, Kāva, captures Ẕaḥḥāk and chains him in a cave in Mount Damāvand for 11,000 years, where he remains hanging, "his heart's blood pouring down on the earth." By the time Farīdūn is 50, two sons have been born of his wife Shahrnāz and one has been born of his wife Arnavāz. "From delicacy," he has not given them names, even when they have the strength to outrun elephants. When they are old enough for thrones of their own, he summons his counselor Jandal and commissions him to go forth and select three maidens of royal birth for his sons' wives. He tells Jandal, "Their father must likewise out of delicacy have refrained from giving them names, so that no one shall have been able to discuss them." The maidens are found, the sons are tested—named Salm, Tur, and Iraj—and their father divides the world between them. But Salm is jealous of Iraj, and later Iraj is killed by his brothers. A son is born to the daughter of Iraj and named Manuchehr (Minuchir). He is reared as a warrior by his grandfather, whose sole aim in life is to exact vengeance for Iraj. Farīdūn sends Manuchehr to war against Tur so that he can be king, and later, after the old king dies and Manuchehr replaces him, the new king kills Salm.

Among Manuchehr's courtiers is the mighty hero Sām, son of Narīmān. During the reign of Manuchehr, a child is born to the nobleman Sām Suwar, who is ruling over a corner of the kingdom. This son, named Zāl, is born with shocking white hair and so is carried off to an Indian mountain and abandoned. Years later, Sām dreams that his son is still alive. He consults the magi, who castigate him for abandoning his son. He travels to India and finds his son alive, having been reared by a bird, the Simorgh (Simurgh). The bird loves Zāl like a son; she gives him a feather and tells him if he ever needs her help, to burn the feather and she will come immediately. Sām puts his son in charge of all his holdings.

On a trip to survey his lands, Zāl meets a Semite potentate, Mehrāb (Mihrab), a descendant of the cruel Ẕaḥḥāk. The two men become friendly, and Zāl falls in love with Mehrāb's daughter, Rudābah. She, only hearing of his beauty, loves him in return. A passage describes Persian wisdom on the subject of women: "Refrain from describing masculine beauty when women are within earshot. / In the heart of every female lurks a living devil / . . . When desire enters a woman's heart, wisdom flies out the window."

Sām, on learning of the couple's plans to marry, consults the magi, who heartily approve of the match. Reluctantly, he gives his consent to the wedding. But the shah, who hates the Semites, orders Sām to burn Mehrāb's palace and kill Mehrāb, his queen Sindokht (Sindhukht), and the daughter Rudābah. Zāl goes to plead with the shah, while Queen Sindokht disguises herself as an Iranian warrior and takes much of Mehrāb's hoarded wealth to try to buy their lives from Sām. Impressed by her courage, Sām consents to spare them and agrees to the marriage.

Meantime, the shah has also consulted astrologers and has found that the proposed marriage will be extremely fortuitous, so he gives his permission. The two are married, but when the time comes for the birth of their first child, Rudābah cannot deliver. As she lies near death, Zāl burns the feather of his bird-mother. The Simorgh appears and instructs him on how the arch-Mage (wise medicine man) should cut open her abdomen to bring the baby out. The newborn child is exceedingly large and powerful, requiring the milk of 20 nurses. His mother, fully recovered from the ordeal, names the child Rostam (Rustam).

After the reign of Manuchehr ends, three shahs reign for short periods. Rostam has grown to young manhood when the third shah dies, and his father sends him on a mission to Mount Elbury to bring back the new shah, Kai-Kobad. Rostam, who is a giant of a man, chooses a giant of a horse, Rakhsh, for the expedition. The magnificent stallion remains with him always and saves his life on many occasions.

Rostam brings back the new shah and then goes to war to drive away Afrāsiyāb, a pretender who has threatened several shahs. Kai-Kobad's reign of 100 years is followed by that of his son Key Kāvus (Kai Kaus), who does not prove to be the wisest of rulers.

Key Kāvus takes advice from a demon disguised as a harpist and leads his warriors to conquer Mažindarān (Maginderan). But after a week of plundering by his warriors, the shah is confronted by the Great White Demon, protector of the kingdom of Māzindarān, who has been summoned from his cave on Mount Damavand. In the storm that follows, Key Kāvus and his warriors are blinded, and 12,000 demons carry them away to a cave.

Learning of the shah's plight, Rostam sets off on his horse Rakhsh to rescue the men. After many harrowing adventures, Rostam kills the White Demon and uses blood from its liver to restore the sight of the shah and his men.

Key Kāvus is restored to his throne, but he soon becomes dissatisfied and decides to launch a war against Yemen. When he has subdued the Yemenites, he decides to marry the king's daughter, Sudaba, who is perfectly agreeable. The Yemen king pretends to desire to visit his daughter, but his plan is to capture Key Kāvus and bring his daughter home. The shah is captured, and Sudaba goes willingly with him into exile.

In order to rescue the shah this time, Rostam must wage war against the combined forces of Yemen, Berberistan, and Egypt. This he does with great courage and skill. Then on behalf of his shah, he leads his forces against Afrāsiyāb, the pretender who has plagued so many rulers. Rostam so intimidates the enemy troops that Afrāsiyāb deserts them and flees for his life.

Meantime, another demon disguises himself as a youth and convinces the restless shah that the proper place for one of his brilliance is in the sky. So the shah has his throne attached to four eagles and flies off into the blue, only to disappear. Again Rostam goes off to rescue him, and when he finds Key Kāvus this time, he and the shah's magi castigate the ruler for his irresponsibility. The shah is genuinely chagrined and does penance for 40 days, promising to be more attentive to duty from now on.

One spring Rostam goes hunting with his steed Rakhsh. While he is sleeping at his campsite near the Turānian border, some Turk nomads steal his "high-stepping mount." Filled with anxiety when he discovers the theft, Rostam thinks, "On foot, running, whither shall I go in my disgrace? . . . How shall I traverse the wilderness? . . ." He goes forward, "his heart full of pain and grief, his body racked with torment and his spirit in agony," searching into the province of Samangān, where he is welcomed by the king, who promises to help the renowned hero find his horse. The king invites Rostam to stay with him in the meantime, and while Rostam is there, the king's daughter Tahmina (Tamineh) falls in love with him. She tells him she wants to give him the gift of a child, so Rostam calls in the king and asks permission to marry the daughter then and there, that very night. The king gladly gives his permission, and for so long as Rostam remains in the province, he and Tahmina are husband and wife. But when Rakhsh is found, Rostam rides away forever, giving his bride an amulet for their unborn child.

The child, a boy, is named Sohrāb (Suhrab) by his mother, and he rapidly grows to be tall and powerful like his father. When Sohrāb learns that he is the son of Rostam, he decides to travel to Iran, team up with his father, and defeat the hapless Key Kāvus so that Rostam can sit on the throne. Then the two, father and son, can go on to Turān and defeat Afrāsiyāb so that Sohrāb can also have a throne. So goes his plan.

But Afrāsiyāb learns of the plan and instructs two of his henchmen, Barman and Human, to go along on the expedition to make sure that Sohrāb and Rostam do not have the opportunity to recognize one another, so that they will unknowingly kill each other: "Perhaps the aged hero will find his death at the hands of this lion-man."

The two henchmen are successful in preventing Sohrāb from learning the true identity of the man whom he challenges to a battle. Through three days of bloodthirsty battles, Rostam and Sohrāb take turns besting one another, but in the end Rostam kills Sohrāb. Only then, from the dying boy's lips, does Rostam learn that Sohrāb is his son: "Someone among the mighty and proud will carry to Rostam the tidings that Sohrāb is slain and overthrown in ignominy, his one desire being only to find him." Heartbroken, Rostam builds a magnificent horseshoe-shaped tomb for his son and mourns him for many months.

The poem ends with additional material that was not part of the original legend. It continues the story from the time of the second reign of Khosrow II (590–628) to the Mohammedan overthrow of the Sasanian king Yazdegerd III in 651.

Portions of the Key Kāvus epic, in which the shah is depicted in a more flattering light, appear in the yashts of the *Avesta,* or, as the Pahlavi translation is called, the *Zend-Avesta,* sacred book of Zoroastrianism. (Levy 1967)

See also Abandonment; Flood Myths; Rostam; Savior.

SHAKA
(Also Chaka)

Shaka is the hero of the great Zulu epic *Emperor Shaka the Great* (ca. 1787–1828). The son of the playboy Zulu king Senzangakhona and the valiant Langeni princess Nandi of Bhibhi, Senzangakhona exiles Shaka as a child, along with his mother and sister, because Nandi's people are angry over the king's shabby treatment of her. Shaka is described as "the fierce-tempered boy" who "never bowed his head." It was said that all feared his anger. Shaka grows to manhood among distant kinsmen, where "rumour tells of his courage and intelligence." He hones his leadership and military skills, and when his father dies, he returns to claim his inheritance. Through a series of brilliant military encounters, he consolidates his power and brings a number of clans into the Zulu nation. His mother remains the most important influence throughout his life. After her death his brothers plot his assassination, and he is killed a year later. The poet said of him, "He grew to overwhelm the earth!"

Shaka is also the name of a Japanese god. (Kunene 1979; Sproul 1991)

See also *Emperor Shaka the Great.*

SHAMASH
(Also Utu)

In Mesopotamian religion, Shamash is the Akkadian sun god who plays an important part in the *Epic of Gilgamesh.* He is the husband and brother of Ishtar (Sumerian Inanna). In the hymns from Nineveh, his aspects of omniscience and judge are expressed in terms of a net: "Spread out is your net to catch the man who covets," and "Thrown down like a net over the land are your rays." It is he who gives Hammurabi his system of laws. For the Sumerians, Utu was principally judge and lawgiver, also possessing some characteristics of a fertility god. The Semites saw him also as a victorious warrior, god of wisdom, son of—and greater than—Sin. When Utnapishtim tells Gilgamesh the story of the flood, he says, "The time that Shamash had ordained was already fulfilled when he said, 'In the evening, when the rider of the storm sends down the destroying rain, enter the boat and batten her down.'" (Saggs 1990; Sandars 1972)

See also *Gilgamesh, Epic of.*

SHAMBA BOLONGONGO, KING
(Also Shamba of the Bonnet)

According to oral tradition, Shamba is the ninety-third king (ca. 1600) of the Bushongo tribes of the Congo in central West Africa. Before he inherits the throne, Shamba tells his mother he wants to travel abroad because the king must be the wisest of men. She warns him of the dangers, but he says he must learn how to prevent evil.

Thus he becomes the wisest and best king. He shows his people how to weave raffia for clothing, instead of using the rough bark to which they have become accustomed. He shows them how to embroider. He shows them how to play the Arabic game of mankala, replacing the gambling games to which his people have been addicted. He introduces tobacco and the cassava plant, and shows them how to get rid of the cassava poisons. He outlaws bows and arrows and the shongo (throwing knife) for warfare, so that the Bushongo become renowned as peaceful people who are welcomed anywhere they travel.

He introduces the oil palm called Shamba. He is a wise king who uses many parables. He compares palm wine to human nature. When the first cut is made in the palm, the sap is sweet but weak, like a young child; as the flow increases, it becomes strong but harsh, like an old man.

He is also a just king. A person who does not appear in court to defend himself is judged guilty on the premise that a guilty man tries to avoid discussing things. When two women quarrel over a man, Shamba tells of a man with two dogs with whom he shares his leftovers equally, except when he has a bone that he cannot break in two. The dogs fight over the bone so viciously that they kill each other. Shamba's moral is that each dog should have his own bone, and each woman her own husband. (Parrinder 1982)

SHAMIRAM

Armenian epic figure. *See* Ara and Shamiram.

SHANG TI

Shang Ti is the Chinese God of the Sky. (Mackenzie 1990)

See also Ch'ih Yu.

SHANGO

Shango is the god of thunder of the Yoruba people of Nigeria in West Africa. (Parrinder 1982)

SHAUSHKA

Shaushka is the Anatolian goddess of love and war, corresponding to the Babylonian goddess Ishtar and the Sumerian Inanna.

SHCHEK

In the *Russian Primary Chronicle,* Shchek is one of three brothers, leaders of the Slavic Polyane tribe, who found the Russian city of Kiev ca. the sixth century. The other brothers are Kiy and Khoriv. By another account in the same work, the brothers are Rurik, Helgi (or Oleg), Scandinavians. (Garraty and Gay 1981; Wilson 1975)

See also *Russian Primary Chronicle.*

SHEMANE

In the Zulu epic *Emperor Shaka the Great,* Shemane is the great Ndwandwe king Zwide's heir after the death of Prince Nomahlanjana. (Kunene 1979)

See also Zwide.

SHEMWINDO

In the *Epic of Mwindo* of the Banyanga of Zaire, Shemwindo is the hero's father, who becomes Mwindo's most dangerous antagonist. Unwilling to have a male child to succeed him on the throne, King Shemwindo seals the newborn Mwindo in a drum and throws it into a river. Mwindo is found and eventually, when he grows to manhood, must fight his father. Shemwindo flees in terror to the subterranean world, where at length Mwindo finds him and reconciles with him. (Biebuyck and Mateene 1969)

SHEN NUNG
(Divine Husbandman)

Legendary second ruler of China, said to have been born in the twenty-eighth century B.C., Shen Nung was able to speak at the age of three days, to walk at the age of one week, and to plow a field at the age of three years. He was a sage who cultivated five grains and established markets in which to sell them. He invented the plow and tamed the ox to pull it. He also invented the cart and cataloged 365 species of medicinal herbs. He was sacrificed on Mount T'ai Shan and given the official name Yen Ti. (Mackenzie 1990)

See also Fu Hsi.

SHIH-CHING

(Book of Songs). This ancient collection of Chinese poetry, the first anthology, was compiled by Confucius (551–479 B.C.). It contains 305 poems consisting of court songs, ballads, and eulogies drawn from various levels of Chou society. (Waley 1960)

See also Book of Songs.

SHILAPPADIKARAM
(The Ankle Bracelet)

See Cilappatikāram.

SHUN

In Chinese mythology, Shun is a legendary emperor (ca. twenty-third century B.C.) whose jealous father tries to murder him. But the boy's virtue and sense of duty do not flag. When he is given chores, Heaven comes to his assistance, sending birds to weed the paddies and animals to pull the plow. King Yao bypasses his own son to name Shun as his successor, and he gives Shun two of his daughters in marriage: Hsiang and Fu-jen. Shun's official name is Yu Ti Shun. Confucius held him up as an example of integrity and piety. (Mackenzie 1990)

SIABURCHARPUT CONCHULAINN
(Cú Chulainn's Demon Chariot)

This tale from the *Ulster Cycle,* not directly related to the *Taín Bó Cúailnge,* describes St. Patrick's attempt to convert Irish king Laegaire to Christianity by summoning up Cú Chulainn's spirit. (Kinsella 1969)

See also *Ulster Cycle.*

SIĀLKOT

Siālkot is a district and city of legendary renown in Lahore, Punjab Province, Pakistan. Siālkot's legendary founder is Raja Sāla, uncle of the Pāṇḍavas of the *Mahābhārata.* From ca. 520 to 530, the Hunnish nomad Mihirakula, whom legend calls "the Attila of India," made the city his base. The accounts of Chinese pilgrim Sung Yün mention a visit there in 820. (Grousset 1970)

SIEGFRIED
(Also Sigurd)

A hero in both Old Norse and Old German legends, it is disputed whether Siegfried's character is of historical or mythical origin. According to tales, he is of noble birth but abandoned and reared in humble surroundings. In the *Völsunga Saga* and the *Poetic Edda,* he is known as Sigurd. In the *Völsunga Saga,* he meets his death at the spurned Brunhild's instigation, but he is depicted as a true hero throughout, having jilted Brunhild only because he drinks a magic potion. In the *Poetic Edda,* Sigurd fights with a dragon, awakens the Valkyrie maiden Brunhild from a charmed sleep, and obtains the treasure of two warring brothers. As Siegfried, he is the hero of the first half of the *Nibelungenlied* and of the second half of Wagner's opera *Der Ring des Nibelungen.*

Like Achilles, Siegfried is invulnerable except for one spot. Achilles, hero of the *Iliad,* has been dipped in the Styx by his mother, which renders him invulnerable except in the heel by which she holds him. Siegfried, after slaying the dragon, bathes in its blood, making his skin impervious except for the one spot where a leaf falls. When Hagen, the king's retainer and enemy of Siegfried, learns of the vulnerable spot, he arranges a hunting party and is able to strike Siegfried there and kill him. (Hatto 1969; Hollander *Edda* 1990)

See also Abandonment; *Edda, Poetic; Nibelungenlied; Völsunga Saga.*

The Norse and Germans included Siegfried in the *Nibelungenlied*. In the *Poetic Edda* and *Völsunga Saga* he is called Sigurd or Sigurth. Here he slays a dragon whose blood he bathes in to make himself invulnerable.

SILAMAKA AND PULURU
(Silimaka et Poullori)

This oral epic (ca. eighteenth to nineteenth centuries) of the Fulani people of Macina, Mali, West Africa, about a friendly pair of adventurers and the conflicts between the Fula and Bambara, is still being performed today. (Okpewho 1992; Westley *RAL* 1991)

SIN
(Also Nanna)

In Mesopotamian religion, and in the *Epic of Gilgamesh,* Sin is the moon god and son of Enlil and Nanlil. His Sumerian counterpart is Nanna. He is the chief Sumerian astral deity, father of Utu-Shamash, the sun, and of Ishtar. (Saggs 1978; Sandars 1972)

See also *Gilgamesh, Epic of;* Nanna.

SINDBAD THE SAILOR

In the Indian, Persian, and Arabian folktale collection *The Thousand and One Nights,* Sindbad (not to be confused with Sindbad the Wise, hero of the *Seven Viziers)* is hero to a cycle of tales dating to the era when Baghdad and Basrah were at their commercial zenith. This cycle probably was originally an independent work, some of which has similarities to the *Odyssey.* Although the tellers of the Sindbad tales (ca. 750–ca. 850) did not know Homer, the Odysseus legends had reached the Arabs by that time.

The cycle begins when Sindbad, an old man, meets a porter whose name is also Sindbad. It is to the porter, discontented with his lot, that Sindbad the Sailor tells the story of his seven voyages.

During his first voyage, the passengers stop at an island, which turns out to be a giant whale. They light a fire, which wakes the creature, and he dives under water. A similar story appears in stories of Pliny and Solenus. Marooned, Sindbad is eventually rescued, finds favor with the local king, and becomes comptroller at the port, where one day his own goods are returned to him by merchant marines.

On his second voyage, he is accidentally left behind during a stop at a desert island. He comes upon an enormous egg and, later, the gigantic Roc that laid it. He hitches a ride with the bird to a craggy hillside. As he makes his way down, he encounters a valley of diamonds (such as Marco Polo, among others, mentions). Merchants come to the crags above the valley and throw meat, to which the diamonds stick. When the eagles carry the meat back to their nests, the merchants scare them away and pick up the diamonds. Sindbad fastens himself to a piece of meat and is carried back to an eagle's nest. He is rescued by the merchants and comes home laden with diamonds.

On his third voyage, his ship is waylaid by a race of vicious dwarfs. He and his fellow sailors escape on the mainland, only to be confronted by a gigantic monster who eats several men before they escape. This account is reminiscent of the Cyclops Polyphemus story in the *Odyssey.* Sindbad is rescued by a ship whose captain has found his lost treasure from the second voyage, and the captain returns the treasure to him.

A storm shipwrecks him and his companions during his fourth voyage, and the men find themselves guests of a group of cannibals who feed them food that affects their mental capacities—except that Sindbad abstains from eating. This episode brings to mind the lotus-eating episode in the *Odyssey.* Sindbad escapes to another kingdom, where he makes a saddle for the king and is rewarded with a beautiful wife. But when the wife dies, Sindbad is also entombed with her, as is the custom. He escapes from the cave in which he is entombed, carrying valuables from the dead bodies. He makes his way to the shore where he is rescued by a passing ship.

On his fifth voyage, he is again shipwrecked and becomes the captive of a monster who makes Sindbad carry him on his back. Sindbad ferments some grapes, and when the monster drinks the wine and passes out, Sindbad kills him. When he is rescued by a passing ship, he learns that his captor was the Old Man of the Sea.

On his sixth voyage, the ship is driven off course and sinks. The survivors are washed ashore on Serendip (Sri Lanka), where they find a riverbank covered with precious jewels. One by one, his companions all die. He fashions a raft and floats down to a kingdom of Indians and Abyssinians, where he presents the king with the precious jewels he has found. The king orders a new vessel built for him so that he can return to Baghdad.

On his last voyage, his ship is swallowed by a giant whale, but he jumps overboard at the last minute and reaches an island. He again fashions a raft of sandalwood and floats down a river. As he is about to be swept over a waterfall, he is rescued by a group of men. A kind old man takes him to his large, fine home. His raft is auctioned off for 1,100 dinars, making him a wealthy man. The old man, having no son, offers Sindbad his daughter for a wife, promising to make Sindbad his heir. Soon all the men of the kingdom grow wings, and Sindbad hitches a ride on the back of a flying friend. They fly so high that he can hear angels. As he praises Allah, he is abandoned by his friend, who drops him on a mountaintop. Later, returning home, he learns that he has been living among a race of the brothers of Satan, save for the family of his new wife. He sells his property and, taking his wife, sets sail for home, having been gone for nearly 27 years. (Dawood 1973)

See also Journey.

SINLEQEUNNINI

(Also Sin-leqe-unini)

This Akkadian poet (fl. ca. 1100 B.C.) of Uruk (Erech) reworked an earlier Babylonian version of the *Epic of Gilgamesh.* (Sandars 1972)

SIR GAWAIN AND THE GREEN KNIGHT

This Middle English (ca. 1370) alliterative poem, compiled from several sources, was composed by an unknown poet who was a contemporary of Chaucer. It is considered the masterpiece of medieval alliterative poetry and the greatest of the Arthurian legends. Some scholars theorize that its author was the poet of "The Pearl and Its Jeweler," possibly John Donne or John Prat; others suggest Hughown, Ralph Strode, and Hugo de Masci (Hugh Mascy).

The poem is divided into four sections, called fits. In fit I, the New Year's revelry at King Arthur's court is interrupted by the appearance of the Green Knight, "an awesome fellow," who is "the handsomest of horsemen" with "hips and haunches" that are "elegant and small." He is dressed in garments of green, "marvelous fur-trimmed material." He rides in on a "mettlesome" green horse, holding an ax "of green hammered gold and steel" and says, "I crave in this court a Christmas game." He dares any knight present to strike him a blow with the ax, on the condition that he can return the blow one year later. The king's nephew, Gawain, sitting beside Queen Guinevere, accepts the challenge and chops off the Green Knight's head. The knight picks up the head, which tells Gawain to meet him at the Green Chapel in one year, and leaves.

After All Saints' Day ten months later (in fit II), Gawain sets off in search of the Green Chapel to fulfill his bargain. On Christmas Eve, he arrives at a marvelous castle whose master, Lord Bertilak (or Bercilak), invites him to stay for the holidays with him, his wife ("most beautiful of body and bright of complexion . . . excelling Guinevere") and an older woman whose body is "stumpy and squat, / Her buttocks bulging and wide. . . ." The Green Chapel is only two miles away, the castellan tells him, an easy ride. The lord of the manor proposes that Gawain rest at the castle each day while he goes hunting, that his wife should entertain Gawain, and that at the end of each day they should exchange what each has won.

In fit III, while three hunts for deer, boar, and fox take place, the wife visits Gawain's bedroom three times, tempting his virtue. But although she tries hard "to win him to wickedness," the two only "laugh and play," and Gawain receives only her kisses, which he gives to his host in exchange for the animals from the daily hunt. On the third visit, he is sorely tempted, for the lady "pressed him so hotly," but he is concerned for his courtesy, "lest he be called caitiff, / But more especially for his evil plight if he should plunge into sin, / And dishonour the owner of the house treacherously." When she fails to seduce Gawain, she persuades him to accept her girdle of green silk, claiming, "As long as he laps it closely about him, / No hero under heaven can hack him to pieces, / For he cannot be killed by any cunning on earth." Gawain accepts the gift but fails to mention it to his host during the evening's exchange of gifts.

On New Year's Day, in fit IV, Gawain is led to the Green Chapel, where he meets the Green Knight. The knight strikes him with three blows to the neck. The first two do not touch him, but the third nicks his neck. The knight reveals himself to be Bertilak, his host, who was sent to Arthur's court in the form of

Sir Gawaine challenges Sir
Launcelot:

Honor, a continuing theme in epics, was personified by Sir Gawain, hero of a fourteenth-century Middle English epic and a character in the Authurian legends. American illustrator Howard Pyle drew Sir Gawain's challenge to Lancelot who had killed Gawain's brothers and sons.

the Green Knight by Morgan le Fay, the old woman, in order "to grieve Guinevere and goad her to death." The first two blows have missed because Gawain has resisted temptation twice. The third blow has nicked Gawain's neck as a reproof for his failure to reveal the gift of the girdle. He begs Gawain to come back to his castle, but Gawain refuses. He returns to Arthur's court, vowing to wear the girdle as a "mark of shame," a reminder of his moral lapses. When his peers hear his story, they judge that he has acted honorably. They gather around to comfort him and vow to also wear green girdles for his sake. (Stone, B. 1974)

See also Arthurian Legend; Morgan le Fay.

SĪRAT AL-AMĪRA DHĀT AL-HIMMA

(Also *Dhū al-Himma* and *Delhemma)*

This Arabic vernacular cycle about Aḥādīth al-Baṭṭāl, dating from ca. A.D. 863, was composed in a spirit of hostility to the crusaders. It recounts deeds of the Arabs against the Byzantians and the ensuing struggles against the Franks. The Egyptian historian al-Kurtī mentions hearing "Aḥādīth al-Baṭṭāl," stories from this epic, in 1160. (Connelly 1986)

SĪRAT AL-NABĪ

This Arabic epic chronicling early Islam recounts deeds and teachings of the Prophet. (Connelly 1986)

SĪRAT 'ANTAR

This Arabian vernacular epic about the pre-Islamic poet-warrior 'Antar ibn Shaddād depicts him as a Bedouin knight who triumphs over all obstacles. 'Antar's adventurous tale spans 500 years in its narratives about expeditions to secure trade routes. The epic was still being sung in coffeehouses throughout the nineteenth century. (Connelly 1986)

See also *'Antar, The Romance of.*

SĪRAT BANĪ HILĀL

(Also *Banī Hilāl Epic* or *Sīrat Abū Zayd* or *Abu Zayd Epic)*

This Arabic epic of the Banī Hilāl tribe of Egypt and Tunisia is still being performed today in Cairo cafes. (Connelly 1986)

See also *Banī Hilāl Epic.*

SĪRAT BAYBARS

(Also *Sīrat al-Ẓāhir Baybars)*

This cycle of Arabic folk literature purports to recount the life of Mamluk Sultan Baybars I (ruled Egypt and Syria from 1260 to 1277) and his wars against the

Mongols, Persians, and Christian crusaders. It is still popular in the Arabic-speaking world today. (Connelly 1986)

SĪRAT SAYF IBN DHĪ YAZAN

This Arabic vernacular epic changes the historical pre-Islamic Himyarite prince Sayf, who expelled the Abyssinians from southern Arabia, into a precursor of the Prophet Muḥammad fighting Abyssinians and Negroes in the name of Islam. (Connelly 1986)

SIRENS

In Greek mythology, in the *Odyssey* (xii), the *Aeneid* (v), and the Argonaut story, the Sirens are creatures who are part woman and part bird. By their seductive singing, they lure sailors to their deaths upon the rocks of Scylla. Odysseus is warned by Circe to stuff wax into the ears of his crewmen so that they cannot succumb to their charms. Odysseus orders himself tied to the mast. The Sirens are so furious that they throw themselves into the sea and perish. In the Argonaut story, when the *Argo* sails past the Sirens, Orpheus sings even more beautifully than the Sirens, drowning them out and saving the men. (Graves 1955; Humphries 1951; Rouse 1937)

See also *Aeneid;* Argonauts; *Odyssey.*

SISYPHUS

In Greek mythology, in the *Odyssey* (xi) and the *Aeneid* (vi), Sisyphus is, according to Homer, "the craftiest of men." He is the king of Corinth who ravishes Anticlea (Autolycus), mother of Odysseus. Since she is the wife of Laertes, Odysseus is reared as Laertes's son. He also ravishes his niece Tyro, but she kills all her children by him. After his death, because he has plundered, killed, insulted Pluto, and accused Zeus of raping Aegina, he is condemned to roll a large stone up to the top of a hill in Hades, only to have it repeatedly roll back down again. In the *Iliad,* he is the son of Aeolus. (Graves 1955)

SĪTĀ

In the *Rāmāyaṇa,* Sītā is the wife of Rāma. She is the epitome of wifely devotion, the ideal of Hindu womanhood. She is not born, but arises from a furrow (sītā) while her father, King Janaka of Videha, is plowing. Her abduction by the demon Rāvaṇa and Rāma's rescue of her from Laṅkā are the key incidents in the epic, but the account of Sītā's test to prove herself unsullied by her captor has elevated her to the position of avatar of the goddess Lakṣmī. (Buck 1976)

See also Hanumān; Lakṣmī; Rāma; *Rāmāyaṇa;* Rāvaṇa.

ŚIVA

Śiva is a Hindu god of many aspects. He is not a god of the *Vedas,* but appears in various of the *Purāṇas.* He is a complex god; as the god of ascetics, he is opposed to Kāma, the god of desire or love; as the god of the linga, Śiva's eroticism overreaches Kāma's. He is the god of dance and the annihilator of the universe at the end of time. His wife is Pārvatī (she from the mountain), likewise a complex god, both generative and destructive. Her destructiveness takes the form of famines or pestilence. She is the daughter of the Himālaya. She seduces Śiva, the ascetic, by becoming an ascetic herself. Śiva courts her, arriving at his father-in-law's house dressed as a beggar. He performs a lewd dance, then asks for Pārvatī's hand. Pārvatī's father is furious when Śiva, a god, refuses to behave with respect toward her family. Śiva and Pārvatī are married in a traditional ceremony. It is a difficult marriage, because he is reluctant to have children. Gaṇeśa, for example, is born from the dirt washed from her body during a bath. Gaṇeśa wears an elephant head because in a fit of jealousy Śiva lops off his head, then replaces it with the head of the first creature he sees. Another son is the six-headed Skanda. In other places Śiva's female consort is manifested as Umā, Sāti, Durgā, and Kālī. Śiva is often depicted as the cosmic dancer Naṭarāja. His many epithets include Mahādeva, Paśupati, and Śaṇkara. (Coomaraswamy 1985; Meister 1984; O'Flaherty *Śiva* 1981)

SKADI
(Also Skathi)

In Norse mythology, in the *Poetic Edda,* Skadi is the giantess wife of Njörd, the sea god, and later, the wife of Óthin. She is the daughter of the giant Thiazi (Thjatsi), whose death by the Aesir she attempts to avenge. To appease her, they offer her a choice of a husband, stipulating that she must choose him by his feet. She believes that she is choosing the handsome Baldr, but she picks Njörd instead. But he wants to live by the sea, while she wants to return to Thrymheim, her mountain home. Later she marries Óthin and has several sons. She appears in the Eddaic "Lays of Grímnir" and "Skírnir," "The Flyting of Loki," and "The Short Seeress's Prophecy." (Hollander *Edda* 1990)

See also *Edda, Poetic.*

SKANDA
(Spurt of Semen)

In Hindu mythology, Skanda, god of war, is the firstborn son of Śiva and Pārvatī. He has six heads or six faces, developed so that he can drink from his six nurses. In South India the war god was originally named Murugaṉ but later was incorporated into the personality of the North Indian god Skanda. He is also called Subrahmaṇya, Dear to the Brahmins, Guha, Kārttikeya, and Kumāra. The *Skanda Purāṇa* tells of how, while Śiva is meditating, the god of

A thirteenth-century bronze from southern India represents the Hindu god Śiva as Naṭarāja, god of dance. The statuette was cast so that it could be carried in processions.

love Kāma enters his heart and he is driven wild with desire for Devī (Pārvatī). However, he abstains from fleshly pleasures for many years, making his seed so strong that it spurts out into the fire in which Śiva burns Kāma. Thus the name Skanda, burst of semen. (Embree 1988)

SMILING GOD

(Also El Lanzon, or the Great Image)

The Smiling God was an icon of the Chavin people of Peru ca. 700 B.C. (Alexander, H. 1964)

SNORRI STURLUSON

(Also Snorre Sturlason)

An Icelandic historian and poet (1178–1241), Snorri is the author of the *Prose Edda* and *Heimskringla,* and possibly of *Egil's Saga.* He also expanded one section of *Heimskringla* into *Olafs Saga.* He based the *Heimskringla* on earlier histories and material from the oral tradition, preserving some original works from the period. (Monsen and Smith 1990; Young 1954)

SOBHUZA I

In the Zulu epic *Emperor Shaka the Great,* Sobhuza is the South African chief who founds the Ngwane nation. He and his clans are forced to flee from Zwide following a dispute over lands, and he establishes a settlement at the present site of Swaziland. He marries a daughter of Zwide in order to secure the peace, and makes a diplomatic visit to Shaka, who has strong marital bonds with Sobhuza. (Kunene 1979)

See also *Emperor Shaka the Great;* Zwide.

SOGA

Soga is the name of a powerful and highly respected Japanese family (A.D. 592–643) whose members are mentioned in the *Nihongi* Chronicle (volume II) accounts of the reigns of Suiko and of Kögyoku, and in the *Kojiki.* Specifically, Soga-no-iname-no-sukune was an opo-omi (governmental title corresponding to Minister of the Right after the Taika Reform) and the father of the powerful minister Umako (d. 626) and of Kitasi-pime, who became the consort of Emperor Kimmei and mother of Emperor Yōmei and Empress Suiko, and of Opo-gitasi-pime, who became a consort of her nephew, Emperor Yōmei. The family descended from Soga-no-isikapa-no-sukune, a son of Takesi-uti-no-sukune. (Aston 1972; Philippi 1968)

SON OF LIGHT

In this Hopi Indian tale, "a frightful monster" named Man-Eagle abducts the young wife of the hero, Son of Light. It is Man-Eagle's custom to seize women and girls in his sharp talons and fly with them to his home above the clouds, where he abuses them for four days before eating them.

Son of Light sets out immediately to rescue his wife. Along the way he meets the Piñon Maidens, accompanied by Spider Woman and Mole. Spider Woman, who knows much magic, offers to help Son of Light. She directs the Piñon Maidens to gather piñon resin and fashion a shirt that looks exactly like the magical impenetrable shirt belonging to Man-Eagle. Then Spider Woman turns herself into a tiny spider and perches on Son of Light's right ear. She says, "Here I am, where I can tell you what to do if you get in trouble."

Mole burrows through the mountain so Son of Light can reach the summit without being seen. But when he reaches the top, he is still far below Man-Eagle's home. Spider Woman calls on the birds for help, and the three are carried up and deposited at the white house of Man-Eagle. But the ladder leading to the door has rungs as sharp as knife blades. Spider Woman directs him to gather berries and feed them to the horned toad. The toad chews them into a paste, which Son of Light spreads on the rungs, making them dull. Mole buries himself in Son of Light's hair, and the three climb up to Man-Eagle's door.

In the front room, they see Man-Eagle's shirt hanging on the rafters. Son of Light quickly exchanges it for the piñon shirt. In the next room, he finds his wife and unties her. Meanwhile, Man-Eagle wakes up, goes to the front room to put on his shirt, then comes in to eat the wife. But he finds Son of Light waiting instead.

He tells Son of Light that before he can take his wife back, he must participate in a smoking contest. Whoever faints is the loser; if Son of Light loses, Man-Eagle will kill him; if he wins, he may take his wife home. Man-Eagle's tobacco is poisonous to anyone who is not accustomed to it, but Mole burrows a hole in the floor under Son of Light, so that Son of Light's smoke will pass right through him to the outside. Thus it is Man-Eagle who feels faint first.

But he subjects Son of Light to a second contest: Each must try to break a rack of elk antlers. But Son of Light's rack is actually made of stone, and Man-Eagle's is made of brittle wood. At the last second, however, Spider Woman exchanges the antlers, and Son of Light breaks his antlers easily.

Man-Eagle subjects Son of Light to a third contest: Each must try to pull up a pine tree by its roots. While they talk, Mole burrows under Son of Light's tree and gnaws through the roots so that he is able to pull up his tree.

Man-Eagle submits Son of Light to a fourth and last test: He must eat an enormous mountain of food. Again Mole burrows beneath Son of Light so that the food goes through him into the earth.

Man-Eagle still refuses to honor his promise. He orders two fires to be built upon which each must climb. Son of Light, wearing the magical shirt belonging to Man-Eagle, is unburned; in fact, the shirt forms a shield of ice that melts and extinguishes the fire. Man-Eagle, wearing the piñon shirt, perishes in the fire. Spider Woman gives Son of Light some magic medicine to spit upon the ashes, and Man-Eagle arises, transformed into a handsome man. He promises never to eat people again.

Son of Light, his wife, Mole, and Spider Woman get on the backs of the birds to return to earth, bringing with them all the Hopi people that Man-Eagle has killed. With her magic, Spider Woman has brought them all back to life. (Erdoes and Ortiz 1984)

SONG OF ROLAND

Epic poem. *See Chanson de Roland.*

SONG OF ULLIKUMMI

An ancient Hurrian myth partially preserved in Hittite in *Theogony,* it describes the conflict between the weather god Teshub and a great stone monster that rises out of the sea. Kumarbi, described as "father of all gods," second god of the netherworld, wants to depose Teshub. After taking wisdom into his mind, he rises from his chair, takes his staff, puts on "as shoes the swift winds" and goes forth to unseat Teshub. To this end he begets a stone monster named Ullikummi, who stands in the sea on the shoulder of the Hurrian equivalent of Atlas, Upelluri, who carries heaven and earth on his shoulders. Ullikummi rises out of the sea only from his waist up, but nevertheless he can touch the sky with his head. Teshub ignores warnings and goes into battle against Ullikummi, who is too mighty for him. Teshub calls for help from Ea, god of wisdom, who orders that the ancient tool once used to sever earth from heaven be brought, and he cuts Ullikummi loose from the shoulders of Upelluri. The end of the epic is lost, but it is presumed that Teshub is able to defeat Ullikummi. (Preminger 1990; Pritchard 1973)

See also Teshub; *Theogony.*

SONG-SEN-GAM-PO

(Also Songtsan Gambo)

In the oral tradition of the tiny kingdom of Ladakh, between present-day India and Pakistan, Song-sen-gam-po is a romantic historical figure about whom many stories have evolved, making fact difficult to distinguish. He is depicted as a tribal chief during the period when Buddhist monks, to protect themselves from warlike tribes, are forced to build fortresses. The tribal clans ban together to form feudal kingdoms, all intent on expanding their influence. To solidify his own position, Song-sen-gam-po contracts marriages with Buddhist princesses from China and Nepal, with the result that he founds the first Buddhist kingdom in Tibet. Later Ladakhi kings wishing to make their independence secure follow the example of Son-sen-gam-po. (Rao 1989; Ward *RAL* 1980)

SONGS OF KOGHT'EN

Part of an Armenian epic celebrating the victory of Prince Artashes over invading Alans, it occurs while the new city Artashat is being built, ca. 185 B.C. Hannibal the Carthaginian, still fleeing from the Romans, seeks hospitality at the Armenian court, and in return plans and supervises the building of the new city Artashat (Artaxata) on the river Araxes. During this time, the Alans invade. Artashes chases them beyond the river Kura, at the same time taking prisoner the son of the Alan chief. He refuses to return the youth, despite the chief's pleas. According to one poem in the cycle, the chief's beautiful daughter Sat'enik steps to the river's bank and pleads, "'Tis unworthy of heroes to enslave their prisoners, / Forever perpetuating / The enmity 'twixt Great Armenia and the Alani." At that, "Brave Artashes" rides his "spirited steed, / Like a winged eagle . . ." and leaps across the stream. From his saddle he unleashes a cord. "Then casting his belt round her lithe waist, / Upon his strong horse bore her to his camp." The two make love, and the king, "gallant groom," marries the princess, "comely bride," while "pearls rained from smiling heaven." (Chahin 1987)

SOTOBE

In the Zulu epic *Emperor Shaka the Great,* Sotobe is the leader of a mission sent by Shaka to King George to find out the white men's intentions in his area. Sotobe continues to be a highly respected political figure even after Shaka's death. (Kunene 1979)

See also *Emperor Shaka the Great.*

SPENTA MAINYU

Spenta Mainyu is the holy spirit, an aspect of the Zoroastrian god Ahura Mazda. (Olmstead 1948)

See also Ahura Mazda; Angra Mainyu.

SPIELMANN

Spielmann was a wandering German minstrel of the Middle Ages. The storytelling Spielleute were keepers of the High Middle German oral traditions and the native vernacular legends, which they performed at fairs, markets, and festivals. Although priests did not approve of the minstrels' songs about the great deeds of heroes of the Frankish race, instead of Christian hymns, Emperor Charlemagne listened to the singers and "wrote out the barbarous and ancient songs, in which the acts of the kings and their wars were sung, and committed them to memory." (Power 1963)

STURLUNGA SAGA

This is the name applied to the group of secular histories of Iceland compiled during the period from ca. 1100 to 1264. The most important work of this group is the *Islendinga saga,* written by Sturla Thórdarson, dealing with the various feuds during the end of the period. (Jones, G. 1990)

SUIKO TENNŌ

In the *Nihongi* and the *Kojiki,* Suiko (554–628) is depicted as the first reigning empress of Japan. The daughter of Emperor Kimmei, she is described as "beautiful, and her conduct was marked by propriety." She marries her brother, Emperor Bidatsu (the second child), who dies of "a disease" and is succeeded by Yōmei (Tachibana no Toyohi), the emperor's younger half brother (the fourth child). But Yōmei becomes afflicted with sores and dies during the second year of his reign. The following month "the army of the Mononobe [another powerful family]" make "a disturbance thrice." The head of the family now hopes "to make use of a hunting party to devise a plan for raising [the Imperial Prince Anahobe] to the throne. . . . The plot leaked out." The Soga clan is victorious against the threat. Soga guardsmen surround Anahobe in his own palace. He is pursued to the top floor, where he is smitten on the shoulder by a guard. He falls from the upper story and runs away into an outhouse. "Then the guardsmen, holding up lights, executed him."

The reign falls to another half brother of the former emperor, Sujun (the twelfth child), Suiko's brother. But Sujun acts contrary to the wishes of the head of the Soga family, Soga no Mŭmako (Umako), who murders him. Suiko is 34 years old when her uncle Umako bypasses Bidatsu's sons, breaks with recent tradition, and places her on the throne. (Aston 1972; Philippi 1968)

SUMANGURU
(Also Soumaoro)

A West African warrior king (fl. thirteenth century), Sumanguru is the subject of an oral tradition who appears in the *Sundiata Epic* (Sunjata) as Sundiata's archenemy. He is the ruthless and cruel king of Susu (Soso) Kaniaga (in present-day southwestern Mali). He sets out to expand his territory, and conquers several outlying tributaries of the Ghana empire. In ca. 1203 he swoops in and takes the Ghanian capital, Kumbi. But the merchants merely abandon the town and establish new trading centers at Djenne and Oualata. Sumanguru usurps the kingship of Mali from Sundiata, forcing the young heir and his mother and sisters into exile. He also takes Sundiata's griot, Balla Fasseke. The griot then has to change his tune to one extolling the supremacy of Sumanguru.

Sundiata's sister, Sugulun Kulunkan, plans to trick Sumanguru into telling her the secret of his magical powers and invincibility, so she goes to his gates and calls, "Come make me your bed companion!" When she learns the ritual by which he can be vanquished, she returns to tell her brother.

The tyrant's subjects begin to rebel, and eventually Sundiata returns, joined by Faa Koli, to attack Sumanguru, who is joined by Jibrila. Early in the clash, Faa Koli bests Jibrila in a contest to prove which man has more physical and magical strength. Faa Koli wins, and he breaks Jibrila's arms and legs one by one, to the horror of the onlookers. However, "Laughter came to Manding, weeping came to Susu." Sundiata goes on to best Sumanguru in combat (ca. 1235) at the Battle of Kirina: "Son-Jara [Sundiata] held him at bladepoint: / 'We have taken you, Colossus! / We have taken you!' / Samarmuru [Sumanguru] dried up on the spot! . . ." (Laye 1984; Niane 1989; Sisòkò 1992)

See also *Sundiata, Epic of.*

SUNDIATA, EPIC OF
(Also Sunjata or Son-Jara)

This is a West African epic of the legendary founder of the Sudanese empire of Old Mali, or Manden, in the thirteenth century. Written versions vary according to which griot's performance has been recorded, for the epic is still being performed today. The epic begins with a genealogy of the kings of Mali, some versions going back to include a story of creation.

Sundiata and his chief adversary, Dankran Tuman, are both sons of the handsome King Nare Maghan (Fara Magan). Dankran Tuman is the puppet of his mother, Sassouma Berete. Sundiata's mother is Sogolon the Konde (Sugulun Konde), a virgin received as a reward by the Tarawere brothers, whom she has turned away with magic powers. The king gets her away from the brothers, but his other wife, Sassouma Berete, is very jealous. In some accounts, she hexes Sundiata and makes him crippled. At the age of three he still crawls on all fours, and he has none of the beauty of his father. His father is disappointed, and none of his mother's magic works. Sassouma Berete uses his affliction to her advantage, for she intends for her own son to be king. Sogolon and her children are moved to the back of the village, and Sundiata is even dispossessed of his griot, Balla Fasseke.

Finally, after many years, Sundiata stands up and walks. He decides to become a great hunter and give up all claim to the throne. Dankran Tuman becomes king and his mother makes him send Sologon and her children into exile. This launches Sundiata on his long journey.

Sundiata travels far, seeking refuge with first one tribe and then another. His first major experience occurs at Djedeba, where he is taken in by King Mansa Konkon, only to realize later that the king, having been bribed by Sassouma Berete, means to kill him. He leaves much wiser, having learned not to be so trusting. They move on to Tabon, but the king does not wish to endanger his relations with Mali by offering them hospitality for too long. They go to Ghana but are forced to move on because of Sogolon's poor health. At one stop, the nine Queens-of-Darkness steal his wraith. Sundiata reclaims his wraith by exchanging it for nine buffalo. They go on to Mema, where King Tunkara gives them sanctuary. From the king's daughter, Mema Sira, Sundiata learns how to play the sigi game, and he plays it successfully with Tunkara. The king, with no heir, grows fond of Sundiata and adopts him as his son and successor. At the age of 15, Sundiata is given the title of Kan-Koro-Sigui, or Viceroy, and the power to perform the king's duties in his absence. But his mother says, "Do not deceive yourself. Your destiny lies not here but in Mali."

Meanwhile, Sumanguru, the sorcerer-king of Sosso, conquers the Manden and puts calabashes over the mouths of the Mandens' heroes. He conquers and subjugates not only Mali but all the neighboring kingdoms. Sundiata's sister, Sugulun Kulunkan, takes the calabashes off the mouths of the Manden heroes.

The Mali people go to the Mema market and discover Sundiata's whereabouts. They send a party to Sundiata, urging him to return to save them from Sumanguru: "The brave await you, come and restore rightful authority to Mali."

Sundiata's mother, who has been ill for so long, has died, and he must threaten the prince in order to get a plot of land on which to bury her. He must also extricate himself from the clutches of the king of Mema, who is very reluctant to let him go. But the delegation from Mali has assured him, "You are the giant who will crush the giant Sumanguru."

He organizes an army and travels to attack Sumanguru in an effort not only to regain his inheritance, but to free the neighboring kingdoms as well. But Sumanguru is invincible, so Sundiata retires and begins founding settlements in the area. His sister goes to Sumanguru's palace, seduces him, and tricks him into revealing the source of his invincibility. Sundiata returns to fight again; this time, after long and bloody confrontations, he is triumphant. He goes on to liberate the surrounding kingdoms and is hailed as the supreme hero. (Laye 1984; Niane 1989; Sisòkò 1992)

See also Mansa Moussa.

SUSANOWO

(Also Sosa no wo)

In Japanese mythology, in the creation myth of the *Nihongi* Chronicles, Susanowo is the storm god. The accepted derivation of the name is from the verb Susamu, "to be impetuous." When his father Izangi no Mikoto gives charges to his children, he tells Susanowo to rule the world. "Nevertheless, he neglected to rule the world, and was always weeping, wailing, and fuming with rage." When asked why he is behaving in such a manner, he answers, "I wish to follow my mother to the Nether Land. . . ." His father's heart is "filled with detestation of him." He says, "Go, even as thy heart bids thee," and he drives him away. (Aston 1972)

See also *Nihongi.*

T

TA RUA

In Hawaiian oral tradition, Ta Rua is the daughter of Ra'i Ra'i who picks the forbidden fruit. (Melville 1990)

See also Ra'i Ra'i; Tani; Teave.

TA YU
(Tamer of the Flood)

Chinese savior-hero. ***See*** Yu the Great, Emperor.

TABUKA EPIC

This Hausa epic of West Africa, which has been taped but not transcribed, concerns a critical battle during the early days of Islamic expansion into West Africa. (Westley *RAL* 1991)

TAGARO

In the Polynesian cycle of the culture hero Qat, Tagaro is the name of all of Qat's 11 brothers. (Dixon 1964)

See also Qat.

TAÍN BÓ CÚAILNGE
(The Cattle Raid of Cooley)

The most important of the eighth-century *Ulster Cycle* of heroic tales, it is Ireland's greatest epic tale.

See also *The Cattle Raid of Cooley.*

THE TALE OF THE HEIKE
(Heike monogatari)

The most famous of the Japanese gunki monogatari, or war epics, it occupies the place in Japanese literature held by Homer's epics in the West. It stems from oral tradition and reached its present form, in 12 books, ca. 1220, during the Kamakura period. It was probably written by a nobleman, originally in three books, but expanded through variations in the telling from accounts recited by priests. The tale concerned the Taira (Heike) samurai clan, which originated in 825 when the name "Taira" was given to Prince Takamune when he was sent into the provinces. Prior to that time, members of the imperial family were not given surnames. Takamune was the grandson of Emperor Kammu, the fiftieth emperor (d. 806). Takamune's nephew Takamochi settled in the Hitachi district to serve as a local official, and his descendants succeeded him in the post.

The epic concerns the prodigious first rise to power of the Taira clan under a great-grandson, Masakado, who in 939 establishes a seat of government in Kanto. A man of great hubris, he establishes himself as "shinno," meaning "New Emperor." Masakado is not above eliminating even his own uncles in order to retain power. The enmity between the Taira and Minamoto families begins with small incidents, but during a clash called the Tengyo no Ran, Masakado is defeated, and he dies (940). When another Taira samurai, Tadatsune, attempts to reestablish domination over Kanto (1028), the imperial court sends a member of the Minamoto family, Yorinobu, to put down the rebellion. With Tadatsune's surrender (1031), the Minamoto clan gained ascendancy over the Taira family in Kanto.

In 1108 another member of the clan, Masamori, who has gained local prominence in the district of Ise, is summoned to suppress a faction of the Minamoto family that has become too powerful in Japanese affairs. The confrontation, which occurs along the Inland Sea, leaves the Minamoto, unaccustomed to sea warfare, defeated. The emperor rewards Masamori with holdings in western Japan, where the family embarks on trade with China.

After Masamori's death, his son Tadamori assists the court by eliminating the pirate menace along the China trade route and quelling challenges by the bothersome Minamotos. His successes gain him new favors from the emperor. He becomes the emperor's personal bodyguard and confidant.

His son Kiyomori continues to expand the Taira family holdings and influence. When a coup attempt erupts between two brothers—the former emperor, Sotoku, supported by the Minamoto family, and the present emperor, Shirakawa II, supported by the Tairas—war becomes inevitable (1156). In the first bloody encounter, called the Hogen War, Kiyomori, aided by Minamoto defectors, is victorious and merciless with his defeated enemies. During the next uprising, the Heiji War (1159), Kiyomori viciously cuts down his former Minamoto allies who aided him in the last war. The war leaves him the most powerful man in Japan. He marries his wife's sister to the former emperor, and Kiyomori becomes prime minister (1167). The Taira family becomes the most prominent family in the country, occupying most of the high offices and owning more than 500 estates.

Kiyomori is content for many years to exercise control from the sidelines, but in 1180 he decides to place his two-year-old grandson Antoku on the throne and move the capital to his own city, Fukuhara. This move proves too much for even his own appointees, and although Kiyomori puts down the rebellion, a counterrebellion is led by a member of the Minamoto clan, Yorimoto.

One of the most famous sections concerns Atsumori, son of Tsunemori, who fights bravely at Ichi-no-tani (1184). When the defeated Taira take flight, Atsumori is left behind and must spur his horse into the sea. Kumagai Naozane, of the Minamoto (Genji) family, sees him and challenges him to combat, during which he cuts off Atsumori's head. Kumagai Naozane is so pained to learn his victim's identity that he enters the priesthood, becoming the priest, Rensei, as related in the Nō play *Atsumori.*

Yoritomo and his brother Yoshitsune, whose father had once been ordered by Kiyomoto to cut off his own father's head, organize the rugged forces from outlying districts, which trounce Kiyomori's army. The final Taira catastrophe is related in a section called "Dan no ura," which describes how warriors, courtiers, and court ladies are all drowned in the sinking ships. Lady Nü takes the seventh emperor in her arms and says, "In the depths of the ocean is our capital," and sinks beneath the waves. Kiyomori retires from the field and from government, intending to raise a new army, but he soon dies. By 1185 the Taira clan has been eliminated from government completely and the Minamoto family has gained supremacy. The former empress, Toku-ko Kenreimon'in, daughter of Kiyomori and wife of Takakura, whose son has perished in the sea, enters a convent and becomes a nun in Kyōto, where she dies in 1213. (Keene 1960)

TAMMUZ
(Also Dumuzi)

In the *Epic of Gilgamesh,* Tammuz is an ancient Mesopotamian fertility god, husband of Inanna (Ishtar), and counterpart of Adonis. In the Sumerian *Inanna's Descent to the Nether World* Inanna sends him as her substitute in the underworld. In this sense Tammuz becomes a savior. His sister Geshtinanna goes to find him, and Inanna decides that the brother and sister may alternate staying in the underworld six months at a time. (Sandars 1972)

See also *Gilgamesh, Epic of; Inanna's Descent to the Nether World;* Savior.

TANGUN

In Korean mythology, the first king of Korea is Tangun, whose reign begins in 2333 B.C. His father Hwanung, the son of Hwanin, the creator, is sent to rule Earth from atop Mount T'aebaek. When two animals, a tiger and a bear, express the desire to become human, he orders them to hibernate in a cave for 100 days. The tiger grows tired of waiting and leaves the cave, but the bear remains for the entire time. When it emerges, it has been transformed into a beautiful woman, who becomes Hwanung's wife. She conceives Tangun after Hwanung breathes upon her. Tangun grows up to found Choson. He may have a historical counterpart who ruled a tribal state in the Taedong River Valley and called himself a grandson of Heaven. (Reischauer and Fairbank 1960)

See also Kija.

TANI

(Also Tane)

In ancient pre-Christian Hawaiian tradition, in the religion of the Mu, or Tahunaism, Tani is the Heavenly Father, Lord of Hawaii. The title actually means man, head of the family, father. According to one tradition, Ra'i Ra'i, the progenitress of the Hawaiian people, is born of the mind of Tane. Although the religion of the native people of Hawaii was abolished in 1819, old-timers have kept Tane's memory alive through oral tradition. (Melville 1990)

See also Ra'i Ra'i; Teave.

TANIT

Chief goddess of Carthage, Tanit is the counterpart of the West Semitic Astarte, and consort of Baal Amon (Hammon), Lord of the Tophet (the sanctuary where sacrifice was made). The likeness of Tanit appears on ancient relics in many Punic cities. She is parent of all, mistress of the elements, goddess of fertility, and queen of the Manes (souls of the dead). Together, Tanit and Baal rule the Punic pantheon. (Ben Khader and Soren 1987)

TAPIO

Tapio is a Finnish forest god who presides over forest game. He is mentioned in the *Kalevala* poems 14, 32, 41, and 48. (Lönnrot 1963)

See also *Kalevala;* Leib-Olmai.

TĀRĀ

Buddhist savior goddess, protectress of travelers, and consort of the bodhisattva of infinite compassion, Avalokiteśvara, Tārā is revered in Nepal, Mongolia, and Tibet. She is born when a tear falls from Avalokiteśvara, forming a lake from which sprouts a lotus. When the lotus opens, the goddess appears. (Similarly, the Egyptian sun god Horus emerges from the lotus-form of Hathor floating on the Nile.) "Tara" means "savioress." The goddess Samaya-Tārā, consort of Amaghasiddha, appears in the *Bardo Thötröl* (Tibetan Book of the Dead). She is Savior of the Blessed Word; his name means "accomplishing all actions, all powers." They are of the family of Karma. (Fremantle and Trungpa 1987)

TARHUN

(Also Taru, Teshub, Tarhunna, and Tarhuis)

In Hittite mythology, Tarhun, weather god, is the supreme deity of the pantheon (ca. 1400–612 B.C.). (Ceram 1990; Chahin 1987)

See also Teshub.

TARPEIA

In Roman mythology, Tarpeia is a vestal virgin, the daughter of Spurius Tarpeius, governor of Rome and commander of the Capitol citadel. During the Sabine War, Tatius, king of the Sabines, bribes her to open the gates to the citadel's fortress in exchange for what the Sabines wear on their left arms: their gold bracelets. But Tatius throws not only his bracelet at her, but his shield as well, knocking her to the ground. The other Sabines throw their shields on her and crush her to death. She is buried in the Capitol, which comes to be called Tarpeian Rock, a cliff from which Roman traitors are thereafter thrown. (Bowder 1984)

TAYCHUIT

In the *Secret History of the Mongols,* the Taychuit are a rival Mongol family who, after the murder of Temüjin's father Yesugei, consider Temüjin too weak to rule and lead the rest of the clan away, abandoning Temüjin's mother and her children. At one time Temüjin is captured by the Taychuit, who do not kill him but place him in a wooden collar and keep him prisoner. Temüjin escapes during a feast by striking his guard a blow with the wooden collar. During the search that follows, one of the Taychuit spots him, but is so impressed by the fire in the boy's eyes that he risks his own life to help Temüjin get away. (Grousset 1970)

See also *Secret History of the Mongols.*

TE WHEROWHERO

A Maori chief of New Zealand celebrated in oral tradition, he was chosen king in the Waikato province, to reign as King Potatau I (r. 1857–1860), primarily over the Waikato and Maniopoto tribes. These tribes joined forces to prevent the further incursion of white settlers in their land. (Dixon 1964; Simmons 1976)

TEAVE

In the pre-Christian Hawaiian creation myth of the Tumuripo, Teave evolves out of chaos when he breathes forth the manna, or animating spirit, of his God Substance and orders confusion to cease. He speaks into space, "Ora," meaning Life of the Sun God Ra, commanding life to begin in the gloomy world of Po. Teave is the Father-Mother, regent over the Kings of Heaven, while Tane is the

Son. All proceeds from the Father-Mother through the Son. The Mother is also called Eri Eri.

Teave decides to establish a royal family for the kingdoms of heaven and earth, so he manifests as his daughter Na' Vahine, the goddess Uri Uri. The Holy Trinity becomes Teave, Eri Eri, and Uri Uri. Na' Vahine and Tane mate and produce three sons—Tanaroa, Rono, and Tu—and three daughters—Rata, Tapo, and Hina. ***See also*** Tumuripo. (Melville 1990)

See also Ra'i Ra'i; Tani; Teave.

TEISHEBA
(Also Tesheba)

Teisheba is an ancient Urartu weather god akin to, but less important than, the earlier Hurrian principal god Teshub (the Destroyer). (Chahin 1987)

See also Teshub.

TEJĀ

This oral folk epic, still recited in Rajasthan in India today, tells about a young hero who learns that as a small child he was married; he sets off for his wife's village to bring his wife home. On the way, he saves a snake caught in a burning tree. When the ungrateful serpent tries to bite him, Tejā begs to be allowed to meet his wife first. The snake agrees, and Tejā continues on to his wife's village, where the father welcomes him but the mother insults him. Indignant, he prepares to leave, but Hīrā, a friend of his wife, asks him to help her recover her cows and her one-eyed bull first. He learns that Hīrā is a reincarnation of Śakti, and by the time he recovers the bull, he is covered with wounds from head to toe. He returns to keep his promise to the snake. Finding no other space on his body not covered with wounds, the snake bites him on the tongue. At the same time, he thus gives Tejā rule over snake venom. Today Tejā is worshiped as a major god who cures snakebites. (Blackburn et al. 1989)

TELEMACHOS
(Also Telemachus)

In Greek mythology, Telemachos is the son of Odysseus and Penelope who plays an important role in the *Odyssey* (i–iv, xv–xvii, xix, xxii, xxiv). As an infant he is thrown in front of his father's plow as a test of Odysseus's sanity. When he grows to manhood, after his father has been gone for nearly 20 years, Telemachos goes to Pylos in search of him. Nestor sends him on to Sparta, where Menelaus tells him of Proteus's prophecy concerning Odysseus. Telemachos returns home to discover that his mother's suitors have been plotting to murder him. He avoids their plot and discovers that his father has reached home before him. The two devise a plan to slay his mother's suitors. (Rouse 1990)

See also Odysseus; *Odyssey;* Penelope.

TELIPINU

Telipinu is the Hittite god of fertility whose much earlier myths are recorded on clay tablets (fifteenth century) found at the ancient Hittite capital of Hattusas, now Boghazkoy, Turkey. Telipinu's sleep is the cause of harsh winters, and in order to wake him and then calm the storms that his anger brings, elaborate rituals must be performed. Telipinu, or Telipinus, is also the name of the last king of the Hittite Old Kingdom in Anatolia (r. ca. 1525–ca. 1500 B.C.), who seized the throne during a power struggle and issued the Edict of Telipinus to regulate laws of succession. (Ceram 1990)

TEMÜJIN

This Mongolian ruler (Genghiz-khan) is the hero of the *Secret History of the Mongols.* (Grousset 1970)

See also *Secret History of the Mongols.*

TENCHI TENNŌ

He is the thirty-eighth emperor of Japan (r. 668–671), whose reign is one of the last detailed in the *Nihongi* Chronicles. (Aston 1972)

TESHUB
(the Destroyer)

Teshub is the ancient Hurrian weather god, principal god of the Hurrians, akin to the Urartian weather god Teiseida, and to the later Hittite weather god, Tarhun. Teshub's consort is Hebat, Queen of Heaven. Their son is Sharruma. Myths about Teshub have survived among Hittite remains. ***See*** *Theogony* and *Song of Ullikummi.* (Ceram 1990; Chahin 1987)

See also Tarhun.

TETEOINNAN

Aztec goddess. ***See*** Coatlicue.

TEUCER

In the *Iliad* (viii) and the *Aeneid* (i), Teucer is the son of Telamon and Hesione, stepbrother of Telamonian Ajax. He goes with the Greeks to the siege of Troy, where he is the best archer. On his return, he is banished by his father for leaving unavenged the death of Ajax at the hands of Odysseus.

Teucer is also the name of a king of Phrygia, and by some accounts, the first king of Troy; in the *Aeneid* (iii), he is called "our forefather." (Humphries 1951; Lattimore 1976)

See also *Aeneid;* Ajax; *Iliad.*

TEZCATLIPOCA
(Also Yoalli Ehécatl, Night Wind; Yaotl, Warrior; and Tepochtli)

In the Aztec creation cycle (fourteenth century) of central Mexico, Tezcatlipoca is a creator and first-era sky god associated with the constellation of the Great Bear. He is often depicted as a jaguar. During Ocelotonatiuh, the first world (the present being the fifth), Tezcatlipoca reigns, followed by Quetzalcóatl, Tlaloc, and Huitzilopochtli. According to one myth regarding the demise of the golden age of the Toltec, Tezcatlipoca ousts the great and virtuous Quetzalcóatl, the Feathered Serpent, from the temple at Tula by first inducing him with magic to stoop to debauchery and drunkenness. The practice of human sacrifice is introduced under Tezcatlipoca. He is associated with the later lightning god Hurakan. (Bierhorst 1974)

See also Tonatiuh.

THEOGONY

This ancient Hurrian myth, preserved in the Hittite tradition, relates the deposition and banishment to the netherworld of the gods of the pantheon Alalu, Anu, and Kumarbi by the weather god Teshub, who alone remains supreme. (Saggs 1978)

See also *Song of Ullikummi;* Teshub.

THEOGONY
(*Divine Genealogy*)

This Greek epic poem attrubuted to the Boeotian poet Hesiod (ca. 800 B.C.) presents in 1,022 lines a cosmogony and account of adventures of the gods, beginning with Uranos and Gaea, Father Sky and Mother Earth, resembling the Hurrian myth by the same name. (Lattimore 1959)

THERSITES

In the *Iliad* (ii), Thersites is "ill-favored beyond all men" that come to fight with the Greeks at the siege of Troy. He is described as "bandy-legged . . . and lame of one foot" with a "warped" head. He reviles Achilles, Odysseus, and even Agamemnon. In a later story (Apollodorus's *Epitome,* v), Achilles hits him so hard that his teeth fall out, and he dies. (Lattimore 1976)

See also *Iliad.*

THESEUS

Theseus is the greatest hero of Attica in Greek legend, celebrated by everyone from Homer to Shakespeare. He appears in the *Odyssey* (xi), the cyclic epic

Cypria, in Ovid's works, and in many others. Theseus is the son of King Aegeus (some legends say Poseidon) and Queen Aethra. He is reared by his mother. When he is strong enough to lift the stone from his father's sword, he is sent to Athens. On the way he has many adventures, confronting and destroying Sinis, Cercyon, Periphetes, Phaea, Procrustes, and Sciron. He arrives in Athens to find his father married to Medea, who tries to convince Aegeus to poison him before the king recognizes him and has him declared heir to the throne.

Among his other deeds are overcoming the Marathonian bull; slaying, with Ariadne's help, the Cretan Minotaur, shut up in the Cretan labyrinth; capturing the Amazon princess Antiope (or Hippolyta); and participating with Herakles in the subsequent war against the Amazons. Hippolyta, who has borne a son, Hippolytus, dies at Theseus's side during the fighting. Another legend says that Theseus kills Antiope when she interferes with his marriage to Phaedra.

In addition to those feats, he participates in the Calydonian boar hunt, joins the expedition of the Argonauts, aids the Lapithae in their war against the Centaurs, and rescues the bodies of those killed in the war of the Seven against Thebes.

He has several loves and wives: Perigone, daughter of the Pine Bender Sinis, who bears a son, Melanippus; Ariadne, daughter of King Minos of Crete, who with a ball of thread helps him escape from the labyrinth where he has been placed to be devoured by the Minotaur, but whom he deserts at Naxos; Antiope (some say Hippolyta), the Amazon queen whom Herakles gives in marriage to Theseus; and Phaedra, who bears two sons, Acamas and Demophon, but becomes infatuated with her stepson Hippolytus. When he rejects her, she hangs herself, leaving a note for Theseus accusing Hippolytus of attacking her. Enraged, Theseus appeals to Poseidon, who sends a sea monster to frighten Hippolytus's horses so that they bolt, and Hippolytus is dragged to death under the wheels of his chariot.

Theseus becomes unpopular in his old age and goes to the island of Scyrus, where King Lycomedes pushes him off a cliff to his death. Other legends tell of his shade rising with the Athenians at the Battle of Marathon. (Graves 1955)

THIÐREKSSAGA

(Also *Thidrik's Saga*)

This mid-thirteenth-century Norse prose saga is a compilation of the legendary life and deeds of Thidrek (Dietrich) taken from narratives told by German merchants who came to Bergen in Norway. In the saga, Sigurd, son of King Sigmund of Tarlungland, is born in a forest where his mother Sisibe, daughter of the king of Spain, places him in a glass pot. He accidentally floats down the river to the sea, where he eventually beaches and is found by a doe, who suckles him. A smith named Mimi finds him and names him Sigurd. When it seems that Sigurd is growing too strong, Mimi asks his brother Regin, a dragon, to destroy him. Sigurd beats the dragon to death, then cooks him and tastes him. Immediately he is able to understand the language of birds, who say that he should kill Mimi. He smears his body with the dragon's blood, except between his shoulder blades, where he cannot reach. The blood makes his skin tough. He returns home, kills Mimi, then starts off on a journey. He arrives at the famed Amazonian Icelandic queen Brynhild's castle, where he asks for the steed Grane, which only he can tame.

Sigurd becomes Thidrek's vassal and marries Grimhild, the Burgundian princess, receiving half her brother Gunnar's kingdom as a dowry. He convinces Gunnar that he should marry Brynhild, whom he himself had promised to marry. He takes Gunnar to Brynhild's castle, and with Thidrek's assistance a marriage is arranged. But Brynhild will not allow Gunnar to touch her, and each night she hangs him on the wall with her girdles. After three nights of this treatment, Gunnar asks Sigurd's aid, but Sigurd explains that, so long as Brynhild is a virgin, she will remain strong. Gunnar requests that Sigurd, disguised as Gunnar, relieve her of her virginity. This Sigurd does, but later, when Brynhild berates Grimhild for not rising before her queen, Grimhild tells her the truth about who deflowered her.

In the meantime, there are accounts of other warriors, including Waltharius's escape with Hildegund and Thidrek's flight from Ermanrik. The story of Sigurd and Brynhild resumes when, during a hunt, she convinces a Hogni, kingman and vassal of the Burgundian kings, to kill Sigurd.

Sigurd's body is returned to Grimhild, and after Hogni tells her that he has been killed by a wild boar, she says, "You and no other were that boar, Hogni."

Learning of Sigurd's death, King Attila sends his nephew, Duke Osid, to woo Grimhild on his behalf. The wedding takes place with much pomp and a great show of affection between Thidrek and Hogni, who has withheld Sigurd's treasure from Grimhild.

Seven years pass, and Grimhild asks Attila to invite her brothers for a visit and to help her get her rightful treasure back. Hogni suspects a trap and doesn't want to go to the land of the Huns, but Gunnar, believing Attila's message that he has grown too old to rule and wants someone to rule in his stead until his son comes of age, ignores Hogni's warning.

The Niflungs arrive and soon learn the true reason for the invitation. When Hogni refuses to turn over the treasure, Grimhild asks Thidrek to join forces in destroying the Niflungs. But Thidrek begs to remain neutral. A tremendous battle ensues, during which Grimhild sets fire to the hall. Eventually Thidrek, challenged by Hogni, must join the battle. He breathes flames on Hogni, forcing him to surrender. Thidrek reminds Attila of all the carnage Grimhild has caused and asks permission to kill her, which he does. (Hatto 1969)

THOR

In Norse mythology, Thor is the thunder or war god. In some traditions, he is the son of the great god Odin, and second only to him. Thor's most prized possessions are his magic returning hammer or thunderbolt Mjollnir, his belt of strength, and his iron gloves. When Thor's hammer falls into the hands of

Thor, hero of Norse mythology and son of Odin, wields his magic hammer and wears a belt of strength in a 1910 illustration by Arthur Rackham for *Das Rheingold,* an opera by Richard Wagner.

the giant Thrym, Thor retrieves it by disguising himself as the goddess Freyja. His chief enemy is Jormungandr, the evil serpent surrounding the world. On Doomsday (the Ragnarök), Thor and Jormungandr will slay each other. Thor appears throughout the *Poetic Edda.* (Hollander 1990)

See also *Edda, Poetic;* Freyja; Óthin.

THUNNUPA

(Also Tonapa Wirakocha Nipacachan)

In the creation cycle of the Aymara Indians of northern Chile and central Bolivia, after the creation of the world and of man, Thunnupa appears. He is a white man with a beard who comes from the north. He discourages man's practice of polygamy and opposes the use of chicha, the national drink of the Aymara. South of Cuzco, he brings forth the Cana nation, but the people, not recognizing him, attack him. He causes fire to fall from the sky, burning a mountain, and the people throw away their weapons and worship him. Thunnupa may have been a historical figure.

Two other tales concerning Tonapa are preserved in old manuscripts. In one, the deity is a wandering preacher whose life story has absorbed some details from the life of Jesus; in the other, he appears as a trickster called Koniraya Wirakocha. (Bierhorst 1988)

TIAMAT

In the Babylonian creation epic *Enuma Elish,* or War of the Gods, Tiamat is the primal seawaters, or primal chaos, mother of all gods and wife of the freshwater god Apsu. In a fight against the younger gods, Tiamat is slain by the warrior god Marduk, who severs her body in two, making heaven of the upper half and earth of the lower half. (Sproul 1991)

See also *Enuma Elish, Epic of.*

TIBETAN BOOK OF THE DEAD

See *Bardo Thötröl.*

TIMURID EPIC

This cycle of tales concerns the barbaric Turkic conqueror known in the West as Tammerlane (1336–1405). Timur comes from Kesh near Samarkaland and leads a band of nomadic warriors to subjugate tribes from Mongolia all the way westward to the Mediterranean. The Timurid dynasty becomes renowned for a revival of artistic and intellectual endeavors, resulting in many fine works of literature, art, and architecture. (Grousset 1970)

TIP-OF-THE-SINGLE-FEATHER

This is one of the Fijian "epic chants," which depict the heroic deeds of warriors and chiefs of the legendary kingdom of Flight-of-the-Chiefs, from whom the present chiefs and their people are said to be descended. The poem, composed by an old seer-poet named Velema, was recorded in the village of Namuavoivoi in the 1930s. The setting of the poem is the village of Flight-of-the-Chiefs, which is ruled by The-Eldest, father of Tip-of-the-Single-Feather. Before the poem opens, the hero Curve-of-the-Whale-Tooth has asked his kinsman The-Eldest to help him make a formal gift to the king of Rotuma.

The poem opens as a large contingent prepares to depart. The-Eldest instructs his son and Curve-of-the-Whale-Tooth to bring a felled poplar for the ship's mast. When the poplar arrives, The-Eldest commands that it be set up and the ship launched. The boat sets out for Rotuma, but sailing is delayed because of lack of wind. The chief commands Curve-of-the-Whale-Tooth to climb the mast and learn their location. Curve-of-the-Whale-Tooth spies a hurricane, but the chief decides to ride with it to Rotuma. As the winds approach, The-Eldest makes preparations, placing his best sailors in key positions. But Branch-of-the-Red-Nettle slackens his hold on the mainsail so that it swings out and drags in the water. Tip-of-the-Single-Feather, at the tiller oar, wants to take full advantage of the wind and commands Branch-of-the-Red-Nettle to shorten the mainsail. But it drags more deeply into the water, submerging the forward point and dragging the bow to the bottom of the sea, where it becomes lodged among rocks. The stern is still above water, and the men take refuge upon it. The people are stricken with terror. They dive repeatedly to try to dislodge the boat, but to no avail. Tip-of-the-Single-Feather is called, but after he fails, he tells his father, "In the light of this day we shall die. / It is our custom to father only on dry land; / Sometimes we fall by the spear, but some of us live on. / Now all of us are forever finished!"

The-Eldest suggests they dress in ceremonial regalia pleasing to their ancestors. He commands Curve-of-the-Whale-Tooth to attempt what his own son has failed to accomplish. Curve-of-the-Whale-Tooth dresses himself in a manner pleasing to his ancestors and dives in. He succeeds in bringing the ship's bow to the surface. As they prepare to tack, Curve-of-the-Whale-Tooth is so arrogant that Tip-of-the-Single-Feather refuses to cooperate. During their argument, the mast is broken. Curve-of-the-Whale-Tooth is so discouraged that he retreats below and feigns sleep. The-Eldest punishes his son by ordering him to scull the ship to Rotuma and then to set anchor.

As Tip-of-the-Single-Feather carries the anchor to shore, he sees King Rotuma leaning down to wash himself. Still fuming with jealousy against Curve-of-the-Whale-Tooth, he kills King Rotuma and brings his legs back to the ship as cleats to mend the broken mast. The-Eldest is dismayed at his son's arrogance. He carries a gift of whale teeth and humiliates himself before Curve-of-the- Whale-Tooth, who grieves over the death of his kinsman but then realizes that there is no longer any reason to present a gift to the Rotumans. He suggests that they destroy Rotuma to avoid retribution by its inhabitants for the death of their king. The-Eldest orders the attack, and his men hurry to the beach to meet the men of Rotuma. But when they are faced with the Rotuma cannon, the men retreat to the ship. The-Eldest chides them for their cowardice and sends Branch-of-the-Red-Nettle ashore to engage in single combat with Rotuma warriors.

Branch-of-the-Red-Nettle meets the son of King Rotuma, Wind-of-the-Open-Sea, and is defeated by him. The-Eldest sends other warriors to face the king's son, but they are also defeated. At length he calls his son, Tip-of-the-Single-Feather, who circles behind the village and charges down upon the army, driving it back. Then the two leaders' sons meet each other in single combat. They charge each other and fight valiantly. During an intermission of the battle, Wind-of-the-Open-Sea retreats for a rest beside his house. While he is resting, he sees a cousin approaching, Lemon-of-the-Sea, who does not know about King Rotuma's death. When the intermission is over, Lemon-of-the-Sea wounds Tip-of-the-Single-Feather, angering him and causing him to attack the opponents with his bare hands, as if they are not worthy of the respect of weapons. He tosses them into the air, and they land at the house of Watcher-of-the-Land, who devours them and commends Tip-of-the-Single-Feather for remembering to make offerings to him. "And the village at Rotuma is destroyed to emptiness. / And now the wild fowl flies upwards in the wild growth there." The-Eldest and his men return home, victorious. (Finnegan 1978)

TĪRTHAṄKARA

In the Jaina religion of India, a Tīrthaṅkara (Ford-maker) is a savior who has successfully crossed the stream of rebirths, leaving a path for others to follow. During each cosmic age, 24 Tīrthaṅkaras appear. If it is an age of descending purity, the first Tīrthaṅkara will be a giant, and each succeeding one will become smaller. In the present age, the last to appear was Mahāvira, great hero (sixth century B.C.), and no more will be born during this present time cycle. It is significant to note that all Tīrthaṅkaras, or Jinas (victors), are of the Kṣatriyas, or warrior caste. An occasional Tīrthaṅkara has been believed by some sects to be a woman: Mallinātha is so labeled by the Śvetāmbara sect. (Sproul 1991)

TITANS

In Greek cosmology, according to Hesiod's *Theogony,* Titans are the 12 sons and daughters of Uranus and Gaea, Heaven and Earth. (Lattimore 1959)

TITUS TATIUS

In the Roman legend of Romulus and Remus, Titus Tatius is the Sabine king who co-rules Rome with Romulus for a few years. (Frazer 1963)

See also Romulus and Remus.

TIWAT

(Also Istanu, Estan, and Shimegi)

In the Luwian religion of ancient Asia Minor, Tiwat is the sun god. Several Anatolian myths found in Hittite literature have to do with the disappearance of a god, which causes blight upon the earth. In one myth, the god Telipinu, son of the weather god Nerik, becomes angry and withdraws while the sun god, the weather god, and the grandmother Hannahanna search for him. In another version, it is the weather god who withdraws, and the search is conducted by the sun god and the weather god's father and grandparents. In another version, the sun god and Telipinu are seized by "Torpor," causing nature to become paralyzed. (Ceram 1990; Saggs 1978)

See also Telipinu.

TLALOC

Tlaloc is the Aztec rain god, ruler of the second world era. (Bierhorst 1974)

See also Tezcatlipoca; Tonatiuh.

TLAZOLTÉOTL

(Also Tlaelquarni)

Tlazoltéotl is the Aztec goddess of carnal love, known as Goddess of Impurity or Devourer of Filth. She is an aspect of Coatlicue, the great nurturer-destroyer earth goddess. (Bierhorst 1974)

See also Coatlicue.

TO-KARVUVU AND TO-KABINANA

These brothers are culture heroes of Melanesia whose stories appear throughout Oceania. In New Britain a god draws figures of men on the ground, then pricks himself with a knife and allows the blood to drip upon the figures. They come to life as To-Kabinana and To-Karvuvu. In another tale the two choose dark and light coconuts, which turn into handsome women. The women bear children, and To-Kabinana berates his brother for bringing in a dark-skinned woman: "You are indeed a stupid fellow. You have brought misery upon our mortal race. From now on, we shall be divided into two classes, into you and us." Later, he tells him again, "alas, you have only ruined our mortal race. If all of us were only light of skin, we should not die." He decrees that dark-skinned men shall marry dark-skinned women. And so he divides mankind into two classes. In another tale from New Britain, the brothers arise from the bloody bandages discarded by an old woman. There are tales of death and resurrection, making rain, and inventing fish. In most of the tales, To-Karvuvu is pictured as foolish or stupid, and responsible for most of the troubles of human life, while To-Kabinana is benevolent and well-intentioned, although often foiled by his brother. (Dixon 1964)

TOCHMARC FERB
("The Courtship of Ferb")

This tale from the *Ulster Cycle*, not directly related to the *Taín Bó Cúailnge*, relates how a son of Queen Medb and King Ailill, Maine Mórgor, woos Gerg's daughter. At the wedding feast, Conchobor kills both Gerg and Maine as well as their followers. (Kinsella 1969)

See also *Ulster Cycle.*

TOCI

Aztec goddess. ***See*** Coatlicue.

TOGAIL BRUIDNE DA-CHOCA
("The Ruin of Da-Choca's Hostel")

This *Ulster Cycle* tale tells of the struggle for succession following Conchobor's death. (Kinsella 1969)

See also *Ulster Cycle.*

TŌLUBOMMALĀṬA

This Telugu shadow-puppet tradition draws on the *Rāmāyaṇa* and the *Mahābhārata* for the major portion of its performances. Tōlubommalāṭa puppeteers present one-night performances that focus on a single episode from an epic, following the narrative structure closely, and reciting many verses directly from the classic text. For *Rāmāyaṇa* performances, they recite verses from the *Ranganātha Rāmāyaṇa* (ca. A.D. 1300, a version composed by a non-Brahmin prince in which Rāma's divinity is emphasized) and the *Bhaskara Rāmāyaṇa* (ca. 1400 by the legendary author Bhāskarācārya) and others. (Blackburn et al. 1989)

TONANTZIN
(Also Coatlicue)

Aztec earth mother goddess, she is also called Cihuacóatl, the goddess of childbirth. (Bierhorst 1974)

See also Coatlicue.

TONATIUH
(Also Ollin Tonatiuh)

Tonatiuh is the Aztec (Nahua) sun god, ruler over the present, or fifth, era. According to Aztec cosmology, the first era was ruled by the sun god Tezcatlipoca; the second by Quetzalcóatl in his aspect as wind god; the third by the rain god Tlaloc; and the fourth by the goddess of water, Chalchiuhtlicue. (Bierhorst 1974)

TOPILTZIN
(Our Dear Prince)

Topiltzin is another name for the Aztec hero-god Quetzalcóatl. (Bierhorst 1974)

See also *Quetzalcóatl, Topiltzin.*

TOSOL-GA

In the Korean *Samguk Sagi,* "Tosol-ga" is mentioned as a Korean poem (ca. first century) written during the reign of the Silla king Yuri (A.D. 24–57); however, the work itself has been lost. Historians have credited it as heralding the arrival of secular poetry. (Preminger 1990; Reischauer and Fairbank 1960)

See also *Samguk sagi* and *Samguk yusa.*

TOTEC
(Also Huitzilopochtli and Ilhuimecatl)

Aztec war god and son of Coatlicue, Totec is described in one section of the *Quetzalcóatl* as "an evil sorcerer," called upon to help defeat the Tollan. (Bierhorst 1974; León-Portilla 1982)

See also *Quetzalcóatl, Topiltzin;* Uitzilapochtli.

TRISTAN
(Also Tristram)

Tristan is the hero of the medieval love cycle *Tristan and Iseult.* His character and the cycle originated with a Celtic cycle about Drystan and Esyllt. Tristan is depicted as a handsome lover, great warrior, hunter and dragon-killer, and poet-musician. In the fifteenth century Malory made him a knight of the Round Table. (von Strassburg 1960)

See also *Tristan and Iseult.*

TRISTAN AND ISEULT
(Also Drystan and Esyllt)

This great medieval cycle of Celtic tales (ca. twelfth century) includes one of the world's greatest love stories. No complete version of the cycle has survived. The story revolves around the elopement of King Mark's nephew with his own Irish bride. The king sends Tristan to Ireland to accompany Iseult the Fair to Cornwall for the wedding. Along the way the two accidentally drink a love potion concocted by Iseult's mother and intended for the bride and groom. Thereafter Tristan and Iseult are bound by an eternal love. The lovers eventually part, and Tristan leaves for Brittany, where he marries another Iseult. When he is wounded by a poisoned spear, he sends for Iseult the Fair, who has healing skills that can save him. However, his jealous wife tells him that Iseult is not coming, and he dies of grief. When Iseult the Fair arrives to find him dead, she dies with him in her arms. From their graves spring two trees with intertwining branches.

Tristan und Isolde is the title of a medieval German epic (ca. 1210) by Gottfried von Strassburg, based on the same material. The story was translated into Old Norse (1226), and called *Tristams saga.* (Heer 1961; von Strassburg 1960)

See also Deirdre; "The Pursuit of Diamuid and Gráinne."

TROJAN HORSE

In the *Odyssey* (viii), the *Aeneid* (ii), and the *Cyclic Epics,* "The Little Iliad" and "The Sack of Ilium," the Trojan horse is a large wooden horse devised by Odysseus and built by Epeus inside which the Greeks are to hide. They pretend to desert the war, while Simon allows himself to be captured so he can convince the Trojans that the horse, as an offering to the goddess Athena, will make Troy impregnable. Cassandra and Laocoon warn against accepting the horse: "I fear the Greeks even when they bring gifts." But King Priam allows the horse to be brought inside the gates of Troy. At nightfall, Simon releases the Greeks hidden in the horse, and the gates of Troy are flung open to all the remaining Greeks to storm and sack the city. (Finnegan 1978; Humphries 1951; Rouse 1991)

See also *Aeneid; Epic Cycle; Odyssey.*

TROJAN WAR

This legendary conflict (ca. 1194–1184 B.C.) between the Aecheans and the Trojans forms the backdrop and material for the three great classical epics—*Iliad, Odyssey,* and *Aeneid*—as well as the *Cyclic Epics,* or *Epic Cycle.* (Finnegan 1978; Humphries 1951; Rouse 1990)

TS'AN NÜ

In the Chinese cultural hero myth of Huang Ti, the Yellow Emperor, Ts'an Nü is his wife, who teaches women to breed silkworms and to weave fabric from the silk thread. She is later canonized as Lady of the Silkworm, Ts'an Nü. (Reischauer and Fairbank 1960)

TSUNI-G//OAB

(Also Tsuni//goab)

In the mythology of the Khoisan people of the Kalahari Desert region of southern Africa, Tsuni-g//oab is the first deity from which all others arise.

Originally a man of great magical skills, he creates man and woman and many other things. He goes through a cycle of births and deaths, eventually becoming pure spirit, who can give life and rain. His adversary is G//aunab, the evil god of death, disease, and misfortunes. (Parrinder 1982; Peires 1982; Sproul 1991)

See also G//aunab.

TÚATHA DÉ DANANN

(Also Túatha Dé Danand, People of Danu)

In the Gaelic mythological cycle as found in *Leabhar Gabhala* (the Book of Invasions), the Túatha Dé Danann are one of the five original races to inhabit Ireland before the arrival of the Milesians, who are ancestors of the modern Irish. They defeat the people before them, the Fir Bolg. They score several victories over the pesky Fomorians, the most notable being the Battle of Moytura. However, the last invaders, the Sons of Mil, first defeat the Túatha, then worship them as gods. Among the Túatha heroes are Dagda (Dagdae), Lug, Mórrígan (Morrigaine or Morrigu), Manannán mac Lir (Manadán, son of Ler), and Ogma (Ogmae). The Túatha are relegated to the underworld, where they live to this day. Popular legend associates them with the fairies who still inhabit the Emerald Isle and who make a particular appearance on the eve of Samhain. (Evans-Wentz 1990; Hubert 1980)

See also Dagda; Lug; Manannán mac Lir; Mórrígan; Samhain.

TU'CHÜEH

(Also Orhon or Orkhon, Blue Turks or Kok Turk)

The Tu'chüeh are Turkish people who settled in Mongolia ca. the fourth to tenth centuries, and are the subject of the Orkhan inscriptions telling their epic history. In old Kosho-Tsaidam inscriptions, the Tu'chüeh call themselves Blue Turks (Kok Turk). The blue comes from the Tängri, the sky, of which the Tu'chüeh khagans believe themselves to be the representative on earth. Literally, "Turk" means "strong." The ancestor of the Tu-chüeh is suckled by a she-wolf. When he grows to manhood, he mates with the she-wolf and has ten sons, born in the wolf cave. The Tu-chüeh decorate their flag with wolves because "Being born of a she-wolf, they do not want to forget their ancient origin."

The Turkic universe consists of many levels: The 17 upper ones form the realm of light, or heaven; the seven or nine lowest ones form the underworld; and in between is earth, where man dwells. At the highest level, Tängri dwells. Tängri is a god who denotes both heaven and hell. At other upper levels the virtuous souls dwell, and the evil souls are relegated to the underworld. An important goddess is Umai, goddess of childbirth. Numerous genies inhabit the earth and waters.

The first great hero is Bumin, who, in payment for assisting the Mongolian Juan-juan khagan A-na-kuei (ca. 546), asks for the hand of a Juan-juan princess.

When the khagan refuses, Bumin allies himself with the Hsi-Wei dynasty of northwest China, which awards him the hand of one of its princesses. The combined force encircles the Juan-juan Mongols and drives the khagan to suicide (552). Bumin assumes the Juan-juan khaganate, but only a year later he dies. His possessions are divided between his two sons. Mu-han receives Mongolia and the title of khagan; Istami receives the western nomadic khanate with its summer camp north of Kara Shahr and its winter camp in the Talas Valley or on the shores of the Issyk Kul. Thus are established the two arms of the Turkish empire. (Grousset 1970)

TUISTO

Tuisto is an ancient god of German creation myth. According to Tacitus's *Germania* (A.D. 98), songs that were ancient in his time told of the Germans' descent from the three sons of Mannus, the offspring of the "earth-born god" Tuisto, the son of Earth. The sons formed three groups: the Ingaevones, "the people nearest the Ocean," to the north; the Herminones to the interior; and the Istaevones, probably those near the Rhine. The first to cross the Rhine and oust the Gauls were called Germans. Tacitus says that Herakles once visited them, so "they chant his praises before those of other heroes on their way to battle." (Campbell *Occidental* 1976)

TUKULTI-NINURTA EPIC

One of only two extant epics of Assyrian origin, the epic commemorates a victory by Tukulti-Ninurta I (r. ca. 1244–ca. 1208 B.C.), who calls himself "the one whose name the god Ashur and the great gods faithfully called, the one to whom they gave the four quarters to administer, and the one to whom they entrusted their dominion." The epic is an account of the clash between Assyria's Tukulti-Ninurta I and Kashtiliash IV (r. ca. 1242–ca. 1235 B.C.), ruler of the Kassites (Babylonia) to the southeast, by the Persian Gulf. According to the epic, it is Kashtiliash who violates the peace by launching raids into Assyria. Tukulti-Ninurta (who in reality has already subjugated several peoples to the north) nevertheless, according to the epic, tries to settle the dispute by diplomacy, but the arrogant Babylonian king leaves him no alternative but war. Tikulti-Ninurta sacks and loots Babylon and its temple (ca. 1225 B.C.), the king is deposed, and for seven years the country is ruled by governors. The epic served the purpose not only of fostering national pride, but also of providing divine blessing for the sacking of a holy city. The epic relates how the gods of Babylon, led by Marduk, express their disapproval of Kashtiliash for his behavior and withdraw from their cities, abandoning him completely. In actuality, Tukulti-Ninurta took the image of Marduk away to Ashur, where it remained for almost 100 years, even after Babylon regained independence. (Saggs 1990)

A relief shows Tukulti-Ninurta, hero of the thirteenth-century B.C. Assyrian epic, approaching and then kneeling before an altar to the fire god Nasku.

TUMURIPO

This pre-Christian Hawaiian cycle of chants tells the Hawaiian story of creation. It was recorded in writing for the first time in the 1860s. The first nine chants recount the nine periods of creation. Many of the chants are chants of "begets." The Tumuripo has been regarded by island royalty as the genealogical chant of the Kalakaua family, the last ruling family of the kingdom of Hawaii. (Melville 1990)

See also Ra'i Ra'i; Ta Rua.

TUPI-GUARANI

The Tupi-Guarani are South American Indians whose religious myth of the "land-without-evil" is responsible for their epic migrations. Over centuries they have moved from place to place in Bolivia, Paraguay, and particularly eastern Brazil, in search of the "land-without-evil," a paradise on earth. The migrations took place even before the arrival on the continent of the white man, although they may have increased since the sixteenth century. (Bierhorst 1988)

TURNUS

In the *Aeneid,* Turnus is the warrior king of the Rutuli (a tribe on the coast of Latium) when Aeneas arrives in Italy. He is Aeneas's rival for the hand of Latinus's daughter Lavinia. After Latinus betrothes her to Aeneas, Turnus marshals the Rutuli and the Latins in a war against Aeneas. When Aeneas clearly is to be the victor, Turnus's sister Juturna and Hera try to save Turnus, and the goddess Juno tries to protect him, but he refuses to declare a truce. Aeneas pursues him and, in single combat, kills him. (Humphries 1951)

TURPIN

Turpin is a legendary figure who appears as one of the 12 paladins in Charlemagne's entourage in the chansons de geste, including the *Song of Roland.* He is identified with the historical archbishop of Reims, Tilpin (fl. eighth century). (Harrison 1970)

See also *Chanson de Roland.*

TWELVE-TABLET POEM

The *Epic of Gilgamesh.* ***See*** *Gilgamesh, Epic of.*

TYPHON

(Also Typhoeus and Typhaon)

In Greek mythology, Typhon is the youngest son of Gaea (Ge, Earth) and a monster from Tartarus (the lowest netherworld). He is the father by Echidna of a number of monsters such as the Chimera, the Lernean Hydra, Ladon,

Orthrus, Cerberus, the Nemean Lion, and the Sphinx. He is taller than the tallest mountain and has a hundred fire-breathing-dragon heads. His body is covered with serpents. He attacks Zeus, cuts the sinews in his hands and feet, and imprisons him in a cave guarded by a dragon. Later Hermes and Pan rescue Zeus; Zeus defeats him with his thunderbolts and buries him under Mount Aetna. Typhon appears in the *Aeneid* (ix) and *Theogony.* (Humphries 1951; Lattimore 1959)

TÝR
(Also Tiw)

One of the most ancient of Germanic gods, Týr is the one-handed god of justice and treaties. In the most famous myth of Týr, as a show of good faith he places his hand in the jaws of the wolf Fenrir. The other gods, pretending to be otherwise occupied in sports, suddenly bind the wolf. When Fenrir realizes he has been tricked, he bites off Týr's hand. By the time of Old Norse literature, stories of Týr, who had probably been a major god in earlier times, were all but forgotten. Norse poetry has him as the son of Óthin (Odin), although one poem makes him the son of a giant. In the Ragnarök (Doomsday), he and the wolf Garmr will slay each other. (Jones, G. 1990)

TYUSNINCHIS, THE TALES OF

In this cycle of oral tales of the Yura Indians of southern Bolivia, "Tyusninchis and the Chullpas" tells of the destruction of the Chullpas culture. Before this world, people lived and worked in a dark world. Their principal divinity was the goddess, the Moon. Tyusninchis, the Sun, appears and destroys the ancient dark world and the Chullpas culture, creating a new earth to be peopled by the ancestors of the Yuras. The people make their offerings to Tyusninchis and to Pacha Mama (Earth Mother).

In "Tyusninchis and the Yawlis" Tyusninchis takes on human characteristics; he is the culture hero representing the Yura people. He lives in the world as a (powerful) child, and his presence angers a group of Yawlis (devils) on horseback who set out to destroy him. One day as he flees from the Yawlis, he passes a field where a man is planting. He asks, "What are you doing there?" The man is ill-tempered and snaps, "What's it look like I'm doing? I'm planting." Tyusninchis travels on until he finds another man planting in a field. When he asks the same question of this man, he receives a courteous reply: "Oh, my lord, I'm planting all the things we eat, maize, potatoes, oqa, broad beans." Tyusninchis is pleased with the answer and instructs the man to tell the Yawlis that he has seen Tyusninchis while he was planting. When the first farmer goes to his field the next day, he finds nothing but rocks everywhere. When the second farmer goes to his field, he finds flourishing, full-grown crops. When the Yawlis come by, he tells them that while he was planting, he saw Tyusninchis. Seeing full-grown crops, the Yawlis presume, "That must have been months ago. Look, the field is ready to be harvested. Let's turn back; he has escaped us."

In another story, which may have historical precedence, "King Inca, the Spaniards, and the Mines," Tyusninchis becomes King Inca, another culture hero. Before the Spaniards arrive, gold and silver lie around on the ground like rocks for anyone to pick up. Then the Spaniards arrive and want to kill King Inca. He becomes angry, orders all the precious metals to disappear inside the mountains, and goes away, leaving only his staff. He will never come back, but the miners sometimes pour libations to him. (Hill 1989)

U

UCHA ARUODO

An oral epic song of the Ohafia people in Nigeria, West Africa, it is the legend of Ucha Aruodo who, in her old age, gives birth to a girl, her only child. She has great difficulty fending for the child. Ucha Aruodo is also the name of the mother of the returning war hero Egbele, in the Ohafia legend of the same name. (Azuonye *RAL* 1990)

UDUDI

In *Watunna,* the creation cycle of the Makiritare Indians of the Orinoco River in Venezuela, Ududi is a hairy dwarf who serves the master of evil, Odosha, who created him. (Civrieux 1980)

See also *Watunna.*

UITZILAPOCHTLI

(Also Huitzilopochtli)

Uitzilapochtli is the Aztec sun and war god. His mother, Coatlicue, finds a ball of hummingbird feathers (the soul of a warrior) that has fallen from the sky. She keeps them in her bosom until Uitzilapochtli is born. He is believed to be the leader who brings the Aztecs from their traditional home, Aztlan, to the Valley of Mexico. (Bierhorst 1974; León-Portilla 1982)

See also Coatlicue; *Quetzalcóatl, Tipiltzin;* Totec.

UKE-MOCHI NO KAMI

(Also Uka no mi-tama no Mikoto, Food August-Spirit)

In Shinto mythology, in the *Nihongi* chronicles, Uke-mochi no kami is the Japanese food goddess. The name means "Goddess Who Possesses Food." In one *Nihongi* version, Izanagi no Mikoto and Izanami no Mikoto, having created the eight-island land, create a God of the Wind, then a Food August-Spirit. Another story in the *Nihongi* tells of Ama-terasu, who is in Heaven, commanding the Moon God Tsuki-yomi no Mikoto to go down to the reed plains and wait upon the Food Goddess. As soon as Tsuki-yomi arrives on the reed plains,

Uke-mochi turns her head toward the land, and from her mouth pours boiled rice. She faces the sea, and from her mouth come "things broad of fin and things narrow of fin." When she faces the mountains, things pour forth "rough of hair and things soft of hair." These things are all prepared and set on 100 tables for the visiting Moon God.

But Tsuki-yomi becomes flushed with anger and says, "Filthy! Nasty! That thou shouldst dare to feed me with things disgorged from thy mouth." He draws his sword and slays her. His act angers Ama-terasu, who berates him, "Thou art a wicked Deity. I must not see thee face to face." So the two are parted, separated by one day and one night.

Next she sends Ame-kuma-bito, the Messenger of the Gods, to go to the reed plains to see Uke-mochi. She is dead, but on the crown of her head have been produced the ox and the horse; on her forehead millet has been produced; over her eyebrows, the silkworm has been produced; within her eyes has been produced panic; in her belly, rice has been produced; in her genitals have been produced wheat and large and small beans. The messenger carries all these things back to Ama-terasu, and she rejoices. "These are the things which the race of visible men will eat and live." (Aston 1972)

See also Izanagi and Izanami; *Nihongi.*

UKKO

(Also Jumala, Heaven God)

Ukko is the Finnish god of thunder, said to dwell in the navel of the sky. He is prominent in the *Kalevala,* appearing in poems 1, 9, 12, 14, 17, 18, 19, 26, 28, 32, 33, 36, 40, 42, 43, 45, 47, and 48. (Lönnrot 1963)

ULAID CYCLE

Gaelic heroic cycle. ***See*** *Ulster Cycle.*

ÜLIGERS

Mongolian orally transmitted epics, they relate the adventures of heroes including Genghiz-khan, Erintsen Mergen, Shansi Tatung governor Engke Bolod-khan (Bolod Temur), and Geser-khan. Geser-khan is the Tibetan king and magic hero who is also the subject of the great Tibetan epic *Rgal-po Ge-sar dgra-'dul gyi rtogs-pa brjod-pa* (The Great Deeds of King Gesar, Destroyer of Enemies; *Gesar Saga).* The Üligers are composed of as many as 20,000 lines or more, in alliterative couplets or quatrains, and are still recited by bards from memory. With few exceptions, Mongolian bards come from the common people rather than from the nobility. Although the characters are historical, the situations are fantasy; the Üligers have in common as a villain the Manggus, a terrible many-headed dragon, always slain by the hero. (Finnegan 1978)

See also *Gesar's Saga*; *Kesar Saga*; *Zong Belegt Baatar*.

ULIXES

Ulixes is the Latin name for Odysseus, hero of the *Odyssey.*

ULL

(Also Ullr)

In Norse mythology, Ull is the handsome warrior-god of hunting, the bow, shield, and snowshoes who is frequently summoned to help in hand-to-hand combat. (Jones, G. 1990)

ULLIKUMMI

In the ancient Hurrian mythological work *Theogony,* written in Hittite, Ullikummi is a stone monster who rises out of the sea to challenge Teshub in the story *Song of Ullikummi.* The monster is the creation of the Hurrian third king of the gods Kumarbi, who hopes to depose Teshub using Ullikummi as his champion. (Preminger 1990)

See also *Song of Ullikummi.*

ULSTER CYCLE

In ancient Gaelic literature, the *Ulster Cycle* is a group of pagan sagas, legends, and romantic tales that survive in the twelfth-century manuscripts *Leabhar na h-Uidre, The Book of the Dun Cow* (ca. 1100) and *The Book of Leinster* (ca. 1160), as well as in the *Yellow Book of Lecan* (fourteenth century). However, the stories deal with the heroic age of the Ulaids, who peopled northeastern Ireland in the first century B.C. Heroic adventures are set in the reigns of two kings: King Conchobar mac Nessa and his knights of the Red Branch in the Ulster capital of Emain Macha, near present-day Armagh, and King Ailill and Queen Medb (Maeve) of Connaught. Other characters in the cycle include Bricriu Poison-Tongue, Cathbad the Druid, Conall Cernach, Conaire, Cú Chulainn (the greatest hero of all), Cu Roi, Da Derga, Deirdre, Emer, Etain, Fergus, Finnabair, Mac Da Thó, and Noísiu. The stories combine prose narrative with verse interspersed. The centerpiece of the cycle is the epiclike tale *Taín Bó Cúailnge* (Cattle Raid of Cooley). Several other tales concern aspects of Cú Chulainn's life. *The Death of Aife's Only Son* describes a duel between father and son in which Cú Chulainn unknowingly slays his own son, a theme that appears in other stories elsewhere in the world, as in the story of Rostam in the *Shāh-Nāmah.* The tale *Bricriu's Feast* describes the beheading game that appears later in *Sir Gawain and the Green Knight.* The story of Deirdre's elopement, found in *Fate of the Sons of Usnech* (Oidheadh Chloinne Uisneach), parallels the *Tristan and Iseult* legend. (Kinsella 1969)

See also *The Cattle Raid of Cooley; Taín Bó Cúailnge.*

ULYSSES

Ulysses is the English name for Odysseus, hero of the *Odyssey* and an important player in the *Iliad*.

See also Odysseus.

UMI-NO-KAMI

In Japanese mythology, in the *Nihongi* Chronicles, Umi-no-kami is God of the Ocean. (Aston 1972)

UMSILIGASI

(Also Mzilikazi and Mozelekatse)

In the Zulu epic *Emperor Shaka the Great,* Umsiligasi is called Mzilikazi and is described as a great Bantu general, leader of the Khumalos. He later broke away and migrated with his people to present-day Zimbabwe, where he founded the Ndebele kingdom (1823 to ca. 1840). He withstood an attack from the Transvaal and forced the South Africans to a peaceful settlement. A local oral tradition has grown around his exploits. (Kunene 1979)

UNCEGILA'S SEVENTH SPOT

(Also *Unktehi)*

Legend of the Brule Sioux recited in 1968 in South Dakota by George Eagle Elk, a Yuwipi medicine man. The story concerns a time when the earth is young, and an evil witch is transformed into a huge snakelike monster named Uncegila. She has one weak spot, the seventh spot behind her head, where lies her ice-cold heart.

Many brave warriors want to kill her, not only to put an end to her evil deeds but to acquire her sparkling heart, which gives great power to whoever owns it. But one look at her causes blindness, then madness, and finally death.

Two brave brothers, one of them blind, discuss killing the monster, and the blind boy says he can kill her if his brother will lead him to her lair. He knows of an Old Ugly Woman in the Paha Sapa (the Black Hills) who has magic arrows that never miss their mark.

The boys set out to find the Old Ugly Woman, who lives in a remote cave. She agrees to give them the arrows if one of them will sleep with her. The blind one, who cannot see how ugly she is, agrees: "I'll sacrifice myself."

But as he embraces her, she turns into a beautiful young girl. She thanks him for freeing her from her wrinkled outer shell. When the other brother returns, he too wants to sleep with her. But she rejects him because he rejected her when she was ugly.

The brothers stay for four days, while the Young Pretty Woman prepares four arrows. When they are ready, she tells the boys, "Be careful when you cut out Uncegila's heart; it's so cold that it will burn your hands right off." She advises them to make leather gauntlets to wear. She also warns them, "The heart will speak, asking you for four things. You must refuse four times; but after that, you must do as the heart wishes." She also commands them to share the power they receive. And to the blind boy, she promises: "One day you will see again. Then come back to me."

The boys travel for many days until they come to a dark lake. Soon Uncegila bursts forth from the foaming water, and the blind brother shoots the four arrows directly into the seventh spot. The monster writhes and groans while the water turns to blood and boils. At last the monster grows still, and the older brother rushes over to take out its icy heart, being careful to first put on his leather gauntlets. He has the sensation of great power emanating from the heart.

The heart speaks, commanding, "Don't cut the horn off my head." But remembering the caution of the Young Pretty Woman, he cuts the horn off at once, or the monster will come to life again. The heart asks him to stick the tip of the horn into his wound, but the brother refuses. The heart tells them to cut a piece of his flesh, roast and eat it, but the boys refuse, for the flesh contains poison. The monster tells them to make a trail of tobacco around the lake's edge, but they refuse, for the tobacco will draw all of Uncegila's monster children.

The blind brother says, "We have refused four times. . . . From now on we must fulfill its requests." So when the heart commands, "Blind one, put some of my blood on your eyelids," he obeys. At once new eyes are formed, and the boy can see.

The boys take the heart back to camp, but they soon become burdened by its power. They can foretell the future. Their house is always full of meat. They are irresistible to women. Soon they are made chiefs. The older brother takes four wives and has many strong sons. But the younger brother still pines for the Young Pretty Woman. He asks his brother to lead him to her cave.

But when they arrive, the cave is gone, and there is no trace of the woman. They return to camp, and the younger brother says, "I'm tired of power; I want to be like other men."

The older brother agrees. "I'm tired of feeding the monster's heart and carrying out its endless wishes." He remembers that the Young Pretty Woman has warned them not to let anyone else set eyes on it or the power will be taken away, so they call in the whole village to look at the heart. At once the heart screams and bursts into flame, consuming itself. The younger brother says, "I feel much better now." The older brother says he is relieved to have the heavy burden removed. Now they both live as other men, taking the bad with the good. (Erdoes and Ortiz 1984)

UNTAMO

In poem 5 of the *Kalevala,* Untamo is a spirit of sleep; in poem 26, he is the name of the owner of some wolves; in poems 31, 34, 35, and 36, as Untamoinen, or Unto, he is Kalervo's brother, with whom he feuds and on whom his nephew

Kullervo wreaks vengeance. Poem 15 mentions Untamo's farm, with which Soppy Hat is associated; this does not appear to be associated with the other Untamos, nor do the farms appear in poems 31 and 36. (Lönnrot 1963)

See also *Kalevala.*

UNUARTO

Unuarto is a culture-hero myth of the Arapaço Indians of the Vaupés basin in the Brazilian Amazon region. The story is told in three parts.

In part 1, Unuarto is the offspring of an illicit union between Dia Pino, a water snake who transforms himself into a man, and a human woman referred to only as Iapo's wife. Iapo finds the lovers together and shoots Dia Pino with a poison blowgun. His body falls into the river and becomes a snake again. Iapo goes fishing and catches, among the fishes, Dia Pino. He cuts off the snake's penis, wraps it with his wife's fish, and tricks her into eating it. Then he plays on his flute a melody that means, "She ended up eating that which she loved most." The wife understands and rushes to the river to drink much water. A kind of fish, like a snake, floats from her mouth, and she believes that the penis has left her body.

But she is pregnant, and the being is not a human. She tells him, "Don't speak, you are not people." When it is time to give birth, the being comes out of her mouth, but the son leaves his tail there, so as not to lose connection with his mother. But while he goes out to climb in the trees, she plots how to get rid of him. She leaves in a canoe, but he flies through the sky until he reaches her house. He lies above her house while, inside, her family expels her, wanting nothing to do with her. She leaves, enters the water, and becomes a fish.

In part 2, Unuarto, who is human by night, journeys downriver to the white city of Manaus, where he socializes with the people. By day, he returns to the river, becoming a snake. But he prefers being human, so he decides to sacrifice his divinity, associated with his father. He asks a white man to meet him at the river one night with a hen's egg, some whiskey, and a gun, the last two being symbols of the white man's world. The white man is to throw the egg at him so that he will become human. But when Unuarto swims up to meet him as a snake, the white man shoots him with the gun.

In part 3, Unuarto, who has sacrificed his divinity, becomes a construction worker in Brasilia. Then, in the form of a submarine laden with weapons and machinery, Unuarto swims upriver. Now, underwater, the snake-beings are building an enormous city. The Arapaço are full of promise: "Now we are few, but he will give us back our prosperity, and our numbers." (Hill 1989)

UPELLURI

In Hittite mythology, in *Theogony,* Upelluri is a dull giant—the equivalent of Atlas—who stands in the middle of the ocean holding both heaven and earth upon his shoulder. When the gods separate the two with a magic knife, he does not notice, nor does he notice when Kumarbi places the still-growing stone monster Ullikummi upon his right shoulder. (Lattimore 1959)

See also *Song of Ullikummi; Theogony.*

'UQBAH IBN NAFI'

(Also Okba)

This semilegendary Islamic Qurayshite warrior plays a large part in the seventh-century raids into the Maghrib (Western Land) of North Africa. In ca. 670 he swoops into Ifriqiyah, present-day Tunisia, and founds al-Quayrawan (Kairouan), which soon becomes the Islamic military stronghold in the region, protecting the Muslims from the Berbers to the south and the Byzantines along the coast. In 683 Uqbah meets the Berber leader Kusaylah (Kassila) near Biskra, and is slain. His forces are defeated, and his stronghold of Ifriqiyah is overrun with Berbers, led by Kusaylah and Kahena (Kahina), queen of the Aures. It was later recaptured under the caliphship of 'Abd al-Malik. A regional oral tradition persists around the figure of 'Uqbah ibn Nafi', elevating him to near–patron-sainthood status in the Maghrib. Similarly, among the Berbers, an oral tradition still celebrates Kahena and Kassila. (Ben Khader and Soren 1987)

URANUS

(Also Heaven)

In Hesiod's *Theogony,* Uranus and Gaea (Earth) mate to create the Titans, the one-eyed Cyclopes, and the giants of 300 hands, the Hecatoncheires. Uranus is ashamed of his children and hides them in Gaea's body. The Titan Cronus answers his mother's call for vengeance and severs Uranus's testicles, thus separating Heaven and Earth. The drops of blood that fall upon her form the Three Furies (Erinyes), the Giants, and the Melian Nymphs who become Zeus's nurses. As the testicles float out to sea, Aphrodite rises from their foam. Elements of the story bear resemblance to stories in an earlier *Theogony* of the Hittites. (Lattimore 1959)

See also Cyclops; *Theogony.*

URASHIMA OF MIZUNOE

In this ancient Japanese legend, a young fisherman rescues an ancient tortoise, which becomes a beautiful princess, Otohime. Urashima returns with her to her underwater palace, but after three years he grows restless and wishes to return home. Otohime gives him a box and admonishes him not to open it, assuring his safe return to her. When he reaches his village, he discovers that 300 years have passed on earth. He forgets his promise and opens the box; he is enveloped in a white mist, which leaves him wrinkled, grey, and dead.

In another version of the story, the young man is sitting beneath a holy tree, and his image is reflected into a dragon well. The daughter of the dragon king, "Abundant Pearl Princess," appears and casts a spell upon him. He returns with her to the palace of the dragon king ("Abundant Pearl Prince"), where they live for three years. Then he becomes homesick for the world of men. She pleads with him not to return, but when she sees he is determined, she decides to accompany him. They return to earth, and he builds her a house by the seashore. When she becomes pregnant, she makes him vow not to look upon her until the baby is born. But he becomes curious and peeks into her bedchamber, to discover that she has become a dragon. As soon as the child is born, she returns to the sea, never to be seen again. The story bears a resemblance to the story of Melusine. (Mackenzie 1990)

See also Melusine.

UṢAS

In the *Ṛg Veda* of India, a number of hymns are addressed to Uṣas, daughter of Dyaus (Sky), sister of Ratri (Night), and mother or consort of Sūrya (Sun). She is the goddess of dawn, who at night's end rides a chariot in the sky to awaken the world. (O'Flaherty *Veda* 1981)

USUKUNKYUM
(Also Sukum)

In Mayan cosmology as practiced by present-day Lacandones, Usukunkyum is a god of the underworld in the center of the earth amid "much fire." He is brother to the sun, Nohotsakyum, who spends each night with him, being nourished and refreshed by sleep. Usukunkyum orders earthquakes and volcanoes, and punishes the sinful "by running hot irons up their penises." He protects his brother from Cizin (Kisin), god of earthquakes. The Lacandones preserve more of their original culture than any other Mayan group. (Toor 1947; Weyer n.d.)

UTENZI WA MWANA MANGA
(Lady from the North)

This famous 52-verse Swahili epic, handed down through oral tradition, is attributed to the poet-hero Fumo Liyongo (ca. ninth to thirteenth centuries). (Shariff *RAL* 1991)

See also Liyongo.

UTGARD-LOKI
(Also Utgartha-Loki)

In Norse myth, Utgard-Loki is chief of the giants in the stronghold of Utgard located at the northernmost edge of the universe, Jötunheim. Disguised as Skyrmir, Utgard-Loki leads three gods to Utgard: Loki, Thor, and Thjalfi. In "Gylfaginning" from the *Prose Edda,* Thor and Loki stop on the way to Utgard and spend the night with a farmer, Egil. Because someone in Egil's household does not follow Thor's instructions in the eating of the evening meal, Thor is angered. To appease him, Egil gives him his son Thjalfi and his daughter Roskva. Once they have arrived at Utgard, Fire, disguised as Loki, eats faster than Loki; Old Age, disguised as Elli, is stronger than Thor; and Thought, disguised as Hugi, runs faster than Thjalfi. Utgard-Loki confesses his trickery to Thor and quickly vanishes before he can be punished. (Young 1954)

UTNAPISHTIM

In the *Epic of Gilgamesh,* Utnapishtim is the Babylonian Noah, a distant kinsman of Gilgamesh whom the king seeks out so as to learn the secret of eternal life. Utnapishtim lives with his wife on an island beyond the ocean of death. He tells Gilgamesh the story of how he survived the Great Deluge, a story almost identical to the story of Noah and the Ark. As a reward for obeying the gods, he is given immortality. He tells Gilgamesh of a magic plant at the bottom of the sea that will restore youth. Gilgamesh finds the plant, but loses it to a serpent while he is bathing. The serpent eats the plant and returns to the sea. The character of Utnapishtim is probably derived from the Sumerian character Ziusudra. (Sandars 1972)

See also Flood Myths; *Gilgamesh, Epic of;* Noah; Ziusudra.

UTU

In Mesopotamian religion, Utu is the Sumero-Akkadian god of the sun and of justice, son of the moon god Nanna and Ningal, husband of Shenirda, and father of Shakan, god of goats and goatherds. In the Sumerian epic *Enmerkar and the Lord of Aratta,* Enmerkar is called "the son of Utu." In *Gilgamesh and the Land of the Living,* before Gilgamesh sets out for the cedar land, he is advised to tell Utu, who is in charge of the cedar land. Utu is ultimately convinced to aid Gilgamesh by immobilizing the seven weather demons so that Gilgamesh can reach his destination. Utu is identified with the Akkadian sun god Shamash. (Kramer 1956)

See also *Enmerkar and the Lord of Aratta, Epic of; Gilgamesh, Sumerian Poems;* Shamash.

VĀC

(Word)

In the *Purāṇas,* Vāc is the Hindu goddess of speech, whose main flaw is ugliness. In the *Ṛg Veda* hymn "The Rape and Return of the Brahmin's Wife," Sāyaṇa says, "Speech was the wife of Bṛhaspati. One day she offended him because she was so ugly, and so he abandoned her. Then the gods . . . made her free from offense (ugliness) and gave her back to Bṛhaspati." (O'Flaherty *Veda* 1981)

VAFTHRÚÐNISMÁL

("The Lay or the Words of Vafthrúdnir")

In the Norse epic Elder or *Poetic Edda,* the wise giant Vafthrúdnir is tested by Óthin, in disguise as Gagnráth, to see if the giant's wisdom is as great as his own. After an initial round of questions, the giant proposes another round with the loser forfeiting his head. In answer to Óthin's questions, the giant tells how the earth was shaped from Ymir's flesh. He tells of the oldest giant of all, Aurgelmir, who is formed when drops of poison fall from the waters Eliagar. From one of his legs a six-headed boy grows; from under his arm grow a maiden and a youth. Óthin finally asks the unanswerable question, "What did Óthin whisper . . . in the ear of his son, / ere Baldr on bale was laid?" Too late, Vafthrúdnir recognizes his opponent and admits, "Of all beings thou art born wisest." (Hollander *Edda* 1990)

See also *Edda, Poetic.*

VÄINÄMÖINEN

(Also Wäinamöinen)

In the Finnish epic *Kalevala,* and in ancient Finnish myth, Väinämöinen is chief of three heroes, sons of Kalevala, the other two being Ilmarinen and Lemminkäinen. He is the most revered because of his wisdom, his strength, and his magical songs, accompanied on the kantele (haro). He has been called the

Finnish Orpheus. The name Väinämöinen actually means "Man of Slack Water Farm." (Lönnrot 1963)

See also Ilmarinen; *Kalevala;* Lemminkäinen.

VÄKĪ

The väkī is a supernatural power that Baltic Finns believe attaches itself to natural or historic sites, objects, and even animals, all of which have evoked strong emotions for some reason, thus attracting the väkī. They are actually spiritual entities, which gifted seers can recognize. Any number of these spirits appear in the *Kalevala.* (Lönnrot 1963)

VALHALLA
(Also Valhöll)

In Norse myth, in the *Poetic Edda,* particularly in "Grímnismál" and in the "Lay of Hyndla," Valhalla is the Hall of the Slain, domicile of the valiant dead, the palace in Ásgard (heaven) for warriors (einherjar) slain in battle, presided over by the god Óthin (Odin), who increases their number because he needs them at his side at the Ragnarök (Doomsday). It is a magnificent hall where warriors can feast every night and never run out of food and drink, and can fight every day, a treat that is mentioned in the "Second Lay of Helgi." When Ragnarök comes, they will fight the giants. (Hollander *Edda* 1990)

See also *Edda, Poetic.*

VALKYRIES
(Choosers of the Slain)

In Norse myth, and mentioned throughout the *Poetic Edda,* Valkyries are the maidens who attend Óthin (Odin) and are sent by him to the battlefields to choose the slain warriors heroic enough to be worthy of a place in Valhalla. The most famous Valkyrie is Brunhild of *Völsunga Saga.* (Hollander *Edda* 1990)

See also *Edda, Poetic; Völsunga Saga.*

VĀLMĪKI

Legendary author of the *Rāmāyaṇa* and inventor of poetry, Vālmīki, in the closing stanzas of the epic, is depicted as seeking the True before he ever becomes a poet. He sings, "I'm still myself, I'm me. / Here is the True, have no fear; / This is for you, for you are dear / To me; I'm still myself." He is said to have composed the *Rāmāyaṇa* after seeing a hunter's arrow fell a mating bird, and "from soka flowed sloka" (from sorrow flowed the poetry). According to legend, born a Brahmin, he makes his way as a thief until Nārada ("a meddlesome sage," messenger between gods and men) sets him on the right path. (Buck 1976)

See also *Rāmāyaṇa.*

VĀMANA

In Hindu religious myth, Vāmana is a dwarf, the fifth of the ten avatars of the god Viṣṇu. He appears while the demon-king Bali rules the universe, having sapped the gods' power. Vāmana requests that the king give him as much land as he can step over in three paces. Once the request is granted, the dwarf becomes a giant; he covers both the world and the mid-world with two steps, and with the third sends Bali to the underworld, ending his tyranny and restoring power to the gods. (Dimmitt and van Buitenen 1978)

VANIR

In Norse mythology, appearing throughout the *Poetic Edda,* Vanir is a benign race of nature gods who bestow fertility and good fortune. Their chief god is Njörd, husband of Skadi and father of Frey and Freya. When the giant gods Aesir torture their goddess Gullveig, they demand reparation, either in the form of elevated status, making them equal with the Aesir, or in the form of money. The Aesir not only do not comply with their demands, they declare war. The Vanir fight valiantly and victoriously. After an exchange of hostages—Njörd and Freyr leave to live with the Aesir, and Hoenir and Mimir come to dwell with the Vanir—the Vanir are received in Asgard. During the peace ceremony the two races mingle their saliva in one vessel, and from this is born the poet god Kvasir. (Hollander *Edda* 1990; Jones, G. 1990)

See also *Edda, Poetic.*

VARĀHA
(Boar or Swine)

Varāha is the third of the ten avatars of the Hindu god Viṣṇu. His myth is the equivalent of the earlier Vedic creation myth of Prajāpati, who takes on the shape of a boar to lift the earth out of the "ocean of Doomsday." In the later version in the *Purāṇas,* the demon Hiraṇyākṣa (Golden Eye; also called Hiranyanetra or Hiranyalocana), takes the earth to the bottom of the sea ("the vast ocean of dissolution"). Brahmā is awakened by the Siddhas to find his bed in the middle of the water. He thinks, "Where is that lovely lady, the broad earth, with her lofty mountains, her streams, towns, and forests?" He remembers Prajāpati and, assuming the form of a mighty boar, parts the water with his tusks and fights the demon. The war lasts for a thousand years, and he finally slays Hiraṇyākṣa. Then he emerges from the netherworld holding the earth aloft in his tusks. Having brought the earth to its proper place, he piles up mountains and makes all just as it was before. (Dimmitt and van Buitenen 1978; Fremantle and Trungpa 1987)

VARUṆA
(All-Enveloping)

In the *Ṛg Veda,* Varuṇa is the Hindu lord of the universe, guardian of sacred law and cosmic order. He despises falsehood and is known for inflicting diseases, particularly dropsy, upon sinners. In post-Vedic times he is god of the waters and guardian of the western quarter. The Zoroastrian god Ahura Mazda is his equivalent. (O'Flaherty *Vedic* 1981)

VE

In Scandinavian creation mythology as told in "Gylfaginning" in the *Prose Edda,* Ve is the brother of Óthin (Odin) and Vili, one of three creators of the world. He is responsible for giving senses to Aska and Embla, the first man and woman. The three brothers slay the demon monster Ymir and drown the entire race of frost giants in his blood. (Young 1954)

VED-AVA

Ved-ava is the Water Mother of the Mordvins of the Volga basin in the Mordvinian Republic, responsible for the bounty to fishermen, and for fertility of land beings as well. Among the Finns, she appears in the *Kalevala* as Vellamo, wife of Ahto, king of the waves; she is also known as Veen ema by Finns. Estonians know her as Vete-ema. She is usually pictured as a mermaid—half woman, half fish—with long, flowing hair. (Embree 1988; Lönnrot 1963)

See also *Kalevala.*

VELES
(Also Volos)

Veles is an early Slavic god of cattle. In the tenth century, Keivan princes took oaths in the names of Perun (god of thunder) and Veles. In Kiev, Boyan the minstrel was called the offspring of Veles. In northern Russia, Veles was the antagonist of Perun. In Christian times, the heir of Veles became St. Vlas. Eastern Slavs erected churches to St. Vlas over old sanctuaries of Veles. (Georgieva 1985)

VENANCIO CAMICO

The famous nineteenth-century millennarian leader Venancio Camico is the hero of an oral cycle of tales among the Wakuénai Indians in the Isana-Guainia drainage area of Venezuela, Brazil, and Colombia. The cycle developed as the Indians were trying to decide how to react to the white men's incursions upon their land and to their plans to develop the region in which the Indians lived. The cycle portrays Venancio as a symbol of the indigenous past, integrating within himself the trickster-creator Inapirrikuli, the primordial man Kuwaii, and powerful shamans (dzawinaitairi).

One tale, called "Venancio Christu and Tomás Funes," makes Venancio, who actually lived in the last century, victor over the tyrant Funes, who terrorized the Venezuelan Wakuénai during the 1920s. Three times Funes puts Venancio into a coffin, ties it shut with rope, nails it shut, weights it with stones, and throws it into the Acque River. Three times Venancio escapes. Funes decides that Venancio really is a saint. Venancio pronounces punishment on Funes, saying he will be killed by his own followers. Funes remains guilty until his death.

"Venancio's Annual Death and Resurrection" concerns the hero's announcement that he is leaving for his house in the sky. His wife tells his followers, "We have to wait for Venancio for two days, until late Sunday afternoon." She tells them to pray and to take care of his body during his spirit's absence. She informs the followers and some soldiers who come out of curiosity that there will be no dancing or drinking aguardiente until Venancio returns. But she forgets her promise and begins dancing with the soldiers on Saturday, instead of leading the people in prayer. When Venancio returns the next day, he asks her what she has been doing. "We prayed the whole time," she says. He punishes her by waiting until she falls ill; instead of healing her, he hands her a slip of paper that says she is permanently denied access to God. Then a devil with no lower body comes and makes love to her. When they finish, she also has no lower body and must dance with the devil forever, using her arms as legs.

Each year, Venancio dies for two days during Holy Week. He warns his followers not to cut wood during his absence, since it would break their souls in two. Three brothers discuss the matter, and one decides to test Venancio's claim. He breaks a piece of wood and nothing happens. He goes to sleep thinking that Venancio has lied. Venancio returns and questions the brothers, and he tells them that a group of men will come and kill them. Later the same day the brothers are killed. (Hill 1989)

VERALDEN-RADIEN

(Also Veralden-olmai, Ruler of the World)

Veralden-Radien, the Lapp creation and fertility deity, dwells closest to the starry heaven and is responsible for maintaining life, delivering the souls of soon-to-be-born infants to the goddess of childbirth Madar-ahkku (Madderakke), and delivering dead souls to Yabme-aimo, the land of the dead. He is often considered the equivalent of the Scandinavian fertility god Frey. He guards the pillar of heaven (mailmen stytto), which may be the inspiration for the Saxon pillar Irminsul, the World Pillar or Column of the Universe, destroyed by the Franks (eighth century). (Holmberg 1964; Weyer n.d.)

See also Madar-ahkku.

VERCELLI BOOK

(Also *Codex Vercellensis)*

This Old English manuscript (tenth century) contains the eighth-century Anglo-Saxon oral poem "The Dream of the Rood" and the poem "Andreas," both purportedly signed by Cynewulf, as well as a number of prose works and the fragment of a homiletic poem. The book was discovered in the library of the Cathedral of St. Andrew at Vercelli, Italy, in 1822. (Alexander, M. 1991)

VERGIL

Roman poet. *See* Virgil.

VÍGA-GLÚMS SAGA

This Icelandic folk saga (thirteenth century) purports to tell the life story of a poet and cruel chieftain named Víga-Glúm. His verses relate the committing of several ruthless murders, and brag of covering his guilt with obscure equivocal oaths. (Jones, G. 1990)

VILI

In Norse creation mythology, Vili, brother of Odin and Ve, is a mighty archer who slays the giant Ymir. The three create the world from Ymir's body. Vili bestows motion and reason upon Aska and Embla, the first man and woman. (Young 1954)

VIRA COCHA

In the Incan creation cycle as recorded in the *Huarochirí Manuscript,* Vira Cocha is one name for the culture hero–creator god who creates man from painted stone dolls. He begets more gods from himself, and these become local gods. When the "Origin People" surface to the earth from their underground caves, he establishes a pattern of living for them. Then the "Wilderness People" come, followed by "Wartime People." After each group of people, a flood appears, and Vira Cocha must re-create man after the flood subsides.

Vira Cocha also appears in the mythology of the Aymara Indians of northern Chile. He rises from Lake Titicaca, creates sky and earth, then man, and disappears under the waters. But man is disobedient, and Vira Cocha leads man to Tiahuanaco and turns him to stone. He re-creates man and this time gives him the sun, moon, and stars so that he will not have to live in darkness.

According to the *Huarochirí Manuscript,* when the Spaniards arrive they are called "Vira Cochas" by the Quechuan Indians. (Salomon and Urioste 1991)

VIRGIL
(Also Vergil)

This famous Roman poet (70–19 B.C.), born Publius Vergilius Maro, brought the legendary founding of Rome to the reader in the 12 books of the epic *Aeneid.* As a work that brings the reader to oral tradition, the *Aeneid,* which is considered a literary epic, is included in this volume. (Humphries 1951)

See also *Aeneid.*

THE VISION OF ADAMNÁN
(Also *Adhamhnán)*

In Irish Gaelic literature, *The Vision of Adamnán,* one of the earliest examples of medieval visions, is preserved in the *Leabhar na h-Uidhre* (Book of the Dun Cow, eleventh century). The prose narrative describes the journey, guided by an angel, of seventh-century Iona abbot Adamnán Ó Tinne's soul to the Land of the Saints ("a fertile and shining land"), the seven stages of purification, and the Land of Torment. (Jackson, K. 1971)

VIṢṆU
(the All-Pervader)

In Hinduism, Viṣṇu, originally a solar god during the Vedic period and later the supreme god, is closely identified with Kṛiṣṇa. He is also known as Vāsudeva, Acyuta, Hari, Jagannātha, Keśava, Mādhava, Madhusūdana, and Nārāyaṇa, among others—a total of 1,000 names in all. He is one of the most popular deities in Purāṇic mythology. While Brahmā is regarded as creator and Śiva as destroyer, Viṣṇu is seen as preserver of the world between each successive emergence and dissolution of the universe. The *Ṛg Veda* celebrates "that very manhood of (Viṣṇu) the savior who / gives not harm but bounty." Viṣṇu's spouse is Lakṣmī or Śrī, goddess of prosperity and good fortune. Another spouse is Bhūmidevi, Earth. Sometimes Viṣṇu and Lakṣmī appear to be a single god. He has had nine avatars (incarnations): the fish Matsya; the tortoise Kūrma; the boar Varāha; the man-lion Narasiṃha; the dwarf Vāmana; the human with an ax, Paraśurāma; the hero of the *Rāmāyaṇa,* Rāma; the divine cowherd of the *Bhagavata-Purāṇa,* Kṛiṣṇa (who is also Arjuna's friend and the charioteer in the *Rāmāyaṇa);* and the Buddha. There is one yet to come: Kalki, a winged white horse who will destroy all enemies of the natural cosmic order. (Dimmitt and van Buitenen 1978; O'Flaherty *Śiva* 1981)

The Hindu god Viṣṇu, represented in an Indian statue from about the fourteenth century, has nine incarnations or avatars and appears in the *Ṛg Veda* and *Bhāgavata-Purāṇa*.

VIŚVAKARMAN
(All-Maker)

In Hindu mythology, Viśvakarman was originally a name of Prajāpati, then of Tvaṣṭr (Architect), artisan of the gods, maker of divine implements. (O'Flaherty 1975)

VIŚVĀMITRA
(Friend of All)

In Hindu mythology, Viśvāmitra is a great sage, originally born as a kṣatriya (warrior), who vies with the sage Vasiṣṭha (Most Excellent) for his wishing-cow and becomes a Brahmin. The *Ṛg Veda,* which is divided into ten books (mandalas), each ascribed to a priestly family, ascribes one to Viśvāmitra and one to Vasiṣṭha. The Dasarajanya hymn, in portraying the battle of ten kings, says that it begins as a result of Bharata king Sudas replacing his chief priest Viśvāmitra with Vasiṣṭha. Viśvāmitra organizes the tribes to wage war upon Sudas. Among the ten are the five famous tribes of the Druhyu, Anu, Puru, Yadu, and Turvasas.

Viśvāmitra also appears in one myth as a king who becomes a Brahmin and, despite the gods, creates a new universe. (O'Flaherty 1975; O'Flaherty *Veda* 1981)

***See also** Ṛg Veda.*

VIŚVANTARA

In Buddhist mythology as told by the astrologer-sage Asita, King Viśvantara is a previous incarnation of Gautama Buddha. As crown prince he gains renown for his generosity, of which his father disapproves. He is banished to the forest, where he lives the life of an ascetic. He gives away his wife, his children, even his eyes, all of which are restored to him. His people demand that he return home to rule. In his subsequent reincarnation (ca. 500 B.C.), he is the infant bodhisattva Shakyamuni (Sakyamuni), the historical Siddhartha Gautama, "teacher of the Shakya (Sakya) clan," whose life, as Asita predicts, follows much the same early pattern until the time of his enlightenment. (Davids 1929; Kyokai 1978)

VODYANOY

Vodyanoy is a malevolent Slavic water spirit who preys on humans, intent on drowning them. Pan-Slavic traditional narrative poetry, including the oldest extant South Slavic form, the bugarštica, embodies various magical elements in accounts of what otherwise appear to be historical incidents. Duke Janko shoots a flying serpent (zmiju) in "Duke Janko Shoots a Serpent in the Air." Novak captures a fairy (vila) and marries her in "Fairy Wife." It is a fairy who informs Mother Margaret of the fate of her brother and son, who have not come home from fighting the Turks in "Mother Margaret." These spirits are kin to the Bulgarian deity Veles, or Volos. (Georgieva 1985; Miletich 1990)

See also Veles.

VOLODYMYR, GRAND PRINCE

(Also Vladimir)

Volodymyr is the subject of a cycle of twelfth-century Ukrainian epic poetry, lost since the sixteenth century, about the court of Volodymyr, similar to King Arthur's Round Table. (Dvornik 1962; Preminger 1990; Vernadsky 1959)

VÖLSUNGA SAGA

The most well-known Icelandic heroic saga (ca. 1270) of the fornaldar sogur (sagas of antiquity) genre, the *Völsunga Saga* describes deeds of heroes purported to have lived in pre-Icelandic times in Scandinavia and Germany. It is based on earlier heroic lays, such as those pre-nineteenth-century lays contained in the *Codex Regius,* which includes the *Poetic Edda.* Related works include the "Lays of Young Siegfried" (fifth or sixth century, possibly Frankish), three "Lays of the Fall of the Burgundians" (fifth-century Burgundian; fifth or sixth century, possibly Frankish; and eighth century, possibly Bavarian), "Lay of Siegfried and Brunhild" (sixth century, possibly Frankish), "Atlakviða" (ninth-century Norse), *Brot* (ca. 1100, Norse), two "Lays of Siegfried and Brunhild" (twelfth-century German), Epic *Diu Nôt* (ca. 1160, Austrian), *Nibelungenlied* (ca. 1205, Austrian), and *Thiđrekssaga* (thirteenth-century Norse). The *Völsunga* itself is the predecessor and chief source of the *Nibelungenlied,* as well as Wagner's *Der Ring des Nibelungenlied.* The saga is named for the hero Sigurd's (Siegfried's) grandfather, Völsung, who is the grandson of the god Odin (Óthin) and the father of Sigurd's father Sigmund.

Many years before the saga begins, the god Loki has stolen the gods' treasure and magic ring, and placed the dragon Fáfnir to guard the treasure. Now Sigurd, out on a heroic quest, slays the dragon and reclaims the treasure, riding the magic horse Grani, a gift from Odin. He soon meets a sleeping Valkyrie, Brunhild (Brynhild), whom he awakens. The two fall in love and become betrothed.

He rides out in search of other conquests, while Brunhild surrounds herself with a circle of fire until his return. He meets three Burgundian princes—Gunnar (Gunther), Gernot, and Kiselher—and their sister Gudrun (Kriemhild in *Nibelungenlied;* Grimhild in *Thiđrekssaga).* After he drinks a magic potion, he forgets Brunhild and falls in love with Gudrun. Sigurd agrees to help Gunnar win the hand of Brunhild in exchange for the hand of Gudrun.

Disguised as Gunnar, he rides through the circle of fire on his magic horse Grani and wins the love of Brunhild. The two friends, Gunnar and Sigurd, and their brides have a double wedding. Later the two women get into an argument, during which Gudrun reveals Sigurd's deception. Enraged, Brunhild arranges for Sigurd to be killed by Hagen and then commits suicide. The Burgundians now have the treasure, which Hagen hides in the Rhine.

At length Gudrun remarries, this time to Atli (Etzel or Attila the Hun). She bears him several sons. Atli wants the fabled treasure for himself and eventually a war breaks out. The Burgundian brothers die defending the treasure, refusing to the last to reveal where it has been hidden. Gudrun takes vengeance by killing Atli and his sons. (Hatto 1969; Siepmann 1987)

See also *Edda, Poetic; Nibelungenlied; Thiđrekssaga.*

VÖLUSPÁ

(Sybil's Prophecy)

This Old Scandinavian poem found in the Elder, or *Poetic Edda,* describes the beginning and prophesies the end of the world. (Hollander *Edda* 1990)

See also *Edda, Poetic.*

VORTIGERN

Vortigern was a ruler of Saxon Britain (ca. 425), first mentioned in Nennius's *Historia Brittonum,* and also cited by Geoffrey of Monmouth in *History of the Kings of Britain* and by Bede in *Ecclesiastical History.* He is the subject of many fabulous episodes, including those connected with the building of his citadel, the materials of which repeatedly disappear overnight. As Merlin prophesies to him, he is slain by the Jute brothers Hengest and Horsa, who invade England ca. 449 and enlist the help of the Picts to oust him. Horsa is believed killed in battle (455), while Hengest continues to rule Kent until 488. (Alcock 1979; Rutherford 1987)

THE VOYAGE OF BRÂN, SON OF FEBAL

(Also *Imran Brain)*

This is a Gaelic tale (seventh century) of the journeys of Brân and his men to a supernatural realm. It is preserved in the fifteenth-century *Yellow Book of Lecan.* Fragments appear in the most ancient of collections containing Old Irish romances, the *Leabhar na h-Uidhre (The Book of the Dun Cow,* ca. 1100). It tells in verse and prose the story of Brân, who one day hears strange music that lulls him to sleep. When he wakes, he finds a blossoming silver branch beside him. He takes it to the royal house, where a strange woman appears. She sings a song that begins, "A branch of the apple-tree from Emain / I bring. . . ." She tells the assemblage, "There is a distant isle, / Around which sea-horses glisten. . . ." When she finishes singing, the branch springs from Brân's hand to hers, and there is no strength in his hand to hold it. A fairy spell has been cast upon him.

The next day, still under the spell, he and his 27 men begin a voyage in a small coracle toward the setting sun. Along the way he meets King Manannan riding over the waves in his magic chariot, on his way home to Ireland after a long absence. Brân and his men sail on until they reach the Island of Joy, where one man is put ashore. They go on to the next island, the Land of Women, where the queen uses a magic claw to draw the men to her realm. She entertains them for what they think is no more than a year, but it chances to be many years.

The men decide to return home, but they are warned not to set foot on earth until they have been sprinkled with holy water. They sail away and arrive at the harbor of Scrub Brain, where a group of people stand. When Brân tells them who he is, they answer, "We do not know such a man, though the Voyage of Brân is in our ancient stories."

In his eagerness to get ashore, one of the men forgets the warning and leaps out of the boat. As soon as he touches the earth of Ireland, he becomes a heap of ashes, as if he has been on the earth for many hundreds of years. Brân then tells the gathering his story. "And he wrote these quatrains in Ogam, and then bade them farewell. And from that hour his wanderings are not known." (Evans-Wentz 1990; Meyer 1987)

See also Brân.

VṚTRA
(Restrainer)

In Hindu mythology from Vedic times, Vṛtra is a dragon who prevents the monsoon rains from coming. The *Ṛg Veda* tale "Indra Slays Vṛtra and Releases the Waters" is the account of Indra's "rejoicing in his virility like a bull," taking up the thunderbolt fashioned for him by Tvaṣṭṛ, and striking Vṛtra, "the shoulderless one." The young dragon is described as "the castrated steer who wished to become the equal of the virile bull." Then Indra hurls his weapon at Vṛtra's demoness mother, and the waters that Vṛtra has enclosed overflow the bodies of both mother and son. (O'Flaherty *Veda* 1981)

VYĀSA
(Compiler; also Kṛiṣṇa Dvaipayāna or Bādarāyaṇa)

Vyāsa is an Indian sage, specifically the legendary, semidivine compiler of the *Mahābhārata*. (Buck 1981)

W

WACE

(b. ca. 1100)

Wace is the Anglo-Norman author of *Roman de Brut* (1155) and *Roman de Rou* (1160–1174), verse chronicles about the founders of Bretons and Normans. The *Brut,* written in octosyllabic verse, borrows from the legends of King Arthur and includes the story of his Round Table. It is based on Geoffrey of Monmouth's *Historia regum Brittanniae,* which purports to trace Breton's history beginning with its founding by the Trojan Brutus. In its turn, Layamon's *Brut* (ca. 1200) is based upon it. The *Rou,* which was never completed, tells the history of Norman dukes from Rollo the Viking (after 911) through Robert II Curthose (1106). (Rutherford 1987)

See also *Brut the Trojan; Roman de Brut;* Layamon.

WÄINAMÖINEN

A hero of the *Kalevala.* ***See*** Väinämöinen.

WAKINYAN TANKA

This oral legend of the Brule Sioux Indians is another version of the Great Deluge tale. It tells of the great thunderbird Wakinyan Tanka, who lives on the top of a mountain in the Black Hills. He hates dirt and loves what is clean and pure. No one can see him; he is clothed in black clouds. But people can hear him—his voice is the great thunderclap. And they can feel his presence. Everything moves in a direction that the white man calls clockwise. But thunder beings move counterclockwise. Thunder beings are guardians of the truth. If a person swears on the sacred pipe and lies, the Wakinyan will kill him with lightning.

In contrast, the water monster Unktehi has never liked humans from the day they were put upon earth. She is shaped like a great scaly snake with feet. She can fill the whole Missouri River from end to end, and she can make it overflow. There are little water monsters in smaller streams and lakes who ask, "What are these blood-clot people creeping out of the red pipestone? We don't want them around!" They too can make the streams and lakes overflow.

The great thunderbird decides that he must help save humans from Unktehi. A great battle ensues, lasting many years, between the thunderbirds and the evil water monsters. During this time, the earth trembles and the waters burst forth in mighty torrents. The night is like day because of the lightning flashes. The water monsters are winning, so the thunderbirds retreat to the mountaintop and take council. The Great Wakinyan says, "Our power comes from the sky. It was wrong to fight the Unktehi on their own ground." He calls the thunderbirds into the sky where they all shoot a thunderbolt at the same instant. The earth turns red-hot, and all the water monsters dry up and die, leaving their bones in the Mako Sicha (the Badlands). A few humans, who have climbed upon a high rock during the battle, praise the Wakinyan for saving them. These few people repopulate the earth. (Erdoes and Ortiz 1984; Walker 1983)

WALDERE

This is an Anglo-Saxon alliterative verse, of which two short fragments are extant. It is related to the Latin heroic poem *Waltharius,* and it is likely that both poems draw from a lost German lay. The characters Hildeguth, Attila, Guthere, and Hagen appear in the poem. As in other versions of this story, Hagen apparently is again to be the villain-turncoat, although the extant fragment does not tell the outcome of the confrontation. In this version, when Guthere and Hagen intercept Waldere and Hildeguth, Waldere says, "King of Burgundians, did you count on / the hand of Hagen? Was it he who was to finish / Waldere's fighting days?" (Alexander, M. 1991)

See also Walter; *Waltharius;* Wayland.

WALTER
(Also Walter of Spain)

Walter is the hero of the epics *Waldere* and *Waltharius,* and the hostage, in *Nibelungenlied,* of King Etzel, from whom he escapes with Hildigund. They are waylaid by Gunther and his men, including Walter's old comrade Hagen, who refuses to fight him until forced to do so. (Alexander, M. 1991)

See also *Waldere; Waltharius.*

WALTHARIUS

This 1,456-line Latin heroic poem (ninth or tenth century) is a variation on the Norse *Thiđrekssaga* and a relative of the Anglo-Saxon *Waldere.* In addition, three of the characters appear in the *Nibelungenlied*: Hagen, Gunther, and Attila. Some scholars believe that the poem may have been composed ca. 930 by a Swiss monk, Ekkehard I the Elder, and revised a century later by Ekkehard IV (980–1069).

The rulers of the Franks, Burgundians, and Aquitaine determine to offer tribute and child-hostages to Attila to prevent their territories from being overrun by the Huns. Heriricus of the Franks gives his daughter Hiltgunt; the Burgundian Gibicho gives his liegeman, Hagano; and Alphere gives his son and Hiltgunt's betrothed, Waltharius (Walter of Aquitaine), all to be brought up in Hunnish court with respect as to their stations.

When Gibicho dies, his successor-son Guntharius announces that he does not intend to pay tribute any longer, so Hagano escapes. Lest Waltharius choose the same route, Attila proposes a match with a Hunnish princess. But Waltharius is true to his betrothed, and he and Hiltgunt also escape, carrying their rightful treasure with them.

As they cross the Rhine into Burgundy, Guntharius is notified. Hagano knows their identity by their description and so informs his leader. But Guntharius decides to hunt them down so as to take their treasure.

Waltharius picks a defensible spot in a narrow canyon, through which only one person can pass at a time. There, he picks off Guntharius's 11 warriors as each one passes through. After the 11 successful battles and a night's rest, he and Hiltgunt continue their escape. However, when they reach open country, they are met by Guntharius himself and Hagano, who has finally had to declare his loyalty to his king by agreeing to fight. The three engage in a brutal clash in which all three are seriously but not mortally wounded. Waltharius and Hiltgunt leave the other two to care for their injuries and continue toward home. (Alexander, M. 1991; Hatto 1969)

See also *Nibelungenlied; Thiđrekssaga; Waldere.*

WANADI

Wanadi is a hero-god of the *Watunna* creation cycle of the Makiritare Indians of Venezuela. (Civrieux 1980)

See also Attawanadi; *Watunna.*

A WAR BETWEEN GODS

This legend-epic of Vietnam is set in the reign of the last emperor of the first royal dynasty, Hung Vuong XVIII, believed to be ca. the third century B.C. It is part of a cycle of epics revolving around Lac Long Quang and Au Co, legendary founders of Vietnam, and their offspring.

Son Tinh, a son of Lac Long Quang and Au Co, is said to have followed his father to sea but later returned to dwell on Mount Tan Vien (the Vietnamese version of Olympus), where he has become known as God of the Mountain, or Mountain Spirit. He is young, handsome, and beloved by all creatures because of his good nature.

One day as he strolls along the beach, he overhears the conversation of six fishermen aboard a boat that has just pulled ashore. They are discussing a beautiful and extraordinary fish. Son Tinh's curiosity is piqued and he boards the boat to look at the fish.

Before his eyes, the fish changes color from blue to green. Then Son Tinh becomes aware of the fish's pleading eyes. He tells the fishermen, "This is no ordinary fish. You must not kill it. Let it go back into the ocean." When the fishermen refuse, he offers to buy the fish; once he has purchased it, he releases it into the sea. The fish leaps out of the water three times, and one of the fishermen says, "Look! It is trying to thank you."

That evening, as Son Tinh relaxes in his mountaintop home, a tall, handsome, young man appears. He is Thuy Tinh, King, or God, of the Water. He explains that while he was swimming that day, he took the form of a fish, leaving behind his magical powers. When the fishermen caught him, he was powerless to escape. In gratitude to Son Tinh for freeing him, he invites him to visit his kingdom at the bottom of the sea.

Son Tinh accepts the invitation and visits the Kingdom of the Sea. Amazed at the wealth he finds there, he tells his host, "My own mountain kingdom does not have such riches and luxury."

Thuy Tinh offers him anything he wants as a gift of gratitude, but Son Tinh refuses, saying that he has all that he needs. Thuy Tinh then begs him to accept a small, worn book, which he inherited from his father. Son Tinh accepts the book so as not to offend his host.

When he returns home and examines the book, he discovers that it is magical, containing the power to make all dreams come true. Nevertheless, since he already has everything he needs, he tosses the book aside.

One day King Hung Vuong announces a contest for the hand of his beautiful daughter, Princess My Nuong. Son Tinh journeys to the king's palace along with hundreds of other suitors to compete for the princess's hand. When the first competition is over, only two contenders remain: Son Tinh and Thuy Tinh. Both are equally suited to be the mate of the princess.

The king decides on a task to determine the winner: He will be the first to bring him ten white elephants, ten giant tunas, ten tigers, ten sailfish, ten 100-meter-tall trees, and ten green pearls. Half of these can be found in Son Tinh's kingdom, half in Thuy Tinh's.

While Thuy Tinh painstakingly assembles the gifts the hard way, Son Tinh rushes home and retrieves his "Book of Wishes." He wishes for everything the king has assigned and is able to deliver them all to the king the following day. The king declares him the winner. On the second day, when Thuy Tinh returns with his gifts, he is furious to discover what Son Tinh has done. He attacks Son Tinh with as much water as he can assemble from both the sky and the ocean. But Son Tinh, who is high on his mountaintop, remains safe.

Thuy Tinh attacks again the next year and the next. Each year he tries again to win the princess away by causing monsoons. (Terada 1989)

See also *Lac Long Quang and Au Co; The Magic Crossbow.*

WAR OF THE GODS

Babylonian epic poem. ***See*** *Enuma Elish, Epic of.*

WATUNNA

This creation cycle of the Makiritare, or so'to, Indians of the upper Orinoco River in Venezuela is still being recited and referred to daily by tribal members. It is the compendium of deeds and actions of the primordial heroes, ancestors of the "true people," or so'to. Four groups of people speak the language of so'to and share the same oral tradition of the *Watunna.* The stories of the deeds of "Old People," or Heavenly Ancestors, are models for the so'tos' conduct. The tradition is handed down to the men through magic religious festivals called Wanwanna, consisting of drinking, dancing, wrestling, and group trances to communicate with the supernatural world.

The first cycle of four tales is entitled *Wanadi,* who is the unseen, unknowable light in Heaven, a combination of God, hero, and shaman. Wanadi is created by Shi, the sun, and it is he who establishes order as the so'to know it. Since he left the earth, he has taken no further part in human affairs.

As examples of the content of the cycle, the first story in the *Wanadi* segment, entitled "Seruhe Ianadi," tells that in the beginning, when there is only Sky and nothing on Earth, Wanadi looks down on Earth and says, "I want to make people down there." He sends a spirit messenger (damodede), a spirit of himself called Seruhe Ianadi, the Wise. Seruhe brings the Earth knowledge, tobacco, the maraca, and the shaman's stone (wiriki), and he makes the first people. He buries his own placenta, which gives birth to an ugly human called Kahu (also called Odosha). The human is evil and jealous of Wanadi. Because of him, there is hunger and sickness and war. He teaches people to kill, and after they kill, they are punished by being turned into animals. Seruhe cannot do anything on Earth because of the evil creature, so he goes back to the Sky. The lesson is: When a baby is born, the placenta should not be buried; another evil Odosha or Kahu will come and kill the baby. (Among the Indians of northern Mexico and the southern United States, the practice of burying the placenta in one's yard ensures that when the child is grown, he will return to his mother.)

In "Nadeiumadi," Wanadi sends another spirit double of himself, Nadeiumadi, because he wants good people on Earth. He brings Huehanna, the stonelike egg, which contains the unborn people to inhabit Earth. To show his power, he dreams his own mother, Kumariawa, to life, then he dreams her to death. He plans to bring her back to life as an example to Odosha of what he is able to do. But first he goes hunting, and while he is gone, Odosha speaks to the monkey Iarakaru in a dream, telling him to open Wanadi's medicine pouch (chakara) and let out the night. While the night escapes and covers the landscape, Odosha instructs his lizard Makaka to pour poison urine upon Kumariawa's body. The urine scorches the body and the bones fall apart. When Wanadi returns, he finds there is nothing left of his mother to resurrect. He hides the stone-egg Huehanna and leaves Earth in darkness, taking his mother's bones with him. He throws her bones into a lake in Heaven, and she comes to life again.

"Attawanadi" is the third incarnation of Wanadi, who comes to Earth to bring light again. He sees that Odosha has ruined the people, so he makes new people, new houses, and whole villages. Thus his name is Attawanadi, meaning House-Wanadi. Odosha tries to counteract his good by starving the new people. On the advice of the shaman Wade, Wanadi disguises himself as an old hunter. In this disguise he is able to supply birds for his people to eat.

In "Kaweshawa," Wanadi is living at Wade's house. One day while he is fishing in the river, he almost catches a mermaid. In the water, she is a fish. Out of the water, she is a woman, and he decides that he wants to marry her. Although he tries several techniques, he cannot catch her. Finally he gets her completely out of the water and makes arrangements for a wedding. But his bride is stolen by Kurunkumo, the curassow, spirit bird of Odosha. When Wanadi cannot find her, the bumblebee Mottodona suggests that he make a new woman out of white clay. He does so, but she falls apart in the stream. He makes another of black resin, but she melts in the sun. He dreams a woman into being from the picture of a frog on his tobacco pouch, but she is no good, so he sends her away. He makes a bird-woman who laughs too much, so he sends her away as well. He wants his first wife back. Finally the bumblebee tells him her whereabouts, but Wade warns him that he must disguise himself again. He and Wade switch identities, and he starts off for Kurunkumo's house. On the way he meets an old woman who tells him that Kaweshawa has just given birth. He goes to the birthday feast and finds that his wife has become old and ugly, but he decides to take her home anyway. In order to escape with her unnoticed, he turns them both into cockroaches. When one man tries to swat them, Wanadi becomes a woodpecker and his wife becomes a frog. He flies away with her and lights in a tree that reaches up to Heaven, where they turn back into man and woman. But Wanadi sees that his wife is still old and ugly, so he decides to kill her and make her again because "she's no good like this." He kills and roasts her, then he ties her up in the cane like a piece of cane. He returns to Earth and exchanges appearances with Wade again. In gratitude for Wade's help, he builds him a grand house. He sends first a squirrel, then an anteater, and finally a lizard up the tree to cut his wife's burnt body down. The lizard succeeds, and Kaweshawa falls into lake Akuena. As she falls, an arm breaks off. When she emerges from the water, new and beautiful, a smaller version of herself, formed from the broken arm, also emerges. Wanadi marries one and gives the smaller one to the lizard as his wife.

Other sections of the *Watunna* concern the trickster Iureke, the younger of twin heroes who come out of the cosmic egg Huehanna; Kasenadu, called Lightning Man, who terrorizes the people with his Arakusa (Lightning Cane) until he is vanquished and replaced by his nephew Wachamadi; Kasenadu's brother Mominaru, who kills Sahatuma, from whose blood is born the first jaguar Mado; Kuamachi, the Evening Star, who, attempting to avenge his mother, drives the star people led by Wlaha into the sky, where they become the Pleiades; Makusani, a boy who travels to the houses of the moon and the sun; Marahuaka, or Little Gourd, the tallest mountain and petrified memory of the first yucca tree; and Wahnatu, the first Makiritare created by Wanadi from the clay of Mount Dekuhana.

Makusani, the boy who travels to the houses of the moon and the sun, is closely related to the culture hero of the Karina and Makushi people, Makunaima (the one who works in the dark). (Civrieux 1980)

See also Adichawo; Ahishama; Akato; Attawanadi; Wanadi.

WAYANG
(Also Wajang, Shadow)

Classical Javanese and Balinese puppet plays, Wayang dramatize episodes from the Hindu epics *Rāmāyaṇa* and *Mahābhārata.* Some extend, with Javanese or Balinese myth, additional elaborations on the legends of the Pandava brothers of the *Mahābhārata.* These ritualized and highly significant presentations last from midnight to dawn and are viewed by a segregated audience of devotees. The male viewers sit behind the puppeteer (dalang) and watch him manipulate, with long sticks or rods, the puppets whose actions are spotlighted against a screen. The female members of the audience sit on the opposite side of the screen and watch a shadow play. When the play begins, the benevolent characters are introduced on the puppeteer's right, while the malevolent ones are introduced on his left.

Wayang Topeng are Javanese masked-dance plays (ca. 1000–1400), popular but highly sophisticated interpretations based on the *Mahābhārata.* Wayang Kulit, dating from the same era and still popular today, are the Balinese versions. (Grosvenor and Grosvenor *Ntl Geo* 1969; Reischauer and Fairbank 1960)

WAYLAND
(Also Weland and Volund)

In Scandinavian, German, and Anglo-Saxon legend, Wayland is an invisible smith of outstanding skill. He is the English equivalent of Volund (Volunder), whose story is told in "Völundarkviđa" (The Lay of Volund), found in the *Poetic Edda.* Here he is lord of the elves, as well as a supernatural smith. He also appears in the Anglo-Saxon poems *Waldere* and *Deor,* and in *Beowulf* (sixth to ninth centuries). Alfred the Great also mentions him in his ninth-century translation of *Boethius.* In *Frithofs saga* (thirteenth century), Volund forges the armor of Frithof's father, Thorsten, including a golden arm ring, which Frithof inherits as one of his most prized possessions. According to legend, Wayland is captured by King Nidud (Nithad, Niduth, Nidung) of Sweden, who lames him by cutting the sinews in his feet to prevent him from escaping. Nidud casts him into prison and forces him to work in the royal smithy. But Wayland kills Nidud's two young sons, and from their skulls fashions drinking bowls, which he sends to the king. He also rapes their sister Bodvild when she brings a ring to be mended. According to one legend he escapes in a feather boat. In *Thiđrekssaga* he makes himself wings of birds' feathers. English legend has it that he lives in a cromlech near Lambouen, Berkshire, now called Wayland Smith's Cave, and that in olden times, if a traveler tethered his horse there, left sixpence, and then departed, when he returned, his horse would be shod. A likeness of Wayland can be found on an eighth-century Franks Casket in the British Museum, London. (Alexander, M. 1991; Hollander *Edda* 1990)

See also *Edda, Poetic.*

WELTHOW, QUEEN

(Also Wealtheow)

In *Beowulf,* Welthow is the wife of King Hrothgar and the mother of sons Hrethric and Hrothmund and daughter Freawaru. She presents a speech following the account of *The Fight at Finnsburh* in which she hints that Hrothgar is growing old and should consider bequeathing his throne to his sons ("sheltered in Hrothulf's gracious protection"), rather than to a savior-foreigner. She gives Beowulf a mail shirt, golden arm bands, and the valuable Brosings' neckpiece, and urges him to "lend these two boys / Your wise and gentle heart! . . . Spread your blessed protection / Across my son, and my king's son!" (Hieatt 1967; Raffel 1963)

See also *Beowulf;* Grendel; Hrothgar.

WIDSITH

("Far Traveled")

This Old English poem (ca. seventh century) can be found in the *Exeter Book.* It purports to be the firsthand account of the wandering scop of the Germanic heroic era who entertains in various great mead halls throughout the Germanic world; however, the heroic figures he claims to have known span from the fourth to the sixth centuries, which would make him far-traveled indeed. (Alexander, M. 1991)

WIGLAC

In the epic of *Beowulf,* Wiglac is a heroic Geat thane who accompanies Beowulf when he goes to fight the dragon. When the other thanes flee, young Wiglac remains behind and tries to help his wounded lord; thus, he becomes a model of courage and heroism. (Hieatt 1967; Raffel 1963)

See also *Beowulf;* Grendel.

WILLIAM OF ORANGE
(Also Guillaume d'Orange)

He is the hero of chansons de geste and of Wolfram von Eschenbach's unfinished epic *Willeholm.* (Harrison 1970; Heer 1962)

See also Chansons de Geste.

WINDIGO
(Also Witiko)

In Algonquian Indian lore, a windigo is a giant man-eating ogre who causes a cannibalistic madness, making the victim as dangerous as the ogre is. Since the seventeenth century, some 70 cases have been observed of "windigo psychosis," and 45 victims have committed cannibalism, 36 against members of their own family. Some describe the windigos as being made wholly of ice, while others claim only their hearts are made of ice. Their hisses can be heard for miles. (Maxwell 1978)

WODEN

Woden is the Anglo-Saxon equivalent of Odin, chief god of the Scandinavians. Wednesday (Woden's day) is named in his honor. (Holmes 1990; Jones, G. 1990)

See also Óthin.

WOI-MENI-PELE
(Woi's Matter-Play)

This is the *Woi Epic* of the Kpelle people of Liberia, West Africa, first recorded from the oral in 1982. Composed of 17 episodes, the epic combines singing, narration, and dramatic and instrumental performance to relate the adventures of the superhuman, bigger-than-life hero and ritual specialist, Woi. The Western reader may be disconcerted by the absence of linearity in the epic and particularly by the lack of closure. The epic has no precise beginning—with the hero's birth, for example—or climax or concluding episode. Rather, the teller is free to begin and end at any point. At the end of an episode, the teller says, "Dried millet, wese [sound of breaking]," and the chorus answers, "Wese [sound of breaking]," signaling the end of an episode.

As recorded in the cited text, episode 1 begins as Woi is preparing for war because, he says, "They have treated me badly." The narrator explains, "One man called Yele-Lawo has caught one of Woi's bulls and raised it behind the sky." Yele-Lawo is a monster spirit who also appears as a bitter rattan plant. Woi is joined in his battle preparation by Squirrel-Monkey, Tsetse-Fly, and Horse-Fly. Yele-Lawo knows that Woi is coming and waits to take him on. Woi climbs and climbs until he arrives "behind the sky." The bull, meanwhile, has "gotten down."

In episode 2, with the pregnancy of Woi's wife, the diviner of the anteater is called to predict the future, because "At that time there was nothing alive. / Sheep didn't exist. Chickens didn't exist. There was nothing / at all alive." The woman delivers people, chickens, ducks, sheep, goats. The only thing left yet to be born is Spider.

In episode 3, an enormous feast is held to feed Spider, the last to be born, so that when he has eaten his fill he can play the Slit-Drum, which marks the beat enabling the bellows to be pumped. The bellows will fire the forge that Kelema-ninga will use to make the needle to sew Woi's battle clothes.

In episode 4, Tuu-tuu-Bird arrives to pump the bellows, and Beetle, Kpayang-Miling, arrives to forge the iron for the needle. However, Tuu-tuu-Bird, "the one who has sleeping sickness badly," keeps falling asleep at his work. Woi takes the cutlass iron and rubs it on Tuu-tuu-Bird's buttocks to wake him. Woi sends one of his wives, who claims that he does not love her, to sit at the fork of the big road and carve bowls with her voice.

In episode 5, because she is jealous of her co-wives, Woi's wife Gelengol has been banished to the fork in the road, where she is carving bowls with her voice. Young men come to buy the bowls "on the bed," meaning that her customers pay for the bowls by sleeping with her.

In episode 6, Woi's house moves into battle. The rooster takes the role of a praise singer, a musician who goes into battle with the hero. Woi is ready for the war.

In episode 7, Woi's sons Zu-kpeei and Woi-boi attempt to cut down Bele-Tree, which is blocking the way of Woi's moving house. His daughter Maa-pu waits to set fire to the tree when it falls, but her husband, the demon Meni-maa-fa, taking the form of a lizard, strikes the ax-cut in the tree with his head and restores it. Woi gives his iron bow and arrow to Zu-kpeei so that he can shoot Male-Lizard out of the fork of the tree.

In episode 8 we learn that Iron Bow and Arrow have been given not only to Zu-kpeei, but to Maa-pu, as well. When Male-Lizard appears, Bow sends an arrow to strike him down. Bele-Tree flies up and becomes one of Woi's houses.

In episode 9, the Bele-House, now containing all the people, is traveling to the distant sky where Woi will battle Yele-Lawo for taking one of his bulls.

In episode 10 the house reaches the foot of a Koing-Tree and cannot pass. The Cutlass and the wise Ax come to cut the tree.

In episode 11 the Cutlass cuts the tree, then Ax splits it. When the tree has been cleared away, Woi's brother-in-law, the demon-lizard Meni-maa-fa, attempts to take his wife, Woi's sister Maa-pu, from the house. He meets Bat and tells him, "Woi has taken my woman from me . . . don't let him pass here." Bat assures him, "They are not equal to me one bit."

In episode 12, Bat assaults the house, but Woi holds out a dried koong-leaf and captures Bat in a bag. The house continues to travel toward its destination in the sky.

In episode 13, as the house, "the vehicle," continues, Meni-maa-fa travels ahead to find "clever Pumpkin," which swells up so that "there is no passageway for anything at all." The house cannot pass. Woi strikes the bag to summon help.

In episode 14 the voice of Woi's Knife, apparently summoned from the bag, announces, "I have split the Pumpkin and passed here."

In episode 15, Poling-Bird comes to fight in the war. Back down on earth, one powerful man, Gemila, is having a feast. The narrator sings, "Gemila is really powerful, he really beats people. / He takes out their eyeballs." Poling is called to go to earth to attend Gemila's feast and oppose him because "Poling is not powerful, but she is smart."

In episode 16, being told that Gemila is down on earth eating people, taking their eyeballs, Woi asks, "Well, what should I do? I am in the sky, and I cannot come down. So what Gemila is doing to people, spoiling their eyes, I am not responsible." After Poling-Bird agrees to fight Gemila, the people dress her in finery and she comes outside to wait for Gemila.

In episode 17, "Poling is stalking outside. . . . She is called a fine, clever thing." She wears beautiful pants, carved beads, and a red headscarf. All the birds gather around her: eagles and hawks, waiting for Poling to battle Gemila. (Stone, R. 1988)

WOLFDIETRICH

In the Middle High German poems of Ortnit and Wolfdietrich in *Das Heldenbuch* (The Book of Heroes), Wolfdietrich is the hero who is the son of Hugdietrich, emperor of Constantinople. Some scholars believe that Hugdietrich may be Frankish king Theodoric; thus Wolfdietrich would be Theodebert (d. 548), whose right to the throne was disputed by his uncles. One extant manuscript begins with the story of how Hugdietrich wins Princess Hildburg, daughter of the king of Salonika. Wolfdietrich is cast out by his father when Hugdietrich is led to the erroneous belief that the child is illegitimate. He is reared by the emperor's faithful servant Berchtung von Meran, who, with his 16 sons, provides for Wolfdietrich when his blood brothers cheat him out of his inheritance. Dietrich lives for many years at the Lombardy court of King Ortnit, until he hears that Berchtung's sons have been imprisoned. He returns to free his adoptive kinsmen and to regain his kingdom. He hunts down and slays the dragon who has killed King Ortnit. (Forster 1957)

See also Heldenlieder; Spielmann.

WOLFRAM VON ESCHENBACH

The greatest epic poet of the German Middle Ages, his epic masterpiece *Parzival* (ca. 1200–1210) introduces the theme of the Holy Grail into German literature.

The epic, containing 25,000 verses in 16 books, was based on Chrétien de Troyes's unfinished *Perceval.* Von Eschenbach also wrote the epic *Titurel,* which enlarged on the tragic love story of Sigune that appears in book III of *Parzival.* He did not finish the epic *Willeholm,* based on the exploits of the crusader Guillaume d'Orange. In the latter work, a woman, Gyburg, attempts to reconcile her Christian and Saracen kinsmen. (Eschenbach 1980; Heer 1962)

See also *Parzival;* Percival.

WOMAN OF POI-SOYA

This Ainu heroic epic, first recorded in writing in 1932, reflects the traditional society that existed for many centuries without change prior to 1669. The Ainu title is *Poi-Soya-Un-Mat Shipitonere Shikamuinere,* which means, approximately, "The Woman of Poi-Soya Exalts Herself and Behaves with Outrageous Arrogance." The epic is an object lesson for the proper conduct of women in Ainu society and details the consequences of deviating from prescribed behavior. It also reinforces the great pride to which warrior-heroes have a right, and the privileges that heroes expect. The epic originates in the Saru area of Hidaka, Japan, where the hero is always Otasam-Un-Kur (meaning "hero who dwells at Otasam"). As is typical of the epics of the region, its verse lines are short but eloquent—pawetac, or elegance, being among the chief manly virtues of the culture. It is sung in first-person without a burden, or refrain, or a chorus. It differs from other epics of the Ainu in that the various books, or sections, are sung by different characters.

The first section is narrated by the hero, Otasam-Un-Kur, who is referred to throughout the epic as "the exalted hero." He tells of his upbringing by his beautiful, older foster sister, who, with his younger sister, "would send out / brilliant flashes of light" as evidence of their comeliness.

He has begun to hear rumors of a woman, Poi-Soya-Un-Mat, who behaves in an outrageous manner, such as dressing in men's clothing and going on hunting trips and fishing excursions. If she sees anyone who has caught a fish, she beats him and takes the fish; if anyone has killed a deer, she beats him and takes the deer. Otasam-Un-Kur describes his reaction to these reports: "Even if a man / had done such things, / I would be terribly angry, / but for a woman to do it / means self-exaltation, / outrageous arrogance!"

He decides to go hunting himself, and on the way "some gods / must have attached themselves to me, / for my companion spirits / sent forth rumblings / above me." He senses, in other words, the terrible trouble ahead. He kills a deer, and while he is skinning it, Poi-Soya-Un-Mat, dressed in men's clothing, appears accompanied by six servants. She obviously does not recognize the exalted hero, for one of her servants demands his deer. In a rage, Otasam-Un-Kur kills him, and the other five servants as well. Then he beats the woman violently, knocks her against trees until she is dead, throws her mangled corpse to the ground, and ties her with vines to the trunk of a tree.

But she is rescued by servants and manages to nurse herself back to life. Meantime, Otasam-Un-Kur's foster sister reveals to him that he and the very same Poi-Soya-Un-Mat who is so arrogant were betrothed to each other in their cradles by their parents. Otasam-Un-Kur is exceedingly outraged to learn that it is his betrothed who has behaved in such an irreverent manner.

Once revived, Poi-Soya-Un-Mat goes back to her needlework. But after a while she tires of the work, and besides, she has accumulated a great deal of it. So she decides to sail off on a trading expedition to sell her embroidery. Because she is an exceedingly beautiful woman, she gets many proposals along the way, but she tells her would-be suitors that she is betrothed, and then she fights them for behaving disrespectfully toward her betrothed, the renowned hero Otasam-Un-Kur.

Otasam-Un-Kur also decides to sail on a trip to trade with the Japanese. On his return trip, he stops at a settlement where he learns of Poi-Soya-Un-Mat's activities: fighting like a man. He says, "At the mere / hearing of it, / a frenzied rage / burst over me." He goes ashore where she is, tracks her down, and strikes her in the neck with his silver club: "At the ends of my arms / there were thudding noises." He ties her to his ankles and drags her mangled corpse to the beach, where he beats her servants soundly, takes her onto his boat, and heads for home. At the shore of the land of Poi-Soya, he unties her and tosses her into the boat of her servants. He returns to his own home and throws himself down on his bed: "I was overcome / with feelings of rage."

Part two is narrated by Poi-Soya-Un-Mat, who says that while she is doing nothing but needlework, it occurs to her that if she continues this boring life, her betrothed may take a dislike to her. She decides to dress in men's clothes, take six menservants, and embark on a hunting trip. She relates the same incidents Otasam-Un-Kur has told in part one. When she reaches the part in the story where she meets him skinning a deer, she senses the force of the presence of a chieftain, a warrior, a force so strong that it drives her backward: "Was he a human, / or was he a god?" She describes how he slashes her, mutilates her, inflicting excruciating pain upon her before tying her to a tree.

When she regains consciousness, she hears her servants whispering, "This is why / it is better / for women / to stay in the house / and to amuse themselves / with needlework / or with women's work." They go on to say that her imitations of men's occupations and behavior are deeds that are punished by the gods. They untie her and take her home, where she heals herself and returns to her needlework.

At length she becomes bored and decides to travel around and trade her embroidery. During her travels she arrives at the land of Repunship, where one chieftain proposes giving her in marriage to his younger brother. She resists and begins "to fight battles / of revenge" until someone whom she can't see begins to beat, slash, and tear her. It is her betrothed, the exalted hero Otasam-Un-Kur. He continues to pummel her until she loses consciousness, then he ties her up and sails away with her toward her native land of Poi-Soya. She is afraid to show that she is in pain, because if he "were to hear / that I was in pain, / he might punish me / all the more intensely." He drops her in her own boat. She eventually heals herself and resumes her needlework.

One day he comes to her home "with his beauty / even more imposing / than before." He tells her that he has been on a trading mission and has brought her some silk for her needlework. If she will come along with him to his ship, he will give it to her. She thinks, "Let me finish / one needle stitch / before I get up." When she does not rise immediately, "fierce rage" flashes across his face. He stamps toward her, saying, "How long, / o evil woman, / o contemptible woman, / are you going to / commit these / unforgivable / indignities against me?" He knocks her against the upper rafters and the lower rafters until she loses consciousness in a pool of blood.

Once again she is able to nurse herself back to life and health, and she returns to her needlework. But again Otasam-Un-Kur appears, and again he commands her to come to his ship to get the silken cloth he has brought. As he speaks, she thinks, "The last time / when he said this to me, / I took too long / in getting up, / and I was slain / as a result!" So she gets up hurriedly before he finishes speaking and follows the "exalted hero" down to his boat. But when they board the boat, it sails away. The man who has been posing as Otasam-Un-Kur unmasks, revealing himself to be a member of the ruling family of the land of Moshirpa. Hearing how the exalted hero has treated her, he has come to rescue her and marry her himself. She shows her abhorrence of his proposal by scratching the "evil wretch" who has kidnapped her. When they reach Moshirpa, his sister befriends her and berates her brother for placing them all in danger by bringing home the betrothed of the exalted hero Otasam-Un-Kur.

At length Otasam-Un-Kur arrives, "stamping fiercely," draws his sword, and attempts to kill Poi-Soya. The Moshirpan sister intervenes, explaining that his betrothed was brought to Moshirpa against her will. When it is clear that Otasam-Un-Kur will not listen to reason, the sister goes flying up the smoke-hole with Poi-Soya, while below a full-blown battle breaks out.

In book three, Otasam is again the speaker. He relates how, against the advice of his foster sister, he decides to go after Poi-Soya. Although she disapproves of his mission, the sister leaps onto the boat with him, takes the oars, and rows powerfully. They sail to the land of Moshirpa, where he stamps into the big house of the rulers. He spies the younger Moshirpan brother, "awe-inspiring in his beauty." In the corner he sees Poi-Soya, "the evil woman," and Moshirpa-Un-Mat, the kidnapper's sister, who is also "awe-inspiring in her beauty." The two women escape him, but he slices the brother into several pieces. Then the older brother appears, "doing a war dance," with offers of indemnities, treasures brought as payment for the wrong done by his late brother to Otasam. The "exalted hero" continues to cut down villagers without mercy until his foster sister takes him by the shoulders and holds him until he comes to his senses. He accepts the indemnities as his due and sails for home.

He hears that Poi-Soya and Moshirpa are traveling around the countryside together, denied lodging in the homes of chieftains of their own class and being forced to stay in the homes of slaves and other low-ranking people.

He reveals that long ago on a trading trip, being angry at Poi-Soya for her past transgressions, he asked for the hand of Retarpira-Un-Mat, an ugly younger sister of the chieftain of White Cliff, Retarpira-Un-Kur. He decides now to go to Retarpira and woo Retarpira-Un-Mat; once again, his foster sister opts to make the trip with him.

Along the way, he hears the eddying waters say, "How pitiful it is / for Otasam-Un-Kur, / the exalted hero, / that his luck / should always / be withdrawn!" But the god ruling the cliffs answers, declaring that the exalted hero has luck stronger than anyone else's: "The eddying waters around the oar / are lying!" The hero wonders which god is telling the truth. He reaches the land of Retarpira, where the chieftain has just finished brewing a large vat of wine. He welcomes the renowned hero, and as a large company gathers around the wine tub for a feast, Otasam hears the froth of the wine say, "How pitiful it is / for Otasam-Un-Kur, / the exalted hero, / that his luck / should be withdrawn / always!" But the god of the rafters refutes the claim of the froth on the wine, calling them lies. Otasam again wonders which god is telling the truth.

During the feast he steps outside to relieve himself and spies a pretty little house nearby. As he approaches it, he overhears from inside the voice of the chieftain of Kunnepot confessing to the woman Retarpira-Un-Mat that he has been deceiving her by pretending to be Otasam and coming to woo her nightly. He asks her to marry him and sail away to Kunnepot, assuring her that he can kill Otasam, if necessary, with one single sword stroke. Retarpira-Un-Mat berates him for deceiving her, saying, "you / lay with me like dogs, / you did wicked things to me!" Nevertheless, it is the woman who receives Otasam's fury, and to whom he refers as evil. He bursts into the house, takes her by the hair, and knocks her against the rafters until she is almost dead. After he has mutilated both her and her suitor, he ties them to either side of the fireplace and sets the thatched house on fire. Retarpira-Un-Mat screams for her older brother to come quickly and save, not her, but the exalted hero. She does not beg to be saved herself, since "my actions were evil."

Book four is spoken by Kunnepet-Un-Mat, the shamaness sister of the man whom Otasam has tied to the fireplace and set afire. One day she receives a servant bearing news of the incident and telling her that the three of them are dead. However, since the exalted hero's death is "bad for the land," if she is unable to restore him to life, "a war of annihilation, / a war of extirpation" will be launched against their land of Kunnepot. She brings out her woman's treasure bag and takes from it a silken hood and a "little shamaness's wand." She puts on the hood and places the wand within her robes. She fastens the robes of her little brother, takes him "by his little hand" and sets out for the land of Retarpira. Along the way she prepares the lad for the bravery he must show.

When they arrive at Retarpira, they find a large crowd of relatives, so thick that they almost block her way. She sees the spirit fence where the charred bones of Otasam are hanging. She imitates a man's speech and behavior and, with her little brother "shaking and quivering [with fear]," she makes her way through the thick crowd. She sits down beside the charred bones and, with her wand, begins the process of restoring Otasam to life. She works both day and night until, little by little, the flesh grows back and he is eventually revived.

Book five is sung by the exalted hero, who describes his feelings upon coming back to life. He opens his eyes to see a beautiful young woman: "The brightness of her face / was like the rising sun, / sending out / dazzling rays of light." She is holding the hand of a little child "of an amazing appearance— / he was awe-inspiring / in his beauty." Far from expressing gratitude for the work of the shamaness, Otasam, the exalted hero, thinks instead, "For what reason / should I leave alive / . . . the offspring of our enemies?" and he darts "a swift sword thrust / at the little child" and kills him. He takes home with him the sister who has saved his life and allows her to cook for him. At one point he reflects, "Why on earth / should I ever have chosen / precisely / an enemy offspring, / the woman of the enemy race, / to cook my meals / for me?" Nevertheless, since she is the one who has restored him to life, he magnanimously allows her to continue to cook for him. He eventually takes her as his wife. She bears "two children, three children," and he now says, "we lead / a superb married life, / a magnificent married life, / and this is the way / we live on." (Philippi 1979)

WOMAN'S EPIC: REPUNNOT-UN-KUR

This epic of the Ainu was recorded in 1932, but probably reaches back for centuries prior to Ainu's subjugation by the Japanese in the seventeenth century. Although it is called a woman's epic, the subtitle is the name of a man, the chief villain of the story. The epic is sung in first-person without a burden. The speaker is a yankur woman; that is, a mainlander, or Ainu, who is being raised by Repunnot-Un-Kur, whom she believes to be her older brother. He is a repunkur; that is, one of the sea people, an enemy clan living in the territory north of the Ainu. Compare the situation in this epic to that of *The Epic of Kotan Utunnai,* where a male mainlander is being reared by a repunkur woman whom he believes to be his sister.

As the epic begins, the heroine Shinutapka-Un-Mat tells that her foster brother raised her "with a magnificent upbringing" until she finally "came to look like a woman." From that time onward, she does nothing but needlework, while her brother does nothing but carve on scabbards, apparently the usual occupations for a couple. One day he brings down from the mountain a bear cub, which they raise for three years, preparing it for an iyomante, or bear ceremony. (By slaying the bear, the humans free the spirit of the god trapped inside, enabling him to return to his own domain. After the bear has been killed, his head lies in state surrounded by offerings of food, wine, and elaborately whittled sticks, inau, dedicated to the god. The people hold a great feast and dance, over which the god presides at the head of the fireplace. When the feast has ended, the god is sent home, and when he arrives home, he finds many gifts that have been sent ahead by humans. Thus the bear ceremony is called iyomante, which means "sending-off.")

The brother decides to go trading with the Japanese for some special wine for the bear ceremony with the idea that, when the ceremony is over, he will take Shinutapka for his wife. During his absence, she continues cooking good food to fatten up the bear. Finally one day she hears the servants whispering to one another that a boat bearing the brother's emblem has come ashore and is unloading at the next village below, at the house of Kotanra-Un-Kur, a relative of the brother. As time goes on, she hears the sounds, both night and day for six days, of drinking and feasting coming from the house of Kotanra. She continues to try to feed the bear, but he will no longer eat; he only growls angrily.

One night she lies down in tears and goes to sleep. A god in the form of a bear cub appears in her dream and tells her that her real father was the ruler of Shinutapka. While her parents were on a trading mission, the mother carrying her on her back while the elder brothers remained behind, her father was killed in Karapto. The bear cub tells her that the mother moved on to Santo where she continued to battle until she was captured. At that time, Repunnot-Un-Kur went to join in the battle against Shinutapka's mother; seeing the mother in chains, he stole the child from her mother's back. The bear cub tells her that Repunnot-Un-Kur ran off with her and took her back to Repunnot, where he raised her secretly, planning to marry her when she was grown. When he saw that she has come "to look like a woman," he decided that the time was ripe to marry her and planned the wine-trading trip to Japan. But, the bear cub tells her, on Repunnot-Un-Kur's way home, he was hailed by the woman Kotampa-Un-Mat, who is jealous of Shinutapka. She has told him that in his absence, Shinutapka and the bear cub "lay together like dogs, / did wicked things together." So Repunnot-Un-Kur has unloaded the wine at the house of his kinsman Kotanra-Un-Kur, where the sounds of "noisy reveling" have been coming from ever since. Now, the bear cub warns, they plan to come and kill them both: Shinutapka and the bear cub. He tells her not to fear, that he will save her life if she will stick close to him.

The next morning she dries her tears and cooks the bear cub a good meal, then dresses in her best embroidered garments. At dawn she hears the sounds of many people running toward the house. At the same time, the bear crashes out of his cage and rushes out to face the companies of armored men, spearmen, and archers. As the bear dives into battle, she sees Repunnot-Un-Kur, not leading the fight, but standing in the back of the crowds, exhorting his forces, "Struggle mightily! Kill them, / the evil-doers."

But the companies of spearmen and archers are no match for the bear cub. He completely lays to waste the entire village of Repunnot. Exhausted, he throws himself down to catch his breath. Meanwhile, Shinutapka tells the audience, she has been "shedding / many sparkling teardrops, / countless sparkling teardrops." In the sounds of the bear cub's breathing she thinks she hears him tell her to stay with him, to hold onto his back no matter what happens, and she will be saved.

They go together to the sandy shore, where he dives into the sea. With Shinutapka clinging onto his back, the bear swims both day and night until he reaches the mainland near a river mouth. Again, as the bear cub rests, she seems to hear words in the sound of his breathing. He tells her that they will go upstream along the course of the river, past a large village, where the people will be of the same enemy clan and will also attack them. He tells her again to stay close to him and she will be saved. The events unfold as the bear has predicted. As before, the bear winds and twists himself "like a soft hoop [made of vines]" and goes raging through the attackers. In a short time the "populous village" is reduced to "charred, bare sticks of wood," and not a single villager is left alive.

Shinutapka and the bear continue their journey, making their way up a steep crag through which a path has been cut. On either side of the path stand stone Buddhas. Atop the crag stands "a divinely made stockade," which is, she says, "exactly / what I would expect / to find only in / the abode of a god." Inside the stockade stands a majestic house. The bear cub seats himself against the spirit fence located outside the sacred window of the house. She sits on a rubbish heap in the yard and waits, shedding "many sparkling teardrops."

From the house, amid "countless flashes of light," a human face appears of such majestic beauty as she has never seen before. The face is surrounded by curly metal hair. (Curly hair is highly prized among the Ainu.) This imposing man hangs a sword-guard treasure onto the neck of the bear cub. They all enter the house together, to face another human sitting at the head of the fireplace. This noble man asks Shinutapka to explain why they have come. In an extremely lengthy passage of 500 lines, she simply repeats the same story she has told the reader up to this point.

After she has told her story, the two men recognize her as their younger sister, and there is great rejoicing at her return. Her elder brother, Kamui-otopush, bows to the bear cub in worship and orders that a cage be built for him. The reunited family lives on uneventfully and peacefully, caring for the bear cub, giving him "a magnificent upbringing, / a splendid upbringing."

After two or three years, Kamui-otopush decides that "it would be / an indignity / to make a weighty god / remain / for a very long time / among humans," so he proposes going to trade with the Japanese for some wine with which to have a bear ceremony. Preparations for the feast begin, and invitations go out to all the relatives nearby and far away. When the appointed day arrives, the guests stream in. Part of the bear ceremony consists of leading the bear cub around on a rope among the crowd just before he is killed. When this part of the ceremony begins, Shinutapka, remembering how the bear saved her life, throws herself down by the spirit fence and sheds "many fierce, sobbing tears, / countless fierce, sobbing tears."

After a while she looks up over the spirit fence and sees a young boy with a godlike appearance who tells her, "As you celebrate the feast, / do not even so much / as to lick the bits [of food] / sticking to your fingers." She follows his directions, being very careful not to get any of the food in her mouth. It is the most splendid bear ceremony ever.

Some time passes, uneventfully, and then one day, amid "countless flashes of light," the exalted hero who had appeared to her by the spirit fence appears in her doorway. He identifies himself as the former bear cub and tells her elder brother that after he ascended to the land of the gods and was honored with the welcoming feast, he told his father, "I want to marry / the human woman." The father consented for him to return to earth. The exalted hero tells the elder brother, "If you think / it would be well / for us to dwell together / as a single family / from now on, / then I would like / to live / together with / your younger sister."

The elder brother acknowledges that they are indebted to him for bringing their sister safely home: "Our younger sister, / though she is unattractive, / though she lacks beauty, / has come back to us / thanks to the weighty god." He does not bother to ask Shinutapka's wishes, but reasons that, were a wedding between the god and their sister to take place, "we would greatly enhance / our standing among the gods / and our position among men." So the two are married, and they live for several years in the majestic house with Shinutapka's two brothers.

At length the elder brother decides that they should have a home of their own, so he builds them a separate lodging next door and fills it with treasures. It is there that they now live and where, the narrator says, "I have nothing / to worry about, / and I am leading / a magnificent married life." (Philippi 1979)

WONGURI-MANDJIKAI SONG CYCLE OF MOON BONE

Australian Aboriginal cycle. ***See** Moon Bone.*

THE WOOING OF ÉTAÍN

This Early Irish saga is told in three independent sections. The first describes how the Dagdae desires Elcmar's wife Baond and tricks him into leaving so that he can sleep with her. She bears a son named Óengus, whom Dagdae takes to be reared in the house of Mider. When he grows older, Óengus, in promise of a boon for Mider, tries to win Étaín away from her father Ailill by performing several tasks that Ailill devises. Finally he buys her and takes her home to Mider, who sleeps with her and thanks his foster son. But Mider's druid wife Fuamnach turns the princess into a pool of water. Mider leaves home, without a woman. The water turns into a worm, then into a scarlet fly, that travels with Mider; he knows it is Étaín. Fuamnach also knows it is Étaín, and she creates a "lashing wind" that blows the fly away until it lands upon Óengus's clothes. He too knows it is Étaín, so he takes her into the house to cherish. Fuamnach learns of the fly's whereabouts, so she tells Mider, "Have your foster son summoned, that I may make peace with the two of you, and I, meanwhile, will go in search of Étaín." While Óengus is gone, Fuamnach unleashes a wind that blows the fly away so that she wanders for seven years throughout Eriu. Finally she falls into a vessel, and Etar's wife swallows the fly as she drinks from the vessel. Étaín is conceived in the woman's womb and is born as her daughter.

Thereafter Étaín is brought up by Etar along with the 50 chieftains' daughters who attend her. One day when all the girls are bathing in the river, a rider in a green cloak fastened with a gold brooch comes toward them. He is so handsome that all the girls fall in love with him. He recites a poem about Étaín and rides away. Meanwhile, Oengus has come home from Mider's, suspecting a trick by Fuamnach, and discovers that Étaín is missing. He follows Fuamnach's trail, and when he finds her, cuts off her head and takes it home with him.

In the second section, Echu Airem (Eochaid), king of Eriu, and his brother Ailill Angubae are rivals for Étaín. Echu has no queen, so he sends messengers out to bring back the fairest woman in the land, who is Étaín. But after Echu has slept with Étaín, Ailill sees her and is smitten with desire. He grows ill, and Echu sends him home to die. When he is making a circuit of his kingdom, he leaves Étaín with Ailill to care for him and perform the funeral rites. After nine days of her ministrations, Ailill is well. The couple makes plans to meet on a certain hill to consummate their desire, but each time Ailill oversleeps. Étaín is met by someone who looks and speaks like Ailill, but is not he. On the third day the man reveals himself to be Mider. He asks her to come with him, but she answers, "I will not exchange the king of Eriu for a man whose race and family I know nothing of." He tells her it is he who quelled Ailill's desire to sleep with her lest she be dishonored. He asks her, "Will you come . . . with me if Echu bids you?" She agrees to do so. Then Echu returns from his rounds and finds his brother alive. He thanks Étaín for what she has done and takes her home.

In the third section, one day Echu sees a young warrior in a scarlet tunic riding toward him. He introduces himself as Mider and proposes a game of fidchell. He has brought his own fidchell board made of silver with gold men. They make a wager that if Echu wins, Mider will give him 50 horses and 50 bridles. Mider loses, and the next day he brings Echu 50 horses and bridles, and proposes another game. This time Mider wagers 50 boars, 50 gold-hilted swords, 50 cows with 50 calves, 50 wethers, 50 ivory-hilted blades, and 50 cloaks. When he loses again, Echu's father is impressed by Mider's great riches; he suggests that Echu impose some difficult tasks upon him. Mider agrees to perform the tasks if Echu will promise that no one under his rule be allowed to walk outside before sunrise the following day. The following day they play again, and Echu loses. Mider asks only for "My arms round Étaín and a kiss from her." Echu promises him that he can have what he wants in one month. Echu encircles the castle with warriors and locks himself and Étaín inside. That night as Étaín is serving the chieftains, Mider comes walking toward her. The people are astonished at his beauty, and astounded that he has gained entrance to the hall. When Echu allows Mider to put his arms around Étaín, Mider abducts her, lifting her up through the skylight. The chieftains look up and see two swans flying away. Echu assembles the best men in Eriu and orders that all the hills be hollowed out. The couple flees from hill to hill. Finally Echu meets Mider coming toward him. He promises that Étaín will return to him by the third hour the next day. At the appointed hour, 50 women looking like Étaín approach, and Mider tells Echu to pick out his wife. Echu says, "My wife is the best at serving . . . and that is how I will know her." Echu picks out his wife by the process of elimination. But later Mider returns and tells him, "Your wife was pregnant when I took her from you, and she bore a daughter, and it is that daughter who is with you now. Your wife is with me. . . ." Echu does not dare dig up Mider's hill again. He is distressed that he has slept with his own daughter and even fathered a daughter by her. He sends two members of his household to take the girl and throw her into a pit with wild beasts. But on the way they stop at a herdsman's house to eat, and decide to throw the girl outside to the dog and its pups. When the herdsman and his wife return, they see the fair-haired child in the kennel and take her in to rear her as their own. She grows to be very beautiful, and one day King Eterscelae learns of her and takes her away by force to be his wife. She becomes the mother of the hero Conare. (Gantz 1988)

WOTAN

Wotan is the Old High German form of Odin, chief god of the Scandinavians. Wotan appears in Wagner's *Ring des Nibelungen.* (Jones, G. 1990)

See also Óthin; Woden.

WOTO

In the creation cycle of the Bushongo and related Congo tribes, Woto is the father of the Bushongos. He is one of twins, the first two children born to the god Bomazi and the daughter of the old man and old woman who are the progenitors of the tribe. When Woto grows up, he has three wives, but one day he finds his nephew with one of his wives. Later he discovers that the nephew has sinned with his other two wives as well. Woto is angry and retreats to the forest, singing of his loneliness. He is a magician, and when the little people hear him, they come out of the trees. They exclaim over his big ears, eyes, and nose. The people are Pygmies. He wanders on, and in time becomes the father of all the Bushongo people. (Parrinder 1982)

WURADILAGU SONG CYCLE

This Australian Aboriginal cycle, consisting of 18 songs similar to the *Moon Bone* cycle, has in common with other Aboriginal cycles the celebration of oneness with nature. It centers around the arrival, after the northwest monsoon season, of the southeast winds. (Wilde et al. 1991)

See also Moon Bone.

WYANDOT CREATION MYTH

This Seneca Indian Ka'kaa, or Ga'kaa, oral tale concerns the people who "lived beyond," called Wyandots. It tells of the chief's only daughter, who is very ill. The old doctor advises the people to lay the girl against a wild apple tree, then instructs them to dig around the tree's roots because they will find something that will cure the girl. The people dig and dig until they have made such a large hole that both tree and girl fall through and disappear into an underworld of water. Two great white swans who are swimming nearby hold the girl on their backs. They consult different animals as to what is to be done in order to make dry land, a place for her to live. Eventually, after many animals have tried to solve the problem, an island is made around the shell of Big Turtle. The island continues to grow until it is big enough for the girl to live on. The swans swim to its edge and she steps off onto it. (Parker 1989)

X

XANTHIUS

(Also Xanthos)

In the *Iliad* (v), Xanthus is the name of a Trojan killed by Diomedes. In the *Iliad* (xvi, xix) Xanthus is a horse, swift as the wind, to whom Hera bestows the power of speech. Poseidon gives the horse to Peleus, the father of Achilles. Xanthus predicts to Achilles that he will return safely from one battle at Troy, but that his death is not far away. In the *Iliad* (xvii) Xanthus and his twin Balius weep when Patroklos is killed by Hektor. Xanthus is also the name of a river in the *Iliad* (vi), and in the *Iliad* (xxi), Xanthus is the name of the river god who floods the river to halt Achilles's ravagement of the Trojans. As the river threatens to drown Achilles, Hera asks Hephaestus to set it afire so that it will return to its banks. (Lattimore 1976)

See also *Iliad.*

XBALANQUÉ

In the *Popol Vuh* of the Maya, Xbalanqué is one of the heroes, along with his brother Hunahpú, whose stories make up a large part of the book. They attack and overcome the devil-like Vucub-Caquix, then kill his sons Cabracán and Zipacná. They avenge themselves on their brothers, who have treated them very badly since they were born. To avenge their father, they travel to the Xibalba, the underworld region of evil, and play a number of ball games with the lords of Xibalba in an effort to gain their freedom. They are eventually killed, but are brought back to life. They slay the lords of Xibalba to avenge the deaths of both Hun-Hunahpú and Vucub-Hunahpú, eventually return to earth, and rise up to the sky. (Recinos, Goetz, and Morley 1983)

See also Hunahpú; Journey; *Popol Vuh;* Xibalba, Lords of.

XIBALBA, LORDS OF

In the *Popol Vuh* of the Maya, the lords of Xibalba are underworld devils who plot the deaths of the hero-brothers Hunahpú and Xbalanqué but are ultimately destroyed by them. (Recinos, Goetz, and Morley 1983)

See also Hunahpú; *Popol Vuh;* Xbalanqué.

XIU, HUN UITZIL CHAC TUTUL

In the Mayan ritual epic *Cuceb,* Xiu is the superior chief (Halach Uinic), as well as a priest, of Cuzamil. Xiu is also the name of his people, who scorn the Itzá people, yet take some regal pride in tracing their ancestry to Mexico. (Bierhorst 1974)

See also The Cuceb.

XIUHTECUHTLI

(Turquoise Lord; also Huehueteotl, Old God)

Xiuhtecuhtli is the ancient Aztec god of fire. (León-Portilla 1982)

XIUHTLACUILOLXOCHITZIN, LADY

In the Aztec cycle of *Quetzalcóatl,* in fragment C, "A Cycle of Transformation," Lady Xuihtlacuilolxochitzin is depicted as the widow of King Huactli, who is given the city of Cuauhtitlan to rule after her late husband's reign of 62 years. The people are nomadic. The uncouth Huactli has not taught them how to plant edible corn. They do not know how to weave, and they dress only in hides. Their food consists of birds, snakes, deer, and rabbits. The lady's house is made of thatch and stands beside the square, "where today it is paved with / stones. . . ." An idol-worshiper, she rules for 12 years before she dies. The account has an authentic ring, supporting the possibility of a historical counterpart. (Bierhorst 1974)

See also Quetzalcóatl, Tipiltzin.

XIUIT

In the Mayan ritual epic *Cuceb,* the dire prophecy is made for the Fifteenth Year concerning their Itzá king: "Death will the wooden mask give to Xiuit for his / insolence to his mother, / his insolence to his father, / for the insolence of his lineage of offspring, of / youths. . . ." The prophet predicts an end of the race of Itzá: "Comes / the misery, the heaping of skulls: . . . of / no profit, are they. . . ." (Bierhorst 1974)

See also The Cuceb.

XMUCANE

In the *Popol Vuh* of the Maya, Xmucane is the grandmother of the hero-brothers Hunahpú and Xbalanqué and the creator of man, whom she makes from yellow and white corn. She is the mother of Vucub-Hunahpú and Hun-Hunahpú, sacrificed by the lords of Xibalba and avenged by Hunahpú and Xbalanqué. (Recinos, Goetz, and Morley 1983)

See also Hunahpú; *Popol Vuh;* Xbalanqué.

In Mesoamerican mythology Xolotl, the evening star, is the twin brother of Quetzalcóatl, the morning star. Here he appears as the lid for a Mixtec incense burner from about 1300. He is patron of the ball game and led the dead to the underworld.

XOCHIQUETZAL
(Flower Feather)

Xochiquetzal is the Aztec goddess of beauty, uxorial arts, and erotic love whose myth is found in the *Codex Fejervary-Mayer.* She is the wife of the rain god Tlaloc until the god of night Tezcatlipoca, stricken by her beauty, abducts her and enthrones her as the goddess of love. She is patroness of the single maidens who accompany young warriors to war. (Alexander, H. 1964)

XOLOTL

In the Aztec creation cycle *Quetzalcóatl,* Xolotl is the evening star, twin brother of the hero–Toltec king–morning star *Quetzalcóatl.* In one variant of the fragment entitled "The Restoration of Life," Xolotl replaces his brother as the protagonist. (Bierhorst 1974)

See also *Quetzalcóatl, Tipiltzin.*

Y

YAM

(Also Rahab and Yamm)

Yam is the Canaanite dragon god of the sea and inland waters. In the *Baal Epic,* Baal, with the help of his sister Anath, defeats Yam, who at the time also has dominion over the earth. Baal then becomes lord of the earth. (Ben Khader and Soren 1987; Pritchard 1973)

See also *Baal Epic.*

YAMA

In Indian Vedic mythology, Yama is the king of death, described in the *Ṛg Veda* as "the first to find the way for us," meaning that Yama is the first mortal to die and reach the other world. He becomes a god and the guide for all who come after, conducting the dead to their ancestors. He has two dogs, regarded as both dangerous and benevolent, because they can guard the departed and assist in leading them to Heaven. Descendants of Sarama, the bitch of Indra, these dogs guard the doorway to the otherworld. In later myth Yama becomes the judge who must weigh the good and evil of the departed and decide their fate. He also appears in the Tibetan *Bardo Thötröl.* In Bali he is called the Lord of Hell. (Dimmitt and van Buitenen 1978; Fremantle and Trungpa 1987; Grosvenor and Grosvenor *Ntl Geo* 1969; O'Flaherty *Veda* 1981)

YAMATO-TAKE

(Also Yamato-takeru)

Yamato-Take is a legendary Japanese hero-prince, ca. second century A.D., who performs many heroic deeds in battle. Before he sets off to make a name for himself, he receives from his priestess-aunt, Yamato-hime, the famous Kusanagi sword and a bag that he is not to open unless his life is in danger. After subduing the Kyūshū "barbarians," he subjugates the "barbarians" of the Kantō Plain. While he is in quest of the "Violent Deity," he is threatened by fire, and he opens the bag to discover a fire-striker. He fights off the fire and slays the wicked rulers who set it. He slays a god who appears in the shape of a white deer. He enters a mountain pass leading to the province of Shinano, besting the deity of the pass, and goes to live in the house of Princess Miyazu "of fragrant and slender arms." He leaves his sword behind at her house and goes forth to slay the deity of evil breath. But he does not recognize the deity, who has disguised himself as a white boar. The boar brings a fatal enchantment upon Yamato-Take, who soon weakens and dies.

His wives eventually come and build a fine mausoleum for him. He is transformed into a white bird that flies away and is never seen again. (Mackenzie 1990; Reischauer and Fairbank 1960)

YAO, TANG TI

Yao is a legendary Chinese emperor (ca. twenty-fourth century B.C.) praised by Confucius in the *Analects* as a model of righteousness, virtue, and devotion. He rules benignly for 70 years, after which the sun and moon shine like jewels and the planets shine like pearls, sparkling springs flow, rice crops thrive, and two unicorns appear in the capitol at P'ing-yang, a symbol of prosperity. During his reign, Yu the Great, one of the savior-heroes of China, contains destructive floodwaters that threaten the country, and the Lord Archer Hou Yi shoots down nine of the ten suns that threaten to burn the earth to ashes. (Creel 1960)

See also Yu the Great, Emperor.

YARIKH

(Also Yareah)

In ancient Semitic religion and in the Ugaritic poem from *Ras Shamra* (Ugarit), Yarikh is the moon god who marries the moon goddess Nikkal (Sumerian Ningal). The first section of the poem describes the courtship and payment of the bride price. The second half of the poem deals with the feminine aspects of marriage, the main purpose being to procreate. (Chahin 1991; Saggs 1990)

YATPÁN

In the Canaanite *Poem of Aqhat*, or *Aqhat Epic,* Yatpan is hired by the goddess Anat to eliminate Aqhat and secure the divine bow, which he has refused to give her. Yatpan kills Aqhat, but he drops the bow and breaks it. After drinking too much wine, he reveals his deed to Aqhat's sister Paghat. (Pritchard 1973)

See also *Aqhat Epic.*

YGGDRASILL

(Also Mimameiđr)

In Norse mythology, in the *Poetic Edda* and the *Prose Edda,* Yggdrasill is the world tree that supports the universe. One of its three roots reaches into the underworld of Niflheim, one to the giants' home of Jotunheim, and one to the gods' dwelling place, Asgard. After Ragnarök (Doomsday), which Yggdrasill

Yao, a legendary ruler of early China, was included in an eighteenth-century album of Chinese emperors. Confucius considered Yao a model of righteousness, virtue, and devotion.

will survive, the world's new life will spring from the tree. (Hollander *Edda* 1990; Young 1954)

See also *Edda, Poetic; Edda, Prose.*

YMIR

In Scandinavian creation myth, Ymir is the primeval giant from whose body the world is created. Two versions exist as to how this came about. One is that Odin and his two brothers Vili and Ve slay Ymir and toss his corpse into an abyss. His blood forms the waters, his skull the heavens, his teeth the rocks, his brains the clouds, his hair the plants, and his eyebrows the wall separating the gods from the giants. The other is that while Ymir is sleeping, a man and woman grow from under his left arm, and sons grow from his feet, thus creating the race of giants. (Jones, G. 1990)

YNGLINGA SAGA

This prose account of the West Norse Ynglinga opens the *Heimskringla* of Snorri Sturluson, which concerns the kings of Norway. They are called Ynglings because they trace their lineage back to the god Frey; another name of Frey is Yngvi. Prior to the fifth century there is no historical credence given to the first 17 Ynglings listed. Snorri writes that he has written what "I have heard wise men, learned in history, tell; . . . some of their family descents even as I have been taught them; . . . some is written according to old songs or lays. . . . And although we know not the truth of these, we know . . . of occasions when wise old men have reckoned such things as true." (Monsen and Smith 1990)

See also *Ynglinga Tal.*

YNGLINGA TAL

(Count or List of the Ynglings)

Old Scandinavian scaldic poem about King Rognvald (Rognvold) the Glorious by Thjodolf of Hvin the Learned, 27 stanzas of which are preserved at the beginning of *Ynglinga Saga.* These bear traces of earlier Swedish heroic poetry no longer extant.

Rognvald is the son of Olag Geirstada-Alf, brother of Halfdan the Black, who is the father of Harald Fairhair. Thirty ancestors and their burial places are mentioned in the poem, including King Helgi, who is the Halga of *Beowulf,* father of Hrothulf, who later becomes king of Denmark. Many cannot be remembered for having performed noble deeds, and many do not fall in battle: Rognvald's father Olav, called a mighty man, dies of a foot disease. King Ingjald, learning that a rival king, Ivor, is on the way, has no strength to fight, so he and Queen Asa the Ill-Minded decide to make their people "dead drunk and afterward setting fire to the hall." Everyone perishes in the blaze. Fjolnir, son of Yngvi-Frey, "heavy with sleep and dead drunk," gets out of bed in the middle of the night "to seek himself a certain place." On his way back to his room, he falls into a vat of mead and "In the mead-vat's / Windless wave / Found his death." Dag, called "so wise a man that he understood the song of birds," learns that his favorite sparrow has been killed by a stone; he orders a great army out to avenge the bird's death. A workman casts a hayfork into the crowd, and it hits Dag on the head, killing him. After a drinking bout one evening, Svegdir and his men see a dwarf standing before a large stone. The dwarf beckons Svegdir to enter the stone if he wishes to meet Odin. Svegdir "leaped after the dwarf, / And Sokkmimi's / Bright abode, / The hall of the giants, / Carried away the king." Sturluson writes of his *Ynglinga Saga:* "[My] lives are written in the first place from Thjodolf's poem and augmented from the accounts of learned men." (Sturluson 1990)

See also Ynglinga Saga.

YOON PAI

("Defeat of the Yoons" or "Defeat of the Yunran")

This Thai half-epic, half-ode similar to the Burmese mawgoon (historical verse) is one of the two earliest extant Thai poems (ca. 1475). (Preminger 1990)

YORIMITSU

(Also Raiko)

Yorimitsu, a Japanese warrior-hero (944–1021) and member of the Minamoto clan, is the subject of a legendary tradition. His exploits, with his four companions—Walanabe no Tsuna, Sakata no Kintoki, Usui no Sadamichi, and Urabe no Suetake—have made him one of the most popular heroes of Japan. He is purported to have shot a large arrow to the rooftop of the imperial palace and killed a fox that was taking refuge there. In one cycle he bests the giant Shuten-dōji (Drunken Boy), who survives by drinking human blood. Yorimitsu and his companions don the robes of priests to gain entrance into Shuten-dōji's hideaway on Ōye-yama, where he lives with his retinue of giants. (In reality, Oi-yama, or Tamba, was a famous bandit slain by the historical Yorimitsu.) They pour a magic potion into the drinks of the giant creatures, making them drunk. Then they toss aside their robes and attack, cutting off Shuten-dōji's head. The head continues to attack, but Yorimitsu's warriors eventually triumph.

Another episode involves a fantastic spider who assumes the shape of a servant in order to poison Yorimitsu, but he too is killed in the end. (Popinot 1972)

YU THE GREAT, EMPEROR

(Tamer of the Flood)

Chinese culture-hero and engineering genius (third millennium B.C.), the myth of Yu appears in *The Shu King* in the chapter entitled "The Tribute of Yu." He is thought to be a possibly historical figure to whom myths have become

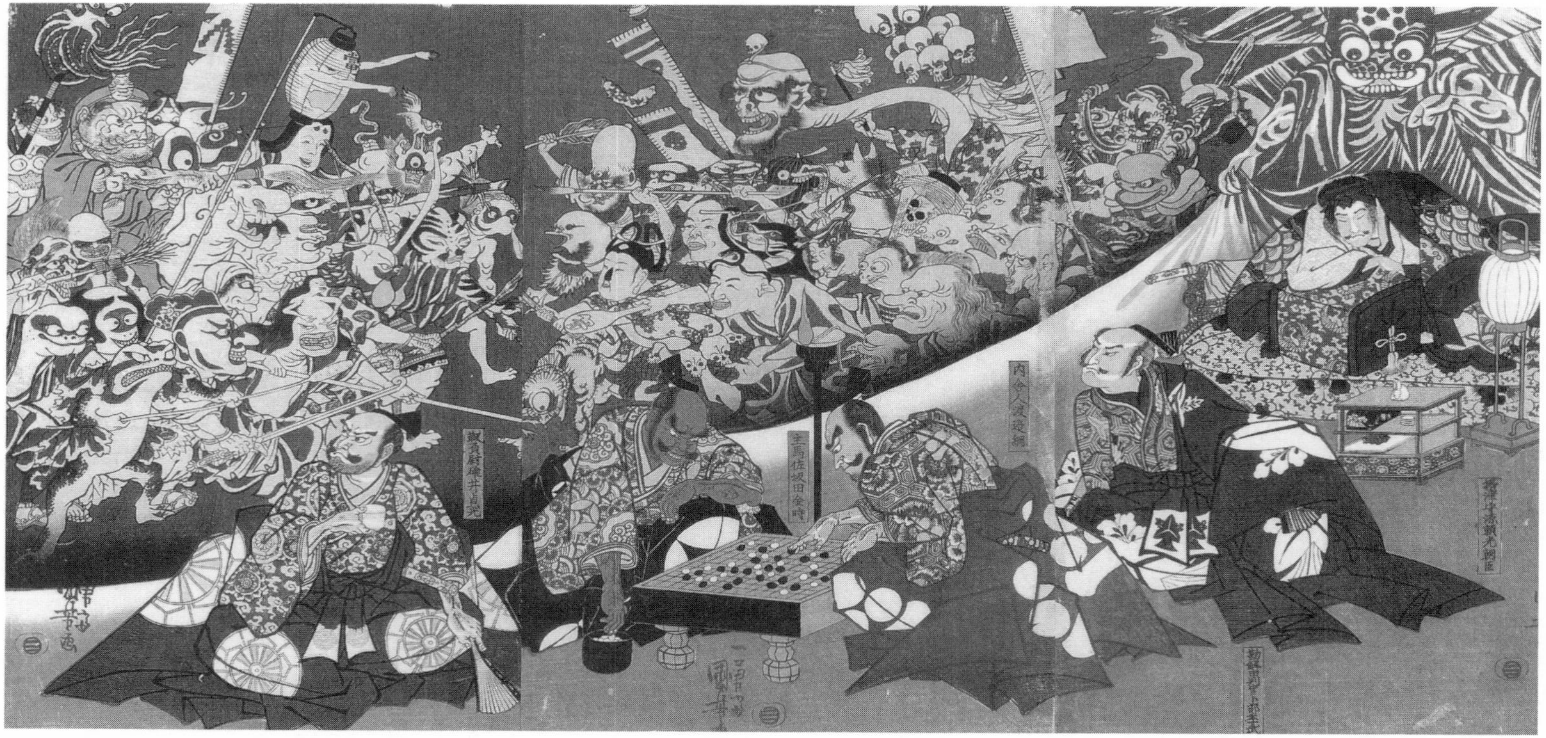

Yorimitsu, upper right, and his companions are fierce medieval Japanese warrior heros whose exploits include battling giants and besting a magical spider.

attached. According to the legend, Emperor Yu is the first monarch of the dynasty of Hea. By one account, he is the son of a star god: One night his mother sees a falling star and becomes pregnant. Later she swallows a pearl dropped by a spirit. In due time Yu is born. At birth, he has the mouth of a tiger. "His ears had three orifices; his head bore the resemblance of the star Kow and K'een." During his youth, he has a dream that while he bathes in the Ho (Yellow River), he drinks up the water. When he grows up, he is a giant of a man.

Another version of his birth is that he or his father is engendered by a three-legged tortoise. Still another version of his birth concerns the son of former emperor Kao Yang (Chuan Hsu) named Kun (Great Fish), who, employed by Emperor Ti Yao to control floodwaters, works for nine years to no avail. He decides to build a dam. For this purpose, he steals from heaven a piece of magic sod. Angered by the theft, the gods cause the waters to rise even higher. Shang Ti, Ruler of Heaven, orders Kun's execution, which takes place on Mount Yu. Three years later, when Kun's incorrupt corpse is slit open, his son, Yu the Great, is born.

Yu is a conscientious man who abstains from drink. He takes up his father's task with such diligence that he stays only four nights with his wife, and for ten years thereafter he doesn't see home. In *The Shu King,* Yu says, "When the floods were lifted to the heavens, spreading far and wide, surrounding the hills . . . I availed myself of four vehicles (boats, carts, sledges, boots), and going up the hills I felled the trees. . . . I dug out ditches and canals and brought them into rivers." *The Shu King* states, "Yu divided the land, following the course of the hills." Along the way, he teaches the people "how to procure the food of toil in addition to flesh meat." He encourages them to trade off accumulated stores, and in this way everyone has grain to eat. After years of labor, Yu provides outlets to the sea. A host of sprites and spirits help him, and dragons and tortoises drag their tails over the most suitable courses for the new water channels. After he has made the world fit for agriculture and human habitation, Heaven presents him with a dark-colored mace. After Emperor Shun resigns, Yu takes his place, becoming ruler of nine provinces. Vegetation becomes lush, and green dragons lie along the borders of the empire. When Yu crosses a river, yellow dragons rise from it. Yu reigns for 45 years. One myth says he is transformed into a bear. (Mackenzie 1990)

See also Flood Myths; P'an Ku; Yao, Tang Ti.

YUDHIṢṬHIRA

In the *Mahābhārata,* Yudhiṣṭhira is the oldest of the five Pāṇḍava brothers, the son of Kuntī and Dharma (God of Justice or Earthly Harmony). Yudhiṣṭhira is wise and strong, but he has one weakness: gambling. When the ambitious Kaurava Duryodhana invites him to a game of dice, Yudhiṣṭhira cannot resist. He loses everything—lands, kingdom, brothers, even Draupadī, wife of the five brothers. In a final game he gambles and loses, condemning the whole Pāṇḍava clan to 12 years in exile in the forest, and a thirteenth in disguise so that no one can recognize them. Although the others reproach him and urge him to action, Yudhiṣṭhira prefers to keep his word and fulfill the terms of the wager. While they are in exile, the other brothers are killed by the water of a poisonous lake. Yudhiṣṭhira restores them to life by answering questions asked by a voice in the lake, such as, Q: What is quicker than the wind? A: Thought. Q: What is madness? A: A forgotten way. Q: What is the cause of the world? A: Love. Much later, after the bloody war, Yudhiṣṭhira decides to renounce the throne and withdraw into the forest, but Bhīṣma reminds him how, even in terrible misfortune, mankind still has hope and "the taste for honey." Yudhiṣṭhira decides that he will reign after all. At the end of their days, Yudhiṣṭhira arrives in paradise carrying a dog, which the gatekeeper tells him he must leave behind if he wishes to enter. Yudhiṣṭhira refuses and is admitted anyway, where he finds none of his family, only his enemies. When he confronts the gatekeeper, he is told, "You've known neither paradise nor hell. . . . Here words end. This was the last illusion." He is rewarded for his attention to duty and his steadfastness by being united with his family. He accepts peace at last, knowing that all is illusion. (Buck 1981)

See also *Mahābhārata.*

YURUPARÍ

Yuruparí is a mythical hero of the Tariana Indians of Brazil. (Bierhorst 1988)

See also *Coadidop.*

Z

ZAQUI-NIM-AC AND ZAQUI-NIMA-TZIIS

In the *Popol Vuh* of the Maya, Zaqui-Nima-Tziis, mother of god, and her consort Nim-Ac (great wild boar) are names given to the Creator. They are the old man and old woman who help to kill Vucub-Caquix the arrogant. (Recinos, Goetz, and Morley 1983)

See also *Popol Vuh.*

ZEUS

(Also Jove and Jupiter)

Zeus is the supreme god, the most powerful of the ancient Greek gods, son of Cronus and Rhea, and husband of Metis, Themis, Eurynome, Demeter, Mnemosyne, Leto, and Hera. He is mentioned throughout the *Iliad* and the *Odyssey.* Although he is known as a just god and is supposedly neutral in the Trojan War, he shows favoritism toward Priam and Hektor and the Trojans in general, agreeing, in the *Iliad* (i), after a visit from Thetis, to aid them against the Aecheans. Although he is all-powerful, he frequently appears to fear his wife Hera's wrath. After the war has been in progress for nine years, he decides that it should be brought to an end. When Hera protests, Zeus sends Athena to bring an end to the truce (iv). In Achilles's quarrel with Agamemnon, he favors Achilles. When Hektor is killed, Thetis is sent to tell Achilles that it is Zeus's will that he give Hektor's body to Priam (xxiv). Stories abound outside the epics about Zeus's lustful exploits; for example, he transforms himself into the Bull of Sidon in order to kidnap Europa. (Calasso 1993; Morford and Lenardon 1977)

See also Abduction; *Iliad; Odyssey.*

ZIHLANDLO

In the Zulu epic *Emperor Shaka the Great,* Zihlandlo is the chief of the Mkhize clan. He is Shaka's close friend who, after Shaka's murder, is killed by King Dingane in an attempt to eliminate any possible opposition to his rule. (Kunene 1979)

See also Dingane; *Emperor Shaka the Great.*

ZIPACNÁ

In the *Popol Vul* of the Maya, Zipacná is the elder son of the Luciferlike Vucub-Caquix the arrogant, born before the time of first man and first woman. When he is young, he plays ball with the large mountains, which he creates in a single night. He and his brother Cabracan argue with their father, who says, "Listen! I am the sun!" Zipacná answers, "I am he who made the earth!" Cabracan says, "I am he who shook the sky and made the earth tremble!" Zipacná goes on a rampage and kills 400 youths, so angering the boys Hunahpú and Xbalanqué that they kill him. (Recinos, Goetz, and Morley 1983)

See also Hunahpú; *Popol Vuh;* Xbalanqué.

ZIUSUDRA

In ancient Sumerian myth, Ziusudra is the Sumerian counterpart of Noah. The extant fragment of the flood story shows it to be similar to the account told in the *Epic of Gilgamesh,* where the ark builder is named Utnapishtim. (Kramer 1956; Sandars 1972)

See also Flood Myths; *Gilgamesh, Epic of;* Noah; Utnapishtim.

ZONG BELEGT BAATAR

This is a short heroic epic of the Mongols. "Hero" is the meaning of the word "baatar." Mongol epics are generally intended for oral performance, although some written versions exist. They are told either entirely in verse, or in some cases in verse with prose passages interspersed. Although some Mongol oral epics may run as many as 5,000 lines, *Zong Belegt Baatar* is usually about 480 lines; a performance lasts only about 17 minutes. Mongol epics are not historical in content, although the persons mentioned may be historical figures. The narrative generally relates fantastic happenings, replete with ogres, talking horses, resurrection from death, and the like.

When the epic begins, Zong Belegt Baatar is ruler of the "eastern continent." He is a strong king: "Whose native body was formed of steel, / Whose born body was formed of iron." He is a good king: "His realm flourished and prospered / . . . His numerous peoples / Flourished and shone." He lives in a magnificent "vitriol-white" palace on "a good firm base." His wife, Okhin Nomin, is a "most wise wife, / Who was equal and companion / To the sturdy hero. . . ." Flowers grow where she steps, and beams of light spurt from the ground after her. The epic relates in great detail the king's possessions, which number in the millions: He has "thirty times ten million camels," for example.

To the northwest of this peaceful land dwells a malevolent ogre named Khuiten Tomor Bust, whose toenails have turned to "hooks of blue iron" and whose fingernails have turned to "hooks of steel." He is in the habit of sucking people's blood and eating children's flesh. His every thought is "how to destroy famous heroes, / Capture their golden seals, / . . . And steal their virgin pastures." He wants to make their people "slaves of his slaves. . . ." He dreams that he slays Zong Belegt Baatar, ravages his people, and plunders his land. He wakes from this happy dream believing that it is a sign from the god Khormusda. He calls his "cruel troops" to mount, and they march, carving out "a terrible and bloody path. . . ." Near the good king's realm, he stops on a knoll to have a smoke. The smoke forms a black fog, through which an eagle flies and lands near the ogre. The eagle turns into Zong Belegt Baatar, "with the strength of ten thousand tigers. . . ." When the hero challenges him, the ogre falls into a rage, and they break into bitter combat. They fight for four years, until Khuiten Tomor Bust feels his strength failing. He withdraws, going back the way he came.

But the hero says, "If we let this murderous ogre / Get away with his life, / He will never leave in peace / The creatures of the golden earth." He blows on his flute to call his horse, mounts, and rides out with shield and armor to rid the country once and for all of the ogre. He reaches a "tall cast-iron fort / With its fence of thorny trees" in which he makes a hole "through which a loaded camel could pass." Flourishing his battle-ax, he charges inside and meets "tens and hundreds of thousands of troops" head-on. He hews to the right and cuts down most of them. He hews to the left and destroys the rest. Then he rushes full speed to the black ogre's palace.

The two wrestle for "seven and eight days," but in the end the hero forces the ogre to his knees. The ogre begs for his life, but Zong says, "Having looked in my father's divination books, / I must kill you." He cuts the ogre to pieces and burns the pieces in a fiery flame. The people who have suffered under the ogre rejoice and praise Zong, "offering / A great scarf of rejoicing." (Finnegan 1978)

ZURVAN

Zurvan is an ancient deity of time, going back to the twelfth century B.C., later incorporated into Zoroastrianism (sixth century B.C.) Zurvan has two aspects: Infinite Time (Zurvan aharana) and Finite Time (Zurvan deregho-chvashata). (Sproul 1991)

ZWANGENDABA

In the Zulu epic *Emperor Shaka the Great,* Zwangendaba (ca. 1785–ca. 1845) is a member of the junior house of the Ndwandwe royal family and the founder of the Angoni kingdom in central East Africa. After he is driven from his land by Shaka's Mfecane (crushing), he leads his Jere people more than 1,000 miles for more than 20 years until they reach the southern end of Lake Tanganyika, where he founds the city of Mapupo. (Kunene 1979)

See also *Emperor Shaka the Great.*

ZWIDE
(Also Uzwide, Zwiti, and Zidze)

In the Zulu epic *Emperor Shaka the Great,* Zwide (ca. 1770s–1825) is the powerful king of the Ndwandwes. Legend holds that he is an "unsavory magician." He tricks Dingiswayo into a trap and has him killed (ca. 1816). At the suggestion of his mother Ntombazi, he is said to have added Dingiswayo's head to a grisly trophy collection. When Zwide hears of Shaka's growing power, he sends an army south to halt him, but his army is repulsed and five of his sons are killed (ca. 1817). The following year he sends his entire army, under the direction of Soshangane, to attack again. He is soundly defeated in one of Shaka's most dramatic conflicts. His mother is captured by Shaka, but he escapes and flees to the Komati River, where he reassembles his forces over the next six years, planning to attack again. But he dies after a prolonged illness (1825) and never regains power. (Kunene 1979; Lipschutz and Rasmussen 1989)

See also *Emperor Shaka the Great;* Ntombazi; Shemane.

APPENDIX A

EPICS LISTED BY GEOGRAPHICAL REGION

AFRICA

ADANGME, THE NATIONAL EPIC OF THE
ADU OGYINAE
AIWEL LONGAR
AMOOGU BI
ANUKILI NA UGAMA
ASKIA MOHAMMED, THE EPIC OF
BAKARIDJAN KONE, A HERO OF SEGU, EPIC OF
BAMBARA EPIC
BANĪ HILĀL EPIC
BASSADJALAN ZAMBELE, EPIC OF
BATTLE OF QADESH
BATTLE OF UHUD
CONTE D'ILBONIA
DA MONZON, EPIC OF
DESTURI ZA WASWAHILI
EBULU IJEOMA
EGBE NRI ADIGHI
EGBELE
THE EGYPTIAN BOOK OF THE DEAD
ELIBE AJA
EMPEROR SHAKA THE GREAT
EZEMU
GASSIRE'S LUTE
GESTE DE HAM-BODEDIO (LA GUERRE ENTRE NDJE FARAH NDJE ET HAMBODEDJO)
LE GESTE DE SEGOU
GIKUYU
HEITSI-EIBIB
IBE OHAFIA ZHIA BIA
IJEOMA EBULU
IKWOGHO
INYAM OLUGU
INYIMA KAALU
KAALU EZE NWA MGBO
KAMBILI, EPIC OF
KAPEPE
KAYARWAR EPIC
KAYOR, EPIC OF
KGODUMODUMO
KIGUMA
KINTU
KOUMBI SALEH, SNAKE OF
LADY FROM THE NORTH/OMAN
LIANJA
LIONGO FUMO
LOFOKEFOKE EPIC
LUBANGO NKUNDUNGULA
MADLEBE AND MADLISA
MBIRE
MOKE MUSSA AND MOKE DANTUNAM
MUBILA
MUJAJI THE RAIN QUEEN
MVET
MWINDO, EPIC OF
MZILIKAZI
NAMBI
NGOLO DIARA
NGUNZA
NNE MGBAAFO, EPIC OF
OGBABA OKORIE
OZIDI SAGA
THE REDISCOVERY OF WAGADU
SAMBA GANA
SÉGOU EPIC
SENKATANA
SHAMBA BOLONGONGO, KING
SILAMAKA AND PULURU
SUMANGURU
SUNDIATA, EPIC OF
TABUKA EPIC
TSUNI-G//OAB
UCHA ARUODO

'UQBAH IBN NAFI'
UTENZI WA MWANA MANGA
WOI-MENI-PELE

ASIA

BALLAD OF THE HIDDEN DRAGON
BARDO THÖTRÖL
CH'U TZ'U
ERINTSEN MERGEN, EPIC OF
GESAR'S SAGA (KESAR SAGA)
HOST OF IGOR, THE LAY OF THE
IKUTA
ILYA OF MUROM
JAHANGIR
KOJIKI
KOTAN UTUNNAI, THE EPIC OF
K'UNG-CHÜEH TUNG-NAN FEI
LAC LONG QUANG AND AU CO
LHA-RINGA
LO-FU HSING
MAN'YŌSHŪ
NIHONGI
THE ORPHAN
RUSSIAN PRIMARY CHRONICLE
SAMGUK SAGI AND SAMGUK YUSA
SASUNTZI DAVITH
SECRET HISTORY OF THE MONGOLS
SHIH-CHING
SONG-SEN-GAM-PO
SONGS OF KOGHT'EN
THE TALE OF THE HEIKE
TANGUN
TIBETAN BOOK OF THE DEAD
TOSOL-GA
URASHIMA OF MIZUNOE
VOLODYMYR, GRAND PRINCE
WOMAN OF POI-SOYA
WOMAN'S EPIC: REPUNNOT-UN-KUR
YORIMITSU
YU THE GREAT, EMPEROR
ZONG BELEGT BAATAR

AUSTRALIA AND OCEANIA

DJANGGAWUL
KIHO
KUMULIPO
MAUI
MOON BONE
RA'I RA'I
TE WHEROWHERO
TIP-OF-THE-SINGLE-FEATHER
TO-KARVUVU AND TO-KABINANA
TUMURIPO

CARIBBEAN, CENTRAL AMERICA, AND MEXICO

THE ANNALS OF THE CAKCHIQUELS
CAVE OF THE JAGUA
CHILAM BALAM, BOOKS OF
THE CREATION OF THE HOE
THE CUCEB
GUAHAYONA
POPOL VUH
QUETZALCÓATL, TOPILTZIN

EUROPE

AENEID
AMIS ET AMILES
ARA AND SHAMIRAM
ARGONAUTICA
ARMES PRYDEIN
ARTHURIAN LEGEND
ATLI, LAY OF
AUCASSIN ET NICOLETTE
THE BATTLE OF KOSOVO
THE BOOK OF LEINSTER
THE BOOK OF THE DUN COW
BRICRIU'S FEAST
BRUNANBURH, THE BATTLE OF
CATH RUIS NA RÍG
THE CATTLE RAID OF COOLEY (TAÍN BÓ CÚAILNGE)
THE CATTLE RAID OF FROECH
CHANSON DE ROLAND
CID, POEMA DEL
CONLE, THE ADVENTURE OF
CULHWCH AND OLWEN
DEOR
DESTRUCTION OF DA DERGA'S HOSTEL
DOON DE MAYENCE
EDDA, POETIC
EGIL'S SAGA
EPIC CYCLE
FAEREYINGA SAGA
THE FATE OF THE SONS OF USNECH
FENIAN CYCLE
FIERY VUK
FINNSBURH, THE FIGHT AT
FLOIRE ET BLANCHEFLOR
FORNALDAR SAGA
FÓSTBRAEÐA SAGA
LE FRESNE
GAMELYN, THE TALE OF
GRETTIS SAGA
GRÍMNISMÁL
GUDRUNLIED
GUIGEMAR
HAMÐISMÁL
HÁVAMÁL
HEIMSKRINGLA

HELEDD
HELIAND
HENGERDD
HILDEBRANDSLIED
HROLFS SAGA KRAKA
HUON DE BORDEAUX
ILIAD
INTERROGATION OF THE OLD MEN
JANKO THE DUKE
JÓMSVÍKINGS, THE SAGA OF THE
KALEVALA
KANTETELAR
KINGS, CYCLE OF
KÖNIG ROTHER
LANVAL
LAXDAELA SAGA
LUDMILA, ST.
MABINOGION
MALDON, THE BATTLE OF
MARKO KRALJEVIĆ
MIORITA
MOCEDADES DE RODRIGO
MORKINSKINNA
NIBELUNGENLIED
NJÁL'S SAGA
ODYSSEY
OĞUZNÂME
ÓLAFS SAGA HELGA
ÓLAFS SAGA TRYGGVASONAR
ORKNEYINGA SAGA
OSSIANIC BALLADS
PARZIVAL
PHARSALIA, EPIC OF
PURSUIT OF DIARMAID AND GRÁINNE
RAGNAR LOTHBROK
REYNARD THE FOX
ROMAN DE RENART
SEVEN SLEEPERS OF EPHESUS
SIABURCHARPUT CONCHULAINN
SIR GAWAIN AND THE GREEN KNIGHT
TAÍN BÓ CÚAILNGE
THEOGONY
TOCHMARC FERB
TRISTAN AND ISEULT
TÚATHA DÉ DANANN
ULSTER CYCLE
VAFTHRÚÐNISMÁL
VERCELLI BOOK
VÍGA-GLÚMS SAGA
THE VISION OF ADAMNÁN
VÖLUSPÁ
VÖLSUNGA SAGA
THE VOYAGE OF BRÂN, SON OF FEBAL
WALDERE
WALTHARIUS
WIDSITH
WOLFDIETRICH
THE WOOING OF ÉTAÍN
YNGLINGA SAGA
YNGLINGA TAL

INDIA AND MIDDLE EAST

AHIKAR, THE STORY OF
ĀLHĀ EPIC
AṆṆAṈMĀR
'ANTAR, THE ROMANCE OF
ANTARAGAṬṬAMMA
AQHAT EPIC
ATRAKHASIS, MYTH OF
BAAL EPIC
BARṢĪṢA, THE LEGEND OF
BASIL DIGENES AKRITAS, EPIC OF
BUDDHACARITA
CANDAINĪ EPIC
CATAKAṆTARĀVAṆAṈ
CILAPPATIKĀRAM
DEDE KORKUT, THE BOOK OF
DEVNĀRĀYAṆ
ḌHOLĀ EPIC
DHŪ AL-HIMMA
ENMERKAR AND ENSUKUSHIRANNA, EPIC OF
ENMERKAR AND THE LORD OF ARATTA, EPIC OF
ENUMA ELISH, EPIC OF
ERIDU GENESIS, EPIC OF
ERRA EPIC
ETANA EPIC
THE FALL OF AKKAD
GILGAMESH, EPIC OF
THE GRATEFUL DEAD
GŪGĀ
INANNA AND BILULU
INANNA AND SHUKALLITUDA
INANNA'S DESCENT TO THE NETHER WORLD
JASHAR, BOOK OF
KĀLAKĀCĀRYAKATHĀ
KĀMAMMA KATHA
KAN PÜDEI
KANYAKĀ AMMAVĀRI KATHA
KĀTAMARĀJU KATHA
KERET EPIC
AL-KHADIR
KORDABBU
LALITAVISTARA
LUDUL BEL NEMEQI
LUGALBANDA AND ENMERKAR
LUGALBANDA AND MOUNT HURRUM
MAHĀBHĀRATA
MAHĀVAṂSA
MAHĀVASTU
MANASĀ-MAṄGALS
MAṆIKKUṞAVAṈ
MANIMEKHALAÏ
NABIBANGSA
PĀBŪJĪ, EPIC OF

PALAVĒCAMCĒRVAIKKĀRAR CĀMI KATAI
PALNĀḌU, THE EPIC OF
PAÑCATANTRA
RĀMĀYAṆA
ṚG VEDA
ŚAKAṬ, THE KATHĀ OF
SANYĀSAMMA KATHA
SEVEN VIZIERS
SHĀH-NĀMAH
SINDBAD THE SAILOR
SĪRAT AL-AMĪRA DHĀT AL-HIMMA
SĪRAT 'ANTAR
SĪRAT BANĪ HILĀL
SĪRAT BAYBARS
SĪRAT SAYF IBN DHĪ YAZAN
SONG OF ULLIKUMMI
THEOGONY
TIMURID EPIC
TU'CHÜEH
TUKULTI NINURTA EPIC
WAR OF THE GODS (ENUMA ELISH)

NORTH AMERICA

BUNGLING HOST
CHILAM BALAM, BOOKS OF
DINÉ BAHANÈ
DZITBALCHE, BOOK OF THE SONGS OF
HIAWATHA
NAPI
PTE CYCLE
QUETZALCÓATL, TOLPILTZIN
SON OF LIGHT
UNCEGILA'S SEVENTH SPOT
WYANDOT CREATION MYTH

SOUTH AMERICA

COADIDOP
FLOOD, GREAT
HUAROCHIRÍ MANUSCRIPT
MALEIWA
ROMI KUMU
THUNNUPA
TYUSNINCHIS, THE TALES OF
UNUARTO
VENANCIO CAMICO
WAKINYAN TANKA
WATUNNA

SOUTHEAST ASIA

ALIM EPIC
BANTUGAN
HAINUWELE
HIKAJAT MALÉM DAGANG
HIKAJAT PRANG KOMPENI
HIKAJAT PRANG SABIL
HIKAYAT BAYAN BUDIMAN
HIKAYAT KHOJA MAIMUN
HIKAYAT RAJA-RAPA PASAI
HIKAYAT SULTAN IBRAHIM IBN ADHEM
HUDHUD
LORD LO
THE MAGIC CROSSBOW
MAHAJATI
NGASAUNGGYAN, BATTLE OF
P'HRA LO-THU
PÒTJOET MOEHAMAT, HIKAJAT
QAT
A WAR BETWEEN GODS
YOON PAI

APPENDIX B

EPICS LISTED CHRONOLOGICALLY

THIRD MILLENNIUM B.C.

ENMERKAR AND ENSUKUSHIRANNA, EPIC OF
ENMERKAR AND THE LORD OF ARATTA, EPIC OF
ETANA EPIC
LUDUL BEL NEMEQI
LUGALBANDA AND ENMERKAR
LUGALBANDA AND MOUNT HURRUM
YU THE GREAT

SECOND MILLENNIUM B.C.

BAAL EPIC
THE EGYPTIAN BOOK OF THE DEAD
ENUMA ELISH, EPIC OF
ERIDU GENESIS, EPIC OF
THE FALL OF AKKAD
GILGAMESH, EPIC OF
INANNA AND BILULU
INANNA AND SHUKALLITUDA
INANNA'S DESCENT TO THE NETHER WORLD
THEOGONY

(NINETEENTH CENTURY)
ATRAKHASIS, MYTH OF

(FOURTEENTH CENTURY)
AQHAT EPIC
KERET EPIC

(THIRTEENTH CENTURY)
BATTLE OF QADESH
ṚG VEDA

(TWELFTH CENTURY)
SONG OF ULLIKUMMI
TUKULTI-NINURTA EPIC

FIRST MILLENNIUM B.C.

(NINTH CENTURY)
ILIAD
ODYSSEY
THEOGONY

(EIGHTH CENTURY)
ERRA EPIC

(SEVENTH CENTURY)
AHIKAR, THE STORY OF
BOOK OF SONGS

(SIXTH CENTURY)
EPIC CYCLE
GASSIRE'S LUTE
SHIH-CHING

(FIFTH CENTURY)
THE GRATEFUL DEAD
MAHĀBHĀRATA

(THIRD CENTURY)
ARGONAUTICA
CH'U TZ'U
A WAR BETWEEN GODS

(SECOND CENTURY)
MAHĀVASTU
RĀMĀYAṆA
SONGS OF KOGHT'EN

(FIRST CENTURY)
AENEID
PAÑCATANTRA

FIRST CENTURY A.D.

LO-FU HSING
THE ORPHAN
PHARSALIA, EPIC OF
TOSOL-GA

SECOND CENTURY

BUDDHACARITA
MANIMEKHALAÏ

THIRD CENTURY

LALITAVISTARA
OSSIANIC BALLADS
QUETZALCÓATL
ULSTER CYCLE

FIFTH CENTURY

ARA AND SHAMIRAM
KOUMBI SALEH, SNAKE OF
K'UNG-CHÜEH TUNG-NAN FEI
MAHĀVAṂSA
SEVEN SLEEPERS OF EPHESUS

SIXTH CENTURY

'ANTAR, THE ROMANCE OF
ARTHURIAN LEGEND
CILAPPATIKĀRAM
HENGERDD
SEVEN VIZIERS
SĪRAT SAYF IBN DHĪ YAZAN

SEVENTH CENTURY

CATH RUIS NA RÍG
THE CATTLE RAID OF COOLEY
FINNSBURH, THE FIGHT AT
HILDEBRANDSLIED
'UQBAH IBN NAFI'
THE VOYAGE OF BRÂN, SON OF FEBAL
WIDSITH

EIGHTH CENTURY

BARDO THÖTRÖL
BEOWULF
BRICRIU'S FEAST
CONLE, THE ADVENTURE OF
THE FATE OF THE SONS OF USNECH
FENIAN CYCLE
KOJIKI
MAN'YŌSHŪ
NIHONGI
PURSUIT OF DIARMAID AND GRÁINNE
SIABURCHARPUT CONCHULAINN
TAÍN BÓ CÚAILNGE
TOCHMARC FERB
TOGAIL BRUIDNE DA-CHOCA
WALDERE
WOLFDIETRICH
THE WOOING OF ÉTAÍN

NINTH CENTURY

DEOR
DOON DE MAYENCE
EDDA, POETIC
GRÍMNISMÁL
HAMÐISMÁL
HÁVAMÁL
HELEDD
HELIAND
JASHAR, BOOK OF
KAYARWAR EPIC
SASUNTZI DAVITH
SINDBAD THE SAILOR
SĪRAT AL AMĪRA DHĀT AL-HIMMA
THEOGONY
UTENZI WA MWANA MANGA
WALTHARIUS

TENTH CENTURY

ARMES PRYDEIN
BARṢĪṢĀ, THE LEGEND OF
BASIL DIGENES AKRITAS, EPIC OF
BRUNANBURH, THE BATTLE OF
IKUTA
ILYA OF MUROM
LUDMILA, ST.
MALDON, THE BATTLE OF
REYNARD THE FOX
SAMGUK SAGI AND SAMGUK YUSA
TU'CHÜEH
VERCELLI BOOK
THE VISION OF ADAMNÁN

ELEVENTH CENTURY

BANĪ HILĀL EPIC
CHANSON DE ROLAND
CULHWCH AND OLWEN

FAEREYINGA SAGA
GESAR'S SAGA (KESAR SAGA)
MABINOGION

TWELFTH CENTURY

AMIS ET AMILES
ATLI, LAY OF
BALLAD OF THE HIDDEN DRAGON
THE BOOK OF THE DUN COW
THE BOOK OF LEINSTER
CID, POEMA DEL
DESTRUCTION OF DA DERGA'S HOSTEL
FLOIRE ET BLANCHEFLOR
FRESNE, LE
GUIGEMAR
HOST OF IGOR, THE LAY OF THE
JÓMSVÍKINGS, THE SAGA OF THE
KĀLAKĀCĀRYAKATHĀ
KINGS, CYCLE OF
KÖNIG ROTHER
LAC LONG QUANG AND AU CO
LANVAL
THE MAGIC CROSSBOW
MORKINSKINNA
NIBELUNGENLIED
ROMAN DE RENART
RUSSIAN PRIMARY CHRONICLE
SHĀH-NĀMAH
SONG OF ROLAND
TRISTAN AND ISEULT
TÚATHA DÉ DANANN
VOLODYMYR, GRAND PRINCE
YNGLINGA TAL

THIRTEENTH CENTURY

AUCASSIN ET NICOLETTE
DEDE KORKUT, THE BOOK OF
EGIL'S SAGA
FÓSTBRAEÐA SAGA
GUDRUNLIED
HEIMSKRINGLA
HUON DE BORDEAU
INTERROGATION OF THE OLD MEN
KAN PÜDEI
KANYAKĀ AMMAVĀRI KATHA
LAXDAELA SAGA
MOCEDADES DE RODRIGO
NGASAUNGGYAN, BATTLE OF
NJÁL'S SAGA
ÓLAFS SAGA HELGA
ÓLAFS SAGA TRYGGVASONAR
ORKNEYINGA SAGA
PARZIVAL
SECRET HISTORY OF THE MONGOLS
SĪRAT BAYBARS
SUMANGURU
SUNDIATA, EPIC OF
THE TALE OF THE HEIKE
VAFTHRÚÐNISMÁL
VÍGA-GLÚMS SAGA
VÖLSUNGA SAGA
YNGLINGA SAGA

FOURTEENTH CENTURY

THE BATTLE OF KOSOVO
THE CREATION OF THE HOE
FIERY VUK
FORNALDAR SAGA
GRETTIS SAGA
HROLFS SAGA KRAKA
JAHANGIR
MBIRE
OĞUZNÂME
PALNĀḌU, THE EPIC OF
SIR GAWAIN AND THE GREEN KNIGHT
TIMURID EPIC

FIFTEENTH CENTURY

CAVE OF THE JAGUA
COADIDOP
DINÉ BAHANÈ
FLOOD, GREAT
GAMELYN, THE TALE OF
GUAHAYONA
HIKAYAT RAJA-RAPA PASAI
KĀTAMARĀJU KATHA
KUMULIPO
MAHAJATI
QUETZALCÓATL
RA'I RA'I
YOON PAI

SIXTEENTH CENTURY

ASKIA MOHAMMED, THE EPIC OF
THE BOOK OF THE DEAN OF LISMORE
CHILAM BALAM, BOOKS OF
THE CUCEB
DZITBALCHE, BOOK OF THE SONGS OF
HUAROCHIRÍ MANUSCRIPT
MANASĀ-MAṄGALS
MARKO KRALJEVIĆ
P'HRA LO-THU
POPOL VUH
URASHIMA OF MIZUNOE
WOMAN'S EPIC: REPUNNOT-UN-KUR

SEVENTEENTH CENTURY

BAMBARA EPIC

DA MONZON, EPIC OF
ERINTSEN MERGEN, EPIC OF
GESTE DE SEGOU, LE
HIKAYAT SULTAN IBRAHIM IBN ADHEM
JANKO, THE DUKE
KAYOR, EPIC OF
LADY FROM THE NORTH/OMAN
LIONGO FUMO
LORD LO
SHAMBA BOLONGONGO, KING
WOMAN OF POI-SOYA
YORIMITSU

EIGHTEENTH CENTURY

BAKARIDJAN KONE
BASSADJALAN ZAMBELE, EPIC OF
EZEMU
HIAWATHA
MADLEBE AND MADLISA
PÒTJOET MOEHAMAT, HIKAJAT
PTE CYCLE
SÉGOU EPIC
SILAMAKA AND PULURU

NINETEENTH CENTURY

ANNALS OF THE CAKCHIQUELS
BATTLE OF UHUD
BUNGLING HOST
DESTURI ZA WASWAHILI
DHŪ AL-HIMMA
EMPEROR SHAKA THE GREAT
GIKUYU
LA GUERRE ENTRE NDJE FARAH NDJE ET HAMBODEDJO
HIKAJAT MALÉM DAGANG
HIKAJAT PRANG KOMPENI
HIKAJAT PRANG SABIL
HIKAYAT BAYAN BUDIMAN
HIKAYAT KHOJA MAIMUN
KALEVALA
KANTETELAR
KOTAN UTUNNAI, THE EPIC OF
LOFOKEFOKE EPIC
MIORITA
MUJAJI THE RAIN QUEEN
MWINDO, EPIC OF
MZILIKAZI
SĪRAT 'ANTAR
SON OF LIGHT
TE WHEROWHERO
TUMURIPO
VENANCIO CAMICO
WYANDOT CREATION MYTH
ZONG BELEGT BAATAR

TWENTIETH CENTURY

ADANGME, THE NATIONAL EPIC OF THE
ADU OGYINAE
AIWEL LONGAR
ĀLHĀ EPIC
ALIM EPIC
AMOOGU BI
AṆṆAṈMĀR
ANUKILI NA UGAMA
BANTUGAN
CANDAINĪ EPIC
CATAKAṆTARĀVAṆAṈ
CONTE D' ILBONIA
DEVNĀRĀYAṆ
ḌHOLĀ EPIC
DJANGGAWUL
EBULU IJEOMA
EGBE NRI ADIGHI
EGBELE
ELIBE AJA
GESTE DE HAM-BODEDIO
GŪGĀ
HAINUWELE
HAMBODJO
HEITSI-EIBIB
HUDHUD
IBE OHAFIA ZHIA BIA
IJEOMA EBULU
IKWOGHO
INYAM OLUGU
INYIMA KAALU
KAALU EZE NWA MGBO
KĀMAMMA KATHA
KAMBILI, EPIC OF
KAPEPE
KGODUMODUMO
AL-KHADIR
KIGUMA
KIHO
KINTU
KORDABBU
LHA-RINGA
LIANJA
LUBANGO NKUNDUNGULA
MALEIWA
MAṆIKKUṞAVAṈ
MAUI
MOKE MUSSA AND MOKE DANTUNAM
MOON BONE
MUBILA
MVET
NABIBANGSA
NAMBI
NAPI
NGOLO DIARA
NGUNZA
NNE MGBAAFO, EPIC OF
OGBABA OKORIE

APPENDIX B

OZIDI SAGA
PĀBŪJĪ, EPIC OF
PALAVĒCAMCĒRVAIKKĀRAR CĀMI KATAI
QAT
THE REDISCOVERY OF WAGADU
ROMI KUMU
ŚAKAṬ, THE KATHĀ OF
SAMBA GANA
SANYĀSAMMA KATHA
SENKATANA
SĪRAT AL-AMĪRA DHĀT AL-HIMMA
SONG-SEN-GAM-PO
TABUKA EPIC
THUNNUPA
TIP-OF-THE-SINGLE-FEATHER
TO-KARVUVU AND TO-KABINANA
TSUNI-G//OAB
TYUSNINCHIS, THE TALES OF
UCHA ARUODO
UNCEGILA'S SEVENTH SPOT
UNUARTO
WAKINYAN TANKA
WATUNNA
WOI-MENI-PELE
ZONG BELEGT BAATAR

APPENDIX C

EPICS LISTED BY SUBGENRE

BALLAD CYCLE

FENIAN CYCLE
OSSIANIC BALLADS

CHANTE FABLE

AUCASSIN ET NICOLETTE

COLLECTION

ANNALS OF THE CAKCHIQUELS
BARDO THÖTRÖL
BOOK OF DRUIMM SNECHTAI *(see* DESTRUCTION OF DA DERGA'S HOSTEL)
THE BOOK OF LEINSTER
BOOK OF SONGS
THE BOOK OF THE DEAN OF LISMORE
THE BOOK OF THE DUN COW
CHILAM BALAM, BOOKS OF
CH'U TZ'U
DESTURI ZA WASWAHILI
DZITBALCHE, BOOK OF THE SONGS OF
EDDA, POETIC
THE EGYPTIAN BOOK OF THE DEAD
FORNALDAR SAGA
HEIMSKRINGLA
DAS HELDENBUCH
HENGERDD
HUAROCHIRÍ MANUSCRIPT
JASHAR, BOOK OF
KANTETELAR
KOJIKI
MABINOGION
MAN'YŌSHŪ
NIHONGI
PAÑCATANTRA
ṚG VEDA
RUSSIAN PRIMARY CHRONICLE

CREATION, MIGRATION, RITUAL, PROPHECY CYCLE, OR EPIC

ADANGME, THE NATIONAL EPIC OF THE ADU OGYINAE
BANTUGAN
CAVE OF THE JAGUA
COADIDOP
THE CREATION OF THE HOE
THE CUCEB
DINÉ BAHANÈ
DJANGGAWUL
EBULU IJEOMA
ENUMA ELISH, EPIC OF
ERIDU GENESIS, EPIC OF
FLOOD, GREAT
GASSIRE'S LUTE
GIKUYU
GRÍMNISMÁL
GUAHAYONA
HAINUWELE
HEITSI-EIBIB
HUDHUD
INANNA AND BILULU
INANNA AND SHUKALLITUDA
INANNA'S DESCENT TO THE NETHER WORLD
KERET EPIC
KIHO
KINTU
KUMULIPO
LAC LONG QUANG AND AU CO
LUGALBANDA AND ENMERKAR

LUGALBANDA AND MOUNT HURRUM
THE MAGIC CROSSBOW
MALEIWA
MAUI
MUJAJI THE RAIN QUEEN
NAPI
PALAVĒCAMCĒRVAIKKĀRAR CĀMI KATAI
POPOL VUH
PTE CYCLE
QAT
QUETZCALCÓATL
RA'I RA'I
ROMAN DE RENART (VERSE TALES)
ROMI KUMU
THUNNUPA
TIP-OF-THE-SINGLE FEATHER
TO-KARVUVU AND TO-KABINANA
TUMURIPO
TYUSNINCHIS, THE TALES OF
VAFTHRÚÐNISMÁL
WATUNNA
WOI-MENI-PELE

EPIC-SAGA

THE CATTLE RAID OF COOLEY
DESTRUCTION OF DA DERGA'S HOSTEL
GESAR'S SAGA (KESAR SAGA)
OZIDI SAGA

FERTILITY EPIC OR MYTH

BAAL EPIC
ETANA EPIC

FOLK CYCLE

ĀLHĀ EPIC
'ANTAR, THE ROMANCE OF
LHA-RINGA
REYNARD THE FOX
VENANCIO CAMICO

FOLK EPIC

ALIM EPIC
AṆṆAṈMĀR
CANDAINĪ EPIC
CATAKAṆTARĀVAṆAṈ
CONTE D'ILBONIA
DEVNĀRĀYAN
ḌHOLĀ EPIC
EGBE NRI ADIGHI
EGBELE
GESTE DE HAM-BODEDIO (LA GUERRE ENTRE NDJE FARAH NDJE ET HAMBODEDJO)
GŪGĀ
HIKAYAT BAYAN BUDIMAN
HIKAYAT KHOJA MAIMUN
IBE OHAFIA ZHIA BIA
IJEOMA EBULU
IKWOGHO
ILYA OF MUROM
INYIMA KAALU
KAALU EZE NWA MGBO
KĀMAMMA KATHA
KAMBILI, EPIC OF
KANYAKĀ AMMAVĀRI KATHA
KAPEPE
KĀTAMARĀJU KATHA
KGODUMODUMO
AL-KHADIR
KIGUMA
KORDABBU
KOTAN UTUNNAI, THE EPIC OF
LIANJA
LIONGO FUMO
LOFOKEFOKE EPIC
LUBANGO NKUNDUNGULA
MADLEBE AND MADLISA
MANASĀ-MAṄGALS
MAṆIKKUṞAVAṈ
MOKE MUSSA AND MOKE DANTUNAM
MUBILA
MVET
MZILIKAZI
NABIBANGSA
NAMBI
OGBABA OKORIE
OĞUZNÂME
PĀBŪJĪ, EPIC OF
PALNĀḌU, THE EPIC OF
SĪRAT 'ANTAR
SĪRAT BANĪ HILĀL
SĪRAT SAYF IBN DHĪ YAZAN
SUMANGURU

HEROIC CYCLE

BAMBARA EPIC
BASIL DIGENES AKRITAS, EPIC OF
BASSADJALAN ZAMBELE
DA MONZON, EPIC OF
DEDE KORKUT, THE BOOK OF
DOON DE MAYENCE
ENMERKAR AND ENSUKUSHIRANNA, EPIC OF
ENMERKAR AND THE LORD OF ARATTA, EPIC OF
EPIC CYCLE
THE FALL OF AKKAD

FIERY VUK
LE GESTE DE SEGOU
JAHANGIR
JANKO THE DUKE
KAYARWAR EPIC
KAYOR, EPIC OF
KINGS, CYCLE OF
MARKO KRALJEVIĆ
NGOLO DIARA
SĪRAT AL-AMĪRA DHĀT AL-HIMMA
SĪRAT BAYBARS
SONGS OF KOGHT'EN
THE TALE OF THE HEIKE
TIMURID EPIC

HEROIC EPIC

AENEID
AMIS ET AMILES
ANUKILI NA UGAMA
AQHAT EPIC
ARGONAUTICA
ASKIA MOHAMMED, THE EPIC OF
BAKARIDJAN KONE, A HERO OF SEGU, EPIC OF
BANĪ HILĀL EPIC
BASIL DIGENES AKRITAS, EPIC OF
BATTLE OF QADESH
BATTLE OF UHUD
BEOWULF
CHANSON DE ROLAND
CID, POEMA DEL
EMPEROR SHAKA THE GREAT
ERINTSEN MERGEN, EPIC OF
ERRA EPIC
EZEMU
GILGAMESH, EPIC OF
HIKAJAT MALÉM DAGANG
HIKAJAT PRANG SABIL
ILIAD
KALEVALA
MAHĀBHĀRATA
MANIMEKHALAÏ
MOCEDADES DE RODRIGO
NIBELUNGENLIED
ODYSSEY
PHARSALIA, EPIC OF
PÒTJOET MOEHAMAT, HIKAJAT
RĀMĀYAṆA
SĪRAT AL-AMĪRA DHĀT AL-HIMMA
SUNDIATA, EPIC OF
ZONG BELEGT BAATAR

HEROIC POEM OR BALLAD

ARMES PRYDEIN
ATLI, LAY OF
BALLAD OF THE HIDDEN DRAGON
DEOR
LE FRESNE
GUDRUNLIED
GUIGEMAR
HAMÐISMÁL
HÁVAMÁL
HELEDD
HELIAND
HIKAYAT RAJA-RAPA PASAI
HILDEBRANDSLIED
HOST OF IGOR, THE LAY OF THE
HUON DE BORDEAU
K'UNG-CHÜEH TUNG-NAN FEI
LANVAL
LO-FU HSING
LORD LO
LUDUL BEL NEMEQI
MAHAJATI
MALDON, THE BATTLE OF
MWINDO, EPIC OF
NGASAUNGGYAN, BATTLE OF
PARZIVAL
P'HRA LO-THU
SIR GAWAIN AND THE GREEN KNIGHT
UTENZI WA MWANA MANGA
VOLODYMYR, GRAND PRINCE
VÖLUSPÁ
WALTHARIUS
YOON PAI
YNGLINGA TAL

HEROIC TALE OR EPIC NARRATIVE

AMOOGU BI
BRICRIU'S FEAST
ELIBE AJA
THE FATE OF THE SONS OF USNECH
GAMELYN, THE TALE OF
HIKAYAT SULTAN IBRAHIM IBN ADHEM
INTERROGATION OF THE OLD MEN
KAN PÜDEI
MAHĀVAṂSA
MBIRE
PURSUIT OF DIARMAID AND GRÁINNE
SINDBAD THE SAILOR
SON OF LIGHT
THE VISION OF ADAMNÁN
THE VOYAGE OF BRÂN, SON OF FEBAL

LEGEND

AHIKAR, THE STORY OF
AIWEL LONGAR
ARA AND SHAMIRAM
ARTHURIAN LEGEND
BARṢĪṢĀ, THE LEGEND OF

CATH RUIS NA RÍG
CONLE, THE ADVENTURE OF
THE GRATEFUL DEAD
HIAWATHA
IKUTA
KĀLAKĀCĀRYAKATHĀ
LALITAVISTARA
MAHĀVASTU
SAMBA GANA
SENKATANA
SEVEN SLEEPERS OF EPHESUS
SONG-SEN-GAM-PO
UNCEGILA'S SEVENTH SPOT
'UQBAH IBN NAFI'
URASHIMA OF MIZUNOE
WAKINYAN TANKA
A WAR BETWEEN GODS
YORIMITSU

MYTH

ATRAKHASIS, MYTH OF
BUNGLING HOST
KOUMBI SALEH, SNAKE OF
MOON BONE
THE REDISCOVERY OF WAGADU
SONG OF ULLIKUMMI
YU THE GREAT, EMPEROR

NARRATIVE POEM

BRUNANBURH, THE BATTLE OF
BUDDHACARITA
MIORITA
THE ORPHAN
ROMAN DE BRUT
TOSOL-GA
VÖLUSPÁ
WALDERE
WIDSITH
WOLFDIETRICH
YNGLINGA TAL

PROSE ROMANCE

CULHWCH AND OLWEN
KÖNIG ROTHER

VERSE ROMANCE

FLOIRE ET BLANCHEFLOR

SAGA

EGIL'S SAGA
FAEREYINGA SAGA
FÓSTBRAEÐA SAGA
GRETTIS SAGA
HROLFS SAGA KRAKA
JÓMSVÍKINGS, THE SAGA OF THE
LAXDAELA SAGA
MORKINSKINNA
NJÁL'S SAGA
ÓLAFS SAGA HELGA
ÓLAFS SAGA TRYGGVASONAR
ORKNEYINGA SAGA
VÍGA-GLÚMS SAGA
VÖLSUNGA SAGA
THE WOOING OF ÉTAÍN
YNGLINGA SAGA

WOMAN'S EPIC

CILAPPATIKĀRAM
COADIDOP
DHŪ AL-HIMMA
INYAM OLUGU
LADY FROM THE NORTH/OMAN
LUDMILA, ST.
NNE MGBAAFO, EPIC OF
SĪRAT AL-AMĪRA DHĀT AL-HIMMA
UCHA ARUODO
WOMAN OF POI-SOYA
WOMAN'S EPIC: REPUNNOT-UN-KUR

BIBLIOGRAPHY

Books

Abrahams, Roger D. *African Folktales.* New York: Pantheon Books, 1983.

Alcock, Leslie. *Arthur's Britain.* Harmondsworth, England: Penguin Books, 1979.

Alexander, David, et al. *Eerdman's Handbook to the Bible.* Carmel, CA: Guideposts, 1973.

Alexander, Hartley Burr. *Mythology of All Races, Latin American.* New York: Cooper Square Publishers, 1964.

Alexander, Michael, trans. *The Earliest English Poems.* New York: Penguin Books, 1991.

Allen, J. W. T., trans. *The Customs of the Swahili People, the Desturi Za Waswahili of Mtoro Bin Mwinyi Bakari.* Berkeley: University of California Press, 1981.

Ashvaghosha. *Buddhacarita.* E. H. Johnston, ed. Calcutta: Baptist Mission Press, 1936.

Aston, W. G., trans. *Nihongi.* Rutland, VT, and Tokyo: Charles E. Tuttle Company, 1972.

Balaban, John, trans. *Ca Dao Việtnam.* Greensboro, NC: Unicorn Press, 1980.

Barber, Karin, and P. F. de Moraes Fariar. *Discourse and Its Disguises. The Interpretation of African Oral Texts.* Birmingham, England: University of Birmingham Centre for West African Studies, 1989.

Barber, R. W. *Arthur of Albion: An Introduction to Arthurian Literature and Legends of England.* London: Cambridge University Press, 1961.

Ben Khader, Aïcha Ben Abed, and David Soren. *Carthage: A Mosaic of Ancient Tunisia.* New York: W. W. Norton, 1987.

Bhaktivedanta, A. C. Swami Prabhupāda. *Bhagavad-Gītā As It Is.* Los Angeles: The Bhaktivedanta Book Trust, 1981.

Biebuyck, Daniel. *Hero and Chief, Epic Literature from the Banyanga (Zaire Republic).* Berkeley: University of California Press, 1978.

Biebuyck, Daniel, and K. Mateene. *The Mwindo Epic from the Banyanga.* Berkeley: University of California Press, 1969.

Bierhorst, John, ed. and trans. *Four Masterworks of American Indian Literature: Quetzalcoatl, The Ritual of Condolence, Cuceb, The Night Chant.* Tucson: University of Arizona Press, 1974.

———. *The Mythology of South America.* New York: Quill/William Morrow, 1988.

Birch, Cyril, ed. *Anthology of Chinese Literature from Early Times to the Fourteenth Century.* New York: Grove Press, 1965.

Bird, Charles, et al., eds. *The Songs of Seydou Camara: Kambili.* Bloomington: Indiana University African Studies Center, 1974.

Blackburn, Stuart H., et al. *Oral Epics in India.* Berkeley: University of California Press, 1989.

Blackburn, Stuart H., and A. K. Ramanujan, eds. *Another Harmony. New Essays on the Folklore of India.* Berkeley: University of California Press, 1986.

Bloodworth, Dennis, and Ching Ping Bloodworth. *The Chinese Machiavelli.* New York: Dell Publishing Co., 1977.

Boone, Sylvia Ardyn. *Radiance from the Waters.* New Haven: Yale University Press, 1986.

Bowder, Diana. *Who Was Who in the Roman World.* New York: Washington Square Press, 1984.

Bownas, Geoffrey, and Anthony Thwaite, trans. *The Penguin Book of Japanese Verse.* Baltimore, MD: Penguin Books, 1968.

Brook, G. L., and R. F. Leslie, eds. *Layamon: Brut.* London: Oxford University Press, 1963.

Brown, Norman O., trans. *Hesiod's Theogony.* New York: Macmillan, 1981.

Buck, William. *Mahabharata.* Berkeley: University of California Press, 1981.

———. *Ramayana.* Berkeley: University of California Press, 1976.

Budge, E. A. Wallis. *The Gods of the Egyptians.* New York: Dover Publications, 1969.

Budge, E. A. Wallis, trans. *The Egyptian Book of the Dead.* New York: Dover Publications, 1967.

Bukko Dendo Kyukai. *The Teaching of Buddha.* Tokyo: Kosaido Printing Co., Ltd., 1978.

Bullchild, Percy. *The Sun Came Down.* San Francisco: Harper & Row, 1985.

Bullfinch, Thomas. *Bullfinch's Mythology: The Age of Fable.* New York: NAL/Mentor, 1962.

Burns, Thomas. *A History of the Ostrogoths.* Bloomington: Indiana University Press, 1991.

Bushnaq, Inea, ed. and trans. *Arab Folktales.* New York: Pantheon Books, 1986.

Calasso, Roberto. *The Marriage of Cadmus and Harmony.* Tim Parks, trans. New York: Knopf, 1993.

Camões, Luis Vaz de. *The Luciads.* William C. Atkinson, trans. New York: Penguin Books, 1952.

Campbell, Joseph. *The Flight of the Wild Gander.* Chicago: Regnery Gateway, 1969.

———. *The Hero with a Thousand Faces.* Princeton, NJ: Princeton University Press/Bollingen, 1972.

———. *Historical Atlas of World Mythology.* Vol. I: *The Way of the Animal Powers.* Part 1: *Mythologies of the Primitive Hunters and Gatherers.* New York: Harper & Row, 1988.

———. *Historical Atlas of World Mythology.* Vol. I: *The Way of the Animal Powers.* Part 2: *Mythologies of the Great Hunt.* New York: Harper & Row, 1988.

———. *Historical Atlas of World Mythology.* Vol. II: *The Way of the Seeded Earth.* Part 1: *The Sacrifice.* New York: Harper & Row, 1988.

———. *Historical Atlas of World Mythology.* Vol. II: *The Way of the Seeded Earth.* Part 2: *Mythologies of the Primitive Planters: The North Americas.* New York: Harper & Row, 1989.

———. *Historical Atlas of World Mythology.* Vol. II: *The Way of the Seeded Earth.* Part 3: *Mythologies of the Primitive Planters: The Middle and Southern Americas.* New York: Harper & Row, 1989.

———. *The Masks of God: Creative Mythology.* New York: Penguin Books, 1976.

———. *The Masks of God: Occidental Mythology.* New York: Penguin Books, 1976.

———. *The Masks of God: Oriental Mythology.* New York: Penguin Books, 1976.

———. *The Masks of God: Primitive Mythology.* New York: Penguin Books, 1976.

———. *The Mythic Image.* Princeton, NJ: Princeton University Press/Bollingen, 1982.

———. *Myths to Live By.* New York: Bantam Books, 1988.

———. *The Power of Myth.* New York: Doubleday, 1988.

Ceram, C. W. *Gods, Graves, and Scholars.* E. B. Garside and Sophie Wilkins, trans. New York: Bantam Books, 1972.

———. *The Secret of the Hittites.* Richard Winston and Clara Winston, trans. New York: Dorset Press, 1990.

Chadwick, Nora. *The Celts.* New York: Penguin/Pelican, 1976.

Chahin, M. *The Kingdom of Armenia.* New York: Dorset Press, 1987.

Charles, Robert H., ed. *The Apocrypha and Pseudepigrapha of the Old Testament in English.* 2 vols. Oxford: Oxford University Press, 1913 and 1976.

Civrieux, Marc de. *Watunna, an Orinoco Creation Cycle.* David M. Guss, trans. San Francisco: North Point Press, 1980.

Clark, John Pepper. *Three Plays.* London: Oxford University Press, 1964.

Clastres, Pierre. *Society against the State.* Robert Hurley, trans., with Abe Stein. New York: Zone Books, 1987.

Cohn, N. *Gold Khan.* London: Secker and Warburg, 1946.

Connelly, Bridget. *Arab Folk Epic and Identity.* Berkeley: University of California Press, 1986.

Cook, Albert. *Myth and Language.* Bloomington: Indiana University Press, 1980.

Coomaraswamy, Ananda K. *The Dance of Śiva.* New York: Dover Publications, Inc., 1985.

Courlander, Harold, with Ousmane Sako. *The Heart of the Ngoni, Heroes of the African Kingdom of Segu.* New York: Crown Publishers, 1982.

Creel, H. G. *Chinese Thought.* New York: Mentor/NAL, 1960.

Daniélou, Alain, trans. *Shilappadikaram.* New York: New Directions, 1965.

Dathorne, O. R., ed. *African Literature in the Twentieth Century.* Minneapolis: University of Minnesota Press, 1975.

Davids, Mrs. C. A. Rhys. *Stories of the Buddha.* New York: Frederick Stokes, 1929.

Davidson, Basil. *Africa in History.* New York: Collier Books, 1991.

Dawood, N. J., trans. *Tales from the One Thousand and One Nights.* New York: Penguin Books, 1973.

Deleuze, Gilles, and Félix Guattari. *Anti-Oedipus.* Robert Hurley, Mark Seem, and Helen R. Lane, trans. Minneapolis: University of Minnesota Press, 1989.

Dimmitt, Cornelia, and J. A. B. van Buitenen, trans. *Classical Hindu Mythology, a Reader in the Sanskrit Purāṇas.* Philadelphia: Temple University Press, 1978.

Diop, Cheikh Anta. *The African Origin of Civilization.* Mercer Cook, trans. Chicago: Lawrence Hill Books, 1974.

Dixon, Roland Burrage. *Mythology of All Races, Oceanic.* New York: Cooper Square Publishers, 1964.

Duerr, Hans Peter. *Dreamtime, Concerning the Boundary between Wilderness and Civilization.* Felicitas Goodman, trans. Oxford: Basil Blackwell, 1985.

Dvornik, Francis. *The Slavs in European History and Civilization.* New Brunswick, NJ: Rutgers University Press, 1962.

Embree, Ainslie T., ed. *Sources of Indian Tradition.* New York: Columbia University Press, 1988.

Erdoes, Richard, and Alfonso Ortiz, eds. *American Indian Myths and Legends.* New York: Pantheon Books, 1984.

Eschenbach, Wolfram von. *Parzival.* A. T. Hatto, trans. New York: Penguin Books, 1980.

Evans-Wentz, W. Y. *The Fairy Faith in Celtic Countries.* New York: Citadel Press, 1990.

Finnegan, Ruth, ed. *A World Treasury of Oral Poetry.* Bloomington: Indiana University Press, 1978.

Forster, Leonard, ed. *The Penguin Book of German Verse.* New York and Harmondsworth, England: Penguin Books, 1957.

Frazer, Sir James George. *The Golden Bough.* New York: Macmillan, 1963.

Fremantle, Francesca, and Chögyam Trungpa, trans. *The Tibetan Book of the Dead.* Boston: Shambhala, 1987.

Frobenius, Leo, and Douglas C. Fox. *African Genesis.* Berkeley: Turtle Island Foundation, 1983.

Gantz, Jeffrey, trans. *Early Irish Myths and Sagas.* New York: Penguin Books, 1988.

———. *The Mabinogion.* New York: Dorset, 1976.

Garcilaso de la Vega, El Inca. *Royal Commentaries of the Incas and General History of Peru.* Harold V. Livermore, trans. Austin: University of Texas Press, 1987.

Garraty, John A., and Peter Gay, eds. *The Columbia History of the World.* New York: Harper & Row, 1972.

Georgieva, Ivanichka. *Bulgarian Mythology.* Vessela Zhelyazkova, trans. Sofia, Bulgaria: Svyat Publishers, 1985.

Gimbutas, Marija. *The Goddesses and Gods of Old Europe.* Berkeley: University of California Press, 1982.

Ginzberg, Louis. *The Legends of the Jews.* 7 vols. Philadelphia: The Jewish Publication Society, 1956.

———. *Legends of the Bible.* Philadelphia: Jewish Publication Society, 1992.

Gleason, Judith. *Oya: In Praise of the Goddess.* Boston: Shambala Publications, 1987.

Glubb, Sir John. *A Short History of the Arab People.* New York: Dorset Press, 1988.

Godolphin, F. R. B., ed. *Great Classical Myths.* New York: Random House, 1964.

Goodrich, Norma Lorre. *The Ancient Myths.* New York: NAL/Mentor, 1960.

———. *The Medieval Myths.* New York: NAL/Mentor, 1961.

———. *Priestesses.* New York: Franklin Watts, 1989.

Grabar, Oleg, and Sheila Blair. *Epic Images and Contemporary History.* Chicago: University of Chicago Press, 1980.

Graham, A. C., trans. *Poems of the Late T'ang.* Harmondsworth, England: Penguin Books, 1970.

Graves, Robert. *The Greek Myths.* 2 vols. Harmondsworth, England: Penguin Books, 1955.

———. *The White Goddess.* New York: Noonday Press, 1966.

Greimas, Algirdas J. *Of Gods and Men. Studies in Lithuanian Mythology.* Milda Newman, trans. Bloomington: Indiana University Press, 1992.

Gretchen, Sylvia, ed. *Hero of the Land of Snow.* Berkeley, CA: Dharma Press, 1990.

Grousset, René. *The Empire of the Steppes, a History of Central Asia.* Naomi Walford, trans. New Brunswick, NJ: Rutgers University Press, 1970.

Hale, Thomas A. *Scribe, Griot and Novelist: Narrative Interpreters of the Songhay Empire.* Gainsville: University of Florida Press/Center for African Studies, 1990.

Hammond, N. G. L. *A History of Greece to 322 B.C.* Oxford: Clarendon Press, 1986.

Hanning, Robert, and Joan Ferrante, trans. *The Laís of Maríe de France.* Durham, NC: Labyrinth Press, 1978.

Harrison, Robert, trans. *The Song of Roland.* New York: Mentor/Penguin, 1970.

Hatto, A. T., trans. *The Memorial Feast for Kökötöy Khan.* Harmondsworth, England: Penguin Books, 1964.

———. *The Nibelungenlied.* New York: Penguin Books, 1969.

Heer, Friedrich. *The Medieval World.* New York: Mentor/NAL, 1962.

Heinberg, Richard. *Memories and Visions of Paradise.* Los Angeles: Jeremy P. Tarcher, 1989.

Hieatt, Constance B., trans. *Beowulf and Other Old English Poems.* New York: Bantam Books, 1967 and 1988.

Hill, Jonathan D., ed. *Rethinking History and Myth, Indigenous South American Perspectives on the Past.* Urbana: University of Illinois Press, 1989.

Hollander, Lee M., trans. *The Poetic Edda.* Austin: University of Texas Press, 1990.

———. *The Saga of the Jómsvíkings.* Austin: University of Texas Press, 1990.

Holmberg, Uno. *Mythology of All Races.* Vol. IV: *Finno-Ugric, Siberian.* New York: Cooper Square, 1964.

Holmes, George, ed. *The Oxford Illustrated History of Medieval Europe.* Oxford: Oxford University Press, 1990.

Hubert, Henri. *The Greatness and Decline of the Celts.* M. R. Dobie, trans. New York: Arno Press, 1980.

Humphries, Rolfe, trans. *The Aeneid of Virgil.* New York: Charles Scribner's Sons, 1951.

Jackson, Guida. *Women Who Ruled.* Santa Barbara, CA: ABC-CLIO, 1990.

Jackson, G. M., ed. *Favorite Fables from around the World.* Houston: Prism Press, 1991.

Jackson, Kenneth Hurlstone, trans. *A Celtic Miscellany.* New York: Penguin Books, 1971.

Jones, Gwyn, ed. *Eirik the Red and Other Icelandic Sagas.* Oxford: Oxford University Press, 1961.

———. *A History of the Vikings.* Oxford: Oxford University Press, 1990.

Jones, Russell, trans. *Hikayat Sultan Ibrahim Ibn Adham.* Lanham, MD: University Press of America, 1985.

Keene, Donald, ed. *Anthology of Japanese Literature.* New York: Grove Press, 1960.

Keith, A. Berriedale, and Albert J. Carnoy. *The Mythology of All Races,* Vol. VI, *Indian, Iranian.* New York: Cooper Square Publishers, 1964.

Ker, W. P. *Epic and Romance.* Cambridge: Cambridge University Press, 1957.

Kinsella, Thomas, trans. *The Tain.* Oxford: Oxford University Press, 1969 and 1990.

Knappert, Jan, trans. *Four Centuries of Swahili Verse.* London: Heinemann, 1979.

Kramer, Samuel Noah. *From the Tablets of Sumer.* Indian Hills, CO: Falcon's Wing Press, 1956.

———. *Sumerian Mythology.* Philadelphia: American Philosophical Society, 1944.

Kunene, Mazisi, trans. *Emperor Shaka the Great.* Portsmouth, NH: Heinemann Educational Books, 1979.

Langer, William. *An Encyclopedia of World History.* Boston: Houghton Mifflin, 1972 and 1980.

Langland, William. *Piers Plowman.* E. Talbot Donaldson, trans. New York: W. W. Norton and Co., 1990.

Lattimore, Richmond, trans. *The Iliad of Homer.* Chicago: University of Chicago Press, 1951 and 1976.

———. *Theogony and Works and Days.* Chicago: University of Chicago Press, 1959.

———. *The Odyssey of Homer.* New York: Harper & Row, 1967.

Laye, Camara. *The Guardian of the Word.* New York: Vintage Books/Random House, 1984.

Leeming, David Adams. *The World of Myth.* Oxford: Oxford University Press, 1990.

León-Portilla, Miguel. *Aztec Thought and Culture.* Jack Emory Davis, trans. Norman: University of Oklahoma Press, 1982.

———. *Time and Reality in the Thought of the Maya.* Charles L. Boilès, Fernando Horcasitas, and author, trans. Norman: University of Oklahoma Press, 1988.

Lerner, Gerda. *The Creation of Patriarchy.* New York and Oxford: Oxford University Press, 1986.

Levy, Reuben, trans. *The Epic of the Kings, Shāh-nāma.* Chicago: University of Chicago Press, 1967.

———. *The Epic of the Kings, Shah-Namah.* Rev. by Amin Banani. New York: Arkana, 1990.

Lewis, Geoffrey, trans. *The Book of Dede Korkut.* New York: Penguin Books, 1974.

Lipschutz, Mark R., and R. Kent Rasmussen. *Dictionary of African History and Biography.* Berkeley: University of California Press, 1989.

Lizot, Jacques. *Tales of the Yanomami.* Ernest Simon, trans. Cambridge: Cambridge University Press, 1991.

Lönnrot, Elias, comp. *The Kalevala.* Francis Peabody Magoun, Jr., trans. Cambridge, MA: Harvard University Press, 1963.

Mackenzie, Donald A. *China and Japan, Myths and Legends.* London: Studio Editions, 1990.

Magnusson, Magnus, and Hermann Pálsson, trans. *Laxdaela Saga.* New York: Penguin Books, 1969.

———. *Njal's Saga.* New York: Penguin Books, 1960.

Markdale, Jean. *Women of the Celts.* A. Mygind, C. Hauch, and P. Henry, trans. Rochester, VT: Inner Traditions International, 1986.

Mascaró, Juan, trans. *The Bhagavad Gita.* New York: Penguin Books, 1962.

Mason, Eugene, trans. *Wace of Jersey.* London: University of London Press, 1962.

Matarasso, Pauline M., trans. *The Quest of the Holy Grail.* New York: Penguin Books, 1984.

Matthias, John, and Vladeta Vučković, trans. *The Battle of Kosovo.* Athens: Ohio University Press, 1987.

Maxwell, James A., ed. *America's Fascinating Indian Heritage.* Pleasantville, OH: Reader's Digest Association, 1978.

Mayer, Fanny Hagin. *The Yanagita Kunio Guide to the Japanese Folk Tale.* Bloomington: Indiana University Press, 1948.

Meister, Michael W., ed. *Discourses on Śiva.* Philadelphia: University of Pennsylvania Press, 1984.

Melville, Leinani. *Children of the Rainbow.* Wheaton, IL: Theosophical Publishing House, 1990.

Merwin, W. S., trans. *Poem of El Cid.* New York: NAL/Mentor, 1962.

Meyer, Kuno, trans. *The Voyage of Brân.* 2 vols. London: Cambridge University Press, 1985–1987.

Miletich, John S., trans. *The Bugarštica.* Urbana: University of Illinois Press, 1990.

Monsen, Erling, and A. H. Smith, trans. *Heimskringla.* Mineola, NY: Dover Publications, 1990.

Morby, John E. *Dynasties of the World.* Oxford: Oxford University Press, 1989.

Morford, Mark P. O., and Robert J. Lenardon. *Classical Mythology.* London and New York: Longman, 1977.

Müller, W. Max, and Sir James George Scott. *Mythology of All Races.* Vol. XII: *Egypt, Far East.* New York: Cooper Square Publishers, 1964.

Narayan, R. K. *Gods, Demons, and Others.* Chicago: University of Chicago Press, 1993.

Niane, D. T. *Sundiata, an Epic of Old Mali.* Harlow, England: Longman, 1989.

Nicholson, R. *A Literary History of the Arabs.* Cambridge: Cambridge University Press, 1962.

O'Flaherty, Wendy Doniger, ed. *Hindu Myths.* New York: Penguin Books, 1975.

O'Flaherty, Wendy Doniger, trans. *The Rig Veda.* New York: Penguin Books, 1981.

———. *Śiva the Erotic Ascetic.* London: Oxford University Press, 1981.

Okpewho, Isidore. *African Oral Literature.* Bloomington: Indiana University Press, 1992.

Olmstead, A. T. *History of the Persian Empire.* Chicago: University of Chicago Press, 1948.

Ostrogorsky, George. *History of the Byzantine State.* Joan Hussey, trans. New Brunswick, NJ: Rutgers University Press, 1969.

Pagels, Elaine. *The Gnostic Gospels.* New York: Random House, 1979.

Pálsson, Hermann, and Paul Edwards, trans. *Egil's Saga.* New York: Penguin Books, 1988.

———. *Orkneyinga Saga*. New York: Penguin Books, 1978 and 1982.

Panikkar, K. Madhu. *The Serpent and the Crescent*. Bombay: Asia Publishing House, 1963.

Papinot, E. *Historical and Geographical Dictionary of Japan*. Rutland, VT, and Tokyo: Charles E. Tuttle Company, 1972.

Parker, Arthur C. *Seneca Myths and Folk Tales*. Lincoln: University of Nebraska Press, 1989.

Parrinder, Geoffrey. *African Mythology*. New York: Peter Bedrick Books, 1982.

Peires, J. B. *The House of Phalo, a History of the Xhosa People in the Days of Their Independence*. Berkeley: University of California Press, 1982.

Perera, Sylvia Brinton. *Descent to the Goddess*. Toronto, Canada: Inner City Books, 1981.

Perrin, Michel. *The Way of the Dead Indians*. Michael Fineberg, trans. Austin: University of Texas Press, 1987.

Philippi, Donald L. *Songs of Gods, Songs of Humans*. Princeton, NJ, and Tokyo: Princeton University Press/University of Tokyo Press, 1979.

Philippi, Donald L., trans. *Kojiki*. Tokyo: University of Tokyo Press, 1968.

Power, Eileen. *Medieval People*. New York: Harper & Row, 1963.

Preminger, Alex, et al., eds. *Princeton Encyclopedia of Poetry and Poetics*. Princeton, NJ: Princeton University Press, 1990.

Previté-Orton, C. W. *The Shorter Cambridge Medieval History*. 2 vols. Cambridge: Cambridge University Press, 1982.

Pritchard, James B. *The Ancient Near East*. Vol I. Princeton, NJ: Princeton University Press, 1973.

Radin, Paul. *The Road of Life and Death*. Princeton, NJ: Princeton University Press/Bollingen, 1973.

Raffel, Burton, trans. *Beowulf*. New York: Mentor/Penguin, 1963.

Rao, Nina. *Ladakh*. New Delhi: Lustre Press Pvt. Ltd., 1989.

Recinos, Adrián, Delia Goetz, and Sylvanus G. Morley, trans. *Popol Vuh*. Norman: University of Oklahoma Press, 1983.

Reischauer, Edwin O., and John K. Fairbank. *A History of East Asian Civilization*. Vol. I: *East Asia: The Great Tradition*. Boston: Houghton Mifflin, 1960.

Rieu, E. V., trans. *The Odyssey*. Harmondsworth, England: Penguin Books, 1961.

Rouse, W. H. D., trans. *Homer, the Odyssey.* New York: NAL/Penguin, 1937 and 1990.

Roys, Ralph L., trans. *The Chilam Balam of Chumayel.* Washington, DC: Carnegie Institute of Washington Publication #483, 1933.

Ruland, Wilhelm. *The Legends of the Rhine.* Andrew Mitchell and H. J. Findlay, trans. Bonn: Verlag Hoursh and Bechstedt, n.d.

Rutherford, Ward. *Celtic Mythology.* Wellingborough, England: Aquarian Press, 1987.

Saggs, Henry W. F. *The Encounter with the Divine in Mesopotamia and Israel.* London: Athlone Press, 1978.

———. *The Might That Was Assyria.* New York: St. Martin's Press, 1990.

Saintsbury, George. *The Flourishing of Romance and the Rise of Allegory.* Cambridge: Cambridge University Press, 1961.

Salomon, Frank, and George L. Urioste, trans. *The Huarochirí Manuscript.* Austin: University of Texas Press, 1991.

Sandars, N. K., trans. *The Epic of Gilgamesh.* New York: Penguin Books, 1972.

Sansom, George. *A History of Japan to 1334.* Stanford, CA: Stanford University Press, 1958.

Sawyer-Lauçanno, Christopher, trans. *The Destruction of the Jaguar, Poems from the Books of Chilam Balam.* San Francisco: City Lights Books, 1987.

Schele, Linda, and David Freidel. *A Forest of Kings, the Untold Story of the Ancient Maya.* New York: William Morrow, 1990.

Schmidt, I. J. *Gessar Khan.* Ida Zeitlin, trans. New York: George H. Doran Co., 1927.

Schwab, Gustav. *Gods and Heroes.* New York: Pantheon Books, 1974.

Schwartz, Howard, ed. *Miriam's Tambourine.* Oxford: Oxford University Press, 1987.

Sélincourt, Aubrey de, trans. *Herodotus, The Histories.* Harmondsworth, England: Penguin Books, 1988.

Shattan, Merchant-Prince. *Mamimekhalaï.* Alain Daniélou, trans. New York: New Directions, 1989.

Siegel, James. *Shadow and Sound, the Historical Thought of the Sumatran People.* Chicago: University of Chicago Press, 1979.

Siepmann, Katherine Baker, ed. *Benét's Reader's Encyclopedia.* New York: Harper Collins 1987.

Simmons, D. R. *The Great New Zealand Myth.* Wellington: A. H. & A. W. Reed, 1976.

Sisòkò, Fa-Digi. *The Epic of Son-Jara.* John William Johnson, trans. Bloomington: Indiana University Press, 1992.

Smith, Edwin W., and Andrew Murray Dale. *The Ila-speaking Peoples of Northern Rhodesia.* New Hyde Park, NY: University Books, 1968.

Snorri, Sturluson. *The Prose Edda.* Arthur Gilchrist, trans. New York: American-Scandinavian Foundation, 1929.

Sproul, Barbara C. *Primal Myths.* San Francisco: Harper Collins, 1991.

Stevens-Arroyo, Antonio M. *Cave of the Jagua.* Albuquerque: University of New Mexico Press, 1988.

Stone, Brian, trans. *Sir Gawain and the Green Knight.* New York: Penguin Books, 1974.

Stone, Ruth M. *Dried Millet Breaking, the Wọi Epic of the Kpelle.* Bloomington: Indiana University Press, 1988.

Suggs, Robert C. *The Island Civilizations of Polynesia.* New York: NAL/Mentor, 1960.

Suny, Ronald Grigor. *The Making of a Georgian Nation.* Bloomington: Indiana University Press, 1988.

Tahara, Mildred, trans. *Tales of Yamato, a Tenth Century Poem-Tale.* Honolulu: University of Hawaii Press, 1980.

Tala, Kashim Ibrahim, ed. *An Introduction to Cameroon Oral Literature.* Yaoundé: SOPECAM, 1984.

Tedlock, Dennis, trans. *Finding the Center, Narrative Poetry of the Zuni Indians.* Lincoln: University of Nebraska Press, 1978.

Terada, Alice M. *Under the Starfruit Tree, Folktales from Vietnam.* Honolulu: University of Hawaii Press, 1989.

Terry, Patricia, trans. *Reynard the Fox.* Berkeley: University of California Press, 1992.

Toor, Frances. *A Treasury of Mexican Folkways.* New York: Crown Publishing, 1947.

Turco, Lewis. *The New Book of Forms: A Handbook of Poetics.* Hanover, NH: University Press of New England, 1986.

Van Buitenen, J. A. B., trans. *Tales of Ancient India.* Chicago: University of Chicago Press, 1969.

Van der Post, Laurens. *The Lost World of the Kalahari.* New York: William Morrow and Company, 1958.

Vernadsky, G. *The Origins of Russia.* Oxford: Clarendon Press, 1959.

Von Srassburg, Gottfried. *Tristan.* A. T. Hatto, trans. Harmondsworth, England: Penguin Classics, 1960.

Waley, Arthur. *The Way and Its Power.* New York: Macmillan, 1949.

Waley, Arthur, trans. *The Book of Songs, the Ancient Chinese Classic of Poetry.* New York: Grove Press, 1960.

———. *Chinese Poems.* London: Unwin Hyman Ltd., 1982.

Walker, James R. *Lakota Myth.* Lincoln: University of Nebraska Press, 1983.

Wallace, Zara. *Gesar!* Berkeley, CA: Dharma Publishing, 1991.

Ward, Philip, ed. *The Oxford Companion to Spanish Literature.* Oxford: Oxford University Press, 1981.

Waters, Frank. *The Book of the Hopi.* New York: Penguin Books, 1977.

Watson, W. J., ed. *Scottish Verse from the Book of the Dean of Lismore.* Edinburgh: University of Edinburgh Press, 1937.

Weiner, James F. *The Empty Place: Poetry, Space, and Being among the Foi of Papua, New Guinea.* Bloomington: Indiana University Press, 1991.

Wender, Dorothea, trans. *Hesiod. Theogony, Works and Days. Theognis. Elegies.* Baltimore: Penguin Books, 1973.

Weyer, Edward, Jr. *Primitive Peoples Today.* Garden City, NY: Doubleday Dolphin, n.d.

Whitten, Norman E., Jr. *Sicuanga Runa.* Urbana: University of Illinois Press, 1985.

Wilde, William H., et al. *The Oxford Companion to Australian Literature.* Melbourne: Oxford University Press, 1991.

Wilson, David M. *The Vikings and Their Origins.* New York: McGraw-Hill, 1975.

Wolkstein, Diane, and Samuel Noah Kramer. *Inanna, Queen of Heaven and Earth.* New York: Harper & Row, 1983.

Wright, Donald R. *Oral Traditions from the Gambia.* 2 vols. Athens: Ohio University Center for International Studies Africa Program, 1980.

Yohannan, John D., ed. *A Treasury of Asian Literature.* New York: NAL/Mentor, 1958.

Young, Jean I., trans. *The Prose Edda of Snorri Sturluson: Tales from Norse Mythology.* Cambridge: Cambridge University Press, 1954.

Zaehner, R. C. *Zurvan: A Zoroastrian Dilemma.* Oxford: Clarendon Press, 1955.

Zimmerman, J. E. *Dictionary of Classical Mythology.* New York: Harper & Row, 1964.

Zolbrod, Paul G. *Diné bahane', the Navajo Creation Story.* Albuquerque: University of New Mexico Press, 1984.

Journals

Research in African Literatures. Vol. 19, no. 4. University of Texas Press, 1988.

Research in African Literatures. Vol. 20, no. 2. University of Texas Press, 1989.

Research in African Literatures. Vol. 20, no. 3. University of Texas Press, 1989.

Research in African Literatures. Vol. 21, no. 3. Indiana University Press, with Ohio State University, 1990.

Research in African Literatures. Vol. 22, no. 1. Indiana University Press, with Ohio State University, 1991.

Research in African Literatures. Vol. 22, no. 2. Indiana University Press, with Ohio State University, 1991.

Research in African Literatures. Vol. 22, no. 4. Indiana University Press, with Ohio State University, 1991.

Articles

Abercrombie, Thomas J. "Cambodia: Indochina's 'Neutral' Corner." *National Geographic* (October 1964): 514–551.

Allen, Jane Addams. "Between India and Islam." *Art in America* (January 1991): 114–123, 149–151.

Azuonye, Chukwuma. "The Performances of Kaalu Igirigiri, an Ohafia Igbo Singer of Tales." *RAL* 21:3 (1990): 17–50.

Chileshe, John. "Literature in English from Zambia: A Bibliography of Published Works to 1986." *RAL* 19:3 (1988): 365–373.

"Early Inhabitants: Who They Are." *Christian Science Monitor* (9 June 1993): 10–11.

Garrett, W. E. "Pagan: On the Road to Mandalay." *National Geographic.* (March 1971): 343–365.

Grosvenor, Donna K., and Gilbert M. Grosvenor. "Bali by the Backroads." *National Geographic* (November 1969): 657–697.

McDowell, Bart. "Thailand: Luck of a Land in the Middle." *National Geographic* (October 1982): 500–535.

MacLeish, Kenneth. "Java, Eden in Transition." *National Geographic* (January 1971): 1–39.

Malaba, Mbongeni Z. "Super-Shaka: Mazisi Kunene's Emperor Shaka the Great." *RAL* 19:4 (1988): 477–488.

Ridehalgh, Anna. "Some Recent Francophone Versions of the Shaka Story." *RAL* 22:2 (1991): 135–152.

Shariff, Ibrahim Noor. "The Liyongo Conundrum: Reexamining the Historicity of Swahilis' National Poet-Hero." *RAL* 22:2 (1991): 153–175.

Ward, Fred. "In Long-Forbidden Tibet." *National Geographic* (February 1980): 219–259.

Westley, David. "A Bibliography of African Epic." *RAL* 22:4 (1991): 99–115.

Film

The Mahabharata by Peter Brooks. Paris: Joinville Studios, 1989. Based on the RST/CICT stage production by Jean-Claude Carrière. Playtext published by Harper & Row. Available on video from Parabola Video Library, New York.

ILLUSTRATION CREDITS

4 Folio from *Bhāgavata Purāṇa* (1525–1550). Denver Art Museum 1964.102.

31 Illustration by Albertine Randall Wheelan. *The Bookshelf for Boys and Girls. Vol. VIII: Stories from Every Land,* page 245. New York: The University Society, 1948.

34 Cover illustration by N. C. Wyeth for *The Boy's King Arthur* (1917). Private collection, courtesy of American Illustrator's Gallery, New York; photograph provided by the Brandywine River Museum, Chadds Ford, Pennsylvania.

40 Acropolis Museum, Athens, Greece. Foto Marburg/Art Resource S0005303, New York.

79 *Brunnhuilde* by Arthur Rackham (1910). From *The Rhinegold and the Valkyrie* by Richard Wagner, translated by Margaret Armour, facing page 102. New York: Garden City Publishing, 1939. Provided by Mary Evans Picture Library, London.

116 Topkapi Palace Museum, Istanbul, Turkey. Giraudon/Art Resource S0048782, New York.

134 National Archaeological Museum, Athens, Greece. Alinari/Art Resource S0048770, New York.

150 *Durgā Slaying Mahisha*, India, Pahari School, Nupur. Mr. and Mrs. William H. Marlatt Fund 60.51, The Cleveland Museum of Art, Cleveland, Ohio.

168 Museo Egizio, Turin, Italy. Scala/Art Resource S0025701, New York.

180 Cylinder seal 202. Pierpont Morgan Library, New York.

205 *Freia, the Fair One* by Arthur Rackham (1910). From *The Rhinegold and the Valkyrie* by Richard Wagner, translated by Margaret Armour, page 23. New York: Garden City Publishing, 1939. Provided by Mary Evans Picture Library, London.

208 The University Museum 29-12-97, University of Pennsylvania, Philadelphia.

218 Louvre, Paris. Giraudon/Art Resource S0042803, New York.

239 From *Rāmāyaṇa of Valmiki,* 07.271 fol. 236 r. *Hanumān Brings the Mountain of Healing Herbs* by Zain-al-Abidin. Freer Gallery of Art, Washington, DC.

245 Anfora di Nessos. National Museum, Athens, Greece. Nimatallah/Art Resource S0048776, New York.

267 Peabody Museum, Cambridge, Massachusetts.

275 National Museum, Athens, Greece. Nimatallah/Art Resource S0025774, New York.

283 Oriental Institute Museum A 27903, University of Chicago.

287 *The Sacrifice of Iphigeneia,* from House of the Tragic Poet, Pompeii. Museo Archeologico Nazionale, Naples, Italy. Alinari/Art Resource S0048771, New York.

289 Denver Art Museum 1955.17.

292 *Izanami and Izanagi Creating the Japanese Islands* by Kobayashi Eitaku. Bigelow Collection, Museum of Fine Arts 11.7972, Boston.

306 Detail of *The Argonauts* by Lorenzo Costa. Museo Civico, Padua, Italy. Scala/Art Resource S0048777, New York.

311 *Lemminkäinen's Mother* by Akseli Gallén-Kallela (1897). The Antell Collection, The Central Art Archives, Ateneum, Helsinki, Finland.

337 *Kṛṣṇa and Arjuna Blow Their Conchshells* from *Bhagavad-gita As It Is,* plate 3. Malmö, Sweden: Bhaktivedanta Book Trust—International, 1983.

356 *Leiv Eirikson Discovering America*. Painting by Christian Krohg (1893). Photograph by J. Lathion, Nasjonalgalleriet, Oslo.

392 Denver Art Museum 1933.26.

418 Denver Art Museum 1964.14.

421 Louvre, Paris. Giraudon/Art Resource S0048765, New York.

437 Musee de l'Homme, Paris. Giraudon/Art Resource S0044557, New York.

441 Staatliche Museen, Berlin. Foto Marburg/Art Resource S0048784, New York.

467 *Parsifal* fol. 49v. mus 19. Staatsbibliothek, Munich, Germany. Foto Marburg/Art Resource S0048783, New York.

475 Denver Art Museum 1979.3.

485 National Museum, Athens, Greece. Alinari/Art Resource S0019346, New York.

509 From *Roman de Renart,* Bibliotheque Nationale, Paris. Giraudon/Art Resource S0042792, New York.

511 *Robin Hood and the Men of Greenwood* by N. C. Wyeth (1917). From the collection of the Central Children's Room, Donnell Library Center, The New York Public Library, New York. Photograph provided by the Brandywine River Museum, Chadds Ford, Pennsylvania.

532 Denman W. Ross Collection; Museum of Fine Arts 30.105, Boston.

541 Illustration by Arthur Rackham (1901) from *The Bookshelf for Boys and Girls, Vol. VIII: Stories from Every Land,* page 311. New York: The University Society, 1948.

545 Illustration by Howard Pyle. Gift of Samuel B. Bird 70.007, Herbert F. Johnson Museum of Art, Cornell University, Ithaca, New York.

549 *Śiva Naṭarāja,* India. Denver Art Museum 1947.2.

567 Illustration by Arthur Rackham (1910). From *The Rhinegold and the Valkyrie* by Richard Wagner, translated by Margaret Armour. New York: Garden City Publishing, 1939. Provided by Mary Evans Picture Library, London.

577 Staatliche Museen, Berlin, Germany. Foto Marburg/Art Resource S0048766, New York.

598 Brass statue, South India ca. fourteenth century. Marianne Brimmer Fund, Museum of Fine Arts 21.1833, Boston.

627 Denver Art Museum 1963.145.

631 Gift of Mrs. Edward S. Harkness, 1947 (47.81.1b). Metropolitan Museum of Art, New York.

634 Print by Utagawa Kuniyoshi. Victoria and Albert Museum, London/Art Resource S0043029, New York.

INDEX

INDEX